LIVING AND WORKING

IN

FRANCE

A SURVIVAL HANDBOOK

by

David Hampshire

SURVIVAL BOOKS • LONDON • ENGLAND

First published 1993
Reprinted 1994 (with revisions)
Second Edition 1996
Reprinted 1998
Third Edition 1999

Survival Books Limited, Suite C, Third Floor
Standbrook House, 2-5 Old Bond Street
London W1X 3TB, United Kingdom
☎ (+44) 207-493 4244, Fax (+44) 207-491 0605
E-mail: info@survivalbooks.net
Internet: survivalbooks.net

British Library Cataloguing in Publication Data
A CIP record for this book is available from the British Library
ISBN 1 901130 55 X

Printed and bound in Great Britain by Page Bros. (Norwich) Ltd., Mile Cross Lane,
Norwich, Norfolk NR6 6SA, UK.

What Reviewers and Readers Have Said About Other Survival Handbooks

We would like to congratulate you on this work: it is really super! We hand it out to our expatriates and they read it with great interest and pleasure.

ICI (Switzerland) AG

Rarely has a 'survival guide' contained such useful advice – This book dispels doubts for first-time travellers, yet is also useful for seasoned globetrotters – In a word, if you're planning to move to the USA or go there for a long-term stay, then buy this book both for general reading and as a ready-reference.

American Citizens Abroad

It's everything you always wanted to ask but didn't for fear of the contemptuous put down – The best English-language guide – Its pages are stuffed with practical information on everyday subjects and are designed to complement the traditional guidebook.

Swiss News

The ultimate reference book – Every conceivable subject imaginable is exhaustively explained in simple terms – An excellent introduction to fully enjoy all that this fine country has to offer and save time and money in the process.

American Club of Zurich

What a great work, wealth of useful information, well-balanced wording and accuracy in details. My compliments!

Thomas Müller

This handbook has all the practical information one needs to set up home in the UK – The sheer volume of information is almost daunting – Highly recommended for anyone moving to the UK.

American Citizens Abroad

A mine of information – I might have avoided some embarrassments and frights if I had read it prior to my first Swiss encounters – Deserves an honoured place on any newcomer's bookshelf.

English Teachers Association, Switzerland

It's so funny – I love it and definitely need a copy of my own – Thanks very much for having written such a humourous and helpful book.

Heidi Guiliani

A concise, thorough account of the DO's and DON'Ts for a foreigner in Switzerland – Crammed with useful information and lightened with humourous quips which make the facts more readable.

American Citizens Abroad

Hats off to Living and Working in Switzerland!

Ronnie Almeida

A very good book which has answered so many questions and some I hadn't thought of – I would certainly recommend it.

Brian Fairman

CONTENTS

ACKNOWLEDGEMENTS

My sincere thanks to all those who contributed to the successful publication of this book, in particular the many people who provided information and took the time and trouble to read and comment on the many draft versions. I would especially like to thank Joanna Styles (who did most of the updating for this edition), John Beaumont (research), Karen (proof-reading) and John Verheul, Janet Macdonald, Ken Maxwell-Jones, John Adams, Alwyn Seppings, John P. Harris, Pat & Ron Scarborough (especially for the delicious meals and wine, which are all too infrequent!), Adèle Kelham and everyone else who contributed in any way who I have omitted to mention. Also a special thank you to Jim Watson (☎ UK 01788-813609) for the superb cartoons, illustrations and cover.

By the same publisher:

The Alien's Guide to France
Buying a Home Abroad
Buying a Home in Florida
Buying a Home in France
Buying a Home in Ireland
Buying a Home in Italy
Buying a Home in Portugal
Buying a Home in Spain
Living and Working in America
Living and Working in Australia
Living and Working in Britain
Living and Working in New Zealand
Living and Working in Spain
Living and Working in Switzerland

What Reviewers Have Said About Living and Working in France

When you buy a model plane for your child, a video recorder, or some new computer gizmo, you get with it a leaflet or booklet pleading 'Read Me First', or bearing large friendly letters or bold type saying 'IMPORTANT -- follow the instructions carefully'. This book should be similarly supplied to all those entering France with anything more durable than a 5-day return ticket. – It is worth reading even if you are just visiting briefly, or if you have lived here for years and feel totally knowledgeable and secure. But if you need to find out how France works then it is indispensable. Native French people probably have a less thorough understanding of how their country functions. – Where it is most essential, the book is most up to the minute.

Living France

Let's say it at once. David Hampshire's *Living and Working in France* is the best handbook ever produced for visitors and foreign residents in this country; indeed, my discussion with locals showed that it has much to teach even those born and bred in *l'Hexagone*. – It is Hampshire's meticulous detail which lifts his work way beyond the range of other books with similar titles. Often you think of a supplementary question and search for the answer in vain. With Hampshire this is rarely the case. – He writes with great clarity (and gives French equivalents of all key terms), a touch of humour and a ready eye for the odd (and often illuminating) fact. – This book is absolutely indispensable.

The Riviera Reporter

Covers just about all the things you want to know on the subject – in answer to the desert island question about *the one* how-to book on France, this book would be it – almost 500 pages of solid accurate reading – this book is about enjoyment as much as survival.

The Recorder (French English-language Newspaper)

A comprehensive guide to all things French, written in a highly readable and amusing style, for anyone planning to live, work or retire in France.

The Times

Covers every conceivable question that might be asked concerning everyday life – I know of no other book that could take the place of this one.

France in Print

12. HEALTH   229

13. INSURANCE   251

16. SPORTS 345

17. SHOPPING 369

18. ODDS & ENDS

393

19. THE FRENCH

415

20. MOVING HOUSE OR LEAVING FRANCE

423

APPENDICES

429

INDEX

449

SUGGESTIONS

459

ORDER FORM

464

IMPORTANT NOTE

France is a large country with myriad faces and many ethnic groups, religions and customs. Although ostensibly the same throughout the country, rules and regulations tend to be open to local interpretation (Paris is a law unto itself!), and are sometimes even formulated on the spot. **I cannot recommend too strongly that you check with an official and reliable source (not always the same) before making major decisions or undertaking an irreversible course of action. However, don't believe everything you're told or read, even, dare I say it, herein!**

To help you obtain further information and verify data with official sources, useful addresses and references have been included in most chapters and appendices A and B. Important points have been emphasised throughout the book **in bold print,** some of which it would be expensive or even dangerous to disregard. **Ignore them at your cost or peril.** Unless specifically stated, the reference to any company, organisation, product or publication in this book *doesn't* constitute an endorsement or recommendation. Any reference to any place or person (living or dead) is purely coincidental. There's no French town named Lyons.

AUTHOR'S NOTES

- Times are shown using the 24-hour clock, e.g. 10am is shown as 1000 and 10pm as 2200, which is the usual way of expressing the time in France (see page 411).

- Prices quoted should be taken only as estimates, although they were mostly correct when going to print and fortunately don't usually change overnight. Although prices are sometimes quoted exclusive of value added tax (*hors taxes/HT*) in France, most prices are quoted inclusive of tax (*toutes taxes comprises/TTC*), which is the method used when quoting prices in this book.

- His/he/him/man/men (etc.) also mean her/she/her/woman/women (no offence ladies!). This is done simply to make life easier for both the reader and, in particular, the author, and isn't intended to be sexist.

- The French translation of many key words and phrases is shown in brackets in *italics*.

- Warnings and important points are shown in **bold** type.

- Frequent references are made in this book to the European Union (EU), which comprises Austria, Belgium, Denmark, Finland, France, Germany, Greece, Ireland, Italy, Luxembourg, the Netherlands, Portugal, Spain, Sweden and the United Kingdom, and the European Economic Area (EEA), which includes the EU countries plus Iceland, Liechtenstein and Norway.

- References are made throughout this book to Minitel, the French telephone information system (see page 125), although it is now being superseded by the Internet (see page 125).

- Lists of **Useful Addresses** and **Further Reading** are contained in **Appendices A** and **B** respectively.

- For those unfamiliar with the metric system of weights and measures, conversion tables are included in **Appendix C**.

- A map of France showing the regions and departments is included in **Appendix D**.

- A **Service Directory** containing the names, addresses, telephone and fax numbers of companies and organisations doing business in France is contained in **Appendix E**.

INTRODUCTION

Whether you're already living or working in France or just thinking about it – this is THE BOOK you've been looking for. Forget about those glossy guide books, excellent though they are for tourists, this amazing book was written especially with you in mind and is worth its weight in truffles! **Living and Working in France** is designed to meet the needs of anyone wishing to know the essentials of French life including immigrants, temporary foreign workers, businessmen, students, retirees, long-stay visitors, holiday-home owners and even extra-terrestrials! However long your intended stay in France, you'll find the information contained in this book invaluable.

In sharp contrast to the abundant information available from French Government Tourist Offices, up-to-date information for foreigners **Living and Working in France** is often difficult to find – particularly in the English language. My aim in writing this book was to help fill this void and provide the comprehensive *practical* information necessary for a relatively trouble-free life. You may have visited France as a tourist, but living and working there's a different matter altogether. Adjusting to a different environment and culture and making a home in any foreign country is usually a traumatic and stressful experience, and France is certainly no exception.

You need to adapt to new customs and traditions and discover the French way of doing things, for example finding a home, paying bills and obtaining insurance. For foreigners in France, finding out how to overcome the everyday obstacles of French life has previously been a case of pot luck. But no more! With a copy of **Living and Working in France** to hand you'll have a wealth of information at your fingertips. Information is derived from a variety of sources, both official and unofficial, not least the hard won personal experiences of the author, his friends, colleagues and acquaintances. **Living and Working in France** embraces the whole gamut of everyday subjects and represents the most comprehensive, up-to-date source of general information available to foreigners in France. It isn't, however, simply a monologue of dry facts and figures, but an entertaining, practical and occasionally humorous look at life in France.

Adapting to life in a new country is a continuous process and although this book will help reduce your 'novice' phase and minimise the frustrations, it doesn't contain all the answers (most of us don't even know the right questions to ask!). However, what it *will* do is help you make informed decisions and calculated judgements, instead of costly mistakes and uneducated guesses. Most important of all, it will help you save money and will repay the average reader's investment many times over.

Although you may find some of the information a bit daunting, don't be discouraged. Most problems occur once only and fade into insignificance after a short time (as you face the next half dozen!). The majority of foreigners in France would agree that, all things considered (bureaucracy aside), they relish living there. A period spent in France is a wonderful way to enrich your life, broaden your horizons and hopefully also please your bank manager. I trust this book will help you avoid many of the pitfalls of life in France and smooth your way to a happy and rewarding future in your new home.

Bonne Chance!

David Hampshire
June 1999

1.

FINDING A JOB

Finding a job in France isn't always as difficult as the unemployment figures may suggest, particularly in Paris and other large cities, depending of course on your qualifications and French language ability. However, if you don't qualify to live and work in France by birthright or as a national of a European Union (EU) country, obtaining a residence permit may be more difficult than finding a job. Americans and other nationalities without the automatic right to work in France must have their employment approved by the French Ministry of Labour and need a long-stay employment visa before entering France.

Foreigners are found in large numbers in almost every walk of life in France, particularly in Paris. France has a long tradition of welcoming immigrants, particularly political refugees, who number over 200,000 (mostly from Eastern Europe, Indo-China, the Middle East and Latin America). However, refugees make up few of France's immigrants compared with the over one million French citizens who have left Algeria since it gained independence in 1962. France has around five million foreign residents (around 6 per cent of the population), of whom some 1¾ million are from EU countries, the vast majority from Italy, Portugal and Spain. There are officially around 1½ million North African immigrants in France, although this figure is possibly doubled by illegal immigration. Immigration is a controversial and emotive subject in France and has been agitated by the xenophobic diatribe of the racist *Front National* party, led by Jean-Marie Le Pen.

EU immigrants are tolerated by most Frenchmen, although the same cannot be said of African and Arab immigrants, mostly from Algeria, Morocco and Tunisia. Due to their race, mainly Muslim religion and lifestyle, North Africans are conspicuous and have been slow to integrate into French society. The majority of North Africans exist in ghettos with large families, on incomes well below the official poverty line. France also has some 700,000 black immigrants, most of whom are French citizens from the country's Caribbean colonies. Many are educated and successful middle-class people and are therefore more easily assimilated than North Africans. High unemployment in France has meant that hiring non-EU workers (or even workers from some EU countries) is a sensitive and emotive issue.

Employment Prospects: Being attracted to France by its weather, cuisine, wine and lifestyle (etc.) is laudable, but doesn't rate highly as an employment qualification. You should have a positive reason for living and working in France; simply being fed up with your boss or the weather isn't the best motive for moving to France (although thoroughly understandable). It's extremely difficult to find work in rural areas and isn't easy in cities and large towns (even Paris), especially if your French isn't fluent. You shouldn't plan on obtaining employment in France unless you have a firm job offer and special qualifications or experience for which there's a strong demand. If you want a good job, you must usually be extremely well qualified and speak fluent French. If you plan to arrive in France without a job, it's advisable to have a plan for finding employment on arrival and to try to make some contacts before you arrive. If you have a job offer, you should try to ensure that it's genuine and isn't going to be revoked soon after you arrive in France.

Many people turn to self-employment or starting a business to make a living, although this path is strewn with pitfalls for the newcomer. **Most foreigners don't do sufficient homework before moving to France.** While hoping for the best, you should plan for the worst case scenario and have a contingency plan and sufficient funds to last until you're established (this also applies to employees). If you're planning to start a business in France, you must also do battle with the notoriously obstructive French bureaucracy (*bonne chance!*).

Before moving to France to work, you should dispassionately examine your motives and credentials. What kind of work can you realistically expect to do? What are your qualifications and experience? Are they recognised in France? How good is your French? Unless your French is fluent, you won't be competing on equal terms with the French (you won't anyway, but that's a different matter!). Most French employers aren't interested in employing anyone without, at the very least, an adequate working knowledge of French. Are there any jobs in your profession or trade in the area where you wish to live? Could you be self-employed or start your own business? The answers to these and many other questions can be quite disheartening, but it's better to ask them *before* moving to France rather than afterwards.

Unemployment: Like most European countries France has high unemployment running at just under three million (around 11 per cent of the workforce). Another million or so people are on special 'training' schemes which avoid the unemployment register and are seen by many as simply 'parking areas for the unemployed'. Unemployment is a catastrophe for those aged under 25, among whom it's more than double the national average at almost 28 per cent. Although unemployment has hit manufacturing industries the hardest, no sector has survived unscathed, including the flourishing service industries in the Paris region. Managers and executives haven't escaped the axe and there are tens of thousands of unemployed managers in France. Many companies have put a total ban on recruitment in the last few years and have expected executives to accept fixed or short-term contracts, rather than life-long security. Some of the worst-hit industries have been construction, electronics, communications, the media and banking, all traditionally strong sectors. More than a quarter of France's working population has a short-term contract (*contrat à durée determinée* or *CDD*).

Apart from the debilitating effects on the French economy, unemployment is also very expensive for the French government (i.e. the taxpayers), due to France's high unemployment benefits and expensive retraining schemes. Most Frenchmen don't dream of becoming entrepreneurs or businessmen, but of working in the public sector, which constitutes some 25 per cent of the workforce (over four million people). Long-term unemployment is a huge problem in France, where the average periods of unemployment is one year (the longest in Europe) and over a million people have been unemployed for over two years. Anyone aged over 50 who loses his job is unlikely to work again unless he's highly qualified and in demand. Unemployment is the biggest crisis facing France in the '90s, where successive governments have done little or ncthing to tackle the real causes, which are the high taxes, crippling social security costs and rigid labour laws that serve to discourage employers from hiring staff. Recent years have seen a marked increase in French investment abroad (around £16 billion in Britain in 1998) and France is experiencing the 'brain-drain' phenomena as executives and entrepreneurs (and football players!) leave the country. Unemployment is also largely responsible for a sharp increase in youth crime, particularly in Paris suburbs, and an ever-growing number of suicides among its youth.

Economy: France experienced something of an economic miracle in the last few decades, during which its traditional industries were thoroughly modernised and a wealth of new high-tech industries were created. In the '60s and '70s, France's growth rate was among the highest in the world and by 1980 it was equal third (with Japan) among world exporters, since when it has fallen back. During the same period the number employed in agriculture declined drastically, as did the numbers in manufacturing and construction. With increasing competition, particularly from the Far East, traditional industries such as steel, shipbuilding, textiles and motor vehicles have all become less competitive. However, manufacturing remains important in France, which has a strong industrial base in the manufacture of motor vehicles, aerospace and defence equipment.

Less labour and capital intensive industries such as electronics and communications flourished in the '80s, although the largest growth in recent years has been in service industries, e.g. banking, insurance and advertising. In 1985, the Socialist government cultivated a free-market economy which proved more liberal than anything attempted by any previous conservative government. French industry has increasingly looked beyond its own borders in the last few decades during which it has been one of the world's leading investors in foreign companies. In 1998, inflation (1.3 per cent) was among the lowest of any industrialised nation, growth was relatively strong (2.8 per cent) and the country had a large trade surplus. The GDP per head is among the highest in Europe and, with the advent of the Euro, France is now regarded as Europe's 'benchmark' economy.

Industrial Relations: There has been a large reduction in strikes (*grèves*) in the last decade, particularly in the private sector. The less confrontational relationship between employers and employees is due both to new legislation, requiring both sides to discuss their differences and imposing a 'cooling-off' period before a strike can be called, and high unemployment. Strikes in private companies are almost unheard of in France, mainly because job security is too fragile and the number of unionised workers has fallen to around 10 per cent of the workforce. However, there's a stark contrast between the private and public sectors, where employees stop work at the drop of a beret. The last few years have seen many strikes in the public sector and also among self-employed groups such as farmers, fishermen and truck drivers. A national strike was staged in autumn 1995 to protest against social security reforms, which ended when the government backed down on its proposals to reduce employees' extravagant unemployment benefits and pensions.

Workforce: French workers enjoy an affluent lifestyle compared with workers in many other western countries and similar to Germany's. The French see the German economy as their role model and main competitor, although ironically it's also fashionable to blame Germany for many of the country's ills. Much of the French working class is comprised of skilled workers and technicians. French engineers are part of the elite (as in Germany) and highly respected, which encourages a positive industrial outlook. France has a well educated and trained workforce, and a strong emphasis is placed on training by employers. Even employees doing what many would consider menial jobs, such as shop assistants and waiters, are well trained and aren't looked upon as semi-skilled or unskilled.

France has a reasonably self-sufficient labour market and doesn't require a large number of skilled or unskilled foreign workers. However, in recent years French companies have been keen to expand into international markets, which has created opportunities for foreign workers, particularly bilingual and tri-lingual employees. French employees enjoy high salaries, especially executives and senior managers, and excellent working conditions. Women have professional and salary equality with men, although they still fill most low-paid jobs. France has a minimum wage (*salaire minimum de Interprofessionnel croissance/SMIC*) of 40.22F an hour, equal to 6,797F per month for 169 hours.

Work Attitudes: French companies have a strict hierarchical management structure with little contact between management and workers, both of whom are reluctant to take on responsibilities outside their immediate duties. Experience, maturity and loyalty are highly valued, and newcomers generally find it difficult to secure a senior position with a French company. Frequently changing jobs (job hopping) is rare in France, particularly as a way of increasing your salary or promotion prospects. French firms have traditionally been expected to care for their employees and most have a paternalistic attitude. It's expensive to both hire and fire employees in France (unlike Britain and the USA), which has led many French companies to modernise and restructure, rather than close down businesses.

When it comes to hiring new employees (particularly managers and executives) and making important business decisions, the process is slower in France than in many other western countries. Many foreigners, particularly Americans, find they need to adjust to a slower pace of working life in France. Most French managers and executives rarely take work home and they *never* work at weekends, which are sacrosanct. However, don't be misled by the Frenchman's apparent lack of urgency and casual approach to business – underneath that relaxed exterior lies a hard-headed businessman.

There are a number of English-language books written for jobseekers in France including *Get a Job in France* by Mark Hempshell (How To Books) and *Working in France* by Carol Pineau & Maureen Kelly (Frank Books).

France and the EU

France was one of the six founding members of the EU in 1957 along with Belgium, Germany, Italy, Luxembourg and the Netherlands. Since then Austria, Denmark, Finland, Greece, Ireland, Portugal, Spain, Sweden and the United Kingdom have increased the number of members to 15. The EU countries plus Iceland, Liechtenstein and Norway make up the European Economic Area (EEA). Nationals of EU (and EEA) countries have the right to work in France or any other member state without a work permit, providing they have a valid passport or national identity card and comply with the member state's laws and regulations on employment. EU nationals are entitled to the same treatment as French citizens in matters of pay, working conditions, access to housing, vocational training, social security and trade union rights, and their families and immediate dependants are entitled to join them and enjoy the same rights. The Single European Act, which came into effect on 1st January 1993, created a single market with a more favourable environment for stimulating enterprise, competition and trade, and made it easier for EU nationals to work in other EU countries.

There are still barriers to full freedom of movement and the right to work within the EU, for example many jobs in various member countries require applicants to have specific skills or vocational qualifications, and qualifications obtained in some member states aren't recognised in others. In most trades and professions, member states are required to recognise qualifications and experience obtained elsewhere in the EU (see **Qualifications** below). There are restrictions on employment in the civil service, when the right to work may be limited in individual cases on the grounds of public policy, security or public health.

QUALIFICATIONS

The most important qualification for working in France is the ability to speak French fluently (see page 42). Once you have overcome this hurdle you should establish whether your trade or professional qualifications and experience are recognised in France. If you aren't experienced, French employers expect studies to be in a relevant discipline and to have included work experience. Professional or trade qualifications are required to work in most fields in France and qualifications are also often necessary to work as self-employed or start a business. It isn't just a matter of hanging up a sign and waiting for the stampede of customers to your door. Many foreign artisans and traders are required to undergo a 'business' course before they can start work in France (see **Self-Employment** on page 35).

Theoretically, qualifications recognised by professional and trade bodies in one EU country should be recognised in France. However, recognition varies from country to country and in some cases foreign qualifications aren't recognised by French employers or professional and trade associations. All academic qualifications should also be recognised, although they may be given less prominence than equivalent French qualifications, depending on the country and the educational establishment. A ruling by the European Court in 1992 declared that where EU examinations are of a similar standard with just certain areas of difference, then individuals should be required to take exams only in those particular areas.

All EU member states issue occupation information sheets containing a common job description with a table of qualifications. These cover a large number of trades and are intended to help someone with the relevant qualifications look for a job in another EU country. You can obtain a direct comparison between any EU qualification and those recognised in France from the French branch of the National Academic Recognition Information Centre (NARIC). NARIC doesn't deal directly with individuals and contact must be made through an ANPE office (see below) in France. For information about equivalent professional qualifications in France you can contact the *Délégation à la Formation Professionnelle*, 31, quai de Grenelle, Immeuble Mercerie 1, 75015 Paris (☎ 01.45.78.45.40). In Britain, information can be obtained from the Comparability Co-ordinator, Employment Department, Qualifications and Standards Branch (QS1), Room E454, Moorfoot, Sheffield S1 4PQ, UK (☎ 0114-259 4144). See also **Language** on page 42)

GOVERNMENT EMPLOYMENT SERVICE

The French national employment service (*Agence Nationale Pour l'Emploi/ANPE*) operates some 600 offices throughout France, providing both local and national job listings (although around 75 per cent of jobs listed are temporary or 'CDD' short-term). Local jobs are advertised on a bulletin board and national listings through a Minitel (see page 125) service and a free weekly newspaper. Offices provide free Minitel terminals and telephones for calling prospective employers (not your mum!). The ANPE also provides a comprehensive career resource library including French company listings, trade publications and a wide range of reference books, plus an individual career counselling service and advice on job opportunities and prospects in certain fields. Counsellors can review and translate your *résumé*, provide information about the French job market, and assist you in evaluating your options and drawing up a job hunting strategy.

If you have a residence permit (*carte de séjour*), without which you may receive no help, a personal counsellor is assigned to your case. Other services available to residents include intensive career workshops, mock interviews (on videotape), psychological testing and French language tuition. For those wishing to start a business, special classes are provided that include writing a business plan, obtaining finance, grants, paperwork and legal requirements. All services are provided free of charge, although they must be approved by your counsellor.

ANPE services are available to all EU nationals and foreign residents in France. However (there's usually a 'however'), offices have a reputation for being unhelpful to foreign job seekers unless they have previously been employed in France or are unemployed and receiving unemployment benefit. Note that if you're officially registered as unemployed and have a residence permit (*carte de séjour*), you can obtain free French lessons (*perfectionnement de la langue Française*), although complete beginners don't qualify. Being a government department, ANPE isn't service-oriented and the quality of service varies depending on the region, office and the person handling your case.

Some ANPE offices specialise in certain fields and industries. For example in Paris there are offices dealing exclusively with hotel and restaurant services, tourism, journalism, public works, civil aviation and the entertainment industry. There's also a special Paris office for handicapped persons and some offices also recruit casual and temporary workers. The ANPE operate the *Association Pour l'Emploi des Cadres* (APEC), 51, bd Brune, 75689 Paris (☎ 01.40.52.20.00) for managers and engineers, and the *Association Pour l'Emploi des Cadres, Ingénieurs, Techniciens de l'Agriculture* (APECITA), 1 rue Cardinal-Merciel, 75009 Paris (☎ 01.44.53.20.20) for professionals in the agriculture industry. The ANPE publishes a free booklet, *Guide de la Recherche d'Emploi*, available from any office. Offices are listed under *Administration du Travail et de l'Emploi* in the Yellow Pages or *ANPE* in the white pages. A list of ANPE offices can be obtained from the ANPE head office, 53, rue Général Leclerc, 92136 Issy-les-Moulineaux (☎ 01.46.45.21.26).

'La Villete' is a careers resource centre at the Cité de Sciences et de l'Industrie, 75930 Paris (☎ 01.40.05.73.53) where you will find information on over 2,500 jobs, magazines and periodicals, mini-computers and staff to help with job applications.

There's also a European Employment Service (EURES) network, members of which include all EU countries. Member states exchange information on job vacancies on a regular basis and you can have your personal details circulated to the employment service in selected countries, e.g. to the ANPE in France. Details are available in local employment service offices in each member country, where advice on how to apply for jobs is provided. In Britain, you can contact the Employment Service, Overseas Placing Unit, Level 2, Rockingham House, 123 West Street, Sheffield S1 4ER, UK (☎ 0114-259 6051), who publish information about working in France.

RECRUITMENT AGENCIES

There are two main types of recruitment agencies in France, temporary agencies (*agence de travail temporaire/agence d'intérim*) and recruitment consultants/ executive search companies (*cabinets de recrutement/cabinets de chasseurs de têtes*).

Temporary Agencies: In addition to general temporary agencies dealing with a range of industries and professions, there are agencies specialising in particular fields such as accounting, banking, computer personnel, construction, engineering and technical staff, hotel and catering staff, industrial recruitment, insurance, nannies and nursing, sales, and secretarial and office staff. Temporary recruitment agencies are a huge growth industry in France, up 400 per cent since 1983, and France has the world's second largest market for temps. Manpower, Adecco (between them the biggest employers in the country with over 400,000 employees), Bis, Kelly and Plus are common in cities and large towns, and generally hire office staff and unskilled or semi-skilled labour. Most secretarial jobs are for bi-lingual or tri-lingual secretaries with word processing experience (an agency will usually test your written language and typing or word processing skills).

To be employed by a temporary agency, you must be legally eligible to work in France and have a social security number (see page 256). You need to register with most agencies, which entails completing a registration form and providing a CV and references (you can register with any number of agencies). Always ensure you know exactly how much, when and how you will be paid. Your salary should include a payment in lieu of holidays and a deduction for unemployment insurance. Because of the long annual holidays in France and generous maternity leave, companies often require temporary staff, and a temporary job can frequently be used as a stepping stone to a permanent position. Note that in France, private recruitment agencies can offer temporary work only. Look in the Yellow Pages under *Agences d'Intérim or Personnel Intérimaire.*

Executives: Executive recruitment and search companies are common in cities and large towns and have traditionally been used by large French companies to recruit staff, particularly executives, managers and professionals. Agents place advertisements in daily and weekly newspapers and trade magazines, but don't usually mention the client's name, not least to prevent applicants from approaching a company directly, thus depriving the agency of its fat fee. Recruitment agencies were hard hit by the recession in the '90s, particularly those dealing with executives and senior managers, and many French companies now do their own recruiting or promote in-house. Unless you're a particularly outstanding candidate with half a dozen degrees, are multilingual and have valuable experience, sending an unsolicited CV to an agent is usually a waste of time. There are also recruitment agencies in many countries specialising in recruiting executives, managers and professionals for employers in France.

SEASONAL JOBS

Seasonal jobs are available throughout the year in France, the vast majority in the tourist industry. Many seasonal jobs last for the duration of the summer or winter tourist seasons, May to September and December to April respectively, although some are simply casual or temporary jobs for a number of weeks. French fluency is required for all but the most menial and worst paid jobs, and is equally or more important than experience and qualifications (although fluent French alone won't guarantee you a well paid job). Seasonal jobs include most trades in hotels and restaurants; couriers and representatives; a variety of jobs in ski resorts; sports instructors; jobs in bars and clubs; fruit and grape picking and other agricultural jobs; and various jobs in the construction industry. Seasonal employees in the tourist industry have traditionally been paid below the minimum wage, although the authorities has clamped down on employers in recent years.

If you aren't an EU national, it's essential to check whether you will be eligible to work in France, before your arrival. You may also be required to obtain a visa (see page 64). Check with a French embassy or consulate in your home country well in advance of your visit. Foreign students in France can obtain a temporary work permit (*autorisation provisoire de travail*) for part-time work during the summer holiday period and school terms (see page 72).

Hotels & Catering: Hotels and restaurants are the largest employers of seasonal workers and jobs are available year round, from hotel managers to kitchen hands. Experience, qualifications and fluent French are required for all the best and highest paid positions, although a variety of jobs are available for the untrained and inexperienced. If accommodation with cooking facilities or full board isn't provided with a job, it can be expensive and difficult to find. Ensure that your salary is sufficient to pay for accommodation, food and other living expenses, and hopefully save some money (see **Cost of Living** on page 306).

The weekly trade magazine *L'Hôtellerie* (5, rue Antoine Bourdelle, 75737 Paris Cedex, ☎ 01.45.48.64.61) is a good source of hotel and catering vacancies, as are *L'Echo Turistique* (☎ 01.45.48.64.64) and *Le Quotidien du Tourisme* (☎ 01.40.34.22.07). Note that seasonal workers have few rights and little legal job protection in France and can generally be fired without compensation at any time. See also **Recruitment Agencies** on page 25 and **Temporary & Casual Work** on page 29.

Summer Jobs

There are numerous summer jobs in France, a number of which are described below:

Grape & Fruit Picking: One of the most popular summer jobs in France is grape picking (*vendange*). Goodness knows why, as it's boring, badly paid and involves hard physical work, although a surprising number of young people find it appealing. Occupational hazards include mosquito and other insect bites, cuts from secateurs, rashes on your arms and legs from chemical sprays, and incessant back pain from bending all day long. Accommodation and cooking facilities can be extremely primitive, and the cost of food and accommodation is usually deducted from your pay.

The grape harvest begins in the south of France in Languedoc-Roussillon in mid-September and moves up towards Alsace by the middle of October. If you're a masochist it's possible to move from area to area, particularly as growers recommend workers to each other. The best or only way to find work in a vineyard is to turn up and ask for a job (it's almost impossible to arrange employment from outside France). It isn't essential to speak French, but it certainly helps.

Fruit-picking jobs vary depending on the season and region and include strawberries (May to mid-June), peaches (June to September), cherries (mid-May to early June), pears (mid-July to mid-November) and apples (mid-August to mid-October). The harvest begins early in the south, so it's possible to start in May and work through until October (or even mid-November if you pick frozen grapes on Mont Ventoux), following the sun as it ripens the fruit. Note that fruit and grape picking is usually paid at below the national minimum wage (see page 22), so you shouldn't expect to get rich (but you should expect to get backache). Camping equipment comes in handy if you're fruit picking (other than grapes), as farmers often don't provide accommodation. Over 100,000 foreigners are employed on

French farms each summer, most of whom are 'professionals' from Morocco, Portugal and Spain who return to the same region each year. Information about farm work can be obtained from the *Service des Echanges et des Stages Agricoles dans le Monde/SESAME*, 9/11, square Gabriel Fauré, 75017 Paris (☎ 01.40.54.07.08).

Holiday Camps: There are many children's and youth holiday centres in France, where French (and many foreign) parents sensibly off-load their offspring during the long summer break from July to August. These offer many job opportunities for children-lovers (or those who can tolerate them in 'small' doses). Information about children's holiday centres is available from local *Administration/Directions Départementales de la Jeunesse et des Sport*, the addresses of which can be obtained from French embassies or from the Yellow Pages. You may also be able to obtain a job at Disneyland Paris or another theme park (see page 324).

One of the largest British recruiters of summer seasonal workers is PGL Young Adventure Ltd. (Alton Court, Penyard Lane, Ross-on-Wye HR9 5NR, UK, ☎ 01989-764211), who operate around ten activity centres in France and recruit some 1,000 staff for work from May to September. They offer a variety of jobs including couriers, group and entertainment organisers, chalet staff, sports instructors (particularly watersports), teachers, caterers and cooks, and various support staff. Applications should be made by March for the following summer season. Some companies, such as Club Méditerranée (25 av. Opéra, 75001 Paris, ☎ 01.42.96.01.29), operate both summer and winter holiday 'villages' throughout France for a period of around five months. Applicants should be aged between 20 and 30, fluent in French and at least one other language, and be reasonably good looking or attractive!

Language Teachers: Although not strictly a seasonal job, teaching is a good source of temporary or seasonal work (many language schools need extra teachers in summer). This may entail teaching English at a language school or privately, or even teaching French to expatriates if your French is up to the task. Language schools don't always require an English-language teaching qualification, and a university degree and a respectable appearance may suffice (although you should take as many educational certificates with you as possible). The British Council in Paris keeps a list of language schools for students, although they won't help you find work. The larger language schools such as Berlitz, usually pay the lowest wages. For more information obtain a copy of *Teaching English Abroad* by Susan Griffith (Vacation Work). You could also try placing advertisements in French newspapers and magazines offering private lessons. **However, you must be careful how you word your advertisement as many Frenchmen think that 'English lessons' implies something quite different** (see the cartoon on page 138). You can also apply directly to state schools for a position as a language *assistant(e)*. Note that full-time teachers in French state secondary schools and universities must be French citizens and possess French teaching qualifications.

Sources of Information: A good source of temporary or part-time work in France, particularly for students, is the *Centre d'Information et de Documentation Jeunesse (CIDJ)*, 101, quai Branly, 75740 Paris Cedex 15 (☎ 01.45.66.40.20). The *Centre d'Information Jeunesse Provence-Alpes*, 4, rue de la Visitation, 1324-8 Marseille Cedex 04, provides details of a wide variety of work in the south. Both of the above organisations must be visited in person, as they don't mail information. The *Centre de Documentation d'Information Rurale*, 92, rue du Dessous-des-Berges, 75013 Paris (☎ 01.45.83.51.68) helps French speakers find work, providing you're already in France. American students can apply to the Council on International Educational Exchange (CIEE), 1, place de l'Odéon, 75006 Paris (☎ 01.44.41.74.74).

Books: There are many books for those seeking holiday jobs including *Summer Jobs Abroad* by David Woodworth and *Work Your Way Around the World* by Susan Griffith (both published by Vacation Work). The Central Bureau for Educational Visits & Exchanges (c/o British Council, 10 Spring Gardens, London SW1A 2BN, ☎ 0171-389 4383) publishes a number of books for seasonal workers including *Home From Home, A Year Between, Teach Abroad* and *Working Holidays*, an annual guide to job opportunities in over 100 countries, including France. If you speak French you may be interested in *Emplois d'été en France* (Summer Jobs in France), which carries advertisements from farmers, co-operatives and others (published by VAC-JOB, 46, avenue René Coty, 75014 Paris, ☎ 01.43.20.70.51) and *1,000 Pistes de Jobs*, which although primarily a guide for the French is an excellent source of holiday jobs (available from *L'Étudiant*, 54, rue St. André des Arts, 75006 Paris).

Winter Jobs

A seasonal job in a French ski resort can be a lot of fun and very satisfying. You will get fit, improve your French, make some friends, and may even save some money. Note, however, that although a winter job may be a working holiday to you (with lots of skiing and little work), to your employer it means exactly the opposite! Ski resorts require an army of temporary workers to cater for the annual invasion of winter sports enthusiasts. Besides jobs in the hotel and restaurant trades already mentioned on page 27, a variety of other jobs are available including couriers, resort representatives, chalet girls, ski technicians, and ski instructors and guides. As a general rule, the better paid the job, the longer the working hours and the less time off there is for skiing. Employment in a winter resort usually entitles employees to a discounted ski-pass. An invaluable book for anyone looking for a job in a ski resort is *Working in Ski Resorts - Europe*, by Victoria Pybus & Charles James (Vacation Work).

TEMPORARY & CASUAL WORK

Temporary and casual work is usually for a fixed period, ranging from a few hours to a few months (or work may be intermittent). Casual workers are often employed on a daily, first-come, first-served basis. Anyone looking for casual unskilled work in France must usually compete with North Africans, who are usually prepared to work for less money than anyone else, although nobody *should* be paid less than the minimum wage (see page 22). Many employers illegally pay temporary staff in cash without making deductions for social security (see **Illegal Working** on page 41). However, legally, pay must be aligned with that of permanent workers and most temporary work found by agencies must have an 18-month renewal contract or in exceptional circumstances, 24 months. Temporary and casual work usually includes the following:

- Office work, which is well paid if you're qualified and the easiest work to find due to the large number of temporary secretarial and office staff agencies.

- Work in the building trade, which can be found by applying at building sites and through industrial recruitment agencies (such as Manpower).

- Jobs in shops and stores, which are often available over Christmas and during sales periods.
- Gardening jobs in private gardens (possibly working for a landscape gardener), public parks and garden centres, particularly in spring and summer.
- Peddling ice cream, cold drinks and fast food in summer, e.g. on beaches.
- Working as a deck-hand on a yacht on the French Riviera (e.g. Antibes or Cannes). You can earn over 1,000F a week (plus tips) as a deckhand.
- Market research, which entails asking people personal questions, either in the street or house to house (an ideal job for nosy parkers with fluent French).
- Modelling at art colleges; both sexes are usually required and not just the body beautiful.
- Work as a security guard (long hours for low pay).
- Nursing and auxiliary nursing in hospitals, clinics and nursing homes (temps are often employed through nursing agencies to replace permanent staff at short notice).
- Newspaper, magazine and leaflet distribution.
- Courier work (own transport required – motorcycle, car or van).
- Driving jobs, including coach and truck drivers, and ferrying cars for manufacturers and car hire companies.
- Miscellaneous jobs such as office cleaners, baby-sitters and labourers, are available from a number of agencies specialising in temporary work.

Temporary jobs are also advertised in ANPE offices (see page 24), on notice boards in expatriate clubs, churches and organisations, and in expatriate newsletters and newspapers. See also **Recruitment Consultants** on page 85 and **Seasonal Jobs** on page 26.

VOLUNTARY WORK

Voluntary work (as described here) is primarily to enable students and young people to visit France for a few weeks or months, and learn about the country and its people at first hand. The minimum age limit for volunteers is 16 to 18 and they must usually be under 30, although some organisations have no upper age limit. No special qualifications are required and the minimum length of service is usually a few weeks. Handicapped volunteers are welcomed by many organisations. Voluntary work is (naturally) unpaid and you must usually pay a registration fee that includes liability and health insurance, and your travel costs to and from France and to the workcamp. Although meals and accommodation are normally provided, you may be expected to contribute towards the cost of board and lodging. The usual visa regulations apply to voluntary workers and you will be informed when applying whether you need one. A work or residence permit isn't necessary.

Much voluntary work in France takes place in international workcamps that provide the opportunity for young people to live and work together on a range of projects including agriculture, archaeology, building, conservation, environmental, gardening, handicrafts, restoration of buildings and monuments, social welfare and community projects. Camps are usually run for two to four weeks between April and October, although some operate year round. Work is unskilled or semi-skilled and is for around five to eight hours a day, five or six days a week. The work is usually physically quite demanding and accommodation, shared with your fellow slaves, is fairly basic. Most workcamps consist of volunteers from several countries and English may be the common language. There are around ten associations in France sponsoring voluntary work programmes (*chantiers de jeunes volontaires bénévoles*) under the administration of Cotravaux, 11, rue de Clichy, 75009 Paris (☎ 01. 48.74.79.20). Many French voluntary organisations are also listed in *Working Holidays* published by the Central Bureau (see page 29), who also publish *Volunteer Work*.

In addition to workcamps there are a variety of unpaid voluntary jobs in France, particularly in Paris and other cities. Voluntary work is an excellent way to improve your French and gain valuable work experience, and may even be an *entrée* to a permanent salaried job. Whatever your motive, whether it's a desire to make new friends, boredom, or a stepping stone to a new career, voluntary work is highly rewarding. Whenever you find yourself wondering what to do with yourself, contact local expatriate organisations – they'll put those idle hands to work!

JOB HUNTING

When looking for a job (or a new job) in France it's best not to put all your eggs in one basket – the more job applications you make, the better your chances of finding the right (or any) job. Contact as many prospective employers as possible, either by writing, telephoning or calling on them in person. Whatever job you're looking for, it's important to market yourself correctly and appropriately, which depends on the type of job or position you're seeking. For example, the recruitment of executives and senior managers is handled almost exclusively by recruitment consultants who advertise in the French 'national' press and trade magazines. At the other end of the scale, manual jobs requiring no previous experience may be advertised at ANPE employment offices, in local newspapers and on notice boards, and the first suitable applicant may be offered the job on the spot. Job hunting includes the following resources:

Newspapers: Obtain copies of Parisian and regional newspapers, all of which have positions vacant (*offres d'emploi*) sections on certain days. The most popular Parisian newspapers for job advertisements are *Le Monde, Le Figaro, France-Soir, Libération, Le Parisien* and *Les Echos* (the daily financial and stock exchange journal). The best newspapers depend on the sort of job you're seeking. If you're looking for a management or professional position you should obtain copies of *Le Monde, Le Figaro, Libération* and *Les Echos*. *Le Figaro* provides a separate publication, *Carrières & Emplois*, on Wednesdays. Professional and executive vacancies are also advertised in the weekly publication *Courrier Cadre* (8, rue Duret, 75783 Paris).

Those seeking employment as technicians, artisans, secretaries, sales clerks, factory workers and manual labourers should try *France-Soir* and *Le Parisien*. *Libération* is a mixture with ads. in all job categories. In addition to the above, there are many important regional newspapers in France, e.g. *Sud-Ouest* and *Ouest-France*. There are also a number of newspapers and magazines devoted to careers and jobs such as *Carrières et Emplois* (which publishes regional issues), *Entreprise et Carrières* and *Rebondir* (who also publish many books for job-seekers).

Most professions and trade associations publish journals containing job offers (see *Benn's Media Directory Europe*). Jobs are also advertised in various English-language publications including the *International Herald Tribune, Wall Street Journal Europe, Paris Free Voice*, and *France-USA Contacts* (fortnightly). You can also place an advertisement in 'employment wanted' (*demandes d'emplois*) columns in most publications. It's best to place an advert in the middle of the week and avoid the summer and other holiday periods. Minitel (see page 125) maintains a job vacancies database and can also be used to advertise your services.

When writing for jobs, address your letter to the personnel director or manager (*Chef de Service du Personnel*) and include your curriculum vitae (in French), and copies of references and qualifications. If possible, offer to attend an interview and tell them when you will be available. Letters should be tailored to individual employers and professionally translated if your French isn't perfect. Note that some 90 per cent of French companies require hand-written letters from job applicants and submit them to graphologists (employers also use astrology, numerology and even wilder methods of selecting staff!).

Employment Offices: Visit local ANPE offices in France (see page 24). Jobs on offer are mainly non-professional skilled, semi-skilled and unskilled jobs, particularly in industry, retailing and catering.

Recruitment Agencies: Apply to international recruitment agencies acting for French companies. These companies chiefly recruit executives and key personnel, and many have offices worldwide including in many French cities. Contact recruitment agencies in France (see page 25). Note that many French agencies will find positions only for French and EU nationals or foreigners with a residence permit (*carte de séjour*).

Internet: The Internet has hundreds of sites for job-seekers including corporate websites, recruitment companies and newspaper job advertisements (you can use a search engine to find them).

International Organisations: Apply to international organisations with offices in France. The largest organisations in France include the Organisation for Economic Co-operation and Development (OECD), the United Nations Education, Science and Cultural Organisation (UNESCO), the World Bank, the International Monetary Fund and the International Labour Office, all located in Paris. The ability to speak French may not be of paramount importance to work for an international organisation. If you're an EU national there are a variety of jobs connected with EU bodies including the Council of Europe, the European Court of Human Rights and the European Parliament (all located in Strasbourg).

Unsolicited Job Applications: Apply to American, British and other multinational companies with offices or subsidiaries in France, and make written applications direct to French companies. Useful addresses can usually be obtained from local chambers of commerce and other organisations. A list of French companies can be obtained from the *Chambre de Commerce et d'Industrie de Paris*, 27, avenue Friedland, 75008 Paris (☎ 01.42.89.70.00). The chamber will provide a list of French companies in a particular field or industry. French companies are listed by products, services and *départements* in *Kompass France*, available at libraries in France and main libraries and French chambers of commerce abroad.

Making unsolicited job applications (*candidature spontanée*) to targeted companies is naturally a hit and miss affair. It can, however, be more successful than responding to advertisements, as you aren't usually competing with other applicants. Some companies recruit a large percentage of employees through unsolicited *résumés*. When writing from abroad, enclosing an international reply coupon may help elicit a response.

Networking: Networking (which originated in the USA) is basically making business and professional contacts. It's particularly useful in France, where people use personal contacts for everything from looking for jobs to finding accommodation. It's difficult for most foreigners to make contacts among the French and therefore many turn to the expatriate community, particularly in Paris. If you're already in France, contact or join expatriate social clubs, churches, societies and professional organisations. A useful resource for English speakers seeking contacts in Paris is *Paris Anglophone* (Frank Books), containing over 2,000 listings. Finally don't forget to ask friends and acquaintances working in France if they know of an employer seeking someone with your experience and qualifications.

WORKING WOMEN

The number of working women in France has increased dramatically in recent years and some 45 per cent of French women (the vast majority under 40) now work full or part-time, representing around 40 per cent of the workforce. Three-quarters of women are employed in distribution and transport, nursing and health care, education, secretarial professions, and service industries such as retailing. More surprisingly, over a quarter of France's 2½ million businesses are run by women, by far the highest in Europe.

French women aren't noted feminists and most are happily subservient to men (overbearing and assertive women are treated with disdain by most Frenchmen). Most aren't ambitious and few are career women. French women didn't receive the vote until 1945 and it wasn't until the '70s that inequalities concerning divorce, employment and property ownership were eradicated. French women are more interested in equal rights in the workplace and rights for pregnant women (such as paid maternity leave) and mothers (e.g. state-run nurseries), than the opportunity to reach the top. French employers are often reluctant to hire women in responsible positions if they think they're planning a family, not least because they must provide generous paid maternity leave.

A woman doing the same or broadly similar work to a man and employed by the same employer is legally entitled to the same salary and other terms of employment. However, despite the Equal Pay Act of 1972, women's salaries are an average of 20 per cent lower than men's. This largely reflects the fact that most women work in lower paid industries and hold lower paid positions than men, rather than discrimination. Nevertheless, although there's no official discrimination, in practice it's often not the case. The fact that 'the best man for the job is often a woman', isn't often acknowledged by French employers, and women must generally be twice as qualified as a man to compete on equal terms. Some 15 per cent of women earn the minimum wage (see page 22) and few belong to trade unions. However, the situation has improved considerably in recent years and women are much less exploited in France than in many other western European countries.

France has traditionally been a minefield for career women and few women are found in senior management positions. The 1983 law on professional equality (*loi Roudy sur l'égalité professionelle*) made it easier for women to break into male-dominated trades and professions. However, women still find it difficult to attain management positions, particularly in technical and industrial fields, where there has long been a tradition of prejudice against them. Women have had some success in reaching the top in the professions and in finance, insurance, the media, personnel, advertising and retailing. Companies with over 300 employees must produce an annual report comparing the positions of male and female employees, which is used to chart the career progress of women compared with their male colleagues. Career women are generally more accepted and taken more seriously in Paris, which has a more progressive outlook than the provinces (particularly the south, where opinions and attitudes lag behind the north).

Male chauvinism is alive and well and thriving in France, where women employees face the additional hazard of sexual harassment. Sexual advances from men are common and flirting is an accepted part of French life and isn't to be taken too seriously (a Frenchman's flirting shouldn't be confused with sexual harassment). If it's any consolation, refusing a sexual advance from your boss rarely results in you losing your job in France as it's difficult to fire employees.

SALARIES

It's often difficult to determine the salary you should command in France, as salaries aren't often quoted in job advertisements, except in the public sector where employees are paid according to fixed grades and salaries are public knowledge. Salaries may vary considerably for the same job in different parts of France. Those working in Paris and its environs are generally the highest paid, primarily because of the high cost of living, particularly accommodation.

If you're able to negotiate your own salary you should ensure that you receive the salary and benefits commensurate with your qualifications and experience (or as much as you can get!). If you have friends or acquaintances working in France or who have worked there, ask them what an average or good salary is for your particular trade or profession. When comparing salaries you must take into account compulsory deductions such as tax and social security, and also compare the cost of living (see page 306). French salaries compare favourably with other western countries and are among the highest in Europe. Note, however, that in recent years university graduates and school-leavers have been willing to accept almost any wage in order to get on the career ladder.

There has been a statutory minimum wage in France since 1950 (see page 22). The cost of living index is reviewed annually and when it rises by 2 per cent or more the minimum wage is increased. Unskilled workers (particularly women) are usually employed at or near the minimum wage, semi-skilled workers are usually paid 10 to 20 per cent more, and skilled workers 30 to 40 per cent more (often shown in job advertisements as SMIC + 10, 20, 30, 40 per cent). Most employees in France receive an extra month's salary at Christmas, known as the 13th month's salary, and some companies also pay a 14th month's salary prior to the summer holiday period.

Salaries in many industries are decided by collective bargaining between employers and unions, either regionally or nationally. When there's a collective agreement, employers must offer at least the minimum wage agreed, although they are exceeded by most major companies. Agreements specify minimum wage levels for each position within main employment categories in a particular industry or company. This means that wage levels are effectively fixed, although it also ensures that they keep pace with inflation.

The average gross monthly salary on 1ˢᵗ April 1998 was 12,300F (9,200F for an unskilled worker and 24,200F for a manager). Typical middle management salaries range from 12,000F to 40,000F per month. French salaries are similar to those in Germany and some 25 to 50 per cent higher than in Britain. Salaries are around the same or slightly lower than in the USA, except for senior management staff, where French salaries tend to be higher (with the exception of CEOs, who are grossly overpaid in the USA). A foreign executive may find that his salary is much higher in France. French executive salaries were lower than the international average in the '70s and early '80s, but have since caught up and even surpassed some of their competitors. Executive salaries rose much faster than the rate of inflation in the '80s and were augmented by lucrative bonuses and profit-sharing schemes.

For many employees, particularly executives and senior managers, their remuneration is much more than what they receive in their monthly pay packets. Many companies offer a range of benefits for executives and managers that may include a company car (although rare in France); private health insurance and health screening; expenses-paid holidays; private school fees; inexpensive or interest-free home and other loans; rent-free accommodation; free or subsidised public transport tickets; free or subsidised company restaurant; sports or country club membership; non-contributory company pension; stock options; bonuses and profit-sharing schemes; tickets for sports events and shows; and 'business' conferences in exotic places (see also **Executive Positions** on page 49).

SELF-EMPLOYMENT

If you're an EU-national or a permanent resident with a *carte de séjour/résident* (see page 67), you can work as self-employed (*travailleur indépendant*) or as a sole trader (*entreprise individuelle*) in France. If you want to work as self-employed in a profession or start a freelance business in France, you must meet certain legal requirements and register with the appropriate organisations, e.g. the *Chambre des Métiers*, the *Registre de Commerce* and social security (*URSSAF*), within 15 days of starting a business.

Under French law a self-employed person must have an official status and it's illegal simply to hang up a sign and start business. Members of some professions and trades must have certain qualifications (see page 24) and certificates recognised in France, and all are required to attend a business administration course (see **Self-Employment** on page 35). Don't be in too much of a hurry to register, as from the date of registration (when you receive your SIRET number) you must pay hefty social security, pension and health insurance payments, and are also liable for income tax and VAT. **However, you should <u>never</u> be tempted to start work before you're registered as there are harsh penalties that may include a large fine (e.g. 100,000F), confiscation of machinery or tools, and even deportation and a three-year ban from entering France.**

As a self-employed person you don't have the protection of a limited company should your business fail and there are few tax advantages (except for a business classified as a *petit commerçant* with a limited turnover). It may be advantageous to operate as a limited company, for example an *Entreprise Unipersonnelle à Responsabilitée Limitée (EURL)*. An EURL is a one-person limited company that allows a self-employed person to be taxed at a more favourable rate. Note that while an EURL protects your personal assets from your creditors, they may ask for a personal guarantee, thus negating this advantage. Always obtain professional advice before deciding whether to operate as a sole trader or form a company in France, as it has far-reaching social security, tax and other consequences. Most new businesses enjoy a tax exemption for the first two years of trading, including sole traders, whose business and personal income are combined by the tax authorities. This means that as a sole trader you're unlikely to pay any income tax during your first two years in business. After the first two years, businesses are granted a tax exemption (*exonération*) of a percentage of their turnover.

There are, however, many drawbacks to being self-employed in France, which may outweigh any advantages. Social security contributions (see page 258) for the self-employed are much higher than for salaried employees and they receive fewer benefits, e.g. doctors' bills are reimbursed at 50 per cent, not the 75 per cent paid to salaried employees. As a self-employed person in France you aren't entitled to unemployment benefit should your business fail and there are no benefits for accidents at work (except for artisans), although you're insured against invalidity. It's advisable to join a professional association as they provide valuable information and assistance and may also offer insurance discounts. One such organisation is the *Confédération pour la Défense des Commerçants et Artisans/CDCA* (Le Capoulie, 6, rue Maguelone, 34000 Montpellier, ☎ 04.67.58.24.90), which was formed to fight for better rights for the self-employed and small businessmen. (In recent years CDCA has encouraged small businesses to register abroad, e.g. in Britain, in order to save taxes.)

STARTING A BUSINESS

The bureaucracy associated with starting a business (*fonds de commerce*) in France is frightening and rates among the most pernicious in the world. France is a red tape jungle and civil servants (*fonctionnaires*) can be inordinately obstructive (endlessly recycling bits of paper to create 'employment' for themselves). For foreigners the red tape is almost impenetrable, especially if you don't speak French, as you will be inundated with official documents and must be able to understand them. It's only when you come up against the full force of French bureaucracy that you understand what it *really* means to be a foreigner! However, despite the red tape, France is traditionally a country of small companies and individual traders, where the economic philosophy actually encourages and even nurtures the creation of small businesses.

Before undertaking any business transactions in France, it's important to obtain legal advice to ensure that you're operating within the law. There are severe penalties for anyone who ignores the regulations and legal requirements. It's also important to obtain legal advice before establishing a limited business in France. All businesses must register for value added tax and there's no threshold below which you don't need to register. Non-EU nationals require a special licence (*carte commerçante étranger*) to start a business in France and no commitments should be made until permission has been granted. Among the best sources of help and information are your local chamber of commerce and town hall (*mairie*).

Generally speaking you shouldn't consider running a business in France in a field in which you don't have previous experience (excluding 'businesses' such as bed and breakfast or *gîtes*, where experience isn't necessary). It's often advisable to work for someone else in the same line of business in order to gain experience, rather than jump in at the deep end. Always thoroughly investigate an existing or proposed business before investing any money. **As any expert can tell you, France isn't a country for amateur entrepreneurs, particularly amateurs who don't speak fluent French!** Many small businesses in France exist on a shoe string and certainly aren't what would be considered thriving enterprises. As in most countries, people are usually self-employed for the lifestyle and freedom it affords (no clocks or bosses!), rather than the financial rewards. It's important to keep your plans small and manageable and work well within your budget, rather than undertaking some grandiose scheme.

A useful guide for anyone starting a business in France is *Setting up a Small Business in France* published by the French Chamber of Commerce, 197 Knightsbridge, London SW7 1RB, UK (☎ 0171-304-4040). International accountants such as Price Waterhouse have offices throughout France and are an invaluable source of information (in English) on subjects such as forming a company, company law, taxation and social security. Many countries maintain chambers of commerce in France that are an invaluable source of information and assistance. The British Business Centre (BP 21, 14700 Falaise, ☎ 02.31.40.05.77) can also help you buy or establish a business in France. You can also enlist the services of a *Centre de Gestion*, a group of accountants, bookkeepers and administrative staff who specialise in assisting and establishing small businesses and providing financial services. See also **Self-Employment** on page 35.

Buying an Existing Business

It's much easier to buy an existing business in France than start a new one and it's also less of a risk. The paperwork for taking over an existing business is also simpler, although still complex. Note, however, that buying a business that's a going concern is difficult as the French aren't in a habit of selling businesses, which are usually passed down from generation to generation.

If you plan to buy a business, obtain an independent valuation (or two). Never sign anything you don't understand 110 per cent and even if you think you understand it, you should obtain professional advice. Always obtain unbiased professional advice, e.g. from local experts such as banks and accountants, before buying a business in France. In fact it's best not to start a business until you have the infrastructure established including an accountant, lawyer and banking facilities. There are various ways to set up a small business and it's essential to obtain professional advice regarding the best method of establishing and registering a business in France, which can dramatically affect your tax position. It's important to employ an accountant (*expert comptable*) to do your books, although you shouldn't expect him to be interested in reducing your social security charges and should question costs that appear to be too high.

When buying a business in France, there are often separate prices for the business or 'goodwill' (*Fonds* or *Fonds de Commerce*) and the building or 'walls' (literally *murs*), e.g. the building housing a hotel or restaurant. If you don't buy the building, a separate rental contract (lease) must be negotiated. If possible, it's best to purchase a business with the building, particularly if you need to raise a loan. You can obtain a mortgage of up to 80 per cent on the bricks and mortar, but you must fund the goodwill yourself. The notary's (*notaire's*) fees when buying a business property are usually around 20 per cent of the purchase price. Note that the protection afforded domestic tenants doesn't extend to business rentals. Therefore if you rent business premises it's essential to take legal advice regarding a lease, which *must* contain a right to rent clause to ensure the future value of the business.

Taking over the assets of a company such as the stock, the client list, business name, premises (etc.) can also be expensive with regard to taxes. Registration duty (around 15 per cent) is payable on the transfer of most of the elements of the *fonds de commerce* such as the immovable property, leasehold rights, furniture, fittings and equipment, business name, client list and licences. Stock is subject to 20.6 per cent VAT. Note that the authorities can reassess the value of the *fonds de commerce* if they consider that they have been undervalued and also impose fines. When taking over an existing and operating company, French labour law compels new owners to respect existing employment contracts (which isn't a bad thing if you require help as experienced staff are priceless). However, you aren't compelled to employ them if you cannot afford it.

You can contact local estate agents and *notaires* for details of businesses for sale in a particular area. The *Centrale Immobilière des Commerçants et des Entreprises* (CICE, Centre de l'Horloge, 49000 Angers, ☎ 02.41.48.56.56) publish a comprehensive magazine listing hundreds of business opportunities throughout France and the National Agency for the Setting up of Companies (*Agence Nationale pour la Création d'Entreprise/ANCE*, 142, rue du Bac, 75007 Paris) publishes a bimonthly bulletin, listing business opportunities. Local and regional chambers of commerce in France are excellent sources of information and operate a regional network called *Bureaux de Rapprochement d'Entreprise (BRE)* to bring together sellers and prospective buyers. They also publish newsletters listing the various opportunities. Businesses are also advertised for sale in many French newspapers and magazines.

Starting a New Business

Most people are far too optimistic about the prospects for a new business in France and over-estimate income levels (it often takes years to make a profit). Be realistic or even pessimistic when estimating your income and overestimate the costs and underestimate the revenue (then reduce it by 50 per cent!). While hoping for the best, you should plan for the worst and have sufficient funds to last until you're established (under-funding is the major cause of business failures). New projects are rarely if ever completed within budget and you need to ensure that you have sufficient working capital and can survive until a business takes off. French banks are extremely wary of lending to new businesses, especially businesses run by foreigners (would you trust a foreigner?). If you wish to borrow money to buy property or for a business venture in France, you should carefully consider where and in what currency to raise finance.

Location: Choosing the location for a business is even more important than the location for a home. Depending on the type of business, you may need access to *autoroutes* and rail links, or to be located in a popular tourist area or near local attractions. Local plans regarding communications, industry and major building developments, e.g. housing complexes and new shopping centres, may also be important. Plans regarding new *autoroutes* and rail links are normally available from local town halls.

Employees: Hiring employees shouldn't be taken lightly in France and must be taken into account *before* starting a business. You must enter into a contract under French labour law and employees enjoy extensive rights. It's also *very* expensive to hire employees, as in addition to salaries you must pay an additional around 50 per cent in social security contributions, a 13th month's salary and five weeks paid annual holiday (see **Social Security** on page 254 and **Chapter 2**). However, there are tax holidays for limited periods for newly formed companies, particularly regarding the first employee. During their first two years' trading, most new businesses enjoy a tax exemption and are required to pay only around 10 per cent of their first employee's wages in social security contributions.

Type of Business: The most common businesses operated by foreigners in France include holiday accommodation (e.g. bed & breakfast, *gîtes*, *chambres d'hôte*, chalets, apartments and cottages); caravan and camping sites; building and allied trades; farming (e.g. dairy, vineyards, fruit, fish, fowl); catering (e.g. bars, cafés and restaurants); hotels; shops; franchises; estate agencies; translation bureaux; language schools; landscape gardening; and holiday and sports centres (e.g. tennis, golf, squash, shooting and horse-riding schools). The majority of businesses established by foreigners are linked to the leisure and catering industries, followed by property investment and development.

Companies: Companies cannot be purchased 'off the shelf' in France and it usually takes a number of months to establish a company. Incorporating a company in France takes longer and is more expensive and more complicated than in most other European countries (those bureaucrats again!). There are around 13 different types of 'limited companies' or business entities in France and choosing the right one can be difficult. Companies in France are either trading (*Société Commerciale*) or non-trading (*Société Civile*) companies. **You must never use a non-trading company to trade.**

The most common form of company created by foreigners in France is a SARL (*Société à Responsabilité Limitée*), a private limited company with a minimum share capital of 50,000F (part of which can be fixed assets) and at least two shareholders and a maximum of 50. Another common type of company is an SCI (*Société Civile Immobilière*), which is a property holding company. Note, however, that if you form a French company (e.g. a SARL) and pay yourself as an employee, you must pay an additional 60 per cent in social security contributions. **Always obtain professional legal advice regarding the advantages and disadvantages of different limited companies.**

Information: The interdepartmental economic agency (*Délégation à l'Aménagement du Territoire et à l'Action Régionale/DATAR*) is the major French government organisation concerned with attracting overseas investment and business ventures. DATAR provides comprehensive information about all aspects of doing business in France. It also implements the French government's policy of providing grants and investment incentives for certain businesses, particularly those located in depressed and under-developed areas. DATAR operates abroad as Invest in France (IFA) and has offices in Belgium, Britain, Germany, Italy, the Netherlands, Spain, Switzerland, the USA (4 offices) and in various Asian countries. Their head office is IFA, c/o DATAR, 1, avenue Charles Floquet, 75007 Paris (☎ 01.40.65.12.34).

Grants: There are over 250 different grants and incentives available for new businesses in France, particularly in rural areas. Grants include EU subsidies, central government grants, regional development grants, redeployment grants, and grants from departments and local communities. Grants include assistance to buy buildings and equipment (or the provision of low-cost business premises), subsidies for job creation, and tax incentives. In areas designated as 'enterprise zones', new businesses may be exempt from corporation tax for up to ten years. Contact IFA (see above) and departmental and communal authorities for information about grants.

AU PAIRS

Single males and females aged between 18 and 27 are eligible for a position as an au pair, officially called a family help (*stagiaire aide-familiale*) in France. The au pair system provides an excellent opportunity to travel, improve your French, and generally broaden your education by living and working in France. The main aim of the au pair system is to give young people the opportunity to learn a foreign language in a typical family environment. Au pairs are accepted from most countries. If you're an EU national you need only a valid passport and aren't required to arrange a position before arriving in France, although it's usually advisable. Some agencies allow you to meet families in France before making a final decision, which is highly desirable as you can interrogate the family, inspect their home and your accommodation, and meet the children who will make your life heaven or hell! However, applicants from non-EU countries need a long-stay visa (see page 64) and require an agreement (*déclaration d'engagement*) with a French family and a certificate of registration for French classes at a language school. These must be presented to your local French embassy or consulate with your passport when applying for a visa (see **Au Pairs** on page 73).

Au pairs are usually contracted to work for a minimum of six and a maximum of 18 months. Most families require an au pair for at least the whole school year, from September to June. The best time to look for an au pair position is therefore before the beginning of the school year in September. You should apply as early as possible and not later than one month prior to your preferred start date or at least two months if you need a visa. There are also summer au pair programmes of one to three months between June 15th and September 15th. Enrolment must usually be made before 31st March. Au pairs employed for the summer only aren't required to attend French lessons.

Au pairs are usually placed in French-speaking families with children, although non French-speaking families without children can also engage an au pair. An au pair's duties consist of *light* housework including simple cooking for children; clothes washing (with a machine) and ironing; washing and drying dishes (if the family doesn't have a dishwasher); making beds; dusting; vacuum cleaning; and other light jobs around the home. To enjoy life as an au pair you should be used to helping around the house and like working with children. An au pair isn't a general servant or cook (*although you may be treated as one*) and you aren't expected to look after physically or mentally handicapped children. As an au pair, you receive all meals and accommodation, usually with a study area, in lieu of a salary. Working hours are officially limited to 30 a week, five hours a day (morning or afternoon), six days a week, plus a maximum of three evenings' baby-sitting. You should be given time off to attend French classes and religious services. In some families, au pairs holiday with the family or are free to take Christmas or Easter holidays at home. Choose a wealthy family and you may be taken on exotic foreign holidays (although they may be less likely to treat you as a family member)!

For your labours you're paid the princely (princessly?) sum of around 1,500F per month 'pocket money'. You're required to pay your own fare from your country to Paris (and back). If you're employed in the provinces, your family will pay the rail fare from Paris to their home and back to Paris at the end of your stay. In Paris, a family may provide a *carte orange*, a monthly public transport pass for the Paris *métro*, buses and suburban trains.

An au pair position can be arranged privately with a family or through an agency. There are au pair agencies in France and many other countries and positions can also be found via magazines (such as the British *The Lady* magazine) and newspapers, but you're usually better off going through an agency. The better agencies vet families, make periodic checks on your welfare, help you overcome problems (either personal or with your family), and may organise cultural activities (particularly in Paris). An agency will send you an application form (questionnaire) and usually ask you to provide character (moral) and child-care references, a medical certificate and school references. Au pairs must usually have had a high school education or the equivalent, have a good knowledge of French and *must* attend French classes (see page 165) organised for foreign students. Agency registration fees vary, although there are maximum fees in some countries, e.g. around £50 in Britain.

Your experience as an au pair will depend entirely on your relationship with your family. If you're fortunate enough to work for a warm and friendly host family, you will have a wonderful experience, lots of free time and possibly some memorable holidays. Many au pairs grow to love their children and families and form lifelong friendships. On the other hand, abuses of the au pair system are common in all countries and you may be treated as a servant rather than a member of the family, and be expected to work long hours and spend most evenings baby-sitting. Many families engage an au pair simply because it costs far less than employing a nanny. If you have any complaints about your duties, you should refer them to the agency that found you your position (if applicable). **There are many families to choose from and you shouldn't feel that you need to remain with a family that treats you badly.** You're usually required to give notice if you wish to go home before the end of your agreement, although this won't apply if the family has broken the contract.

Prospective au pairs should contact a number of agencies and compare registration fees and pocket money, both of which may vary considerably (although the terms of employment should be the same). Pocket money is usually higher in Paris than in the provinces. Many British agencies are listed in the *Au Pair and Nanny's Guide to Working Abroad* by Susan Griffith (Vacation Work). Note that it's possible for responsible French-speaking young women without experience or training to obtain employment as a nanny in France. Duties are basically the same as an au pair, although a position as a nanny is a proper job with full employee rights and a real salary!

ILLEGAL WORKING

Illegal working (*travail au noir* or *travail clandestin*) thrives in France, particularly among sections of the expatriate community and immigrants from North Africa. It has been conservatively estimated that the loss of tax revenue due to the 'black' or 'underground' economy (*l'économie souterraine*) totals around 30 billion francs a year, with up to a million people regularly working illegally. It's estimated that some 30 per cent of all work in France isn't declared to the tax authorities! Many unscrupulous employers use illegal labour in order to pay low wages (below the minimum wage) for long hours and poor working conditions. Abuse is common in industries that traditionally employ casual labour such as building, farming, service and textile industries. Another aspect of illegal working is avoiding payment of value added tax (TVA) of 20.6 per cent.

In recent years there has been a clamp down on black labour with greater powers given to the police, gendarmerie, courts and work inspectors (*inspecteurs de travail*), and increased penalties. Illegal working is punishable by up to two years in prison and fines of between 2,000F and 200,000F (which are doubled for a second offence). If you employ someone who's an illegal immigrant, you can be fined 3,000F to 30,000F and can be imprisoned for up to three years.

It's strictly illegal for non-EU nationals to work in France without a work permit. Note that if you use illegal labour or avoid paying VAT (TVA), you will have no official redress if goods or services are substandard. If you work illegally you have no entitlement to social security benefits such as insurance against work injuries, public health care, unemployment pay and a state pension.

LANGUAGE

Although English is the *lingua franca* of international commerce and may help you secure a job in France, the most important qualification for anyone seeking employment is the ability to speak fluent French. While it's a myth that the French don't speak English (most French children learn English at school and the majority of educated Frenchmen speak English), many Frenchmen have an irrational fear of feeling foolish and are reluctant to speak English. The French are also extremely proud (or arrogant) where their language is concerned and quite rightly expect anyone living or working in France to speak it.

If you don't already speak good French, don't expect to learn it quickly, even if you already have a basic knowledge and take intensive lessons. It's common for foreigners not to be fluent after a year or more of intensive lessons in France. If your expectations are unrealistic you will become frustrated, which can affect your confidence. It takes a long time to reach the level of fluency needed to be able to work in French and understand the various accents. If you don't speak French fluently, you should begin French lessons on arrival in France and consider taking a menial or even an unpaid voluntary job, as this is one of the quickest ways of improving your French.

If necessary you should have French lessons before arriving in France. A sound knowledge of French won't only help you find a job or perform your job better, but makes everyday life much simpler and more enjoyable. If you come to France without being able to speak French you will be excluded from everyday life and will feel uncomfortable until you can understand what's going on around you. The most common reason for negative experiences among foreigners in France, both visitors and residents alike, is because they cannot or won't speak French. However terrible your French, your bad grammar, poor vocabulary and terrible accent will be much better appreciated than your fluent English. Don't, however, be surprised when the

French wince at your torture of their beloved tongue! You *must* learn French if you wish to have French friends.

When doing business in France or writing letters to French businesses, communications should always be in French. Many Frenchmen have a phobia about writing letters (most are unable to write grammatically correct French) and postpone replying to letters for as long as possible. However, if you write a letter to a French company applying for a job you should ensure that it's grammatically correct, even if it means employing a professional translator. A book that explains precisely how to write letters in French is the *Handbook of Commercial French* (Routledge).

When stating your French language ability, it's important not to exaggerate as it's easy to confirm. If you state that your French is very good or fluent, you will almost certainly be interviewed in French (which is also possible even if you have only a little knowledge). Overstating your fluency is just a waste of your and a prospective employer's time. Your language ability in French and other languages must be listed on your *résumé* and the level of proficiency stated as follows: some knowledge (*notions*), good (*bien*), very good (*très bien*), excellent or speak, read and write (*parle, lis, écris*), fluent (*courant*) and mother tongue (*langue maternelle*).

Many Frenchmen are horrified at the cultural colonialism of France by America (American TV, Coke, McDonalds, Disneyland Paris, et al), although the young eagerly embrace everything American including the language. There has long been a campaign by the (often pedantic) traditionalists to keep French pure and unadulterated by English words and expressions (*franglais*). The *Académie Française* (established in the 17th century) aided and abetted by the *Société pour la Défense de la langue Française*, the *Comité Consultatif de la Langue Française* and the *Commissariat Général de la langue Française*, are dedicated to maintaining the purity of the French language.

Together they battle to keep the French language free of foreign adulterations and defilement. The *Académie Française* (with just 40 elected members) controls the national dictionary and votes on whether to accept foreign words (usually English), and invariably invents new French words to replace foreign words such as *stationnement* (parking), *bande video promotionelle* (video-clip) and *stylique* (design). Nevertheless some foreign words are permitted, e.g. bulldozer, cowboy, drugstore and dead-beat. However, new French words are often ignored by the French, particularly the young, who delight in speaking *franglais* and slang (*argot*).

In the last few years the French government has been ridiculed by the media with its attempt (the Taubon law) to enforce the use of French and ban the use of foreign languages or *franglais* in official communication (e.g. business, government and the media). However, the plan was neutered in 1994 when the Constitutional Council ruled that the choice of language couldn't be forced on citizens. The French government is trying to stem the global hegemony of English by encouraging French students to learn other foreign languages.

France also has a number of regional languages including Alsatian (spoken in Alsace), Basque (Pyrénées), Breton (Brittany), Catalan (Roussillon), Corsican (Corsica), Flemish (Flanders) and Occitan (Languedoc), which are taught as optional subjects in some schools. Note that however fluent your French, you will still have problems understanding some accents and local dialects (*patois*). See also **Language** on page 144 and **Language Schools** on page 165.

2.
WORKING CONDITIONS

Working conditions in France are largely dependent on the French labour code (*code du travail*), collective agreements (*conventions collectives de travail*), an employee's individual employment contract (*contrat de travail*) and the employer's in-house regulations (*règlements intérieurs/règlements de travail*). Salaried foreigners are employed under the same working conditions as French citizens, although there are different rules for certain categories of employees, e.g. directors, managers and factory workers. As in many countries, seasonal and temporary workers aren't protected by employment laws and have few legal rights. However, part-time employees receive the same rights and benefits (on a pro rata basis) as full-time employees.

French employees (particularly state employees) enjoy excellent employment conditions and social security benefits (at a price!), and have extensive rights under the labour code. The code details the minimum conditions of employment including working hours, overtime payments, holidays, trial and notice periods, dismissal, health and safety regulations, and trade union rights. France has had a statutory minimum wage (*Salaire Minimum de Interprofessionnel Croissance/SMIC*) since 1950 (see page 22). The French labour code is described in detail in a number of books including the *Code du Travail* (VO Editions).

Collective agreements are individually negotiated between employee unions and employers' associations in many industries. These specify the rights and obligations of both employees and employers in a particular industry or occupation, and cover around 75 per cent of the workforce. Agreements specify minimum wage levels for each position within the main employment categories in a particular industry or company. If an employer doesn't abide by the laws or the regulations in a particular industry, employees can report him to unions or work syndicates (see page 61). Where there's no union the case is heard before an industrial tribunal (*Conseil de Prud'hommes*) comprising employer and syndicate representatives (elected by the workforce). When an employee is wrongfully dismissed he's awarded damages based on his length of service.

Employment laws cannot be altered or nullified by private agreements, and employment courts, trade unions and employee representatives work together to ensure that the law isn't broken. Matters concerning employment regulations are also supervised by local work inspectors (*Inspecteur du Travail*) and the *Direction Départmentale du Travail et de l'Emploi*. French law forbids discrimination by employers on the basis of sex, religion or race, and there are specific rules regarding equal job opportunities for men and women.

TERMS OF EMPLOYMENT

When negotiating your terms of employment for a job in France, the checklists on the following pages will prove invaluable. The points listed under **General Positions** (below) apply to most jobs, while those listed under **Executive Positions** (on page 49) usually apply to executive and senior managerial appointments only.

General Positions

- Salary:
  - Is the salary adequate, taking into account the cost of living (see page 306)? Is it index-linked?

- Is the total salary (including expenses) paid in French francs or will the salary be paid in another country in a different currency, with expenses for living in France?
- When and how often is the salary reviewed?
- Does the salary include a 13th (or 14th) month's salary and annual or end-of-contract bonuses (see page 51)?
- Is overtime paid or time off given in lieu of extra hours worked?

● Relocation expenses:
- Are removal expenses or a relocation allowance paid?
- Does the allowance include travelling expenses for all family members? Is there a limit and is it adequate?
- Are you required to repay relocation expenses (or a percentage) if you resign before a certain period has elapsed?
- Are you required to pay for your relocation in advance? This can run into tens of thousands of francs for normal house contents.
- If employment is for a limited period only, will your relocation costs be paid by the employer when you leave France?
- If you aren't shipping household goods and furniture to France, is there an allowance for buying furnishings locally?
- Do relocation expenses include the legal and agent's fees incurred when moving home?
- Does the employer use the services of a relocation consultant (see page 85)?

● Accommodation:
- Will the employer pay for a hotel or pay a lodging allowance until you find permanent accommodation?
- Is subsidised or free, temporary or permanent accommodation provided? If so, is it furnished or unfurnished?
- Must you pay for utilities such as electricity, gas and water?
- If accommodation isn't provided by the employer, is assistance provided to find suitable accommodation? If so, what sort of assistance?
- What will accommodation cost?
- Are your expenses paid while looking for accommodation?

● Working Hours:
- What are the weekly working hours?
- Does the employer operate a flexi-time system (see page 53)? If so, what are the fixed working hours? How early must you start? Can you carry forward extra hours worked and take time off at a later date, or carry forward a deficit and make it up later?
- Are you required to clock in and out of work?
- Can you choose whether to take time off in lieu of overtime or be paid?

- Leave entitlement:
  - What is the annual leave entitlement? Does it increase with length of service?
  - What are the paid public holidays? Is Monday or Friday a free day when a public holiday falls on a Tuesday or Thursday respectively?
  - Is free air travel to your home country or elsewhere provided for you and your family, and if so, how often?
- Insurance:
  - Is extra insurance cover provided besides obligatory insurance (see **Chapter 13**)?
  - Is free life insurance provided?
  - Is free health insurance provided for you *and* your family (see page 264)?
  - For how long will your salary be paid if you're sick or have an accident?
- Company or supplementary pension:
  - What percentage of your salary must you pay into a pension fund (see page 264)?
  - Are you required or able to pay a lump sum into the fund in order to receive a full or higher pension?
  - Is the pension transferable to another employer?
- Employer:
  - What are the employer's future prospects?
  - Does he have a good reputation?
  - Does he have a high staff turnover?
- Are free or subsidised French lessons provided for you and your spouse?
- Is a travelling allowance (or public transportation) paid from your French residence to your place of work?
- Is free or subsidised parking provided at your place of work?
- Is a free or subsidised company restaurant provided? If not, is an allowance paid or are luncheon vouchers provided? (Some companies provide excellent staff restaurants which save employees both money and time.)
- Will the employer provide or pay for professional training or education, if necessary abroad?
- Are free work clothes or overalls provided? Does the employer pay for the cleaning of work clothes?
- Does the employer provide any fringe benefits, such as subsidised banking services, low interest loans, inexpensive petrol, employees' shop or product discounts, sports and social facilities, and subsidised tickets?
- Do you have a written list of your job responsibilities?
- Have your employment conditions been confirmed in writing? For a list of the possible contents of your employment conditions, see page 50.

- If a dispute arises over your salary or working conditions, under the law of which country will your employment contract be interpreted?

Executive & Managerial Positions

The following points generally apply to executive and top managerial positions only:

- Is private schooling for your children financed or subsidised? Will the employer pay for a boarding school in France or abroad?
- Is the salary index-linked and protected against devaluation? This is particularly important if you're paid in a foreign currency that fluctuates wildly or could be devalued. Are you paid an overseas allowance for working in France?
- Is there a non-contributory pension fund besides the supplementary company scheme? Is it transferable and if so, what are the conditions?
- Are the costs incurred by a move to France reimbursed? For example the cost of selling your home, employing an agent to let it for you or storing household effects.
- Will the employer pay for domestic help or towards the cost of a servant or cook?
- Is a car provided? With a chauffeur?
- Are you entitled to any miscellaneous benefits, such as membership of a social or sports club or free credit cards?
- Is there an entertainment allowance?
- Is there a clothing allowance? For example if you arrive in France in the winter from the tropics, you will probably need to buy new winter clothes.
- Is extra compensation paid if you're made redundant or fired? Redundancy or severance payments (see page 59) are compulsory for employees in France (subject to length of service), but executives often receive a generous 'golden handshake' if they're made redundant, e.g. after a takeover.

EMPLOYMENT CONTRACTS

Employees in France usually have an employment contract (*contrat de travail/ contrat individuel*) stating such details as job title, position, salary, working hours, benefits, duties and responsibilities, and the duration of employment. There are two main types of employment contract in France, an indefinite term contract (*contrat à durée indéterminée*) and a term contract (*contrat à durée déterminée*). All contracts must be written in French.

An **indefinite term** contract is the standard employment contract for permanent employees. Somewhat surprisingly it isn't necessary for it to be in writing (unlike a term contract), although you should insist on a written contract. It usually includes a trial period of one to three months (three months is usual), depending on collective agreements, before it becomes legal and binding on both parties.

A **term contract** is, as the name suggests, a contract for a fixed term up to a maximum of two years (there's no minimum term), which applies to around 25 per cent of French employees. A contract for longer than two years comes under the rules for indefinite term contracts, particularly regarding the dismissal of employees. A term contract must be in writing and for a fixed term or, in the case of temporary employment, for a specific purpose that must be stated in the contract. A fixed term contract ends on the date specified, although it can be renewed twice for a term no longer than the original contract, providing it doesn't exceed two years in total.

The salary of an employee hired on a term contract mustn't be less than that paid to a similarly qualified person employed in a permanent job. The employee has the right to an end of contract bonus (*indemnité de fin de contrat*) equal to 5 per cent of his salary in addition to other agreed bonuses, although this doesn't apply to seasonal and temporary employees. A term contract can be terminated before the end of its period only in specific circumstances, i.e. when either the employer or employee has committed a serious offence (*faute grave*), an event beyond the control of both parties (*force majeure*), or with the agreement of both parties. If the employer commits a serious offence or illegally dismisses the employee before the end of his contract, the employee is entitled to be paid in full for the remaining period of the contract, plus 5 per cent of his salary and bonuses. If the employee commits a serious offence or unilaterally breaks the contract, he may need to pay damages and loses his right to any bonuses. No compensation is payable if termination is due to *force majeure*.

There are special contracts for seasonal (*saisonnier*) and temporary (*temporaire*) workers, who have few rights. Contracts for seasonal and temporary workers can be issued when a permanent employee is on leave of absence (including maternity or sick leave), if there's a temporary increase in business, or at any time in the construction industry or for youth employment schemes. If you're thinking of employing a part-time or temporary employee, e.g. domestic help in your home, take care that you don't get embroiled in French employee legislation, particularly when terminating employment (see **Dismissal & Redundancy** on page 59).

All employment contracts are subject to French labour law and references may be made to other regulations such as collective agreements. Anything in contracts contrary to statutory provisions and unfavourable to an employee may be deemed null and void. There are usually no hidden surprises or traps for the unwary in a French employment contract. Nevertheless, as with any contract you should know exactly what it contains before signing it. If your French isn't fluent, you should try to obtain a translation, as your French must be excellent to understand the legal jargon in some contracts. If you cannot obtain a written translation (which is unlikely), you should at least have it translated verbally so that you don't receive any nasty surprises later. If you're an employee, your employment contract must be produced when applying for your residence permit (*carte de séjour*).

EMPLOYMENT CONDITIONS

Employment conditions (*règlements intérieurs/règlements de travail*) contain an employer's general rules and regulations regarding working conditions and benefits that apply to all employees (unless stated otherwise in your employment contract). Employment conditions are explained in this chapter or a reference is made to the chapter where a subject is covered in more detail.

Validity & Applicability

Employment conditions usually contain a paragraph stating the date from which they take effect and to whom they apply.

Salary & Benefits

Your salary (*salaire*) is stated in your employment contract and salary reviews, planned increases, cost of living rises (etc.) may also be included. Salaries may be stated in gross or net terms and are usually paid monthly, although they may be quoted in contracts as hourly, monthly or annually. If a bonus is paid, such as a 13th or 14th month's salary, this is stated in your employment contract. General points such as the payment of your salary into a bank or post office account and the date of salary payments are usually included in employment conditions. Salaries above 120,000F a year must be paid by cheque or direct transfer (not cash). You receive a pay slip (*bulletin de paie*) itemising your salary and deductions.

There has been a statutory minimum wage in France since 1950, known as *Salaire Minimum Interprofessionnel de Croissance (SMIC)*. This is 40.22F an hour (1999), equal to 6,797F per month for 169 hours. The cost of living index is reviewed every six months and when it rises by 2 per cent or more, the SMIC is increased. The SMIC is lower for juveniles and disabled employees. Cost of living increases for salaries above the SMIC aren't regulated by the government. Note, however, that many employees, particularly seasonal workers in the farming and tourist industries, are traditionally paid below the minimum wage (although the French government is clamping down and forcing employers to comply with the law). Salaries in France must be reviewed once a year (usually at the end of the year), although employers aren't required by law to increase salaries which are above the SMIC, even when the cost of living has increased. Salary increases usually take effect from 1st January. See also **Salaries** on page 34.

The introduction of the 35-hour week (see page 52) isn't expected to reduce salaries, although they will probably remain static and pay rises will be fewer and far between.

13th Month's Salary & Bonuses

Most employers in France pay their employees a bonus month's salary in December, known as the 13th month's salary (*13ème mois*). A 13th salary isn't mandatory unless part of a collective agreement or when it's granted regularly, and it should be stated in your employment contract. In practice its payment is universal and taken for granted by most employees. In your first and last years of employment, your 13th salary and other bonuses should be paid pro rata if you don't work a full calendar year. Some companies also pay a 14th month's salary, usually in July prior to the summer holiday period. A few companies, e.g. banks and other financial institutions, may pay as many as 15 or 16 months' salary. Where applicable, extra months salary are guaranteed bonuses and aren't pegged to the company's performance (such as with profit-sharing). Senior and middle managers often receive extra bonuses, perhaps linked to profits, equal to around 10 to 20 per cent of their annual salary.

Employees of many French companies are also entitled to participate in bonus schemes (perhaps tied to productivity) and profit-sharing schemes (*participation des salariés aux résultats de l'entreprise/système d'intéressement aux bénéfices*), which must be provided by any company with over 100 employees. Companies are obliged to contribute a minimum amount of their total payroll (which may be up to 20 per cent) to a special fund. Some employers also operate optional investment plans (*plan d'épargne d'entreprise*), where the company holds a portfolio of securities on behalf of its employees, and share option schemes (*options sur actions*). If you're employed on a term contract for a fixed period, you're paid an end of contract bonus (*indemnité de fin de contrat*) equal to 5 per cent of your salary, in addition to other agreed bonuses.

Working Hours & Overtime

From the 1st January 2000, France will introduce a mandatory 35-hour working week. The long-term objective is to dramatically reduce unemployment. Companies with over 20 employees must have a 35-hour week in place by 1st January 2000, while those with fewer than 20 have a further two years in which to reduce working hours. The distribution of the 35 hours will be flexible with the possibility of a seven-hour day, a four and a half day week, or even varying weeks within the same month, and will be determined by negotiations between employers, employees and unions. The government is offering employers financial incentives such as a reduction in social security contributions and annual payments for new employees. Some large companies such as Renault and Carrefour have already implemented the new legislation. Optimistic (government!) sources predict the creation of one million jobs, while more pessimistic (realistic?) sources claim the scheme will, at best, create only a quarter of a million jobs.

Overtime: Until 1st January 2000, when the 35 hour week is officially introduced, if you work over 39 hours a week you must usually be paid overtime. Employees can be asked to do overtime, but cannot be compelled to do more than a certain number of hours each year (130 in 1999), although this can be altered by collective agreements. The total hours worked per week mustn't exceed an average of 46 over 12 consecutive weeks or an absolute maximum of 48 hours a week. Over 50 per cent of French workers (excluding executives) regularly work over 39 hours a week, although new legislation will reduce this.

The minimum legal pay for overtime is the normal rate plus 25 per cent for the first eight hours above the standard 39-hour week (i.e. up to 47) and plus 50 per cent for additional hours (i.e. above 47). The working week for round-the-clock shift workers is limited to 25 hours and night work and shift working is usually paid at higher rates as specified in collective agreements. Employees cannot be obliged to work on Sundays unless collective agreements state otherwise. If an employee agrees to work on a Sunday, normal overtime rates apply. Official authorisation is usually required for employees to work on Sundays and time off in lieu must be granted during the normal working week.

Salaried employees, particularly executives (*cadres*) and managers, aren't generally paid overtime, although this depends on their employment contracts. Managers and executives generally work long hours, even allowing for their occasionally long lunch breaks. For example, in Paris executives often work from 0830 or 0900 to 1900 or 2000. Senior staff in the south generally work shorter hours than those in Paris and the north, particularly on hot summer days (when they sensibly go home early and jump in the pool!). Weekends are sacrosanct and almost nobody works on Saturdays and Sundays (except when necessary, e.g. shop staff). Taking a long lunch break, perhaps for a game of tennis or a swim, isn't frowned upon, providing you put in the required hours and don't neglect your work. The idea of fixed office hours are alien to French executives and managers. It isn't unusual for a parent to leave work early to collect children from a nursery and some employees work only a half-day on Wednesdays when children aren't attending school. These are statutory rights granted to both parents.

There are usually no scheduled coffee or tea breaks in France, although drinks can usually be taken at an employee's workplace at any time. Many workers traditionally have a two-hour lunch break, particularly in the provinces, although this isn't standard practice. Lunch may be anything from a two-hour marathon (don't overdo the wine!) to a quick bite at a café. Eating at your desk is generally frowned upon unless you have urgent work to complete. In Paris, lunch breaks commonly start at 1300, while in the provinces it's usually noon or 1230.

It may come as a nasty surprise to some foreigners to discover that many French employers (including most large companies) require employees to clock in and out of work. If you're caught cheating the clock you could be liable to dismissal.

Flexi-Time Rules

Many French companies operate flexi-time (*horaire mobile/horaire flexible*) working hours. A flexi-time system requires employees to be present between certain hours, known as the block time (*temps bloqué/heures de présence obligatoire*). For example from 0830 to 1130 and from 1330 to 1600. Employees may make up their required working hours by starting earlier than the required block time, reducing their lunch break or by working later. Most business premises are open between around 0630 and 1900, and smaller companies may allow employees to work as late as they like, providing they don't exceed the maximum permitted daily working hours. Because flexi-time rules are often quite complicated, they may be contained in a separate set of regulations.

Travel & Relocation Expenses

Travel (*frais de voyage*) and relocation expenses to France depend on your agreement with your employer and are usually included in your employment contract or conditions. If you're hired from outside France, your air ticket and other travel costs to France are usually booked and paid for by your employer or his local representative. In addition you can usually claim any extra travel costs, for example the cost of transport to and from airports. If you travel by car to France, you can usually claim a mileage rate or the equivalent air fare. Most French employers pay your relocation costs to France up to a specified amount, although you may be required to sign a special contract stipulating that if you leave the employer before a certain period (e.g. five years), you must repay a percentage of your removal costs.

An employer may pay a fixed relocation allowance based on your salary, position and size of family, or he may pay the total cost of removal. The allowance should be sufficient to move the contents of an average house (*châteaux* aren't usually catered for) and you must normally pay any excess costs yourself. If you don't want to bring your furniture to France or have only a few belongings to ship, it may be possible to purchase furniture locally up to the limit of your allowance. Check with your employer. When a company is liable for the total cost, they may ask you to obtain two or three removal estimates.

Generally you're required to organise and pay for the removal in advance. Your employer usually reimburses the equivalent amount in French francs *after* you have paid the bill, although it may be possible to get him to pay the bill directly or give you a cash advance. If you change jobs within France, your new employer may pay your relocation expenses when it's necessary for you to move house. Don't forget to ask, as they may not offer to pay (it may depend on how desperate they are to employ you).

Social Security

All French employees, foreign employees working for French companies and the self-employed must contribute to the French social security (*sécurité sociale*) system. Social security includes health care (plus sickness and maternity); injuries at work; family allowances; unemployment insurance; and old age (pensions), invalidity and death benefits. Contributions are calculated as a percentage of your gross income and are deducted at source by your employer. Social security contributions are high and total an average of around 70 per cent of gross pay, some 20 per cent of which is paid by employees (the balance by employers). For full details, see **Social Security** on page 254.

Medical Examination

Most French employers require prospective employees to have a pre-employment medical examination (*médecin du travail*) performed by a doctor nominated by the employer. An offer of employment is usually subject to a prospective employee being given a clean bill of health. However, this may be required only for employees over a certain age (e.g. 40) or for employees in certain jobs, e.g. where good health is of paramount importance for safety reasons. Thereafter a medical examination may be required periodically, e.g. every one or two years, or may be requested at any time by your employer. A medical examination may also be necessary as a condition of membership of a company health, pension or life insurance scheme. Some companies insist on certain employees having regular health screening, particularly executives and senior managers.

Health Insurance

Many industries, occupations and professions have their own supplementary (*mutuelle*) health insurance schemes that pay the portion of doctors' and hospital medical bills not covered by social security (usually 20 or 30 per cent). Membership may be obligatory and contributions may be paid wholly by your employer. Some employers, particularly foreign companies, provide free comprehensive private health insurance for executives, senior managers and their families. For further information about health insurance see page 264.

Company Pension Fund

In addition to contributing to social security, which provides a state pension, most employees in France contribute to a supplementary company pension fund (*caisse complémentaire de retraite*). Managerial staff usually contribute to a supplementary managerial company pension fund (*caisse de retraite des cadres supérieurs*). Almost every trade or occupation has its own scheme and in many companies it's obligatory for employees to join. For further information see **Supplementary Pensions** on page 264.

Unemployment Insurance

Unemployment insurance (*allocation d'assurance chômage*) is compulsory for employees of French companies and is covered by social security contributions. For details see **Unemployment Insurance** on page 261.

Salary Insurance

Salary insurance (*assurance salaire*) pays employees' salaries during periods of sickness or after accidents and is provided under social security. After a certain number of consecutive sick days (the number varies depending on your employer), your salary is no longer paid by your employer but by social security, which is one reason why you pay those astronomical contributions. Employees in France don't receive a quota of sick days as in some countries (e.g. the USA) and there's no limit on the amount of time you may take off work due to sickness or accidents. Employees also have the right to take paid time off work to care for a sick child. The regulations allow 12 days a year for each child, although a doctor's certificate (*fiche médicale pour enfant*) must be provided. Some employers operate their own unemployment insurance schemes and pay their employees' full salaries for a limited period, usually depending on their length of service.

You're normally required to notify your employer immediately of sickness or an accident that prevents you from working. If you're away from work for longer than two days, you're required to produce a doctor's certificate (*certificat d'absence*). The actual period is stated in your employment conditions. For information see **Sickness & Maternity Benefits** on page 260.

Annual Holidays

Under French labour law an employee employed for one month or more is entitled to 2.5 days paid annual holiday (*congé/vacances*) for each full month he works. This totals five weeks annually for full-time employees. Employers cannot include official French public holidays (see below) as annual holidays. Some collective agreements grant extra vacation days, usually from one to three, for long service. French employees are legally entitled to take four weeks paid holiday between 1st May and 31st October, unless business needs dictate otherwise (although other agreements are possible). Most employees take three or four weeks summer holiday between July and August and one or two weeks in winter (often around the Christmas and New Year holiday period). Traditionally August was the sole month for summer vacations, with many businesses closing for the whole month. When a company closes down during summer, employees are obliged to take their vacation at the same time.

The government is trying to encourage companies to stagger their employees' holidays throughout the summer, although this isn't popular with employees. Despite enticements and pleas from employers and the government, many French employees refuse to surrender their August annual holiday. Almost half of French companies close down during August, which naturally has adverse effects on the economy, resulting in a drop of some 30 per cent in industrial production and exports. Many large manufacturers are forced to close because their component suppliers shut during this period and they don't carry large enough stocks.

However, there has been some progress in the Paris area, where only around 20 per cent of companies shut during August. Unlike the provinces, Paris is more in tune with the international business scene and more aware of how the French economy is tied to the rest of Europe. The August shutdown varies from industry to industry. Around 80 per cent of companies close in the textile and garment industry, almost 70 per cent of timber companies, and some 60 per cent of steelworks and metal plants.

Before starting a new job, check that any planned holidays will be honoured by your new employer. This is particularly important if they fall within your trial period (usually the first three months), when holidays may not be permitted.

Public Holidays

The only public holiday (*jour férié*) that an employer in France is legally obliged to grant with pay is 1st May. However, most collective agreements include the following 11 public holidays:

Date	Holiday
January 1st	New Year's Day (*nouvel An/Jour de l'An*)
March or April	Easter Monday (*Lundi de Pâques*)
May 1st	Labour Day (*Fête du Travail*)
May 8th	Victory Day WWII/1945 (*Fête de la Libération/Victoire 1945/Anniversaire 1945*)
May	Ascension Day (*Ascension*) – Thursday 40 days (6th Thursday) after Easter
May/June	Pentecost/Whitsuntide (*Pentecôte*) – ten days (2nd Monday) after Ascension Day
July 14th	Bastille Day/National Day (*Fête Nationale*)
August 15th	Assumption (*Fête de l'Assomption*)
November 1st	All Saints' Day (*Toussaint*)
November 11th	Armistice Day (*Fête de l'Armistice*)
December 25th	Christmas Day (*Noël*)

When a holiday falls on a Saturday or Sunday, another day isn't usually granted as a holiday unless the number of public holidays in a particular year falls below a minimum number. However, when a public holiday falls on a Tuesday or Thursday, the day before or the day after (i.e. Monday or Friday respectively) may be declared a holiday, depending on the employer. This practice is called making a bridge (*faire le pont*). If a holiday falls on a Wednesday, it's common for employees to take the two preceding or succeeding days off, a practice known as *faire le viaduc*. In May there are usually three or four public holidays and it's possible to have a two-week break while using only a few days of your annual holiday.

All public offices, banks, post offices, etc., are closed on public holidays, when only essential work is carried out. Note that foreign embassies and consulates in France usually observe French public holidays *plus* their own country's national holidays.

Compassionate & Special Leave of Absence

Most French companies provide additional days off for moving house, your own or a family marriage, birth of a child, death of a family member or close relative, and other compassionate reasons. Grounds for compassionate leave (*congé spécial*) are usually defined in collective agreements. The number of days special leave granted vary depending on the particular event, e.g. four days off for your own wedding (but not if you get married during your regular annual holidays!) and one day off to attend a child's wedding or the funeral of a grandparent. Employees who have worked for a company for a minimum of three years are entitled to take a one-time, year's sabbatical (naturally *without* pay!).

Paid Expenses

Expenses (*frais*) paid by your employer are usually listed in your employment conditions. These may include travel costs from your home to your place of work, usually consisting of a second class rail season ticket or the equivalent amount in cash (paid monthly with your salary). In the Paris area, most employers pay 50 per cent of the cost of an employee's *carte orange*, a monthly public transport pass for the Paris *métro*, buses and suburban trains. Travelling expenses to and from your place of work are tax deductible.

Companies without an employee restaurant or canteen may pay a lunch allowance or provide luncheon vouchers (*chèque restaurant*). Expenses paid for travel on company business or for training and education may be detailed in your employment conditions or listed in a separate document.

Trial & Notice Periods

For most jobs in France there's a trial period (*période d'essai*) of one to three months, depending on the type of work and the employer (three months is usual). The trial period isn't required by law, although there's no law forbidding it. The length of a trial period is usually stated in collective agreements that impose restrictions on the maximum period. During the trial period either party may terminate the employment contract without notice or any financial penalty, unless otherwise stated in a collective agreement. If at the end of the trial period an employer hasn't decided whether he wishes to employ someone permanently, he may have the right to repeat the trial period, but only once. After this period, if he doesn't officially dismiss the employee, he's deemed to be hired permanently, irrespective of whether an employment contract exists.

Notice periods usually vary with length of service and are governed by law and collective agreements. The minimum notice period is usually one month for clerical and manual workers, two months for foremen and supervisors, and three months for managerial and senior technical staff. The minimum notice period for employees with over two years' service is two months.

Although many employers prefer employees to leave immediately after giving notice, employees have the right to work their notice period. However, both parties can agree that the employee receives payment in lieu (*indemnité compensatrice de préavis*) of notice. Compensation must also be made for any outstanding paid annual holidays (*indemnité compensatrice de congés payés*) up to the end of the notice period. See also **Dismissal** on page 59.

Education & Training

Employee training is taken seriously in France, whether it's conducted in your own office or factory or some exotic location. Training may include management seminars, special technical courses, language lessons or any other form of continuing education. If you need to learn or improve your French or another language in order to perform your job, the cost of language study is usually paid by your employer. Employers with ten or more employees must allocate a percentage of their gross payroll for employee education and training (*formation continue*).

Employers who are keen to attract the best employees, particularly those engaged in high-tech fields, usually allocate extra funds and provide superior training schemes (large companies commonly spend an amount equal to around 10 per cent of their payroll on training). Not all employees benefit equally from training, which is decided by the employer. It's in your own interest to investigate courses of study, seminars and lectures that you feel will be of direct benefit to you and your employer. Most employers give reasonable consideration to a request to attend a course during working hours, providing you don't make it a full-time occupation.

Companies with 50 or more employees must have an enterprise committee (*comité d'entreprise*) comprising elected employees. The company pays an amount equal to 1 per cent of its payroll into the committee's fund, to be used at the discretion of the employees to provide benefits such as private day-care, vacations, theatre discounts, holiday gifts, employee Christmas party, etc. As with training, some companies allocate extra funds to their *comité d'entreprise* as a means of attracting employees.

Pregnancy & Confinement

Female employees are entitled to excellent employment benefits under French labour law with regard to pregnancy (*grossesse*) and confinement. The family is of fundamental importance in France and employers are flexible regarding time off work in connection with a pregnancy. Social security benefits are generous and are designed to encourage large families. Maternity leave is guaranteed for all women irrespective of their length of employment. The permitted leave period is 20 weeks, six weeks prior to birth and 14 weeks after (leave is extended for the third and subsequent children). A doctor may authorise additional time off, either before or after the birth, in which case a company must continue to pay your salary.

A mother and her husband also have the right to an additional year of unpaid parental leave (*congé parental*), which also applies to parents with adopted children. Providing you don't extend your leave beyond the permitted period, your employer *must* allow you to return to the same job at the same or a higher salary, taking into account general increases in wages and the cost of living. Fathers are entitled to three months unpaid paternity leave (*pregnant* fathers receive the Nobel prize for medicine). State-run nurseries (*crèche*) are provided for children from the age of three months. See also **Working Women** on page 33, **Sickness & Maternity Benefits** on page 260 and **Childbirth** on page 241.

Part-Time Job Restrictions

Restrictions regarding part-time employment (*travail à mi-temps*) may be detailed in your employment conditions. Most French companies don't allow full-time employees to work part-time (i.e. moonlight) for another employer, particularly one in the same line of business. You may, however, be permitted to take a part-time teaching job or similar part-time employment (or you could write a book!).

Changing Jobs & Confidentiality

Companies in a high-tech or highly confidential business may have restrictions (*clause de non-concurrence*) on employees moving to a competitor in France or within Europe. You should be aware of these restrictions, as they are enforceable under French law, although it's a complicated subject and disputes often need to be resolved by a court of law. French law regarding industrial secrets and general employer confidentiality are strict. If you breach this confidentiality you may be dismissed and could be unable to find further employment in France.

Acceptance of Gifts

Employees are normally forbidden to accept gifts (*accepter des dons*) of more than a certain value from customers or suppliers. Many suppliers give bottles of wine or small gifts at Christmas that don't breach this rule (if you accept a bribe, make sure it's a big one and that you have a secret bank account!).

Retirement

Your employment conditions may be valid only until the official French retirement age (*retraite*), which is 60 for both men and women in most trades and professions and 65 for civil servants (although some state employees can retire on a full pension as early as 50 or 55). If you wish to continue working after you have reached retirement age, you may be required to negotiate a new employment contract (you should also seek psychiatric help!).

Dismissal & Redundancy

The rules governing dismissal and severance pay depend on the size of a company, the employee's length of service, the reason for dismissal (e.g. misconduct or redundancy), and whether the employee has a protected status, such as that enjoyed by union and employee representatives who can be dismissed only for 'gross misconduct'. The two main reasons for dismissal are personal or economic, i.e. when a company is experiencing serious financial problems. After the trial period (see page 57), an employee can be dismissed only for personal reasons for a valid and serious offence (*cause réelle et sérieuse*), e.g. stealing from an employer. It's difficult for an employer to dismiss an employee unless he has blatantly proved his total incompetence or is guilty of some form of gross misconduct.

If an employee is accused of misconduct, a strict procedure must be followed before he can be disciplined or dismissed. The employee must be summoned by registered letter to attend a formal preliminary hearing with the employer, during which the alleged misconduct is discussed. The employee has the right to bring another person to the interview, either a colleague or an employee representative (whose name must appear on an official list). If dismissal could result, the employer must mention this as a possibility during the hearing. If the employer decides that the offence warrants dismissal, there's usually a cooling off period before he can effect the dismissal. The grounds for dismissal must be stated in the dismissal letter.

A dismissed employee is entitled to accrued holiday pay, severance pay (*indemnité de licenciement*) if he has at least two years' service, and compensation in lieu of notice when a notice period cannot be observed. Payment must also be made in lieu of any outstanding paid holiday (*indemnité compensatrice de congés payés*) up to the end of the notice period. However, severance pay isn't payable when an employee is dismissed for a serious breach of conduct. Severance pay is 10 per cent of the employee's average monthly salary during his last three months, for each year of service. This is increased by one-fifteenth of average monthly pay for each year of service over ten years. Collective agreements may provide for increased severance pay. An employee can be dismissed at any time during his trial period, usually the first one to three months, without notice or compensation.

An employee dismissed for misconduct can appeal against the decision to a union or labour court. If the employer didn't abide by the law or the regulations in a particular industry, the employee can have his case heard by his union or syndicate (*syndicat*). If there's no union the case is heard before an industrial tribunal (*conseil des Prud'hommes*) comprising both employer and syndicate representatives (elected by the workforce). If the employee wins the case, he's entitled to severance pay and compensation (e.g. six months' salary or more) for breach of his labour contract, but he may not be reinstated. In order to avoid the expense and publicity of legal proceedings, most employers come to an out-of-court settlement.

When an employee is dismissed for economic reasons, i.e. made redundant, the procedures are strictly regulated. Certain administrative authorities must be consulted or informed before any steps are taken. If the employer subsequently needs to hire someone to fill a position in which an employee was made redundant, the previously dismissed employee must be offered the job first. Under new rules which came into effect in 1993, a company considering redundancies is obliged to table a 'social plan' offering employees internal or external redeployment, a generous retraining package, or funding for new local employment initiatives.

If you're thinking of employing a part-time or temporary employee, take care that you don't get embroiled in French employee legislation, particularly if you wish to terminate the employment. You should get an employee to sign a written statement agreeing to the terms of the termination of employment, otherwise you could be sued for unfair dismissal.

Union Membership

There are numerous trade unions in France, many grouped into confederations. Unions in France aren't as highly organised as in many other western countries and their power and influence has been reduced considerably since the late '70s, when labour disputes and strikes (*grèves*) were common. Since the '70s, union membership has declined dramatically, with membership of the *Confédération Générale du Travail (CGT)* dropping from over 2½ million to around one million today. Union membership is insignificant and includes less than 10 per cent of the private sector workforce and only around a fifth of the total workforce. Unions remain strongest in the older traditional industries such as mining, railways and automobile manufacturing, and have had little success in new high-tech industries. However, they are still capable of causing widespread disruption, as has been demonstrated in recent years.

Under French law, unions are allowed to organise on any company's premises and 'closed shops' are banned. Workers' rights are protected by labour laws and workers are organised in individual companies through labour organisations. All businesses with over ten employees must have a workers' council or a labour management committee comprising employee delegates (*délégués du personnel*) elected by and from among the employees. The number of delegates increases in proportion to the number of employees, up to 50. Delegates represent employees with management when they have questions or complaints concerning, for example, working conditions, job classification, wages, and the application of labour laws and regulations.

In companies with over 50 employees, employee delegates must be elected to the board of directors and a labour management committee (*comité d'entreprise*) must be formed. Companies with separate locations (e.g. factories or offices) employing over 50 employees must have a local labour management committee (*comité d'établissement*), with representatives of this committee sitting on a central labour management committee (*comité central d'entreprise*). In addition to dealing with matters relating to terms and conditions of employment, major changes relating to the operation, organisation and management of a company must be discussed with the committee before they can be initiated. However, a company isn't usually required to act on the opinion of the labour management committee.

With the exception of certain public sector employees, e.g. the police, employees are guaranteed the right to strike under French law and cannot be dismissed for striking.

3.
PERMITS & VISAS

Before making any plans to live or work in France, you must ensure that you have a valid passport (with a visa if necessary) and the appropriate documentation to obtain a residence permit. Citizens of the neighbouring EU countries can visit France with a national identity card only. Other foreigners require a passport. A non-EU national usually requires a long-stay visa (*visa de long séjour*) to work, study or live in France. Note that there's no such thing as a work permit in France, where foreigners receive a residence permit (*carte de séjour*) permitting them to work, if applicable. All foreigners need a residence permit to live in France and nationals of some countries require a visa to visit France (see below). While in France, you should carry your passport or residence permit (if you have one). You can be asked to produce your identification papers at any time by the French police or other officials and if you don't have them you can be taken to a police station and interrogated. A residence permit serves as an identity card, which Frenchmen must carry by law.

Immigration is an inflammatory issue in France. The government introduced new laws to curb non-EU immigration in recent years, which were coupled with a crackdown on illegal immigrants, including forcible repatriation. The new laws give the police wider powers to prevent illegal immigration and they can make random checks up to 40km (25mi) inside frontiers and at airports, docks, and road and rail terminals handling international traffic.

Immigration is a complex and ever-changing subject and the information in this chapter is intended only as a general guide. You shouldn't base any decisions or actions on the information contained herein without confirming it with an official and reliable source, such as a French consulate. Permit infringements are taken very seriously by the French authorities and there are penalties for breaches of regulations, including fines and even deportation for flagrant abuses.

Bureaucracy

French bureaucracy (*l'administration*) is a nightmare and you should be prepared for endless frustration, time-wasting and blatant obstruction on the part of officials (this isn't necessarily xenophobia – they treat their countrymen in the same brusque manner!). Often you may wonder whether the right hand knows what any other part of the body is up to (it usually doesn't) and you should expect to receive conflicting information from consulates, government departments, *préfectures* and town halls. Red tape is a way of life in France, where every third person is employed by the state. In order to obtain a permit you must complete numerous forms, answer hundreds of irrelevant questions and provide mountains of documents with official translations (the paperchase is designed to keep as many redundant civil servants in 'employment' as possible). Never take anything for granted where French civil servants (*fonctionnaires*) are concerned and make sure that you understand all communications. If in doubt have someone translate them for you. When dealing with officialdom in France you must persevere, as the first answer is always *non*! You can sometimes speed up proceedings by employing a lawyer, although this is unusual in France.

VISAS

Non-EU nationals may need a visa to enter France, either as a visitor or for any other purpose. Visas may be valid for a single entry only or for multiple entries within a limited period. A visa is stamped in your passport, which must be valid for at least 60 days *after* the date you intend to leave France. EU nationals and visitors from a number of other countries don't require visas (see **Visitors** on page 66). All non-EU nationals wishing to remain in France for longer than three months must obtain a long-stay visa (*visa de long séjour/longue durée*). A long-stay visa is also required for non-EU nationals coming to France to work, study or live. Holders of a long-stay visa must apply for a residence permit (*carte de séjour*) within one week of their arrival in France (see page 67).

Short-Stay Visas (*visa de court séjour*): A short-stay visa is valid for 90 days and is usually good for multiple entries. Another type of short-stay visa, often issued to businessmen, is a *visa de circulation*. It allows multiple stays of up to 90 days over a period of three years, with a maximum of 180 days in any calendar year. Transit visas valid for three days are issued to rail passengers travelling through France.

Long-Stay Visas: A non-EU national intending to remain in France for more than 90 days, whether to work, study or reside, must obtain the appropriate long-stay visa (*visa de long séjour* or *visa de plus de trois mois*) before arriving in France. If you arrive in France without a long-stay visa, it's impossible to change your status after arrival. If you wish to remain in France for longer than 90 days, e.g. to study or work, you must return to your country of residence and apply for a long-stay visa. A long-stay visa isn't necessary for EU nationals planning to take up residence in France, e.g. retirees, although a residence permit is required (see page 67).

Applications for visas must be made to the French consulate with jurisdiction over your place of residence. Applicants for long-term visas living in a country other than their country of nationality must have been resident there for at least one year. You can usually apply for a visa in person or by mail. If you apply in person, you should bear in mind that there are long queues at consulates located in major cities (take a thick book). The documentation required for a visa application depends on the purpose of your visit to France. All applicants require a valid passport plus a number of black and white passport-size photographs on a white background (usually one for each application form, of which there may be up to eight!). Depending on the purpose of the visa, a number of the following documents are required:

- a certified copy of your birth certificate and those of your spouse and other members of your family;
- proof of financial resources (see below);
- a medical examination by an approved doctor is necessary for most long-term visa applicants including employees and their family members, students and au pairs. It must be carried out during the three months before taking up residence in France. Applicants must pay the doctor's fee.
- a health insurance certificate if you aren't eligible for health treatment under French social security (see page 232);
- employees require a work contract (*certificat d'emploi*) approved by the French Ministry of Labour (see below);
- students require proof of admission from an approved educational establishment (see below);
- au pairs require an agreement (*déclaration d'engagement*) with a French family and a certificate of registration for French-language classes (see page 165).

- a non-EU national married to a French citizen or to a foreigner who's resident in France, requires a marriage certificate (see page 402).

- an affidavit stating that you have never been convicted of a criminal offence or declared bankrupt;

- written authorisation from a parent or guardian for those aged under 18.

Proof of Financial Resources: Proof of financial resources or financial support may take the form of bank statements, letters from banks confirming arrangements for regular transfers of funds from abroad, letters from family or friends guaranteeing regular support, or a 'certificate of accommodation' (*certificat d'hébergement*) from a French family or friends with whom you will be staying in France. Letters should be notarised. Students may submit a letter from an organisation or institution guaranteeing accommodation or evidence of a scholarship or grant. Proof of financial resources isn't required by someone coming to France to take up paid employment. Retirees must provide a copy of a pension book, some other proof of regular income or confirmation from a French bank that their monthly income is no less than 6,000F for a couple or 3,300F if single.

Employees: A non-EU national wishing to work in France requires an employment contract approved by the French Ministry of Labour or the District Labour Department where the business is registered. This must be obtained by the prospective employer in France. It's sent to the *Office des Migrations Internationales (OMI)* for transmission to the appropriate French consulate abroad.

Students: Students require proof of admission from an approved educational establishment stating that they will be studying for at least 20 hours a week. This is usually a letter of admission (*attestation de pré-inscription*) when registering for the first time or other evidence of registration (e.g. *certificat d'inscription* or *autorisation d'inscription*), depending on the level and type of studies (see page 72).

Documents: Various documents are required depending on the purpose of the visa, many of which must be translated into French. All translations must be made by a translator approved by your local consulate, a list of whom (*liste de traducteurs*) is provided on request by French consulates.

If you require a visa to enter France and attempt to enter without one, you will be refused entry. If you're in doubt as to whether you require a visa to enter France, enquire at a French consulate before making travel plans. Visa applications usually take six to eight weeks to be approved, although they can take much longer.

Visitors

Non-residents can visit France for a maximum of 90 days at a time. Visitors from EU countries plus Andorra, Canada, Cyprus, the Czech Republic, Hungary, Iceland, Japan, Malta, Monaco, New Zealand, Norway, Singapore, the Slovak Republic, South Korea, Switzerland and the USA *don't* require a visa for stays of up to three months. All other nationalities need a visa to visit France. French immigration authorities may require non-EU visitors to produce a return ticket and proof of accommodation, health insurance and financial resources.

EU nationals who visit France to seek employment or start a business have three months in which to find a job or apply for a residence permit. After three months they must apply for a residence permit to remain in France (see below). If they haven't found employment nor have sufficient funds, the application will be refused. If you're a non-EU national, it isn't possible to enter France as a tourist and change your status to that of an employee, student or resident. You must return to your country of residence and apply for a long-stay visa. It's possible to leave France, e.g. by crossing the border to a neighbouring country, before the 90-day period has expired and return again for another 90-days. However, if you wish to prove you have left, you must have your passport stamped. This is legal, although your stay mustn't exceed a total of six months (180 days) in a year.

RESIDENCE PERMITS

All foreigners residing in France for longer than 90 days in succession (for any reason) require a residence permit. Where applicable, a residence permit holder's dependants are also granted a permit. Children can be listed on a parent's permit until the age of 18, although they require their own residence permit at age 16 if they are working. Different types of residence permits are issued depending on your status including long-stay visitors (*visiteur*), salaried employees (*salarié*), transferees (*détaché*), family members (*membre de famille*), students (*étudiant*) and traders (*commerçant*). There are two main categories of residence permit in France: a *carte de séjour* and a *carte de résident*. To avoid confusion the *carte de séjour* is referred to below as a temporary residence permit and the *carte de résident* as a permanent residence permit. There's no fee for the initial residence permit.

Temporary Residence Permit (*carte de séjour*): A temporary residence permit is issued to all foreign residents aged 18 and above, both to EU and non-EU nationals. Non-EU parents with children aged under 18 must obtain a long-stay visa for their children before their arrival in France. A temporary residence permit for non-EU residents is valid for up to one year and is renewable. A permit is valid only for the period of employment if it's less than 12 months. Residence permits for EU nationals (*carte de séjour de ressortissant d'un état membre de l'UE*) are valid for ten years and are automatically renewable for further ten-year periods. However, EU nationals who are unemployed and have no proof of income are issued with a one-year temporary residence permit.

A residence permit for a non-EU employee (*carte de séjour temporaire salarié*) is valid for a maximum of one year and can be renewed two months before its expiration date, upon application and presentation of a new employment contract. It has the annotation *salarié* or the professional activity for which the contract was approved and lists the department(s) where the holder can be employed. After three years of continuous residence in France, the holder of a temporary residence permit can obtain a permanent residence permit. A combined residence and work permit (*carte unique de séjour et de travail*) is issued to certain categories of workers.

Permanent Residence Permit (*carte de résident*): A permanent residence permit is usually issued to foreigners who have lived in France for three consecutive years (the exception is the foreign spouse of a French citizen, who's automatically granted a permanent residence permit). It's valid for ten years and renewable providing the holder can furnish proof that he's practising a profession in France or has sufficient financial resources to maintain himself and his dependants. A permanent residence permit authorises the holder to undertake any professional activity (subject to qualifications and registration) in any French department, even if employment was previously forbidden.

Applications

An application for a residence permit must be made to your local town hall (*mairie*) in small towns, the police (*gendarmerie/commissariat de police*) in large towns and cities (e.g. Paris), and direct to the *Préfecture de Police* in prefectoral towns. In large towns and cities many offices have a special 'foreigners office' (*bureau des étrangers*). If you arrive in France with a long-stay visa, you must apply for a residence permit within one week, although students can delay their application for up to 30 days. EU nationals who visit France with the intention of finding employment or starting a business have three months in which to find a job and apply for a residence permit. Once employment has been found an application must be made for a residence permit. If you don't have a regular income or adequate financial means, the application will be refused. Failure to apply for a residence permit within three months of your entry into France is a serious offence and can result in a fine. It isn't possible to obtain a *carte de séjour* while living in temporary accommodation such as a hotel or caravan site.

Paris: In Paris, applications must be made to the appropriate police centre (*centre d'accueil des étrangers*) for the area (*arrondissement*) where you reside. Centres are open from 0845 to 1630 Mondays to Fridays. You must provide the necessary documentation (with translations if necessary), complete a number of forms and provide a local address. You're given a date (usually from 2 to 12 weeks after your application) when you can collect your permit from the *Préfecture de Police*.

Provinces: In the provinces an application for a residence permit should initially be made to your local town hall (*mairie*). If permits aren't issued locally you must apply to the *Direction de la Réglementation* of your department's *préfecture* or the nearest *sous-préfecture*.

Documents: Your local town hall or *préfecture* will notify you of the documentation required to apply for a residence permit. It depends on your particular situation and nationality and includes some of the following:

- *a valid passport, with a long-stay visa if necessary, or a national identity card (certain countries only);
- a birth certificate;
- *a number (usually three) of black and white (white background) or colour passport-size photographs;
- *proof of residence (see below);
- *two stamped and self-addressed envelopes;
- *proof of financial resources (see page 66);
- *details of your French bank account;
- *health insurance or a medical certificate (e.g. students) if you aren't covered under French social security. British retirees must produce a form E121 available from the DSS Overseas Branch. If you covered by French social security, you need your social security number.
- a marriage or divorce certificate or other papers relating to your marital status (this isn't usually required by EU nationals, but British applicants require a copy of their marriage certificate because the maiden name of a married woman isn't included in a British passport);

- an employment contract (see page 49);
- an affidavit stating that you have never been convicted of a criminal offence or declared bankrupt;
- a pre-registration or admission letter to an educational institution (students only);
- an au pair contract (see page 40) and a certificate of registration for French-language classes (au pairs only);

* Required by all applicants, including those from EU countries. If you're accompanied by any dependants, they also require a passport, birth certificate and photographs. Note that British dependants under 16 must have their own passport.

If you don't have the required documents you will be sent away to obtain them. If you don't have all the necessary documents to apply for a renewal of your residence permit, you should apply for an extension (*prolongation*). Certain documents must be translated by a notarised translator (listed under *Traducteurs - traductions officielles certifiées* in the Yellow Pages). It isn't advisable to get documents translated in advance as it's expensive and the requirements often vary depending on the area or office and your nationality. Certain documents must be notarised by a public notary (*notaire*) and all copies should be stamped 'official copy' (*copie certifiée conforme*) at your local town hall or *préfecture*.

When it isn't possible to issue a residence permit immediately, you're given a temporary authorisation (*récipissé de demande de carte de séjour* or an *attestation d'application de résidence*) valid for up to three months and renewable. You should keep this as evidence that you have applied for your residence permit. You're notified by mail when your residence permit is ready for collection. Where applicable, your local town hall submits your documents to the local *préfecture*, which usually issues a residence permit within six months (the period varies depending on where you live).

Proof of Residence: Proof of residence may consist of a copy of a lease or purchase contract or an electricity bill (*facture EDF*). If you're a lodger, the owner must provide an attestation (*certificat d'hébergement*) that you're resident in his home.

Moving House: When you move house you must inform the local town hall with jurisdiction over your new place of residence and produce proof of your new address. Your residence permit is updated with your new address. This is particularly important if you're in the process of renewing your residence permit, as the change of address must be recorded before a new permit can be issued.

Renewals: An application for renewal of a residence permit should be made one or two months before its expiry date. When you renew your residence permit, you must reconfirm your status and provide documentary evidence, as for the original application. There's a fee for the renewal of a residence permit. For renewal of a *carte de séjour salarié*, you must provide proof that you have declared your income and paid your taxes for the previous year. If the renewal is refused you must leave France when your permit expires. A residence permit automatically becomes invalid if you spend over six months outside France.

Change of Status: If you're a non-EU national and want the status of your residence permit changed to allow you to work in France, you must undergo a process called *régularisation*. An application must be made to your *préfecture* with proof of residence, a written job offer, and a letter explaining why a French or EU employee cannot do the job. The application is sent to the *Direction Départementale du Travail* for approval and can take up to six months.

Residence permits are issued for various categories including employees, the self-employed, businessmen, fiancé(e)s and spouses, students, au pairs, non-employed residents and refugees, all of which are described below.

Employees

If you're a national of an EU country (your passport must show that you have the right of abode in an EU country) you don't require official approval to live or work in France, although you still require a residence permit. If you visit France to look for a job you have three months to find employment or set up in business. Once employment has been found you must apply for a residence permit within one week. When you have been offered a job, you should obtain an employment contract (*certificat d'emploi*) or a letter of employment (*déclaration d'engagement*).

France has had a virtual freeze on the employment of non-EU nationals for many years, which has been strengthened in recent years due to the high unemployment rate. The employment of non-EU nationals must be approved by the French labour authorities (*Agence Nationale Pour l'Emploi/ANPE*), who can propose the employment of a French national in place of a foreigner (although this is rare). The prospective employer must obtain authorisation to employ a non-EU national from the French Ministry of Labour or the District Labour Department where the business is registered. The authorisation is a prerequisite to obtaining a long-stay visa and is sent to the *Office des Migrations Internationales* (OMI, 44, rue Bargue, 75732 Paris Cedex 15) for transmission to the appropriate French consulate abroad. The consulate notifies the applicant who can then proceed with the visa application. When the proposed monthly salary is above that for senior managers, the application is usually approved, although it's difficult for non-EU nationals to obtain a permit for employment paying a lower salary.

A non-EU national is subject to restrictions on the type of work he can do and the department(s) where he can work. Exceptions are foreigners with a permanent residence permit (see page 67), spouses of French citizens, and students who have studied in France for the preceding two years and have a parent who has lived in France for at least four years.

Self-Employed

An EU-national or a non-EU national with the status of a permanent resident (*carte de résident*) can work as self-employed (e.g. *travailleur indépendant* or *profession libérale*) or as a sole trader (*entreprise individuelle*) in France. It's difficult for non-EU nationals (without permanent residence) to obtain a residence permit to work as self-employed in France. There are three main categories of self-employed people in France: *profession libérale* (e.g. accountants, doctors, lawyers), *commerçants* (traders and shopkeepers) and *artisans* (craftsmen). To work in some professions and trades you must have particular qualifications (see page 24) and certificates that are recognised in France. If you're self-employed, you must register with the appropriate organisation for your particular profession or trade, e.g. the *Chambre de Commerce,* the *Chambre des Métiers* or the *Chambre d'Agriculture*. You can obtain the address of the relevant body from your local town hall.

Before being permitted to register as self-employed, you must attend a business course (*cours/stage de gestion*) run by the relevant local organisation for your trade or profession, covering all aspects of business administration. Courses last from four to six days and cost around 800F. At the end of the course you're issued with a certificate (whether you understood anything or not!), which is a prerequisite for starting a business. Some courses are held with English translators, although in certain cases you may also need to pass an exam (in French) to obtain a trading licence. The various chambers issue a certificate that must be presented to your local chamber of commerce when registering your business. For information about French chambers of commerce contact the *Assemblée Permanente des Chambres de Commerces et d'Industrie (APCCI)*, 45, avenue d'Iéna, Paris 75016 (☎ 01.47.23.01.11). To work as a self-employed person in France, you need:

- qualifications and diplomas that are recognised in France for professions and trades requiring certification (see page 24);
- contracts or letters of intent from prospective clients (for those in service industries only);
- a social security number (see page 256);
- to register for value added tax (TVA) at the office nearest to your business location;
- to register with the appropriate organisation for your profession or trade, e.g. the *Chambre de Commerce*;
- a tax registration certificate (*l'avis d'imposition*);
- a residence permit;
- a *carte de commerçant* and to register at your local *tribunal de commerce* (for a commercial business).

See also **Self-Employment** on page 35.

Businessmen

Non-EU nationals wishing to start or manage a business in France, including any commercial activity or business selling goods (e.g. retailing), must obtain a business permit (*carte de commerçant*). Business permits aren't required by EU nationals, holders of permanent residence permits (*carte de résident*), owners and investors in companies (not managers), and self-employed workers performing a service (rather than a commercial activity).

An application for a business permit should be made abroad at a French consulate when applying for a visa. Your residence permit is stamped *non-salarié, profession libéi ale* and you aren't permitted to work as a salaried employee in France. If you're already resident in France, you can apply for a business permit at your local town hall or *préfecture*. You must provide details relating to the incorporation of the prospective business, a detailed description of the proposed business activity, proof of financial resources, and an affidavit stating that you have never been convicted of a criminal offence or declared bankrupt. It may take up to six months to obtain a business permit, although a temporary permit can be issued within a shorter period.

For further information contact your country's embassy in France or the commercial attaché at a French consulate. See also **Starting a Business** on page 36.

Fiancé(e)s & Spouses

The status of the fiancé(e) or spouse of a French resident depends on the nationality and status of the fiancé(e) or spouse who's resident in France.

Fiancé(e): Non-EU nationals coming to France to marry a French citizen, EU-national or a non-EU resident of France, and planning to remain in France for longer than three months must obtain a long-stay visa for marriage (*visa de long séjour pour mariage*) before their arrival.

Spouse: Non-EU nationals married to a French citizen for less than one year require a long-stay visa to enter France and cannot obtain an extension (beyond 90 days) if they enter France as a visitor. This rule also applies to non-EU nationals married to foreign residents of France. Foreigners who have been married to a French citizen for over one year may be permitted to enter France as visitors then apply for a residence permit, although a long-stay visa is recommended (check with a French consulate abroad). The foreign spouse of a French citizen is automatically granted a permanent residence permit (*carte de résident*). The non-EU spouse of an EU-national is granted a temporary five-year residence permit (*carte de séjour*) permitting him or her to live and work in France.

The spouse and children aged under 18 of a non-EU national with a visa to work in France (*visa de séjour salarié*) may usually accompany him to France, although a visa is required for each family member. Applications for visas for family members must be made at the same time as the main applicant's visa application. Family members don't have the right to work in France unless they have their own *visa de séjour salarié*. The spouse of a French citizen or foreigner resident in France must produce his or her marriage licence (*acte de mariage*) when applying for a residence permit.

Students

Non-EU nationals planning to study in France for less than six months (e.g. language students) are issued with a special six-month student visa (*visa d'étudiant pour six mois avec plusieurs entrées*). With this temporary visa it's usually unnecessary to obtain a residence permit. The visa must, however, state that a residence permit is unnecessary, i.e. *le titulaire de ce visa est dispensé de solliciter une carte de séjour* or *le présent visa vaut autorisation de séjour*. If you're a non-EU national planning to study in France for longer than six months, you require a *visa de long séjour pour études*. You must obtain a visa before arriving in France and cannot change your status later, e.g. after entering France as a visitor.

If you're a student living in Paris, you must apply for a residence permit at the *Centre Etudiants*, 13, rue Miollis, 75015 Paris, open from 0900 to 1615, Mondays to Fridays. Outside Paris, applications should be made to your local *mairie* or *préfecture*. To renew your residence permit you require a certificate (*certificat d'assiduité*) stating that you have attended classes during the past year and passed your exams.

After completing your first year of study you can obtain a temporary work permit (*autorisation provisoire de travail*) for part-time (*mi-temps*) work. You may work for a maximum of 20 hours a week during school terms or for 39 hours a week (35 from 1st January 2000) during the summer holiday period. The French government issues instructions regarding student employment during the last term of the academic year. The rules apply to tertiary level students and students in secondary and technical schools aged 16 or older. Students at educational institutions that don't provide students with French social security health cover or students with a French scholarship (or *bourse*) aren't eligible for temporary work permits. Summer work cannot exceed three months and must take place between 1st June and 31st October. Students can also work for a maximum of 15 days during the Christmas and Easter holiday periods. Most students, including those in secondary education aged 14 or older, are eligible for a permit for part-time summer employment, although students aged 14 or 15 are permitted to do only light work and may work for just half the summer holiday period.

To apply for a work permit, you must submit your student card (*carte d'étudiant*), residence permit, and a letter from the prospective employer (stating his name and address, job title and description, salary, working hours, place of work and length of employment) to your local *Direction Départementale du Travail et de l'Emploi*. Secondary and technical school students aged under 18 also need a letter of authorisation from their parents and a *certificat de scolarité*. Foreign students aged 14 or 15 must provide proof that their parents are legally resident in France.

Au Pairs

A non-EU national must obtain a long-stay visa for an au pair (*stagiaire aide-familial*) position before arriving in France. To obtain a long-stay visa you must usually have an agreement (*déclaration d'engagement*) with a French family and a certificate of registration for French-language classes. A French family or au pair agency must complete the application forms (*accord de placement au pair d'un stagiaire aide-familial*) available from the Foreign Labour Department of the Ministry of Labour (*Direction Départementale du Travail et de la Main d'Oeuvre*) office in the *département* where the au pair will be resident. Two copies of the form are returned to the family or agency, one of which must be sent to a non-EU au pair abroad so that she can apply for a visa. An au pair's residence permit (*permis de stagiaire aide-familiale*) is valid for six months and renewable for up to 18 months. For further information see **Au Pairs** on page 40.

Non-Employed Persons

Retired and non-active EU nationals don't require a long-stay visa before moving to France. A residence permit is still necessary and an application should be made within one week of your arrival in France. Retirees have their permit stamped 'retired' (*retraité*) allowing for automatic social security cover. Non-EU nationals require a long-stay visa (*visa de long séjour*) to live in France for longer than three months and should make a visa application to their local French Consulate at least four or five months before their planned departure date. All non-employed residents must provide proof that they have an adequate income or financial resources to live in France without working (see page 66).

4.

ARRIVAL

On arrival in France, your first task is to negotiate immigration and customs. Fortunately this presents few problems for most people, particularly European Union (EU) nationals after the establishment of 'open' EU borders on 1st January 1993. However, with the exception of EU nationals and visitors from a number of other countries, all persons wishing to enter France require a visa (see page 64).

France is a signatory to the Schengen agreement (named after a Luxembourg village on the Moselle River where the agreement was signed) which came into effect on 1st January 1995 and introduced an open-border policy between member countries. These now comprise Austria, Belgium, France, Germany, Greece, Iceland, Italy, Luxembourg, the Netherlands, Portugal, Spain and Sweden. Under the agreement, immigration checks and passport controls take place when you first arrive in a member country, after which you can travel freely between member countries. However, France invoked a special 'safeguard' clause in the agreement to preserve frontier controls because of fears over illegal immigration and cross-border drug trafficking.

In addition to information regarding immigration and customs, this chapter also includes suggestions for finding local help and information and contains a list of tasks that must be completed before or soon after arrival in France.

IMMIGRATION

When you arrive in France from another EU country, there are usually no immigration checks or passport controls, which take place when you arrive in an EU country from outside the EU. If you're a non-EU national and arrive in France by air or sea from outside the EU, you must go through immigration (*police des frontières*) for non-EU citizens. If you have a single-entry visa (see page 64) it will be cancelled by the immigration official. **If you require a visa to enter France and attempt to enter without one, you will be refused entry.** Some people may wish to get a stamp in their passport as confirmation of their date of entry into France. If you're a non-EU national coming to France to work, study or live, you may be asked to show documentary evidence.

Immigration officials may ask non-EU visitors to produce a return ticket, proof of accommodation, health insurance and financial resources, e.g. cash, traveller's cheques and credit cards. The onus is on visitors to show that they are genuine and that they won't violate French immigration laws. Immigration officials aren't required to prove that you will breach the immigration laws and can refuse you entry on the grounds of suspicion only. Young people may be liable to interrogation, particularly long-haired youths with 'strange' attire. It's advantageous to carry international credit and charge cards, a return or onward travel ticket, a student identity card, and a letter from an employer or college stating that you're on holiday.

French immigration officials are usually polite and efficient, although they are occasionally a little over zealous in their attempts to exclude illegal immigrants, and some racial groups (e.g. Africans and Arabs) may experience harassment and persecution.

CUSTOMS

The Single European Act, which came into effect on 1st January 1993, created a single trading market and changed the rules regarding customs (*douanes*) for EU nationals. The shipment of personal (household) effects to France from another EU country is no longer subject to customs formalities, although an inventory must be provided. Note, however, that those arriving in France from outside the EU (including EU citizens) are still subject to customs checks and limitations on what may be imported duty-free. There are no restrictions on the import or export of French or foreign banknotes or securities, although if you enter or leave France with 50,000F or more in cash or negotiable instruments (see page 276), you must make a declaration to French customs.

If you require general information about French customs regulations or have specific questions contact the *Centre Renseignement des Douanes*, 238, quai de Bercy, 75572 Paris Cedex 12 (☎ 01.40.01.02.06). Information about duty-free allowances can be found on page 390, pets on page 404 and vehicles on page 195.

Visitors

Visitors' belongings aren't subject to duty or VAT when they are visiting France for up to 90 days. This applies to the importation of private cars, camping vehicles (including trailers or caravans), motorcycles, aircraft, boats and personal effects. Goods may be imported without formality providing their nature and quantity doesn't imply any commercial aim. All means of transport and personal effects imported duty-free mustn't be sold or given away in France and must be exported before the expiration of the 90-day period.

If you enter France by road you may drive (at a walking pace) through the border without stopping. However, any goods and pets that you're carrying must fall within the exemptions and mustn't be the subject of any prohibition or restriction (see page 78). Customs officials can still stop anyone for a spot check, e.g. to check for drugs or illegal immigrants. Occasionally (although rarer nowadays) you will come across an obstructive customs officer who will insist on inspecting everything in your car, which is often pure obstruction as they usually aren't looking for anything. However, if you enter France from Spain, particularly if you're a single male in an old car, your vehicle is likely to be searched and be 'inspected' by a drugs 'sniffer' dog.

If you arrive at a seaport by private boat there are no particular customs' formalities, although you must show the boat's registration papers if asked. If you arrive at a river port or land border with a boat, you may be asked to produce registration papers for the boat *and* its out-board motor(s). A foreign-registered boat may remain in France for a maximum of six months in a calendar year, after which it must be exported or permanently imported (and duty and tax paid). Foreign-registered vehicles and boats mustn't be lent or hired to anyone while in France.

Non-EU Residents

If you're a non-EU resident planning to take up permanent or temporary residence in France, you're permitted to import your furniture and personal effects free of duty. These include vehicles, mobile homes, pleasure boats and aircraft. However, to qualify for duty-free importation, articles must have been owned and used for at least six months. Value Added Tax (VAT) must be paid on items owned for less than six months that weren't purchased within the EU. If goods were purchased within the EU, a VAT receipt must be produced.

To import personal effects, an application must be made to the *Direction Régionale des Douanes* in the area where you will be resident. Customs clearance can be carried out by a customs office in an internal town in France, rather than at the border, in which case you should obtain a certificate (*carte de libre circulation*) proving that you have declared your belongings on entry into France and are entitled to travel with them.

All items should be imported within one year of the date of your change of residence, either in one or a number of consignments, although it's best to have one consignment only. After one year's residence in France, you must pay French VAT (TVA) on further imports from outside the EU, except in certain exceptional circumstances such as property resulting from an inheritance. A complete inventory of items to be imported (even if they're imported in a number of consignments) must be provided for customs officials, together with proof of residence in your former country and proof of settlement in France. If there's more than one consignment, subsequent consignments should be cleared through the same customs office.

If you use a removal company to transport your belongings to France, they will usually provide the necessary forms and take care of the paperwork. Always keep a copy of forms and communications with customs officials, both French customs officials and officials in your previous or permanent country of residence. You should have an official record of the export of valuables from any country in case you wish to re-import them later.

Prohibited & Restricted Goods

When entering France certain goods are subject to special regulations and in some cases their import (and export) is prohibited or restricted. This applies in particular to animal products; plants (see below); wild fauna and flora and products derived from them; live animals; medicines and medical products (except for prescribed drugs and medicines); firearms and ammunition; certain goods and technologies with a dual civil/military purpose; and works of art and collectors' items. If you're unsure whether any goods you're importing fall into the above categories, you should check with French customs.

To import certain types of plants into France, you must obtain a phytosanitary health certificate (*certificats sanitaires*). Information can be obtained from the *Service de la Protection des Végétaux*, 175, rue du Chevaleret, 75646 Paris Cedex 13 (☎ 01.45.84.13.13) or your country's customs department. There's usually a limit on the number of plants that can be imported into France. However, as plants can be imported as part of your personal effects, they won't usually be subject to any controls.

If you make it through customs unscathed with your car loaded to the gunnels with illicit goods, don't be too quick to break out the champagne in celebration. France has 'flying' customs officials (*douane volante*) with the power to stop and search vehicles at random anywhere within its borders (they often stop vehicles at *autoroute* toll gates and roundabouts on national highways).

RESIDENCE PERMIT

All foreigners (legally) residing in France for longer than 90 days must register with the local authorities and obtain a residence permit. Whether you're an employee, student, or a non-employed resident, you must usually register within one week of taking up residence in France. EU nationals who visit France with the intention of finding employment or starting a business have three months in which to find a job and apply for a residence permit. Once employment has been found, an application must be made for a residence permit. If you don't have a regular income or adequate financial resources, your application will be refused. Failure to apply for a residence permit before three months have expired is a serious offence and may result in a fine. For further information see **Residence Permit** on page 67.

EMBASSY REGISTRATION

Nationals of some countries are required to register with their local embassy or consulate after taking up residence in France. Registration isn't usually mandatory, although most embassies like to keep a record of their country's citizens resident in France (it helps to justify their existence).

FINDING HELP

One of the biggest difficulties facing new arrivals in France is how and where to find help with day-to-day problems, for example finding accommodation, schooling, insurance and so on. **This book was written in response to this need.** However, in addition to the comprehensive information provided herein, you will also need detailed *local* information. How successful you are at finding help depends on your employer, the town or area where you live (e.g. residents of Paris are better served than those living in rural areas), your nationality, French proficiency and your sex (women are better served than men through numerous women's clubs).

There's an abundance of information available in French, but little in English and other foreign languages. An additional problem is that much of the available information isn't intended for foreigners and their particular needs. You may find that your friends and colleagues can help, as they can often offer advice based on their own experiences and mistakes. **But take care!** Although they mean well, you're likely to receive as much false and conflicting information as accurate (it may not necessarily be wrong, but may be invalid for your particular situation).

Your local community is usually an excellent source of reliable information, but you need to speak French to benefit from it. Your town hall (*mairie*) is often the local registry of births, deaths and marriages; passport office; land registry; council office; citizens advice bureau; and tourist office. Some companies employ staff to help new arrivals or contract this job out to a relocation consultant (see page 85). However, most French employers are totally unaware of (or disinterested in) the problems and difficulties faced by foreign employees and their families.

An organisation of particular interest to foreigners moving to France is the 'National Union for Welcome in French Towns' (*Union Nationale des Accueils des Villes Françaises/AVF*). The AVF is a national organisation comprising over 600 local volunteer associations who provide a welcome for individuals and families, and help them settle into their new environment. Each association operates an information centre where information and advice is available free of charge. The address of local associations in France can be found via Minitel (3615 AVF-ACCUEIL) terminals at any post office (see page 125). Foreigners planning to move to France can obtain information about particular areas from the *Union*

Nationale des AVF, Relations Internationales, Secrétariat Administratif, 20, rue du 4 Septembre, 75002 Paris (☎ 01.40.17.02.36). Write to them indicating the town, department and region where you're planning to live and the reason for moving to France, e.g. work, retirement, study or training.

There's a wealth of valuable information and expatriate organisations in major French cities, particularly in Paris, where foreigners are well-served by English-speaking clubs and organisations. Contacts can be found through many expatriate magazines and newspapers (see page 384). In Paris, the American Church (65, quai d'Orsay, 75007 Paris, ☎ 01.40.62.05.00), runs an annual newcomer's orientation series in October called 'Bloom Where You Are Planted'. The programme is designed to help foreigners adjust to life in France and consists of seminars on topics such as overcoming culture shock, survival skills, personal and professional opportunities, networking, enjoying France/food, fashion, travel and wine. The Women's Institute for Continuing Education (20, bd du Montparnasse, 75015 Paris, ☎ 01.45.66.75.50) also operate a 'Living in France' programme for newcomers, as do expatriate clubs and organisations throughout France.

Note that in France it isn't what you know, but who you know that can make all the difference between success or failure. String-pulling or the use of contacts is widespread in France and is invaluable when it comes to breaking through the numerous layers of bureaucracy, when a telephone call on your behalf from a French neighbour or colleague can work wonders. In fact any contact can be of help, even a professional acquaintance, who may not even charge you for his time.

Most consulates provide their nationals with local information including details of lawyers, interpreters, doctors, dentists, schools, and social and expatriate organisations. The British Community Committee publishes a free *Digest of British and Franco-British Clubs, Societies and Institutions*, available from British consulates in France (see **Appendix A**).

CHECKLISTS

Before Arrival

The following checklist contains a summary of the tasks that should (if possible) be completed before your arrival in France:

* Obtain a visa, if necessary, for you and your family members (see **Chapter 3**). Obviously this *must* be done before arrival in France.

* Visit France prior to your move to compare communities and schools and to arrange schooling for your children (see **Chapter 9**).

* Find temporary or permanent accommodation and buy a car. If you purchase a car in France, register it and arrange insurance (see pages 196 and 201).

* Arrange for shipment of your personal effects to France (see page 95).

* Arrange health insurance for yourself and your family (see page 264). This is essential if you aren't covered by a private insurance policy and won't be covered by French social security.

* Open a bank account in France and transfer funds (you can open an account with many French banks while abroad, although it's best done in person in France). It's

advisable to obtain some French francs before arriving in France as this will save you having to queue to change money on arrival.

● Obtain an international driver's licence, if necessary.

● If you don't already have one, it's advisable to obtain an international credit or charge card, which will be invaluable during your first few months in France.

Don't forget to bring all your family's official documents including birth certificates; driver's licences; marriage certificate, divorce papers or death certificate (if a widow or widower); educational diplomas, professional certificates and job references; school records and student ID cards; employment references; medical and dental records; bank account and credit card details; insurance policies; and receipts for any valuables. You will also need the documents necessary to obtain a residence permit (see page 67) plus certified copies, official translations and numerous passport-size photographs (students should take at least a dozen).

After Arrival

The following checklist contains a summary of tasks to be completed after arrival in France (if not done before arrival):

● On arrival at a French airport or port, have your visa cancelled and your passport stamped, as applicable.

● If you aren't taking a car with you, you may wish to rent one for a week or two until buying one locally (see page 222). Note that it's practically impossible to get around in rural areas without a car.

● Apply for a residence permit at your local *mairie* or *préfecture* within one week of your arrival (see page 67).

● register with your local consulate (see page 79).

● make courtesy calls on your neighbours and the local mayor within a few weeks of your arrival. This is particularly important in villages and rural areas if you want to be accepted and become part of the local community.

● Do the following in the days following your arrival:

  – apply for a social security card from your local social security office (see page 256);

  – open a bank account at a local bank and give the details to your employer (see page 279);

  – arrange schooling for your children (see **Chapter 9**);

  – find a local doctor and dentist (see **Chapter 12**);

  – arrange whatever insurance is necessary (see **Chapter 13**) including:

    * health insurance (see page 264);
    * car insurance (see page 201);
    * household insurance (see page 266);
    * private liability insurance (see page 268).

5.

ACCOMMODATION

In most areas of France accommodation (to buy or rent) isn't difficult to find, although there are a few exceptions. For example, in Paris, rental accommodation is in high demand and short supply and rents can be astronomical. Accommodation accounts for around 20 to 25 per cent of the average French family's budget and can be much higher in expensive areas. Property prices rose considerably in the '80s in many areas, fuelled by a high demand for holiday homes, particularly from foreigners. When the recession hit France in the early '90s, property prices plummeted by up to 50 per cent as buyers disappeared, although they have since returned to their previous levels (or higher) in most regions.

Property prices and rents in France vary considerably depending on the region and city. For example, a 50m² (538ft²) two-bedroom apartment in a reasonable area of Paris rents for between 5,000 and 10,000F per month, and around 50 per cent less in a city such as Bordeaux. In cities and large towns, apartments are much more common than houses, particularly in Paris, where houses are rare and prohibitively expensive. Property in Paris and on the French Riviera is among the most expensive in the world, although prices are reasonable in most regions.

Home ownership in France is around 55 per cent compared with some 40 per cent in Germany, 70 per cent in Britain and Italy, and 80 per cent in Spain. However, although ownership of principal homes in France is below the European average, French ownership of holiday homes (mostly located in France) is the world's highest, with around one in six people owning a holiday home. In cities and many towns it's simply too expensive for most people to buy and many families prefer to rent and don't see property as a good investment (added to which tenants in France have security of tenure and rents are strictly controlled). Many Parisians rent their principal home but may own up to three holiday homes, e.g. one in the country for weekends, one on the French Riviera for summer holidays and another in the Alps for skiing. The French aren't particularly mobile and tend to move home much less frequently than people in some other countries, e.g. Britain and the USA.

In rural France there's a depopulation crisis due to the mass exodus of people from the land to the cities and factories in the last 30 years. Provincial France is losing its population to the cities at the rate of around 100,000 people a year. It's estimated that around one in every 12 French properties is vacant and the number is even higher in some areas. Some communities offer inexpensive or even free housing to families with school-age children in an attempt to preserve local schools and keep communities alive.

TEMPORARY ACCOMMODATION

On arrival in France, you may find it necessary to stay in temporary accommodation for a few weeks or months, e.g. before moving into permanent accommodation or while waiting for your furniture to arrive. Some employers provide rooms, self-contained apartments or hostels for employees and their families, although this is rare and usually for a limited period only.

Many hotels and bed and breakfast establishments cater for long-term guests and offer reduced weekly or monthly rates. In most areas, particularly in Paris and other main cities, service and holiday apartments are available. These are fully self-contained furnished apartments with their own bathrooms and kitchens, which are cheaper and more convenient than a hotel, particularly for families. Service apartments are usually rented on a weekly basis. In most provincial regions self-catering holiday accommodation (see page 318) is available, although this is prohibitively expensive during the main holiday season (June-August). One of the easiest ways to find temporary accommodation in Paris is through an agent such as *Allô Logement Temporaire*, 64, rue du Temple, 75003 Paris (☎ 01.42.72.00.06).

For information about hotels, bed and breakfast, self-catering, hostels, dormitories and YMCA/YWCAs, see **Chapter 15**.

RELOCATION CONSULTANTS

If you're fortunate enough to have your move to France paid for by your employer, it's likely that they will arrange for a relocation consultant to handle the details. There are fewer relocation consultants in France (most are based in Paris) than in many other European countries and they usually deal only with corporate clients with lots of money to pay their fees. Fees depend on the services required, with packages usually ranging from around 8,000F to 20,000F. The main service provided by relocation consultants is finding accommodation (either to rent or purchase) and arranging viewing.

Other housing services include conducting negotiations, drawing up contracts, arranging mortgages, organising surveys and insurance, and handling the move. They also provide reports on local schools, health services, public transport, sports and social facilities, and other amenities and services. Some companies provide daily advice and assistance and help in dealing with French officials, e.g. residence procedures. Finding rental accommodation for single people or couples without children can usually be accomplished in a few weeks, while locating family homes may take up to four weeks, depending on the location and requirements. You should usually allow two to three months between your initial visit and moving into a purchased property.

FRENCH HOMES

Most French families live in detached homes and apartments, and semi-detached and terraced properties are relatively rare. Some 45 per cent of the French population live in apartments (although less than 10 per cent in tower blocks), which are more common in France than in most other European countries. In cities and suburbs, most people have little choice as houses are in short supply and prohibitively expensive. In the major cities there are many *bourgeois* apartments built in the 19th or early 20th century, with large rooms, high ceilings and huge windows. Unless modernised they have old fashioned bathrooms, kitchens and non 'public' rooms (the rooms visitors don't see), and are expensive to decorate, furnish and maintain. Many apartments don't have their own source of hot water and heating, which is shared with other apartments in the same building.

French homes are usually built to high structural standards and whether you buy a new or an old home, it will usually be extremely sturdy. Older homes often have metre-thick walls and contain numerous rooms. Many have a wealth of interesting period features including vast fireplaces, wooden staircases, attics, cellars (*caves*) and a profusion of alcoves and annexes. Many houses have a basement (*sous-sol*), used as a garage and cellar. In most old houses, open fireplaces remain a central feature even when central heating is installed. In warmer regions, floors are often tiled and walls are painted rather than papered, while in cooler northern regions, floors are carpeted or bare wood and walls are more likely to be papered. When wallpaper is used, it's often garish and may cover everything including walls, doors and even the ceilings! Properties throughout France are usually built in a distinct local (often unique) style using local materials. There are stringent regulations in most areas relating to the style and design of new homes and the restoration of old buildings.

In older rural properties, the kitchen (*cuisine*) is the most important room in the house. It's usually huge with a large wood-burning stove for cooking and providing hot water, a huge solid wood dining table and possibly a bread oven. French country kitchens are worlds apart from modern fitted kitchens (called American kitchens in France) and are devoid of shiny formica, plastic laminates and pristine order. They are often stark in comparison with modern kitchens, with stone or tiled floors and a predominance of wood, tiles and marble.

Refrigerators (*frigos*) and stoves (*cuisinières*) are usually quite small in French homes. Stoves in rural homes usually run on bottled gas or a combination of bottled gas and electricity. Many homes have a gas water heater (*chaudière*) which heats the water for the bathroom and kitchen. Most French homes don't have a separate utility room and the washing machine and dryer are usually housed in the kitchen. Homes often have a separate toilet (*toilette* or *WC/waters*) and the bathroom (*salle de bains*) often has a toilet, a *bidet*, a bath (*baignoire*) and/or a shower (*douche*). Baths are more common than showers in older homes, although showers are found in most modern homes. Note that many old, unmodernised homes don't have a bath, shower room or an inside toilet.

Although new properties are often lacking in character, they are usually spacious and well endowed with modern conveniences and services, which certainly cannot be taken for granted in older rural properties. The standard fixtures and fittings in modern houses are more comprehensive and of better quality than those found in old houses. The French generally prefer modern homes to older houses with 'charm and character', which to the locals means that it's expensive to maintain and is in danger of falling down. You do, however, often find pseudo period features such as beams and open fireplaces in new homes. Central heating, double glazing and insulation are common in new houses, particularly in northern France, where they are essential. Central heating may be electric, gas or oil-fired. However, on the French Riviera, where winter temperatures are higher, expensive insulation and heating may be considered unnecessary (don't you believe it!). Air-conditioning is rare, even in the south of France.

Many French properties have shutters fitted, both for security and as a means of insulation. Often external shutters are supplemented by internal shutters, which are fixed directly to the window frames. French casement windows open inwards, rather than outwards as in most other countries. In the south and southwest, many homes have outdoor swimming pools and homes throughout France have a paved patio or terrace that's often covered.

BUYING PROPERTY

Buying a house or an apartment in France is usually a good long-term investment and preferable to renting. However, if you're staying for only a short term, say less than three years, then you're usually better off renting. For those staying longer than this, buying is usually the best option, particularly as buying a house or apartment is generally no more expensive than renting in the long term and could yield a handsome profit (or a loss!).

The French don't generally buy domestic property as an investment but as a home for life and you shouldn't expect to make a fast profit when buying property in France. Generally property values increase at an average of around 4 or 5 per cent a year (or in line with inflation), meaning you must usually own a house for around three years simply to recover the high costs associated with buying. House prices rise much faster than average in some fashionable areas, although this is generally reflected in higher purchase prices. The stable property market in most areas acts as a discouragement to speculators wishing to make a fast profit, particularly as many properties require a substantial investment in restoration or modernisation before they can be sold at a profit. Note that capital gains tax (see page 301) can wipe out a third of any profit made on the sale of a second home.

Many foreigners buying property in France buy a second home for holidays or as a weekend retreat, perhaps with a view to retiring or living there permanently in the future. However, an increasing number of people are moving to France to retire, work or start a business, or even to commute to a job in another country. For many foreign buyers, France provides the opportunity to buy a size or style of home that they couldn't afford in their home countries.

There has been resistance to foreigners buying property in some areas, although few towns have actually blocked sales to foreigners to deter speculators. Understandably, the locals don't want property prices driven up by foreigners to levels they can no longer afford. However, foreigners are generally welcomed by the local populace because they boost the economy and in rural areas often buy derelict properties that the French won't touch. Permanent residents in rural areas who take the time and trouble to integrate into the local community are invariably warmly welcomed.

Before buying a property in France, you should be clear about your long-term plans and goals. One of the most common mistakes when buying a rural property in France is to buy a house that's much larger than you need with acres of land, simply because it seems to offer such good value. Don't, on the other hand, buy a property that's too small! Bear in mind that extra space can easily be swallowed up and when you have a home in France you will inevitably discover that you have many more relations and friends than you ever thought possible!

Buying a huge house with a few acres may seem like a good investment, but bear in mind that should you need to sell buyers may be thin on the ground, particularly when the price has doubled or trebled after the cost of renovation. In most areas there's a narrow market for renovated rural property. Although there are usually plenty of buyers in the lower 300,000F to 500,000F price range, they become much scarcer at 1,000,000F or more unless a property is exceptional, i.e. outstandingly attractive, in a popular area and with a superb location. In some areas even the most desirable properties remain on the market for a number of years.

Although it's tempting to buy a property with a lot of land, you should think carefully about what you're going to do with it. After you've installed a swimming pool, tennis court and croquet lawn, you still have a lot of change left out of even a few acres. Do you like gardening or are you prepared to live in a jungle? A large garden needs a lot of upkeep (i.e. work!). One of the most common pitfalls for new buyers is buying too much land. Of course you can always plant an orchard or vineyard, create a lake or take up farming.

If you're looking for a holiday home (*résidence secondaire*), you may wish to investigate mobile homes or a scheme that restricts your occupancy of a property to a number of weeks a year. These include sale-and-leaseback (*nouvelle propriété*), co-owner finance (*copropriété financière*), time-sharing (*time-propriété/multi-propriété*), a holiday property bond and shared ownership. Don't rush into any of these schemes without fully researching the market, and before you're absolutely clear about what you want and what you can realistically expect to receive for your money. Note that a leaseback scheme should provide vacant possession at the end of the lease period without you having to pay an indemnity charge, which could mean that you end up paying more than the property's worth.

As when buying property anywhere, it's never advisable to be in too much of a hurry. Have a good look around in the area you have chosen and make sure you have a clear picture of the relative prices and the types of properties available. The average cost per square metre of apartments in France is around 10,000F, with the lowest prices in the Lorraine and the highest in Paris. There's a huge range of property available, ranging from derelict farmhouses to a modern townhouses and apartments with all modern conveniences, from crumbling *châteaux* requiring complete restoration to brand new chalets. You can also buy a plot of land and have an individual architect-designed house built to your own specifications. If, however, after discussing it at length with your partner, one of you insists on a new luxury apartment in Cannes and the other a 17th century *château* in the Loire Valley, the easiest solution may be to get a divorce!

It's a wise or lucky person who gets his choice absolutely right first time. Although property in France is relatively inexpensive compared with many other European countries, the professional fees associated with the purchase of properties older than five years are the highest in Europe and add an average of around 15 per cent to the cost. To reduce the chances of making an expensive error when buying in an unfamiliar region, it's often prudent to rent for six to 12 months, taking in the worst part of the year (weather-wise) if you're planning to become a resident. This allows you to become familiar with the region and the weather and gives you plenty of time to look around for a permanent home at your leisure.

There's no shortage of properties for sale in France (indeed, in most areas there's a glut) and whatever kind of property you're looking for you will have an abundance from which to choose. Wait until you find something you fall head over heels in love with and then think about it for another week or two before rushing headlong to the altar! One of the best things about buying property in France is that there's always another 'dream' home around the next corner – and the second or third 'dream' home is often even better than the others. It's better to miss the 'opportunity of a lifetime' than end up with an expensive pile of stones around your neck.

The most important point to bear in mind when buying property in France is to obtain expert professional advice from someone who's familiar with French law. It isn't advisable to rely solely on advice given by those with a financial interest in selling you a property, although their advice may be excellent and entirely unbiased. You will find the relatively small cost (in comparison with the cost of a property) of obtaining expert advice to be excellent value for money, if only for the peace of mind it affords. **If you don't know the country well and don't speak French fluently, obtain legal advice before signing a contract!**

Many people have had their fingers burnt by rushing into deals without proper care and consideration. It isn't that France is full of crooks out to rob unsuspecting foreigners, although like most countries, it has its fair share. In fact, buyers in France have a much higher degree of legal protection than in many other European countries. However, it's too easy to fall in love with the beauty and ambience of France and sign a contract without giving it sufficient thought. You can find professionals who speak English and other languages in most areas of France, and many expatriate professionals (e.g. architects, builders, surveyors) also practise there. **However, don't assume when dealing with a fellow countryman that he'll offer you a better deal or do a better job than a Frenchman (the opposite may be true).** It's also wise to check the credentials of professionals you employ, whether French or foreign.

The more homework you do before buying a property the better, including obtaining advice from existing expatriate homeowners in France. Buying a property in France is a complex and vast subject and to cover it in depth is beyond the scope of this book. Fortunately there's a wealth of information and books on the market for French property buyers, including *Buying a Home in France* (Survival Books) written by yours truly David Hampshire (and highly recommended!). A comprehensive list of other books is contained in **Appendix B**.

In the last decade or so a number of specialist English-language French property magazines and newspapers have sprung up in Britain including *Focus on France*, *French Property News* and *Living France* (see **Appendix B** for addresses). In France, property is advertised for sale (under *vente maisons/appartements*) in all major Parisian and provincial newspapers plus many free newspapers. Weekly property newspapers such as *De Particulier à Particulier*, *Le Journal des Particuliers*, *La Centrale des Particuliers* and *La Semaine Immobilière* are also good sources of information. A good overview of the types of properties available and the prices in different areas is contained in *Your Home in France* (in French), a monthly catalogue of properties for sale throughout France (and available on subscription) published by *Indicateur Lagrange*, 163, av. G. Clémenceau, 92022 Nanterre Cedex (☎ 01.47.24.63.63).

RENTED ACCOMMODATION

If you're staying in France for only a few years (say less than three), then renting is usually the best solution. It's also the answer for those who don't want the trouble, expense and restrictions associated with buying a property. Renting is common in France, where some 45 per cent of the population lives in rented accommodation (many French families prefer to rent and don't see property as a good investment). Tenants have security of tenure and rentals are strictly controlled under French law. France has a strong rental market and it's possible to rent every kind of property, from a tiny studio apartment (bedsitter) to a huge rambling *château*. In large cities most rental properties are apartments, which are preferred by many renters. Note that large apartments and houses are more difficult to find than small one or two-roomed apartments, particularly in Paris and other cities.

Most rental properties in France are let unfurnished (*non-meublé*), particularly for lets longer than one year, and furnished (*meublé*) properties are difficult to find. If you're looking for a home for less than a year, then you're better off looking for a furnished apartment or house. However, you don't have the same legal protection in a furnished property, although for short-term renters this isn't usually so important.

Note that in France, 'unfurnished' doesn't just mean without furniture. An unfurnished property usually has no light fixtures, curtain rods or even an outdoor TV aerial. There's also no cooker, refrigerator or dishwasher and there may even be no kitchen units, carpets or kitchen sink! Always ask before viewing, as you may save yourself a wasted trip. If the previous tenant has fitted items such as carpets and kitchen cupboards, he may ask you for a rebate (*reprise*) to reimburse him for the cost. You should negotiate the rebate and ensure that you receive value for money. A *reprise* isn't enforceable, although if the tenant has the approval of the landlord it's difficult to avoid paying it, even though it may amount to little more than a bribe.

Many apartment blocks have a caretaker or porter (*concierge* or *gardienne*), who usually lives in a tiny apartment at the entrance to grand apartment blocks, particularly in Paris. Her job (it's usually a woman, perhaps assisted by her husband) includes cleaning the entrance hall and stair wells, brass polishing, receiving goods and packages, distributing mail, doing minor repairs, tending the gardens and surrounds, and ensuring that the rubbish is collected. She will also keep a spare set of keys to your apartment, which is handy if you lose yours. The *concierge* is an important person in the daily life of an apartment block and it's wise to establish and maintain a good relationship with her, tipping her generously for extra services.

Although paid meagre salaries, *concierges* are increasingly being replaced by the ubiquitous 'digi-code', a pad on which you enter a number to obtain entry to an apartment block. Apart from the loss of extra services provided by the *concierge*, the *digi-code* 'security' system is extremely insecure. The code number is invariably given to anyone and crime has risen as a result. Although not everyone loves their *concierge*, often referred to as dragons, many would gladly pay a premium for her services rather than suffer the dreaded *digi-code*. There are less than 20,000 caretakers left in Paris and some 2,000 disappear each year.

Finding a Rental Property

Your success or failure in finding a suitable rental property depends on many factors, not least the type of rental you're seeking (a one-bedroom apartment is easier to find than a four-bedroom detached house), how much you want to pay and the area where you wish to live. There are a number of ways of finding a property to rent, including the following:

• ask your friends, relatives and acquaintances to help spread the word, particularly if you're looking in the area where you already live. A lot of rental properties are found by word of mouth, particularly in Paris, where it's almost impossible to find somewhere with a reasonable rent unless you have connections.

• check the ads. in local newspapers and magazines (see below);

• visit accommodation and letting agents. Most cities and large towns have estate agents (*agences immobilières*) who also act as letting agents for owners. Look under *Agences de Location et de Propriétés* in the Yellow Pages. It's often better to deal with an agent than directly with owners, particularly with regard to contracts and legal matters.

• look for advertisements in shop windows and on notice boards in shopping centres, supermarkets, universities and colleges, and company offices;

• check newsletters published by churches, clubs and expatriate organisations, and their notice boards.

To find accommodation through advertisements (*offres de locations/location offres*) in local newspapers you must usually be quick off the mark. Buy newspapers as soon as they are published and start phoning straight away. You must be available to inspect properties immediately or at any time. Even if you start phoning at the crack of dawn, you're still likely to find a queue when you arrive to view a property in Paris. The best days for advertisements are usually Fridays and Saturdays. Advertisers may be private owners, real-estate managers or letting agencies (particularly in major cities). You can insert a 'rental wanted' (*demandes de locations/location demandes*) advertisement in many newspapers and on notice boards, but don't count on success using this method.

Finding a property to rent in Paris is similar to the situation in London and New York, where the best properties are usually found through personal contacts. The worst time to look is during September and October when Parisians return from their summer holidays and students are looking for accommodation. In Paris, rental accommodation is listed according to area (*arrondissement* or *banlieue*). The best newspapers for rental property in Paris are the daily *Le Figaro* and weekly newspapers such as *De Particulier à Particulier* (Thursdays) and *J'annonce* (Wednesdays), both of which also provide Minitel services (see page 125). Other sources for accommodation in Paris for English-speaking foreigners are *France-USA Contacts* and *Paris Free Voice*, both available free at English-language bookshops, restaurants and public offices in Paris (see also **Newspapers, Magazines & Books** on page 384).

Street numbers in cities and towns may have a suffix such as *bis* or *ter*. This means that the property is attached or adjacent to a property taking the whole number, e.g. 15bis, rue de France is next to 15, rue de France. If you're given directions, obtain information such as the stairway (*escalier*), floor (*étage*) and whether it's on the left or right (*à gauche/à droite*). If a building has a door code (*digi-code*), make sure you obtain the code if there's no bell.

Rental Costs

Rental costs vary considerably depending on the size (number of bedrooms) and quality of a property, its age and the facilities provided. However, the most significant factor affecting rents is the region of France, the city and the particular neighbourhood. Rental accommodation in Paris is in high demand and short supply, and rents are among the highest in Europe and often double those in other French cities. Like everywhere, rents in France are dictated by supply and demand and are higher in Cannes, Grenoble, Lyon, Nice and Paris than in Bordeaux, Marseille, Strasbourg and Toulouse.

Rents are lowest in small towns and rural areas, although good rental accommodation is often difficult to find. As a general rule, the further a property is from a large city or town (or town centre), public transport or other facilities, the cheaper it is. Rents for short-term lets, e.g. less than one year, are higher than for longer lets, particularly in popular holiday areas where many properties are let furnished as self-catering holiday accommodation. Rents are calculated according to the number of rooms (*pièces*) and the floor area (in square metres). A one-room apartment with a separate kitchen and bathroom is called a *studio* rather than one-room (*une-pièce*). A two-room (*deux-pièces*) apartment usually has one bedroom, a living room, kitchen and bathroom. A three-room (*trois-pièces*) apartment has two bedrooms, a four-room (*quatre-pièces*) apartment three bedrooms and so on.

Rents are also based on the prevailing market value of a property (*indice*). In Paris, a tiny studio apartment of around 20m² (215ft²) in a good area costs around 3,000F a month, while a two or three bedroom apartment in a fashionable residential area can cost from 15,000F to 30,000F a month. In the provinces you can rent a two-bedroom apartment for 4,000F or less per month. Anything with a terrace or balcony is usually more expensive. Generally the higher the floor the more expensive an apartment will be (you pay for the view, the extra light, the absence of street noise and the rarified air). However, if a block doesn't have a lift, apartments on lower floors are the most expensive. Rents are often open to negotiation and you may be able to secure a 5 to 10 per cent reduction.

If you rent a property through an agent, you must pay the agent's commission, typically 10 to 15 per cent of a year's rent, or 10 per cent of the first year's rent plus 1 per cent for subsequent years. Providing that rent isn't paid in advance at more than two-monthly intervals, the landlord can ask for a deposit (*caution*) equal to two months rent. The deposit must be returned within two months of the termination of the lease, less any amount due to the landlord (for damages, redecoration, etc.). Although it's illegal, many tenants don't pay their last two months' rent and forfeit their deposit. Rent is normally paid one month in advance and you cannot be required to pay your rent by direct bank deposit.

Note that in addition to rent, tenants must have compulsory insurance (see page 266) and pay service charges. Service charges include services such as heating, hot water, rubbish removal, upkeep of grounds and gardens, use of lift, communal lighting and maintenance, swimming pool maintenance, and possibly a caretaker's services. The rent may also include *taxe d'habitation* (see page 298). Other utilities such as gas and electricity are usually paid separately by tenants. Always check whether rent is inclusive or exclusive of charges, which is usually stated in advertisements. Service charges are calculated monthly (payable with the rent) and are usually higher in a new building than an old one.

Rental Contracts

A rental contract or lease (*bail/ contrat de location*) is usually a standard document in France and must be for a minimum period of three years if it's for a named individual (*Bail un Nom Propre/personne physique*) and cannot be for an unspecified period. Make sure your contract is as complete as possible and includes an exact description of what you're renting and for what use, plus the exact dates and length of the lease. Two originals should be provided (one for the tenant and the other for the landlord) and the cost of the contract should be met equally. Company leases are usually for a minimum of six years. It's common for a lessee to be asked to sign an inventory, particularly for a furnished property (see page 94), which should be annexed to the lease. A tenant is responsible for any damage caused and must take out insurance against damage to a property (see page 266). Note that rental laws and protection don't extend to holiday lettings, furnished lettings or sub-lettings.

A lease (*bail*) is deemed to have been renewed automatically for a further three years if the landlord doesn't give notice to quit. If the landlord wishes to renew the lease but change the terms, he must give notice and provide the new terms at least six months before the lease is due to expire. The tenant must accept the new lease at least three months before the lease expires, otherwise he's deemed to have accepted notice to quit. He can, however, challenge the new rent or terms. If neither the landlord nor the tenant gives notice to alter the existing lease during the time limits imposed, it's automatically renewed for a further three years with the same rent and terms.

If an owner decides to sell a property at the end of or during a rental contract, the tenant has first option to purchase. If the tenant declines to buy and the landlord sells the property, the tenant cannot be evicted if his agreement is for a fixed term. At the end of an agreement a landlord can ask a tenant to vacate a property only when he wishes to sell it, to use it for himself or his family (but he *must* use it for this purpose), or if the tenant hasn't fulfilled his obligations, e.g. he hasn't regularly paid the rent. In order to evict a tenant the landlord must obtain a court order and give him six months notice to quit. Should he do so, the tenant can move out before the six months notice has expired and isn't required to pay the rent after moving out. Note that it isn't possible to evict a tenant during the winter months, usually between mid-November and mid-March.

A tenant may terminate the lease at any time providing he gives three months notice by registered letter (*lettre recommandée avec accusé de réception*). He must pay rent for the full three-month notice period, even if he moves out early. All important communications to your landlord *must* be sent by registered mail and you must also keep a copy. The notice period can be shortened to one month under certain circumstances, e.g. when a tenant is transferred by his employer at short notice, becomes unemployed or due to ill health (providing the tenant is over 60 years old).

The landlord may want proof that you're able to pay the rent such as a bank statement or pay slips (proof of your income), or an employer's attestation of employment stating your salary. If your salary isn't four times the amount of the rental, the owner may insist that your employer signs the lease or provides a guarantee. Students may require a letter from a parent or sponsor stating their financial support and must be aged 18 or over to sign a lease in France. Your landlord may also require bank references, income tax receipts, references from previous landlords and a photocopy of your passport showing your name, date and place of birth, the date of issue and the expiry date.

INVENTORY

One of the most important jobs when moving into rented accommodation is to complete an inventory (*inventaire détaillé/état des lieux*) of the contents and a report on its condition. This includes the condition of fixtures and fittings, the state of furniture and carpets (if furnished), the cleanliness and state of the decoration, and anything missing or in need of repair. Don't sign the inventory until after you have moved in. If you find a serious fault after signing the inventory, send a registered letter to your landlord asking for it to be attached to the inventory. You normally have one month to do this after moving in. Note that appliances such as central heating are exempt from the one month limit until they are used (*sous réserve de bon fonctionnement en période de froide*). An inventory document is normally provided by your landlord or letting agent and usually includes every single item in a furnished property. If an inventory isn't provided, you should insist on one being prepared and annexed to the lease.

This can be done by a *huissier* (for around 1,000F), who's an official authorised to prepare factual legal documents, or can be drawn up by the landlord and tenant. If you have an inventory drawn up by a *huissier* you have a better chance of getting your deposit back, as in the event of a dispute his evidence overrides that of all other parties. An inventory should be drawn up both when moving in (*état des lieux d'entrée*) and when vacating (*état des lieux de sortie*) rented accommodation. If the two inventories don't correspond, the tenant must make good any damages or deficiencies or the landlord can do so and deduct the cost from your deposit. Although French landlords are generally no better or worse than landlords in most other countries, some will do almost anything to avoid repaying a deposit.

When moving into a property that you have purchased, you should also make an inventory of the fixtures and fittings, and check that the previous owner hasn't absconded with anything included in the contract or paid for separately, e.g. carpets, light fittings, curtains, fitted cupboards, kitchen appliances or doors.

SECURITY

When moving into a new home it's often wise to replace the locks (or lock barrels) as soon as possible and fit high security locks, as you have no idea how many keys are in circulation for the existing locks. Some apartments and houses may be fitted with special high security door locks that are individually numbered. Extra keys for these locks cannot be cut at a local store and you must obtain details from the previous owner or your landlord to have additional keys cut or change the lock barrels. At the same time as changing the locks, you may wish to have an alarm system fitted, which is the best way to deter intruders and may also reduce your home contents insurance (see page 266).

If you have a holiday home in France, your insurance company may insist on extra security measures such as two locks on external doors (one of a deadlock mortise type) and internally-lockable shutters (or grilles) on windows, which must be locked when a property is vacant. In high risk areas you may be required to fit extra locks and shutters, security blinds or gratings on windows. However, no matter how secure your home, a thief can usually break in if he's determined enough, e.g. through the roof or by knocking a hole in a wall! In isolated areas thieves can strip a house bare at their leisure and an alarm won't be much of a deterrent if there's nobody around to hear it. If you have a holiday home in France, it isn't advisable to leave anything of real value (monetary or sentimental) there. If you vacate a rented house or apartment for an extended period, it may be obligatory to notify your caretaker, landlord or insurance company, and leave a key with the caretaker or landlord in case of emergencies.

If you have a break-in, you should report it immediately to your local *gendarmerie*, where you must make a statement (*plainte*), of which you receive a copy. This is required by your insurance company if you make a claim. Note that a generous donation to the local police at Christmas may 'encourage' them to keep a watchful eye on your home when you're away.

Another important aspect of home security is ensuring you have early warning of a fire, which is easily accomplished by installing smoke detectors. Battery-operated smoke detectors can be purchased for around 50F and should be tested weekly to ensure that the batteries aren't exhausted. You can also fit an electric-powered gas detector that activates an alarm when a gas leak is detected.

MOVING HOUSE

After finding a home in France it usually takes just a few weeks to have your belongings shipped from within continental Europe. From anywhere else it varies considerably, e.g. four weeks from the east coast of America, six weeks from the west coast and the Far East, and around eight weeks from Australasia. Customs clearance is no longer necessary when shipping your household effects from one EU country to another. However, when shipping your effects from a non-EU country to France, you should enquire about customs formalities in advance, as if you fail to follow the correct procedure you can encounter numerous problems and delays and may be charged duty or even fined. The relevant forms to be completed by non-EU citizens depend on whether your French home will be your main residence or a holiday home. Removal companies usually take care of the administration and ensure that the right documents are provided and correctly completed (see also **Customs** on page 76).

For international removals, you should use a company that's a member of the International Federation of Furniture Removers (FIDI) or the Overseas Moving Network International (OMNI), with experience in France. Members of FIDI and OMNI usually subscribe to an advance payment scheme that provides a guarantee. If a member company fails to fulfil its commitments to a customer, the removal is completed at the agreed cost by another company or your money is refunded. Some removal companies have subsidiaries or affiliates in France, which may be more convenient if you encounter problems or need to make an insurance claim. Obtain at least three written quotations before choosing a company. Costs vary considerably, although you should expect to pay from 15,000F to 25,000F to move the contents of a three to four-bedroom house.

Make a complete list of everything to be moved and give a copy to the removal company. Don't include anything illegal (e.g. guns, bombs, drugs, pornographic videos, etc.) with your belongings, as customs checks can be rigorous and penalties severe. Give the shipping company *detailed* instructions how to find your French address from the nearest *autoroute* (or main road) and a telephone number where you can be contacted. If you're flexible about the delivery date, most removal companies will quote a lower fee based on a 'part load', where the cost is shared with other deliveries. This can result in savings of 50 per cent or more compared with an 'individual' delivery.

Be sure to fully insure your belongings during removal with a well established insurance company. Insurance premiums are usually 1 to 2 per cent of the declared value of your goods, depending on the type of cover chosen. It's prudent to make a photographic or video record of valuables for insurance purposes. Most insurance policies cover for 'all-risks' on a replacement value basis. Note that china, glass and other breakables can usually be included in an 'all-risks' policy only when they're packed by the removal company. If you need to make a claim, be sure to read the small print as some companies require you to make a claim within a few days, although seven is usual. Send a claim by registered mail. Some insurance companies apply an 'excess' of around 1 per cent of the total shipment value when assessing claims. This means that if your shipment is valued at 200,000F and you make a claim for less than 2,000F, you won't receive anything.

If you plan to transport your belongings to France personally, check the customs requirements of the countries you must pass through. If you're importing household goods from another European country, it's possible to hire a self-drive van in France. Hiring a van outside France isn't advisable, as you must usually return it to the country where it was hired. Most people find it isn't advisable to do their own move unless it's a simple job, e.g. personal effects only. It's no fun heaving beds and wardrobes up stairs and squeezing them into impossible spaces. If you're taking pets with you, you may need to get your vet to tranquillise them, as many pets are frightened (even more than people) by the chaos and stress of moving house.

Bear in mind when moving home that everything that can go wrong often does, so allow plenty of time and try not to arrange your move from your old home on the same day as the new owner/tenant is moving in. That's just asking for fate to intervene! Last but not least, buy a house allowing access to a large removal truck. If it has poor access (or soft ground) you will need to inform the shipping company! See also **Customs** on page 76 and the checklists in **Chapter 20**.

ELECTRICITY

Electricity throughout most of France is supplied by the state-owned *Électricité de France (EDF)*, although there are local electricity companies in some areas. EDF is combined with *Gaz de France* (GDF) and the two companies are often referred to as EDF-GDF. Unlike other western countries, France generates some 75 per cent of its electricity from nuclear power, with the balance coming mostly from various hydro-electric schemes. This ensures that France's electricity is among the cheapest in Europe and it supplies electricity to its neighbours for less than they can produce it themselves. Due to the moderate cost of electricity and the high degree of insulation in new homes, electric heating is more common in France than in other European countries.

Connection: The first thing to check before moving into a home in France is whether there are any light fittings. When moving house, some people remove not just the bulb, but bulb-holders, flex and even the ceiling rose! You must usually apply to your local EDF office to have your electricity connected and to sign a contract specifying the power supply (see below) installed and the tariff (see page 98) required. To have your electricity connected, you must prove that you're the owner by producing an *attestation* or a lease if you're renting. You must also show your passport or residence permit (*carte de séjour*). If you wish to pay your bill by direct debit from a bank or post office account, don't forget to take along your account details (*relevé d'identité bancaire*).

When moving house, most people simply tell the EDF the day they are leaving (although EDF requests two weeks notice) and EDF assumes that someone else is taking over the property. To ensure your electricity supply is connected and that you don't pay for someone else's electricity, you should contact your local EDF office and ask them to read the meter (*relevé spécial*) before taking over a property. If the property has an existing electricity supply, you must pay a registration (*mise en service*) fee of around 75F. New residents don't usually pay a deposit, although non-residents may be required to pay one. When payable, the deposit is refundable against future bills.

EDF publish a useful free booklet, *EDF répond à vos questions*, available from any EDF office. Your local electricity board may also have a booklet (*livret de l'usager de l'électricité*) explaining the electricity supply and apparatus. If you have any questions regarding the electricity supply contact *Electricité de France (EDF)*, 2, rue Louis Murat, 75384 Paris (☎ 01.40.42.22.22).

Power Supply: The electricity supply in France is delivered to homes at 380/440 volts through three separate phases (not one as in some countries) and is then shared across the three phases at 220/240 volts with a frequency of 50 hertz (cycles). Some appliances such as large immersion heaters or cookers draw power from all three phases. Older buildings may still have 110/120 volt supplies, although these have been converted to 220/240 in most areas. In many rural areas the lights often flicker and occasionally go off and come back on almost immediately (just long enough to crash your computer!). If you live in an area with an unstable electricity supply, it's prudent to obtain a power stabiliser for a computer or other vital equipment to prevent it powering off when the power drops. If you use a computer, it's also advisable to fit an uninterrupted power supply (UPS) with a battery backup which allows you time (around five minutes) to save your work and shut down your computer after a power failure. Power cuts are fairly frequent in some areas, particularly during thunderstorms, and you should keep torches, candles and preferably a gas lamp handy.

If the power keeps tripping off when you attempt to use a number of high-powered appliances simultaneously, it probably means that the power supply of your property is too low to operate all the appliances simultaneously. This is a common problem in France. If this is the case, you must ask EDF to uprate the power supply to your property. If you have an integrated electrical heating system, you can have a gadget called a *délesteur* installed. This momentarily cuts off convectors, under-floor heating and water-heater (etc.) when the system is overloaded when other high-consumption appliances are in use, but without noticeable temperature fluctuations. It may therefore be possible to avoid a higher supply rating that could save you up to 40 per cent on your standing charge. The power setting is usually shown on your meter (*compteur*). The possible ratings are 3, 6, 9, 12, 15, 18, 24, 30 and 36Kva or KW. The three lower rates (3, 6 and 9KW) don't cater for electric heating, which needs a power supply of 12KW to 18KW (if you have numerous high-wattage electrical appliances and electrical heating you may need the maximum 36KW supply).

To calculate the power supply required, you need to list all the electrical appliances you have (plus any you intend installing, such as an electric shower or dishwasher) and the power consumption of each. Add the power consumption of the appliances you're likely to operate simultaneously to obtain the total kilowatt power supply required. If you have appliances such as a washing machine, dishwasher, water heater and electric heating in an average sized house (e.g. two to three bedrooms), you will probably need an 18KW supply. Your standing charge (*abonnement*) depends on the power rating (*puissance*) of your supply. Unless you use very little or a great deal of electricity, the most appropriate rating is 18KW operating under the Tempo tariff (see below). When buying electrical appliances in France, the label PROMETELEC (*Association pour le développement et l'amélioration des installations intérieures*) indicates that they are safe. The safety of electrical materials is usually indicated by the French safety standards association's initials 'NF' (*normes françaises*). EDF-GDF publish a number of leaflets detailing their services and tariffs including one in French and English (*Le Service du Gaz et de l'Électricité*).

Tariffs: EDF offers two domestic tariffs: Blue Tariff (*tarif bleu*) divided into two options, normal tariff (*option base*) and reduced tariff (*option heures creuses*), and *Tempo*. It is worth noting that EDF in common with many European countries is reducing the price of electricity on an annual basis.

Blue Tariff: With the normal tariff (*option base*) there's no difference between day and night rates and the meter has just one dial. This system isn't recommended unless you use little or no electricity! The standing charge per year (1999) is from 129F (3KW power supply) to 4,650.72F a year (36KW power supply). There is also the possibility of paying the standing charge monthly. The price per kWh is 0.6441F for a 3KW supply and 0.5311F above this.

With the reduced rate tariff (*option heures creuses*), you can select your own reduced rate period, e.g. from 2230 to 0630, or 0230 to 0730 *and* 1330 to 1630 for a maximum of eight hours daily. The low night tariff is generally used to heat hot water and charge night storage heaters. You can have relays installed by EDF to switch on your immersion water heater, tumble dryer or dish washer during the cheap period. The meter has two dials, one for normal tariff, marked *heures pleines* (HP) with an image of the sun on it, and one for night tariff marked *heures creuses* (HC) with an image of the moon on it. Your bill will show your day-time and night-time consumption separately. The standing charge per year is from 588.96F (6KW power supply) to 7428.12F a year (36KW power supply). The off-peak tariff doesn't apply to a 3KW supply. The price per kWh is 0.3242F off-peak (*creuses*) and 0.5311F at peak rate (*pleines*).

Tempo: The Tempo tariff (*option tempo*) is designed to encourage users to conserve electricity during severe weather when demand is at its highest. It allows you to use off-peak rates throughout the year with the exception of peak demand days. Under the Tempo scheme, the year is divided into three periods, blue (*bleu*) for 300 days, white (*blanc*) for 43 days and red (*rouge*) for 22 days of the year. Within these periods the day is also divided into peak and off rate consumption like the *option heures creuses*. The standing charge per year is from 907.44F (9KW power supply) to 3117.72F a year (36KW power supply). There's no monthly payment option for the tempo tariff, which applies only to power supplies rated at 9, 12, 15, 18 and 36KW, in homes with a viable alternative to electrical heating. The *bleu* rate per kWh is 0.2198F off-peak and 0.2753F peak. The *rouge* rate per kWh is 0.4532F off-peak and 0.5394F peak. For the remaining 22 'peak days' (*jour rouge*) you're required to pay around *four* to *eight* times the normal off-peak rate for your electricity, i.e. 0.8416F per kWh off-peak and 2.3182F peak. The 22 peak days are selected by EDF between 1st November and the 31st March and are determined by the meteorological centre in Toulouse.

You can have a special light and/or buzzer installed by an electrician giving you a 30-minute warning of the start of the higher rate. You can also have your heavy consumption appliances connected to a remote control switch (*Télécommande*) so that they switch off automatically during the high rate period and switch on again when the period ends. There's no charge for switching to the Tempo scheme and a special meter is installed free of charge, although you must pay for the installation of the warning light or buzzer and the remote control switch. There's also a lower standing charge under the Tempo scheme. Obviously if you have a second home in France that's unoccupied during the winter, you should choose the Tempo tariff.

Billing: You're billed for your electricity every two or four months, depending on your electricity company and the size of your bills. A number of bills (*facture*) received throughout the year, e.g. alternate bills, are estimated. Bills include a standing charge (*abonnement*), value added tax (TVA) and local taxes (*taxes locales*). TVA is levied at 20.6 per cent on the standing charge and 19.5 per cent on the total power consumption. Local taxes (*taxes commune/département*) are around 12 per cent and where applicable are levied before TVA is added.

All your utility bills (plus telephone) can be paid by direct debit (*prélèvement automatique*) from a bank or post office account. It's also possible to pay a fixed amount each month by standing order based on your estimated usage. At the end of the year you receive a bill for the amount owing or a rebate of the amount overpaid. These methods of payment are preferable, particularly if you spend a lot of time away from home or you're a non-resident. If you don't pay a bill on time, interest (*majoration*) can be charged at 1½ times the current interest rate and if your bills still aren't paid after a certain period your electricity company can cut your service. If you're a non-resident, you can have your bills sent to an address outside France.

Meters: Meters are usually installed in a box on an outside wall of a property. However, if your meter isn't accessible or a house isn't permanently occupied, make sure you leave the keys with a neighbour or make special arrangements to have your meter read, which is done every four months. If your meter cannot be read, you will receive an estimate based on your previous bills, although it *must* be read at least once a year.

GAS

Mains gas (*gaz de ville*) in France is available only in towns and cities and is supplied by the state-owned *Gaz de France (GDF)*, part of the same company as *Électricité de France (EDF)*. If you buy a property without a mains gas supply, a new connection (*raccordement*) within 35 metres of the nearest supply will cost around 5,500F for tariffs *base* and B0 (see below), providing of course mains gas is available in the area. Contact *Gaz de France* for an accurate estimate. When moving into a property with mains gas, you must contact GDF to have the gas switched on and/or have the meter read, and to have the account switched to your name. This can usually be done at the same time as you arrange for your electricity supply (see page 97). If you're taking over a property with an existing gas supply, there's a registration fee (*mise en service*) of around 75F.

Billing: As with most utilities in France, you're billed every two months and if your electricity is supplied by EDF, your gas is included on the same bill as your electricity. As with other utility bills, gas bills can be paid by direct debit (*prélèvement automatique*) from a French bank or post office account or a fixed amount can be paid each month. Meters are read every four or six months.

Tariffs: As with electricity, you can choose the gas tariff that best suits your requirements. There are four standing charge rates depending on the amount of gas you use: Base (less than 1,100 kWh a year), B0 (between 1,100 and 7,300 kWh), B1 (between 7,300 and 17,000 kWh) and 3GB (between 17,000 and 30,000 kWh). The *base* rate is for those who cook by gas only, the BO rate for cooking plus hot water and the other rates are necessary for homes with gas central heating. The cubic metres of gas you use are converted to kilowatt hours for invoicing. In some apartment buildings where gas is used only for cooking and apartments are owned *en copropriété*, a standard charge for gas may be included in your service charge. As with heating and hot water charges, this isn't advisable if you own a holiday home in France.

Bottled Gas: Most rural homes have cookers and possibly water heaters that use bottled gas. Cookers often have a combination of electric and (bottled) gas rings (you can choose the mix). If your gas rings are sparked by electricity, keep some matches handy for power cuts. Check when moving into a property that the gas bottle isn't empty. Keep a spare bottle or two handy and make sure you know how to change bottles (get the previous owner or the real estate agent to show you). A bottle used just for cooking will last an average family around six weeks. Note that the rubber cover over the gas outlet turns clockwise, in contrast to most other threaded devices.

Bottled gas is more expensive than mains gas. You can buy it at most petrol stations and super/hypermarkets, but should trade in an empty bottle for a new one, otherwise it's much more expensive. An exchange bottle costs around 130F. If you need to buy new gas bottles, a retailer will ask you to register and pay a bottle deposit. Some village shops also sell bottled gas. Some houses keep their gas bottles outside, often under a lean-to. If you do this you must buy propane gas rather than butane, as it can withstand a greater range of temperatures than butane, which is for internal use only. Ignore those who say this doesn't matter on the Côte d'Azur, as even there temperature variations can be huge (it even snows occasionally!).

Gas central heating is common in France, although in rural areas the gas supply comes from a gas tank (*citerne*) installed on the property, rather than a mains supply. Tanks are hired from gas suppliers such as Total and Antargaz, who will install a tank free of charge in return for a contract to provide gas for a fixed period. Note that having a gas tank on your property will increase your insurance premiums.

WATER

Mains water in France is supplied by a number of private companies, the largest of which are Vivendi, Lyonnaise des Eaux, Cise (group St-Gobaun) and Saur (group Bouygues), who between them supply some three-quarters of the water in France. Most properties in France are metered, where you pay only for the water you use. If you need to have a water meter installed, there's a small non-refundable charge. When moving into a new house, ask the local water company to read your meter. It's usual to have a contract for a certain amount of water and if you exceed this amount you incur a higher charge. There's no flat fee (*forfait*), which has been abolished, although 'special charges' may be levied.

Cost: The price of water in France varies considerably from region to region, depending on its availability or scarcity, and is among the most expensive in the world. In the most expensive towns water can cost as much as 30F per cubic metre, although the national average is around 13F per cubic metre or 16.50F when a town employs a private company to provide the service. Note that if you have a septic tank (*fosse septique*) as opposed to mains drainage (*tout à l'égout*), your water bill will be much lower, e.g. 3F to 4F per cubic metre. You're billed by your local water company annually or every six months and can pay by direct debit. If an apartment block is owned *en copropriété*, the water bill for the whole block is usually divided among the apartments according to their size. Hot water may be charged by adding an amount per cubic metre consumed by each apartment to cover the cost of heating the water, or may be shared among apartments in proportion to their size.

Reliability: Water shortages are rare in towns (although they do occur occasionally), but are fairly common in some rural areas during long hot summers, when the water may periodically be switched off. It's possible to have a storage tank installed for emergencies and you should also keep an emergency supply for watering the garden or recycle your house water. If you rely on a well (*puits*) or spring (*source*) for your water, bear in mind that they can dry up, particularly in parts of central and southern France which have experienced a drought in recent years. Always confirm that a property has a reliable water source. If a property takes its water from a spring or well (possibly on a neighbour's land), make sure that there's no dispute about the ownership of the spring and your rights to use it, e.g. that it cannot be stopped or drained away by your neighbours.

Mains Supply: If you own a property in or near a village, you can usually be connected to a mains water system. Note, however, that connection can be expensive as you must pay for digging the channels required for pipes. Obtain a quotation (*devis*) from the local water company for the connection of the supply and the installation of a water meter. Expect the connection to cost at least 5,000F, depending on the type of terrain and soil (or rock!) which must be dug to lay pipes. If you're thinking of buying a property and installing a mains water supply, obtain an estimate before signing the purchase contract. You don't pay water charges for well water or water from a stream or river running through your property. If you need to install a hot water boiler and immersion heater, make sure it's large enough for the size of your property, e.g. one room studio (100 litres), two rooms (150 litres), three to four rooms (200 litres) and five to seven rooms or two bathrooms (300 litres).

6.

POST OFFICE SERVICES

There's a post office (*la poste*) in almost every town and village in France, where in addition to the usual post office services, a range of other services are provided. These include telephone calls, telegrams, fax and telex transmissions, domestic and international cash transfers, payment of telephone and utility bills, and the distribution of mail-order catalogues. The post office also provides financial and banking services including cheque and savings accounts, mortgage and retirement plans, and share prices. Post offices usually have photocopy machines, telephone booths and Minitel terminals (see page 125).

The identifying colour used by the French post office (and most European countries) is yellow, which is the colour of French post boxes, post office signs and mail vans. The post office logo looks like a blue paper aeroplane or swallow on a yellow background. Signs for post offices in towns vary widely and include *PTT, PT, P et T, bureau de poste* or simply *poste*. Post offices are listed in the Yellow Pages under *Poste: Services*. Post offices in France are always staffed by post office employees and there are no post offices run by private businesses, e.g. as in Britain, where village post offices are located in general stores.

Main post offices usually have different counters (*guichets*) for different services, e.g. *CCP, mandats, poste restante* and *timbres en gros*, although some counters provide all services (*tous services/toutes operations*). Before joining a queue make sure that it's the correct one, because if you join the wrong queue you'll need to start over again (there are often long queues). If you need different services you must queue a number of times if there's no window for all services. Stamps are sold at most windows and most handle letters and packages (*Envoi de lettres et paquets*), except perhaps very large parcels.

The French mail (*courrier*) delivery service has a reputation of being one of the slowest in Europe, although services have improved markedly in recent years. Delivery times in Europe vary considerably depending on the countries concerned, e.g. two days for a letter from France to the Netherlands or Germany and around six days to Italy. Air mail (*par avion/poste aérienne*) from major French cities to the USA takes five to ten days. Letters may arrive quicker when sent from main post offices. Surface mail is much cheaper than airmail, but takes eons. In the marshlands northeast of St. Omer (Pas-de-Calais), mail is delivered by boat (probably the same boat that delivers mail to Britain).

In addition to slow deliveries, mail often arrives in tatters. If you're sending anything remotely fragile, make sure that you pack it *very* carefully. Naturally the PTT takes no responsibility for late delivery or damaged mail (they would be bankrupt in no time at all!). However, although it isn't highly rated, the French post office isn't as bad as it's sometimes portrayed and service is usually efficient (if not friendly). The post office, like all government departments, is over-staffed and there are plans for restructuring and a reduction of manpower.

The post office produces numerous leaflets and brochures including *Tarifs France et étranger, Les P.T. sont heureux de vous souhaiter la bienvenue* and *Bienvenue en France* or telephone 08.01.63.02.01 (local rate). Note that French companies are usually slow to reply to letters and it's often necessary to follow up a letter with a telephone call. For information about telegrams, telex and fax, see page 127).

BUSINESS HOURS

Business hours for main post offices in towns and cities in France are usually from 0800 or 0900 to 1900, Mondays to Fridays and from 0800 or 0900 to noon on Saturdays. Main post offices in major towns don't close for lunch and may also provide limited services outside normal business hours. In small towns and villages post offices close for lunch, e.g. from noon to 1330. Post office opening hours in villages vary considerably and some open for just three hours a day from 0900 to noon Mondays to Saturdays, while others are open from 0800 to noon and 1330 to 1630 Mondays to Fridays and from 0800 to 1130 on Saturdays. In some villages opening hours are irregular, e.g. 0700 to 1030, 1345 to 1530 and 1630 to 1800 Mondays to Fridays, and 0700 to 1100 on Saturdays.

In Paris, a post office is open in each *arrondissement* from 0800 to 1100 on Sundays. The central post office at 52, rue du Louvre, 75001 Paris (☎ 01.40.28.20.00) is open 24 hours a day, every day (although after 1900, only *poste restante* mail collection, cash withdrawals, letters and telegrams are dealt with), but it's best to avoid Saturday afternoons and Sundays unless you're desperate. The post office at 71, avenue des Champs-Elysées, 75008 Paris is open from 0800 to 2200 Mondays to Saturdays, and from 1000 to noon and 1400 to 2000 on Sundays. In other major cities and large towns, selected post offices also provide limited opening hours on Sundays.

LETTER POST

There are two categories of internal letter post in France and to French territories overseas (DOM-TOM), normal tariff (*service rapide*), which is supposed to ensure delivery the next working day, and reduced tariff (*service économique*/ECOPLI) for non-urgent letters, which take much longer. For elsewhere normal tariff (*service prioritaire*) and reduced tariff (*service économique*) exist. The maximum weight for domestic letter post is 3kg and for international letters it's 2kg. The cost of posting a letter in France is as follows:

Weight	Inland*	EU#	Other Europe**	Africa	N.America/ Near East	Other Countries
up to 20g	3.00/2.70	3.00	3.80	3.90	4.40	4.90-5.20
up to 40g	4.50/3.50	4.60	7.00	7.80	8.20	9.00-9.70
up to 100g	6.70/4.20	8.00	12.00	12.50	15.00	17.00-19.00

*   The 'up to 40g' rate for domestic mail includes mail weighing up to 50g. The second rate shown is for *service économique* (*Ecopli*).

\#   The EU rate includes letters to Liechtenstein and Switzerland.

** Other European countries not included under the EU rate plus Algeria, Morocco and Tunisia.

Postal tariffs can be displayed via a Minitel terminal (3614 La Poste).

General Information

Note the following general information concerning the French mail service:

- If you live in an apartment block with a caretaker (*concierge* or *gardienne*), he or she may receive and distribute mail (including parcels) to tenants. Otherwise mail is placed in your mail box in the foyer (make sure that it has a lock). Often mailboxes aren't big enough for magazines and large packets, which are left in a common storage space. In some apartment blocks in main cities it isn't unusual for mail to be stolen, so if possible you should procure a mail box large enough to hold all your mail (or rent a post office box).

- Stamps can be purchased at local *tabacs* or from coin-operated vending machines outside main post offices. Main post offices also have machines that print postage labels for the amount required (*vignettes d'affranchisement* or *etiquettes*). Stamps for local (and EU) letters are sold in packs of ten and are of the 'peel-off' type, i.e. they don't need to be moistened or licked. It's usually more convenient to buy stamps from a *tabac* (see page 383) and village post offices than a main post office. Official fiscal stamps (*timbres fiscals*), used to legalise documents, pay government taxes and motoring fines, must be purchased from a *tabac* or tax office, **not a post office**. Car road tax discs (*vignettes*) are also available only from *tabacs*.

- A domestic express service (*en service rapide*) called *Distingo* is provided for important documents. Documents must be inserted in a special envelope of which there are two sizes: small (*petit format*) for up to 12 A4 pages (20F) and large (*grand format*) for up to 30 A4 pages (25F). There are reduced rates for more than four items. France also has an international express (*express*) service costing 28F plus postage. See also the *Chronopost* service on page 109.

- You should affix an airmail (*par avion*) label or use airmail envelopes for international air mail, although this isn't necessary for mail between western European countries, as all mail is automatically sent by air. Aerogrammes (*aérogramme*) are available from post offices and cost 5F for anywhere in the world. Pre-stamped domestic postcards (*cartes postales préaffranchissement*) are also available.

- Post boxes (*boîte à lettres*) in France are yellow and are usually on a pillar or set into (or attached to) a wall. They can sometimes be difficult to locate, although there's always one outside a post office or railway station and outside *tabacs*. It's advisable to post urgent letters at a main post office or railway station, as collections are more frequent and delivery is expedited. In cities and at main post offices, there's often a choice of boxes, for example local mail (the name of the local town or *département*), other destinations outside the local area (*autres destinations* or *départements étrangers*) and airmail (*avion*). Other boxes may include reduced tariff (*tarif réduit*), packets/periodicals (*paquets - journaux périodiques*) and in Paris, suburbs (*banlieue*) and city (*Paris*). In Paris, there are also special post boxes labelled *pneumatique*, where mail for addresses within the city and to some suburbs is delivered within three hours (mail is sent by compressed air under the streets of Paris).

- In rural areas there's one mail collection and delivery a day. The postperson isn't obliged to deliver right to your front door unless it's on the street. If it isn't, you must install a letterbox at the boundary of your property on the street.

- The international postal identification for French postal or zip codes (*code postal*) is 'F', which is placed before the code (as shown below), although its use isn't mandatory. France uses an obligatory five-digit post code, where the first two digits indicate the *département* and the last three the town or a district (*arrondissement*) in Paris, e.g. 75005 is the fifth *arrondissement*. Often Paris addresses are shown with the *arrondissement* written as 6ème/6e or 14ème/14e. To translate this into the post code, simply add 7500 or 750 to the area number, e.g. 6ème becomes 75006 and 14ème 75014. Small villages often use the post code of a nearby town and the village name should be included in the address before the post code. A typical French address is shown below:

  > M. Rougenez
  > 69, rue du Vin
  > F-12345 Grenouilleville
  > France

  Many people include the department name after the post code, although this isn't necessary. Cedex (*Courrier d'Entreprise à Distribution Exceptionnelle*) is a special delivery service for business mail and where applicable is included in addresses after the town. Companies and individuals can rent a post box (*Boîte postale/BP*) at main post offices (shown in addresses as, e.g. BP 01). All French post codes are listed by *commune* in alphabetical order in a yellow *Code postal* booklet, available at any post office. Free post (*Libre réponse*), where the addressee pays the cost of postage, is available in France, but isn't widely used.

- If a letter is unable to be delivered due to being wrongly addressed or the addressee having moved, it will be returned with a note stating this, e.g. *n'habite pas à l'adresse indiquée - retour à l'envoyeur*.

- If you want your mail to be redirected by the post office temporarily, you must complete a temporary change of address card (*ordre de réexpédition temporaire*) at least one week in advance. Identification is required. Mail can be redirected for up to one year and costs around 110F. If you're moving house, you should complete a permanent change of address card (*ordre de réexpédition définitif*). Change of address cards are available from post offices.

- Brochures describing special stamps and first day covers for philatelists are available from main post offices. Some post offices have a special window (*Timbres de Collection*) for commemorative stamps and first-day covers. For information about services for philatelists, contact the *Service Philatélique des PTT*, 18, rue F. Bonvin, 75758 Paris Cedex 15 (☎ 01.40.61.52.00).

- Some stamps, usually collector's stamps, have a surtax (*avec surtaxe*) which goes to the Red Cross or another charity.

- Your postperson may present you with a calendar each year around Christmas, designed to encourage you to tip him for thoughtfully delivering your mail (albeit late and often mangled).

Finally, carefully check your mail and don't throw anything away unless you're certain it's junk mail (unsolicited mail, circulars, free newspapers, etc.). It isn't unknown for foreigners to throw away important bills and correspondence during their first few weeks in France. Look between the pages of junk mail for 'real' mail.

REGISTERED MAIL

You can send a registered (*recommandée*) letter with (*avec*) or without (*sans*) proof of delivery (*avis de réception*). Proof of delivery costs 8F for both domestic and international mail. The sender's address must be written on the back of registered letters. You receive a receipt for a registered letter or parcel. There are three levels of compensation (*indemnité forfaitaire*) for domestic registered letters and parcels: 50/100F (15.50F letter 50F compensation/10.50F parcel 100F compensation), 1,000F (19F letter/14F parcel) and 3,000F (24F letter/22F parcel). These costs are in addition to postage. The registration fee for international letters and parcels is 24F plus postage. International letters and parcels can also be insured for a fee of 2.50F per 500F (or fraction) of the declared value (*valeur déclarée*).

Ordinary (*ordinaire*) registered letters require a signature and proof of identity on delivery, normally the person to whom they're addressed. If the addressee is absent when delivery is made, a notice is left and the letter must be collected from the local post office (see **Mail Collection** on page 109). When a registered letter has a receipt (*avis de réception*), it's returned to the sender as proof of delivery. Registration is commonly used in France when sending official documents and communications, when proof of despatch and receipt is required.

PARCEL POST

The post office provides a range of parcel (*colis*) services, both domestic and international. Parcel services are also provided by French railways and airlines and international courier companies such as DHL and UPS. First-class letters and packets are limited to a maximum weight of 3kg and parcels containing printed matter (e.g. books and magazines) are limited to 5kg. Parcels heavier than 5kg must be taken to a main post office. International parcels are usually limited to a maximum of 30kg, although some countries have lower limits, e.g. 20kg. Parcels to addresses outside the EU must have an international green customs label (*déclaration de douane*) affixed to them.

Parcels posted in France must be securely packaged. Rather than fall foul of the post office it's advisable to buy the yellow cardboard boxes sold in various sizes at post offices. Post offices also sell padded postal packets (*emballages*). These come in four sizes and are sold in self-service machines at main post offices. The Post Office sells a wide range of domestic (often pre-paid) packaging for specific contents such as envelopes for books (*poste livre*/25F), reinforced boxes for bottles (*Diligo Bouteille*/41F) and packaging for CDs (*Diligo CD*/27F). Boxes, padded bags and large envelopes are also sold in stationery stores.

The standard (*service économique*) domestic parcel service (*Colieco*) takes three to five days. Sample rates are up to 250g (13.50F), 500g (19.50F), 1kg (24.50F), 2kg (29.50F), 5kg (45F) and 10kg (65.50F). An express domestic parcel service called *Colissimo* was introduced in 1992 for parcels up to 10kg. There are two rates: one for guaranteed delivery within 24 hours in your own department and the other for delivery within 48 hours to any other department. Sample rates are up to 250g (13.50F for your own department and 19,50F for other departments), 500g (19.50F/27.50F), 1kg (24.50F/34F), 2kg (29.50F/39F), 5kg (45F/54.50F) and 10kg (65.50F/75F).

A standard international parcel service (*en service économique*) is available to all countries. Sample costs to EU countries plus Liechtenstein and Switzerland are 100g (6.80F), 200g (13F), 500g (20F), 1kg (35F) and 2kg (49F). To North America the cost is 100g (8.80F), 200g (15.50F), 500g (25F), 1kg (46F) and 2kg (67F). For other destinations and weights ask at a post office or enquire via Minitel (see page 125). When mailing small parcels, newspapers, magazines, books, brochures or other printed matter, use a window marked *paquets*. In larger branches there's an automatic coin-operated weighing machine that issues the correct postage for packages.

The fastest way to send letters or parcels is via the *Chronopost* (called EMS in most other European countries) express mail service serving around 160 countries. Within France packages up to 25kg are guaranteed to arrive at their destination within 24 hours, while mail sent to EU countries is guaranteed delivery within 24 or 48 hours (depending on the country) and mail sent to New York is guaranteed to arrive within 48 hours. The maximum time for delivery to any country is three or four days. *Chronopost* is relatively expensive, but cheaper than other international courier services.

French railways (SNCF) also operate an express package and parcel service (SERNAM) within France and to most European countries. The 'special express' service operates from door-to-door and the 'direct express' service from station-to-station. Charges vary depending on the speed of delivery, the distance, and whether the package is to be collected or delivered at either end. Air Inter, DHL and UPS also provide a domestic freight service guaranteeing airport-to-airport delivery within four hours, plus optional delivery at the receiving end.

MAIL COLLECTION

If the postperson calls with mail requiring a signature or payment when nobody is at home, he will leave a collection form (*avis de passage du facteur*). Mail is kept at the post office for 15 days, after which it's returned to the sender, therefore if you're going to be away from home for longer than 15 days, you should ask the post office to hold your mail.

To collect mail, you must present the collection form at your local post office, the address of which is written on the form. In large post offices there may be a window marked *retrait des lettres et paquets*. You need some form of identification (*pièce d'identité*), for example your passport, *permis de séjour* or French driving licence. A post office may refuse to give letters to a spouse addressed to his or her partner, or to give letters to a house owner addressed to his tenants or guests. You can give someone authorisation to collect a letter or parcel on your behalf by entering the details on the back of the collection form in the box marked (*vous ne pouvez pas vous déplacer*), for which both your identification and that of the 'collector' is required.

You can receive mail at any post office in France via the international *poste restante* service. If you choose a large town or city, address mail to the main post office (*Poste Centrale*) to avoid confusion. Letters should be addressed as follows:

Blenkinsop-Smith, Marmaduke Cecil
Poste Restante,
Poste Centrale
Post Code, City Name (e.g. 75000 Paris)
France

Mail sent to a poste restante address is returned to the sender if it's unclaimed after 30 days. Identification (e.g. a passport) is necessary for collection. There's a fee of 2.50F for each letter received. Mail can be forwarded from one post office to another.

If you have an American Express card or use American Express traveller's cheques, you can have mail sent to an American Express office in France. Standard letters are held free of charge, but registered letters and packages aren't accepted. Mail, which should be marked 'client mail service', is kept for 30 days before being returned to the sender. Mail can be forwarded to another office or address, for which there's a charge. Other companies also provide mail holding services for customers, e.g. Thomas Cook and Western Union.

You can obtain a post office box at main post offices for an annual fee. If you have a post office box, all your mail will be stored there and the postperson will no longer deliver to your home. You can arrange to be informed when registered or express mail arrives.

POSTCHEQUE ACCOUNTS

The French post office provides a range of cheque and savings accounts and is the largest banking facility in France. In rural areas, where the nearest bank is often many kilometres away, many people use the post office as their local bank. Post office accounts provide the same services as bank accounts including international money transfers (by mail and telegraph to many countries), payment of bills, and cheque, cash and debit cards. One of the main advantages of the post office, in addition to the vast number of outlets, is that they are open for longer hours than banks. Post office account holders are issued with a (free) cash card for withdrawals from cash machines (ATMs) located outside main post offices. Every transaction is confirmed with a receipt by mail.

Postal cheque accounts (*Compte Chèques Postal*) are referred to by the initials CCP. The post office provides a wide range of savings accounts (CCP Service Plus) through the national savings bank (*caisse nationale d'épargne*) including tax-free savings accounts (*livret A*), house purchase savings plans (*plan d'épargne logement*) and retirement plans. You can check the balance of your post office account via telephone (*Audioposte*) 24 hours a day, including purchases made with your *Carte Bleue* (*différé*) and the last five transactions or all transactions during the last ten days. You're given a personal access code to access your account, which costs 3.65F for each call.

Cash transfers can be made both within France and internationally, when a pink *mandat de poste international* card must be completed. International transfers can often be made via telegraph. Where there's no telegraphic service (e.g. between France and Britain), cheques take around ten days to arrive. Post cheques (*chèques postaux*) must be cashed within two months in France. The maximum value of each cheque is 4,000F, although larger amounts can be sent by using more than one cheque. Personal postcheques can be cashed at any post office in France (and other western European countries) with a cheque guarantee card. Foreign currency change facilities are provided at some 150 post offices in major towns, indicated by a *CHANGE* sign. If you have a Visa, American Express or Eurocheque guarantee card, you can withdraw money at around 800 post offices indicated by the *CB/VISA* or *EC* sign.

A leaflet (*Conditions et Tarifs des principales prestations financières applicables aux particuliers*) is available from post offices listing the range of services and the costs associated with postcheque accounts, savings account interest rates and money orders (*mandats*). Information about post office accounts is also available via Minitel (3614 Videoposte) and a free telephone number (08.00.02.50.25).

7.

TELEPHONE

The French telephone service is operated by France Télécom, partially privatised in 1998 in France's biggest ever sell-off, when two private companies (Cegetel and Omnicom) were created. France Télécom still maintains a monopoly on 'local' calls up to 52km (32mi) but all three companies offer services for inter-department and overseas calls. France has one of the most modern and efficient telephone services in the world and is fully automated. Calls invariably go through first time, lines are clear, crossed lines are virtually unknown, and tariffs are reasonable by European standards. France also has an efficient car telephone service, encompassing the most populous areas of the country. France Télécom is in the forefront of telephone technology and provides a wide range of services including the Internet.

In the '70s the number of telephone lines in France tripled and today it has over 25 million subscribers and the third largest network in the world. Over 90 per cent of French households have a telephone and nine out of ten new customers have a telephone installed within two weeks. The French aren't, however, such habitual telephone users as some people, particularly North Americans, and they don't usually spend hours on the telephone. Many businessmen prefer to meet in person or exchange letters, rather than conduct business over the telephone. Where applicable, costs listed in this chapter are inclusive of value added tax (*toutes taxes comprises/TTC*). **A list of EMERGENCY NUMBERS is provided on page 126.**

INSTALLATION & REGISTRATION

When moving into a new home in France with a telephone line, you must have the account transferred to your name. If you're planning to move into a property without an existing telephone line, you will need to have one installed. To have a telephone installed or reconnected, contact your local France Télécom agent (*Agence Commerciale*), a list of which is available in telephone directories. If you're taking over a property from the previous occupants, you should arrange for the telephone account to be transferred to your name from the day you take possession. **However, before you can do this the previous occupant must have already closed his account, so check in advance that this has been done.** If you move into a property where the telephone hasn't been disconnected or transferred to your name, you should ask France Télécom for a special reading (*relevé spécial*).

To contact your local Télécom agent dial 1014 and you will be connected. If you're applying to have a line connected or installed for the first time in France, i.e. you don't have an existing account with France Télécom, you must visit your local agent. To have a telephone connected or installed, you must prove that you're the owner or tenant of the property in question, e.g. with an electricity bill, confirmation of purchase (*attestation d'acquisition*) or a lease. You also require your passport or residence permit (*carte de séjour*). France Télécom publish a 'Set Up Guide' in English. If you wish to use Cegetel (☎ 08.00.77.77.77) or Omnicom (☎ 08.01.55.00.55) for long-distance and international calls (see page 121), you will need to subscribe to open a separate account with them (note, however, that you must still have an account with France Télécom for line rental and local calls).

You need to know what kind of plugs are already installed in the property, how many telephones you want, where you want them installed and what kind of telephone you want (if you're buying or renting them from France Télécom). You will be asked whether you want a listed or unlisted number (see **Directories** on page 122) and must inform France Télécom where you want your bill sent and how you wish to pay it (see page 120). If you wish to pay your bill by direct debit from a bank or post office account, you must provide your account details (*relevé d'identité bancaire*). You can also request an itemised bill and apply for a Minitel (see page 125) terminal at the same time.

You may be given a telephone number on the spot, although you should wait until you receive written confirmation before giving it to anyone. Note that France Télécom always changes the telephone number when the ownership or tenancy of a property changes. You will receive a letter stating that you have a mixed line (*ligne mixte*), which is simply a line allowing both incoming and outgoing calls. If you own a property and are letting it for holidays, you can have outgoing calls limited to the local area only, but you cannot limit the service just to incoming calls.

To have a line installed takes from a few days in a city to weeks or possibly over a month in a remote rural area, although the average is around two weeks. If you're taking over an existing line, you can usually have it connected within 48 hours. In certain areas there's a waiting list and you can get a line installed quickly only if you have priority, e.g. if you're an invalid, when a medical certificate is required. Business lines may be installed quicker than domestic lines. Note that if you buy a property in a remote area without a telephone line, it may be expensive to have a telephone installed, as you must pay for the line to your property. Contact France Télécom for an estimate. If you're restoring a derelict building or building a new house, you should have trenches dug for the telephone cable if you want a below ground connection (you may be able to have an above ground connection via a wire from the nearest pylon).

The cost of installing a new line is 250F. If a line has been disconnected for less than six months, the cost of reconnection is 200F. The cost of installation includes the installation of two telephones, the maximum number permitted per line. Each additional telephone line and installation costs 83.02F plus 154.18F for the France Télécom agent's services. If you want a number of telephone points installed, arrange this in advance. Note that there are regulations regarding the positioning of points and if you have only one telephone point installed it should usually be located in the main living room or entrance hall.

You can have a basic telephone installed or you can choose from a wide range of all-singing, all-dancing models, which can be rented or purchased. You can buy a telephone from France Télécom or any retailer (e.g. a telephone shop), but it must be approved (*agréé*) by France Télécom (non-approved telephones can cause line problems).

USING THE TELEPHONE

Using the telephone in France is simplicity itself. All French telephone numbers have ten figures. Since 1996 numbers have incorporated the regional code (the first two digits, see below). Numbers beginning with 0800 are free (called a *Numéro Vert*), those beginning with 0801 (*Numéro Azur*) are charged at local rates and 0802/3 (*Numéro Indigo*) announce the rate at the start of the call.

If you're a Cegetel client you must replace the first zero of the area code with a 7 e.g. 01.40.20.70.00 becomes 71.40.20.70.00 and dial 70 instead of 00 for international calls. If you subscribe to Omnicom then you replace the first zero of the area code with a 5 and for international calls you dial 05 instead of 00.

Code	Region	Departments
01	Paris	Essonne, Hauts-de-Seine, Paris, Seine-et-Marne, Seine-Saint-Denis, Val-de-Marne, Val-d'Oise, Yvelines
02	Northwest	Calvados, Cher, Côtes-d'Armor, Eure, Eure-et-Loir, Finistère, Ille-et-Vilaine, Indre, Indre-et-Loire, Loir-et-Cher, Loire-Atlantique, Loiret, Maine-et-Loire, Manche, Mayenne, Morbihan, Orne, Sarthe, Seine-Maritime, Vendée
03	Northeast	Aisne, Ardennes, Aube, Bas-Rhin, Côte-d'Or, Doubs, Haute-Marne, Haute-Saône, Haut-Rhin, Jura, Marne, Meurthe-et-Moselle, Meuse, Moselle, Nièvre, Nord, Oise, Pas-de-Calais, Saône-et-Loire, Somme, Territoire-de-Belfort, Vosges, Yonne
04*	Southeast	Ain, Allier, Alpes de Hte-Provence, Alpes-Maritimes, Ardèche, Aude, Bouches-du-Rhône, Cantal, Corse, Drôme, Gard, Hautes-Alpes, Haute-Loire, Haute-Savoie, Hérault, Isère, Loire, Lozère, Puy-de-Dôme, Pyrénées-Orientales, Rhône, Savoie, Var, Vaucluse
05	Southwest	Ariège, Aveyron, Charente, Charente-Maritime, Corrèze, Creuse, Deux-Sèvres, Dordogne, Gers, Gironde, Haute-Garonne, Hautes-Pyrénées, Haute-Vienne, Landes, Lot, Lot-et-Garonne, Pyrénées-Atlantiques, Tarn, Tarn-et-Garonne, Vienne
06	Mobile Phones	

* Note that Monaco now has its own country code of 377 instead of the regional code 04.

The second pair of digits of the ten is the area code, as listed below.

20 Nord	48 Cher	75 Ardèche; Drôme
21 Pas-de-Calais	49 Deux-Sèvres; Vienne	76 Isère
22 Somme	50 Ain; Haute-Savoie	77 Loire
23 Aisne	51 Vendée	78 Ain; Puy-de-Dôme; Rhône
24 Ardennes	53 Dordogne; Lot-et-Garonne	79 Ain; Savoie
25 Aube; Haute-Marne	54 Indre; Loir-et-Cher	80 Côte-d'Or
26 Marne	55 Corrèze; Creuse; Haute Vienne	81 Doubs
27 Nord	56 Gironde	84 Jura; Haute-Saône; Terr. De Belfort
28 Nord	57 Gironde	85 Ain; Saône-et-Loire
29 Meuse; Vosges	58 Landes	86 Ain; Nièvre; Yonne
31 Calvados	59 Pyrénées-Atlantiques	87 Ain
32 Eure; Oise	61 Ariège-Pyrénées; Haute-Garonne	88 Bas-Rhin;
33 Manche; Orne	62 Gers; Hautes-Pyrénées	89 Haut-Rhin
35 Seine-Maritime	63 Tern; Tarn-et-Garonne	90 Bouches-du-Rhône; Gard; Vaucluse
37 Eure-et-Loir	65 Aveyron; Lot	91 Bouches-du-Rhône
38 Loiret	66 Gard; Lozère	92 Alpes-de-Haute-Provence; Hautes-Alpes
40 Loire-Atlantique	67 Hérault	93 Alpes-Maritimes; Monaco
41 Maine-et-Loire	68 Aude; Pyrénées-Orientales	94 Var
42 Bouches-du-Rhône	70 Allier	95 Corse
43 Mayenne; Sarthe	71 Cantal; Haute-Loire	96 Côtes-d'Armor
45 Charente	72 Rhône	97 Morbihan
46 Charente-Maritime	73 Puy-de-Dôme; Rhône	98 Finistère
47 Indre-et-Loire	74 Ain; Isère; Rhône	99 Ille-et-Vilaine

If after dialling, you hear a recorded message (which is often incomprehensible), it may be telling you that all lines are engaged and to try again later. It's advisable to try again immediately and if you cannot get through, redial after five or ten minutes. The message may also be telling you that the number you have dialled doesn't exist (e.g. *le numéro que vous demandez n'est plus en service actuellement*). If this happens, check that the number is correct and redial. If you're dialling an international number, make that sure you haven't dialled the first zero of the area code. To make an international call, first dial 00 to obtain an international line then dial the country code, e.g. 44 for Britain, the area code *without* the first zero and the subscriber's number.

It isn't possible to make a reverse charge (collect) call (*communication en PCV/payable chez vous*) within France, although you can make them abroad. To make a reverse charge call, dial 00, then dial 33 for the international operator, followed by the country code. Person-to-person (*avec préavis*) calls can also be made via the operator. These calls can also be made to certain countries via the Home Direct service (see page 122). As with anything requiring interaction with the operator, this can be a slow process and it may be easier to make a short call and ask someone to call you back.

The usual French greeting on the telephone is simply *allô*, said as a question (*allô?*). If the operator tells you to wait or hang on, he will say *ne quittez pas*. I'm trying to connect you is '*j'essaie de vous passer l'abonné*' and go ahead may be simply '*parlez*' (speak!). A telephone call in French is *coup de téléphone* or *appel*.

Telephone numbers (*numéro*) are dictated on the telephone in France in the same way as they're written, two digits at a time. For example 04.15.48.17.33 is *zéro quatre, quinze, quarante-huit, dix-sept, trente-trois*. The French don't say double when two digits are the same. e.g. 22 is *vingt-deux* and not *double-deux* (double-two). If someone asks you to spell something (*Comment ça s'écrit?*) on the telephone, such as your name, you should use the telephone alphabet. To use it you must be able to pronounce the alphabet in French and the names listed below. For example if your name's Smith you say, S (ess) pour Suzanne, M (em) pour Marcel, I (ee) pour Irma, T (tay) pour Thérèse et H (arsh) pour Henri.

A (ah)	Anatole	N (en)	Noémie
B (bay)	Berthe	O (oh)	Oscar
C (say)	Camille	P (pay)	Pierre
D (day)	Désiré	Q (ku)	Quintal
E (er/eh)	Eugène	R (air)	Roger
F (eff)	François	S (ess)	Suzanne
G (zhay)	Gaston	T (tay)	Thérèse
H (arsh)	Henri	U (oo)	Ursule
I (ee)	Irma	V (vay)	Victor
J (zhee)	Jean	W (doobl-vay)	William
K (kah)	Kléber	X (ix)	Xavier
L (el)	Louis	Y (ee-grec)	Yvonne
M (em)	Marcel	Z (zed)	Zoé

CUSTOM & OPTIONAL SERVICES

France Télécom provides a range of custom and optional telephone services (*services confort*). To take advantage of them your telephone must be connected to a digital exchange and you must have a touch-tone telephone. If you aren't on a digital exchange, France Télécom can change your number and connect you electronically should you require any of these services. Custom calling or optional services can be ordered individually or as part of a package deal and include the following:

Call transfer (*Transfert d'Appel*) allows you to divert calls to another telephone number automatically, e.g. from home to office (or vice versa) or to a mobile telephone. Dial *21* followed by the number to which you wish your calls to be transferred, followed by a hash sign (#).

Third party call signal (*Signal d'Appel*) or 'call waiting' lets you know when another caller is trying to contact you when you're already making a call and allows you to speak to him without terminating your call. To activate press the 'R' button followed by 2.

Three-way conversation (*Conversation à trois*) allows you to hold a three-way conversation, either within France or overseas.

The subscription cost for each of the above services varies. Contact France Télécom for details. For some services such as 'call memo' (see below) there's no monthly subscription charge, but a fixed charge each time the service is used.

Call Memo (*Mémo d'Appel*) allows you to programme your telephone to ring at a preset time, for example to wake you, or remind you of an appointment or to make an important call. To make a memo call dial *55* followed by the time you wish to be called, using the 24-hour clock. For example, if you wish to be woken at 0730, you dial *55*0730 followed by a hash sign (#). To have a reminder call at 1530 dial *55*1530#.

CHARGES

Telephone charges in France include line charges; telephone, Minitel and other equipment rentals; credit card calls; Internet charges; and general call charges. The monthly line rental or service charge (*abonnement*) is 49.08F per month. If you use Cegetel or Omnicom, you must pay an additional 10F or 8F per month respectively. Tariffs depend on the time of calls (and the destination) as follows:

Tariff (*tarif*)	Period
Peak (*heures pleines/ tarif normal*)	Mondays to Fridays from 0800 to 1900 and Saturdays from 0800 to noon;
Reduced (*heures creuses/ tarif réduit*)	Mondays to Fridays from 1900 to 0800, weekends from noon on Saturdays and public holidays.

France Télécom's charge for local calls is based on a unit cost of 0.74F, which for a local call is equal to three minutes at full tariff (*normal*). Competition in the telephone market has brought much needed competition to 'long-distance' (inter-department) and international calls. For example, for long-distance calls France Télécom charges 1.14F per minute, Cegetel 1.02F and Omnicom 0.97F. Each company offers a range of packages and incentives and you should shop around for the best deal. For example, France Télécom offers a 'light user scheme' (*abonnement modéré*) with a lower service charge but higher call rates. See also **International Calls** on page 121.

BILLS

France Télécom bills its customers every two months and allows you two weeks to pay your bill (*facture*). Bills include value added tax (TVA) at 20.6 per cent. If you're connected to a digital exchange you can request an itemised invoice (*facturation détaillée/annexe à la facture*). An itemised bill lists all calls with the date and time, the number called, the duration and the charge, and is particularly useful if you let a second home in France or lend it to your friends (it isn't worth losing friends over a telephone bill). If you wish to find out how much you have spent on calls between bills, Âllofact (☎ 3653) will tell you for 0.74F.

Bills can be paid by post by sending a cheque to France Télécom, at a post office or at your local France Télécom office. Simply detach the bottom (pink) part of your bill and send or present it with payment. You can pay your telephone bill by direct debit (*prélèvement automatique*) from a bank or post office account or have payments spread throughout the year. These last two methods are recommended if you spend a lot of time away from home or are a non-resident, as they will ensure that you won't be disconnected for non-payment. If you're a non-resident, you can have bills sent to an address outside France. If you pay your bills by direct debit, your invoice will specify the date of the debit from your account, usually around 20 days after receipt of the invoice. Contact your local France Télécom agent for information. FT are trying to encourage customers to pay by direct debit, telepayment by telephone or Minitel (see page 125), or by TIP (*Titre Interbancaire de Paiement*), whereby your bank account details are pre-printed on the pink part of the bill which you simply date and sign and return to France Télécom.

If you don't pay your bill by the date due, you will receive a reminder (either a letter or a telephone call) around one week after the date due. Late payment of a bill automatically incurs a 10 per cent penalty. If payment still hasn't been made two weeks after the date due, France Télécom may progressively reduce your telephone service (*service restreint*), depending on your payment record. If a reduced service is implemented, first the international service will be terminated, followed by a restriction to local calls and finally to emergency calls only. You will receive a letter before your service is totally disconnected and must pay the bill immediately to prevent being cut off. If you're cut off, you must pay the outstanding bill, a reconnection fee of 250F (as for a new connection) and you may also need to pay a deposit. France Télécom bills include the following details:

Item	Description
No. d'Appel	your telephone number
No. de Compte	your account number
Relevé	statement of accounts for the current year
Date Facture	date of invoice
Facture Précédente	previous invoice total
*Prochaine Facture vers le:	date of next bill due on:
*Situation de votre compte au:	date of this bill:
Services et produits facturés	Services and rentals provided
Montant H.T.	itemised bill excluding TVA (HT = *hors taxes*)

Montant Facture H.T.   invoice total excluding TVA

Montant Total de la TVA   invoice total TVA

Montant Totale Facture TTC   total payable, including TVA, before 'date' (the
                                date shown is two weeks after the invoice
                                period)

＊ Underneath these two dates (previous page) is the balance carried forward from
your previous bill (if you haven't paid it or are paying in instalments).

If you receive an unusually large bill with which you don't agree, you should pay
your usual charge and contest the bill with your telephone company. They will
investigate it and won't disconnect you while it's in dispute, providing you pay
something. Check also for counterfeit bills produced by foreign companies. The give-
away is the address to which to send the money, which is usually abroad.

INTERNATIONAL CALLS

It's possible to make direct IDD (International Direct Dialling) calls to most
countries from both private and public telephones. A full list of country codes is
shown in the information pages (pages info) of your local white and Yellow Pages,
plus area codes for main cities and tariffs. To make an international call you must
first dial 00 to obtain an international line. Then dial the country code, the area code
(without the first zero) and the subscriber's number. For international dialling
information and directory enquiries ☎ 00.33.12.

Deregulation of the telecoms market has resulted in an intense price war and
considerable savings can be made on international calls by shopping around for the
lowest rates. France Télécom has 16 tariff levels for international calls, listed in
telephone directories, and are usually the most expensive. Calls to EU countries,
Liechtenstein and Switzerland come under tariff one (the cheapest) and cost 2.10F
per minute during normal tariff and 1.65F per minute during reduced tariff (réduit).
Cegetel and Omnicom both charge the same rates of 1.59F normal (from 0800 to
2100 Mondays to Fridays and 0800 to noon on Saturdays) and 1.27F reduced (all
other times). Calls to North America via France Télécom come under tariff 6 and cost
2.25F per minute during normal tariff, 1.80F per minute during reduced tariff.
Cegetel and Omnicom charge 1.80F to North America during normal tariff (from
1300 to 1900 Mondays to Fridays) and 1.44F during reduced tariff (all other times).

Indirect Access or Callback Companies: The cheapest companies for
international calls are usually indirect access companies (also called 'callback'
companies when you need to ring a number and receive a call back to obtain a line),
where you dial a freephone number to connect to the company's leased lines or dial a
code before dialling a number. They may offer low rates for all calls or just national
and international calls. Some charge a subscription fee. Calls are charged at a flat rate
24 hours a day, seven days a week. Calls may be paid for with a credit (charge or
debit) card, either in advance when you must buy a number of units, or by direct
debit each month. Alternatively you may be billed monthly in arrears. There are a
number of indirect access companies in France including Riviera Communications
SARL, BP 227, 92205 Nueilly-sur-Seine Cedex (☎ 04. 93.67.39.31).

France subscribes to a Home Direct (*pays direct*) service that allows you to call a number giving you direct and free access to an operator in the country that you're calling, e.g. for Britain dial 08.00.99.00.44 (BT) or 08.00.99.09.44 (Mercury). The operator will connect you to the number required and can also accept credit card calls. To obtain an operator from one of the four major US telephone companies ☎ 08.00.99.00.11 (AT&T), 08.00.99.00.19 (MCI), 08.00.99.00.87 (Sprint) or 08.00.99. 00.13 (IDB Worldcom). For a list of countries served by the Home Direct service consult your telephone directory or ☎ (free) 08.00.20.22.02. You can also use a France Direct service from some 50 countries allowing you to make calls to France via a France Télécom operator.

France Télécom publish a useful free booklet, *Guide du Téléphone International*, containing information in both French and English. Business users can save up to 50 per cent on international calls by using France Télécom's Global Virtual Private Network (VPN).

DIRECTORIES

Telephone directories (*annuaires/bottins*) in France are published by department and are numbered with the department number, e.g. 33 for Gironde. Not all directories are published at the same time (the issue dates for new directories is listed at the front of directories). Some departments have more than one volume (*tome*), e.g. the Paris white pages (*Les Pages Blanches*) have five volumes and the Yellow Pages (*Les Pages Jaunes*) two volumes. Telephone directories (both white and Yellow Pages) contain a wealth of information (*pages info*) including emergency information and numbers; useful local numbers; France Télécom numbers and services; tariffs; international codes and costs; how to use the telephone (in English, French, German, Italian and Spanish); public telephone information; bills; directories; Minitel; Télécom products; administration numbers; and maps of the department(s) covered by the telephone book.

When you have a telephone installed, your name and number is usually automatically included in the next issue of your local telephone directory and is included within a few weeks in the Minitel directory (see page 125). You can choose to have an unlisted number (*liste rouge*), for which there's a charge of 15.26F per month (to discourage you!). The bonus is that it saves you from the affliction of telephone marketing. You can also ask to be placed free of charge on the 'orange list' (*liste orange*), meaning that although your number will be listed in both the Minitel and paper directories, you won't be sent any advertising material. Like most telephone companies, France Télécom sells its list of subscribers to businesses, but if you're on the orange list your name is excluded. Subscribers are listed in the white pages under their town or village (*commune*) and not alphabetically for the whole of a department. In Paris, entries are listed by area (*arrondissement*). It isn't enough to know that someone lives, for example, in the department of Dordogne, you must know the town. You will receive little or no help from directory enquiries (who aren't always helpful at the best of times) unless you know the town or village where the subscriber is located.

When your application for a telephone line has been accepted, you're given a voucher (*bon*) for a copy of your local department telephone directory; the issuing office is usually housed in the same building as the Télécom agent. You can choose between two sizes, the standard international size in use throughout the world and a smaller more compact size. Most people choose the standard size, as the print in the smaller directories is more difficult to read (particularly for anyone without perfect eyesight). If you cannot obtain a directory, ☎ 08.00.30.23.02.

Dial 12 for domestic directory enquiries, for which there's a charge of 3.71F. If you hear music or a recorded message, all lines are busy (wait or call back later). Trying to obtain international numbers from directory enquiries is time-consuming and costly, and it may be easier to call someone abroad and ask them to find the number for you. Alternatively you can go to any post office and use a Minitel terminal free of charge (see page 125) or use the Internet. For international directory enquiries (fee 5.57F), dial 00 followed by 33 + 12 and the country code, e.g. 44 for Britain. Note that for the USA, Canada and other countries whose code starts with '1', you should dial '11'.

Yellow Pages are published for all departments and contain only business and official (e.g. government) telephone numbers. They are included with the white pages in one volume for departments with few subscribers or published in a separate volume or volumes, e.g. Paris has two volumes. When there's more than one volume, the index is included at the front of the first volume. You can obtain a copy of white or Yellow Pages for other departments for a fee of around 50F per volume. There are also local Yellow Pages (*Les Pages Jaunes Locales*) in some areas (e.g. Paris) and business to business directories (*Professionnels à Professionnels/PAP*) are published in national and regional editions.

MOBILE TELEPHONES

After a relatively slow start in introducing mobile phones (*le mobile/ téléphone mobile*), France has one of Europe's fastest growing cellular populations. In addition to being a necessity for travelling business people, a mobile phone is a vital status symbol for yuppies and the young. On the negative side, mobile phones are now so widespread that some businesses (e.g. restaurants, cinemas, theatres, concert halls, etc.) ban them and some even use mobile phone jammers that can detect and jam every handset within 100m. **Note that in recent years there has been widespread publicity regarding a possible health risk to users from the microwave radiation emitted by mobile phones.**

There are over ten million mobile phone users in France, whereas in 1997 there were 'just' 3½ million. Lower prices and increased market competition have ensured rapid growth and France Télécom, SFR and Bouygues Télécom provide mobile phone services. Buying a mobile phone is an absolute minefield as, not only are there three networks from which to choose, but a wide range of tariffs covering connection fees, monthly subscriptions, insurance and call charges. Before buying a phone shop around and compare phone prices and features; installation and connection charges; rental charges; and most importantly, charge rates. Most mobile phone numbers have the prefix 06.

PUBLIC TELEPHONES

Public call boxes (*cabines téléphoniques/téléphones publiques*) can be found in all towns and villages, post offices, bus and railway stations, airports, bars, cafés, restaurants and other businesses, and of course, in the streets. All payphones allow International Direct Dialling (IDD) and international calls can also be made via the operator. Most old-style call boxes have been replaced by (over 100,000) new perspex kiosks, many of which accept telephone cards (*télécartes*) only. Generally when there are a number of public call boxes together, one accepts coins, although single or double call boxes may accept telephone cards only. The proliferation of card telephones is to prevent coin box robberies, which are common in some areas.

Telephone cards are available from post offices, railway stations, *tabacs*, cafés, news' kiosks, banks and various shops where the sign *TELECARTE EN VENTE ICI* is displayed. The *télécarte* is available in four versions: 33,67F, 40,60F, 80,85F and 97,50F. When using a public telephone, a unit costs 1F and for local calls is equal to three minutes during full tariff. *Télécartes* are used as an advertising medium by companies and therefore have different designs (many people collect them and some issues are valuable and much sought after). The procedure when using a *télécarte* in most public telephones is as follows:

1. First lift the receiver; *Décrochez* is displayed.

2. Insert your *télécarte* in the slot or dial a free number; *Introduire carte ou faire numéro libre* is displayed. In some telephone boxes you must close the compartment where the card is inserted; the message *Fermez le volet SVP* is displayed.

3. Wait; *Patientez SVP* (be patient please) is displayed while your card is checked.

4. Your card's remaining credit is displayed, e.g. *crédit: 0040 unité(s). Numérotez.* You can now dial your number.

5. Hang up when you're finished; *Raccrochez SVP* is displayed.

6. If you don't 'immediately' retrieve your card you will hear a bleep and the message 'retrieve your card' (*retirez votre carte*) is displayed.

Coin telephones usually accept 5, 2, 1 and ½ franc coins or 10, 5, 1 and ½ franc coins. You must lift the receiver and insert at least 1F before dialling (2F when making a long-distance call). In older coin boxes, unused coins are visible in coin holders, while in new boxes the amount in reserve is shown on a digital display, which also displays the number as it's dialled. When making a long-distance call, it's best to insert small coins, e.g. ½ franc and one franc coins. If you insert a two or five franc coin and hang up without fully using them, any partly used coin is lost. Calls can be received at most telephone boxes, indicated by a blue 'ringing' bell sign on a yellow background (the number is displayed inside the booth). Public telephone booths are also available at post offices, where you're allocated a booth and pay for your calls at the counter afterwards.

Public telephones in bars, cafés and restaurants usually accept one franc coins for local calls, although some still have telephone booths where the bartender activates the line for you and you pay at the bar afterwards (usually between 1F to 2F per unit). Even rarer than the old booths are telephones accepting only tokens (*jetons*), which can be bought at the bar for around 2F. When using a *jeton* telephone, you must press a rectangular button to the right of the telephone when your party answers. Many cafés and restaurants (particularly in Paris) use a new telephone service called *téléphone bleu*, where a local call costs from 1.50F to 2F.

To make a call from a hotel room, you may be able to dial direct (after dialling a '0' or '1') or you may need to make calls via the hotel receptionist. Note that hotels make a surcharge (which can be 100 or 200 per cent!) in addition to the cost of calls; cafés and restaurants also set their own charges. Most hotels have public telephones in the foyer, although some along with many cafés and restaurants have a 'Pointphone'. Pointphones require that you deposit 2F to dial but you can get half of that back if you make a short call and use two 1F coins. To make another call with your credit, press the *reprise crédit* button. Public telephones are provided on TGV trains and allow both domestic and international calls (Europe, North America and Japan). They can be operated with a *télécarte* or a *Carte France Télécom* (see below). There are usually three telephones on each TGV train, one in 1st class, one in 2nd class and one in the bar.

There are free SOS (e.g. breakdown) telephones on *autoroutes* and at main intersections in Paris and other large cities (marked *Services Médicaux*), for use in the event of accidents or medical emergencies. When making an emergency call from a standard public telephone, you must insert one franc or a *télécarte*. Your money is returned when the emergency service answers.

You can obtain a telephone credit card from France Télécom, called a *Carte France Télécom (CFT)*, that can be used both domestically and in over 40 other countries to make calls to France. The CFT costs 81.35F per year and permits international calls to be made from France to foreign countries and from foreign countries to France, but not from a foreign country to a country other than France. Cards can be used from any public or private telephone, with calls being charged to your French telephone account. When phoning from France using a card telephone, you insert your CFT in the card slot, enter your personal identification (ID) number followed by the code and number of your party. When you aren't using a touch-tone phone, calls must be made via the operator. You receive a detailed invoice for calls made with a CFT with your telephone bill every two months.

In major French airports such as Charles de Gaulle (Paris), Lyon and Nice, there are public telephones that accept international credit cards, e.g. American Express, Diners Club, Eurocard, Mastercard and Visa. The cost of calls is automatically debited to your credit card account. Note that while using telephone credit cards is convenient, it can be *very* expensive. There's a charge of 12 units (around 12F) each time a card is used, although telephones have a button allowing you to make multiple 'follow on' calls without paying this charge each time.

MINITEL

Minitel (launched in 1985) is a computer-based videotex/teletext information system that can be linked to any telephone. For many years Minitel was in the vanguard of technology, although it's slowly but surely on its way out, having succumbed to the relentless march of the Internet. It is, however, still in widespread use and references to Minitel numbers are commonplace (even in this book). In order to access Minitel you need to buy or rent a terminal from France Télécom, who will happily advise you on the various options. They may, however, prefer to sell you their Internet service!

INTERNET

The Internet in France has got off to rather a slow start due to Minitel competition and the relative lack of computers. However, the government is keen to catch up with other European countries (such as Britain and Germany) and is injecting vast sums of money into the Internet. 'Internet Days' and venues are commonplace in large cities, where you can try the Internet free of charge. In 1998 there were less than two million Internet users in France (around 2 per cent of households), but predictions for 2002 run to over ten million users or some 20 per cent of households.

This dramatic increase in the market has led to the prolific growth of servers (*fournisseurs d'accès/ FAI*) with over 200 in early 1999 with a variety of products and prices. To find out which are the best you can consult the many computer magazines, some of which are dedicated to the Internet such as *Planète Internet* or *Démarrer sur Internet*. France Télécom offers *Wanadoo*, a package that includes e-mail, Minitel (of course) and on-line shopping. Vivendi AOL France and Compuserve are two other big Internet contenders. Between them, Wanadoo and AOL have some two-thirds of the market.

Unlimited access to Internet costs around 100F a month although with ever-increasing competition, prices are likely to fall dramatically. The French search engine (*moteur de recherche*), equivalent to *Yahoo* or *Altavista*, is called *Voila* and was established in April 1999 in Sophia Antipolis with France Télecom as a partner. Once the French have got over the shock of Minitel losing out to the Internet, they should have a lot to contribute through their Minitel experience to improving the practical use of search engines for everyday use. In France you don't surf the web, you navigate it (*naviguer*) and a surfer is a *navigateur*. A new interesting option is one provided by CanalNet whose *Darty* service allows you to surf (navigate) the Internet from your TV screen by attaching a decoder and keyboard. The connection kit costs 250F, plus a returnable deposit (*depôt de garantie*) of 500F. Unlimited surfing time costs 99F a month with the telephone charge at local rate of 0.28F per minute (also for PC owners).

Useful telephone numbers and websites in France include Club Internet (☎ 01.55.45.45.00, Internet: www.club-internet.fr), France Net (☎ 01.43.92.14.49, Internet: www.francenet.fr) and Worldnet (☎ 01.40.37.90.90, Internet: www. worldnet.fr).

EMERGENCY NUMBERS

Emergency numbers (*Services d'Urgence et d'Assistance*) are listed at the front of telephone directories. In addition to the emergency numbers for police and fire shown below, you should also make a note of the number of your local ambulance service, police station (*gendarmerie*) and fire service (*pompiers*), for which a space is usually provided in telephone books. Calls to emergency numbers are free from private telephones. You need to insert 1F (or a *télécarte*) when using a public telephone, although your money is returned when the emergency service answers.

There are free SOS call boxes on *autoroutes* and some other roads. In Paris and other main cities there are emergency telephone boxes at major intersections marked *Services Médicaux* with direct lines to emergency services. The following numbers should be used in emergencies only:

Number	Service
15	SAMU (*Service d'Aide Médicale d'Urgence*) Ambulance
17	Police (*police-secours*)
18	Fire (*sapeurs-pompiers/feu centrale d'alarme*)
01.47.07.77.77	SOS medical (Paris)
01.43.37.51.00	SOS dental (Paris)

In addition to the above, numbers for your local poison emergency service (*centre anti-poisons*), the Samaritans (*SOS Amitié*) and various help organisations are listed at the front of telephone directories. An English-language Samaritan service (SOS Help) is provided in Paris from 1500 to 2300 daily (☎ 01.47.23.80.80). For gas and electricity emergency numbers, look in your local directory under *EDF/GDF*. Dial 13 to report telephone breakdowns or line problems. See also **Emergencies** on page 231.

TELEX & FAX

Telex: In Paris, there are public telex offices at 7, place de la Bourse, 2e and 7, rue Feydeau, 2e, open from 0800 to 2000 daily. Telexes can be sent and received via post offices, where subscribers are assigned a telex number for sending and receiving messages (the post office notifies subscribers by telephone when messages are received). Telexes can also be sent from major hotels and offices providing 'business services' in cities and towns. The telex (or fax) number of any French company can be obtained via Minitel (3616 SCRIP).

Fax: There has been a huge increase in the use of fax (facsimile) machines in France in the last decade, boosted by lower prices and the failings (and frequent strikes) of the French post office. Fax machines can be purchased (but not rented) from France Télécom and purchased or rented from private companies and shops. Shop around for the best price. Before bringing a fax machine to France, check that it will work there (i.e. is compatible or *agréé*) or that it can be modified. Note, however, that getting a fax machine repaired in France may be impossible unless the same machine is sold there. Public fax services (*Postéclair*) are provided by central post offices in most towns, although you can only send faxes and cannot receive them. The cost in France is 30F for the first page and 18F for subsequent pages. An international service is available to some 50 countries.

Beware of bogus fax bills (usually for thousands of francs) purporting to be from France Télécom. This is a Europe-wide scam and often includes 'the right to inclusion in an annual directory of fax owners'. The give-away is usually the address, which is often abroad!

8.

TELEVISION & RADIO

Until 1974, all French television (TV) and radio stations were state-owned and under the tight control of the government. However, there has been a minor revolution in the last few decades, particularly since 1981 when the Socialists came to power, although two of the three principal TV stations remain under government control. Cable TV is available in the main French cities and towns, although it's less common in France than in many other western European countries. Satellite TV is largely ignored by the French and is mainly watched by expatriates. Almost every French household has a TV and there are some 20 million in France, most of which are colour.

The French complain endlessly about their TV, particularly its lack of quality, surfeit of advertising, dependence on trashy foreign programmes, moronic game shows and endless repeats, although it's generally no worse than most other European countries. Although France prides itself on its culture, this isn't evident from its TV programmes (at least they were spared *A Year in Provence!*). Many Frenchmen prefer to listen to the radio rather than watch TV, particularly the educated middle classes, many of whom don't watch TV at all. The most popular TV programmes include films, sport, theatre, variety, serials and game shows in that order. The daily TV viewing time in France is about average for Western Europe.

TV and radio programmes are listed in daily newspapers, some of which provide free weekly programme guides with reviews and comments (e.g. the Saturday edition of *Le Figaro* and the Sunday edition of *Le Monde*). Weekly TV magazines include *Télé 7 Jours*, *Télé Loisirs*, *Télé Poche*, *Télé Star* and *Télé Z*, published two weeks in advance.

TELEVISION

The standards for TV reception in France **aren't the same as in some other countries**. Due to the differences in transmission standards, TVs and video recorders operating on the PAL system or the North American NTSC system won't function in France. Most European countries use the PAL B/G standard, except for Britain, which uses a modified PAL-I system that's incompatible with other European countries. Naturally France has its own standard called SECAM-L, which is different from the SECAM standard used elsewhere in the world, e.g. SECAM B/G in the Middle East and North African countries, and SECAM D/K in eastern European and many African countries.

If you want a TV that will work in France and other European countries, and a VCR that will play back both PAL and SECAM videos, you must buy a multi-standard TV and VCR. These are widely available in France and contain automatic circuitry that can switch from PAL-I (Britain), to PAL-B/G (rest of Europe) to SECAM-L (France). Some multi-standard TVs also handle the North American NTSC standard and have an NTSC-in jack plug connection allowing you to play American videos. If you have a PAL TV, it's also possible to buy a SECAM to PAL transcoder that converts SECAM signals to PAL. Some people opt for two TVs, one to receive French TV programmes and another (i.e. PAL or NTSC) to play their favourite videos. A British or US video recorder won't work with a French TV unless it's dual-standard (with SECAM). Although you can play back a SECAM video on a PAL VCR, the picture will be in black and white. Most video machines sold in France are multi-standard PAL and SECAM. Video recordings can be converted from PAL to SECAM or vice versa, although the cost is prohibitive.

If you decide to buy a TV in France, you will find it advantageous to buy one with teletext, which apart from allowing you to display programme schedules, also provides a wealth of useful and interesting information. A portable colour TV can be purchased in France from around 1,200F for a 36cm (14in) with remote control. A 55cm (21in) TV costs between 3,000F and 4,500F depending on the make and features, and a 70cm (27in) model 5,000F to 6,500F. Special offers can be up to 50 per cent cheaper than the prices quoted, particularly at hypermarkets such as But, Cora, Mammouth and Rallye.

TV Stations

France has six terrestrial stations broadcasting throughout the country: TF1, France 2, France 3, Canal Plus, M6 and Arte. Reception is poor in some areas, particularly if you're in a valley or surrounded by tower blocks. There's advertising (*publicité* or *pub*) on all French channels, although the public channels aren't permitted to raise more than 25 per cent of their revenue from advertising. Limits are imposed on the amount of TV advertising permitted, which may not average more than six minutes per hour per day, with a maximum of 12 minutes in any single hour. The public channels France 2 and France 3 are permitted to show advertisements between programmes only, whereas private channels (TF1, Canal-Plus, M6 and Arte) may have an advertising break during films and other major programmes.

The two main TV stations, TF1 and France 2, broadcast their main evening news at 2000 for half an hour. Newsreaders are huge celebrities in France and receive vast salaries. They are chosen for their intelligence, personality and in some cases their good looks. Some TV weathermen are incredible and speak faster than DJs – perhaps they are allocated a 1-minute slot to give a 2-minute weather report! News is followed by a film on most channels starting between 2030 and 2100 (the highlight of the evening's viewing). One of the aims of the 1982 broadcasting law was to encourage the production of French programmes, thus reducing the reliance on foreign, particularly American, imports. However, there remain a large number of American films and other programmes, many very old. French TV has a huge number of talk shows, probably because they are inexpensive to produce. Television channels compete vigorously for audience ratings and sometimes prime time programmes may be broadcast at the same time or changed at the last minute.

TF1 (*Télévision Française 1*) was France's first private channel (privatised in April 1987) and is its premier channel with around 40 per cent of the viewing audience or double its nearest rival France 2. Its programming is conservative although usually of good quality, with the notable exception of the mindless game shows and soaps. Its news reporting is generally weak, although popular.

France 2 (previously Antenne 2) is quite liberal and progressive in its programming. Programmes include special events, interviews and cultural events. News coverage is fairly nondescript and similar to TF1's. It has a good film series on Friday evenings with original soundtracks (*version originale/VO*), often in English. France 2 (like France 3) is state-owned and operated by France Télévision.

France 3 is state-owned like France 2, with whom it shares much of its programming, augmented by regional news, documentaries and environmental programmes. The quality of programmes has improved in the last few years and is generally more intellectual than TF1 or France 2. One programme of particular interest to expatriates is *Continentales*, a news and documentary programme broadcast five days a week containing original news broadcasts from around Europe in the original language with French subtitles.

France 2 and 3 share some 40 per cent of the audience and have benefited from a large injection of public funds in recent years in order to carry fewer advertisements and return to 'quality' (open to interpretation) public service programming.

Canal-Plus (channel 4) was launched in 1984 and is Europe's biggest pay channel with some 50 per cent of the market. Apart from a few unscrambled (*en clair*) programmes, indicated in newspapers and programme guides by a + or * sign, the signal is scrambled. To receive Canal Plus (or Canal +) you must buy a decoder (*décodeur*) costing around 500F from a local TV shop or rent one from Canal + for 45F monthly, and pay a subscription of between 130F and 170F per month depending on the length of your contract. There is also a 250F returnable deposit (*depôt de garantie*). Although financed mainly by subscriptions from over five million subscribers in France (plus a further 1½ million in Belgium, Germany, Poland and Spain), it also carries ads. It specialises in films and sports programmes, particularly live soccer matches. It shows many second-rate films, although they are more up-to-date than other channels and most new films are eventually screened (some of which are unsuitable for your maiden aunt or young children). It also screens unscrambled CBS Evening News from the previous evening at 0700 or 0800 each day (depending on the time of year) with French subtitles.

Arte (pronounced 'artay') and **La Cinq** broadcast on the same frequency. Arte (from 1900 until around 0030) is a Franco-German station funded by the respective governments. Many programmes have German or other foreign-language soundtracks with French subtitles. Arte provides a welcome cultural alternative to commercial broadcasting and its output largely consists of documentaries and cultural transmissions (e.g. classical music, operas, debates, concerts, and ballets), foreign films with subtitles, English comedy and *no game shows*. Not surprisingly, it's considered by most people to be too highbrow and attracts only around 2 per cent of viewers. La Cinq broadcasts standard and educational programmes from 0600 to 1900.

M6 has been broadcasting since 1987 and broadcasts mostly general entertainment programmes, show business and video clips. It screens many American series and other mainstream shows plus soft-porn movies. It often has surprisingly good programmes considering its low profile and budget. Note that M6 is difficult to receive in some areas.

France has a seventh channel, **La Sept**, that's available only on cable TV, plus a number of satellite stations (see page 133). If you live close to a French border, you can also receive foreign stations with the appropriate aerial. In the northern border regions of France, Nord, Pas-de-Calais, Alsace and Lorraine, many viewers tune into foreign stations. In the Nord/Pas-de-Calais region it's possible to receive British and Belgian stations. Northern Lorraine viewers tune to Luxembourg TV and in Alsace many people watch German and Swiss TV stations. Those in border areas can also receive foreign programmes, e.g. Belgium, German, Italian or Spanish TV, and if you have a special aerial and live on the French Riviera west and north of Marseilles, you can receive Télé Monte Carlo.

Cable Television

Cable TV is available only in large towns and cities in France although the number of subscribers increases annually. The percentage of homes with cable TV in France is low compared with some 95 per cent in Belgium, 85 per cent in the Netherlands and over 40 per cent in Germany. Most of Paris is covered by cable TV and some towns or areas have their own local cable TV network. If your locality is cabled, Reseau Cable de France (RSF) offer over 30 different channels (mostly in French) for 132F a month for the basic option and 242F a month for full access. Foreign channels such as Sky, CNN, BBC, Eurovision and MTV are also available. Programme listings for the most popular French cable stations are included in French TV guides.

Satellite Television

Although most people complain about the poor quality of TV in their home countries, many find they cannot live without it when abroad. Fortunately the advent of satellite TV in the last few decades means that most people can enjoy TV programmes in English and a variety of other languages almost anywhere in the world. France is well served by satellite TV and a number of satellites are positioned over Europe carrying over 200 stations broadcasting in a variety of languages.

Astra: Although it wasn't the first in Europe (which was Eutelsat), the European satellite revolution really took off with the launch of the Astra 1A satellite in 1988 (operated by the Luxembourg-based *Société Européenne des Satellites* or SES), positioned 36,000km (22,300mi) above the earth. TV addicts (easily recognised by their antennae and square eyes) are offered a huge choice of English and foreign-language stations which can be received throughout France with a 60 or 85cm dish. Since 1988 a number of additional Astra satellites have been launched, increasing the number of available channels to 64 (or over 200 with digital TV). An added bonus is the availability of radio stations via satellite, including all the national BBC stations (see **Satellite Radio** on page 137).

Among the many English-language stations available on Astra are Sky One, Movimax, Sky Premier, Sky Cinema, Film Four, Sky News, Sky Sports (three channels), UK Gold, Channel 5, Granada Plus, TNT, Eurosport, CNN, CNBC Europe, UK Style, UK Horizons, The Disney Channel and the Discovery Channel. Other stations broadcast in Dutch, German, Japanese, Swedish and various Indian languages. The signal from many stations is scrambled (the decoder is usually built into the receiver) and viewers must pay a monthly subscription fee to receive programmes. You can buy pirate decoders for some channels. The best served by clear (unscrambled) stations are German-speakers (most German stations on Astra are clear).

BSkyB Television: You must buy a receiver with a Videocrypt decoder and pay a monthly subscription to receive BSkyB or Sky stations except Sky News, which isn't scrambled. Various packages are available costing from around £12 to £30 a month for the premium package offering all movie channels plus Sky Sports. To receive scrambled channels such as Movimax and Sky Sports you need an address in Britain. Subscribers are sent a coded 'smart' card (similar to a credit card) that must be inserted in the decoder to switch it on (cards are updated every few years to thwart counterfeiters). Sky won't send smart cards to overseas viewers as they have the copyright for a British-based audience only, and overseas homeowners need to obtain a card through a friend or relative in Britain. However, a number of satellite companies in France (some of which advertise in the expatriate press) supply BSkyB cards.

Digital Television: Digital TV was launched on 1st October 1998 by BSkyB in the UK. The benefits include a superior picture, better (CD) quality sound, widescreen cinema format and access to many more stations. To watch digital TV you require a Digibox and a (digital) Minidish, which in 1998 could be purchased at a subsidised price by existing Sky customers in the UK. Customers had to sign up for a 12-month subscription and agree to have the connection via a phone line (to allow for future interactive services). In addition to the usual analogue channels (see above), digital TV offers BBC 1, BBC 2 and Channel 4 (but not ITV or ITV2), plus many new digital channels (a total of 200 with up to 500 possible later). ONdigital launched a rival digital service on 15th November 1998, which although it's cheaper, provides a total of just 30 channels (15 free and 15 subscription) including BBC 1 and 2, ITV, ITV2, Channel 4 and Channel 5. Widescreen digital TVs cost around £1,000, but will inevitably become cheaper as more models become available and the demand increases. At the time of writing, digital satellite TV wasn't officially available in France, although it's offered by some expatriate satellite companies.

Eutelsat: Eutelsat was the first company to introduce satellite TV to Europe (in 1983) and it now runs a fleet of communications satellites carrying TV stations to over 50 million homes. Until 1995 they had broadcast primarily advertising-based, clear-access cable channels. Following the launch in March 1995 of their Hot Bird satellite, Eutelsat hoped to become a major competitor to Astra, although its channels are mostly non-English. The English-language stations on Eutelsat include Eurosport, BBC World and CNBC Europe. Other channels broadcast in Arabic, French, German, Hungarian, Italian, Polish, Portuguese, Spanish and Turkish.

BBC Worldwide Television: The BBC's commercial subsidiary, BBC Worldwide Television, broadcasts two 24-hour channels: BBC Prime (general entertainment) and BBC World (24-hour news and information). BBC World is free-to-air and is transmitted via the Eutelsat Hot Bird satellite, while BBC Prime is encrypted and transmitted via the Intelsat satellite. BBC Prime requires a D2-MAC decoder and a smartcard costing around £25 and an annual £75 subscription fee (plus VAT). Smartcards are available from TV Extra, PO Box 304, 59124 Motala, Sweden (☎ 46-141-56060). For more information and a programming guide contact BBC Worldwide Television, Woodlands, 80 Wood Lane, London W12 0TT, UK (☎ 0181-576 2555). The BBC publishes a monthly magazine, *BBC On Air*, giving comprehensive information about BBC Worldwide Television programmes. A programme guide is also listed on the Internet (www.bbc.co.uk/schedules) and both BBC World and BBC Prime have their own websites (www.bbcworld.com and www.bbcprime.com). When accessing them, you need to enter the name of the country (e.g. France) so that schedules appear in local time.

French Satellite TV: There are no French-language channels on Astra. If you wish to receive French satellite TV you need to tune in to French satellites such as the Télécom 2A and 2B satellites, which between them carry around 20 French-language stations. A SECAM standard TV isn't required to receive most French satellite broadcasts, which are different from terrestrial broadcasts, but a decoder (e.g. Syster) is required to unscramble most signals.

Equipment: A satellite receiver should have a built-in Videocrypt decoder (and others such as Eurocrypt, Syster or SECAM if required) and be capable of receiving satellite stereo radio. A 60cm dish (to receive Astra stations) costs from around 2,000F plus the cost of installation (which may be included in the price). Shop around as prices vary enormously. You can also install a motorised 1.2 or 1.5 metre dish and receive hundreds of stations in a multitude of languages from around the world. If you wish to receive satellite TV on two or more TVs, you can buy a system with two or more receptors. To receive stations from two or more satellites simultaneously, you need a motorised dish or a dish with a double feed (dual LNBs) antenna. **When buying a system, ensure that it can receive programmes from all existing and planned satellites.**

Location: To receive programmes from any satellite, there must be no obstacles between the satellite and your dish, i.e. no trees, buildings or mountains must obstruct the signal, so check before renting or buying a home. Before buying or erecting a satellite dish, check whether you need permission from your landlord or the local authorities. France has strict laws regarding the positioning of antennas in urban areas, although in rural areas they are more relaxed. Dishes can be mounted in a variety of unobtrusive positions and can be painted or patterned to blend in with the background.

Programme Guides: Many satellite stations provide teletext information, which includes programme schedules. Satellite programme listings are provided in a number of British publications such as *What Satellite, Satellite Times* and *Satellite TV* (the best), available on subscription and from some international news kiosks in France. The annual *World Radio and TV Handbook* (Billboard) contains over 600 pages of information and the frequencies of radio and TV stations worldwide.

Television Licence

A colour TV licence (*redevance pour télévision couleur*) is required by TV owners in France, costing 744F a year for a colour TV and 475F for a black and white TV. The licence fee covers any number of TVs (owned or rented), irrespective of where they are located in France, e.g. holiday homes, motor vehicles or boats. The licence fee subsidises France 2 (40 per cent) and FR3 (80 per cent), and also contributes towards the Radio-France and Radio-France International public radio stations.

If you buy a TV in France the retailer must inform the authorities and a TV licence fee bill will follow automatically after a few months (which not surprisingly leads to many Frenchmen paying in cash and giving fictitious addresses). If you import a TV capable of receiving French TV programmes, you should report it within 30 days to your local *Centre Régional de la Redevance Audiovisuelle* (you can obtain the address from your local post office). You will be fined if you're discovered to have a TV without a licence when an inspector calls. If you don't pay the annual fee on time, you must visit the local *commisariat* to explain why and pay an extra fee (*aggrandisement*) for late payment. If you sell or otherwise dispose of your TV and don't replace it you must notify the authorities, otherwise you remain liable to pay the licence fee. You may be asked what you did with your TV to ensure that the licence is being paid by the new owner (if applicable).

Videos

Video films are expensive in France and there's little available in English. French video rental shops may have only a few English-language titles. However, there are specialist English-language rental shops in the main cities, and mobile and mail-order services in rural areas. English-language videocassette films can be rented from around 30F a day from video shops and postal video clubs. Rental costs can often be reduced by paying a monthly membership fee or a lump sum in advance. PAL videotapes can be converted to SECAM (and vice versa), although it's prohibitively expensive. If you have a large collection of PAL videotapes, you should buy a multi-standard TV and VCR or have a separate TV and video to play back your favourite videos, e.g. PAL or NTSC. If you wish to improve your French before arriving in France, French-language films are sold or can be rented in many countries.

BBC Television has also leapt on the profitable video bandwagon and produces three-hour videos of its best programmes (including entertainment, humour, sport, natural history, news and current affairs), available on subscription. For information write to Video World, Subscription Dept., 680 Romford Road, London E12, UK.

RADIO

Radio was deregulated in France in the '80s, since when there have been commercial local radio (*radio libre*) stations. Deregulation led to scores of radio stations springing up overnight, representing diverse ethnic groups, lifestyles and communities. Consequently the wavebands were flooded with stations and the only ones that could be received clearly were the large commercial stations with powerful transmitters such as NRJ, Radio Luxembourg and Radio Monte Carlo. This led to the introduction of new regulations, although less stringent than in the '70s. Local radio stations (*Radio Locales Privées*) often have limited audiences due to their small catchment areas and low transmitting power, and many have been grouped together into national networks. The largest is operated by NRJ, a popular Paris music station. With an estimated 35 million radios in France (plus ten million car radios) embracing some 99 per cent of the population, France has one of Europe's largest radio markets and it's much more popular than TV. A radio licence isn't required in France.

Music Stations: There's a wealth of excellent FM stations in Paris and other cities, although in some rural areas you may be lucky to receive a few FM stations clearly, e.g. one chat show and one playing nothing but folk music! French radio stations are often original and progressive, particularly in Paris, and play a wide variety of music. Among the most popular FM stations are Kiss FM (89.0), France Info (105.5), Radio Classique (101.1), RTL (104.3) and Europe 1 (104.7). Radio Classique is also available throughout France on other wavelengths. France has many excellent music stations, which previously played mostly American and British pop songs. However, from the 1st January 1996 at least 40 per cent of radio musical broadcasts have had to consist of songs sung in French. Stations that don't comply can be fined or even closed. This has led to talk shows replacing the 40 per cent French music, as in the words of one French DJ, 'no-one wants to listen to 40 per cent of Sacha Distel'!

Radio France: Radio France public radio is divided into three networks: France-Inter, France-Musique and France-Culture. France-Inter is the main channel and broadcasts news bulletins, current events, magazine programmes, discussions, light music and plays (many foreigners tune in to improve their French). During the summer it broadcasts news bulletins in English (at 0900 and 1600). France-Musique broadcasts mostly classical music with some jazz and contemporary music. Much of

France-Culture's output is highbrow and somewhat pretentious and includes talks, debates and interviews on arts and literature.

Other Stations: Many French people tune into foreign radio stations such as Europe One, Radio Luxembourg (RTL), Radio Monte-Carlo and Radio Sud, all broadcasting from outside French territory, having been established many years ago to circumvent the earlier French government monopoly on radio stations. Together they have a larger audience than Radio France. Other popular stations include France Info, a continuous news channel available throughout France, Radio Bleue, targeted at mature listeners, and Fun Radio, part of a new wave of youth-oriented radio stations that have saturated French airwaves in recent years. Radio France International (RFI) is France's world service station, broadcasting 24 hours a day in some 15 languages. There are also a number of expatriate English-language radio stations in France, such as Riviera Radio (FM stereo 106.3 and 106.5) in the south of France.

BBC: The BBC World Service is broadcast on short wave on several frequencies (e.g. 12095, 9410, 7325, 6195, 3955, 648 and 198 khz) simultaneously and you can usually receive a good signal on one of them. The signal strength varies depending on where you live in France, the time of day and year, the power and positioning of your receiver, and atmospheric conditions. You can also receive BBC radio stations in some northern and western areas of France. All BBC radio stations, including the World Service, are also available on the Astra satellite (see below). The BBC publish a monthly magazine, *BBC On Air*, containing comprehensive information about BBC World Service radio and TV programmes. For a free copy and frequency information write to BBC On Air, Room 205 NW, Bush House, Strand, London WC2B 4PH, UK (☎ 0171-240 3456).

Satellite Radio: If you have satellite TV, you can also receive many radio stations via your satellite link. For example, BBC Radio 1, 2, 3, 4 and 5, BBC World Service, Sky Radio, Virgin 1215 and many foreign-language stations are broadcast via the Astra satellites (see page 133) Satellite radio stations are listed in British satellite TV magazines such as the *Satellite Times*. If you're interested in receiving radio stations from further afield you should obtain a copy of the *World Radio TV Handbook* (Billboard).

9.

EDUCATION

France is noted for its high academic standards and has an excellent state-funded school system (*écoles publiques*). This is supported by a comprehensive network of private schools (*écoles privées*), including many distinguished international schools. Around 15 per cent of French children attend private schools, most of which are co-educational day schools (education in France is almost exclusively co-educational). Higher education standards are only average, with the notable exception of the elite *grandes écoles*, that are rated among the world's best educational establishments.

Education in France is compulsory between the ages of 6 and 16 and entirely free from nursery school through to university (free state schools have existed in France for over a century). Some 80 per cent of children continue their schooling beyond the age of 16 and by the year 2000 there's expected to be some two million students in *lycées*, private institutions, *grandes écoles* and universities. Free education is also provided for the children of foreign residents, although non-resident, non-EU students require a student visa (see **Chapter 3**).

It was Napoleon who decided that French children should study the same subject, at the same level, at the same time in a particular region. Some 200 years later the system is largely unchanged and the syllabus and textbooks are broadly the same in all schools of the same level throughout France. This means that children moving between schools can continue their education with the minimum disruption. Regions do, however, have a certain amount of autonomy in setting their own school timetables. The French are proud of their schools and resent government interference, although there are almost continual 'reforms' of the educational system. They have a respect, even a love of learning, and reforms are argued at great length and with surprising passion.

Critics of the French education system complain that its teaching methods are too traditional and unimaginative, with most learning by rote. It's also accused of being inflexible and discouraging self-expression and personal development. French schools place a great emphasis on the French language (particularly grammar), arithmetic and the sciences. Schools usually impose more discipline than most foreign children are used to, including regular homework (*devoir*) that increases with the age of the child. French teachers generally have high expectations of pupils and the system is hard on slow learners and the not so bright. However, despite the generally high standards, there have been reports of an increasing number of children entering secondary education unable to read or write adequately.

Generally the younger your child is when he enters the system, the easier he will cope. Conversely the older he is, the more problems he will have adjusting, particularly as the school curriculum is more demanding. Teenagers often have considerable problems learning French and adjusting to French school life, particularly children from America or Britain who haven't already learnt a second language. In some schools, foreign children who cannot understand the language may be neglected and just expected to get on with it. In your early days in France it's important to check exactly what your children are doing at school and whether they are making progress (not just with the language, but also with other lessons).

As a parent, you should be prepared to support your children through this difficult period. If you aren't fluent in French, you will already be aware how frustrating it is being unable to express yourself adequately, which can easily lead to feelings of inferiority or inadequacy in children (and adults!). Note that it's also important for parents to ensure that their children maintain their English or other native language, as it can easily be neglected (surveys show that the children of English residents in France are losing their ability to read and write English).

If pupils fall behind they have traditionally been required to repeat a year (*redoublement*), although this has changed in recent years in nursery and primary schools with the introduction of a more flexible system of cycles (see page 148). Truancy is a heinous and rare offence in France, where a child can be expelled for forging a parent's signature to skip classes. Parent-teacher meetings are held regularly in schools, where parents can discuss a child's progress with teachers.

France has a highly competitive and selective examination system that separates the brighter students from the less academically gifted at around age 14. A strong emphasis is placed on training and few school-leavers go directly into a job without prior training. It's normal practice for those leaving school at 16 to attend a technical college or train as an apprentice. In the highly competitive labour market of the '90s, most parents and students are acutely aware that academic qualifications and training are of paramount importance in obtaining a good job (or any job). Although the French state school system is more disciplined and less flexible than in many other countries, the results speak for themselves, with every child given the opportunity to study for a trade, diploma or degree.

For many children, the experience of schooling and living in a foreign land is a stimulating challenge they relish, providing invaluable cultural and educational experiences. Your child will become a 'world' citizen, less likely to be prejudiced against foreigners and foreign ideas. This is particularly true if he attends an international school with pupils from many different countries (many state schools also have pupils from a number of countries and backgrounds). However, before making major decisions about your child's future education, it's important to consider his ability, character and individual requirements.

Information about French schools, both state and private, can be obtained from French embassies and consulates abroad, and from foreign embassies, educational organisations and government departments in France. Local information can be obtained from town halls (*mairies*). The *École des Parents et des Educateurs (Interservice Parents)*, 5, Impasse du Bon Secours, 75543 Paris Cedex 11 (☎ 01.44.93.44.70) provides free advice for parents regarding all aspects of education and careers. The French Ministry of Education provides a nationwide free information service through local *Centre d'Information et d'Orientation (CIO)* offices. For the address of your local CIO office, contact your *mairie*. The Association of American Wives of Europeans (AAWE), BP 127, 92154 Suresnes Cedex (☎ 01.47.28.46.39) publishes a comprehensive *Guide to Education* in the Paris area.

In addition to a detailed look at the French state school system and private schools, this chapter also contains information about apprenticeships, higher and further education, and language schools.

STATE OR PRIVATE SCHOOL?

If you're able to choose between state and private education in France, the following checklist will help you decide:

- How long are you planning to stay in France? If you're uncertain, then it's probably better to assume a long stay. Due to language and other integration problems, enrolling a child in a French state school is advisable for a minimum of one or two years only, particularly for teenage children who aren't fluent in French.

- Bear in mind that the area where you choose to live will affect your choice of school(s). For example, it's usually necessary to send your child to a state school near your home and if you choose a private day school you must take into account the distance from your home to the school. Note that in some areas (e.g. some Parisian suburbs), schools are plagued by violence (directed against fellow pupils and teachers), vandalism and drugs.

- Do you know where you're going when you leave France? This may be an important consideration with regard to your child's language of tuition and system of education in France. How old is your child and what age will he be when you plan to leave France? What future plans do you have for his education and in which country?

- What educational level is your child at now and how will he fit into a private school or the French state school system? The younger he is, the easier it will be to place him in a suitable school.

- How does your child view the thought of studying in French? What language is best from a long-term point of view? Is schooling available in France in his mother tongue?

- Will your child need help with his studies, and more importantly, will you be able to help him, particularly with his French?

- Is special or extra tutoring available in French or other subjects, if necessary?

- What are the school hours? What are the school holiday periods? Many state schools in France have compulsory Saturday morning classes. How will the school holidays and hours affect your family's work and leisure activities?

- Is religion an important aspect in your choice of school? There's no compulsory religious instruction in French state schools and most international schools are non-denominational. Note that state schools ban religious apparel at school, which has upset Moslems and other religious groups, and some Moslem children have even been expelled for wearing a headscarf (not a veil). Jewish kippa 'hats' and Catholic crucifixes are also banned.

- Do you want your child to go to a co-educational or a single-sex school? French state schools are usually co-educational.

- Should you send your child to a boarding school? If so in which country?

- What are the secondary and further education prospects in France or another country? Are French examinations or the examinations set by prospective French schools recognised in your home country or the country where you plan to live after leaving France? If applicable, check whether the French *baccalauréat* examination is recognised as a university entrance qualification in your home country.

- Does a prospective school have a good academic record? Most schools provide exam pass rate statistics.

- How large are the classes? What is the pupil-teacher ratio?

Obtain the opinions and advice of others who have been faced with the same decisions and problems as yourself, and collect as much information from as many different sources as possible before making a decision. Speak to teachers and the parents of children attending the schools on your shortlist. Finally, most parents find it pays to discuss the alternatives with their children before making a decision. See also **Choosing a Private School** on page 158.

STATE SCHOOLS

Although state-funded schools are termed public schools (*écoles publiques*) in France, the term 'state' has been used in preference to public in this book. This is to prevent confusion with the term 'public school', used in the USA to refer to a state school, but which in Britain refers to a private fee-paying school (confusing isn't it!). The state school system in France differs considerably from the school systems in, for example, Britain or the USA, particularly regarding secondary education.

The Ministry of National Education, Youth and Sport is responsible for most of France's state education system. The state educates some 13 million students (6.6 million in nursery and primary schools, 5 million in secondary schools and 1.3 million in higher education) in some 58,000 nursery and primary schools, 7,400 *lycées* and *collèges*, and 72 universities. The French education system divides the country into 26 regions or districts (*académies*), which is a group of several *départements* headed by a superintendent (*recteur*) and attached to at least one university. The *académies* set the curriculum and examinations, and a high degree of consultation ensures that standards vary little from region to region. Although the state provides a large proportion of the funding for the French education system, in recent years some of the responsibility has been transferred to departments (for *collèges*) and the regions (for *lycées*).

French state education is highly rated and is well organised, efficient and adequately funded (not that teachers would ever agree!), and over 80 per cent of students claim they are well motivated and want to succeed. France is particularly well endowed with free nursery schools and the primary and secondary education system provides a solid foundation for university or a career. State education in France is perceived by many to be (in general) of a higher quality than private education (among the most famous schools in Paris are the Henri IV and Louis le Grand *lycées*, both state schools). French parents usually send their children to a private school only for religious reasons or when they need extra assistance that's unavailable in a state school. In recent years, however, there has been disquiet particularly among *lycée* students of whom half a million took to the streets in October 1998 in protest against class overcrowding and a shortage of teachers. The government has promised reform and set up an investigation committee.

Attending a state school helps children integrate into the local community and to learn the local language. Pupils usually go to local nursery and primary schools, although attending secondary school often entails travelling long distances. One of the consequences of the depopulation of rural areas in the last few decades has been the closure of many schools, resulting in children having to travel long distances to school. This has led some communities to offer inexpensive or even free housing to families with school-age children, in an attempt to preserve local nursery and primary schools and keep communities alive.

A general criticism of French state schools often made by foreigners is the lack of extracurricular activities such as sport, music, drama, and arts and crafts. State schools have no school clubs or sports teams and if your child wants to do team sports he must join a local club. This means parents need to ferry children back and forth for games and social events (Americans will be used to this!). However, although not part of the curriculum, a variety of sports activities are organised through local sports associations (*associations sportives*), which may also organise non-sporting activities such as dance and music. Fees are low and activities usually take place directly after school.

Note that grades in French state schools differ considerably from the American and British systems. The French system is almost the exact reverse of the American system. Instead of counting from 1 to 12, the French start with the 11th grade at age six and end with the *classe terminale*, the last year of a secondary high school (*lycée*) at age 18 or 19.

Having made the decision to send your child to a state school, you should stick to it for at least a year to give it a fair trial. It may take a child this long to fully adapt to a new language, the change of environment and the different curriculum. State schools have special education sections (*Sections d'Education Spéciale/SES*) for children with learning difficulties due to psychological, emotional or behavioural problems and for slow learners.

Language

There are many considerations to take into account when choosing an appropriate school in France, not least the language of study. The only schools in France using English as the teaching language are a few foreign and international private schools. A number of multilingual French schools teach students in both English and French (but not simultaneously!). If your children attend any other school, they must study all subjects in French. For most children, studying in French isn't such a handicap as it may appear at first, particularly for those aged below ten. The majority of children adapt quickly and most become reasonably fluent within three to six months (if only it were so easy for adults!). However, all children don't adapt equally well to a change of language and culture, particularly children aged over ten (at around ten years of age children begin to learn languages more slowly), many of whom encounter great difficulties during their first year. Nevertheless, foreign children often acquire a sort of celebrity status, particularly in rural schools, which helps their integration.

It should be born in mind that the French state school system generally makes little or no concession to non-French speakers, for example by providing intensive French lessons. This can make the first few months quite an ordeal for non French-speaking children. However, some state schools do provide free intensive French lessons (*classes d'initiation/CLIN*) for foreign children, although this depends on the school and the department. It may be worthwhile inquiring about the availability of extra French classes before choosing where to live. Note that while attending a CLIN, children may fall behind in other subjects.

Once your child has acquired a sufficient knowledge of spoken and written French, he's integrated into a regular class in a local neighbourhood school. Foreign children are tested (like French children) and put into a class suitable to their level of French, even if this means being taught with younger children or slow-learners.

However, a child of six or seven must be permitted to enter the first year of primary school (*cours préparatoire/CP*), even if he speaks no French. An older child can be refused entry to the CP or another class and can be obliged to attend a CLIN against his parents' wishes.

If your local state school doesn't provide extra French classes, your only choice will be to pay for private lessons or send your child to another (possibly private) school, where extra tuition is provided. Some parents send a child to an English-speaking school for a year, followed by a move to a bilingual or French school. Other parents find it's easier to throw their children in at the deep end, rather than introduce them gradually. It depends on the character, ability and wishes of the child. Whatever you decide, it will help if your child has some intensive French lessons before arriving in France. It may also be possible to organise an educational or cultural exchange with a French school or family before coming to live in France, which is a considerable help in integrating a child into the French language and culture (see page 165).

Many state schools teach regional languages including Alsatian, Basque, Breton, Catalan, Flemish, Corsican and Occitan, in addition to French. Where applicable these are optional and are taught for around three hours a week, generally outside normal school hours.

Enrolment

Information about schools in a particular area can be obtained from the schools information service (*service des écoles*) at the local town hall (*mairie*). If you wish to arrange your child's education before arriving in France, you should write to the *Inspecteur d'Académie* of the *département* where you're going to live, with details of a child's age, previous schooling and knowledge of French. In France, a child must attend a state school within a certain distance of his home, so if you have a preference for a particular school, it's important to buy or rent a home within that school's catchment area (which change periodically to take into account the changes in population). Town halls can provide a list of local schools at all levels.

If you wish your child to attend a different school from the one assigned by your *mairie*, you may make a request (*dérogation*) for your child to attend another school. You must usually have good reasons for such a request, e.g. another of your children already attends your preferred school, the preferred school is located close to your home or place of work, or it teaches a unique course that you wish your child to study, e.g. certain foreign languages. The transfer must be approved by the *directeurs* of both schools. To enrol your child in a French school you must visit your *mairie* with the following documents:

- Your child's birth certificate or passport, with an official French translation (if necessary). If your child was born in France, you must take along your family record book (*livret de famille*) or birth certificate (*extrait de l'acte de naissance*).

- Proof of immunisation. In France, immunisations are recorded in a child's health book (*carnet de santé*), which is issued to parents when a child is born in France. When you arrive in France, you should bring proof of your child's immunisations with you. You're issued with a *carnet de santé* by your *mairie* for all school age children. For more information see **Children's Health** on page 243.

- Proof of residence in the form of an electricity or telephone bill in your name. If you don't have any bills (lucky you!), a rent receipt, lease or proof of ownership (*attestation d'acquisition*) is acceptable.

School Hours

Most French state schools have adopted the four-day week (*semaine de quatre jours*) with Wednesday remaining free and the lack of Saturday lessons compensated for by reducing holiday periods (which was the option favoured by most parents in a recent survey). The changes are now official, although you may find the odd *département* still instituting Saturday morning classes. Contact your local education department to find out the official position regarding school hours in your area.

School hours vary depending on the type of school. Nursery school hours are from 0830 or 0900 to 1130 or noon and from 1330 or 1400 to between 1600 and 1700, on Monday, Tuesday, Thursday and Friday, plus Saturday mornings. There's a 15-minute break in the mornings and afternoons. Primary school consists of 26 hours per week, usually from 0830 to 1130 and 1330 to 1630. Secondary schools have the longest hours, which vary depending on the kind of school. In a *collège* students attend school for 27 or 28 hours a week and in a *lycée* for around 30 to 36 hours (depending on the type of *lycée*). The school hours for a *collège* and a *lycée* are usually from 0800 to noon and 1400 to 1700, although some start at 0900 and finish at 1800.

Some schools have a minibus, which collects children from outlying regions and returns them home at the end of the day. However, due to the roundabout journey, this often adds considerably to the school day. Many parents prefer to take children to and from school or take them to school and allow them to get the bus home. State schools and communities usually provide an after school nursery (*garderie*) for working mothers on Wednesdays and during school holidays.

Holidays

French school children have the longest school holidays (*vacances scolaires*) in the world. They generally attend school for some 160 days a year only, from early September until late June, although they compensate with longer school hours and abundant homework. French school term dates have been fixed for a number of years, although they may be modified to take account of local circumstances. The school year is made up of five terms, each averaging around seven weeks. The following table shows the school calendar (*calendrier scolaire*) for 1999/2000 (all dates inclusive):

Holiday	Dates
All Saints (*Toussaint*)	30th October to 7th November (1999)
New Year (*Noël*)	18th December to 2nd January (2000)
Winter* (*Hiver*)	Zone A: 19th February to 5th March, Zone B: 12th to 27th February, Zone C: 5th to 20th February
Spring* (*Printemps*)	Zone A: 15th April to 1st May, Zone B: 8th to 28th April, Zone C: 1st to 16th April
Summer (*Été/grandes vacances*)	2nd July to 8th September

* Winter and spring school holiday periods are based on a system of zones (see below) to enable holiday resorts (particularly ski resorts) to cope with the flood of children during these periods.

Zone	Cities/Towns
A	Caen, Clermont-Ferrand, Grenoble, Montpellier, Nancy-Metz, Nantes, Rennes and Toulouse
B	Aix-Marseille, Amiens, Besançon, Dijon, Lille, Limoges, Lyon, Nice, Orléans-Tours, Poitiers, Reims, Rouen and Strasbourg
C	Bordeaux, Créteil, Paris and Versailles.

Schools are also closed on public holidays when they fall within term time. School holiday dates are published by schools and local communities well in advance, thus allowing parents ample time to schedule family holidays during the school holidays. Normally you aren't permitted to withdraw your children from classes during the school term, except for visits to a doctor or dentist, when the teacher should be informed in advance. In primary school a note to the teacher is sufficient, while in secondary school an official absence form must be completed by the teacher concerned and submitted to the school office.

Provisions

Education is free in France but pens, stationery and sports clothes/equipment must be purchased by parents. Most provisions are provided in primary school (ages 6 to 11) and in *collège* (ages 12 to 15), although parents may need to buy some books, but everything must be purchased by parents for children attending a *lycée*. The average parent can expect to pay around 2,500F a *lycée* year per student (or even more for technical subjects). This can be hard on low-income families, although it's possible to buy secondhand books at the start of the term, when schools hold secondhand book sales (*bourse aux livres*). Grants are also available for parents with financial difficulties. A number of passport-size photographs are required for secondary school students. Primary school children require the following articles:

● school bag or satchel or a small bag for a kindergarten snack;

- a pencil case, pencils and crayons, stationery, etc.;
- slippers, gym shoes (plimsolls), shorts and a towel for games and exercise periods;
- sports bag for the above if the satchel is too small.

At nursery school, children usually take a snack for both morning and afternoon breaks (hungry work studying!). Children may also take a packed lunch if they don't go home for lunch or eat at a school canteen. The cost of lunch at a nursery or primary school varies depending on the area, the parents' income and whether they live within the school's catchment area. The cost is usually around 10F per meal, paid one month in advance (i.e. 20 meals). Lunch at a secondary school, e.g. a *lycée*, costs around 650F per term. Children are usually expected to eat everything when they have school lunch.

With the exception of a few 'exclusive' schools, school uniforms are non-existent in France. Students usually devise their own 'uniform' of jeans, T-shirt or sweater and trainers. In some areas the theft (e.g. by 'mugging') of designer clothes by 'gangs' is widespread and has resulted in children being told to dress down and not wear expensive clothes to school.

Nursery & Primary School Cycles

Major educational reforms (*loi d'orientation*) launched in the 1989-90 school year divided nursery and primary schooling into educational stages (*cycles pédagogiques*). These were designed to allow pupils to progress at their own speed, but at the same time provide individual help in order to reduce the number of pupils required to repeat a year (*redoublement*). Attainment targets are set for each stage to provide the necessary flexibility and restrict the number of children repeating years. The reforms introduced a series of three cycles, each of three years duration:

1. *Cycle des Apprentissages Premiers*: The first cycle includes the three sections of nursery school from the age of three to six (*petite, moyenne* and *grande*).

2. *Cycle des Apprentissages Fondamentaux*: The second cycle includes the final year of nursery school and the first two years of primary school (*cours préparatoire/CP* and *cours élémentaire 1/CE1*).

3. *Cycle des Approfondissements:* The third cycle includes the primary school years *cours élémentaire 2/CE2, cours moyen 1/CM1* and *cours moyen 2/CM2*.

Although each cycle lasts an average of three years, each can be completed in two or four years, depending on each individual child's progress. The decision whether a child is ready to progress to the next cycle is made jointly by a teachers' council on cycles (*conseil des maîtres de cycles*), the school director, the pupil's teachers and the psycho-pedagogical group. It's no longer possible to fail a grade and repeat a year, as the new system allows pupils to progress at their own speed and doesn't require them to repeat the same work as in the previous year. Parents are able to appeal against a school's decision regarding progression to the next cycle. A scholastic record book (*livret scolaire*) is maintained for each child during the three cycles.

Nursery School

France has a long tradition of free, state-funded, nursery schools (usually termed *écoles maternelles*) and has one of the best programmes in the world. Around 30 per cent of children attend nursery school at the age of two, 90 per cent at age three and virtually all by the time they are four – a level of attendance matched only by Belgium. Before the age of two or three, working mothers often place their children aged from three months in a state or private nursery or kindergarten (*crèche* or *jardin*) while they are working. Nursery schooling from the age of two to six is optional. However, under the 1989 Education Act, a place must be available in nursery school for every three-year-old whose parents request one. The place must be in a nursery school or an infant class (*classe enfantine*) in a primary school as close as possible to the child's home. Priority is given to providing places for two-year-olds living in socially underprivileged areas. Nursery school is held in a local nursery school or the local primary school.

Nursery school hours are generally from 0830 or 0900 to 1130 or noon and 1330 or 1400 to 1600 or 1630, with the exception of Wednesdays, when there's no school. Young children usually sleep for two hours after lunch. Children can attend for just half a day, which many foreign parents prefer, particularly at first when a child doesn't speak French. There's usually a morning session on Saturdays, depending on the *département*, although this is optional. Children may have lunch at the school canteen (*cantine*) by arrangement, where gourmet-style, three-course lunches are available for around 10F per day, usually paid a month in advance. Priority is given to children with two working parents, children from families with three or more young children and children who live too far from school to go home for lunch. If parents are unable to collect their children when school is over, there's usually a supervised nursery (*garderie*) outside school hours for a small fee (e.g. starting at 0730 and ending at 1830 in the evening). When it's necessary to limit numbers, children of working mothers have priority.

Nursery school has traditionally been divided into three sections, depending on age, which together form the introduction to the basic stage of primary education:

● lower section (*petite*) from 2 to 4 years;

● middle section (*moyenne*) from 4 to 5 years;

● upper section (*grande*) from 5 to 6 years.

The three years of primary school from age three to six are included in the first cycle (*cycle des apprentissages premiers*) of the new *cycles pédagogiques* and the last year is incorporated in the second cycle (*Cycle des Apprentissages Fondamentaux*).

Nursery school is designed to introduce children to the social environment of school and to concentrate on the basic skills of coordination. It encourages the development of self-awareness and provides an introduction to group activities. Exercises include arts and crafts (e.g. drawing, painting and pottery), music, educational games, perceptual motor activities and listening skills. During the final years of nursery school, the rudiments of reading, writing and arithmetic are taught in preparation for primary school. Nursery school is highly recommended, particularly if your children are going to continue with a state education. After one or two years of nursery school they will be integrated into the local community and will have learnt French in preparation for primary school.

Primary School

Primary school (*école primaire*) attendance is compulsory from the age of six to 11 for 26 hours a week. Schools are established and maintained by local communities, although the overall responsibility lies with the state. Since the '80s the primary school population has been decreasing, leading to a reduction in the number of classes. In many rural areas this has led to the closure of schools and children having to travel to schools in neighbouring towns or schools having to share teachers and expensive equipment such as computers. There are several pilot schemes in operation around the country to find better ways of organising primary education, particularly staff, half of whom are over 50 and reluctant to change. One scheme makes part-time use of graduates to assist teachers in an attempt to inject new blood into the system.

Each primary school has a director (*directeur/directrice*) who presides over the school council (*conseil d'école*). The council makes decisions regarding school regulations, communication between teachers and parents, school meals (canteen), after school care, extracurricular activities, security and hygiene. The school council usually meets twice a year and comprises a teachers' committee (*comité des maîtres*), a parents' committee (*comité des parents*), and representatives of the local education authority and municipality. The parents' committee is the equivalent of the parent-teacher association (PTA) in many other countries.

The five years of primary school each represent a particular course or level (*cours/cycle*), as shown below. Before the introduction of the new cycles (see page 148) it was fairly common for children to repeat a year, particularly the CP (first) or last (CM2) year.

- preparatory course (*cours préparatoire/CP*) from 6 to 7 years (11th class);
- first year elementary course (*cours élémentaire/CE1*) from 7 to 8 years (10th class);
- second year elementary course (CE2) from 8 to 9 years (9th class);
- first year middle/intermediate course (*cours moyen 1/CM1*) from 9 to 10 years (8th class);
- second year middle/intermediate course (CM2) from 10 to 11 years (7th class).

The subjects taught at primary school are divided into three main groups:

1. French, history, geography and civic studies;
2. Mathematics, science and technology;
3. Physical education and sport, arts and crafts, and music.

Minimum and maximum numbers of tuition hours are set for each group of subjects, up to the total school hours of 26 per week. Teachers are allowed some flexibility in determining the actual hours so that they can place more emphasis on certain subjects for particular pupils, based on their strengths and weaknesses. The main objectives of primary school are the learning and consolidation of the basics such as reading, writing and mathematics (language skills are accorded a special status). There are no examinations at the end of primary school, although a child's primary record is forwarded to his secondary *collège*. However, all children are expected to be able to read and write French by the end of their first term in primary school and are tested to see whether they're up to standard. If they aren't they must repeat the whole year.

Since 1989-90, the teaching of a foreign language has been included in primary school years CM1 and CM2. Most pupils (over 80 per cent) choose to learn English, although the French government is trying to encourage them to learn other foreign languages (all part of the plot to reduce the growing influence of the English language in France). Primary language tuition is, of necessity, fairly basic, and English-speaking parents shouldn't rely on it to improve their child's English. Primary school children have a notebook (*cahier de texte*) that they bring home each day. Parents sign the book to verify that a child has done his homework and teachers use it to convey messages to parents, e.g. special items a child requires for school next day.

One of the unique aspects of French primary education is the discovery 'class' (*classe de découverte*), when pupils spend one to three weeks in a new environment. It may be held in the country (*classe verte/classe de nature*), mountains (*classe de neige* or ski class), by the sea (*classe de mer*) or even abroad. It isn't a holiday camp and pupils follow their normal lessons, augmented by field trips and other special activities. The most popular discovery class is the skiing trip, which usually takes place in January or February. Financial assistance is available for parents who are unable to pay for a child's trip.

Secondary School

Secondary education is compulsory until the age of 16 and includes attendance at a *collège* (similar to an American junior high school) until age 15. At 15, secondary education is decided by examination, with the top students going to a *lycée* (high school) until they are 18 (*cycle long*) to study for the *baccalauréat* (see page 154). Students who don't succeed in being entered for the traditional three-year general or technology *baccalauréat* may follow shortened studies (*cycle court*) in a vocational course. These include the study for a *Brevet d'Enseignement Professionnel (BEP)*, *Certificat d'Aptitude Professionnelle (CAP)* or the *baccalauréat professionnel* in a vocational *lycée* (see page 153). At the end of technical college a certificate of competence is issued for particular skills, providing a certain level of language ability has also been attained. Students can repeat a year until they pass the final examinations and few leave school without a certificate.

As in all countries, the schools with the best reputations and exam results are the most popular and are therefore the most difficult to gain entry to. Parents should plan well ahead, particularly if they want a child to be accepted by a superior *collège* or *lycée*. Some *collèges* are attached to *lycées*, with *collège* students granted preferential entrance to the *lycée*. The secondary school(s) your child may attend is primarily determined by where you live. In some rural areas there's little or no choice of schools, while in Paris and other cities there are usually a number of possibilities. Secondary schools usually provide excellent school meals for around 25F a day.

Collège

At the age of 11 all children attend a *collège* (formally known as a *collège d'enseignement secondaire/CES*), headed by a *principal*. Each *collège* has a school council (*conseil d'établissement*) composed of administrative staff and representatives of teachers, parents, students and the local authorities. Its task is to make recommendations regarding teaching and other matters of importance to the school community.

The four years of *collège* education are numbered from the 6th to the 3rd (6ème, 5ème, 4ème, 3ème). The school year is organised on a trimester basis (a period of three months equating to a term), with students being evaluated by teachers (*conseil des professeurs*) at the end of each trimester. This valuation is particularly important, as it determines the future studies open to a student and the type of *baccalauréat* he may take. Parents' organisations (*associations des parents/délégués des parents*) also play an important role in determining a student's future studies. It's common for school class councils (*conseil de classes*) to recommend that a student repeat a year of *collège*, although this can be done only with the parents' permission. If parents don't agree, they can appeal against the decision, although if they lose the appeal they must abide by the appeal commission's decision. *Collège* education is divided into two, two-year stages:

The Observation Cycle (*cycle d'observation*) is the name given to the first two years of *collège* (the sixth and fifth forms or 6e/5e), where all students follow a common curriculum. General lessons total around 24 hours per week and include French, mathematics, a modern foreign language, history, geography, economics, civics, physics and chemistry, biology and geology, technology, artistic subjects, physical education and sport. An extra three hours (*heures de soutien*) of lessons are set each week in subjects selected by the *collège* (usually French, mathematics and a foreign language), depending on individual students' needs. At the end of the fifth form students move to the orientation cycle (fourth form) or repeat the fifth form.

The Orientation Cycle (*cycle d'orientation*) is the name given to the last two years of *collège* (the fourth and third forms or 4e/3e). It's so called because students are allowed some choice of subjects and can thus begin to decide the future direction (orientation) of their studies. Students follow a common curriculum of around 25 hours of lessons a week in the same subjects as in the sixth and fifth forms. In addition to the core subjects, there are compulsory lessons in an optional obligatory subject (*options obligatoires*) chosen from a second modern foreign language, intensive study in the first modern foreign language, a regional language or a classical language (Greek or Latin). Students may also choose an optional (voluntary) additional subject. The majority of students choose to study a second modern foreign language, which is officially encouraged. Decisions regarding future studies are made at the end of the third form (at around age 14), when exams are taken to decide whether students go on to a *lycée* and sit the *baccalauréat* (see page 154), attend a vocational *lycée* or take an apprenticeship.

In 1984, technology fourth and third year forms were established in an effort to reduce the number of students leaving school without a certificate or qualification. These are designed to offer a more practical educational approach for students suited to a less academic form of learning. Students who attain the age of 14 or 15 and haven't reached the necessary level to move on to the fourth form are taught in small pre-vocational classes (*Classes Préprofessionnelles de Niveau/CPPN*). Here they receive extra lessons and special assistance, particularly in French and mathematics, in order to help them continue their studies. Others move into preparatory apprenticeship classes (*Classes Préparatoires à l'Apprentissage/CPA*). See **Vocational Schools** on page 154.

At the end of their last year at *collège*, students sit a final written examination (*brevet des collèges*) in French, mathematics and history-geography. The *brevet* is the entrance examination to a *lycée*, although failure doesn't exclude students from going on to higher secondary education.

Lycée

A *lycée* is either a sixth form college or a school with a sixth form, as opposed to a *collège*, which educates students up to the age of 15. It's similar in standard to an English grammar or high school (but higher than an American high school or two-year college) and provides an excellent secondary education that's the equal of any school system in the world. It's the aim of all ambitious students to attend a *lycée* and competition for places is fierce. There are far fewer *lycées* than *collèges* and consequently there's less choice of schools. In rural areas, *lycées* take students from a wide area and because of the travelling distances involved, many offer weekly boarding from Mondays to Fridays. At a *lycée*, students are treated more like university students and aren't required to remain in school if they don't have a lesson. However, the informal, often casual air contrasts with the constant pressure of monthly tests (*interrogations*) and the writing of formal dissertations in most subjects. It goes without saying that unless a student is prepared to work hard, it's a waste of time attending a *lycée*.

A general and technology *lycée* (*lycée d'enseignement général et technologique* prepares students for the general or technology *baccalauréat* (see page 154) or the technical certificate (*Brevet de Technicien/BT*). There are also professional *lycées* (*lycées professionnels/LP*) offering courses leading to vocational certificates (see **Vocational School** on page 154). The *lycée* course is divided into second (*seconde/2ème*), first (*première/1er*) and terminal (*terminale*) years. Second form or *classe de seconde de détermination* is so called because it prepares students to choose the type (*série*) of *baccalauréat* they are going to take. At the initial stages of second form, few students specialise and work for a specific *baccalauréat*. Exceptions are music or dance and certain technology diplomas (*Brevet de Technicien/BT*). During their second form, students study French, mathematics, a modern foreign language, history, geography, physics, chemistry, biology and geology, and have physical education and sports lessons. They also choose compulsory subjects from one of the following two groups:

- compulsory introduction to economics and social studies, and one or two other subjects chosen by students from: a second modern language, regional language, classical language, management, office automation, automation technology, artistic subjects and specialised sporting activities;

- one or two specialised technology subjects such as industrial technology, science and laboratory technology, medical and social science, or applied arts. The choice of at least one technology subject is compulsory for students planning to progress to the first form leading to the corresponding technology *baccalauréat* series.

After the second form, students move on to one of the courses leading to one or several of the types of *baccalauréat* examination. It's possible to transfer from a practical to an academic section or vice versa by way of a transition class (*classe passerelle*).

General and technology *lycées* also offer post-*baccalauréat* classes to students who have obtained a technology *baccalauréat* (usually series E, F or G) or a *Brevet de Technicien (BT)*. These students can study for a further two years for the *Brevet de*

Technicien Supérieur (BTS), encompassing some 90 areas of specialisation. Holders of the BTS are capable of entering a trade or occupation and assuming a responsible technical or administrative position. The BTS programme has developed rapidly since its introduction due to good employment prospects and the enthusiasm of parents, and it's often chosen in preference to attending a university.

Vocational Schools

In addition to general and technology *lycées* (see above), there are also vocational *lycées* (*lycées professionnels/LP*) where courses lead to vocational certificates. These include the *Brevet d'Études Professionel (BEP)* and the *Certificat d'Aptitude Professionelle (CAP)*. The BEP certificate covers the broad range of knowledge required in a particular trade, industrial, commercial, administrative or social sector, rather than a specific skill. The CAP is more specialised and is awarded for skill in a particular trade, e.g. carpentry, plumbing or dressmaking. In addition to school lessons, the BEP and CAP programmes include practical periods with companies providing students with an introduction to the workplace.

Students with a BEP or CAP can also take a technology or vocational *baccalauréat*, known as a *baccalauréat professionnel*, after a further two years' study. The majority of those who pass the vocational *baccalauréat* go straight into employment, although it also entitles them to enter higher education. A major feature of the vocational *baccalauréat* course is that students spend a quarter of their time training in industry. The vocational *baccalauréat* is chosen by an increasing number of students each year and has enjoyed huge success since its introduction. After passing the CAP, students may be permitted to enter the special second (*seconde spéciale*) where they attend three years of technological studies leading to the Technical Certificate (*Brevet de Technicien/BT*).

Almost every occupation in France has some form of recognised apprenticeship or certificate, including filing clerks, shop assistants and waiters, without which it's difficult to get a job in a particular field. See also **Apprenticeships** on page 160.

The Baccalauréat

The *baccalauréat* (commonly called the *bac*) is taken at a *lycée* at the age of 18 or 19 and is an automatic entrance qualification to a French university. Those who pass the *baccalauréat* are known as *bacheliers*. The *baccalauréat* is taken in two parts, the first of which consists of an examination in French language and literature (*baccalauréat de français*) taken during the *première* year. This must be passed before any other exams can be taken. The second part of the *Bac* is taken in the *terminale* year. Students who fail the *Bac* can retake it again the following year.

The general *baccalauréat* is a general diploma and doesn't prepare students directly for a trade or profession, but for higher education. It enables students to continue their studies at university, in preparatory classes for a *grande école*, in a higher technicians' section (STS), in a university institute of technology (*Instituts Universitaires de Technologie/IUT*) and in specialised schools. The technology *baccalauréat* is awarded for both general knowledge and training in modern technologies. It's the first stage of higher technical training, usually at a university institute of technology or higher technicians' section, and occasionally at a university or *grande école*.

The different types of *Bac* are rated according to their difficulty and importance. The type of *Bac* a student takes determines to a certain extent his future prospects and is usually decided by his career plan. For example those wishing to study medicine usually take *Bac* D, and *Bacs* C and D are the most common among those wishing to attend a *grande école* (see page 163). Among students planning to go to university, *Bacs* A and B are common. Students can always lower their expectations, but once started on a lower track (e.g. *Bac* A or B), it's difficult to change to a higher track, for example to a *Bac* C or D.

Students can choose to follow the vocational (*système d'orientation*) or selection (*système de sélection*) system of further education. Those who choose the vocational system must pass the *baccalauréat* in subjects such as law, science, medicine, dentistry, pharmacy, management and economic sciences, social sciences and fine arts. The selection system is designed for students who wish to attend superior institutions of higher education. These students must pass the *baccalauréat* and a competitive examination, or pass the *baccalauréat*, provide a school record and attend an interview with an examining board. The selection system applies to university institutes of technology (IUT), institutes of political studies (IEP), post-*baccalauréat* establishments preparing students for the *Brevet de Technicien Supérieur (BTS)* and for entry to a *grande école* preparatory school (see below).

The courses taken during a student's final two years at a *lycée* depend on the type of *baccalauréat* selected. There are seven sections (major subjects) in *première* (penultimate year) and eight in *terminale* (final year), and a total of around 30 types of *baccalauréat* from which to choose. The types of *baccalauréat* are divided into two main groups: the general *baccalauréat* and the technology *baccalauréat*. The French *baccalauréat* examination is marked out of 20, as are all French exams. An average of 10 is a pass, 12/13 is quite good (*mention assez bien*), 14/15 is good (*mention bien*) and 16 and over is very good/excellent (*mention très bien*). Marks of 16 or over are extremely rare, so in reality a mark of 12 to 14 can be considered as good or very good and anything above 14 as excellent.

All European universities and most American colleges recognise the French *baccalauréat* diploma as an entrance qualification, although foreign students must provide proof of their English language ability to study in Britain or the USA. An American university may grant credits to a *bachelier* allowing him to graduate in three years instead of the usual four. The international baccalaureate option (*Option Internationale du Baccalauréat/OIB*) and International Baccalaureate (IB) examinations are also offered by some French International *lycées* and *lycées* with international sections (see page 157).

Grandes Écoles Preparatory School

Grandes écoles preparatory schools (*Classes Préparatoires aux Grandes Écoles/CPGE* or *prépa* for short) are the first step for anyone with ambitions to attend a *grande école* (see page 163), France's elite higher education institutions. Admission to a *prépa* is based on a student's grades in his final *terminale* year at *lycée* and the subjects chosen. For example to attend a science CPGE a student must take a C or D science *baccalauréat*. If a student's grades aren't good enough, his *baccalauréat* results may be taken into account. Usually students require an average of 14 (*mention bien*) to be accepted.

Applications must be made by 1st May, i.e. before actually sitting the *baccalauréat*, with provisional selection based on school reports for the terminal (final) year of *lycée* and teachers' reports. Successful students spend two years (one in the case of veterinary students) in a CPGE, which is generally an integral part of a *lycée*, although it may be housed within a *grande école*. Entrance to a *prépa* constitutes a first selection procedure prior to the actual competitive examination (*concours*) for the *grande école*, taken at the end of the two-year period. This exam has a failure rate of around 90 per cent!

Students who fail the entrance examination may be permitted to remain at a preparatory school for another year and retake the exam if their grades are high enough. If they fail again they must change track, which for most students means going to a university. However, even partial success in one of the CPGE examinations can bring exemption from all or part of the *Diplôme d'Etudes Universitaires Générales (DEUG)*, the examination taken at the end of the second year at university (see page 160).

PRIVATE SCHOOLS

There's a wide range of private schools (*écoles privées*) in France including parochial (mostly catholic) schools, bilingual schools, international schools and a variety of foreign schools, including American and British schools. Together they educate around 15 per cent of French children. Most private schools in France are co-educational, non-denominational day schools (Catholic private schools usually admit non-Catholics). Most private schools operate a five-day Monday to Friday timetable, unlike French state schools where children usually have Wednesdays free and may attend school on Saturday mornings. There are few boarding schools in France, although some schools provide weekly (Monday to Friday) boarding or board children with 'host' families.

There are two main types of private schools in France, those that have a contract with the French government (*sous contrat d'association*) and those that don't (*hors contrat* or *école libre*). A private school that has a contract with the government must follow the same educational programme as state schools, for which it receives government subsidies and is therefore less expensive than a *hors contrat* school. A private school without a contract with the government is free to set its own curriculum, although it receives no state subsidies and is consequently more expensive. In 1983 the socialist government threatened to end the payment of teachers' salaries in private religious schools (*confessionnel* or parochial/Catholic schools). Parents were incensed and organised mass demonstrations, with the result that the proposal was quickly dropped and the minister forced to resign (the Ministry of Education portfolio is generally regarded as a poisoned chalice in France). People power is important in French education and woe betide any politician who forgets it!

Private schools in France teach a variety of syllabi, including the British GCSE and A level examinations, American High School Diploma and college entrance examinations (e.g. ACT, SAT, achievement tests and AP exams) and the International Baccalaureate (IB). However, many schools offer bilingual children the French *baccalauréat* only. Among private schools in France are a number that follow special or unorthodox methods of teaching such as Montessori nursery schools and Rudolf Steiner schools. There are also private schools in some areas for children with special language requirements.

Some schools are classified as bilingual (*sections bilingues* or *classes bilingues*) or international (e.g. *lycée international* or *section internationale*) and certain bilingual schools, such as the *École Active Bilingue* in Paris, have American, British and French sections. Note, however, that the curriculum in most bilingual schools is tailored to French children, rather than foreign children whose mother tongue isn't French. Most private schools teaching in French provide intensive French tuition for non-French speakers. The few American and English schools in France are mostly located in the Paris area and on the French Riviera. Most English-language private schools offer a comprehensive English-as-a-Second-Language (ESL) programme and number students from many countries.

There are international schools at Bordeaux, Cannes, Grenoble, Lyon, Nice, St. Etienne, Strasbourg, Toulouse and many in the Paris area. The *Lycée International* at Saint-Germain-en-Laye (near Paris) has nine national sections (American, British, Danish, Dutch, German, Italian, Portuguese, Spanish and Swedish). Each section aims to teach children about the language, literature and history of the particular language/country selected. All other lessons are taught in French. The *École International de Paris* is bilingual and teaches in both French and English. Where applicable, students who don't speak French are usually given three to six months intensive French lessons. Places in bilingual and international schools are in strong demand and there are usually stiff entrance requirements. Private sixth form colleges are provided for students aged 16 or older who need additional help with their *baccalauréat* studies or who wish to study subjects unavailable at their local *lycée*.

Some private schools, such as some international *lycées*, offer the international baccalaureate option (*Option Internationale du Baccalauréat/OIB*) in addition to the French *baccalauréat* examination. The OIB is intended for bilingual French students or foreign students with fluent French who are planning to enter a French university. The OIB is a French exam and shouldn't be confused with the International Baccalaureate (IB) examination, which is classed as a foreign diploma in France. The IB, which originated in Switzerland and has its headquarters in Geneva, is an internationally recognised university entrance qualification. It's taught in over 500 schools in around 65 countries and is accepted as an entrance qualification by the world's top universities. As an international examination it's second to none. Many North American universities grant students with an IB diploma up to one year's credit.

Private school fees vary considerably depending on, among other things, the quality, reputation and location of a school. Not surprisingly, schools located in the Paris area are the most expensive. Fees at a Catholic private school that's *sous contrat* (where teachers' salaries are paid by the state), may be as low as 2,000F a year, whereas fees at an independent (*hors contrat*) international senior day school can be as high as 75,000F or 100,000F a year. Fees aren't all-inclusive and additional obligatory charges are made, such as registration fees, in addition to optional extras. Lunches may be included in school fees or charged separately, e.g. 500F to 1,000F a month.

Private schools have smaller classes and a more relaxed, less rigid regime and curriculum than French state schools. They provide a more varied and international approach to sport, culture and art, and a wider choice of academic subjects. Many also provide English-language summer school programmes, combining academic lessons with sports, arts and crafts and other 'extra-curricular' activities. Their aim is the development of the child as an individual and the encouragement of his unique talents, which is made possible by the small classes that allow teachers to provide students with individually tailored lessons and tuition. The results are self-evident and many private secondary schools have a near 100 per cent university placement rate. Make applications to private schools as far in advance as possible. You're usually requested to send previous school reports, exam results and records. Before enrolling your child in a private school, ensure that you understand the withdrawal conditions in the school contract.

The *Office de Documentation et d'Information de l'Enseignement Privé*, 45, avenue Georges Bernanos, 75005 Paris (☎ 01.43.29.90.70) provides information about private schools from nursery to university level. UNAPEL, 277, rue St. Jacques, 75005 Paris (☎ 01.52.73.73.90) provides information about parochial schools. The *Centre National de Documentation sur l'Enseignement Privé*, 20, rue Fabert, 75007 Paris (☎ 01.47.05.32.68) publishes a guide listing all French private schools. A free list of American and British schools teaching entirely in English, international sections in French *lycées*, and bilingual and international schools can be obtained from the British Council, 9-11, rue de Constantine, 75007 Paris (☎ 01.49.55.73.00).

Choosing a Private School

The following checklist is designed to help you choose an appropriate private school in France.

● Does the school have a good reputation? How long has it been established?

● Does the school have a good academic record? For example, what percentage of students obtain good examination passes and go on to top universities? All the best schools provide exam pass-rate statistics.

● What does the curriculum include? What examinations are set? Are examinations recognised both in France and internationally? Do they fit in with your future education plans? Ask to see a typical student timetable to check the ratio of academic to non-academic subjects. Check the number of free study periods and whether they are supervised.

● How large are the classes and what is the student/teacher ratio? Does the class size tally with the number of desks in the classrooms?

● What are the classrooms like? For example their size, space, cleanliness, lighting, furniture and furnishings. Are there signs of creative teaching, e.g. wall charts, maps, posters and students' work on display?

● What are the qualification requirements for teachers? What nationalities are the majority of teachers? Ask for a list of the teaching staff and their qualifications.

● What is the teacher turnover? A high teacher turnover is a particularly bad sign and usually suggests badly paid teachers with poor working conditions.

● What extras must you pay? For example, lunches, art supplies, sports equipment, outings, clothing, health and accident insurance, textbooks and stationery. Some schools charge parents for absolutely everything.

● Which countries do most students come from?

● Is religion an important consideration in your choice of school?

- Are intensive English or French lessons provided for children who don't meet the required standard?

- What standard and type of accommodation is provided? What is the quality and variety of food provided? What is the dining room like? Does the school have a dietician?

- What languages does the school teach as obligatory or optional subjects? Does the school have a language laboratory?

- What is the student turnover?

- What are the school terms and holiday periods? Private school holidays are usually longer than state schools (e.g. four weeks at Easter and Christmas and ten weeks in the summer) and they often don't coincide with state school holiday periods.

- If you're considering a day school, what are the school hours? Is transport provided to and from school?

- What are the withdrawal conditions, should you need or wish to remove your child? A term's notice is usual.

- What sports instruction and facilities are provided? Where are the sports facilities located?

- What are the facilities for art and science subjects, for example, arts and crafts, music, computer studies, biology, science, hobbies, drama, cookery and photography? Ask to see the classrooms, facilities, equipment and some students' projects.

- What sort of outings and school holidays are organised?

- What medical facilities does the school provide, e.g. infirmary, resident doctor or nurse? Is medical and accident insurance included in the fees?

- What sorts of punishments are applied and for what offences?

- What reports are provided for parents and how often?

- Last but not least – unless someone else is paying – what are the fees?

Before making a final choice, it's important to visit the schools on your shortlist during term time and talk to teachers and students (if possible, also speak to former students and their parents). Where possible, check out the answers to the above questions in person and don't rely on a school's prospectus or director to provide the information. If you're unhappy with the answers, look elsewhere. If necessary take someone with you who speaks fluent French.

Finally, having made your choice, keep a check on your child's progress and listen to his complaints. Compare notes with other parents. If something doesn't seem right, try to establish whether the complaint is founded or not, and if it is, take action to have the problem resolved. Never forget that you're paying a lot of money for your child's education and you should ensure that you receive good value. See also **State or Private School?** on page 141.

APPRENTICESHIPS

Many young people in France look forward to starting work and learning a trade, and the vast majority who don't go on to higher education enter an apprenticeship or another form of vocational training. A French apprenticeship (*apprentissage*) aims to give young people who have completed compulsory schooling a general, theoretical and practical training, leading to a certificate of vocational or technological education at secondary or a higher level. The French apprenticeship scheme is recognised as one of the best in the world.

An apprenticeship is a combination of on-the-job training and further education, where one or two days a week are spent at an apprentice training centre (CFA), covering a minimum of 400 hours a year. An apprenticeship lasts from one to three years, depending on the type of profession and the qualification sought. It can be in almost any vocation from a carpenter to an electrician, a nurse to a waitress. School careers officers are available to advise parents and students on a choice of career. Employers pay a small salary that increases with age and experience, and also pay for apprenticeship schooling and possibly the cost of travel to and from school.

Other types of vocational training include sandwich courses comprising a training course and work contracts (which also include training). Introductory courses to working life (SIVP) are provided to allow young people between 16 and 26 without work experience to work in a company and develop an aptitude for work. An SIVP course lasts from three to six months. Qualification contracts are intended to allow young people under 26 to obtain a vocational qualification with a company. They last from six months to two years and a minimum of 25 per cent of the contract period is spent on general, technological and vocational training leading to a recognised vocational qualification. Adaptation contracts provide for training during working hours and allow young people aged between 16 and 26 to adapt their qualifications to their position in a company. The contract can be for a fixed period of at least six months or an indefinite duration. Training lasts for a total of 200 hours and includes practical on-the-job training and general, vocational and technological education off the job. See also **Vocational School** on page 154.

HIGHER EDUCATION

France has numerous higher education (*enseignement supérieur*) institutions including over 70 traditional universities (13 in Paris) and around 250 *grandes écoles* and *écoles supérieures* colleges (see page 163). Anyone who passes the French *baccalauréat* examination is guaranteed entry to a university, which are attended by 30 per cent of secondary students (around one million). French universities include Aix-Marseille, Amiens, Angers, Avignon, Besançon, Brest, Caen, Chambéry, Dijon, Clermont-Ferrand, Grenoble, Le Havre, Lille, Limoges, Lyon, Le Mans, Metz, Montpellier, Mulhouse, Nancy, Nantes, Nice, Orléans, Paris, Pau, Perpignan, Poitiers, Reims, Rennes, Rouen, Saint-Etienne, Strasbourg, Toulon et Var, Toulouse, Tours and Valenciennes. Although still famous (particularly among foreigners), the 13th century (est. 1253) Paris Sorbonne is little more than a building housing part of the sprawling *Université de Paris*, and it has lost much of its eminence within France to the *grandes écoles* (in fact it's so overcrowded that conditions are said to be 'of third world standards').

Schools of medicine, dentistry and pharmacy are attached to certain universities and entry is restricted to the top 25 per cent of students with a *baccalauréat C*. Other restricted entry schools include economics and law. However, one of the most difficult schools to gain acceptance to is a veterinary school, a popular and lucrative profession in France (France has over ten million dogs!). There are just four veterinary schools in France, all with a highly competitive entrance examination.

French universities are the weakest part of the French education system and are obliged to accept more students each year (since 1987 the annual intake has grown by around 100,000 a year). There's no selection process and universities must accept anyone who passes his *baccalauréat*. They have failed to keep pace with the huge student population and overcrowding, poor facilities and under-funding have resulted in a general lowering of standards. Lecture halls are packed and students have no tutorial system and little supervision. Most courses aren't tailored to specific careers and not surprisingly a huge number of students fail to obtain a degree. However, despite the dropout rate, most people are opposed to limiting admissions, which they feel would compromise the principle of equality. An added problem is the length of time it takes to obtain a degree in France, where the average leaving age is 29.

Foreign students number around 120,000 or some 12.5 per cent of the intake. Most are from Africa (mainly the Maghreb), although there's a large number from EU countries, South America and China. There are quotas for foreign students at certain universities and for particular courses. For example foreign students are limited to 5 per cent of the number of French students in medical and dental studies at universities in and around Paris. Foreign students are admitted to French universities on the basis of equivalent qualifications to the French *baccalauréat*. French universities accept British A-levels as an entrance qualification, but an American high school diploma isn't usually accepted. American students must usually have spent a year at college or have a BA, BBA or BSc degree. All foreign students require a thorough knowledge of French, which is usually examined unless a *baccalauréat* certificate is provided. French language preparatory courses are provided. There's a special university entrance examination for mature students without a *baccalauréat*, although mature students are rare in France, where the idea of going back to school after working isn't popular.

During their first two years at university (termed stage I), students study a core curriculum, after which they take the Diploma in General University Studies (*Diplôme d'Études Universitaires Générales* or DEUG). The DEUG has a high failure rate, with almost half of undergraduates failing to complete their degrees. Those who fail may be given a third year to pass, but no longer. Those who pass the DEUG can take their *licence* in arts and science (equivalent to a BA or BSc) after a further year, or a further two years in the case of economics and law. The *licence* is classified as the first year of stage II studies. A *Diplôme Universitaire de Technologie (DUT)* is awarded on completion of a course of study at a university institute of technology. A two-year DEUG or three-year *licence* has little value in the French job market, where competition for top jobs is fierce. Unemployment among graduates is high and most universities have little prestige. Universities in France don't offer their own degrees and most bachelor degrees, with the exception of law and medicine, carry little weight with employers.

A *maîtrise*, roughly equivalent to an MA, is awarded after completion of the second year of stage II studies, one year after gaining a *licence*. In certain subjects, e.g. science and technology, business studies and computer science, a *licence* isn't awarded, and after obtaining a DEUG students study for a further two years for a *maîtrise*. Students can study for a further three or four years after receiving their *maîtrise* for a doctorate (*doctorat*) or stage III degree. A relatively new degree, called a *magistère*, is awarded in certain subjects for a further three years' study after obtaining a DEUG or DUT. The *magistère* course combines the acquisition of basic knowledge, an introduction to research and its practical application within a professional framework.

Students must complete an initial registration form (*dossier de demande de première admission en premier cycle*) and lodge their application by 1st February for entry the following October (the academic year runs from October to June). Application forms are available from the cultural sections of French embassies. Applicants must present a residence permit valid for at least one year or that of their parents if the latter are in possession of a three-year residence permit. Applicants must name three universities of their choice, at least two of which must be in the provinces, i.e. outside Paris.

There's no central clearing system and applicants must apply to each university separately. Students don't pay tuition fees and costs for foreign students are minimal. Between 1,000F and 2,000F, depending on the options chosen, is sufficient to cover registration fees, including obligatory fees for health insurance and social security. Students over 26 are required to take out health insurance in their country of origin or insurance under the French social security system on arrival in France. Government grants (*bourses*) are awarded to some 20 per cent of students. The maximum grant is around 15,000F a year, although most are for just a few thousand francs. Scholarships are also provided by international organisations and foreign governments. French parents are obliged by law to support their children at university until they are aged 20, after which age they're officially financially self-reliant. Most students support themselves during their studies by working part-time during terms and over holiday periods.

Foreign students must make their own arrangements for accommodation. Students are eligible for a room in a university hall of residence, although places are limited and accommodation is generally of poor quality. Students should expect to pay around 1,000F per month for a room in a hall of residence and between 1,500F and 2,000F per month for a private room (or more in Paris). Foreign students need around 4,000F and 6,000F per month to live in Paris (less in the provinces). Note that students require numerous black and white passport-size photographs (usually on a white background) and photocopies and translations of assorted documents.

Many French students attend the nearest university to their home and treat university as an extension of school, particularly in Paris and other large cities where accommodation is expensive. Most students face the choice of either living with their parents or subsisting in a depressing university residence or cheap room. As with most French schools, universities offer few extracurricular sports and social activities (the most popular extracurricular activity is the pursuit of love!). There are no inexpensive student university bars in France and drinking in public bars is expensive (and female students can be exposed to sexual harassment).

In addition to French higher education establishments, there are also a number of US colleges and universities in France including the American University in Paris (AUP). All classes at the AUP are taught in English and its 1,000 strong student body comes from over 70 countries. It offers both BA and BSc degrees and students can study for a BA in seven fields including international business, art, history and

European culture. Fees for the full academic year are around 75,000F a year, excluding health insurance, accommodation and deposits. A popular American college in Paris is the Parsons School of Design (a division of New York's New School for Social Research), where students take a four-year Bachelor of Fine Arts (BFA) degree. The Paris American Academy also has a good reputation and specialises in fine arts, fashion, languages and interior design. There are many other American colleges in Paris offering courses in a range of subjects and degrees (from a BA to an MBA).

For information about any aspect of student life in France, contact the *Service National d'Accueil aux Étudiants Étrangers* (SNAEE), 69, Quai d'Orsay, 75007 Paris. The *Centre Régional des Oeuvres Universitaires et Scolaires* (CROUS), 39, av. Georges Bernanos, 75231 Paris Cedex 05 (☎ 01.40.51.36.00) is responsible for foreign students in France and provides information about courses, grants and accommodation. CROUS subsidies university accommodation and restaurants, but not all are subsidised and therefore if finance is a factor you should contact CROUS before choosing a university. In Paris, students can contact the *Centre National des Oeuvres Universitaires* (CNOUS), 69, quai d'Orsay, 75007 Paris (☎ 01.40.79.91.00). For general information about French universities, contact the *Office National des Universités et Écoles Françaises*, 96, boulevard Raspail, 75272 Paris Cedex 06 (☎ 01.42.22.26.95). The cultural sections of French embassies also provide information about higher education in France. A complete list of all state and private universities in France, entitled *Le Guide des Études Supérieures*, is published annually by *L'Étudiant* magazine.

Grandes Écoles

Somewhat surprisingly in a country boasting of its commitment to equality (*égalité*), France has the most elitist higher education system in the world. *Grandes écoles* (and *écoles supérieures*) are university colleges specialising in professional training, where entrance is by competitive examination (*concours*). Before being selected for a *grande école*, students spend two years at a *grande école* preparatory school (*Classes Préparatoires aux Grandes Écoles/CPGE*, see page 155). *Grandes écoles* were founded under Napoleon to provide the engineers and administrators of the Republic, and today number around 250 colleges enrolling some 70,000 students. They are dedicated to training high-level specialists, particularly in engineering, applied science, administration and management studies. *Grandes écoles* are outside the university system and controlled by the ministry to which their speciality is linked.

Although they are required to work hard, with little time for play, students at *grandes écoles* enjoy a pampered and privileged existence. Compared with the impoverished and over-crowded universities, *grandes écoles* have an embarrassment of riches and are lavishly funded and equipped. The state spends around 250,000F educating a student at a *grande école*, compared with just 75,000F at a university. They are castigated for elitism, propagating the class system, and comprising an exclusive (largely male) club for the rich and privileged. Only 1 per cent of *grande école* students come from a working class background compared with around 15 per cent in universities, and only 10 per cent are women. Virtually no foreigners are admitted. Critics of *grandes écoles* also complain that they undermine France's universities, which as a result are the weakest part of the country's educational system.

The most celebrated schools include the *École Polytechnique* (usually known simply as *l'X* from its badge of crossed cannons) and *Ponts et Chaussées* (both engineering), *École des Hautes Etudes Commerciales/HEC* (business), *École Normale Supérieure/ENS* (research and teaching) and *École Nationale d'Agronomie* (agriculture). The cream of *grandes écoles* and the most recent is the *École Nationale d'Administration/ENA*, the post-graduate nursery of France's civil service mandarins and political elite (graduates are called *énarques*). At each *grande école* students take the same subjects, with no courses offered outside a school's speciality.

A magnificent career is virtually guaranteed to graduates of *grandes écoles*, who fill the top positions in government, the civil service and most industries in France. Many companies appoint only *grande école* graduates to management positions and they are usually preferred to business school graduates with an MBA. It's common practice for newspaper articles to state the *grande école* attended by a prominent academic, executive or politician, and many graduates include it on their business cards. Attending a *grande école* is of lifelong benefit and graduates are regarded with awe and reverence.

FURTHER EDUCATION

Further education generally embraces everything except first degree courses taken at universities, *grandes écoles* and other institutions of higher education, although the distinction between further and higher education (see page 164) is often blurred. Each year many thousands of students attend further education courses at universities alone, often of short duration and job-related, although courses may be full or part-time and include summer terms. France has many private colleges and other university level institutions, some affiliated to foreign (usually American) universities. These include business and commercial colleges, hotel and restaurant schools, language schools and finishing schools.

Many educational institutions offer American MBA degree courses, including the European University in Paris and Toulouse. The most popular MBA subjects include banking, business administration, communications, economics, European languages, information systems, management, marketing, public relations, and social and political studies. Tuition costs are high and study periods strictly organised. Although most courses are taught in English, some schools require students to be fluent in both English and French, e.g. the European Institute for Business Administration (INSEAD) at Fontainebleau, one of Europe's most prestigious business schools.

Many further education courses are of the open learning variety, where students study mostly at home. These include literally hundreds of academic, professional and vocational correspondence courses offered by private colleges. Many universities offer correspondence courses to students wishing to study for a degree, but are unable to attend a university due to their circumstances, e.g. health, distance, job or family commitments. These courses are particularly targeted at mature students. Over 30,000 students take part in university correspondence courses taught through universities with distance learning centres, and through the *centre national d'enseignement à distance* that prepares students for competitive exams and provides specific training. Another type of course offered by universities and schools allows those in employment to enrol in evening courses and take advantage of specially planned timetables. The *Conservatoire National des Arts et Métiers (CNAM)* and its regional centres admits students without any formal qualifications in a wide range of courses, many leading to a degree.

General information about local adult education and training is available in most towns and cities from town halls and libraries, and the French Ministry of Education provides a free information service through departmental *Centre d'Information et d'Orientation (CIO)* offices. See also **Day & Evening Classes** on page 343.

LANGUAGE SCHOOLS

If you don't speak French fluently, you may wish to enrol in a language course. If you want to make the most of the French way of life and your time in France, it's absolutely essential to learn French as soon as possible. For people living in France permanently, learning French isn't an option, but a necessity. Although it isn't easy, even the most non-linguistic person can acquire a working knowledge of French. All that's required is a little hard work, some help and perseverance, particularly if you have only English-speaking colleagues and friends. **Note that your business and social enjoyment and success in France will be directly related to the degree to which you master French.**

Most people can teach themselves a great deal through the use of books, tapes, videos and even computer-based courses. However, even the best students require some help. Teaching French is big business in France, with classes offered by language schools, French and foreign colleges and universities, private and international schools, foreign and international organisations (such as the British Institute in Paris), local associations and clubs, and private teachers. Tuition ranges from language courses for complete beginners, through specialised business or cultural courses to university-level courses leading to recognised diplomas. Most French universities provide language courses and many organisations offer holiday courses year-round, particularly for children and young adults (it's best to stay with a local French family). If you already speak French but need conversational practice, you may prefer to enrol in an art or craft course at a local institute or club (see **Day & Evening Classes** on page 343). You can also learn French via a telephone language course, which is particularly practical for busy executives and those who don't live near a language school.

There are many language schools (*écoles de langues*) in French cities and large towns. Most schools run various classes depending on your language ability, how many hours you wish to study a week, how much money you want to spend and how quickly you wish to learn. For those for whom money is no object (hopefully your employer!), there are total immersion courses where you study for up to nine hours a day, five days a week. The cost for a one-week (45 hours) total immersion course is usually between 15,000F and 20,000F depending on the school. Rates vary so shop around. Language classes generally fall into the following categories:

extensive	4 to 10	hours per week
intensive	15 to 20	"
total immersion	20 to 40+	"

Don't expect to become fluent in a short time unless you have a particular flair for languages or already have a good command of French. Unless you desperately need to learn French quickly, it's better to arrange your lessons over a long period. However, don't commit yourself to a long course of study, particularly an expensive one, before ensuring that it's the right course. Most schools offer free tests to help you find your appropriate level and a free introductory lesson.

You may prefer to have private lessons, which are a quicker, although more expensive way of learning a language. The main advantage of private lessons is that you learn at your own speed and aren't held back by slow learners or left floundering in the wake of the class genius. You can advertise for a teacher in your local newspapers, on shopping centre/supermarket bulletin boards, university notice boards, and through your or your spouse's employer. Don't forget to ask your friends, neighbours and colleagues if they can recommend a private teacher. Private lessons by the hour cost from around 350F at a school or 100F to 200F with a private tutor. In some areas a *Centre Culturel* provides free French lessons to foreigners. If you're officially registered as unemployed and have a residence permit (*carte séjour*), you can obtain free French lessons (*prefectionnement de la langue Française*), although complete beginners don't qualify (contact your local ANPE office for information).

One of the most famous French language teaching organisations is the *Alliance Française*, 101, boulevard Raspail, 75270 Paris Cedex 06 (☎ 01.45.44.38.28), a state-approved, non-profit organisation with centres in over 100 countries and throughout France. *Alliance Française* run general, special and intensive courses, and can also arrange a homestay in France with a host family. Another non-profit organisation is *Centre d'Échanges Internationaux* (104, rue de Vaugirard, 75006 Paris, ☎ 01.45.49.26.25), offering intensive French language courses for juniors (13 to 18 years) and adults throughout France. Courses include accommodation in their own international centres, with a French family, or a hotel, bed and breakfast, or self-catering studio. Junior courses can be combined with tuition in a variety of sports and other activities including horse riding, tennis, windsurfing, canoe-kayak, diving and dancing.

Parents with young children who are planning to move to France may be interested in *En Famille International*, an exchange organisation founded in the late '70s by Frenchman Jacques Pinault. It specialises in six-month exchange visits for children aged 9 to 13 between European countries and France. Children stay with a French family, attend a French school and return speaking fluent French. One of the most important aspects of the scheme is that children must be enthusiastic about the exchange. It can take up to a year to match two families, so you should make enquiries as early as possible. For further information contact Jacques and Katherine Pinault, 'Savarias', Salignac, 33240 St André de Cubzac (☎ 05.57.43.52.48).

A comprehensive list of schools, institutions and organisations providing French language courses throughout France is contained in a booklet, *Cours de français langue étrangère et stages pédagogie du français langue étrangère en France*. It includes information about the type of course, organisation, dates, costs and other practical information, and is available from French consulates or from the ADPF, 9, rue Anatole de la Forge, 75017 Paris (☎ 01.44.09.27.40). A useful book for anyone wishing to visit France to study the French language and culture is *Study Holidays* (Central Bureau for Educational Visits & Exchanges, c/o British Council, 10 Spring Gardens, London SW1A 2BN, UK, ☎ 0171-389 4383) containing practical information on accommodation, travel, and sources of bursaries, grants and scholarships. For further information about the French language, see **Language** on pages 42 and 144.

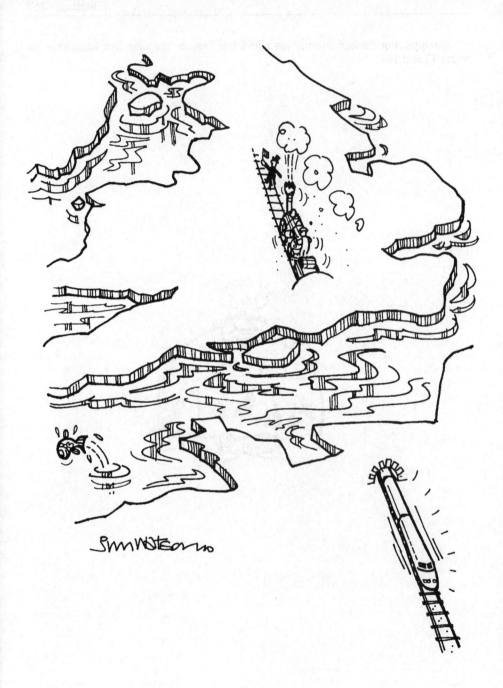

10.

PUBLIC TRANSPORT

Public transport (*transport public*) services in France vary considerably depending on where you live. Public transport is generally excellent in French cities, most of which have efficient local bus and rail services, many supplemented by *métro* (underground railway) and tram networks. French railways (SNCF) provide an excellent and fast rail service, particularly between cities served by the TGV, one of the world's fastest trains. It's a pleasure to travel in France by train, particularly if you have plenty of time and can take the slow, local trains that criss-cross the country. With the opening of the Channel Tunnel in 1994, rail travellers have been able to travel directly between France and Britain without changing trains. SNCF offer a range of special tickets and passes for commuters and travellers who book in advance. France is also served by excellent international and domestic airline services and extensive international ferry services. On the negative side, bus and rail services are poor or non-existent in rural areas and it's generally essential to have your own transport if you live in the country.

Paris has one of the most efficient, best integrated and cheapest public transport systems of any major city in the world. In addition to its world-famous *métro*, public transport services include the RER express *métro*, an extensive suburban rail network and comprehensive bus services. The system is totally integrated and the same ticket can be used on all four services. Thanks to government subsidies, it's also inexpensive, although this doesn't stop the French from complaining about the cost (they have obviously never heard of British railways!). A range of commuter and visitor tickets are available.

Students visiting or living in France should obtain an International Student Identity Card (ISIC) and non-students an International Youth Card (IYC), both of which offer students and youths a range of travel discounts. They are available from most student travel offices and student organisations. The French Government Tourist Office publishes a booklet, *France Youth Travel*, for those aged under 26.

TRAINS

The French railway network was inaugurated in 1832 and today extends to every corner of France. French railways are operated by the state-owned SNCF (*Société Nationale des Chemins de fer Français*) company, formed in 1938 when the five major private railways were nationalised. Despite the closure of 10,000km (6,213mi) of uneconomic lines during the '50s and '60s and another 7,000km (4,349mi) during the early '70s, the SNCF network remains the largest in Western Europe with over 34,000km (21,100mi) of track. SNCF operates over 7,000 locomotives, some 15,000 passenger carriages (*voitures*) and serves around 5,000 stations. It carries over 800 million passengers a year to over 6,000 destinations and has an excellent reputation for safety and punctuality.

Many things in France emanate from or are routed via Paris and this is also true of the rail system. Paris and the Ile-de-France region provide SNCF with around two-thirds of its passengers, some 550 million passengers a year, travelling on 5,000 trains a day. There aren't many cross-country train routes in France and it's often necessary to travel via Paris to reach a destination. There are direct trains from French cities to many major European cities including Amsterdam, Barcelona, Basle, Berlin, Brussels, Cologne, Florence, Frankfurt, Geneva, Hamburg, London, Madrid, Milan, Munich, Rome, Rotterdam, Venice, Vienna and Zurich. Some international services run only at night and daytime journeys may involve a change of train.

SNCF operates one of the most efficient rail systems in Europe and both employees and the French public take great pride in their trains. French railways are operated as a public service and charge reasonable fares and offer a wide range of discounts and special fares (see page 176), all of which help increase passenger numbers, thus reducing road congestion and environmental damage. French high-speed trains compete successfully with road and air travel over long distances, both in cost and speed. However, despite huge government subsidies, SNCF still manages to run up an annual deficit. To reduce the debt the government has sold off 32,000km (19,884mi) of track to *Réseau Ferre de France* (RFF), and invested hugely in advertising to encourage more passengers with the slogan 'It's up to us to make you prefer the train' (*À nous de vous faire préférer le train*).

The SNCF operates TGV (*Train à Grande Vitesse*) trains on its main lines, which are among the world's fastest trains, capable of reaching speeds of over 550kph (around 350mph). TGV services operate to over 50 French cities, carrying more than 40,000 passengers a day. The TGV ('a legend in its own timetable') has revolutionised domestic travel in France and air travel on TGV routes has fallen significantly, e.g. Paris-Lyon, on which route there are around some 35 trains a day in each direction with over 75 per cent seat occupancy carrying more than 20,000 passengers a day. The TGV has sparked a new golden age of train travel throughout Europe and in the new millennium high-speed trains are set to largely replace air travel in continental Europe.

To run at maximum operating speed a TGV must run on special lines, although TGVs presently run to many destinations on a mixture of dedicated TGV lines and mixed traffic lines. The TGV high-speed rail network totals some 5,500km (3,400mi) on three lines, TGV Meditérranée (southeast), TGV Atlantique and TGV Nord Europe. A recent line circumventing Paris means that some services (e.g. Lyon-Nantes and Bordeaux-Lille) are now direct and don't involve changing trains in Paris. Double-deck TGVs (*Duplex*) were introduced in 1995 with around 45 per cent more capacity than standard trains and no reduction in speed. The TGV also runs operates between Paris and Switzerland (Berne, Geneva, Lausanne and Neuchâtel). Paris to Geneva takes around 3½ hours. The TGV is almost totally silent and smooth, even when running at its maximum operational speed of around 300kph (186mph). Trains are often long with 20 carriages and four engines (each train of ten carriages usually has two engines, one pulling and one pushing). The spike on the front of engines is part of a coupling device to secure two engines together.

Trains are air-conditioned and include 1st and 2nd class carriages, a bar/relaxation area, a stationery and tobacco shop, and sometimes a nursery. Train compartments are colour-coded: red for 1st class carriages, blue-green for 2nd class and yellow for the bar. In 2nd class carriages, seats are arranged in airline fashion and are comfortable with reasonable space, pull down trays and foot rests. First class seats are naturally more comfortable and roomy, although much more expensive. Luggage space is provided above seats and at the end of carriages. All seats must be reserved and no standing passengers are permitted.

The basic fare on the TGV is the same as on ordinary trains, except that there's a reservation fee that varies depending on the day and time of travel. Bookings can be made up to two months in advance. Depending on the route and the time of travel, you may need to book weeks, days or just minutes before your departure. Some non-TGV international trains such as *Trans-Europ-Express (TEE)* and *Trans-Europ-Nuit* (TEN) are 1st class only. Reservations are necessary and a supplement is payable in addition to a 1st class fare. Reservations are recommended on long-distance trains, particularly during peak periods, e.g. during school and public holidays.

Standard non-TGV trains have either electric (*Corail*) or gas turbine (*Turbotrain*) locomotives, which although not in the TGV league, are fast and comfortable. Some branch lines operate *express* and *rapide* diesel trains. The slowest trains are the suburban *omnibus* services (some with double-decker coaches) stopping at every station. A *direct* train is a through train, usually classified as an *express*, stopping only at main stations and second in speed to the TGV. A *rapide* is faster than an *omnibus* but slower than an *express*. SNCF also operates an extensive *Motorail* service (see page 178).

Channel Tunnel: The Channel Tunnel is the world's most expensive hole in the ground, joining France with Britain by rail from Sangatte in France to Folkestone in England. Since its opening in 1994, Eurostar trains have operated from Paris to London taking around three hours (it would be quicker, but French TGV trains must slow to a 'snail's' pace once they reach British soil). Since the start of Eurostar services, over 25 per cent of business travellers between Paris and London have switched from air to rail. Airlines have tried to play down the affect that Eurostar has had on their business, although for many travellers Eurostar is cheaper overall when the cost of getting to and from airports is taken into account. In 1998 passenger use rose by 13 per cent and the Eurostar is now making a profit. See also **Eurotunnel** on page 185.

Little Trains: Despite their love of high-speed trains, the French still have a soft spot for their little trains (*petits trains*). These include the *petit train jaune* running from Perpignan to the high Cerdagne plateau in the western Pyrénées, the *petit train de L'Artouste* in the Ardèche, and *le train de la Mer de Glace* which wends its way from Chamonix to Montenvers in the Alps. The *Pinecone Express* or *Chemin de fer de Provence* (operated by Provence Railways) is a spectacular narrow-gauge mountain railway running between Digne les Bains and Nice. *Le Train Jaune* operating between Tour de Carol and Villefranche in the Pyrénées includes the highest SNCF station (1,592m/5,223ft) at Bolquere Eyne. A rack railway hoists a train to the peak of La Rhune in the Basque country. The *Metrazur* train is the key to the Côte d'Azur and runs through the main resorts and into Italy. All Corsica's trains run on narrow-gauge track and are a delight for train fans. A guide to little tourist trains, *Guide des Petits Trains Touristiques*, is published every two years and is available from Thomas Cook Publications in Britain.

The SNCF head office is at 127, avenue des Champs-Elysées, 75008 Paris (☎ 01.47.23.54.02) and it also has offices in many countries including Britain (Rail Europe Ltd., 177 Piccadilly, London W1V 0BA, UK, ☎ 0171-647 4900 or 0990-848 848). SNCF publishes a free quarterly magazine in some countries, e.g. *Top Rail* in Britain plus a wealth of free brochures and booklets detailing its services including *Le Guide du Voyageur*, available from French stations. It also organises hotel accommodation, bus and coach services, boat cruises and package holidays.

General Information

- All TGV and most other fast trains have a bar-buffet and/or a restaurant car (*wagon-restaurant*) with waiter service. All rail catering is expensive and with the exception of a restaurant car, it's of poor quality by French standards (it's better to provide your own 'picnic'). Expect to pay at least 150F for a meal in a restaurant car. On TGV and Corail trains, 1st class passengers can order a tray meal at their seat, which should be booked when making your reservation. Some Corail services provide a Grill-Express and/or self-service restaurant and inter-city trains have a mobile drinks and snacks service (*minibar*) at your seat.

- Most railway stations have a restaurant located in or near them and Paris' main stations have a choice of restaurants, brasseries and snack bars, most serving good food at a reasonable price. Some, such as the Gare de Lyon restaurant in Paris, are famous for their cuisine. Station restaurants in small towns are often well-patronised by locals, which is always a good sign. Take care when buying snacks and drinks at cafés and bars in stations, as they can be expensive, e.g. over 25F for a large *café crème*, and poor quality, e.g. stale rolls.

- There are toilets on inter city trains. If you accidentally drop something down one, be careful how you try to retrieve it. A man who dropped his wallet down a TGV toilet got his hand trapped when he tried to recover it and had to be rescued by firemen after sounding the alarm!

- Main railway stations provide wash, shower and brush-up facilities, including hair dryers. Some provide nappy (diaper) changing rooms.

- There are photocopiers and instant passport photograph machines at most inter-city and international railway stations.

- Most trains have smoking (*fumeurs*) and non-smoking (*non-fumeurs*) carriages. However, suburban trains out of Paris are non-smoking and other major cities are also following this lead.

- Public telephones are available on TGV trains and permit both domestic and international calls with a *télécarte* (see page 123). There are three telephones on each TGV train: one in 1st class, one in 2nd class and one in the bar.

- Note that station platforms (*quais*) aren't always clearly numbered, so make sure you're waiting at the correct one. Lines (*voies*) often have different numbers from platforms and this can be confusing. TGV platforms have a yellow line marked on the surface, outside which passengers must stand for safety. The destination of trains is usually written or displayed on the outside of carriages. At smaller stations you may need to cross the line to exit the station. If you're seeing someone off from a platform at a main station, you must sometimes purchase a platform ticket, although it's unlikely that anyone will check that you have one.

- Car parks are often provided close to railway stations, where long-term parking costs around 25F to 30F a day.

- You can rent an Avis rental car from around 200 main railway stations in France (see page 222) and leave it at any other stations operating the scheme. Cars can be reserved at the same time as your rail journey.

- Bicycles can be hired from many railway stations and transported on trains (see **Cycling** on page 353). The SNCF publishes a brochure, *Guide Train + Vélo*.

- Beware of baggage thieves when travelling on trains and try to store your bags in an overhead rack where you can keep an eye on them.

- Baggage offices (*consigne*) are provided at most stations, where you're charged around 30F per item for 24 hours. Many stations also have luggage lockers *(consigne automatique)*, costing from 15F to 30F for up to 72 hours, depending on the size. If you lose your key, you must pay five times the cost of the locker rental to replace it. Baggage trolleys are available free at main stations, although you need a 10F coin which is refunded when the trolley is returned to a storage location (as in supermarkets). Porters are available at main stations and charge around 5F per bag.

Baggage can be sent unaccompanied from any SNCF station to any destination in France or the rest of Europe, on production of your ticket. SNCF don't accept responsibility for lost baggage or baggage stolen from lockers, unless you can prove there was negligence on their part or that the locker was faulty. Even then the compensation is likely to be derisory. However, you can register *(enregistrement des bagages)* your baggage (including skis or bicycles) for a fee, in which case you're entitled to compensation based on the weight of your baggage. You must inspect your baggage when you collect it and make a claim by registered mail within three days.

Buying Tickets

Tickets *(billets)* can be purchased by telephone, via Minitel (3615 SNCF) and the Internet (www.sncf.fr), at station ticket offices, rail travel centres, rail appointed travel agents and via ticket machines *(billetteries automatiques)*. A ticket must be purchased and validated *before* boarding a train. Single tickets are *aller simple* and return tickets *aller-retour*. There are two classes on most trains, 1st class *(première classe)* and 2nd class *(deuxième classe)*, with the exception of TEE and TEN international trains, which are 1st class only. At main stations, ticket reservations *(locations)* may need to be made at a special window *(guichet)* and there may also be an information *(renseignements)* window. At major stations staff may speak English or other languages, e.g. German, Italian or Spanish. All tickets are valid for two months.

Children: Children under four who don't require a separate seat travel free and children aged from 4 to under 12 travel for half-fare. Children and youths aged from 12 to 25 can save 20 or 50 per cent (depending on the tariff period) with a *La Carte 12-25* card (see page 177). Children aged from 4 to under 14 can travel in the care of a *Jeune Voyageur Service* (JVS) hostess on selected routes for an additional fee of 240F. For information see the booklet *Votre enfant voyage en train*.

Pets: You must buy a half-fare 2nd class ticket for a dog if it weighs over 6kg, which is also valid in 1st class. If your dog or other small pet is transported in a bag or basket no bigger than 45cm x 30cm x 25 cm, the single fare is a flat 32F, irrespective of distance.

Tariffs: There are two tariffs *(tarif)*, depending on the day and the departure time of a journey, although they don't apply to TGV trains:

- **Blue Period:** Usually from midnight on Fridays to 1500 on Sundays and from 1000 Mondays to noon Fridays. This is the reduced tariff period.

- **White Period:** Usually from noon to midnight on Fridays, 1500 Sundays until 1000 Mondays, and on a few special days and public holidays.

A travel calendar *(Calendrier voyageurs)* is published by SNCF and is available at stations. Fares are determined by the tariff applicable at the start of a journey, therefore a journey that starts in the blue (off-peak) period and runs into the white period is charged at the blue period tariff. If you're discovered travelling in the white period with a ticket that only entitles you to travel in the blue period, you must pay the higher fare and a fine on the spot. A range of further discounts are available (see **Season & Special Tickets** on page 176).

Reservations: Seats can be reserved on most trains (the reservation price is included in the ticket price) and *must* be reserved on TGV trains. There's a fee for a TGV reservation, which varies depending on the time and day of the week. However, you can travel on the TGV following or preceding the one you reserved on without changing your ticket. When reserving a seat you can choose 1st or 2nd class, smoking (*fumeurs*) or non-smoking (*non-fumeurs*), and a window (*fenêtre*) or corridor (*couloir*) seat. All TGV tickets include a seat number. Reservations can be made up to two months prior to travel or just a few minutes before departure. Seats can be reserved via telephone (☎ 08.36.35.35.39 in English although it costs 2.23F per minute!) and both reserved and paid for via Minitel (3615 SNCF) or on the Internet (www.sncf.fr). Tickets for seats that aren't paid for in advance must be collected from an SNCF station within 48 hours. If a TGV train is over 30 minutes late, SNCF will refund your reservation fee. Other trains must be at least one hour late before a reservation fee is refunded. TGV drivers have their bonus reduced if a train is late without good reason. Tickets can also be reserved via automatic ticket machines (see below).

Ticket Machines: Tickets can be purchased via ticket machines (*billetterie automatique*) at SNCF stations (the French love ticket machines and using them is usually preferable to queueing). There are special machines (*billetterie automatique grandes lignes*) for main line tickets, e.g. a TGV. Machines have touch-sensitive screens and some can be set to operate in various languages by pressing the appropriate flag symbol, e.g. the Union Jack for English (Americans must defer to the union flag in this rare instance). Payment can be made in cash for tickets costing up to 100F and coins from 10 centimes to 10F are accepted. Tickets costing from 40F to 4,999F can be paid for with a credit or debit card (e.g. *Carte Bleue*, Diners Club, Eurocard, Mastercard and Visa), which you insert in the machine when requested. Your ticket is ejected along with your credit card or change.

Ticket Validation: With the exception of tickets purchased outside France and passes already annotated with their validity dates, tickets *must* be date stamped in a stamping machine (*composteur*) before boarding a train. This includes 'Resa' TGV reservation tickets and the return ticket of a day return. Stamping machines are painted orange (with a sign 'COMPOSTEZ VOTRE BILLET') and mounted on pillars located at the entrance to platforms (*accès aux quais*). At large stations the stamping machine may be placed at the main entrance to platforms and there may not be one on each platform. Insert one end of your ticket in the machine face up and the date and time is stamped on the reverse (if it's illegible, just stamp it again).

Failure to validate your ticket will result in a fine equal to 20 per cent of the fare or a minimum of 40F (if you have no ticket or an invalid ticket you will be fined 100F or 150F). Most trains have ticket inspectors, so you should expect to have your ticket checked. If you break a journey and continue it the same day, your ticket remains valid. However if you break a journey overnight (or longer), you must re-stamp your ticket before continuing your journey. If you validate your ticket and then miss your train, and there are no more trains that day or you decide not to travel, you must go to the ticket office and have your ticket 'un-validated'.

If you refuse to pay a fine the ticket inspector can seek the assistance of the police at the next station, but cannot insist that you leave the train. If you were unable to buy or stamp your ticket for reasons beyond your control, e.g. the ticket office was closed or the *composteur* was out of order, inform the ticket inspector *before* he approaches you (this is also important if you think that you ticket is incorrect). If you ticket is incorrect you must pay any extra due plus a 'handling fee' of 40F (if you're found guilty of fraud you can be fined 625F).

Finding Your Seat: To find your carriage, check the number on your ticket against the notice board showing the layout of trains (*Composition des Trains*) or the number on the outside of carriages. TGV carriage numbers are marked on the platform surface and displayed next to doors. Seat numbers are marked on tickets (VOIT 18: 32 = carriage 18 seat number 32) and displayed on the top of seats.

Refunds: If you buy a ticket and then decide not to use it, you can obtain a refund from any SNCF ticket office within its two-month validation period, plus the following two months. There's a service charge of 20F for a refund, which isn't levied if the service you planned to use didn't run, although you must have written proof from a member of the station staff.

Paris Stations: Paris has six main railway stations and six main lines (*grandes lignes*) covering the whole of France and radiating out from Paris:

Station	Regions and Countries Served
Gare d'Austerlitz	Central and Southwest (Bordeaux, Toulouse), except TGV Atlantique routes, Spain, Portugal;
Gare de l'Est	East (Nancy, Strasbourg), Germany and East Europe, including Moscow;
Gare de Lyon	South and Southeast (Lyon, Marseille, Côte d'Azur) including TGV Meditérranée routes, Switzerland, Italy, the former Yugoslavia states and Greece;
Gare Montparnasse	West (Brittany) plus TGV Atlantique routes including Bordeaux;
Gare du Nord	North, TGV Nord Europe to Lille and London, and Northern Europe (Belgium, Holland and Scandinavian countries);
Gare St. Lazare	Northwest (Normandy) including Dieppe and Cherbourg.

If you buy a ticket for a journey starting in Paris, the departure station is indicated on it. All the above stations are on the *métro* and some are also on the RER (see page 180). Allow around one hour to travel between stations, except between Gare du Nord and Gare de l'Est. Paris' main stations also provide access to the city's comprehensive suburban rail service (*réseau banlieue*).

Season & Special Tickets

Many season tickets (*Abonnement*) and special discount tickets are available in France, including discounts for families and couples; students and youths (16 to 25); senior citizens; commuters and groups; and holiday and excursion tickets. Information is available from the information or ticket office at any railway station. Some of the tickets described below are offered by regional transport authorities and may be available in certain regions only. **SNCF has a complicated fare structure and you should check to ensure that you pay the lowest possible fare.**

Commuters (*trajets fréquents/trajets domicile-travail*): A season ticket (*abonnement Modulopass*) is available for 6 or 12 months and allows a 50 per cent reduction. An annual season ticket can be paid in monthly instalments. Weekly (*hebdomadaire*) and monthly (*mensuel*) commuter tickets are also available in all regions. The cost varies depending on whether you want a ticket between two pre-designated stations (*trajets domicile-travail*) or a go-anywhere card (*Carte de libre circulation*). You must provide a passport photo and present your passport or *carte de séjour*.

Occasional Journeys (*voyages occasionnels*): You can buy a holiday return (*billet séjour*) allowing a 25 per cent reduction on a single, return or circular journey of over 1,000km (621mi) or an annual holiday ticket (*billet de Congé Annuel*) allowing a one-time 25 per cent reduction on a single or return ticket for a journey over 200km (124mi). Both tickets are valid for two months and journeys must start during a blue tariff period and the period between the outward and return journeys must include a Sunday.

Senior citizens: Those over 60 (or as the French delicately put it, those of *troisième age*) can buy a *Carte Senior*, which costs 285F and provides a 50 per cent reduction during the blue period and a 25 per cent reduction during the white period. There is also a 30 per cent reduction on international journeys to over 20 European countries and it can also be used internally on the national railway networks of several European countries. The *Carte Senior* is valid on all 1st or 2nd class trains except Paris regional trains and can be purchased from SNCF offices abroad as well as in France. *Carte Senior* holders are also entitled to discounts of up to 50 per cent on entertainment and museum fees and other travel discounts. Discounts are often listed in entertainment publications such as *Pariscope* (see page 311). Alternatively there's the *Tarif Découverte Senior* providing a 25 per cent reduction on all 1st or 2nd class trains on journeys started in the blue tariff period.

Families: Families with three or more children aged under 18 can purchase a family card (*Carte Familles Nombreuses*) for each member of the family. The first card or a renewal costs 85F and duplicates 55F. Cards are valid for three years and entitle holders to discounts on all rail fares, whether travelling independently or as a family. Discounts start at 30 per cent for a family with three children and rise to 75 per cent for families with six or more children. The *Carte Famille Nombreuse* is available only to French residents as it's a social service subsidised by the French government.

Groups: Parties of ten or more people (no age limit) travelling together receive discounts of varying amounts. Information is provided at SNCF stations. In all groups, children aged 4 to 11 pay half the reduced fare.

Youths: Children and youths aged from 12 to 25 can purchase *La Carte 12-25* card. It provides a 50 per cent reduction during the blue tariff period and a 25 per cent reduction during the white tariff period. It's valid for one year and costs 270F. There is also the *Tarif Découverte 12-25* entitling youths to a 25 per cent reduction on journeys started in the blue tariff period.

Children: A *Carte Enfant* + (350F) is valid for one year and entitles a child aged under 12 (who's the holder) and one to three other people (one of whom must be an adult) to travel at a 50 per cent reduction at all times except during white tariff periods, when a 25 per cent discount is given. It also permits a family dog or cat to travel free. A *Carte Enfant* + doesn't include travel on Paris' suburban railways.

Couples: Two adults (not necessarily related) travelling together have two options for reduced rail travel. The first, *Découverte à deux*, provides a 25 per cent reduction on all 1st or 2nd class trains on journeys starting in the blue tariff period. The second, *Découverte séjour*, gives a 25 per cent reduction on return journeys of less than 200km (124mi) and must include a Saturday night stay.

Congress Ticket: A *billet congrès* is available on presentation of your congress card and provides a 20 per cent reduction on a single or return ticket on all trains except TGV trains during peak times. Journeys must start during a blue tariff period.

Handicapped: Handicapped passengers are entitled to a range of special reductions, depending on the extent of their invalidity. In certain cases a person accompanying a handicapped person is entitled to travel free. Information is provided in SNCF's booklet, *Guide pratique du voyageur à mobilité réduite*.

Advance Purchase Discounts: The *Découverte J8* and *Découverte J30* tickets allow you to take advantage of special 2nd class fare reductions if you book and pay for your ticket 8 or 30 days in advance. The ticket is available only for the train reserved and cannot be exchanged and refunds are possible only up to four days before travel. Fares include ordinary seats (*place assise*) and 'beds' (*place couchée*) on overnight trains.

Motorail

Motorail is a European network of special trains, generally overnight, carrying passengers and their cars or motorbikes over distances of up to 1,500km (900mi). Caravans cannot be taken on car trains. SNCF provides an extensive motorail network of some 130 routes linking most regions of France. The principal internal Motorail routes are between Paris and Avignon, Biarritz, Bordeaux, Briançon, Brive, Evian, Fréjus-St. Raphaël, Gap, Grenoble, Lyon, Marseille, Narbonne, Nice, Nîmes, St. Gervais, Strasbourg, Tarbes, Toulon and Toulouse. The principal Motorail services from Britain operate from Calais and Dieppe to Avignon, Biarritz, Bordeaux, Brive, Fréjus-St. Raphaël, Narbonne, Nice, Moutiers and Toulouse. Trains don't run every day and on most routes operate during peak months only.

A wide range of sleeping accommodation (see below) is available. Breakfast is included in the price and is served in the station buffet on arrival at your destination, although there are interminable queues and it's usually more convenient to buy breakfast at a local café. Check your car carefully for damage before driving off, particularly the exhaust, which can be damaged on ramps. Any damage must be reported before leaving the station. Motorail journeys are expensive and it's cheaper for most people to drive, although it's usually slower and not as relaxing. The main advantage of Motorail is that you travel overnight without losing time and (hopefully) arrive feeling refreshed after a good night's sleep. Note that there's a big difference between fares during the off-peak (blue tariff) and peak (white tariff) periods (see page 174).

A comprehensive timetable (*Guide Trains Autos et Motos accompagnées*) is published for bookings made through a railway station or travel agent in France, containing routes, tariffs, general information and access maps for motorail stations. Passengers in Britain can obtain a brochure, *Motorail for Motorists - the Expressway into Europe*.

Sleeping Accommodation

A range of sleeping accommodation is provided on night trains, depending on your budget and the size of your party. Bookings can be made at SNCF offices, travel agents and motoring organisations abroad, and at railway stations, rail travel centres and rail appointed travel agents in France. Accommodation includes six-berth, second-class *couchettes*; four-berth, 1st class *couchettes*; and sleeping compartments with 'real' beds and en suite washing facilities. You may just wish to sleep on a reclining seat (*siège inclinable*), which can be reserved for a fee of 20F.

Couchettes: *Couchettes* (*places couchées*) are provided in 4-berth compartments in 1st class and in 6-berth compartments in 2nd class, for which there's a 90F reservation fee. Although a sleeping-bag sheet, pillow and blankets are provided, passengers don't usually undress as compartments aren't segregated according to sex. Washrooms and toilets are provided at the ends of carriages. *Couchettes* are non-smoking, although smoking is permitted in corridors.

Sleepers: Sleepers (*voiture-lits*) provide sleeping accommodation for one to three people with a proper bed and private washing facilities. Single and double sleepers are provided in 1st class, and double and triple sleepers in 2nd class. Each sleeper carriage has an attendant who serves snacks and drinks. Trains display the TEN (*Trans Euro Nuit*) emblem on carriages when they cross borders. Sleepers cost between 259F and 907F.

You should beware of thieves and armed robbers on overnight trains. After a spate of robberies a number of years ago special security locks were fitted to sleeping compartments; however, you should still take care before opening the door as crooks sometimes pose as attendants. Cars have also been robbed of their contents on motorail trains.

MÉTRO

A number of French cities have an underground railway or subway (*métro*) including Lille (the world's first fully automatic system without drivers!), Lyon, Marseille, Paris and Toulouse. In most French cities public transport tickets and passes permit travel on all modes of public transport including the *métro*, bus and suburban rail services. No smoking is permitted on *métro* trains or in stations. The following information relates to the Paris *métro*, although the range of tickets and the operation of trains is similar to other French *métro* systems.

The Paris *métro* dates from 1898 and is one of the world's oldest and most famous underground railways, ranking alongside the London underground and the New York subway. It has 199km (123mi) of track, 322 stations and 13 main lines plus two short supplementary lines. In the centre of Paris, you're never more than around 500 metres from a *métro* station. Some 4½ million people use the *métro* daily, although it falls to around three million in July and August when many Parisians are on holiday. Despite its age, the *métro* is one of the most efficient and cheapest urban transport systems in the world.

Trains run from 0530 until around 0100 and there's a frequent service during the day with trains running every 40 seconds during peak times and every 90 seconds at other times. The *métro* is operated by RATP (the Paris public transport authority) and a single all-purpose ticket is valid for all Paris' public transport (*métro*, RER, buses and suburban trains). A flat fare is charged for journeys irrespective of distance, although you aren't permitted to break your journey and cannot make a round trip. Tickets are sold at *métro* stations, bus terminals, tobacconists (*tabac*), RATP offices and machines. A ticket for a single journey costs 8F and ten tickets, called a *carnet*, cost 52F (a huge saving). Children under four travel free and those under ten for half fare. See also **Season & Visitors' Tickets** on page 181.

Ticket control is automated at all stations and you must insert your ticket in a 'turnstile' date/time stamping machine (*composteur*) to gain access to platforms. Always retain your ticket until you have completed your journey and pass the point marked *Limite de Validité des Billets*. If you travel without a valid ticket and are discovered during a random check by a ticket inspector (*contrôleur*), you must pay a fine of around 100F on the spot (there's a fine of 200F if you're caught jumping over a turnstile at a station). Ticket checks are often made at the beginning of the month when monthly tickets are renewed.

Métro stations are easily recognisable by a huge 'M' sign (some have distinctive art nouveau designs) with *métro* and neighbourhood maps (*plan de quartier*) displayed outside. There are computerised maps (*système d'information de trajets urbains/SITU*) at many stations. To use them you simply enter the name of the street you want and are given a print-out showing the quickest way to get there, including by foot. Main lines are numbered from 1 to 13 plus two supplementary lines numbered 3b and 7b. Lines are usually referred to by their terminating stations (*direction*), e.g. line four travelling south is indicated *Direction Porte d'Orléans* and north is *Direction Porte de Clignancourt*. Follow the illuminated orange signs for the *direction* you want and when changing trains at intersections (*correspondance*). Up to six lines may 'join' at an intersection. When changing lines there's often a long walk, although some stations have moving walkways.

To open the door on older trains you push the silver handle upwards (on the inside and outside). New trains have pushbuttons. Doors on trains close automatically and a warning signal is sounded just before they close. Certain seats are reserved for the disabled, elderly or pregnant. You should be wary of pickpockets when travelling on the *métro*. However, serious crime and violence is rare, although it's wise to avoid empty carriages and some stations at night (such as Château Rouge, Châtelet-Les-Halles, Gare du Nord, Réaumur, Saint Denis, Sébastopol and Strabourg), which may be frequented by muggers. There are alarms (*borne d'alarm*) on stations.

RER: The RER (*Réseau Express Régional*) is an express underground rail system (opened in 1969) that's independent of the *métro* and links most suburbs with the centre of Paris. It's much quicker than the *métro* as there are fewer stops. There are four RER lines (designated A, B, C and D) operating from 0530 until around 0030, with trains around every 15 minutes. RER lines A and B are operated jointly by the SNCF and RATP, and lines C and D are operated exclusively by the SNCF.

Line B3 goes to Charles de Gaulle airport, line C2 to Orly airport and line C5 to Versailles-Rive-Gauche. Line A runs to a specially built station at Marne-la-Vallée-Chessy for Disneyland Paris. The journey from central Paris to Disneyland takes around 40 minutes and trains run every ten minutes during normal periods and every 20 minutes during off-peak periods. The RER also links Roissy-Charles de Gaulle airport with the Gare du Nord, and the Gare du Nord with the Gare de Lyon.

RER tickets can be purchased only at RER station ticket offices. Within the central area (Ville de Paris), a *métro* ticket is valid on RER trains. Outside this area the RER has a different ticket system from the *métro*, with prices increasing according to the distance travelled. A ticket for the central zone costs 8F. If you wish to make a combined *métro* and RER journey outside the central area, you must buy separate tickets. Like *métro* tickets, RER tickets must be machine stamped before journeys are commenced and when exiting an RER station. If you have completed your journey the machine will display 'proceed' (*passez*) and retain your ticket. Where you're able to continue your journey, a machine will return your ticket and display 'take your ticket' (*prenez votre ticket*).

Disabled Passengers: Disabled passengers who aren't in wheelchairs can book a free travel companion (*voyage accompagné*) a day in advance for *métro* and RER (and many bus) journeys between 0800 and 2000, Mondays to Fridays (☎ 01.44.54.40.40). The *métro* isn't suitable for wheelchairs, although RER lines A and B allow wheelchair access. An RER access guide is published for wheelchair users and is available from the RATP head office, 54, quai Rapée, 75012 Paris (☎ 01.44.68.20.20). A leaflet for handicapped travellers (*Touriste quand même*) is available from CNFLRH, 38, boulevard Raspail, 75007 Paris.

Season & Visitors' Tickets

The Paris RATP (public transport authority) provides weekly, monthly and annual season tickets, plus tickets for visitors, groups of children and certain other categories of passengers. These include the following:

Carte Orange: The *Carte Orange* was created in 1975 and allows unlimited travel within the one to eight zones that comprise the Ile-de-France. Central Paris (as far as the *Périphérique*) consists of zones one and two, and zones three to five encompass the outer suburbs and the airports. A further three zones (six to eight) extend to the rest of the Ile-de-France. A monthly *Carte Orange* is valid for a calendar month, irrespective of when you buy it. To buy a weekly or monthly card, you need a *Carte Orange*, which is an identity card with your photograph, full name, address and signature. To obtain a *Carte Orange* identity card you need a passport-size photograph, available from instant photo booths at many Paris rail and *métro* stations. You must complete a *coupon vert* for a weekly (*hebdomadaire*) card or a *coupon orange* for a monthly (*mensuelle*) *Carte Orange* the first time you buy one. After obtaining your *Carte Orange* identity card, travel cards can be bought from ticket machines.

You should carry your weekly or monthly card in a slot in the plastic wallet provided along with your identity card and write the number of your *Carte Orange* on the card. This prevents cards from being used by someone else, as they aren't transferable. Failure to do this can result in a fine if it's discovered during a spot check. Weekly and monthly cards can be used on all four levels of Paris public transport (*métro*, RER, SNCF and buses) within the applicable zones and includes buses operated by private operators that are affiliated to the two main groups of companies, APTR and ADATRIF. A weekly card costs from 80F for zones 1 and 2 (central Paris) and a monthly card from 271F. The card can be purchased for the current week up until Wednesday and from Friday onwards for the following week. SNCF publish a *Plan des Zones Carte Orange*.

Carte Intégrale: The *Carte Intégrale* is an annual season ticket costing around 2,871F for zones one and two and 8,316F for all eight zones. It can be paid annually or monthly by standing order (*prélèvement*) at no extra cost. If you pay monthly, the first month costs 50F.

Visitors' Tickets: Visitors to Paris can buy a *Paris Visite* ticket for central Paris (zones one to three) or for zones one to five plus Orlybus, Orlyrail, Roissyrail and Marne-la-Vallée-Chessy (for Disneyland Paris). Tickets can be purchased for two (90F for three zones, 175F for five zones), three (120F/245F) or five days (175F/300F). A *Paris Visite* ticket allows unlimited travel on all public transport including the *métro*, RER, the SNCF Paris network, the bus network (including Montmartrobus, Noctambus and Orlybus), and the Montmartre funicular. It also entitles holders to discounts (worth around 200F) on admission fees to various tourist attractions and a 50 per cent reduction on the cost of bike hire. A one-day *Mobilis* ticket is also available, the price of which depends on the number of zones required (from 30F for zones one to two, up to 70F for zones one to five). Note that the Orlybus, Orlyrail and Roissyrail services aren't included in the *Mobilis* ticket.

Visitors' tickets are available from main *métro* and RER stations, Paris tourist offices, Paris' main SNCF railway stations, Paris airports and the Paris tourist office. Note that unless you travel extensively on public transport, it's cheaper to buy a *carnet* of ten *métro*/bus tickets than a visitor's ticket. This is particularly true if you spend most of your time in central Paris, where walking between areas and attractions is possible (and enjoyable).

Since 1983, half the cost of commuter tickets has been refunded by employers with ten or more employees. This is largely a social benefit and is a loss-maker for the transport operators. The price paid by passengers accounts for just 40 per cent of the price of the ticket, with 40 per cent paid by employers and the remaining 20 per cent paid in the form of a grant by central and local governments.

All prices for RATP bus and rail tickets are listed in a leaflet, *Du Ticket à la Carte*, available from *métro* stations and RATP offices. For RATP information telephone 08.36.68.41.14 (in English) between 0600 and 2100, use Minitel (3615 RATP) or consult the Internet (www.ratp.fr).

BUSES & TRAMS

There are excellent bus services in Paris and other major cities, some of which also have trams or trolley buses. However, in rural areas, buses are few and far between, and the scant services that exist are usually designed to meet the needs of schoolchildren, workers and housewives on market days. This means that buses usually run early and late in the day with little or nothing in between, and may cease altogether during the long summer school holiday period (July to August). Private bus services are often confusing and uncoordinated, and usually leave from different locations rather than a central bus station. Note that a city bus is generally called an *autobus* and a country bus a *car* or *autocar*. Smoking isn't permitted on buses.

The best place to enquire about bus services is at a tourist office or railway station. In large towns and cities, buses run to and from bus stations (*gare d'autobus/routière*) usually located next to railway stations. In rural areas, bus services are often operated by the SNCF and run between local towns and the railway station. An SNCF bus, on which rail tickets and passes are valid, is shown as an *Autocar* in rail timetables. The SNCF also provides bus tours throughout France. Some towns provide free or discount bus passes to senior citizens (over 60) on production of an identity card, passport, or *carte de séjour* and proof of local residence.

There are no national bus companies in France operating scheduled services, although many long-distance buses are operated by foreign companies such as Euroways/Eurolines, Riviera Express, Europabus, Miracle Bus and Grey-Green Coaches. Eurolines operate regular services from Britain to over 50 French cities including Bordeaux, Cannes, Lyon, Montpellier, Nice, Orléans, Paris, Perpignan, Reims, St. Malo and Strasbourg. Discounts are provided for students and youths on some routes. For information about internal inter-city services contact the *Fédération Nationale des Transports Routiers*, 6, rue Ampères, 75017 Paris (☎ 01.44.29.04.29).

The following information relates to Paris buses, although tickets and the operation of buses is similar in other French cities. Paris has over 112km (70mi) of bus lanes, so buses move at a reasonable speed, although they are inevitably slower during rush hours and slower than the *métro*. Timetables are displayed at most stops. Operating hours vary, although buses are in service on most routes from 0700 to between 2030 and 2100. On main routes, evening buses (*Autobus du Soir*) run until at least midnight. From Mondays to Saturdays there's a 10 to 15 minute service during peak hours, with a reduced service after 2030. On Sundays and public holidays services are severely restricted on most routes. Night buses (*Noctambus*) provide a one-hour service on ten routes (a night bus map is available from *métro* stations).

A ticket for a single journey costs 8F and ten tickets, called a *carnet*, cost 52F. The metro and the bus use the same ticket. A single ticket is valid for two sections or fare stages, marked *fin de section* at stops. Two tickets are needed for trips encompassing two fare stages and up to four tickets for trips to the suburbs (or six or seven if you're going from one side of Paris to the other). Each stop displays the numbers of the buses stopping there, a map showing all stops along a given route, and the times of the first and last buses. Route maps are displayed on buses and stops may be announced as they are approached. Free maps are available at bus terminals, *métro* stations, tourist offices and RATP offices. There are numerous private sight-seeing bus tours in Paris, although it's much cheaper to use scheduled RATP buses (RATP recommend certain routes for sightseers) or a RATP excursion bus.

Paris bus stops (many with shelters) are indicated by a post with red and yellow panels marked with the name of the stop (e.g. a street or corner), as shown on route plans. The route number and destination is displayed on the front of buses and the route on the sides. To stop a bus, you must signal to the driver by waving your arm. On boarding a bus you *must* stamp (*oblitérer/composter*) your ticket by inserting it in the stamping machine (*composteur*) located next to the driver. A ticket inspector (*contrôleur*) may ask to see your ticket and if it isn't stamped you will be fined. If you have a *Carte Orange* or other pass (see page 181) valid on Paris buses, show it to the driver as you board. When you want a bus to stop, you signal the driver by pressing a button or pulling a cord. A stop requested (*arrêt demandé*) sign will light up above the driver. Buses usually have separate entrance (*montée*) and exit (*sortie*) doors.

RATP publish a wealth of free leaflets and maps including a *Petit Plan de Paris*, a *Grand Plan de Paris*, a *Grand Plan Ile-de-France* and other Paris regional maps. They also publish *Paris Patchwork*, a pocket-sized guide filled with maps and useful information that's available free from RATP offices and *métro* stations. Many bus guides are available from bookshops including P*lan de Paris par Arrondissements*, containing detailed diagrams of all bus routes, and *Guide Paris Autobus* (Ponchet Plan Net).

FERRIES & EUROTUNNEL

International services operate year round between France and Britain, Ireland and the Channel Islands. There's a wide choice of routes for travellers between France and Britain, depending on where you live, your ultimate destination and the best road connections. There are scheduled car ferry services from the French ports of Boulogne, Caen, Calais, Cherbourg, Dieppe, Le Havre, Roscoff, St. Malo to a number of British ports including Dover, Folkestone, Newhaven, Plymouth, Poole, Portsmouth and Weymouth, plus the Irish ports of Cork and Rosslare. There are also ferry services between St. Malo and the Channel Islands of Jersey, Guernsey and Sark (foot passengers only). The major ferry companies operating international services are P&O (which also operates as P&O Stena Line on some routes) and Brittany ferries, which dominates the routes in the western Channel (from Caen, Cherbourg, Roscoff and St. Malo) with around 40 per cent of the market. Hoverspeed operates a hovercraft service between Calais and Dover and catamaran (Seacat) services on the same route plus Boulogne to Folkestone. A larger Hoverspeed superseacat service operates from Dieppe to Newhaven and Condor operate a fast service (five hours) from St. Malo to Weymouth.

Some ferry services operate during the summer months only, e.g. May to September, and the frequency of services varies from dozens a day on the busiest Calais-Dover route during the summer peak period, to one a week on longer routes. Services are less frequent during the winter months, when bad weather can also cause cancellations. Most Channel ferry services employ large super ferries with a capacity of up to 1,800 to 2,000 passengers and 700 cars. Ferries carry all vehicles, while hovercraft take all vehicles except HGVs, large trucks and buses. All operators except Hoverspeed offer night services, which may be cheaper. Berths, single cabins and pullman seats are usually available, and most ships have a restaurant, self-service cafeteria, a children's play area and duty-free shopping. Generally the longer the route, the better and wider the range of facilities provided, which often makes it worthwhile considering alternative routes to the Calais-Dover crossing. Although Calais-Dover is the shortest route and offers the most crossings, longer passages are generally less crowded and more relaxing, and fares are often lower.

On longer routes, most ships provide hairdressing, fast-photo developing, pools, saunas, live entertainment, cinemas and discos. Most ferries have a range of shops, including duty-free shops, which are huge money-spinners and the reason ferry companies offer such low winter fares (ferry companies make up to 50 per cent of their profits from on-board sales). However, duty-free (see page 390) is set to end in mid-1999. after which fares are expected to increase to compensate for the lost revenue. Most ferries provide day cabins with en suite facilities that provide somewhere to leave luggage, shower and change, or just have a nap. When travelling on a cross-Channel ferry with your car, take any items required during the crossing with you as you aren't allowed access to the car decks during journeys. Many ships cater for children and mothers, and have play areas, baby-feeding and changing rooms. All major ferry operators offer a business class (e.g. P&O's club class) typically costing an extra 70F to 100F per person, per trip. It includes a quieter lounge; free tea, coffee and newspapers; and fax, photocopier and other facilities. Ferry companies also provide ship-to-shore telephone, telex, fax (shore only), and photocopiers on both ships and at ports.

It isn't always necessary to make a booking, although it's advisable when travelling during the summer peak period, particularly on a Friday or Saturday (and when you require a berth on an overnight service). Like air travel, ferry services are sometimes subject to delays due to strikes, out of service ferries, or simply the large number of passengers. If possible, it's best to avoid travelling during peak times. Check-in times depend on the particular crossing and are from 20 to 60 minutes for motorists and from 20 to 45 minutes for foot passengers. Comprehensive free timetables and guides are published by shipping companies and are available from travel agents (although it's *much* quicker to book direct).

Fares: Peak fares are high, e.g. a standard Calais-Dover return with P&O for a vehicle up to 5m in length costs around 3,000F (1,500F single) including the driver and one passenger. This drops to around 900F for a five-day return during the cheapest period. If you want a single ticket only, it may be cheaper to take advantage of a special offer and throw away the return ticket. Ferry companies offer a range of fares including standard single and return fares, apex fares, and 5 and 10-day returns. Children under four years old travel free and those aged from 4 to 14 travel for half fare. Students may be entitled to a small discount during off-peak periods. Bicycles are transported free on most services. Whenever you travel, always check for special offers. Last minute tickets can be purchased at up to 50 per cent discount from 'bucket' shops. P&O shareholders who own at least GB£600 worth of P&O concessionary stock receive a 50 per cent discount on Calais-Dover crossings and 40 per cent off Cherbourg-Portsmouth and Le Havre-Portsmouth crossings. Some ferry lines have clubs for frequent travellers, e.g. the Brittany Ferries French Property Owners Clubs, offering savings of up to 30 per cent on single and standard return fares.

Day Trips: A huge boost to ferry companies in the low winter season in recent years has been the explosion in popularity of low-cost shopping trips to Calais and Boulogne from Britain. However, this is having a detrimental affect on summer crossings, as many people baulk at paying up to 3,000F (over £300) for a summer crossing when a winter day trip costs as little as 100F (£10) return for a car and just 10F (around £1) for foot passengers! Most special offers are usually available only through coupons, published in British daily newspapers. Half of the travellers who take return crossings from Dover to Calais are simply taking day trips or making one-night stays. **Note that the above day trip fares are for day trips originating in Britain, although day trip fares from France to Britain are also available from French ports.**

The proportion of passengers travelling to and from Britain by sea has fallen considerably since the early '60s due to the reduced cost of air travel and competition from Eurostar trains (see page 172) and Eurotunnel (see below). However, ferry companies have been investing in cruise-style super-ferries to compete with the tunnel and are busy promoting a ferry trip as an enjoyable part of a holiday or journey and a relaxing break for motorists. Most ferry companies publish brochures for holidays in France and offer a range of accommodation from *gîtes* and cottages to luxury villas and hotels.

Eurotunnel: Eurotunnel (formally Le Shuttle) started operating its shuttle car train service from Coquelles (near Calais) to Folkestone (England) in 1995. It provides a 15-minute service during peak periods, taking just 35 minutes. Each train can carry around 180 cars. Fares are similar to ferries, e.g. a peak (summer) club class return costs around 3400F and an off-peak (January to March) return 1,700F for a vehicle and all passengers. It's advisable to book in advance, although you should note that reservations are for a particular day, not a particular train or time. Don't expect to get a place in summer on the 'turn up and go' service in the UK, particularly on Fridays, Saturdays and Sundays. Demand is usually lighter on services from France to Britain, when bookings may be unnecessary. Trains carry all 'vehicles' including cycles, motorcycles, cars, trucks, buses, caravans and motorhomes. Vehicles carrying gas are banned.

Domestic Ferries: Car ferries provide daily services between Marseilles, Nice and Toulon and the Corsican ports of Ajaccio, Bastia, Calvi, Ile Rousse, Porto-Vecchio and Propriano (crossing times are from 5 to 12 hours). Car ferry services also operate between Royan and Le Verdon (Gironde estuary) and between Blaye and Lamarque (Gironde). Services operate during daylight hours throughout the year and crossings take around 30 and 25 minutes respectively. A summer hydrofoil service operates from Nice to Cannes and Monaco. In some cities there are river ferry services such as the *Batobus* on the Seine in Paris (May until September), although this is mainly for tourists.

One of the first things you should do after boarding a ferry is to study the safety procedures (announcements are also made). Although travelling by ferry within Europe is one of the safest means of transport, there have been a number of major ferry disasters on roll-on, roll-off (ro-ro) ferries in recent years. This has highlighted safety procedures and ship design, and a number of safety measures have been introduced and more are in the pipeline.

TIMETABLES

French timetables (*horaire*) are usually accurate, particularly rail timetables for TGV and other fast trains. At major airports and rail stations, arrivals (*arrivées*) and departures (*départs*) are shown on large electronic boards. It's wise to double-check departure times and not to rely on announcements (that's if you can understand the often garbled messages). When you buy a rail ticket with a reserved seat, e.g. for a TGV train, the departure time is printed on your ticket. Before planning a trip, check that your planned travel dates aren't 'special days' (*jour particulier*) such as a public holiday (unless you have no option). Note that many services operate only from Mondays to Saturdays (*Semaine*) and not on Sundays and holidays (*Dimanches et Fêtes*). If you wish to save money when travelling by rail or air, avoid travelling during a peak tariff (white) period (see page 174). An SNCF bus on which rail tickets and passes are valid is shown as an *Autocar* in rail timetables.

If you're a regular user of public transport, the first thing you should do when you arrive in a new city is obtain a map of the local public transport system and a timetable. Rail timetables are published in national, regional and local versions, and also for individual routes or lines. SNCF also publish a wealth of special guides and information. The official SNCF timetable (*Indicateur Horaires Ville à Ville*) costs around 100F and contains schedules for trains linking some 280 French and European towns and cities. It also includes a network map and information about fares, reservations and supplementary services. Two editions are published each year from around 1st June to 23rd September and from 24th September to 1st June (actual dates vary annually). It's available from SNCF stations, bookshops and kiosks.

SNCF also publish three regional timetables for the Nord Est, Atlantique and Sud Est et Corse. There are separate timetables and guides (*Horaires et Guide Pratique*) for the TGV lines. Pocket timetables are published for main lines (*Grandes Lignes*) and a *Lignes Affaires* timetable is published containing times for a selection of the most popular trains linking major centres from Monday to Friday. In most regions, a *Guide Régional des Transports* is available from local rail and bus stations.

Train information and reservations can be obtained and made by telephone via 08.36.35.35.39 in English for main stations (at 2.23F a minute!). Rail information is also available via Minitel (3615 SNCF), the Internet (www.sncf.fr) and by telephone for each department. Local department information and reservation telephone numbers are listed in a free booklet, *le Guide du Voyageur*.

TAXIS

Taxi ranks (*station de taxi/tête de station*) are usually located outside rail stations, at airports and at main intersections in towns and cities. At some taxi ranks, e.g. at Charles de Gaulle airport, a button is provided to call a taxi when none are waiting. You can hail a taxi in the street, but it must be at least 50 metres from a taxi rank where people are waiting. You can also call a radio-taxi by telephone (usually provided at taxi ranks), but you must pay for the taxi's journey to the pick-up point. Some radio-taxi companies operate a system where customers pay an annual fee for priority service.

Taxi drivers are one of the most unscrupulous, rudest and unruly groups in France (some achievement!) and they have a strong union. Common practices include refusing a fare unless it's above 30F, loading as many as three strangers in a cab and charging each full fare to be dropped off at different locations, and charging supplements of up to 100F for a few suitcases. It isn't advisable to tell a driver your destination until you get into a taxi, as if it doesn't appeal to him he may refuse the fare and drive off without you. You may pick up one other person along the way for no extra charge, although drivers often try to charge a higher fare. A driver can refuse to take more than three adults (two children under age ten count as one adult), although some allow an extra passenger. The driver may not smoke unless there's a glass partition between him and passengers, and passengers may not smoke if a 'no smoking' sign is displayed.

Paris: Parisian cabs are among the cheapest in Europe and are ordinary cars fitted with a meter and a light on top (unlike purpose-built London taxis). Although there are around 15,000 taxis in Paris, it's often difficult to find one, particularly during lunch times, rush hours and when it's raining! In Paris, taxi ranks are indicated by blue and white 'taxi' signs. A taxi for hire in Paris is indicated by a white light on the roof. A driver must take you if the light on top of his vehicle is lit, unless he's on the last half hour of his shift indicated by a meter inside the taxi on the rear window shelf. An orange light means a taxi is engaged and when no lights are on or the meter is covered by a black cover, then the driver is off duty.

There are three fare rates in Paris and the prevailing rate is indicated by a small light on a taxi's roof beneath the main light. Rate A (3.40F per km) operates from 0700 to 1900 and is the daytime rate for Mondays to Fridays as far as (and including) the *Périphérique*. Rate B (5.40F per km) runs from 1900 to 0700 and is also the day rate for journeys to the Hauts-de-Seine, Seine-Saint-Denis and Val-de-Marne departments from 0700 to 1900. Rate C (7.16F per km) is the rate for the suburbs (*tarif banlieue*) and airports beyond the *Boulevard Périphérique*, including the departments listed above outside the hours of 0700 to 1900. Drivers are supposed to reset the meter tariff when crossing from the suburbs into the central area of Paris (marked by the *Boulevard Périphérique*).

Rates are displayed on the meter inside the taxi and extra charges are shown on a notice affixed to the rear left window. These include pick up charges (*prix en charge*, around 13F in Paris), plus supplements for pick-ups at main railway stations and airports, baggage heavier than 5kg (5 to 10F), a fourth adult (8F) and pets. **Taxi drivers cannot claim a return fare, whatever the destination.** Fares are shown on meters and it's customary to add a tip of around 10 to 15 per cent (more at night) and round fares up to the nearest 5F. For information or to make a complaint about a Paris taxi driver, write to the *Service des Taxis de la Préfecture de Police*, 36, rue des Morillons, 75015 Paris Cedex (☎ 01.55.76.20.00). If you intend to make a complaint, obtain a receipt (*bulletin de voiture*) and indicate the taxi number, and the date and time of the fare.

Taxi drivers can refuse to carry animals and most taxi drivers don't accept dogs. However, if you're handicapped a taxi driver cannot refuse to take you and must help you into the taxi and transport a guide dog for the blind. Specially adapted taxis for the disabled are available in major cities, but must be booked in advance (☎ 01.41.29.01.29/ 01.41.83.15.15 in Paris). Note that taxis in rural areas often double as ambulances, so don't be surprised if you see a taxi-driver wearing a white coat. In many cities there are simply too many cabs and the situation is exacerbated by unlicensed 'cowboy' operators. Beware of illegal unlicensed and unmetered cabs operating in main cities and preying on foreign visitors. If you're obliged to take one of these, always agree the fare in advance. You can also hire chauffeur-driven cars (*voiture de place*) in most towns and cities, either by the hour or for a fixed fee for a particular trip.

AIRLINE SERVICES

All major international airlines provide scheduled services to Paris and many also fly to other main French cities such as Lyon, Nice and Marseille. The French state-owned national airline, Air France, is France's major international carrier, flying to around 190 destinations in over 70 countries. It has a fleet of over 100 aircraft including seven Concordes (dubbed the world's fastest white elephant by jealous competitors) and carries some 16 million passengers annually. Air France operates main routes in Europe, North and South America and Japan, and has a majority stake in UTA, France's second international airline, which concentrates on serving the Ivory Coast, South Africa, Singapore and Australia. Air France provides a high standard of service and, as you would expect, provides excellent in-flight cuisine.

Like most national (and nationalised) carriers, Air France makes huge losses and will need huge injections of public cash for years to come, without which it would be bankrupt (it has aptly been described as a Gallic version of Aeroflot, albeit with a much better safety record). The EU has stated that it won't allow further state funding for nationalised airlines and in spite of opposition from pilots (who staged a strike just prior to the World Cup in 1998) the French government partially privatised (20 per cent) Air France in November 1998. The striking pilots not only found themselves ignored, but their salaries were frozen for seven years (a complete restructure of the airline is planned).

Air France and their domestic airline Air France Europe (known collectively as Groupe Air France) have a virtual monopoly of French airspace. Air France shares its monopoly on many international routes with just one foreign carrier and is thus able to charge high fares. The lack of competition means that international flights to and from most French airports, and French domestic flights, are among the world's most expensive (business fares are the biggest rip-off). However, some opposition is starting to appear and high fares on some routes, e.g. transatlantic flights, have been reduced in recent years by cut-price travel agents such as *Nouvelles Frontières* and cut-price, no-frills airlines such as EasyJet and Virgin Express. Competition on some routes from TGV trains (e.g. Paris-Lyon and Paris-London, the world's busiest international air corridor) has also helped reduce fares. Smoking is banned on French domestic flights and on Air France international flights of less than two hours duration.

Domestic Flights: There are a number of airlines offering domestic services including Air France, Air France Europe, UTA, TAT (Touraine Air Transport), Air Liberté (the latter two are owned by British Airways), Air Outre-Mer, Euralair, Aigle Azur, Air Littoral, Air Vendée and Europe Aero Service. Competition has intensified on France's domestic routes in recent years where there has been a big improvement in regional services, partly as a result of a price war between airlines. Air Inter is France's largest domestic airline, operating 400 flights a day and carrying over 18 million passengers a year. It operates a comprehensive network of routes to around 40 regional airports and links regions both with Paris and with each other.

Air France also operates domestic services between major cities such as Paris, Bordeaux, Lyon, Marseille, Mulhouse/Basel, Nice, Strasbourg and Toulouse. Many domestic flights are timed to connect (*correspondance*) with international arrivals in Paris. Domestic air travel is being squeezed on some routes by TGV trains, although flying is sometimes cheaper than travelling by train and quicker on most routes. Any destination in France can be reached in less than 90 minutes (average one hour) by air and check-in times are just 15 to 30 minutes before departure. Private 24-hour air taxi services also operate from many French airports.

Buying Tickets: When buying a ticket in France for an international or domestic flight it pays to shop around for the best deal. Whatever your destination it's advisable to consult a travel agent, who can explain the various options available and may be able to offer a range of inexpensive flights. In addition to regular first, business and tourist class tickets, airlines offer a variety of discount fares including superpex, apex, superapex, weekend returns, youths and senior citizens (60), students, families, children and groups. Note that regular flights booked at short notice can increase a fare by 200 to 300 per cent, irrespective of the availability of seats.

Although slower, it's often cheaper to fly to Paris and continue your journey in France by train or a domestic flight. If you're able to stay from between 10 and 35 days at your destination, you can get an inexpensive flight from Paris to a range of domestic destinations. If you're under 26 or an academic working in an educational institution (regardless of age), you can take advantage of the *Le Fly France* flexible airpass, which combines travel to France with unlimited travel on domestic flights for four days within a calendar month, usually with Air France Europe.

Special offers for frequent fliers are provided by most European and international airlines. Air France operates a frequent flier scheme (*Fréquence Plus*) targeted at business travellers that has over 150,000 members. However, points are offered only on full-fare tickets and must be used within 18 months. With a commuter ticket (*carte d'abonnement tous vols*) you can save 30 per cent on Air France, UTA and Air France Europe domestic flights on certain routes, and 20 per cent on combined air and 1st class rail journeys. Holders of an SNCF season ticket can also obtain discounts on domestic flights.

After London, Paris is one of the cheapest European destinations from North America and it rarely pays to fly to France from North America via London or another European city, as is often the case with other European destinations. From other intercontinental cities, it's worthwhile comparing the cost of a direct flight to Paris with a flight via London or another European city. Air France is one of the most expensive airlines for intercontinental flights to France. Apart from special offers, the cheapest way to get to Paris from North America is with an Apex fare, which must usually be booked 21 days in advance, travelling midweek and staying at least seven days. As in Europe, the best deals are usually available from travel agents specialising in discount fares, such as STA Travel, Council Travel and *Nouvelles Frontières*. Thanks to the strong link between France and Québec, there are frequent air services between France and Canada, mostly from Paris to Toronto or Montréal. **If you're planning a trip abroad during school holidays, book <u>well</u> in advance, particularly if you're heading for a popular destination such as London or New York.**

The reservation numbers for the major French airlines are: Air France (☎ 08.02.80.28.02, Internet: www.airfrance.com), Air Inter (☎ 08.02.80.28.02) and Air Liberté/TAT (☎ 08.03.80.58.05).

Airports

The main French gateway airports serving intercontinental flights are Paris Roissy-Charles-de-Gaulle, Paris Orly, Lyon-Satolas, Nice-Côte-d'Azur and Marseille-Provence. Paris is served by direct flights from almost every major capital city in the world and there are also direct flights from over 30 US and Canadian cities (Paris is the only French transatlantic gateway) operated by around 12 airlines. Many of France's regional airports have flights to a number of European destinations, particularly London. Flights to North African countries are also common from regional airports, mainly to cater for migrant workers. Nice is France's busiest provincial airport with direct scheduled flights to around 80 cities worldwide, closely followed by Marseille serving around 70 international destinations.

Among the many French cities and towns served by international flights are Biarritz, Bordeaux, Brest, Brive La Gaillarde, Caen, Cherbourg, Clermont-Ferrand, Dijon, Fréjus, Grenoble, Hyères, Le Havre, Le Touquet, Lille, Lourdes, Lyon, Marseille, Montpellier, Mulhouse/Basel, Nancy-Metz, Nantes, Nice, Paris, Perpignan, Pontoise, Quimper, Rennes, Rouen, Strasbourg, Tarbes, Toulouse and Tours-Poitiers. There are also international flights to Ajaccio, Bastia, Calvi and Figari in Corsica. Depending on your ultimate destination, it's sometimes cheaper or quicker to fly to an international airport outside France, such as Luxembourg for northeastern France and Mulhouse-Basle for eastern France. The most important French airports are Paris' Roissy-Charles de Gaulle and Orly airports:

Roissy-Charles de Gaulle airport is located 23km (14mi) northeast of the centre of Paris. There are two terminals (*aérogare*): terminal two serves Air France plus Air Inter, Air Bremen, Air Madagascar, Air Seychelles, Alitalia, Austrian Airlines,

Brymon Airways, Canadian Airlines, Crossair, CSA, Interflug, LOT, Luxair, MALEV, Sabena and Tyrolean Airways. Terminal one serves all foreign airlines not listed above. The terminals are linked by a free bus service. The quickest way to travel between central Paris and Roissy airport is to take the RER line B (see page 180) taking 35 minutes. A free shuttle bus operates from the RER station at Châtelet Les Halles and from Roissy SNCF rail station to the terminals. A new TGV station opened at Charles de Gaulle airport in September 1995 with connections to Lyon (two hours and 20 minutes) and Lille (55 minutes). There are also a variety of bus services to and from central Paris operated by Air France, RATP (the Paris public transport authority) and private operators. Most services operate from around 0500 until 2300 and run every 15 or 30 minutes, taking around fifty minutes. Single fares are around 45 to 65F. Roissy-Charles de Gaulle and Orly airports are linked by bus. For Roissy-Charles de Gaulle airport information telephone 01.48.62.22.80. Airport and flight information is available via Minitel (3615 HORAV).

Orly airport is located 14km (9mi) south of central Paris and has two terminals: *Sud* serving international flights and *Ouest* serving Air Inter domestic flights. The quickest way to get to Orly from central Paris is to take RER line B in the direction of St. Rémy Les Chevreuses and change at Antony for a special *Orlyval* train. Trains also run every 15 minutes (30 minutes after 2000) from Orly SNCF station to the Gare d'Austerlitz on RER line C. Bus services from central Paris are similar to those for Roissy-Charles de Gaulle (see above), costing around 30F and taking some 40 minutes. For Orly airport information telephone 01.49.75.15.15.

Long and short term parking is available at major airports, including reserved parking for the disabled, and car hire is also available at Paris and principal provincial airports.

11.

MOTORING

France has an extensive motorway (*autoroute*) network of over 8,000km (some 5,000mi) supplemented by a comprehensive network (around 30,000km/18,500mi) of excellent trunk roads (*routes nationales*). French *autoroutes* are mostly toll roads built by private companies and are among Europe's finest roads. However, they are also among the world's most expensive and consequently main trunk roads (*routes nationales*) are jammed by drivers who are reluctant to pay or who cannot afford the high *autoroute* tolls. Driving is usually cheaper than taking the train, particularly when your car runs on diesel fuel, the costs are shared between a number of people *and* you avoid the *autoroutes*. However, if you're travelling long distances, you'll find it quicker and certainly less stressful to take a TGV train or fly. If you live in a city, particularly Paris, a car is usually a liability, while in rural areas it's a necessity. Driving is usually enjoyable in remote rural areas, particularly outside the tourist season, where it's possible to drive for miles without seeing another motorist (or a caravan).

France has seen a huge increase in goods transported by road in recent years (some 70 per cent of the total) and has around one vehicle for every two inhabitants. Traffic density and pollution in French cities is increasing and parking can be a problem (dealing with parking takes up 60 per cent of Paris' Highway Department's workload). Paris is one of Europe's most traffic-polluted cities and it often experiences poor air quality in summer. Some cities have drastically cut the number of vehicles entering the central area with dramatic results. For example Bordeaux has seen a reduction of 80 per cent in accidents since restricting traffic and instituting a system of buses and taxi-buses, and encouraging cyclists and pedestrians. France is in the forefront of the development of electric vehicles, which are now commercially available (see *pastille verte* on page 204).

Rush hours are from around 0630 to 0830 and 1630 to 1830, Mondays to Fridays, when town centres are best avoided. Paris is to be avoided by motorists at any time, where traffic moves at about the same speed as a hundred years ago (except for between 0200 and 0400). Friday afternoons are particularly busy on holiday weekends and also the period immediately before and after the lunch period, usually from around noon to 1500. Bottlenecks and traffic jams (*bouchons/embâcles*) are notorious at the start and end of holiday periods, particularly on roads out of Paris and other northern cities. Some areas and roads (particularly the *Autoroute du Soleil/de la Mort*) are to be avoided in July and August, when some six million Frenchmen and around over a million foreigners set off on their annual holidays. The most important days to stay at home are the first Saturday in August, when Parisians escape the city (*départ*) on their *grandes vacances*, and the last Sunday of August when they return (*la rentrée*). The 1st and 15th of July and the 15th August are also best avoided.

Anyone who has driven in France won't be surprised to learn that it has a high accident record, totalling some 8,000 to 9,000 deaths (16,000 in 1984!) and over 200,000 serious injuries a year – or around double that of Britain, Japan and the USA (in proportion to the number of vehicles). Given the Frenchman's *penchant* for a glass or two of *vin rouge* at lunchtime (or anytime), it isn't surprising that some 40 per cent of accidents involve drunken drivers (although the permitted alcohol level for motorists has been reduced). Somewhat surprisingly, France actually has *less* accidents than many other countries. However, if you have an accident in France your chances of reaching the next world are considerably increased.

CAR IMPORTATION

A new or used vehicle (including boats and planes) on which VAT (TVA) *has* been paid in another EU country can be imported into France free of French VAT by a French resident. If you buy a new or secondhand car abroad on which VAT *hasn't* been paid, VAT is due immediately on arrival in France. VAT is calculated on the invoice price if the vehicle is less than three months old or has clocked less than 3,000km (1,864mi), otherwise a reduction is made depending on its age (e.g. 25 per cent after three months) and VAT is payable on the balance. Many people buy a duty-free car and use it abroad for up to six months to reduce their French tax liability. However, if you're resident in France and buy a tax-free car abroad, you have a limited time to export it, e.g. two months when buying a car in Britain.

VAT rates are 28 per cent for imported motor vehicles and motorcycles over 240cc, and 20.6 per cent for caravans and motorcycles up to 240cc. VAT for imported motor-caravans is 28 per cent on two-thirds of their value and 20.6 per cent on the remaining one-third. In addition to VAT at 28 per cent, customs duty must be paid on cars imported from outside the EU. The rate of duty varies depending on the country of origin; some countries have reciprocal agreements with the EU resulting in lower duty rates. The amount of duty payable depends on the value of a vehicle in France, calculated using the *L'argus* guide to secondhand car prices (see page 199).

Tax must be paid in cash or by banker's draft at the point of importation or at the local tax office (*Hôtel/Recette des Impôts*) where you live in France. If you have a choice, it's preferable to pay at your local tax office. After you have paid VAT or confirmed that VAT isn't payable, you receive a customs certificate (*Certificat de Douane* 846A) permitting you to register the vehicle in France (see page 196). Note that you still require form 846A even when there's no VAT to pay, e.g. when importing a vehicle from another EU country. An imported vehicle must be registered in France within three months. However, before you can register it you must contact your local *Direction Régionale de l'Industrie, de la Recherche et de l'Environnement (DRIRE)*, who will send you a checklist of the documentation required, which may include:

● The customs certificate (*Certificat de Douane 846A*) mentioned above.

● A manufacturer's certificate of construction (*certificat/attestation de conformité*), obtainable from a local car dealer, the French importer or the manufacturer. This can cost as much as 700F! It's supposedly no longer required for cars manufactured within the EU, although in practice it's usually required even for left-hand drive French cars!

● A completed request for a registration card form (*Demande de Certificat d'Immatriculation d'un Véhicule*), available from your local *préfecture* or *préfecture de police*.

● Proof of origin of the vehicle (*justification de l'origine du véhicule*) or a certificate of sale (*certificat de vente*). These may not be required.

● The foreign registration document (*titre de circulation étranger*).

● A test certificate (*rapport de contrôle technique*), if necessary (see page 197). If a vehicle fails any of the tests it must be rectified and documentation provided to prove that this has been done (*justifications permettant d'établir qu'il à bien été*).

- The fee for the certification varies depending on the department and is around 200F, payable with a fiscal stamp (*timbre fiscal*) purchased from a *tabac*.
- You will also be asked for proof of your identity and residence in France.

When you have acquired the above documents and sent them to the DRIRE, an appointment will be made to inspect the vehicle at the local vehicle control centre (*centre de contrôle de véhicules* or *Inspecteur des Mines*). They will examine your car to ensure that it conforms to French construction and use regulations (type approval). After successfully negotiating this examination, the DRIRE issues a certificate (*procès verbal de réception à titre isolé*), which is necessary to apply for a registration certificate (*Certificat d'Immatriculation* or *carte grise*) from your local *préfecture* (see below). If you can provide an *attestation de conformité* with your car, then you won't need to go to the local vehicle control centre.

Note that some foreign cars don't conform to French construction and use regulations, and are expensive or even impossible to import. If you import a camper van, even one manufactured in France, the fixtures and fittings are likely to need modifying to conform with French regulations (unless it was equipped in France). It isn't usually wise to import a right-hand drive car, as it may be expensive to import and you will probably need to re-export it when you want to sell it.

CAR REGISTRATION

When you import a car into France or buy a new or secondhand car, it must be registered at the *préfecture* or *sous-préfecture* in the department where you're resident. In Paris, the registration is done by the *préfecture de police* or the town hall (*mairie*) of your *arrondissement*. If you import a car you must obtain customs clearance and have it inspected by the DRIRE before it can be registered (see above). When you buy a new car in France, the dealer usually arranges for the issue of the registration certificate (*carte grise*). When you buy a secondhand car you must apply for a new *carte grise* within 15 days of purchase, which can be done in person or by post. The fee for a *carte grise* varies depending on the size of a vehicle's engine, e.g. 1,100cc (400F), 1,250cc (500F) and 2,000cc (1,600F).

When you buy a secondhand car you must send or present the sales certificate (*certificat de vente*) that you received from the seller and the cancelled *carte grise* with your *carte de séjour* or passport. Never buy a car without a *carte grise* as it could be stolen. If you buy a car that isn't registered in your department, you also require a *certificat de non-gage* stating that the car isn't subject to a hire purchase agreement.

The last two digits of a car's registration number (*numéro d'immatriculation*) is the department number where it's registered. It's possible to obtain a sort of personalised registration number, e.g. a number that starts with a 1, 10 or 100 (the French President's is '1 PR 75'). If you move to a new address in the same department, you must inform your *préfecture* of your change of address. However, if you move to a new department you must re-register your car with the new *préfecture* within three months. You must present your old *carte grise*, *carte de séjour* and proof of residence and you may also be asked for a *certificat de résidence* obtainable from your local town hall.

When you receive a *carte grise* with a new registration number, e.g. after importing a car or moving to a new department, you must fit new registration plates within 48 hours. Plates are made on the spot by supermarkets and ironmongers (*quincaillerie*) on production of your *carte grise* (the cost is around 150F a pair). The small plate goes at the front and the larger one at the rear. Note that reflective number plates (white background at front, orange at rear) are obligatory on new vehicles and those requiring a new registration. A French registered car must, depending on its age, undergo a control test (see below), and be insured (see page 201) and taxed (see page 204).

If a woman marries and changes her name, it's unnecessary for her to replace her *carte grise*. If you lose your *carte grise* or have it stolen, you must report it to the police, who will issue you with a certificate allowing you to obtain a replacement from your *préfecture*.

CONTROL TEST

From 1st January 1996 cars over four years old have been required to have an official control test (*contrôle technique*) every two years, carried out at an authorised garage. Previously tests weren't exhaustive or rigorous and the only things that were required to pass the test were adequate brakes, lights and tyres. However, from 1996 the test (covering over 50 points) has been expanded to include steering, suspension, fuel tank, bodywork, seats, seatbelts, mirrors, windscreen, windscreen wipers and horn, all of which must be in good repair and functional. Around one-third of vehicles tested are found to be in unsatisfactory condition. The cost of the test is 350F and tested items are listed on a report (*certificat d'inspection/autobilan*). When you pass the test you receive a badge (*macaron*) which you must affix to your windscreen next to your tax *vignette* and insurance sticker (any more stickers and you won't be able to see out!). The test must be re-taken when a car over four years old is sold if the last test was completed more than six months previously. The fine for not having a test is 900F, which increases to 2,500F after one month!

Cars over 25 years old are classified as collector's items (*véhicule de collection*) and are exempt from the control test. Note that even if your car passes the control test, you can be stopped at any time by a routine police check and can be fined heavily if it isn't roadworthy, e.g. up to 900F for each tyre without 1.6mm of tread over its entire surface. Since January 1992, tyres purchased in France have incorporated a 'reference slug' to enable motorists to check tyre wear.

BUYING A CAR

If you've done much driving in France, you will no doubt have noticed that most Frenchmen drive French manufactured cars. This isn't simply chauvinism as French cars are usually very good and when they need servicing or break down you can get them repaired at reasonable cost at any local garage. Buying a German car is acceptable in France, particularly a BMW or Mercedes (although the neighbours will be insanely jealous), and in recent years Japanese cars have become more acceptable (particularly since Toyota are building a manufacturing plant in Valenciennes to open in 2001). Peugeot-Citroën has around 35 per cent of the French market, followed by Renault with some 30 per cent. The remaining 35 per cent is taken by importers with Fiat and Audi/VW the most dominant.

Whatever model you choose, unless you have got lots of money or are bent on driving a particular sports model, you should consider buying a diesel car, as diesel fuel costs around one-third less than petrol in France (see page 218). Note that the cost of running a car (e.g. insurance, taxes, petrol, maintenance and depreciation) in France is among the highest in the European Union.

New Cars

New car prices are lower in France than in many other European countries, particularly Britain, Holland, Ireland, Italy and Scandinavian countries. Most British-manufactured cars can be purchased in France for less than in Britain. However, many Frenchmen buy their cars in Belgium, where most cars are 10 to 15 per cent cheaper than in France. It's often cheaper to buy a new car from the factory of a European manufacturer or from an exporter in some countries, e.g. Belgium, Holland and Denmark. In some countries you can buy a tax-free car up to six months before exporting it. This can save you a significant sum, even when buying a French car. Personally importing a car from the USA is usually much cheaper than buying the same car in France or elsewhere in Europe. Before importing a car into France, you should ensure that it's manufactured to French specifications or you will encounter problems getting it approved by the DRIRE (see page 195).

Making comparisons between new car prices in different countries is often difficult, due to fluctuating exchange rates and the different levels of standard equipment. Most new cars are sold at list price in France, although you should still shop around for the best deal. The French government occasionally provides a subsidy of 10,000F for owners of old bangers who buy new cars (designed to help French car manufacturers).

Used Cars

Used cars (*voiture d'occasion*) in France are usually good value for money. It often pays to buy a car that's around two years old, as depreciation in the first two years is considerable. If you intend to buy a used car in France, whether privately or from a garage, check the following:

- that it has passed the official control test (see page 197), if applicable;

- that it hasn't been involved in a major accident and suffered structural damage. A declaration that it's accident free (*sans accident/non-accidenté*) should be obtained in writing;

- that the chassis number tallies with the *carte grise*, which should be in the name of the seller when sold privately;

- that the service coupons have been completed and stamped, and that servicing has been carried out by an authorised dealer;

- that the price roughly corresponds to that shown in the weekly *L'argus* guide (see below);

- that you receive a guarantee, signed by the vendor, stating that the car isn't under a hire purchase agreement (*certificat de non-gage*). This was introduced because many cars were being sold while still under a hire purchase agreement, leaving buyers with cars they didn't own.

- whether a written guarantee is provided.

Car dealers give warranties on used cars of from 3 to 24 months, depending on the age of the car and the particular model. Used car dealers, rather than franchised dealers, have the same dreadful (and well-deserved) reputation as in other countries and caution must be taken when buying from them. If you're buying a used car from a garage try to negotiate a reduction, particularly when you're paying cash and aren't trading in another vehicle.

The best journals for finding a used car are *La Centrale des Particuliers* and *Auto Journal*, both published monthly. All national and local (including free) newspapers carry advertisements for used cars. A weekly guide to secondhand car prices is provided in the *L'argus* magazine, which also lists thousands of cars for sale. *Argus* values are updated every six months and are used throughout the industry, for example by dealers when buying or selling cars and by insurance companies when calculating values for insurance premiums and claims. You should pay within around 10 per cent of the *Argus* value either way, depending on a car's condition. Secondhand prices vary depending on the region of France and are generally higher in remote areas than in Paris and other major cities.

SELLING A CAR

Before selling a car in France you must obtain a certificate of sale (*certificat de vente*) form from your town hall, *préfecture* or a garage selling cars. The certificate of sale must be completed in duplicate, a copy of which is given to the buyer and the other is sent to the registration office. When selling a car you must give the buyer the purchase invoice, the control test badge (see page 197), the tax vignette (with the receipt) and the registration certificate (*carte grise*). Before handing over the *carte grise*, write 'sold to' and the buyer's name (*Vendu à 'name of buyer'*), and sign and date it. Don't forget to remove your insurance vignette (*vignette d'assurance*) from the windscreen. You must also provide a signed guarantee (*certificat de non-gage*) that the car isn't under a hire purchase or lease agreement. Other points to note when selling a car are:

● Inform your insurance company.

● When selling a car privately, insist on payment in cash or with a banker's draft (*chèque de banque*), which is standard practice in France. If you cannot tell a banker's draft from a personal cheque, insist on cash. **Never accept a personal cheque.**

● Include in the receipt that you're selling the car in its present condition (as seen) without a guarantee (*sans garantie*), the price paid and the car's kilometre reading. The new owner may ask for a declaration in writing that the car is accident free (*sans accident/non-accidenté*). This refers to major accidents causing structural damage and not slight knocks.

● The best place to advertise a car for sale is in local newspapers, on free local notice boards, and in the Friday and Saturday editions of major newspapers. Many people also put a for sale (*à vendre*, often reduced to AV) notice in their car with a telephone number and park it in a prominent place.

DRIVING LICENCE

The minimum age for driving in France is 18 for a motor car or motorcycle over 125cc and 14 for a motorcycle (moped) below 50cc. Holders of most foreign driving licences can drive in France for one year on a foreign or international driving licence from the date of receipt of their residence permit (*carte de séjour*). If you or any members of your family hold a foreign driving licence and intend to remain in France longer than one year, then the procedure is as follows:

EU Members: The Second EU Driving Licence Directive provides, among other things, for the mutual recognition of driving licences issued by EU Member States. If EU citizens move from one Member State to another, it's no longer necessary to obtain a local driving licence after one year. **However, a resident who commits a motoring offence in France involving a loss of licence points (see below) is obliged to exchange his foreign licence for a French one so that the penalty may be applied.**

Non-EU Members: After residence of one year, a French driving licence is required by non-EU residents. You should expect the procedure to take at least two months, so should apply to the *Préfecture* or *Sous-préfecture* well before the year is up. You will need a valid, translated driver's licence; proof of domicile; your *carte de séjour*; two passport-size photographs; and the fee in the form of fiscal stamps (*timbre fiscal*). Some countries and some states within the United States have reciprocal agreements with France to waive the driving test, but applicants must take the written exam concerning rules of the road (including road sign recognition). If you need to take a driving test, it's advisable to take a course through a certified driving school, some of which have sections for English speakers. The French Highway Code (*Code de la Route*) is available at most bookshops. The French authorities will confiscate your foreign driving licence and return it to the country of issue or retain it and return it to you when you leave France permanently. It's advisable to make a copy of your foreign licence before surrendering it, as your French licence will show that you have only been driving since it was issued (which may make life difficult if you want to rent a car). A French driving licence is pink in colour and contains a photograph.

You can have your licence suspended in France for 7 to 28 days for minor offences and for up to six years or longer for manslaughter. Suspensions of a French driving licence for six months or longer are based on a controversial points system that came into effect on 1st December 1992. All drivers start with 12 licence points and from one to six points are deducted for offences, depending on their gravity. Typical offences are failing to dip headlights and minor speeding (one point, although speeding can 'earn' up to four points); parking on the hard shoulder of an *autoroute* or accelerating while being overtaken (two points); driving on the wrong side of the road (Britons beware!) and dangerous overtaking (three points); injuring somebody or failure to observe a stop sign or red light (four points); and for killing somebody or driving under the influence of alcohol (six points). The points system is explained in a booklet *permis à points* available from police stations.

When an offence is registered, you receive a letter of notification from the *préfecture* stating the number of points lost and the number remaining. All points are regained if no offences are committed within three years of your last conviction. When all 12 points have been lost, you receive a demand to hand over your licence within one week to your local *préfecture* and you're usually banned from driving for a minimum of six months. Depending on the circumstances, you may need to pass a written test, a practical driving test (e.g. drivers with less than three years' experience) or a medical examination to regain your licence. If you lose your French driving licence or it's stolen, you must report it to the police. They will issue you with an acknowledgement (*récépissé de déclaration de perte ou de vol de pièces d'identité*) that's valid until a replacement is issued. Note that a replacement licence may cost twice as much as the original.

For more information on the subject of licences, contact the *Ministère de l'Équipement, des Transports et du Logement,* Arche de la Défense, 92055 La Défense CEDEX (Internet: www.equipement.gouv.fr).

CAR INSURANCE

Under French law, all motor vehicles plus trailers and semi-trailers must be insured when entering France. However, it isn't mandatory for cars insured in most European countries to have an international insurance 'green' card (*carte internationale d'assurance automobile/carte verte*) in France. Motorists insured in an EU country or the Czech Republic, Hungary, Liechtenstein, Norway, the Slovak Republic and Switzerland are automatically covered for third party liability in France. If you arrive in France with a vehicle without valid insurance, you can buy a temporary policy valid for 8, 15 or 30 days from the vehicle insurance department of the French customs office at your point of entry. The following categories of car insurance are available in France:

Third Party (*responsabilité civile/minimale/tiers illimitée*): Third Party insurance is compulsory and includes unlimited medical costs and damage to third party property.

Third Party, Fire & Theft (*tiers personnes/restreinte/intermédiaire*): Third party, fire and theft (TPF&T) insurance, known in some countries as part comprehensive, includes cover against fire, natural hazards (e.g. rocks falling on your car), theft, broken glass (e.g. windscreen) and legal expenses (*défense-recours*). TPF&T includes damage (or theft) to contents and radio.

Multi-risk Collision (*multirisque collision*): Multi-risk collision covers all risks listed under TPF&T plus damage caused to your own vehicle in the event of a collision with a person, vehicle, or animal belonging to an **identifiable person.**

Fully Comprehensive - all accidents (*multirisque tous accidents/tous risques*): Fully comprehensive insurance covers all the risks listed under TPF&T and multi-risk collision and includes damage to your vehicle however caused and **whether a third party can be identified or not.** Note, however, that illegally parked cars automatically lose their comprehensive cover. Fully comprehensive insurance is usually compulsory for lease and credit purchase contracts.

Driver protection (*protection du conducteur/assurance conducteur*) is usually optional in France and can be added to insurance policies. It enables the driver of a vehicle involved in an accident to claim for bodily injury to himself, including compensation for his incapacity to work or for his beneficiaries should he be killed.

Premiums: Insurance premiums are high in France – a reflection of the high accident rate and the large number of stolen cars. Premiums vary considerably depending on numerous factors including the type of insurance; your car, age and accident record; and the area where you live. Premiums are highest in Paris and other cities and lowest in rural areas. Premiums are lower for cars over three years old.

Some premiums are based on the number of kilometres (*kilométrage*) driven each year. Always shop around and obtain a number of quotations. Value added tax (TVA) is payable on insurance premiums in France.

You can reduce your premium by choosing to pay an excess (*franchise*), e.g. the first 2,000F to 5,000F of a claim. Special insurance can be purchased for contents and accessories such as an expensive car stereo system. A car with a value of over 100,000F must have an approved alarm installed and the registration number must be engraved on all windows. A surcharge is made when a car isn't garaged over night. Drivers with less than three years' experience usually pay a penalty (*malus*) and drivers under 25 pay higher premiums. However, the maximum penalty for young drivers due to their age is 100 per cent or double the normal premium. If you're convicted of drunken or dangerous driving, your premium will be increased considerably, e.g. by up to 150 per cent. It's possible to insure a vehicle for less than one year (e.g. three months) and you can also insure a vehicle for a single journey over 1,000km (621mi).

No-Claims: A foreign no-claims bonus is usually valid in France, but you must provide written evidence from your present or previous insurance company, not just an insurance renewal notice. You may also need an official French translation. Always insist on having your no-claims bonus recognised, even if you don't receive the same reduction as you received abroad (shop around!). If you haven't held car insurance for two years, you're usually no longer entitled to a no-claims bonus in France.

The no-claims bonus isn't as generous as in some other countries and is usually 5 per cent for each year's accident-free driving up to a maximum of 50 per cent after ten years. If you have an accident, you're usually required to pay a penalty (*malus*) or your bonus is reduced. Your premium will be increased by 25 per cent each time you're responsible for an accident or 12.5 per cent if you're partly to blame, up to a maximum penalty of 150 per cent after six accidents. However, if you have had the maximum bonus for three years, one accident won't reduce it. If you're only partly to blame for an accident, e.g. less than 50 per cent, your premium increase is reduced by half. There's no premium increase if your car is damaged while parked (although you must be able to prove it and identify the party responsible) or as a result of fire, theft, or glass breakage, and you should still receive your bonus for the current year.

Claims: In the event of an accident, claims are decided on the information provided in accident report forms (*Constat à l'Amiable/Constat Européen d'Accident*) completed by drivers, reports by insurance company experts and police reports (see **Accidents** on page 215). If you're judged to be less than 30 per cent responsible, you won't usually lose your no-claims bonus. You must notify your insurance company of a claim within a limited period, e.g. two to five days. If you have an accident, the damage must usually be inspected and the repair sanctioned by your insurance company's assessor, although sometimes an independent assessment may be permitted. For minor repairs, an inspection may be unnecessary. After reporting your car stolen, 30 days must elapse before an insurance company will consider a claim. Note that it often takes a long time to resolve claims in France and a number of years isn't unusual!

Cancellation: French insurance companies are forbidden by law to cancel third party cover after a claim, except in the case of drunken driving or when a driver is subsequently disqualified from driving for longer than one month. A company can, however, refuse to renew your policy at the end of the current period, although they must give you two months' notice. If you have an accident while breaking the law, e.g. drunken driving or illegal parking, your comprehensive insurance may be automatically downgraded to third party only. This means that you must pay for your own repairs and medical expenses. If you find it difficult to obtain cover, the *Bureau Central de Tarification* can demand that the company of your choice provide you with cover, with the premium being fixed by the *Bureau*.

If you wish to cancel your car insurance at the end of the current term, you must notify your insurance company in writing by registered letter and give three months notice. You may cancel your insurance without notice if the premium is increased, the terms are altered, or your car has been declared a total loss or stolen. Policies can also be cancelled for certain personal reasons such as moving house, divorce or retirement.

Green Card: All French insurance companies and most other insurance companies in Western Europe provide an automatic 'green' card (yellow in France!), extending your normal insurance cover (e.g. fully comprehensive) to most other European countries. This doesn't, however, include cars insured in Britain, where most insurance companies (the Prudential Assurance Co. is one exception) usually provide a free green card for from 30 or 45 days to a maximum of three months a year. Nevertheless, you should shop around as some companies allow drivers a green card for up to six months a year. This is to discourage the British from driving on the continent, where they are a menace and a danger to other road users (most don't know their left from their right, particularly the politicians!). If you're British and have fully comprehensive insurance, it's wise to have a green card when visiting France.

If you drive a British-registered car and spend over six months a year on the continent, you may need to take out a special (i.e. expensive) European insurance policy or obtain insurance with a European company. Note that many French insurance companies will insure foreign-registered cars, although it may be for a limited period only. French regulations have traditionally required French-registered cars to be insured with a French insurance company. However, theoretically from 1st January 1993, EU residents can insure their cars in any EU country.

Breakdown Insurance: French insurance companies provide an optional accident and breakdown service, e.g. with Mondial Assistance, for policyholders for a fee of around 200F a year. This is adopted by some 90 per cent of French motorists. The breakdown service usually covers the policyholder, his spouse, single dependant children, and parents and grandparents living under the same roof. The 24-hour telephone number of the breakdown service's head office is shown on the insurance tab affixed to your windscreen. If you break down anywhere in France, you simply call the emergency number, give your location and a recovery vehicle is sent to your aid. Although accidents are covered anywhere in France, in the event of a breakdown you need to be a certain distance from your home, e.g. 25 or 50km (15 to 31mi).

The service provides for towing your vehicle to the nearest garage and contributes towards the expenses incurred as a result of a breakdown or an accident, e.g. alternative transportation and hotel bills. If your car is unusable for more than 48 hours in France and over five days abroad, your insurance company will usually pay for alternative transport home, e.g. 1st class rail travel or car hire in France or tourist class air fare abroad. The retrieval of your vehicle is also guaranteed from within France or abroad.

In France, an insurance certificate has a stick-on tab or vignette (*vignette d'assurance*) that must be displayed on your windscreen next to the road tax vignette (see below). Driving without insurance is a serious offence, for which you can be fined up to 50,000F and imprisoned for up to six months. France has a national fund (*Fonds de garantie automobile*) that pays compensation to victims of hit-and-run drivers (see page 216). See also **Insurance Contracts** on page 253.

ROAD TAX

All French registered vehicles must display a road tax certificate (*vignette automobile*), introduced in the early '60s (not to raise money for new roads, but to help finance the national pension scheme!). The amount payable each year varies depending on the horsepower (*puissance fiscale*) of a vehicle, its age and the department where it's registered. The tax rate is fixed each year by each department and can vary by 25 per cent or more. The amount payable ranges from zero (certain owners/vehicles are exempt) to over 4,000F a year for a top-category limousine. Most cars fall into the bottom two rates (A1/A2) which range from 146F (Marne) to 328F (Cantal) for category A1 and from 278F (Marne) to 596F (Cantal) for category A2. The average rates are around 275F (A1) and 500F (A2). The rate is halved for vehicles over five years old at the start of the year and vehicles over 25 years old, classified as *véhicules de collection*, are exempt.

The tax vignette for the following year must be purchased by 30th November from a *bureau de tabac* and must be displayed by the 1st December. There are fines for late payment and you must buy your vignette from the nearest préfecture and pay 10 per cent extra. If you purchase a new or previously untaxed car after December but before 15th August, you pay a portion of the fee that's decided by your *préfecture*. If you buy a car after 15th August, you don't pay road tax until the following year. When you buy a secondhand car that has been used in the current year the vignette should be provided with it.

The tax vignette must be displayed at the right-hand edge of the windscreen with your insurance vignette and control test badge. Vignettes don't contain a car's registration number (a terrible system!) and are therefore frequently stolen. Theft of vignettes is particularly common in November and December when they are new, and some motorists even leave their cars unlocked so that vignette thieves won't break a window to gain access! Keep the receipt for your vignette with your other car papers, as this proves that you didn't acquire it illegally and also enables you to obtain a replacement should it be stolen. If you need to replace your vignette, visit any tax office (*recette des impôts*) and produce your receipt. If you lose your receipt, you can obtain another from the issuing office, which keeps a record of payments.

In 1998, a green disc (*pastille verte*) was introduced for electric and gas-operated vehicles, catalysed, petrol-driven vehicles manufactured since 1993, and diesel vehicles manufactured since 1997. The disc is provided by the car distributor for new cars or can be obtained for the *préfecture*. The disc must be displayed on the windscreen and cars displaying it receive fiscal benefits and are the only vehicles allowed to circulate in cities such as Paris on bad air quality days (level 3). Discs should be renewed every two years.

When vehicle and petrol taxes are included, the French are the highest taxed motorists in Europe, even without the high *autoroute* tolls (which can be considered a form of taxation as in many countries the construction of motorways is financed from vehicle or general taxes).

GENERAL ROAD RULES

The following general road rules may help you adjust to driving in France. Don't, however, expect other motorists to adhere to them (many French drivers invent their own 'rules').

● You may have already noticed that the French drive on the right-hand side of the road (*serrez à droite*). It saves confusion if you do likewise! If you aren't used to driving on the right, take it easy until you're accustomed to it. Be particularly alert when leaving lay-bys, T-junctions, one-way streets, petrol stations and car parks, as it's easy to lapse into driving on the left. It's helpful to display a reminder (e.g. 'think right!') on your car's dashboard.

● All motorists must carry a red breakdown triangle and a full set of spare bulbs and fuses. It's advisable, but not mandatory, to carry a fire extinguisher and a first-aid kit.

● In towns you may be faced with a bewildering array of road markings, signs and traffic lights. If you're ever in doubt about who has priority, always give way to trams, buses and all traffic coming from your RIGHT. Emergency (ambulance, fire, police) and public utility (electricity, gas, telephone, water) vehicles attending an emergency have priority on all roads.

● Most main roads are designated priority roads (*passages protégés*), indicated by one of three signs. The most common priority sign is a yellow diamond on a white background, in use throughout most of Europe. The end of priority is shown by the same sign with a black diagonal line through it. The other two signs are a triangular crossroad sign with the words *passage protégé* underneath and a triangular sign showing a broad vertical arrow with a thinner horizontal line through it. On secondary roads *without* priority signs and in built-up areas, you must give way to vehicles coming from your RIGHT. **Failure to observe this rule is the cause of many accidents.**

The priority rule was fine when there was little traffic, but nowadays most countries (France included) realise the necessity of having 'stop' or 'give way' (*Cédez le Passage*) signs. Most French motorists no longer treat *priorité à droite* as a God-given right, although some still pull out without looking. The priority to the right rule usually also applies in car parks, but never when exiting *from* car parks or dirt tracks. If you're ever in doubt about who has the right of way, it's wise to give way (particularly to large trucks!).

● On roundabouts (*giratoires*), vehicles on the roundabout have priority and not those entering it, who are faced with a give way sign (*cédez le passage* or even *vous n'avez pas la priorité*). Traffic flows anti-clockwise round roundabouts and not clockwise as in Britain and other countries driving on the left. Although the British think roundabouts are marvellous (we spend most of our time going round in circles), they aren't so popular on the continent of Europe, although in recent years the French have taken to them with great enthusiasm (although many drivers still haven't a clue how to use them) and new ones are springing up everywhere.

- The wearing of seatbelts is *compulsory* in France and includes passengers in rear seats when seatbelts are fitted. Front belts are mandatory on cars registered after January 1965 and rear seatbelts on cars registered after October 1978. Children under the age of ten may ride in the front of a vehicle only when an approved seat is fitted (facing rearwards) or when a vehicle has no back seat. Children aged under ten riding in the rear must use a special seat or a safety belt suitable for children. A baby under nine months old must be strapped into a cot or special car seat on the rear seat and an infant from nine months to three years old must have an approved child safety seat. You can be fined up to 500F for not wearing a seatbelt. Note that if you have an accident and weren't wearing a seatbelt, your insurance company can refuse to pay a claim for personal injury.

- Don't drive in bus, taxi or cycle lanes (you can be fined for doing so) unless necessary to avoid a stationary vehicle or another obstruction. Bus drivers get irate if you drive in their lanes, identified by a continuous yellow line parallel to the kerb. Be sure to keep clear of tram lines and outside the restricted area, delineated by a line.

- The use of horns are forbidden in towns at night, when lights should be flashed to warn other motorists or pedestrians. In towns, horns should be used only in emergencies, day or night.

- It's illegal to drive on parking (side) lights at any time. Headlamps must be dipped (low beam) when you're following a vehicle or when a vehicle is approaching from the opposite direction. Failure to dip your lights can cost you a penalty point on your licence. Note that headlight flashing has different meanings in different countries. In some countries it means "after you" in others "get out of my way" or "I have priority" (usually the case in France). It may also mean "I am driving a new car and haven't yet worked out what all the switches are for!" Drivers sometimes warn other motorists of police radar traps and road-blocks by flashing their headlights. This is illegal and you can be fined for doing it (it also prevents the police from catching 'real' criminals such as armed robbers). A vehicle's hazard warning lights may be used to warn other drivers of an obstruction, e.g. an accident or a traffic jam.

- The sequence of French traffic lights (*feux tricolores/feux de circulation*) is red, green, yellow (amber) and back to red. Yellow means stop at the stop line; you may proceed only if the yellow light appears after you have crossed the stop line or when stopping may cause an accident. Traffic lights are often suspended above the road, although most are on posts at the side, with smaller lights lower down at eye level for motorists who are too close to see the main lights (an excellent idea). In Paris and other cities there's a two-second delay after one set of lights change to red before the other set change to green, to allow time for those who don't care to stop at red lights or cannot tell the difference between red and green. You can be fined around 2,000F for running a red light, which also earns you four penalty points on your licence (or a ticket to the next life!).

  A yellow or green filter light, usually flashing and with a direction arrow, may be shown in addition to the main signal. This means that you may drive in the direction shown by the arrow, but must give priority to pedestrians or other traffic. If you get into the wrong lane by mistake, you will no doubt be informed by the irate honking of motorists behind you! Flashing yellow lights are a warning to proceed with caution. Occasionally you will see a flashing red light, meaning stop or no entry, e.g. at a railway level crossing.

● Always come to a complete stop when required at intersections and ensure that you stop behind the white line (intersections are a favourite spot for police patrols waiting for motorists to put a wheel a few centimetres over the line).

● White or yellow lines mark the separation of traffic lanes. A solid single line or two solid lines means no overtaking (*dépasser*) in either direction. A solid line to the right of the centre line, i.e. on your side of the road, means that overtaking is prohibited in your direction. You may overtake only when there's a single broken line in the middle of the road or double lines with a broken line on your side of the road. No overtaking may also be shown by the international sign of two cars side by side (one red and one black). Processions, funerals or foot soldiers mustn't be overtaken at more than 30kph (18mph).

Always check your rear view and wing mirrors carefully before overtaking as French motorists seem to appear from nowhere and zoom past at a 'zillion' miles an hour, especially on country roads. If you drive a right-hand drive (RHD) car, take extra care when overtaking – the most dangerous manoeuvre in motoring. It's wise to have a special 'overtaking mirror' fitted to a RHD car.

● Many motorists seem to have an aversion to driving in the right-hand lane on a three-lane *autoroute*, in effect reducing it to two lanes. It's illegal to overtake on an inside lane unless traffic is being channelled in a different direction. Motorists must indicate before overtaking *and* when moving back into an inside lane after overtaking, e.g. on an *autoroute*.

● Studded tyres may be used from 1st November to 31st March (although this can be extended in bad weather conditions) on vehicles weighing under 3.5 tonnes. Vehicles fitted with studded tyres or snow chains are restricted to a maximum speed of 90kph (56mph) and a '90' disc must be affixed to the rear. Note that you can be fined for not having snow chains (in your car) in winter in mountain areas, even when there's no snow!

● Take care when crossing railway lines, particularly at crossings with no barriers, which can be *very* dangerous. Approach a railway level crossing slowly and **STOP**:

– as soon as the barrier or half-barrier starts to fall;

– as soon as the red warning lights are illuminated or flashing, or the warning bell is ringing;

– when a train approaches!

Your new car may be built like a tank, but it won't look so smart after a scrap with a 70-tonne locomotive.

● Be particularly wary of moped (*vélomoteur*) riders and cyclists. It isn't always easy to see them, particularly when they're hidden by the blind spots of a car or are riding at night without lights. Many young moped riders seem to have a death wish and tragically hundreds lose their lives each year in France (maybe 14 years of age is too young to let them loose on the roads!). They are constantly pulling out into traffic or turning without looking or signalling. **Follow the example set by French motorists, who, when overtaking mopeds and cyclists, ALWAYS give them a wide . . . . WIDE berth.** If you knock them off their bikes you may have a difficult time convincing the police that it wasn't your fault; far better to avoid them (and the police).

- An 'F' nationality plate (*plaque de nationalité*) must be affixed to the rear of a French-registered car when motoring abroad and drivers of foreign registered cars in France must have the appropriate nationality plate affixed to the rear of their cars. You can be fined on the spot for not displaying it, although it isn't often enforced judging by the number of cars without them.

- Cars mustn't be overloaded, particularly roofracks, and luggage weight shouldn't exceed that recommended in manufacturers' handbooks. Note that carrying bicycles on the back of a car is illegal if they obscure the rear lights or the registration number. French police make spot checks and fine offenders around 500F on the spot. If you want to transport bikes in France you should have a roof-mounted rack and (if necessary) a boot rack for transportation on a ferry.

- It's illegal to use car telephones in foreign-registered private cars, unless they are licensed for use in France, e.g. those that conform to GSM standards. CB radios operating on 26,960 to 27,410 Mhz may be used by visitors with a national licence, providing it bears the licencee's agreement number, the power doesn't exceed four watts and the maximum number of channels is 40. Not surprisingly, French and other continental CB users cannot be contacted with equipment using a different frequency.

- The maximum dimensions for caravans or trailers are 2.5m (8.2ft) wide and 11m (36ft) long, or a combined length of 18m (59ft) for car and caravan/trailer combined. No passengers may be carried in a moving caravan. On narrow roads, drivers towing a caravan or trailer are (where possible) required to slow or pull into the side of the road to allow faster vehicles to overtake (although they rarely do). The speed limits for a towing car depends on the weight of the trailer or caravan (see **Speed Limits** on page 219).

- All motorists in France must be familiar with the French highway code (*Code de la Route*), available from bookshops throughout France.

TRAFFIC POLICE

In France, the *gendarmerie nationale/gardes-mobiles* (*gendarmes* for short) are responsible for road patrols and use both cars and motorcycles (*motards*). On-the-spot fines can be imposed for a range of traffic offences including speeding, not being in possession of your car papers and not wearing a seatbelt. The police can insist on a fixed penalty fine being paid on-the-spot in cash. This is common when dealing with non-resident foreigners, whose vehicles are usually impounded if they're unable to pay a fine on the spot. French police are totally indifferent to anyone without cash, although they may take you to a bank to get some. It's well-known that French traffic police target foreigners, although it's naturally officially denied (if France's highwaymen don't get your money the *gendarmes* will). It certainly looks a bit suspicious when police produce pre-written tickets in English! One of the latest money-making schemes is fining motorists for transporting bicycles on the rear of a car.

Residents who are unable to pay fines on the spot are given 30 days to pay and fines are automatically increased (significantly) if they aren't paid on time. A 30 per cent reduction is granted to residents who pay a fine on the spot or within 24 hours. You can choose to go to court rather than pay a fixed penalty, in which case you must usually pay a deposit (*amende forfaiture*). If a court subsequently finds you guilty, you must invariably pay a higher fine. Fines can be *very* severe, e.g. up to 5,000F for speeding and as much as 30,000F for drunken driving.

Police can demand a maximum 'fine' of 900F on-the-spot, although strictly speaking this isn't a fine but a deposit against a fine that may be imposed by a court at a later date. Where applicable, you receive a receipt showing that a payment is a deposit. The papers are sent to a police court (*tribunal de police*) where the case is dealt with in your absence. The case can be dismissed (extremely rare), the 900F fine confirmed (actually an 850F fine plus 50F costs) or the fine increased. You receive the verdict in the form of an *ordonnance pénale* and have 30 days to appeal against the judgement, should you wish to do so.

The police can stop motorists (called a *contrôle*) and ask for identification and car papers at any time (and also check your car tyres, etc.). You should always carry your passport or residence permit (*carte de séjour*), driving licence (French if held), vehicle registration papers (*carte grise*) and insurance certificate. If a vehicle isn't registered in your name, you will also need a letter of authorisation from the owner. If you're driving a rented foreign-registered vehicle, you should ask the rental company for a 'hired/leased vehicle certificate'. It's advisable to make a copy of your car papers and keep the originals on your person or lock them in the glove box of your car.

FRENCH ROADS

France has a good road system that includes everything from motorways (*autoroutes*) to forest dirt tracks. French *autoroutes* are excellent and most other main roads are also very good, although roads are generally poorer in the more remote departments with a low traffic density. Some 20 years ago France had fewer miles of motorways than many other western European countries. Since then there has been a huge investment in *autoroutes*, mainly by the private sector, and today France boasts one of the best motorway networks in Europe totalling over 8,000km (some 5,000mi). Because of the continuous expansion of the network, you shouldn't use a motoring atlas that's more than a few years out of date. A good guide to French *autoroutes* and their services is *Bonne Route!* by Anna Fitter (Anthony Nelson).

However, on the negative side, French *autoroutes* are toll roads (*autoroutes à péage*) and are among the most expensive in Europe. *Autoroute* travel costs an average of 0.40F per kilometre for a light car, e.g. 385F from Calais to Montpellier and 445F from Calais to Menton (not a great deal less than what it costs to fly with a budget airline from London to Nice!). A new system of tolls has been introduced in some areas with higher tolls during peak periods (an *autoroute tarifs* leaflet is available from the Association des Sociétés Françaises d'Autoroutes, 3 rue Edmond Valentin, 75007 Paris, ☎ 01.47.05.90.01). Goods vehicles over 7.5 tonnes are banned from roads between 1000 Saturday and 2200 Sunday, and from 2200 on the eve of a public holiday to 2200 on the day of the holiday. In Paris, goods vehicles aren't permitted to travel out of the city from 1600 to 1900 on Fridays to allow car drivers to get a head start for the weekend. However, although you may need to take out a second mortgage to drive on them, *autoroutes* are France's safest roads (e.g. you cannot get hit by a Frenchman overtaking on a blind bend).

There are five vehicle categories on most *autoroutes*, and caravans and motorhomes are more expensive than cars. Rates aren't standardised throughout the country and vary depending on the age of the *autoroute* and the services provided (some are twice as expensive as others). There are no tolls on the sections of *autoroutes* around cities. Most European currencies (banknotes only) are accepted in payment and tolls can also be paid by Carte Bleue, Mastercard or Visa (some accept Eurocheques, but not traveller's cheques). You can also have an account that permits you to use special *Télépéage Automatique* exits.

On most *autoroutes* a ticket is issued at the entrance or shortly afterwards. At the toll-booth (*péage*) you may need to press a button to obtain your ticket or it may be ejected automatically. When you reach another toll-booth or exit from the *autoroute*, hand your ticket to the attendant; the toll due is usually shown on a display. Tolls may also be levied at intermediate points. On some stretches, tickets aren't issued and a fixed toll is charged. On these roads there may be unmanned toll-booths for those with the correct change, shown by the sign *Monnaie Exacte*. Throw the correct amount into the basket and wait for the light to change green. If you don't have the correct change, choose a lane with the sign *Sans Monnaie* (which means no change and not no money!).

Most *autoroutes* and *routes nationales* have rest stops (*aires de repos*) every 10 to 20km (6 to 12mi) with toilets, drinking water and picnic tables. Toilets and public telephones are also provided at *autoroute* toll booths. Rest stops aren't alternative camping sites for caravans and toll charges are valid for 24 hours only. Note that *autoroute* exit points are usually few and far between and there can be large distances between service stations. Twenty-four hour service areas (*aires de service*) are provided every 30 to 50km (19 to 31mi) on *autoroutes*, with filling stations, vending machines, shops (selling newspapers, gifts, food, snacks and hot drinks), a café or self-service restaurant, and possibly an *à la carte* restaurant. Service areas cater for babies, young children, the elderly and the handicapped, and some also have motels and provide tourist information services. In the summer, roadside attractions are set up at service areas aimed at reducing stress and tiredness. These may include bouncy castles and clown shows for children, free nappies and meals for babies, and massages for drivers!

Note that although they're usually of a high standard, *autoroute* restaurants are mainly self-service rather than *haute cuisine* and don't offer the best value. They should be avoided between noon and 1500 when *all* of France eats. You will save money by leaving the *autoroute* and finding an inexpensive and friendly local establishment. Petrol prices on *autoroutes* are the highest in France and it's much cheaper to fill up at supermarkets. Not surprisingly, service stations have better (i.e. cleaner) toilet facilities than rest stops. Service stations often have facilities for minor car repairs. Signs on *autoroutes* inform you about interesting local sights and features, and regional *autoroute* maps are distributed free by operators. On *autoroutes* there's an excellent system of electronic information boards on overhead gantries, where everything from the temperature to accident reports are displayed.

If you break down on an *autoroute* you must park your car on the hard shoulder and place an emergency triangle 30 metres behind it. Emergency telephones (*poste d'urgence*) are mounted on orange posts every 2km (1.24mi) on *autoroutes* and you may walk along the hard shoulder to the nearest phone, indicated by arrows. Each telephone is individually numbered and directly connected to the *autoroute* security centre (*Centre de Sécurité*). Just tell them whether you have broken down (*panne*) or have had an accident (*accident*), and give the number of your telephone and the location of your car, i.e. before (*avant*) or after (*après*) the emergency telephone. They will arrange for either a breakdown truck (*dépanneur*) or first-aid help (*service de secours*) to be sent, as required. A multi-language service is provided in English, German, Italian and Spanish on some *autoroutes*, e.g. the A7 between Lyon and Marseilles.

Minor repairs of up to around half an hour are usually done on the spot. For anything more serious you will need to be towed to a garage. There are fixed charges for emergency repairs and towing, e.g. 411F for requesting a breakdown service and 528F for repairing a vehicle on the spot (up to 30 minutes work) or towing it up to 5km (3mi) beyond the next *autoroute* exit. There's a 25 per cent supplement at nights and at weekends. If you're unable to continue your journey, breakdown companies must provide free transport to take you and your passengers off the *autoroute*, and provide assistance in finding accommodation and alternative transportation.

For many Frenchmen, driving on *autoroutes* is a luxury and consequently they have the lowest traffic density of any European motorways. Unlike motorways in most other countries, French *autoroutes* have few access points and exits, which coupled with the high tolls, tends to discourage casual and local users. The same cannot be said of main trunk roads (*routes nationales*), which are jammed by drivers who are reluctant to pay or cannot afford the high *autoroute* tolls. If you must get from A to B in the shortest possible time, then there's no alternative to the *autoroute* (apart from taking a plane or train). However, if you aren't in too much of a hurry, want to save money *and* wish to see something of France, you should avoid *autoroutes*. The money saved on tolls can pay for a good meal or an (inexpensive) hotel room and you'll arrive feeling much better. *Routes nationales* and other secondary roads are often straight (and dual carriageways) and you can usually make good time at (legal) speeds of between 80 and 110kph. Tolls are also levied to use the Mont Blanc (Chamonix-Entrèves, Italy, 11.6km/7.2mi), Fréjus (Modane-Bardonecchia, Italy, 12.8km/8mi) and Bielsa (Aragnouet-Bielsa, Spain, 3km/1.86mi) tunnels, and the Tancarville, St. Nazaire and Pont de Normandie bridges.

Driving in Paris is the motoring equivalent of hell – it's a beautiful city, but should be avoided at all costs when driving. If you cannot avoid driving in Paris, at least give the *Place Charles de Gaulle/Étoile (Arc de Triomphe)* a wide berth, which is one of the worst free-for-alls in the whole of Europe. This is a vast roundabout where 12 roads converge, all with (theoretical) *priorité à droite*. Because of the impossibility of apportioning blame in this circus, if you have an accident responsibility is automatically shared equally between the drivers concerned, irrespective of who had right of way (you have been warned!). The *Périphérique* is an eight lane race track around Paris, which although better than actually driving in Paris, is to be avoided if possible, particularly if you aren't sure which exit to take. Paris accommodates some three million vehicles a day, a third on the *Périphérique* ring road, although an advanced electronic traffic management system ensures that traffic keeps moving most of the time.

All 'N' and 'D' class roads (see below) have white kilometre stones on the right and some have smaller stones every 100 metres. On 'N' class roads the tops of kilometre stones are painted red and have the road number painted on the side. Kilometre stones on 'D' class roads have yellow tops. In general, signposting in France is good, even in the most remote rural areas, thanks largely to the vast numbers of tourists who invade France each year. However, in some areas you will find that signs disappear or everywhere is signposted except where you want to go, and signs out of towns may be non-existent. Usually only large towns or cities are signposted as you approach a ring road system, so you should plan your journey accordingly and make a note of the major destinations on your route. Road signs in cities are often mind-boggling in their number and variety. Note that signposts indicating straight ahead usually point at or across the intended road, i.e. to the left or right, rather than 'up in the air' as in most other countries.

In towns, only the town centre (*centre ville*) and 'all directions' (*toutes directions*) may be signposted. If you don't want the town centre, simply follow the *toutes directions* or 'other directions' (*autres directions*) sign until you (hopefully) see the sign for where you want to go. French roads are classified as follows and are identified by their prefix:

Prefix	Classification
A (*autoroute*)	motorways - mostly toll roads (*autoroute à péage*) – usually marked red/yellow on maps
E (*route européenne*)	European 'motorway' standard highways traversing a number of countries, e.g. the Autoroute de l'Est (A4) is also the E25
N (*route nationale*)	national trunk roads (financed by the central government); shown in red on most maps
D (*route départementale*)	main departmental roads (funded by departments); marked in yellow or white on maps
V (*chemin vicinal*)	minor roads; white on most maps
RF (*route forestière*)	forest tracks; shown on local maps only

In June each year, the French Ministry of Transport issues a map (*Carte de Bison Futé*) showing areas of congestion and providing information about alternative routes (*itinéraire bis*), indicated by yellow or green signs (*bison futé* means literally 'wily buffalo' and uses a Red Indian as its symbol). The map is available free from filling stations and tourist offices in France and from French government tourist offices abroad. There are around 90 *Bis* information rest areas throughout France, indicated by a black 'i' and an *Information Bison Futé* sign. Green-arrowed holiday routes (*flèches vertes*) avoiding large towns and cities are also recommended (indicated on Michelin map 911).

Up-to-date information about French roads can be obtained by phoning the National Road Information Centre (*Centre National d'Information Routière*, ☎ 08.36.68.20.00). For information about *autoroutes* contact the *Centre de Renseignements Autoroutes* (☎ 01.47.05.90.01) or tune into *Autoroute Info* on 107.7FM. An advice line in English is operated by France Inter (☎ 01.13.06.13.13). For information in Paris phone 01.40.55.43.00. Information about *autoroutes*, tolls and driving in France can also be obtained from French government tourist offices abroad (see page 312).

An *autoroute* guide for handicapped travellers, *Guide des Autoroutes à l'Usage des Personnes à Mobilité Réduite*, is available free from the Ministère des Transports, Direction des Routes, Service du Contrôle des Autoroutes, La Défense, 92055 Paris Cedex (☎ 01.40.81.21.22). See also **Road Maps** on page 221.

FRENCH DRIVERS

A Frenchman's personality changes the moment he gets behind the wheel of a car, when even the most gentle person becomes an aggressive, impatient and intolerant homicidal maniac with a unshakeable conviction in his own immortality. The French revere racing drivers (Alain Prost et al) and only the French could have invented the suicidal Paris-Dakar race (although it's a stroll compared with driving on French roads!). Some people (including a few foreigners) declare that the French aren't bad drivers at all, and simply innocent victims of a bad press and xenophobic foreigners (your own opinion will obviously depend on your personal experiences).

French drivers certainly aren't incompetent and must pass rigorous written and practical tests before they receive their licences. However, once they've discarded their '90' plates, the majority of French drivers are assailed by an uncontrollable urge to drive everywhere at maximum speed (young women often drive faster than men) and they are among the world's most pathologically aggressive drivers. The French have a passion for fast cars (although their ardour doesn't extend to cleaning them) and abhor driving slowly and slow drivers. They are among the most impatient drivers in Europe and have no time for drivers who stick to speed limits, especially when driving through country towns. To a Frenchman, the racing line on a bend is *de rigueur* (which usually means driving on the wrong side of the road!) and overtaking is an obligation; me first (*moi d'abord*) is the Frenchman's motto.

You would think that with all the practice they get, the French would have mastered the art of overtaking safely. Unfortunately this isn't so. When it comes to reckless overtaking, France has some of the most dangerous drivers in Europe, who seem to use their brakes only when their horn doesn't work. They often hang out in the middle of the road, a few metres behind the vehicle they're planning to overtake and come perilously close to both the vehicle being overtaken and approaching vehicles – **BEWARE!** Foreigners (particularly *les rosbifs*) should be aware that many French drivers become apoplectic when overtaken by them.

When not overtaking, French drivers sit a few metres (centimetres) from your bumper trying to push you along irrespective of traffic density, road and weather conditions, or the prevailing speed limit. They are among Europe's worst tail-gaters and there's no solution short of moving out of their way or stopping, which is often impossible. Always try to leave a large gap between your car and the one in front. This isn't just to give you more time to stop should the vehicles in front decide to get together, but also to give the inevitable tail-gater behind you more time to stop. **The closer the car is behind you, the further you should be from the vehicle in front.** On *autoroutes* and trunk roads, you must keep a safe distance (*distance de sécurité*) from the vehicle in front and you can be fined for not doing so. The safe distance on *autoroutes* is sometimes shown by arrows marked on the road surface.

The French have little respect for traffic rules, particularly anything to do with parking (in Paris, a car is a device used to create parking spaces). French drivers wear their dents with pride and there are many (many) dented cars in France (particularly in Paris, where the '75' registration number acts as a warning to other motorists). What makes driving in France even more of a lottery is that (apart from the unpredictability of French drivers) for many months of the year French roads are jammed with assorted foreigners. Their driving habits vary from exemplary to suicidal and include many (such as the British) who don't even know which side of the road to drive on! Beware of trucks on narrow roads, as truck drivers believe they have a divine right to three-quarters of the road and expect you to pull over. Don't, however, pull over too far, as many rural roads have soft verges and ditches.

If you drive in winter in areas that experience snow and ice – **take it easy!** In bad conditions you will notice that most French slow down considerably and even the habitual tail-gaters leave a larger gap than usual. Even a light snowfall can be treacherous, particularly on an icy road. When road conditions are bad, you should allow two to three times longer than usual to reach your destination (if you're wise, you'll stay at home). Note that many mountain passes are closed in winter (check with a French motoring organisation).

Don't be too discouraged by the road hogs and tail-gaters. Driving in France can be a pleasant experience (Paris excepted), particularly when using country roads that are relatively traffic-free most of the time. If you come from a country where traffic drives on the left, most people quickly get used to driving on the 'wrong' side of the road. Just take it easy at first and bear in mind that there are other foreigners around just as confused as you are!

MOTORCYCLES

The French generally like motorbikes and aren't prejudiced against bikers, as motorists are in many other countries. However, bikers do tend to get stopped more often by the police than motorists and should therefore take care to remain within the law. Approved crash helmets must be worn by moped and motorcycle riders and passengers, and dipped headlamps must be used at all times by all motorcyclists except moped riders. When parking a bike in a city, lock it securely and if possible chain it to an immovable object. Take extra care when parking in a public place overnight, particularly in Paris, where bike theft is rife.

Mopeds: From the age of 14, children in France can ride a moped (*cyclomoteur*) with an engine capacity below 50cc capable of a maximum speed of 45kph (28mph). No licence, registration or road tax is required. Third party insurance is necessary and a metal tab with the insurance policy number must be affixed to the handlebar locking nut. Mopeds aren't permitted on *autoroutes* and riders must use cycle paths where provided. Two-stroke petrol (*mélange deux-temps*) is available at most petrol stations. Mopeds can be lethal in the wrong hands (most teenagers have as much road sense as hedgehogs and rabbits) and hundreds are killed each year in France. If you have a child with a moped, it's important to impress upon him the need to take care (particularly in winter) and not take unnecessary risks, e.g. always observe traffic signs and signal before making manoeuvres. Car drivers often cannot see or avoid moped riders, particularly when they weave in and out of traffic, speed out of side streets without looking or ride at night without lights. To reduce accidents the government has introduced new rules for 14-year-olds, who in future will be required to pass a written test (in school) plus a three-hour practical test.

Motorcycles: At 16 youths can ride a light motorcycle (*vélomoteur/moto légère*) of 51 to 80cc with a maximum speed restriction of 75kph (47mph). At age 18 a medium motorcycle (81cc to under 125cc) may be ridden, for which a full driving licence is required. Bigger bikes (*motocyclette* or *moto*) can also be ridden at 18, although a special motorcycle licence is required for bikes from 125 to 400cc and a heavy motorcycle licence for bikes above 400cc. Speed limits are the same as for cars. A full driving licence and third party insurance is necessary for bikes over 50cc, plus passenger insurance. They must also be registered, have registration plates and carry an international sticker (*plaque de nationalité*). Motorcycles above 50cc are permitted to use *autoroutes* (tolls are lower than for cars, although the cost of a long journey can still be astronomical).

ACCIDENTS

If you're unfortunate enough to be involved in a car accident (*accident d'auto*) in France, the procedure is as follows:

1. Stop immediately. Switch on your hazard warning lights or place a warning triangle at the edge of the road 30 metres behind your car with a visibility of 100 metres. If necessary, for example, when the road is partly or totally blocked, turn on your car's headlights and direct traffic around the hazard. In bad visibility, at night, or in a blind spot, try to warn oncoming traffic of the danger, e.g. with a torch or by waving a warning triangle up and down.

2. If anyone is injured, immediately call the fire service (*sapeurs-pompiers*) by dialling 18. They will send an ambulance and doctor if necessary. If someone has been injured more than superficially or extensive damage has been caused, the police must be called to the scene (dial 17). Emergency phones (orange pillars with SOS written on them) are placed at 2km (1.2mi) intervals on autoroutes and every 4km (2.5mi) on other roads. To use them press and release the button marked 'summon help' (*pour demander au secours*) and speak into the metal grill. Give the number of the telephone and as many other details as possible. Don't move an injured person unless it's absolutely necessary to save him from further injury and don't leave him alone except to call an ambulance. Cover him with a blanket or coat to keep him warm.

3. If there are no injuries and damage to vehicles or property isn't serious, it's unnecessary to call the police to the accident scene. Contacting the police may result in someone being fined or prosecuted for a driving offence. If another driver has obviously been drinking or appears incapable of driving, call the police. Note that you must never leave the scene of an accident, however minor, as this is a serious offence.

4. If either you or the other driver(s) involved decide to call the police, don't move your vehicle or allow other vehicles to be moved. If it's necessary to move vehicles to unblock the road, mark their positions with chalk. Alternatively take photographs of the accident scene or make a drawing showing the position of vehicles involved before moving them. There's a space for this on the French insurance accident report form (see below).

5. Check whether there are any witnesses to the accident and take their names and addresses, particularly noting those who support *your* version of what happened. Write down the registration numbers of the vehicles involved and their drivers' names, addresses and insurance details. If asked, give any other drivers involved your name, address and insurance details.

6. If you have caused material damage, you must inform the owner of the damaged property as soon as possible. If you cannot reach him, contact the nearest police station (this also applies to damage caused to stationary vehicles, e.g. when parking).

7. If you're detained by the police, ask someone you're travelling with to contact anyone necessary as soon as you realise you're going to be detained. **Don't sign a statement, particularly one written in French, unless you're <u>certain</u> you understand and agree with every word.**

8. In the case of an accident involving two or more vehicles, it's standard practice for drivers to complete an accident report form (*Constat à l'Amiable*) provided by French insurance companies (keep one in your car). As the name implies, this is an 'amicable statement', where drivers agree (more or less) on what happened and who was at fault. It isn't obligatory to complete an accident report form and if your French isn't up to it you should refuse. You can, however, complete it in English or another language if you wish. It's important to check the details included on forms completed by other drivers against official documents, particularly those relating to a driver's identity, driving licence, car registration and insurance details. At the bottom of the form there are a number of statements describing the circumstances of the accident. You should tick the boxes that apply, add up the number of ticks and enter the number in the box at the bottom. This prevents the form from being altered later. Drivers must sign each other's forms. Always check exactly what the other driver has written before signing. In the event of a dispute a local bailiff (*huissier de justice*) should be called to prepare an independent report (*constat d'huissier*). If the police attend the scene of an accident, they will also make their own report.

9. Your insurance company must be notified of an accident within 24 to 48 hours and a delay may affect your claim. All accidents should also be reported to the *Bureau Central Français des Sociétés d'Assurances contre les Accidents Automobiles*, 36, ave du Général de Gaulle, 93171 Bagnolet Cedex (☎ 01.49.93.65.50).

France has a national fund (*Fonds de Garantie Automobile*, 64, rue Defrance, 94300 Vincennes) that pays compensation to victims injured by hit-and-run drivers. However, you can claim for damage to your car only if the person responsible can be identified and is uninsured or insolvent. Accident prevention in France is promoted by *Prévention Routière*, 5, rue Gager Gabillot, 75015 Paris (☎ 01.48.56.60.90).

DRIVING & DRINKING

As you're no doubt well aware, driving and drinking don't mix. Alcohol is a major factor in some 40 per cent of France's road accidents. Random breath tests (*alcooltest/dépistage*) can be carried out by the police at any time and motorists who are involved in accidents or who infringe motoring regulations are routinely breathalysed. Officially you 'only' lose six points on your licence (see page 200) for refusing to take a breathalyser test or are over the limit, although you will usually have your licence withdrawn on the spot and receive a suspension.

In 1995, the permitted blood alcohol concentration in France was lowered to 50mg of alcohol per 100ml of blood (it remains 80mg in Monaco), which is lower than most other European countries (although it's the proposed limit for the EU as a whole), in an attempt to discourage drunken driving. The amount you can drink and remain below the limit depends on whether you regularly imbibe, and your sex and weight. Your alcohol level rises considerably when you drink on an empty stomach, which is why the French eat lots of bread! Under the new rules, an average male can drink a maximum of two (12cl) glasses of wine, two *small* glasses of beer or two 4cl measures of spirits only (if he's to remain below the limit). For women the safe limits are usually even lower. **Note, however, that drinks vary in strength and these are only guidelines.**

The law regarding drunken driving is strict, with penalties usually depending on the level of alcohol in your blood and whether you're involved in an accident. Offenders apprehended with 50 to 80mg of alcohol per 100ml of blood are fined between 900F and 2,000F and receive three penalty points on their licences. Above 80mg fines can go up to 30,000F and licences can be revoked for up to five years. Drivers can be jailed for up to two years if a serious accident is caused. **If you have an accident while under the influence of alcohol, your car and health insurance could be nullified. This means that you must pay your own and any third party's car repairs, medical expenses and other damages. Your car insurance will also be increased by up to 150 per cent.**

CAR THEFT

Car theft is rampant in France, which has one of the highest numbers of vehicle thefts in Europe (the thefts of contents or accessories from motor vehicles is even more commonplace). If you drive anything other than a worthless heap, you should have theft insurance that includes your car stereo and personal belongings. It's wise to have your car fitted with an alarm, an ignition disabling system or other anti-theft device, plus a visible deterrent, such as a steering or gear lock.

It's particularly important to protect your car if you own a model that's desirable to car thieves, e.g. most new sports and executive cars, which are often stolen to order by professional crooks. On the French Riviera stolen cars often find their way to Africa and may already be on a ferry by the time the owners report them stolen. A good security system won't stop someone breaking into your car (which usually takes most thieves a matter of seconds) and may not prevent your car being stolen, but it will at least make it more difficult and may persuade a thief to look for an easier target. Radios, tape and CD players attract a lot of the wrong attention in most French cities (especially Paris) and coastal resorts. If you buy an expensive stereo system, buy one with a removable unit or with a removable control panel that you can pop in a pocket. However, never forget to remove it, even when stopping for a few minutes. Some manufacturers provide stereo systems that won't work when they're removed from their original vehicles or are inoperable without a security code being entered.

When leaving your car unattended, store any valuables (including clothes) in the boot or out of sight. If you leave your car papers in your car, make sure you have a copy. If possible avoid parking in long-term car parks, as these are favourite hunting grounds for car thieves. Foreign-registered cars, particularly camper vans and mobile homes, are popular targets, particularly when parked in ports. When parking overnight or when it's dark, parking in a well-lit area may help deter car thieves. If your car is stolen or anything is stolen from it, report it to the police in the area where it was stolen. You can report it by telephone, but must go to the station to complete a report. Don't, however, expect the police to find it or even take any interest in your loss. Report a theft to your insurance company as soon as possible.

Highway Piracy: Highway piracy (*les pirates de la route*) is becoming an increasing problem in some areas, where foreign drivers are often the targets. Gangs deliberately bump or ram cars to get drivers to stop, usually late at night when there's little traffic about. A driver may also pose as a plain clothes policeman and try to get you to stop by flashing a 'badge' or setting up bogus road blocks. In the worst cases thieves take not just the car and its contents, but even the victims' clothes they are wearing. Travelling at night in France is becoming increasingly hazardous and should be avoided if possible.

PETROL

Leaded petrol in France is now available only in *super/carburant* (4-star/98 octane) grade. Unleaded petrol is usually available in two grades, *sans plomb* (95 octane) and *sans plomb 98/super sans plomb* (98 octane). Diesel fuel is *gasoil* or *gazole* and is available at all service stations. Note that *pétrole* or *fuel* is paraffin and not petrol. From 1ˢᵗ January 2000, leaded petrol will no longer be sold throughout the European Union. Some cars may need modification to run on unleaded fuel, which usually involves a simple adjustment to the ignition timing (although some may need hardened valve seats and the fuel pump and fuel-line seals changed).

The cost of petrol has risen dramatically in recent years, although prices vary considerably depending on the area, town and the particular filling station. It can vary by up to a franc a litre for super and unleaded. The cheapest source is hyper/supermarkets, which are around 15 to 20 per cent lower than average, while rural filling stations are the most expensive and should be used only in emergencies. The lowest cost per litre is *roughly* 5F (diesel), 6F (unleaded, 95 octane) and 6.25F (super). To help tourists and travellers on *autoroutes* locate inexpensive supermarket filling stations, the French Government Tourist Office produces a leaflet, *La carte de l'essence moins chère*, showing supermarkets a short detour from main routes. Diesel fuel is much cheaper than petrol and makes it advantageous to run a diesel vehicle in France (despite the fact that tests have shown it to be a bigger source of pollution than petroleum). Liquid petroleum gas (LPG) is also available and there are many LPG (Gepel/GPL) filling stations, particularly on *autoroutes* (a free map is available from filling stations). LPG costs around 4F per litre.

Self-service filling stations (*libre service* or *servez-vous*) are common and include most *autoroute* and supermarket stations. Manned filling stations are common in small towns and villages. To fill-up ask for *faites le plein s'il vous plaît* or *le plein s'il vous plaît*. Tips aren't expected for cleaning the windscreen and checking oil and tyre pressures, although they won't be rejected. There are 24-hour filling stations on *autoroutes*. When paying at self-service petrol stations, simply tell the cashier your pump number. Carte Bleue and major credit cards are accepted by most filling stations. Some stations have automatic pumps accepting banknotes or credit cards when a station is closed.

If you accidentally fill a car fitted with a catalyser with leaded fuel, you can have the tank and fuel system drained without it causing any damage, providing you don't drive it. (This also applies to filling a diesel car with petrol or a petrol car with diesel.) To prevent errors, petrol pumps and pipes are colour coded, green for unleaded, red for leaded and black for diesel. The nozzles of leaded (super) petrol pumps in France are also usually larger than those of unleaded pumps and won't fit the petrol filler hole of a car fitted with a catalyser. Nevertheless, pay attention, particularly when a garage attendant is filling your car.

Most filling stations have toilets, sometimes located outside the main building, when it may be necessary to ask an attendant for the key. Many filling stations provide services such as a car wash, vacuum cleaners and air, and often have a shop selling confectionery, basic foods (e.g. fresh bread), newspapers and magazines, canned drinks, motoring accessories and sundry other items. Routine servicing and repairs are also carried out by some filling stations.

SPEED LIMITS

The following speed limits are in force in France:

Road	Speed Limit*
Autoroutes	130/110kph (81/69mph)
Dual Carriageways	110/100kph (69/62mph)
Other Roads	90/80kph (56/50mph)
Built Up Areas/Towns	50kph (31mph) or as signposted, e.g. 40 or 45kph

* Speed limits are reduced in rain (*par temps de pluie*), when the second limit shown above applies. In thick fog, speed limits are automatically reduced to 50kph on all roads when visibility is less than 50 metres.

Speed limits also apply to cars towing a trailer or caravan, providing the trailer's weight doesn't exceed that of the car. Cars towing a trailer are limited to 45kph (28mph) if the trailer exceeds the car's weight by over 30 per cent or 65kph (39mph) if less than 30 per cent. A plate showing the permitted maximum speed must be displayed at the rear of the trailer. Cars towing trailers with restricted speeds aren't permitted to use the outside (overtaking) lane on a three-lane *autoroute*. There's a minimum speed of 80kph (50mph) on *autoroutes* in the outside (overtaking) lane during daylight, in dry weather on level surfaces and in good visibility, i.e. perfect conditions. Vehicles fitted with studded tyres or snow chains are restricted to 90kph (56mph) and a '90' plate must be displayed at the rear.

Speed restrictions in built-up areas (*agglomérations*) such as small towns and villages often aren't posted. Unless a lower speed limit (such as 40 or 45kph) is posted, the speed limit in towns is 50kph and starts with the town's name sign, which usually has blue letters on a white background, possibly with a red border. The end of the speed limit is indicated by the town's sign with a diagonal red line through it. A village sign with white letters on a dark blue background isn't an *agglomération* sign and there's no speed restriction unless otherwise indicated. The word *rappel* (reminder) is often displayed beneath speed restriction signs to remind motorists that the limit is still in force. Sleeping policemen (speed humps) are common on many major and minor roads and if you don't slow down you risk damaging your vehicle or having an accident.

French drivers routinely speed everywhere and the usual speed is often around 50kph above the posted speed limit on rural roads. Frenchmen rarely slow down for villages, e.g. 40 to 50kph, and are usually irritated by motorists who do so. The use of radar traps is widespread (including on *autoroutes*) and you're usually warned by signs when you're driving through a radar-controlled zone. Radar-warning devices are illegal in France. Note, however, that radar controls must be published in advance and you can check them via Minitel by dialling 3615 (*Auto Défense*) and entering your date of travel and route (this isn't, however, designed to encourage you to break the law!). Police also use concealed cameras to snap speeding motorists. French drivers often flash their headlights to warn other motorists of speed traps, although it's illegal to do this. Speed limits are enforced by motorcycle traffic police operating in pairs.

Speeding fines depend on an offender's speed above the legal speed limit. Usually you're allowed to be 10 per cent above the limit, so if you're clocked at 55kph in a 50kph zone, or 88kph in an 80kph zone, you won't normally be fined for speeding. A fine can be anywhere between 600F and 5,000F, average 900F and if it isn't paid within a certain period it's automatically increased. If you're a non-resident the police may insist on a fine being paid on-the-spot and if you're unable to pay your car may be impounded. You're free to contest a demand for an on-the-spot fine, although unless you have a foolproof case you would be wise to pay the fine. Not speaking French won't get you off with a warning and although policemen rarely speak English or other foreign languages, they thoughtfully have their charge sheets printed in foreign languages.

Under the licence points system (see page 200), motorists lose one to four points for speeding, depending on how many kph they were driving above the legal speed limit: up to 20kph (one point), between 20 and 30kph (two points), between 30 and 40kph (three points) and over 40kph (four points).

For two years after passing your driving test in France, you're designated a 'young' driver (*jeune conducteur*), irrespective of your age, and must display a 80kph (50mph) *disque réglementaire* on the back of any car being driven (magnetic 80kph discs are available and can be swapped between vehicles). During this period you mustn't exceed 80kph on any road, except for 100kph (62mph) on urban *autoroutes* and 110kph (69mph) on rural *autoroutes*. If you're apprehended for speeding in your first year or for not displaying the '80' disc, you will be fined and penalised four points on your licence. Visitors who have held a licence for less than two years are also subject to these speed restrictions, but aren't required to display a disc.

GARAGES

When buying a car in France, you would be wise to take into account local service facilities. Citroën, Peugeot and Renault dealers abound in every large town and there are a fair number of Fiat, Ford, Mercedes, Opel (General Motors) and Volkswagen dealers. Outside these makes dealers may be few and far between. It's difficult to find garages that can repair American, British and some Japanese cars, and the nearest dealer may be a long way from your home or workplace. If you drive a rare car, it's advisable to carry a basic selection of spare parts, as service stations in France may not stock them and you may need to wait several days for them to be sent from abroad.

Garages in France are required to display a list of their charges for routine repairs and servicing, and many also display their hourly rate for different types of work, e.g. mechanical, electrical or bodywork. The quality of work is usually of a high standard and charges compare favourably with other European countries (they are usually much cheaper than in Britain). It's generally cheaper to have your car serviced at a local village garage than at a main dealer, although the quality of work may vary considerably from garage to garage. Note that when a car is under warranty it must usually be serviced by an approved dealer in order not to invalidate the warranty. However, if you need urgent assistance, particularly with an exotic foreign car, you're more likely to receive sympathetic help from a small local garage than a large dealer. Garages in France are generally open from 0800 to 1900 and close for lunch between noon and 1330. Note that many garages close for the whole month of August. In major cities there are garages providing a 24-hour breakdown assistance (at a price).

Service stations in France don't usually provide a free 'loan car' (*véhicule de remplacement*) while yours is being serviced or repaired, although you can usually hire a car from a garage for a reasonable fee. Some garages will collect your car from your home or office and deliver it after a service, or alternatively will drop you off at a railway or bus station or in a local town, and pick you up when your car is ready for collection.

ROAD MAPS

A huge variety of road maps (*cartes routières*) are available in France, including the following:

- Michelin red maps of France (scale: 1cm = 10km) can be purchased as a single sheet (989), in booklet form (915), as a reversible sheet (916), or in two halves; north (998) and south (999). Michelin also produce a route planning map (911) showing *autoroutes* and alternative routes, distances and journey times, 24-hour service stations and peak periods to avoid. When using minor country roads, Michelin yellow maps (scale: 1cm = 2km) are indispensable. Towns and places mentioned in the Michelin red guide (see page 310) are underlined in red on Michelin yellow maps, and the names of towns with a plan in the red guide are enclosed in a rectangle. Alternatively, the Michelin red guide directs you to the appropriate yellow map. The Michelin red guide is much more than a 'tourist' guide and includes numerous detailed town plans and references to main routes. The Michelin green tourist guides (see page 310) also contain more detailed town plans than those in the red guide. Michelin maps and guides are inexpensive (particularly yellow maps) and available throughout France.

- The Michelin *Motoring Atlas of France* and *Road Atlas of France* (Hamlyn) are priceless and contain the complete Michelin yellow maps (see above) plus town plans, and are much cheaper than buying all the yellow maps. The spiral bound version is best.

- Excellent regional road maps are published by the *Institut Géographique National* (IGN), which include town plans, tourist information and an index of places of interest. These include the red series of 16 regional road maps with a scale of 1:250,000 or 1cm = 2.5km (1in = 4mi), containing town plans and an index. Larger scale IGN maps include the green series of 74 maps with a scale of 1:100,000 or 1cm = 1km (1.5in = 1mi). IGN also produce a single road map (IGN 901) of France (scale: 1cm = 10km).

- In June each year the French Ministry of Transport issues a free map (*Carte de Bison Futé*) showing areas of congestion and providing information about alternative routes (see page 212).

- Among the most indispensable Paris maps are the Editions Leconte *Plan de Paris* and *Paris par Arrondissement* (Editions L'Indispensable) containing detailed street maps for each district plus *métro* and bus service maps.

- *Autoroute* maps are distributed free by *autoroute* operators. *Bonne Route: Discovering French Motorways* by Anne Fitter (Anthony Nelson) is also useful.

- Free local town maps are available from tourist offices (e.g. the FGTO). More detailed town maps are available from bookshops, newsagents and kiosks. Local village maps can usually be obtained from town halls.

Unfortunately France has no large-scale maps for rural areas with comprehensive street indexes. You must put your trust in 'St.' Christopher the patron saint of travellers, although he may not be able to help much, since he's had his sainthood revoked by the Pope (if he fails you, try St. Jude, the patron saint of lost causes). If it's any consolation, a map often won't be much help in rural areas as streets often have no names and houses have no numbers. The good news is that the more willing you are to risk getting lost, the more likely you are to see the real France! A map showing the regions and departments of France is shown on page 444.

CAR RENTAL

Car rental companies such as Avis, Budget, Citer, Eurodollar, Europcar, Hertz, Solvet and Thrifty have offices in most large towns and major airports. Look under *location de voitures* in your local Yellow Pages. If you're a visitor, it's advisable to reserve a rental car before arriving in France. Fly-drive deals are available through most airlines and travel agents. French railways (SNCF) offer inclusive train and car rental deals and their *France Vacances Pass* provides car rental. You can rent an Avis car from some 200 SNCF stations and leave it at any station operating the scheme (*Train + auto* leaflets are available at SNCF stations and include a map of participating stations).

Car rental in France is expensive, particularly for short periods, and includes value added tax (TVA) at 20.6 per cent. For example Budget charge around 600F (including optional insurances and taxes, plus almost 3F per km above 100km a day) for a one day rental of their cheapest models, e.g. Peugeot 106 KID or Renault Clio. Rates reduce considerably over long periods, e.g. a week or a month. Note that a diesel car is much cheaper to run than a petrol-engined car. Special rates are available for weekends, usually from noon on Friday to 0900 on Monday. Local rental companies are usually cheaper than the nationals, although cars must be returned to the pick-up point. Car rental rates usually include Collision Damage Waiver (CDW) and Personal Accident Insurance (PAI). If required, check in advance that you're permitted to take a car out of France (usually prohibited).

To hire a car in France you must be a minimum of 18 years old, although most companies have increased this to 21 (e.g. Budget, although drivers under 25 must pay an extra 100F per day of rental) or even 25 (e.g. Hertz). For certain categories of car the limit is 25. Drivers must have held a full licence for a minimum of one year and most companies have an upper age limit of 60 or 65. International companies require payment by credit card, although local firms may allow you to pay a cash deposit of 1,000F to 2,000F (although the whole rental period may need to be paid in advance). You may also require a residence permit (*permis de séjour*) and an identification check will be made.

Rental cars can be ordered with a portable telephone, a luggage rack, snow chains and child seats can be fitted for an extra charge. You can also hire a 4-wheel drive car, station wagon, minibus, luxury car, armoured limousine or a convertible, possibly with a choice of manual or automatic gearbox. Minibuses accessible to wheelchairs can also be hired, e.g. from Hertz. Older cars can be hired from many garages at lower rates than those charged by the national car-hire companies. Vans and pick-ups are available from the major rental companies by the hour, half-day or day, or from smaller local companies (which, once again, are cheaper).

Note that cars can be rented in France through major international rental companies such as Alamo (☎ 00-1-800-327-9633), Avis (☎ 00-1-800-331-1212), Budget (☎ 00-1-800-527-0700) and Hertz (☎ 00-1-800-654-3131) by booking through their American offices and paying by credit card. This is a legitimate practice and can save 50 per cent or more on local hire rates. At present the car hire companies have no way of knowing where the calls were made and therefore cannot prevent this practice. Toll-free (800) numbers of other US-based rental companies can be obtained from international directory enquiries, although you pay international rates when phoning from abroad.

MOTORING ORGANISATIONS

There are a number of motoring organisations in France, although membership isn't as large as in many other European countries. Breakdown insurance is also provided by insurance companies in France and most motorists take advantage of their low rates (see page 201). French motoring organisations, like insurance companies, don't usually operate their own breakdown rescue vehicles and appoint approved garages to assist motorists.

Motoring organisations offer membership for individuals, couples and families and many also provide 'premium' levels of membership providing additional services. For example *Europ Assistance* (1, promenade de la Bonnette, 92230 Gennevilliers, ☎ 01.41.85.85.85) offers three membership levels: individual (852F with vehicle), couple (960F a year) and family (1,128F), which include breakdown and travel assistance in around 45 European countries. Other services provided by motoring organisations include vehicle serviceability checks; health and legal assistance; insurance and financial services; tourism, pastime and sports services (e.g. camping carnet, petrol coupons and ticket services); an information service (via Minitel); and expert advice.

Other French motoring organisations include the *Automobile Club de l'Ile de France* (14, avenue de la Grande Armée, 75017 Paris, ☎ 01.40.55.43.00), the *Automobile Club de France*, 6-8, place de la Concorde, 75008 Paris (☎ 01.43.12.43.12), the *Automobile Club National (ACN)*, 5, rue Auber, 75009 Paris (☎ 01.44.51.53.99) and the *Touring Club de France (TCF)*, Parc Champs Elysées, 75008 Paris (☎ 01.42.65.90.70).

PARKING

Parking in most French towns and cities (Paris excepted) isn't such a problem or as expensive as in many other European countries. However, parking is usually restricted in cities and towns and prohibited altogether in certain areas. Parking regulations may vary depending on the area of a city, the time of day, the day of the week, and whether the date is odd or even. In many towns, parking is permitted on one side of the street for the first half of the month, usually the side with even-numbered houses, and on the other side for the second half of the month. This is called *stationnement alterné semi-mensuel* and is shown by a sign. Parking may also alternate weekly. Parking on alternate days is indicated by a sign stating *Côté du Stationnement – jours pairs* (even) or *jours impairs* (odd). In Paris, signs may indicate that parking is forbidden on one side of the street at certain times due to street cleaning.

Blue zones: In many cities and towns there are blue zones (*zones bleues*), indicated by blue street markings. Here you can park free for one hour between 0900 and noon and from 1400 or 1430 until 1900 from Mondays to Saturdays, with no limit on Sundays and public holidays. Parking isn't controlled between noon and 1400, meaning you can park free from 1100 until 1400 or from noon until 1500. You must display a parking disc (*disque de contrôle/stationnement*) behind your windscreen. These are available free or for a small fee from garages, travel agents, motoring organisations, tourist offices, *tabacs*, police stations and some shops. Set your time of arrival in the left box and the time you should leave is displayed in the right box, e.g. if you set 1000 in the left box, 1100 is displayed in the right box. If you overstay your free time you can be fined. Parking in blue zones is unrestricted between 1900 and 0900 Mondays to Saturdays and on Sundays and public holidays.

Meters: In most French cities, parking meters have been replaced by ticket machines (*horodateurs*). Parking must usually be paid for between the hours of 0900 and 1900, although it's free from noon to 1400 (meter attendants also have lunch). If a parking sign has the word *horodateur* (machine) beneath it or there's a *stationnement payant* sign, perhaps with *payant* also marked on the road, it means that you must obtain a ticket from a nearby machine. The cost is around 4F to 6F per hour (more at railway stations) and machines usually accept 2, 5 and 10 franc coins. In some towns the first 30 minutes is free, one hour costs 2F, 90 minutes 5F and two hours (often the maximum) 10F. Buy a ticket for the period required and place it behind your windscreen where it can be seen by the parking attendant.

Car Parks: Apart from on-street parking there are many car parks (*parking/parc de stationnement*) in cities and towns. Here parking rates vary from 2F to 10F an hour or 15F to 80F for 24 hours. Car parks in central Paris charge 10F to 20F per hour and 75F to 110F for 24 hours. Long term parking, e.g. at railway stations, is available in most towns for around 30F to 50F per day. If you park in a multi-storey car park, make a note of the level and space number where you park your car (it can take a long time to find your car if you have no idea where to start looking). On entering most car parks you take a ticket from an automatic dispenser (usually you must press a button). You must pay *before* collecting your car, either at a cash desk (*caisse*) or in a machine and cannot usually pay at the exit. Machines may accept both coins and banknotes, e.g. 100F. After paying you usually have around 15 minutes to find the exit, where you insert your ticket in a machine in the direction shown by the arrow on the ticket. Headlights should be used in underground and badly lit car parks.

In most cities, residents can pay reduced parking fees by obtaining a residence permit from the local town hall. This must be affixed to the right-hand side of your windscreen. Parking meter subscription cards are also available for residents and commuters in most cities. Disabled motorists are provided with free or reserved parking in most towns, shopping centres and at airports, but they must display an official disabled motorist's badge inside their windscreen.

Fines: Fines for illegal parking are based on the severity of the offence. In Paris, you're fined around 75F for not paying or for overstaying your time in a legal parking spot, which increases to 220F if it isn't paid within three months. You can be fined 230F, 450F or 900F for parking illegally, which increase to 600F, 1,200F and 2,500F respectively if it isn't paid within three months. You can usually agree a payment schedule for a large fine, rather than pay it in one lump sum. Parking fines can often be paid by buying a special fiscal stamp (*timbre-fiscal*) from a *tabac*, that's affixed to the notice and sent to the relevant authority. If your car is given a ticket and isn't moved within an hour, it will be given a second ticket and after two hours a wheel clamp may be affixed or it may be towed way.

Paris has six car pounds (*fourrières*) and in addition to your parking fine of from 230F to 900F you must pay a fee to release your car from a pound (or to have a clamp removed), plus a daily storage charge. However, if you don't collect your car within 10 to 45 days it may be sold (so don't park illegally before taking a long trip abroad!). Most pounds are open from around 0800 to 2000, Mondays to Saturdays. You can pay in cash or with a cheque drawn on a French bank.

On-street parking is forbidden in many streets in the centre of Paris and other cities. Parking is forbidden in Paris on main access routes designated as red routes (*axes rouges*). No parking may be shown by a *stationnement gênant* sign with a picture of a truck towing away a vehicle. If you park in a taxi rank or in front of a private garage, you're likely to find your car towed away or your tyres slashed! *Stationnement interdit* means parking is forbidden and may be accompanied by the sign of a 'P' with a line through it. No parking may also be indicated by yellow kerb markings. It's forbidden to park in front of a fire hydrant. In Paris, it's illegal to leave a car in the same spot on a public highway for more than 24 hours. Parking a caravan on roads is forbidden at any time in Paris and some other towns and cities, and overnight parking in a lay-by isn't permitted anywhere in France, although you can stop for a rest if you're falling asleep at the wheel. On roads outside town limits, you *must* pull off the road to stop.

Parisians are parking anarchists and are world champions at the art of creative parking (you will often see a number of cars squeezed illegally into a space just large enough for one car!). Parking on street corners is a favourite spot. Note, however, that if you park illegally, you aren't covered by comprehensive insurance should your car be damaged. Many Parisians refuse to pay parking fines. It's a tradition in France that there's an amnesty on fines for minor offences such as parking when a new president takes office and many people deliberately collect or delay paying parking fines in the months leading up to a presidential election (although you will have to wait until 2002 for the next one!).

PEDESTRIAN ROAD RULES

Pedestrian crossings (*passages à piétons*) in France are distinguished by black and white or red and white stripes on the road, but aren't normally illuminated, e.g. by flashing or static lights. Many also have humps to encourage motorists to slow down. In towns, pedestrian crossings are incorporated with traffic lights. Motorists are required by law to stop for a pedestrian waiting at a pedestrian crossing *only* if he signals his intention to cross, e.g. by giving a clear hand-signal or placing one foot on the crossing. Take extreme care when using pedestrian crossings in France, particularly in Paris, as French motorists are reluctant to stop and may even try to drive around you while you're on a crossing (it's said that French pedestrian crossings function as a form of population control!). However, you will be pleased to hear that running over pedestrians on pedestrian crossings (or anywhere else for that matter) is taken seriously in France.

At a crossing with lights, pedestrians must wait for a green light (or green man) before crossing the road, regardless of whether there's any traffic. You can be fined for crossing the road at the wrong place or ignoring pedestrian lights and crossings. Pedestrians in France are generally better disciplined than those in many other countries and they usually wait for the green light. Pedestrians must use footpaths where provided or may use a bicycle path when there's no footpath. Where there's no footpath or bicycle path, you should walk on the left side of the road facing the oncoming traffic. Many towns and cities have pedestrian areas (*secteur piétonnier*) barred to traffic, although some roads are also barred to pedestrians (indicated by an *interdit aux piétons* sign).

ROAD SIGNS

Although France generally adheres to international standard road signs, there are also many unique signs with instructions or information in French. Some of the most common are listed below:

absence de marquage	no road markings (usually after resurfacing)
accotements non stabilisés	soft shoulders/verge
allumez vos feux/lanternes/phares	switch on your lights, e.g. for a tunnel
attention travaux	beware roadworks
autres directions	other directions or all directions other than those signposted
cédez le passage	give way (usually shown underneath the international 'give way' sign)
chaussée déformée	bumpy or uneven road surface/road edgings
Déviation	diversion
éteignez vos feux/lanternes/phares	switch off your lights, e.g. after leaving a tunnel
Gravillons	loose gravel or chippings (after road resurfacing)
Impasse	Cul-de-sac or dead end
nids de poules	potholes
poids lourds	route for heavy traffic
Ralentir	slow down
Ralentisseur	a speed hump designed to slow motorists, usually accompanied by a 20 or 30kph speed restriction sign
Rappel	reminder of a speed limit or other restriction
route barrée	road closed
sens interdit	No-entry
sens unique	One-way street
serrez à droite/gauche	keep to the right/left

sortie de camions	exit for lorries
sauf riverains	except residents, e.g. below a 'no entry' sign
stationnement interdit	no parking
toutes directions	all directions, usually meaning all directions except the town centre (centre ville)
véhicules lents	slow vehicles (which are usually confined to the right-hand lane on a gradient)
verglas	risk of ice on road
vitesse réduite	reduced speed limit

12.

HEALTH

The quality of health care and health care facilities in France are excellent and rate among the best in the world. There are virtually no waiting lists for operations or hospital beds and the standard of hospital treatment is second to none. Public and private medicine operate alongside one another and there's no difference in the quality of treatment provided by public hospitals and private establishments. However, local hospital services, particularly hospitals with casualty departments, are limited in rural areas.

France has an excellent, although expensive, national health system, providing free or low cost health care for all who contribute to French social security, plus their families and retirees (including those from other European Union countries). Those who don't automatically qualify for health care under the French national health system can contribute voluntarily or take out private health insurance. The French spend around 10 per cent of their national income on health care and are the world's second largest spenders after the USA. However, funding of the public health service is spiralling out of control and spending could increase to 20 per cent of GDP in a decade if it isn't checked. In France there's a cosy relationship between the doctors and unions, who between them control health spending, with the state's role being simply to cover the deficit. France needs to drastically reform its health care system and cut some 50,000 hospital beds. However, while most people recognise the need for reform, they are reluctant to lose hospitals, unlimited second opinions and an endless supply of free pills.

France devotes a greater proportion of its GDP to health than to defence or education, the lion's share being spent on medicines and drugs rather than hospitals. France has long been a nation of hypochondriacs and the French visit their doctors more often than most other Europeans and buy large quantities of medicines, health foods and vitamin pills. Despite the common stereotype of the French as wine-swilling gourmets stuffing themselves with rich foods, many have become health freaks in recent years. Fitness and health centres flourish in most towns and even jogging has become fashionable in recent years. Smoking has declined considerably and is now a minority habit, although higher than in many other European countries. Air pollution (caused by vehicles not smokers!) is an increasing problem in Paris and other French cities such as Grenoble, Lyon and Strasbourg, where it's blamed for a sharp rise in asthma cases. There's also a high and increasing rate of stress in French cities. The average life expectancy is 81 for women (the highest in Europe) and 73 for men.

In general, French medicine places the emphasis on preventive medicine, rather than treating sickness. Alternative medicine is popular (*médecine douce*), particularly acupuncture and homeopathy. These treatments are recognised by France's medical council (*Ordre des Médecins*) and reimbursed by social security when prescribed by a doctor. France is the world leader in homeopathy and some 15 per cent of the population regularly consults homeopathic doctors.

The incidence of heart disease in France is among the lowest in the world, a fact that has recently been officially contributed in part to their (largely Mediterranean) diet and high consumption of red wine. They do, however, have a high incidence of cirrhosis of the liver and other problems associated with excess alcohol. Among expatriates, sunstroke, change of diet, too much rich food and (surprise, surprise) too much alcohol are the most common causes of health problems. When you've had too much of *la bonne vie* you can take yourself off to a French spa for a few weeks to rejuvenate your system (in preparation for another bout of over indulgence). Among the most popular treatments offered is thalassotherapy, a sea water 'cure' recommended for arthritis, circulation problems, depression and fatigue.

A useful booklet, *Health Care Resources in Paris*, is published by the Women's Institute for Continuing Education (WICE), 20, bd du Montparnasse, 75015 Paris (☎ 01.45.66.75.50). You can safely drink the water in France unless it's labelled as non-drinking (*eau non-potable*), but the wine (especially the 1973 Château Mouton Rothschild) and beer are more enjoyable. *Santé!*

EMERGENCIES

The action to take in a medical 'emergency' depends on the degree of urgency. The emergency medical services in France are among the best in the world. **Keep a record of the telephone numbers of your doctor, local hospitals and clinics, ambulance service, poison control, dentist and other emergency services (fire, police) next to your telephone.** If you're unsure who to call, telephone your local police station, who will tell you who to contact or call the appropriate service for you. In Paris and other main cities there are emergency medical telephone boxes at major intersections marked *Services Médicaux*, with direct lines to emergency services. Whoever you call, give the age of the patient and if possible, specify the type of emergency.

● In a life-threatening emergency such as a heart attack or a serious accident, dial 15 for your nearest SAMU (*Service d'Aide Médicale d'Urgence*) unit. SAMU is a special emergency service that works closely with local public hospital emergency and intensive care units. Its ambulances are manned by medical personnel and equipped with small emergency rooms with cardiac and resuscitation equipment. SAMU has a central telephone number for each region of France and the duty doctor decides whether to send a SAMU mobile unit, refer the call to another ambulance service, or call a doctor for a home visit. In the most critical emergencies, SAMU can arrange transportation to hospital by aeroplane, helicopter or boat. If you call the fire brigade or police services, they will request a SAMU unit if they consider it necessary.

● You can also call the local fire brigade (*sapeurs-pompiers* or *pompiers*) in an emergency by dialling 18. The *pompiers* are equipped with cardiac arrest equipment and will arrive with a doctor. In France, the fire brigade and public ambulance services are combined, and the fire brigade is equipped to deal with accidents and emergency medical cases and operates its own ambulances.

● If you need an ambulance, call the local public assistance (*assistance publique*) or municipal ambulance (*ambulances municipales*) service. There are also private ambulances in most towns providing a 24-hour service, listed by town under *Ambulances* in your Yellow Pages. Ambulance staff are trained to provide first-aid and oxygen. In an emergency an ambulance will take a patient to the nearest hospital equipped to deal with the particular type of emergency. In small towns the local taxi service also provides an 'ambulance' service.

● If you're physically capable, you can go to a hospital emergency or casualty department (*urgences*). Check in advance which local hospitals are equipped to deal with emergencies and the quickest route from your home. This information may be of vital importance in the event of an emergency, when a delay could mean the difference between life and death.

● If you're unable to visit your doctor's surgery, your doctor will visit you at home. If your doctor is unavailable a telephone answering machine or answering service will give you the name and telephone number of a substitute (locum) doctor on call. In France, doctors make house calls at any time of day or night. If you need a doctor or medicines in a non-urgent situation and are unable to contact your doctor, your local police station (*commissariat de police*) will give you the telephone number of a doctor on call or the address of a pharmacy that's open. Local newspapers also usually contain a list of doctors, pharmacies and vets who are on call over the weekend, under the heading *Urgences*.

● There are 24-hour, on-call medical and dental services in major cities and large towns (numbers are listed in telephone directories). For example, in Paris, you can call *SOS Médecins* (☎ 01.47.07.77.77) for medical emergencies, and *SOS Dentaire* (☎ 01.43.37.51.00) for dental emergencies. SOS doctors and dentists are equipped with radio cars and respond quickly to calls. A home visit in Paris costs from around 200F before 1900 and 300F after 1900, plus the cost of any treatment. If someone has swallowed poison, the number of your local poison control centre (*centre anti-poison*) is listed at the front of telephone directories.

You will be billed for the services of SAMU, the fire service or the public ambulance service, although the cost will be reimbursed by social security and your complementary insurance policy (*mutuelle*) in the same way as other medical costs (see below). In an emergency any hospital must treat you, regardless of your ability to pay.

SOCIAL SECURITY HEALTH BENEFITS

If you contribute to French social security (*sécurité sociale*), you and your family are entitled to subsidised or (in certain cases) free medical and dental treatment. Benefits include general and specialist care, hospitalisation, laboratory services, drugs and medicines, dental care, maternity care, appliances and transportation.

To qualify for health benefits under social security, you must have been employed in France for 600 hours during the last six months or for six months at the minimum wage, or for 200 hours in the last quarter or 120 hours in the last month. When a person no longer meets these qualifying conditions, benefits are extended for a maximum of one year from the applicable date. Benefits are extended indefinitely for the long-term unemployed providing they are actively seeking employment. Retirees living in France and receiving a state pension from another EU country are entitled to free health benefits. Note, however, that if you have taken early retirement and aren't working in France or receiving a state pension from your country of origin, you aren't entitled to free health benefits and should ensure you have adequate health insurance to cover any health bills.

Under the social security health system, health treatment is assigned a basic monetary value (*tarif de convention*), of which social security pays a proportion (see the table below). The actual amount paid depends on your social security status, the kind of treatment received and whether the practitioner is approved (*agréé*) by social security. Most people are reimbursed for doctors' bills at 75 per cent, although the self-employed receive 50 per cent only. Certain patients are classified as needing serious long-term treatment, e.g. diabetic, cancer and cardiac patients, and receive 100 per cent reimbursement. The balance of medical bills, called the *ticket modérateur*, is usually paid by a complementary health insurance (*mutuelle*) scheme to which most people belong (see **Health Insurance** on page 264). The standard social security reimbursements are as follows (n.b. these are intended only as a guide and should be confirmed with social security and practitioners):

Reimbursement	Practitioner/Treatment
100 per cent	Maternity-related care
80 per cent	Hospitalisation
75 per cent	Doctors, dentists and midwife services; consultations as an out-patient; basic dental care
70 per cent	Miscellaneous items, e.g. laboratory work, apparatus, spectacles, ambulance services
65 per cent	medical auxiliaries, e.g. nurses, chiropodists, masseurs, therapists
35 to 100 per cent*	drugs and medicines

* The level of reimbursement for medicines is usually 65 per cent, although medicines for 'common' ailments are reimbursed at 35 per cent and certain essential medication at 100 per cent, e.g. insulin or heart pills.

When choosing a medical practitioner, e.g. a doctor or dentist, it's important to verify whether he has an agreement (*convention*) with social security. If he has an agreement he's known as *conventionné* and will charge a fixed amount for treatment as specified under the *tarif de convention*. If he *hasn't* signed an agreement with social security he's termed *non-conventionné* and the bill may be two to five times that set by the *tarif de convention*. Note that some *non-conventionné* practitioners are approved (*agréé*) by social security, but only a small proportion of fees are reimbursed. The reimbursement you receive applies only to the standard medical charges (*tarif de convention*). For example if a blood test costs 500F and the *tarif de convention* is 400F, you would pay the difference of 100F plus 30 per cent of 400F (120F) after social security has refunded its 70 per cent (280F), leaving you with a total bill of 220F. You can, however, take out insurance to pay the portion that isn't paid by social security (see page 232).

There are also special classes of medical professionals classified as *conventionné honoraires libres*, who although they are *conventionné*, are permitted to charge higher fees than the standard rates. These include practitioners who perform special services (*dépassement exceptionnel*) and those with a special title or expertise (*dépassement permanent*). If you're in any doubt, you should ask exactly what the fee is for a consultation or treatment and what percentage will be reimbursed by social security.

Medical treatment must usually be paid for in advance and a claim for reimbursement made to social security and your *mutuelle* later. When paying bills, cash is preferred to cheques, particularly when dealing with non-resident foreigners, although cheques drawn on a French bank are acceptable. One benefit of the payment in advance system, is that it reduces the number of time wasters and hypochondriacs (*malades imaginaires*). If you're unable to pay your portion of the bill (the *ticket modérateur*), you can apply to your social security payment centre (*Caisse Primaire d'Assurance Maladie*) for a waiver (*prise en charge*). In the case of urgent or necessary treatment, approval is a formality.

To be reimbursed by social security for certain medical treatment, you must obtain prior approval from your *caisse*. This may include physical examinations, special dental care, contact lenses and special lenses for glasses, certain laboratory and radiology tests, and thermal and therapeutic treatments. Your medical practitioner will give you a proposal form (*demande d'entente préalable*) and you should apply at least 21 days before the proposed treatment and obtain a receipt for your application (if made in person) or send it by registered mail. If you don't receive a reply from your *caisse* within ten working days or two weeks, they are deemed to have agreed to the request. For information about social security see page 254.

Reimbursement Procedure

Each medical practitioner you see whose fees are wholly or partly refundable by social security completes a treatment form (*feuille de soins*). These may be different colours, for example doctors use a brown and white form and dentists a green and white form. The treatment provided, medicines prescribed and the cost are listed on the form. The same form can be used for subsequent visits to the same practitioner, e.g. a doctor or dentist, in connection with the same illness or problem. You must pay the medical practitioner for the treatment received on each visit.

If your doctor has prescribed medicine, take the treatment form (*feuille de soins*) to a pharmacy with the prescription form (*ordonnance*). The pharmacist will enter the amount and cost of medicines listed on the *feuille de soins*. Each medicine container has a detachable colour-coded label (*vignette*) listing the name and cost of the medicine. These must be affixed to the *feuille de soins* next to where the pharmacist has written the name and price of each medicine. This may be done by the pharmacist. The pharmacy will return the duplicate of the prescription form, which must be attached to the *feuille de soins*. You pay the pharmacist the full cost of medicines and reclaim the cost from social security and your *mutuelle* (as applicable).

Don't forget to sign and date the *feuille de soins* at the bottom right before sending it to your social security office (*caisse*), the address of which is shown on your social security card. If you're requesting a reimbursement for auxiliary services prescribed by a doctor, you must accompany the treatment form with a copy of the doctor's original prescription. You can save a number of *feuille de soins* forms and send them together. Note that if forms aren't correctly completed, they will be returned. The refund will be paid directly into the bank or post office account that was designated when you registered with social security. It's possible to receive payment in cash, although this isn't encouraged. You will receive your reimbursement any time from a few days to a few months after application, depending on the office and the amount involved.

Always keep a copy of your *feuilles de soins* and check that reimbursements are received and correct. When a reimbursement has been paid into your account, you will receive notification from social security detailing the amount and the reason for the payment. This document is necessary to claim reimbursement of the *ticket modérateur* (the amount that isn't reimbursed by social security) from your complementary insurance company.

The social security system is currently replacing the pink *feuille de soins* cards with an electronic medicard (*carte à puce*), called *Vitale*, that covers all members of a family. It's expected to be in widespread use by the end of the year 2000 (some medical practises have been slow to introduce it due to the new equipment required). *Vitale* will enable local medical services to link with Health Boards to process reimbursements and bypass the postal system, thus speeding up the payment process. A *Vitale* card is valid for three years and by the year 2005 is expected to be replaced by a new version, *Vitale 2*, containing your medical records and vital information such as blood group and allergies.

DOCTORS

There are excellent doctors (*médecins*) throughout France, although finding a doctor who speaks good (or any) English can be a problem, particularly in rural areas. Many embassies and consulates in France maintain a list of English-speaking doctors and specialists in their area (or doctors speaking their national language) and your employer, colleagues or neighbours may also be able to recommend someone. Local town halls keep a list of local practitioners and local pharmacies also have a list of local doctors and may recommend someone. You can also obtain a list of doctors registered with social security from your local social security office or by consulting Minitel (see page 125). General practitioners (GPs) or family doctors are listed in Yellow Pages under *médecins généralistes* and specialists under *médecins qualifiés* and their speciality, e.g. *gynécologie médicale*.

You can choose to see any doctor, specialist or consultant at any time in France, and you aren't required to register with a doctor or visit a doctor within a certain distance of your home. This means that you have total freedom of choice and can choose to see a general practitioner (*médecin généraliste*) or a specialist (*spécialiste*), depending on your needs. This also makes it easy to obtain a second opinion, should you wish to do so. Many French doctors are specialists in acupuncture and homeopathy, both of which are reimbursed by social security when performed or prescribed by an approved (*conventionné*) doctor or practitioner. Note that it's normal practice to pay a doctor or other medical practitioner after each visit, whether you're a private or social security patient (see **Reimbursement Procedure** on page 234). A routine doctor's visit usually costs between around 115F and 150F (more for home visits), of which social security pays 110F.

If you need the services of a medical auxiliary such as a nurse, physiotherapist or chiropodist, you must obtain a referral or prescription from a doctor in order to be reimbursed by social security. You may then select your own practitioner, although if you need to see a medical specialist such as a gynaecologist, ophthalmologist or paediatrician, you don't usually need to be referred by your doctor. However, unless you know exactly what the problem is, it's advisable to see your family doctor first and obtain a referral to a specialist (which most specialists prefer). The fee for a consultation is from around 150F, which is the social security reimbursement.

In addition to private and group practises, family doctors also practise at local out-patient health care centres (*centres médicaux et sociaux, dispensaires*), offering services that are usually unavailable at doctors' surgeries. Centres usually provide health screening, vaccinations and a wide range of health care services including dental (*soins dentaires*) and nursing care (*soins infirmiers*). Some specialise in a particular field of medicine such as cancer, cardiac or tuberculosis care. Although it isn't always necessary to make an appointment, it's advisable (unless you like waiting for hours). As when visiting a doctor, check whether the centre is *conventionné* (see page 232). In some areas there are outpatient services (*centres de soins*) run by private organisations such as the Red Cross. You can obtain a list of local health care centres from your town hall.

Surgery hours may vary from day-to-day, e.g. morning surgery from 0900 to 1130 or noon Tuesdays to Saturdays and afternoons from 1400 to 1630 Mondays to Fridays. It isn't usually necessary to make an appointment and you can usually just turn up during surgery hours, although Saturdays may be by appointment only. Lists of doctors receiving patients on Sundays and public holidays are posted on pharmacy doors and can be obtained from local police stations. Local newspapers also usually contain lists of doctors, pharmacies and vets who are on call over the weekend (under the heading *Urgences*). If your doctor is unavailable, his surgery will give you the name of a standby doctor. If you're unable to attend the surgery, your doctor will make a house call. Note, however, that doctors charge higher fees for house calls, particularly at night, and therefore are usually quite happy to be called out.

When you visit a French doctor, you're invariably given a number of prescriptions (*ordonnances*), which are freely dispensed in France. The standing of a doctor with his patients often depends on the number of prescriptions he prescribes and therefore French doctors commonly prescribe a potpourri of medicines (for the same complaint you may be offered an aspirin in other countries). Often this will be in the form of a rectal suppository (*suppositoire*), used by the French to treat everything from a common cold to a sore throat. This isn't because French doctors have an obsession with bottoms, but because it's the fastest way of getting drugs into the bloodstream (via the bowel or lower intestine). Never take a suppository orally – they are usually difficult to confuse with oral pills, due to their size and shape.

It's also common practice in France to have your temperature taken rectally, so if you're bashful you may prefer to choose a doctor of a particular sex. You can request that your temperature be taken orally, although you may need to provide your own oral thermometer. Injections (*piqûres*) and powders (*poudres*) are also frequently prescribed. If medicine needs to be administered by a nurse, e.g. by injection, or other nursing services are necessary, your doctor or pharmacist will give you the name of a local nurse. Treatment can be administered at your home or at a nurse's office and is paid by social security.

Employees in France must (by law) have a medical examination (*médecin du travail*) when they are hired and annually thereafter. If you're a member of social security, you will be issued with a medical certificate (*certificat de santé*). This must be produced before participation in certain sports and must be obtained privately if you aren't covered by social security. A more thorough medical check (*bilan de santé*) is available free on demand every five years (a total of nine during a person's adult life) under social security. Technically it's mandatory for everyone to have a physical examination between the ages of 25 and 35 and between the ages of 45 and 55. Before marrying in France, a couple must undergo a mandatory physical examination no more than two months prior to marriage, which includes a blood test and chest X-ray. In France, the results of medical tests (e.g. blood, urine, heart, smear, etc.) and X-rays are the property of the patient, who receives a copy.

Each child in France is issued with a health record book (*carnet de santé*) in which is recorded every medical occurrence in his life, including vaccinations, childhood illnesses, general medical care and surgery. It should always be taken with you on a medical visit with your child. If you give birth in France, you will be issued with a *carnet de santé* by your town hall. Foreigners can obtain a *carnet de santé* for a child from their town hall on production of the child's passport. There's a small charge if you aren't covered by social security. The *carnet* is obligatory for all school-age children and must be produced when starting school (see **Children's Health** on page 243).

DRUGS & MEDICINES

Drugs and medicines (*médicaments*) prescribed by a doctor are obtained from a pharmacy (*pharmacie*) denoted by a sign depicting a green cross on a white background, often circled in red. Most pharmacies are open from 0900 to 1900 or 1930 from Mondays to Saturdays, although many close for lunch from noon or 1230 to 1400. Some are closed on Mondays. Outside normal opening hours, a notice giving the address of the nearest duty pharmacy (*pharmacie de garde*) is displayed in the windows of pharmacies (the telephone numbers of local doctors on call may also be posted). They are also published in local newspapers and listed in monthly bulletins issued by town halls. In most cities, several pharmacies are open until late evening or early morning and in Paris a 24-hour service is provided by the Pharmacie Les Champs, 84, avenue des Champs-Elysées, 75008 Paris (☎ 01.45.62.02.41). There are also American and British pharmacies in Paris, stocking familiar American and British medicines and drugs. A pharmacist in France must own and run his own pharmacy (chain pharmacies are illegal) and their numbers are strictly controlled.

The French take a lot of drugs and medicines (the national average is around 14 per person, per year), particularly tranquillisers and anti-depressants such as Prozac and Valium, and are the hypochondriacs of Europe. Drugs prescribed by doctors represent over 80 per cent of sales and doctors habitually prescribe three or four different remedies for each ailment. The cost of prescription drugs is controlled by the government (prices are reviewed twice a year) and the per capita cost is some 40 per cent higher than in Germany. There are no price controls on non-prescription drugs. Many French doctors prescribe homeopathic medicines, stocked by all pharmacies, many of which specialise in homeopathy. Pharmacies may need your name and address before they will dispense certain drugs. Note that *drogues* are narcotics, which aren't sold in pharmacies in France!

You must pay the full cost for medicines, a percentage of which will be reimbursed if you're a member of social security. The amount reimbursed depends on the medicines prescribed. Social security pays the whole cost (100 per cent) of essential medication for certain illnesses or conditions (such as insulin for diabetics) with labels marked 100 per cent; 65 per cent of medicines designated as important (with white labels); and 35 per cent for others (with blue labels, termed *médicaments de confort*). You're reimbursed when you return the treatment form (*feuille de soins*) with the labels (*vignettes*) from the medicines to your local social security office (see **Reimbursement Procedure** on page 234). If you belong to a complementary (*mutuelle*) insurance scheme, it will reimburse the amount that isn't paid by social security. Note that there's no refund for some prescribed medicines or for medicines purchased without a doctor's prescription. If you must pay for your own drugs and medicines it can be expensive, e.g. 700F for a course of antibiotics.

Pharmacists in France are trained and obliged to give first aid and they can also perform tests such as blood pressure. They can supply a wider range of medicines over the counter without a prescription than is available in Britain and the USA, although some medicines sold freely in other countries require a doctor's prescription in France. A pharmacist will recommend non-prescription medicines for minor ailments and can also recommend a local doctor, specialist, nurse or dentist. Pharmacists in France are trained to distinguish between around 50 species of edible and poisonous fungi, and will tell you whether those you have picked are delicious mushrooms or deadly toadstools. They are also trained to identify local snakes to enable them to prescribe the correct antidote for bites.

Note that the brand names for the same drugs and medicines often vary from country to country, so if you regularly take medication, you should ask your doctor for the generic name. If you wish to match medication prescribed abroad, you need a current prescription with the medication's trade name, the manufacturer's name, the chemical name and the dosage. Most foreign drugs have an equivalent in France, although particular brands may be difficult or impossible to obtain. It's possible to have medication sent from abroad and no import duty or value added tax (TVA) is payable. If you're visiting France for a limited period, you should take sufficient drugs to cover the length of your stay. In an emergency a local doctor will write a prescription that can be filled at a local pharmacy or a hospital may refill a prescription from its own pharmacy.

French pharmacies aren't cluttered with the non-medical wares found in American and British pharmacies, although many do sell cosmetics and toiletries (called *parapharmacie*). Pharmacies are cheaper than a *parfumerie* for cosmetics, but more expensive than a supermarket or hypermarket. Non-prescription medicines can also be purchased in supermarkets and hypermarkets. A *droguerie* is a sort of hardware store selling toiletries, cleaning supplies, a wide range of general household goods, paint, garden supplies, tools and do-it-yourself supplies. A French *droguerie* shouldn't be confused with an American drug store, a general store come fast food outlet. There are American-style drug stores in Paris selling books, newspapers, magazines, tobacco goods, alcohol, pharmaceuticals, clothes, groceries and souvenirs (they also have restaurants). A health food shop (*magasin de produits diététiques*) sells health foods, diet foods and eternal-life-virility-youth pills and elixirs. A well-known chain is *Naturalia France*.

HOSPITALS & CLINICS

All French cities and large towns have at least one hospital (*hôpital*) or clinic (*clinique*), indicated by the international hospital sign of a white 'H' on a blue background. Hospitals are listed in Yellow Pages under *hôpitaux et hospices*. There are many different categories of hospitals, both public and private.

Public Hospitals: There are generally three categories of public hospitals in France: hospital centres or short-stay hospitals (*hôpitaux de court séjour*), medium-stay centres (*centres de moyen séjour*) and long-term treatment centres (*centres et unités de long séjour*). Hospital centres include general hospitals, *Assistance Publique (AP)* hospitals in Paris, specialist hospitals and regional centres (*Centre Hospitalier Régional/CHR* or *Centre Hospitalier Universitaire/CHU* when associated with a university). Rural community hospitals are also classified as hospital centres, although they are usually less well-equipped than other short-stay hospitals.

Medium-stay hospitals are usually for patients who have previously been treated in a short-stay hospital centre. They contain facilities for convalescence, occupational and physical therapy, and recuperative treatment for drug and alcohol abuse and mental illness. Long-term treatment centres are for those who are unable to care for themselves without assistance and include psychiatric hospitals and nursing homes for the aged (*maisons de retraite*). AP hospitals in Paris are rated among the best in France and professors and senior staff must undergo intensive training to secure their appointments. The majority of teaching and research in France is carried out at AP hospitals and public hospitals attached to universities. Public hospitals must accept all patients irrespective of their ability to pay.

Private Hospitals and clinics: Most private hospitals (*hôpitaux privés*) and clinics (*cliniques*) in France specialise in in-patient care in particular fields of medicine such as obstetrics and surgery, rather than being full-service hospitals (the American Hospital in Paris is a rare exception). Some non-profit, private hospitals participate in French social security and operate in the same way as public hospitals. These include the British (Hertford) and International hospitals in Paris. The cost of treatment in a private hospital or clinic is generally much higher than in a public hospital, where a large proportion of costs are reimbursed by social security.

If your French is poor, you may prefer to be treated at a private hospital or clinic with English-speaking staff, as most French hospitals make little or no allowance for foreigners who don't speak French. There are a number of expatriate hospitals in the Paris area including the American Hospital in Paris (63, boulevard Victor Hugo, 92202 Neuilly, ☎ 01.46.41.25.25 or 01.47.47.70.15 (emergencies)) and the Hertford British Hospital (3, rue Barbès, 92300 Lavallois-Perret, ☎ 01.46.39.22.22), which specialises in maternity cases. Most staff at all levels in these hospitals speak English. Fees at the American hospital are much higher than French hospitals, although they are recognised by most American medical insurance companies.

Except for emergency treatment, you're admitted or referred to a hospital or clinic for treatment only after a recommendation (*attestation*) from a doctor or a specialist. Normally you're admitted to a hospital in your own *département*, unless specialist surgery or treatment is necessary which is unavailable there. If you wish to be treated in hospital by your personal doctor, you must check that he's able to treat you at your preferred hospital. You can usually leave hospital at any time without a doctor's consent by signing a release form (*décharge de responsabilité*).

The basic hospital accommodation in public hospitals (*conventionné*) that's reimbursed by social security is two or three-bed rooms (*régime commun*). Sometimes the facilities provided in public hospitals are limited compared with private hospitals and there may be no private rooms. If available, a supplement must be paid for a private room, although it may be paid in part or in full by your complementary or other private health insurance. You can usually rent a radio, TV or telephone for a small daily fee if they aren't included in the room fee. The best hospital accommodation is similar to five-star hotels with food and wine (and prices!) to match. A bed is also usually provided for relatives if required. You must normally provide your own pyjamas, robes, towels and toiletries.

Upon admission to a hospital you usually receive an information booklet (*livret d'accueil*) containing meal schedules, visiting hours, floor plan, doctors' names, hospital rules, and a description of the uniforms and name tags worn by hospital staff. Visiting hours are usually from 1330 or 1400 to 2030 or 2100 daily. Visits can also be made outside these hours in exceptional circumstances. In a private clinic there may be no restrictions on visiting hours.

Like doctors and other medical practitioners, hospitals are either *conventionné* or *non-conventionné* (see **Social Security Health Benefits** on page 232). Every large town has at least one convention hospital (*hôpital conventionné*), which may be public or private, usually with a direct payment agreement with social security. Private hospitals and clinics that are *non-conventionné* may also have an agreement (*agréé*) with social security. Usually around 30 per cent of the fees at private *non-conventionné* hospitals or clinics that are *agréé* are paid by social security (supplemented by a *mutuelle*). For non-urgent hospital treatment, check in advance the reimbursement made by social security and if applicable, the amount your *mutuelle* or other private health insurance will pay. Except in the case of emergencies, you must provide the following documents on admittance to a public hospital in order to receive reimbursement from social security:

- your social security card (*carte d'immatriculation*);

- a doctor's certificate (*attestation*) stating the reason for hospitalisation;

- documents provided by your social security office (*caisse*) stating the conditions under which you're insured, e.g. if you're unemployed, you need a document stating that you're entitled to unemployment benefits.

If you aren't covered by social security, you must provide evidence of your health insurance, salary or ability to pay. If you're unable to pay you may be refused treatment at a private hospital or clinic, except in the case of emergency treatment. If a woman is hospitalised to give birth or in connection with a pregnancy, she must have a *carnet de maternité* (see **Childbirth** below). An employer must provide an *accident du travail* form when an employee is hospitalised due to an accident at work.

Certain patients, classified as needing serious long-term treatment, receive 100 per cent reimbursement, e.g. cardiac, diabetes and cancer patients. Pensioners receive free hospital treatment under social security, although up to 90 per cent of their pension may be deducted to compensate for the cost of treatment (while in hospital). A stay at a spa is usually reimbursed at 70 per cent or higher when recommended by a doctor and approved by social security. Convalescence after a serious illness is often paid 100 per cent by social security.

Hospital bills can be *very* high, e.g. 1,000F to 1,500F per day for medicine, accommodation and meals plus 1,500F to 2,000F for surgery, or much more for a major operation. If you're paying a bill yourself for elective surgery, you should shop around, not just in France but in other countries, as the price can vary considerably. Note, however, that some operations are performed in France for half or less than a third of the price in some other European countries. Most French people subscribe to a complementary (*mutuelle*) insurance scheme that pays the portion of bills that isn't paid by social security (see page 232). If you're covered by social security, 80 to 100 per cent of your hospital bill will be paid by them direct to the hospital. You must pay the balance of the bill (if applicable) when you leave hospital, unless you have made prior arrangements for it to be paid by social security or your insurance company. You must pay for hospital out-patient treatment in the same way as a visit to a doctor or specialist (see **Reimbursement Procedure** on page 234).

If a medical bill is expected to be above a certain amount, which is increased annually in line with inflation, you can apply to social security for a waiver (*prise en charge*). This means that social security will pay the full bill direct to the hospital.

Social security patients are charged a fixed daily fee (*forfait journalier/indemnité journalière*) for meals of around 70F per day, unless hospitalisation was due to an accident at work or you're exempt on the grounds of low income. This daily fee is usually reimbursed by complementary health insurance.

CHILDBIRTH

Childbirth in France usually takes place in a hospital, where a stay of 5 to 12 days is normal, depending on factors such as the number of beds available and the mother's health and home conditions. Most maternity units are equipped with single and double bedrooms. When admitted to hospital, you must provide a *carnet de maternité* in addition to the documents listed above. Note that it's expensive to have a child in a hospital in France if you aren't covered by French social security or don't have private medical insurance, in which case it may be cheaper to have your child at home or in a hospital abroad. Social security pays 100 per cent of most medical expenses relating to a pregnancy including medical examinations and tests, antenatal care and the delivery. It even pays for a physical examination for the father – to check whether he's well enough to survive the ordeal!

A hospital bed must usually be booked in advance, usually before the tenth week of pregnancy, although this isn't always feasible or necessary (babies have a habit of popping out at the most unexpected times). You can also have a baby at home. Ask your family doctor or obstetrician for information and advice. Before booking a bed in a hospital or clinic, you should ask if it's *conventionné* (see page 232). Other things you may wish to investigate are whether your husband is allowed to attend the delivery, whether breast-feeding is practiced, and what clothes and other articles you need to provide. Mothers must usually provide clothes and accessories (which are *very* expensive in France) for new-born babies in French hospitals, although supplies are provided.

In a public hospital, expectant mothers are supervised by an obstetrician, although he will become closely involved in a birth only if complications are expected or when it's classified as 'high-risk'. You can, of course, engage a private obstetrician to attend you before, during and after giving birth, although this won't be paid for by social security, but may be covered by private health insurance. Your doctor will give you a booklet, *Vous Attendez un Enfant*, containing a number of forms to be completed as your pregnancy progresses.

To qualify for social security benefits, mothers-to-be must undergo four antenatal examinations during their third, sixth, eighth and ninth months of pregnancy. Routine scans (*échographies*), where examinations are made using sound waves, are used to check foetal growth and to detect abnormalities (usually after four and seven months). After your first examination you receive a certificate (*attestation de premier examen prénatal obligatoire*) that must be sent to your *Caisse d'Allocations Familiales* to ensure you receive your social security benefits.

Midwives (*sages-femmes*), who are qualified nurses with special training, handle most routine pregnancies in France and play an important part in childbirth. They are responsible for educating and supporting women and their families during the childbearing period, including giving natural childbirth lessons. Midwives can advise women before they become pregnant, in addition to providing moral, physical and emotional support, both during pregnancy and after a birth. A midwife may also advise on parent education and antenatal classes for mothers. All public hospitals and many private clinics offer natural childbirth classes. French social security also pays for free 'gymnastic lessons' (*kinésithérapie*) with a physical therapist after giving birth. Pharmacists can provide advice for pregnant women and new mothers concerning nutrition and supplements, and the care and feeding of babies. In some areas there are mother and child protection centres (*Centre de Protection Maternelle et Infantile/PMI*) providing free services to pregnant women and children aged under six covered by social security. A list of local PMI centres is available from your local town hall.

France used to have a restricted list of Christian names taken from the Christian calendar, to which parents were limited when naming a child. However, the law was recently changed and you can now name your child anything from Ambrosia to Zacharia (with reckless disregard for the poor kid who has to live with it!). All births must be registered within three days at the town hall in the district where a child is born (see **Births & Deaths** on page 247). If you give birth in France you receive a health record book (*carnet de santé*) from your town hall in which is recorded every medical occurrence in a person's life, including vaccinations, childhood illnesses, general medical care and surgery. It should always be taken with you on a medical visit with your child. Your family doctor or obstetrician will advise you about postnatal examinations and check-ups, listed in the *carnet de santé*. If you have private health insurance, don't forget to notify your health insurance company about your new arrival. Also notify social security and make sure that you receive the correct child allowance benefit (see page 260), if applicable.

There are information (*établissements d'information*) and family planning centres (*centres de planification familiale*) staffed by specialised counsellors and medical professionals throughout France. These provide information and counselling (usually free) about contraception, abortion, and sexual and marital problems. Family planning centres also prescribe contraceptives, diagnose pregnancies, and provide gynaecological examinations and treatment. Family planning centres such as *Le Planning Familial* provide information on contraception and have centres in all areas. A prescription is necessary for certain contraceptive devices and birth control pills (*pilule*), although there are no age restrictions. Condoms (*préservatifs*) and sponges (*ovules*) can be purchased without a prescription from a pharmacy.

Abortions (*interruption volontaire de grossesse/IVG*) are legal in France and must be performed before the tenth week of pregnancy in a hospital or clinic. Therapeutic abortions are allowed at any time during a pregnancy if the life of the mother is at risk or there's a high probability that a child will be born with a serious or incurable disorder. Abortion is available on demand for all except minors under the age of 18, who require the consent of a parent or guardian or a children's judge. A single woman doesn't need the consent of the father and a married women doesn't need her husband's consent to have an abortion. The cost of an abortion is paid for by social security. There are no abortion clinics in France and abortions are performed in a public hospital or an authorised private hospital or clinic. Note that as in most other Catholic countries, abortion is a controversial subject in France.

Many organisations provide counselling services for pregnant women including the *Association Grossesse Secours*, 51, rue Jeanne d'Arc, 75013 Paris (☎ 01.45.84.55.91), the *Mouvement Français du Planning Familial*, 4, square St.-Irénée, 75011 Paris (☎ 01.48.07.29.10) and the English-speaking International Counselling Service, 65, quai d'Orsay, 75007 Paris (☎ 01.45.50.26.49). A book of interest to mothers-to-be is *ABCs of Motherhood in Paris* published by Message (to order contact Sallie Chaballier on ☎ 01.48.04.74.61).

CHILDREN'S HEALTH

France provides excellent health treatment for children, for whom it provides a comprehensive programme of preventive medicine and a variety of special medical facilities. Children born in France are issued with a health record (*carnet de santé*) in which is recorded every medical occurrence in their lives including vaccinations, childhood illnesses, general medical care and surgery. It should always be taken with you on a medical visit with your child. You can obtain a *carnet de santé* for children who weren't born in France from your local town hall on production of the child's passport. If you're covered by social security it's provided free, otherwise there's a small fee. Postnatal examinations and check-ups required during a child's first six years are also listed in the *carnet de santé*. The *carnet* is obligatory for school age children and must be produced when starting school.

Vaccinations against diphtheria (*diphtérie*), polio and tetanus (*tétanos*), collectively called DPT, and whooping cough (*coqueluche*) are given between the third and fifth months after birth. DPT boosters are administered at 12 to 15 months and again at 5 to 6 years and are repeated thereafter at 5 to 6-year intervals. Although it isn't compulsory, a multiple vaccination called ROR (or *rudirouvax*) against measles (*rougeole*), mumps (*oreillons*) and German measles (*rubéole*) is recommended between the age of 12 and 15 months. Vaccinations are provided free and are compulsory for DPT and tuberculosis (called BCG), which must be administered before the age of six. When you arrive in France, you should bring proof of your child's immunisations with you.

Not all French hospitals have paediatric units, particularly private hospitals. In an emergency you should take your child to a hospital catering for paediatric emergencies. Children aged 15 and under are usually treated in a special children's unit well stocked with games, toys, books and other children. Children who require long-term hospitalisation, may, depending on their health, be given school lessons in hospital. Many hospitals permit a parent to stay with a child in hospital and some allow children, depending on their health, to attend during the day and return home at night. A free booklet, *L'Hôpital et l'Enfant*, is available (in French) containing information and advice for parents with children in hospital.

DENTISTS

There are excellent dentists (*dentistes*) throughout France, although few speak fluent English (*Aaargh!* is the same in any language). Many embassies keep a list of English-speaking dentists in their area (or a list of dentists speaking their national language) and your employer, colleagues or neighbours may be able to recommend someone. Town halls maintain a list of local dentists and local pharmacies may recommend someone. You can also obtain a list of dentists registered with social security from your local social security office or by consulting Minitel (see page 125). Dentists are listed in telephone directories under *Dentistes* and by town. Usually only names, addresses and telephone numbers are listed, and information such as specialities, surgery hours and whether they treat children (some don't) isn't provided. Many family dentists in France are qualified to perform special treatment, e.g. endodontics (*endodontie*) or periodontics (*paradontie*), carried out by specialists in many other countries.

Dentists' surgery hours vary considerably, but are typically 0900 to noon and 1400 to 1900. Some dentists have Saturday morning surgeries, e.g. 0900 to noon. You must make an appointment. Many dentists provide an emergency service and there are special emergency services in Paris and other major cities. In Paris, there's a 24-hour home emergency dental service called *SOS Dentaire* (☎ 01.43.37.51.00). Dentists are equipped with radio cars, carry portable equipment and respond quickly to calls. The cost of a house call by a dentist is from around 200F before 1900 and 300F after 1900, plus the cost of treatment.

As with doctors, check whether a dentist is *conventionné* if you wish to be treated under social security (see **Social Security Health Benefits** on page 232). Social security pays 34.5 per cent of the cost of dental care and hygiene and 48 per cent of the cost of prosthetic treatment, e.g. crowns and bridges. The maximum amount reimbursed varies depending on the actual work completed, e.g. 1,200F for a partial metal crown, 2,200F for a ceramic crown and 2,500F for a complete crown. You must obtain a written description of treatment plus an estimate of the cost for social security. Orthodontic treatment, e.g. the straightening of teeth, also requires prior approval and is generally restricted to children aged under 12. Sometimes it pays to have private treatment, as social security pays dentists only a small amount for some jobs (such as cleaning teeth) and they are therefore less likely to do a thorough job.

As when visiting a doctor, a dentist will give you a statement of treatment (*feuille de soins*) on which is listed the treatment provided and the cost. The same *feuille* can be used for subsequent visits until treatment is completed. When the course of treatment is complete, send or take the *feuille de soins* to your local social security office (*caisse*) to obtain reimbursement (see **Reimbursement Procedure** on page 234). It's normal practice to pay a dentist after a course of treatment is completed, although if you're having expensive treatment such as a crown or bridge made, your dentist may ask for a deposit.

Always obtain a written estimate before committing yourself to a large bill and double it to get a more realistic idea of the cost. If you or your family require expensive cosmetic dental treatment, e.g. crowns, bridges, braces or false teeth, it may be cheaper to have treatment abroad (e.g. in Britain) where it may cost 50 per cent less. Alternatively, ask your dentist if he can reduce the cost by reducing the work involved. Dental treatment can be expensive in France, e.g. 8,000F for a crown, so it will pay you to keep your mouth shut during dental visits. See also **Dental Insurance** on page 266.

OPTICIANS

As with other medical practitioners in France, it isn't necessary to register with an optician or optometrist (*opticien*). You simply make an appointment with the optician of your choice. Ask your colleagues, friends or neighbours if they can recommend someone. Opticians are listed in the Yellow Pages under *Opticiens* and eye specialists under *Ophtalmologues*.

The optician business is competitive in France and prices for spectacles and contact lenses aren't controlled, so it's wise to shop around and compare costs. In Paris and other cities, there are large optical chains where spectacles can be made within an hour. Always obtain an estimate for lenses and ask about charges for such things as eye tests, fittings, adjustments, lens-care kit and follow-up visits. Note that the cost of special lenses can increase the cost of spectacles considerably. Ask the cost of replacement lenses; if they're expensive, it may be worthwhile taking out insurance. Many opticians and retailers offer insurance against the accidental damage of spectacles for a nominal fee. The cost of spectacles and contact lenses in France is generally higher than in some other European countries, e.g. soft contact lenses are cheaper in Britain and Germany.

Disposable and extended-wear soft contact lenses are widely available, although medical experts believe they should be treated with extreme caution, as they can greatly increase the risk of potentially blinding eye infections. **Obtain advice from an ophthalmologist before buying them.**

To obtain reimbursement from social security, it's necessary to have your eyes examined by an ophthalmologist (*ophtalmologue*). An ophthalmologist is a specialist medical doctor trained in diagnosing and treating disorders of the eye, performing sight tests, and prescribing spectacles and contact lenses. If glasses are necessary, the ophthalmologist will write a prescription which you then take to an optician. An optician is trained to test eyesight and to manufacture spectacles. If you're obtaining spectacles under social security, you must choose an optician who's approved (*agréé*) by social security. Social security pays for 70 per cent of the cost of lenses and a 'basic' frame, providing your vision has changed or your spectacles are broken beyond repair. You need prior approval from your *caisse* if you need contact lenses, bifocals or tinted lenses. If applicable, your optician will complete the necessary documents for social security.

It's advisable to have your eyes tested before you arrive in France and to bring a spare pair of spectacles and/or contact lenses with you. You should also bring a copy of your prescription in case you need to obtain replacement spectacles or contact lenses urgently.

COUNSELLING & SOCIAL SERVICES

Counselling and help for special health and social problems is available throughout France and include drug rehabilitation; alcoholism and related problems; gambling; dieting; smoking; teenage pregnancy; attempted suicide and psychiatric problems; rehabilitation; homosexual related problems; youth problems; parent-child problems; child abuse; family violence (e.g. battered wives); runaways; marriage and relationship counselling; and rape. There are self-help groups in all areas for problems such as alcoholism (e.g. Alcoholics Anonymous), gambling and weight control (e.g. Weight Watchers).

One of France's major health problems is alcoholism, which is directly responsible for the loss of some 17,000 lives a year, mostly in poor urban and rural areas (usually as a result of drinking cheap red wine rather than spirits). The legal age for drinking alcohol in France is 16, although there's virtually no enforcement and children are readily served and sold alcohol everywhere. There are a number of English-speaking Alcoholics Anonymous (*Alcooliques Anonymes*) groups in Paris (☎ 01.48.06.43.68 for information) and other areas, and French-speaking groups throughout France.

Although it's a serious health problem, the use of illegal drugs is less widespread in France than in North America and some other European countries such as Britain, Germany and the Netherlands. For nationwide free information about drug-related problems contact 08.00.23.13.13. A list of regional organisations providing information and treatment for drug abuse can be obtained from *Mission Interministérielle de Lutte contre la Toxicomanie*, 71, rue St. Dominique, 75007 Paris (☎ 01.45.55.92.30).

The telephone numbers of various local counselling and help services (*Services d'Assistance*) are listed at the front of telephone books and include numbers for *SOS amitié*, drug related problems and Aids. *SOS amitié* provide a free telephone counselling service in times of personal crisis and is the French equivalent of the Samaritans. SOS-Help is an English-speaking Paris-based telephone crisis line in operation from 1500 to 2300 daily (☎ 01.47.23.80.80).

SEXUALLY-TRANSMITTED DISEASES

As in most western countries, the spread of Aids in France continues to cause anxiety. France has the highest incidence of Aids (Acquired Immune Deficiency Syndrome) in the European Union, largely as a result of its large African population (Aids has reached epidemic proportions in some African countries). Aids, called *Syndrome Immuno-Déficitaire Acquis/SIDA* in French, is transmitted by sexual contact, needle sharing among drug addicts, and less commonly, through transfused blood or its components (the French government was rocked by an Aids-infected blood scandal in 1985). The spread of Aids is accelerated by prostitutes, many of whom are also drug addicts, and hypodermic syringe vending machines have been installed in some towns to combat it. Many French heterosexuals don't take the threat of Aids seriously, particularly as most of its victims to date (at least in the western world) have been homosexuals and drug addicts. There's no cure for Aids, which is always fatal.

The most common protection against Aids is for men to wear a condom (supported by Catholic bishops in France), although they're not foolproof (against Aids or pregnancy) and the only real protection is celibacy. In an attempt to combat Aids, the use of condoms (*préservatifs*) has been widely encouraged through a comprehensive (if obscure) advertising campaign, although it has taken a long time to get the message across on safe sex. Condom machines have been installed in various public places including *métro* stations and high schools. Condoms can be bought cheaply in supermarkets and other stores. The English and French credit (blame?) each other with the invention of the condom, called *la capote anglaise* in France and a 'French letter' in Britain (although only the French have a town named after it!). Although condoms are called 'preservatives' in French, don't expect to find them in the food section of supermarkets in different flavours!

Public health centres throughout France provide free information and confidential tests (*dépistages*) for Aids and other venereal diseases. Treatment of venereal diseases is provided free or at a nominal cost. General information about venereal diseases can be obtained from the *Ligue Nationale contre les Maladies Vénériennes*, Institut Alfred-Fournier, 25, bd Saint-Jaques, 75014 Paris (☎ 01.40.78.26.00). Information about Aids is available on Minitel (3615 Sida) and there are many information and support groups in France. Telephone information is available 24 hours a day on 08.00.84.08.40 and there's also an Aids Helpline in English (☎ 01.44.93.16.69) on Mondays, Wednesdays and Fridays from 1800 to 2200. Written information and advice is also available from *Centre Régional d'Information et de Prevention du Sida*, 192, rue Lecourbe, 75015 Paris (☎ 01.53.68.88.88).

SMOKING

France has some 12 million smokers and the cheapest cigarettes in Europe. The sale of cigarettes is strictly controlled by the state, which owns the French cigarette manufacturers and collects 30 billion francs in taxes annually (taxes have been dramatically increased in the last few years to encourage people to stop smoking). Cigarettes can be purchased only at a licensed *tabac* in France. Although smoking has declined in France in recent years, it remains higher than in most other European countries. It's estimated that over 50,000 deaths a year are directly attributable to smoking and that it adds some 50F billion to medical costs.

France has traditionally been extremely tolerant of smokers, with most people indifferent or oblivious to the needs or rights of non-smokers. Passive smoking isn't much of an issue in France, where you may even see signs proudly proclaiming *This is a smoking area – non-smokers are tolerated*. French non-smokers don't declare their offices non-smoking zones and asking people not to smoke is likely to attract indifference or even abuse.

However, the passive smoking issue was brought starkly into the spotlight with the introduction of new and controversial anti-smoking laws in 1992, the most radical in Europe. They prohibited smoking in all enclosed or covered public spaces including schools, shops, public offices, public transport and work places. Restaurants and cafés must provide an area for non-smokers. If they cannot do this, then under the law they are considered to be entirely non-smoking. However, many establishments either ignore the new law or create a remote non-smoking section or floor (in 'Siberia') where most customers wouldn't wish to be seen dead. Before the new law, few restaurants in France voluntarily created a non-smoking area (McDonald's was one exception, although most Frenchmen don't consider it a restaurant). Apart from the 30 per cent of seats reserved for smokers, smoking is banned on trains, including bars and restaurant cars. Smoking is forbidden on French domestic flights and on Air France international flights of less than two hours' duration.

Individuals who break the no-smoking laws can be fined between 600F and 1,300F, and employers who fail to enforce it can be fined between 3,000F and 6,000F. However, most restaurants and workplaces in France don't enforce smoking bans and police don't bother to follow up complaints. Only the police have the authority to impose a penalty (or SNCF inspectors on French trains) and the law is openly flouted and prosecutions practically unknown.

For information and advice on smoking prevention and 'quit smoking' programmes (many run by hospitals), contact SOS Tabac, 4, imp. Mathieu, 75015 Paris (☎ 01.40.47.00.47).

BIRTHS & DEATHS

Births in France must be registered within three days (weekends and holidays excluded) at the town hall of the district where they take place. Registration applies to everyone irrespective of their nationality or whether they are residents of France or just visitors. In the case of a birth, registration may be completed by the hospital or clinic where the child was born. Note, however, that parents are responsible for ensuring that this is done and must usually do it themselves. When registering a birth, you must produce a certificate signed by a doctor or midwife and the parents' passports or identity cards. If a hospital registered the birth, the birth certificate (*acte de naissance*) is given to you when you leave hospital, otherwise you receive it at the time of registration. When a birth is registered, you also receive a health record card (*carnet de santé*) for your child from the town hall.

When a death takes place in a hospital, the attending doctor completes the death certificate (*acte/constatation de décès*). Note that the medical cause of death is treated as confidential in France and doesn't appear on death certificates. This can lead to problems if the body is to be sent abroad for burial. If a death takes place at home in Paris, a coroner (*médicin de l'état civil/médecin légiste*) must be called, although in the provinces a family doctor can complete the death certificate. An inquest (*enquête judiciaire*) must be held when a death occurs in a public place or when it could have been caused by a criminal act.

A death must be registered within 24 hours at the town hall in the district where it took place. If the deceased was a foreigner, the town hall will require his passport or *permis de séjour*. The family record book (*livret de famille*) is required for a French citizen. Cemeteries in France are usually owned by local authorities, who license a local undertaker (*pompes funèbres*) to perform burials. Before a burial can take place, the town hall must issue a burial or cremation permit (*permis d'inhumer*).

Dying is expensive in France and is best avoided if at all possible. However, the cost has been reduced in the last few years with the opening of 'supermarkets for the dead' by the Roc'Eclerc chain (not without considerable opposition from undertakers). Always check the cost of a funeral in advance and make sure you aren't paying for anything you don't want. The cost of a basic funeral is set by the *commune* and is usually around 4,000F, although the average French funeral costs around 7,000F and top-of-the-range funerals some 20,000F (undertakers can bury you once only and have to make the most of it!). Many Frenchmen take out an insurance policy to pay for their funerals.

Most burials take place in vaults except where there are still plots available. It's possible to reserve a plot or a vault. Burials also take place in communal ground (*terrain communal*), where graves are maintained free of charge by the local authority for a period of five years. After this period the remains are disinterred and buried in a common grave or a private vault. Until recently there weren't many crematoria in France, although they can now be found in most large cities. The cost of cremation is around half that of a burial. A body can also be sent abroad for burial or cremation.

When someone who was resident in France dies, all interested parties must be notified (see **Chapter 19**). A doctor will provide a certificate specifying the cause of death for presentation to insurance companies and other interested parties (this may be done automatically). You should make several copies, as they are also required by banks and other institutions. Births and deaths involving foreign nationals in France should be registered at your local consulate or embassy. This is necessary to obtain a national birth certificate and passport for a child. In the case of a death, an embassy or consulate can advise and assist you with any special arrangements necessary, e.g. to ship a body home for burial.

MEDICAL TREATMENT ABROAD

If you're entitled to social security health benefits in France or another European country, you can take advantage of reciprocal health care agreements in other European countries. Everyone insured under French social security is covered for medical expenses while travelling abroad, providing certain steps are taken to ensure reimbursement. In some cases you must obtain a form from your social security office (*caisse*) before leaving France.

Full payment (possibly in cash) must usually be made in advance for treatment received abroad, although you will be reimbursed on your return to France. This applies to all EU countries except Britain, where everyone receives free health care. You're also reimbursed for essential treatment in many non-EU countries, although you must obtain detailed receipts. Note that reimbursement is based on the cost of comparable treatment in France, which may be far below what you're charged abroad. In certain countries, e.g. Canada, Japan, Switzerland and the USA, medical treatment is *very* expensive and you're advised to take out travel or holiday insurance (see page 269) when visiting these countries. This is advisable wherever you're travelling, as it provides considerably wider medical cover than reciprocal health care agreements and includes many other things such as repatriation. If you do a lot of travelling abroad, it's worthwhile having an international health insurance policy.

Visitors to France: If you're an EU resident visiting France, you can take advantage of reciprocal health care agreements. You should apply for a certificate of entitlement to treatment (form E111) from your local social security office (or a post office in Britain) at least three weeks before you plan to travel to France. An E111 is open-ended and valid for life. However, you must continue to make social security contributions in the country where it was issued and if you become a resident in another country (e.g. in France) it becomes invalid. It covers emergency hospital treatment but doesn't include prescribed medicines, special examinations, X-rays, laboratory tests, physiotherapy and dental treatment. If you use the E111 in France, you must apply for reimbursement to French social security (instructions are provided with the form), which can take months. **Note, however, that you can still receive a large bill from a French hospital, as your local health authority assumes only a percentage of the cost!**

If you travel to France or to another EU country *specifically* for medical treatment or maternity care, you need form E112, and prior authorisation is required from your country's social security department. Form E112 authorises treatment in a French public hospital without pre-payment. Note that if you're retired and going to live permanently in France you need form E121 (see page 257). EU nationals transferred to France by an employer in their home country can continue to pay social security abroad for one year (forms E101 and E111 are required), which can be extended for another year in unforeseen circumstances (when forms E102 and E106 are needed).

British visitors or Britons planning to live in France can obtain information about reciprocal health treatment in France from the Department of Social Security, Overseas Branch, Newcastle-upon-Tyne, NE98 1YX, UK.

13.

INSURANCE

The French government and French law provide for various obligatory state and employer insurance schemes. These include health, sickness and maternity; work injuries; state and supplementary pensions; disability; and unemployment insurance. Most employees and their families receive health treatment under the French social security system. French employees have considerable protection under social security and are entitled to higher benefits than employees in most other European Union (EU) countries, although you would be unwise to rely solely on social security to meet your needs. However, it doesn't come cheap and France is one of the highest taxed countries in the EU, where over 30 per cent of GDP is spent on 'welfare' or 'social protection' (e.g. health, pensions, family allowances, unemployment benefits, etc.).

You should ensure that your family has full health insurance during the interval between leaving your last country of residence and obtaining health insurance in France. One way is to take out a travel insurance policy. However, it's better to extend your present health insurance policy, rather than take out a new policy (most policies can be extended to provide international cover). This is particularly important if you have an existing health problem that won't be covered by a new policy.

There are a few occasions in France where insurance for individuals is compulsory, including third party car insurance, third party liability insurance for tenants and homeowners, and mortgage life insurance if you have a mortgage (depending on the amount borrowed). If you lease a car or buy one on credit, a lender will insist that you have comprehensive car insurance. Voluntary insurance includes supplementary pensions, disability, health, household, dental, travel, car breakdown and life insurance.

It's unnecessary to spend half your income insuring yourself against every eventuality from the common cold to being sued for your last *centime*, but it's important to insure against any event that could precipitate a major financial disaster, such as a serious accident or your house falling down. As with anything connected with finance, it's important to shop around when buying insurance. Just collecting a few brochures from insurance agents or making a few telephone calls, **could save you a lot of money.** Regrettably you cannot insure yourself against being uninsured or sue your insurance agent for giving you bad advice.

In all matters concerning insurance, you're responsible for ensuring that you and your family are legally insured in France. Bear in mind that if you wish to make a claim against an insurance policy, you may be required to report the incident to the police within 24 hours (in some cases this may be a legal requirement). Obtain legal advice for anything other than a minor claim. French law is likely to differ from that in your home country or your previous country of residence, so never *assume* that it's the same. See also **Car Insurance** on page 201.

INSURANCE COMPANIES & AGENTS

Insurance is one of France's major business sectors and the fifth largest in the world. There are some 550 French insurance companies and mutual benefit organisations from which to choose, many providing a range of insurance services, while others specialise in certain fields only. Many of the largest companies in France such as *Groupement d'Assurances Nationales* and *Assurances Générales de France* are nationalised. The major insurance companies have offices or agents throughout

France, including most large towns. Most French insurance companies provide a free appraisal of your family's insurance needs.

A mutual benefit organisation or *mutuelle* is an association made up of individuals who are grouped together, e.g. by profession or area, in order to insure themselves for a favourable premium. Theoretically a *mutuelle* is a non-profit organisation and after all costs and claims have been paid any excess is shared equally among its members, held in reserve or reinvested. However, losses must also be shared equally among members. Most trades and occupations in France have their own *mutuelle*, commonly providing supplementary health insurance and pensions.

Insurance companies and *mutuelles* sell their policies in a number of ways. These include through general agents (*agents généraux*) representing a single company and selling the policies of that company only. A person who sells policies from a number of insurance companies and *mutuelles* is a broker (*courtier*). Most *mutuelles* and some insurance companies sell their policies direct to the public, with transactions often taking place wholly by telephone and mail. Note that as in many countries, it's often difficult to obtain independent unbiased insurance advice in France and brokers may be 'influenced' by the high fees offered for selling a particular policy. Insurance agents, brokers and companies are listed in the Yellow Pages under *Assurances*.

When buying insurance, particularly car insurance (see page 201), shop until you drop! Obtain recommendations from friends, colleagues and neighbours (but don't believe everything they tell you!). Compare the costs, terms and benefits provided by a number of companies before making a decision. Note that premiums (*cotisations*) are often negotiable. You should bear in mind that in some countries, e.g. Britain, if you inform your insurance company that you're moving abroad permanently they may automatically cancel your insurance policies without notifying you!

The insurance business in France is governed by regulations set out in the 'insurance code' (*code des assurances*) and insurance companies are supervised by the *Direction Générale des Assurances*. For general information about insurance in France contact the *Centre de Documentation et d'Information de l'Assurance*, 3 bis, rue de la Chaussée d'Antin, 75009 Paris (☎ 01.48.24.96.12 or 01.47.70.89.39).

INSURANCE CONTRACTS

Read insurance contracts carefully before signing them. If you don't understand written French, get someone to check a policy and don't sign it until you clearly understand the terms and the cover provided. Like insurance companies everywhere, some French insurance companies will do almost anything to avoid paying out in the event of a claim and will use any available loophole. Therefore it pays to deal only with reputable companies (not that this provides a guarantee). Policies often contain traps and legal loopholes in the small print, and it's essential to obtain professional advice and have contracts checked before signing them.

Always check the notice period required to cancel (*résilier*) a policy. Note that in France, insurance policies are usually automatically extended (*tacite reconduction*) for a further period (usually a year) if they aren't cancelled in writing by registered letter two or three months before the expiry date. You may cancel an insurance policy before the term has expired if the premium is increased, the terms are altered, e.g. the risk is diminished, or an insured object is lost or stolen. This must, however, still be done in writing and by registered post. Cancellation is also permitted at short notice under certain circumstances including when changing jobs, redundancy, retirement, marriage and divorce (and death!).

Note that if you don't cancel a policy, you must still pay the next year's premium, even if you no longer require it. If you don't pay you will be sued for the whole premium plus the credit agency's fees and interest. Your name may also be added to a debtor's list, your bank account frozen and the bailiffs called, resulting in even more costs! Insurance premiums should be paid within ten days of the due date. If they aren't, you will be notified and if it's still unpaid after 30 days your policy may be suspended. You will, however, still be liable to pay the premium. Bear in mind that French insurance companies often take eons to bill new customers and in the meantime you should obtain documentary evidence that you're insured, e.g. from an agent.

If you wish to make a claim, you must usually inform your insurance company in writing by registered letter within two to five days of the incident (e.g. for accidents) or 24 hours in the case of theft. Thefts should also be reported to the local police station within 24 hours, as the police report (*déclaration de vol*) usually constitutes irrefutable evidence of your claim. An insurance company will normally send an adjuster to evaluate the extent of damage, e.g. to your home or car. If you need to make a claim, you can hire a French assurance expert to negotiate with your insurance company on your behalf. Note that in certain cases, claims for damaged property (such as storm damaged buildings or vehicles damaged by hailstones) aren't considered by insurance companies unless the government declares the situation a natural catastrophe or Act of God.

It's possible to take out certain insurance in another country, e.g. property insurance, although the policy must usually be written under French law. The advantage is that you will have a policy you can understand (apart from all the legal jargon!) and can make claims in your own language. This is usually a good option for the owner of a holiday home in France. However, bear in mind that insuring with a foreign insurance company may be more expensive than insuring with a French company. Theoretically from 1993, EU residents have been able to obtain insurance from any EU country.

French insurance companies loathe foreign competition and the Parisian insurance exhibition, Assurexpo, has been cancelled in recent years because French companies objected to the presence of competitors from Britain, Germany and other EU and international countries! **Maybe they fear that the French public will discover that they are paying far too much for their insurance?** If you find it difficult to obtain insurance cover, the *Bureau Central de Tarification* can demand that the company of your choice provide you with cover, with the premium fixed by the Bureau.

SOCIAL SECURITY

France has a comprehensive social security (*sécurité sociale*) system covering health care (plus sickness and maternity); injuries at work; family allowances; unemployment insurance; and old age (pensions), invalidity and death benefits. Social security benefits in France are among the highest in the EU, as are social security contributions. The total contributions per employee (to around 15 funds) average around 60 per cent of gross pay, some 60 per cent of which is paid by employers (an increasing impediment to hiring staff). With the exception of sickness benefits, social security benefits aren't taxed.

Total social security revenue is around 1,200 billion francs a year and the social security budget is higher than the Gross National Product, i.e. social security costs more than the value of what the country produces! The French social security system is under severe financial strain with an ageing population and increasing unemployment, which have contributed to a huge increase in spending on health care (which increased five-fold between 1977 and 1997 from 119F to 574F billion), pensions and unemployment benefits in recent years. France's health spending alone is around 10 per cent of its GNP – the highest in Europe. The average French household receives around one-third of its income from social support payments such as family allowances, state benefits and pensions.

In France, as in many other EU countries, a shrinking working population is being asked to support an increasing social security debt. The government is reducing social security costs and in order to safeguard tax/social security revenue into the public coffers it was decided to shift most of the employees' health insurance contribution out of the *Patrimoine* section into the general section. Now *all* taxpayers are liable and not just those committed to paying into the social security system. The employee contribution (*instauration du remboursement de la dette sociale/RDS*), introduced in 1996, is 0.5 per cent of the total salary and is intended to erase some 250F billion of social security debt within 13 years (by 31st January 2009). This is in addition to an existing employee levy (CSG) of 5.1 per cent.

The *Caisse Nationale d'Assurance Maladie/CNAM* comes under the Ministry of Health and Social Security and is the public authority responsible for ensuring that social security policy is carried out on a national level, and for the negotiation of conventions and agreements with medical professions. Sixteen regional sickness insurance fund offices (*Caisse Régionale d'Assurance Maladie/CRAM*) coordinate the actions of CPAMs (see below) and deal with questions regarding accidents at work and retirement. Local social security offices (*Caisse Primaire d'Assurance Maladie/CPAM*), of which there are around 130 throughout the country (at least one in each department), deal with everyday matters and reimbursements.

For general information about social security contact *Les Renseignements sur la Sécurité Sociale*, 21, rue Georges Aurie, 75948 Paris Cedex 09 (☎ 01.53.38.70.00). Information about social security is also available via Minitel (3615, SEC SOC). There are a number of books (in French) about social security including *Tous les Droits de l'Assuré Social* (VO Editions).

Eligibility & Exemptions

All foreign employees working for French companies and self-employed foreigners in France must contribute to French social security. Generally if you work for an employer in France, you will be insured under French social security legislation and won't have any liability for social security contributions in your home country or country of domicile.

However, agreements exist between France and over 40 countries, including all EU countries and the USA, whereby expatriates may remain under their home country's social security scheme for a limited period. For example, under an agreement between the USA and France, an American employee of a US company who's transferred to France for up to five years can continue to pay US social security contributions. Similarly, EU nationals transferred to France by an employer in their home country can continue to pay social security abroad for one year which can be extended for another year in unforeseen circumstances. This also applies to the self-employed. However, after working in France for two years, EU nationals *must* contribute to the French social security system. If you qualify to pay social security contributions abroad, it's usually worthwhile doing so, as contributions in most countries are much lower than those in France.

If you're resident in France but aren't employed, you can make voluntary social security contributions in order to qualify for benefits, with contributions based on your income (which must be confirmed by your tax return). Note, however, that if you require just health insurance, it's *much* cheaper to take out private health insurance than pay high French social security payments. Apart from being cheaper, private health policies offer a greater choice of health facilities and may provide a wider range of benefits than social security. EU retirees aren't required to contribute to social security.

If you or your spouse work in France but remain insured under the social security legislation of another EU country, you will be able to claim social security benefits from that country. If you need to claim benefits in France and have paid contributions in another EU country, these contributions are taken into account when calculating your qualification for benefits. There's a mutual agreement between EU countries, whereby contributions made in any EU country count as contributions in your country of origin when calculating benefits. Contact your country's social security administration for information. In Britain information is provided in two booklets, *Social Security for Migrant Workers* and *Your social security, health care and pension rights in the European Community* (SA29). Both are available from the Department of Social Security, Contributions Agency, Newcastle-upon-Tyne NE98 1YX, UK (☎ 0191-213 5000).

Registration

If you're working in France, your employer will usually complete the necessary formalities to ensure that you're covered by social security. If he doesn't, you must obtain an attestation that you're employed in France (*déclaration d'emploi*) and register at the nearest social security office (*Caisse Primaire d'Assurance Maladie/CPAM*) to your home. Your local town hall will give you the address of your local CPAM or it will be listed under *Sécurité Sociale* in your local Yellow Pages. In certain cases you may need to visit the *Relations Internationales* department of social security, for example if you're retired with a pension in another EU country and wish to obtain a French social security card. You must provide your personal details including your full name, address, country of origin, and date and place of birth. You will also need to produce passports, *carte de séjour* and certified birth certificates for your dependants, plus a marriage certificate (if applicable). You may need to provide copies with official translations, but check first as translations may be unnecessary. You will also need proof of residence such as a rental contract or an EDF bill.

When you have registered, you receive a registration card (*carte d'assuré social*) containing your social security number (*No. d'immatriculation de l'Assuré*), a list of beneficiaries (*Bénéficiaires*) and the address of the office (*No. et adresse de votre centre de sécurité sociale*) where you must apply for reimbursement of your medical expenses. Don't forget to sign your card in the box (*Code Gestion 1*) to the left of your address above the validity date. If you move home, you must inform your local social security office, who will issue a new card.

The date when your entitlement to social security benefits expires is shown on your card (*droits jusqu'au*), which is also the expiry date of your social security card. You should automatically receive a new card each year before your existing card expires. If you're entitled to 100 per cent reimbursement for treatment in connection with a specific illness or complaint, there will be a date under *100 per cent jusqu'au*. If a claim has never been made for a child, he may not be listed on the card. A married couple with one partner working are covered by the same social security card and number, as are all dependants, e.g. children under 16, who are listed on the card. If both parents are working, children under 16 are usually listed on the mother's social security card. When applying for benefits or for social security reimbursements, you must apply to the office listed on your social security card and quote your social security number or produce your card.

Note that there's a compulsory waiting period before a new subscriber can claim certain social security benefits. There's a three-month waiting period for foreigners with the exception of students, apprentices, and political refugees, and nationals of EU and other countries with social security agreements with France. The USA doesn't have a reciprocal health agreement with France and therefore Americans and other students who aren't covered by social security *must* have private health insurance. Those coming to France under an exchange scheme must be covered for health care by the exchange authorities. Residents who don't benefit from French social security can subscribe voluntarily, although it isn't advisable as it's prohibitively expensive. For information contact the *Service d'Assurance Volontaire*, 84, rue Charles-Michel, 93625 St. Denis.

To qualify for social security benefits, you must have been employed in France for a limited period and have made minimum contributions. When you no longer meet the qualifying conditions, benefits are extended for a maximum of one year from the applicable date. In the case of long-term unemployed persons actively seeking employment, benefits are extended indefinitely. If you're retired and living in France and receive a state pension from another EU country or from a country with a social security agreement with France, you and your spouse are automatically entitled to health benefits under French social security. You must prove your entitlement to a pension. For example if you're British you must obtain social security form E121 in Britain and produce it when registering with French social security.

If you retire to France before reaching the French retirement age of 60, you must either contribute voluntarily to French social security or take out private health insurance. However, EU citizens who retire early before qualifying for a state pension can receive free health cover for two years by obtaining a form from their country's social security department (e.g. form E106 in Britain). You need to register at your local CPAM and require a copy of your *carte de séjour/résident* or your temporary authorisation (*récipissé de demande de carte de séjour*); proof of relationship between the applicant and any dependants who don't qualify in their own right (e.g. a marriage certificate); and your bank account details (*relevé d'identité bancaire*). If the temporary cover expires before you reach retirement age, you need to make voluntary social security contributions or take out private health insurance (which is the least expensive option).

If you contribute to social security, your dependants will receive the same benefits and will be listed on your card. Dependants include your spouse (if she isn't personally insured); your children supported by you under the age of 16 (or under the age of 20 if they are students or unable to work through illness or invalidity); and ascendants, descendants and relatives by marriage supported by you and living in the same household. Separated, divorced and widowed persons continue to receive benefits for at least one year, or in the case of separated persons, for as long as their spouse is employed providing they aren't eligible for benefits from other sources.

Contributions

Social security contributions (*cotisations*) are calculated as a percentage of your taxable income, although for certain contributions there's a maximum salary level. Note that contributions start as soon as you're employed or start work in France and not when you obtain your residence permit (*carte de séjour*). Social security contributions are paid directly to the *Union de Recouvrement des Cotisations de Sécurité Sociale et d'Allocations Familiales (URSSAF)*, which has 105 offices throughout France. URSSAF offices collect contributions for their area and send them to the central social security agency (*Agence Centrale des Organismes de Sécurité Sociale/ACOSS*) that distributes funds to the various benefit agencies (e.g. CNAF, CNAV and CRAM).

Employees (*employé/employée*): The total social security contributions for employees are an average of around 60 per cent of gross pay, some 60 per cent of which is paid by employers. Salaried employees come under the general regime for salaried workers (*régime général des travailleurs salariés*). There are special regimes for agricultural workers (*régime agricole*), called MSA or GAMEX, and self-employed or non-salaried, non-agricultural workers (*régime des travailleurs non-salariés et non-agricoles*), such as CAMONS, RAM and others. Other special regimes cover miners, seamen, railway workers and various other state employees. All these are termed obligatory regimes (*régimes obligatoires*).

Self-Employed (*travailleurs indépendants*): Before you can be recognised as a self-employed person (sole-trader) in France you must register with the appropriate organisation (see **Self-Employment** on page 35). As a self-employed person you're treated as an employer and must deduct social security contributions from your earnings and pay them directly to URSSAF. Once registered you may choose from a selection of recognised *mutuelle* health insurance organisations (see page 264).

Recent legislation has provided some more than welcome respite for the newly self-employed, who instead of paying crippling social security contributions from their start-up, now pay tax and social security as their business generates income. In the first years you can choose the MicroBic route if your earnings are under 100,000F a year and receive 50 per cent tax-free earnings and generous TVA (see page 290) exclusions. Contributions are payable in two lump sums on 1st April and 1st October each year. Within a limited period of starting a business (shown below), you must register with the *Caisse d'Allocations Familiales/CAF* (family allowance), the *Caisse Nationale de l'Assurance Maladie/CNAM* (sickness), and the *Caisse Nationale d'Assurance Vieillesse/CNAV* (old-age pension).

If you have a limited company, you can decide the salary you pay yourself and therefore limit your social security contributions. However, your total contributions are higher than for a sole trader, although you receive higher benefits than a self-employed person. If you're the boss (*gérant*) of a company employing members of your family and own over 50 per cent of the shares, you're treated as self-employed and must pay social security contributions as a sole trader. Note that if you earn less than 120,000F from a commercial but non-salaried source, you can declare it as 'MICRO-BIC' or 'BNC' income on your tax return (see page 296) and aren't required to pay social security contributions on this income.

The following table shows the percentage of gross income paid in social security contributions by employers and salaried employees, and the payments for an employee based on an annual gross salary of 300,000F.

Type of Contribution	Contribution (%)		Employee's Contributions on 300,000F
	Employer	Employee	
Social Security Contributions (URSSAF)			
Health Assurance	12.80	0.80	2,400 (total salary)
Widow's Assurance	-	0.10	300 (total salary)
Family Allowance	5.40	-	
Old Age Pension	8.20	6.55	948 (first 14,470F)
	1.60	-	- (total salary)
Contribution to Social Security Debt			
General (CSG)	-	5.10	15,300 (total salary)
Reimbursement (RDS)	-	0.50	1,500 (total salary)
Unemployment Fund (ASSEDIC)			
Tranche A	5.13	3.01	435 (first 14,470F)
Tranche B	5.26	3.60	1,563 (14,470F to 57,880F)
Obligatory Complementary Pension (Managers)			
Tranche A (ARRCO)	4.50	3.0	434 (first 14,470F)
Tranche B (AGIRC)	12.50	7.50	3,256 (14,470F to 57,880F)
Tranche C (AGIRC)*	12.50	7.50	4,341 (57,880F to 115,760F)
Exceptional Charge (CET)	0.13	0.08	93 (first 115,760F)
Total Contributions on 300,000F			**30,570F**

* The percentages paid by the employer and the employee on tranche C are variable.

Benefits

Most social security benefits (*allocations*) are paid as a percentage of your salary, rather than as a flat rate, subject to minimum and maximum payments. You must earn a certain minimum salary to qualify for benefits. Under French social security you're entitled to Health; Sickness and Maternity; Work Injury; Family Allowance; Unemployment Insurance; and Old Age, Invalidity and death benefits, each of which is described in more detail below.

Health Benefits: To qualify for health benefits you must have been employed for 600 hours in the last six months or for six months at the minimum wage, 200 hours in the last quarter or 120 hours in the last month. There's no minimum qualifying period during the first three months after entry into the insurance. Social security contributions for health benefits are 12.8 per cent of gross salary for employers and 0.8 per cent for employees. For more information see page 232.

Sickness & Maternity Benefits: To qualify for sickness and maternity benefit you must have made social security contributions for a minimum period. Employees who aren't automatically covered by sickness and maternity benefits can contribute voluntarily. To qualify for sickness benefits you must have been employed for 200 hours in the last three months or six months at the minimum wage. To qualify for extended cash sickness benefits you must have been insured for 12 months before your incapacity and for 800 hours of employment in the last 12 months. This includes 200 hours in the first three months of the last 12 months or 2,080 hours at the minimum wage, including 1,040 hours during the first six months of the last 12 months.

To qualify for maternity benefits you must have been insured for at least ten months prior to your confinement and have been employed for 200 hours in the first three months of the last 12 months or have six months' contributions. Benefits are payable for an additional two weeks prior to confinement if there are complications and 2 to 12 weeks for multiple births. A nursing benefit consisting of a monthly allowance or milk coupons is available for four months after confinement. Benefits are also paid for adoptions.

Work Injury Benefits: Industrial accident insurance pays all medical and rehabilitation costs associated with work injuries and provides a pension for you or your dependants in the case of injury or death. Insurance starts from your first day at work, with the variable contributions paid wholly by your employer. Self-employed workers are excluded and are covered under the state sickness insurance programme. A temporary disability benefit of 60 per cent of earnings is paid (up to a maximum amount) during the first 28 days of disability and thereafter 80 per cent of earnings.

In the case of permanent injury resulting in total disability, a permanent disability pension is paid equal to 100 per cent of average earnings during the last 12 months. Benefits are payable from the day following an accident. In the case of partial disability, average earnings are multiplied by half the degree of incapacity for the portion of disability between 10 and 50 per cent, and by 1.5 times the degree of incapacity for the portion above 50 per cent. A lump sum payment is made if a disability is below 10 per cent. All necessary associated medical treatment, surgery, hospitalisation, medicines, appliances, rehabilitation and transportation are paid 100 per cent by social security.

Family Allowance Benefits: France is a great place for large families, as there are high family allowances and other benefits (including lower taxes) to encourage couples to have more children. However, the qualifying ceiling was recently raised to 25,000F for families with a single income and two children, and to 32,000F with a double income and two children. To qualify for family allowance benefits (*allocations familiales*) you must have a *carte de séjour* and one member of the family must be employed full-time, i.e. for a minimum of 128 hours or 18 days per month. Employees pay no contributions towards family allowances, while employers pay 5.4 per cent of an employee's gross salary. Family allowances include a basic family allowance for families with two or more children, a family supplement (income-tested) for families with one or more children, a prenatal and birth grant for mothers, and a guaranteed minimum family income for families with three or more dependant children. There are special schemes for agricultural, railway and public utility employees, and special allowances for one-parent families and families with handicapped children. Certain allowances are subject to income, i.e. are 'means-tested'.

To qualify for family allowance, a child must usually be aged under 16. This is extended to 18 years if a child is unemployed or employed but earning no more than 55 per cent of the legal minimum wage (SMIC) and to 20 years if a child is a student, apprentice or an invalid. The **basic family allowance** per month in 1999 was 682F for two children, 1,556F for three children and 874F for each additional child. There's no allowance for the first child. A **supplementary benefit** of 192F per month is paid for each child between the ages of 10 and 15 and 341F for each child over 15. However, if a couple have two children, the supplementary benefit *isn't* paid for the eldest child. A family with three children receives this benefit for all children who qualify, providing they live at home.

Other family-oriented benefits include a 'young child allowance' (*allocation pour jeune enfant*), a 'family supplement' (*complément familial*), a 'school start allowance' (*allocation de rentrée scolaire/ARS*), a 'single parent allowance' (*allocation de parent isolé/API*), a 'family support allowance', a 'prenatal 'education' allowance' and a 'child care benefit'.

If you're entitled to family allowance in another EU country, you must provide a certificate of termination of family allowance in that country. Family allowance is granted in France irrespective of whether you're employed. Some family allowances are 'exportable' and paid to families with parents resident in France and children abroad, e.g. for education or health reasons. If one parent lives abroad with the children and is unemployed and the other lives and works in France, the parent in France is entitled to claim family allowance. If the parent abroad works and is paid family allowance by his country of residence, the difference is paid to the parent working in France (providing this is less than the French family allowance, which is most likely). For information enquire at your local CAF in France or at a social security office abroad.

Unemployment Insurance Benefits: Employers pay contributions of 5.13 per cent and employees 3.01 per cent of their salary up to 14,470F per month, and 5.26 per cent and 3.6 per cent respectively on the amount between 14,470F and 57,880F per month. In order to qualify for unemployment benefits (*allocation d'assurance chômage*) you must be registered at your local unemployment office (*Agence Nationale pour l'Emploi/ANPE*), be capable of work and be actively seeking employment. The ANPE sends your details to the *Associations pour l'Emploi dans l'Industrie et le Commerce régime d'assurance chômage (ASSEDIC)* who will send you the appropriate forms to complete. It usually takes two to three months before you receive your first payment, made by direct transfer into a bank or post office account, although payments are backdated. Once you're receiving unemployment benefits you're sent a form each month on which you must declare that you're still unemployed. If unemployment was due to voluntarily leaving a job without a legitimate reason, dismissal due to misconduct, or you refuse a suitable job offer, unemployment benefits won't be paid or will be discontinued.

The maximum period for which you can claim unemployment benefits depends on your length of contributions. There are special schemes for building and dock workers, merchant seamen and aviators. Domestic and seasonal workers aren't covered. In the last few years the French government has had an unemployment payments crisis due to the high number of unemployed (around 11 per cent). Under an agreement between social security, employers and unions, many people lost their entitlement to unemployment benefits and employee contributions were also increased. To qualify for unemployment insurance you must be aged under 60 and must have been employed for at least three months during the last year to receive the minimum benefit, and for two of the last three years.

If you're entitled to unemployment benefits from another EU country and have been claiming unemployment for at least four weeks, you can continue to receive unemployment benefit (at your home country's rate) in France for up to three months while looking for work. You must inform the unemployment office in your own country that you intend to seek work in France well in advance of your departure. If you qualify for transfer of benefits to France, your home country's unemployment service will provide a certificate of authorisation, which is required to register in France.

You must register for work at the nearest office of the ANPE (see page 24) in France within seven days of leaving your home country, so that your eligibility for benefits isn't interrupted. Note, however, that there may be a delay of up to three months before you actually start to receive benefits, so you must be able to finance yourself during your job search in France. During this period you're entitled to health care in France, for which you require a certificate of entitlement (form E119). Note that French bureaucrats aren't very co-operative with this scheme (i.e. even more obstructive than usual!) and you must persevere to obtain your rights. If after three months you don't have a job you must leave France, as you're permitted to remain only for three months without a residence permit (*carte de séjour*). A residence permit is unlikely to be granted if you don't have a job (see page 67) or an adequate income.

Old Age, Invalidity & Death Benefits: The French state pension is paid at 60 for both men and women (in the EU, only Italy pays state pensions at a lower age – 57 for women). Contributions are paid by both employers and employees and vary depending on income. Certain non-employed persons can contribute voluntarily to the state pension scheme. The French state pension scheme comprises both basic and supplementary schemes (see page 262). Employers pay 8.2 per cent and employees 6.55 per cent of their salary up to a maximum salary of 14,470F per month.

The basic scheme covers employees in business and industry and there are special schemes for the civil service, French railway employees, government manual workers, miners, French electricity and gas (EDF/GDF) employees, farmers, shopkeepers, small businessmen (artisans), and the self-employed. The national retirement insurance fund (*Caisse Nationale d'Assurance Vieillesse/CNAV*) for employees is the largest pension fund in France. Certain categories of civil servants receive full pension benefits after just two-thirds of the time required for those working in the private sector and the self-employed. For example primary school teachers, nurses and postal workers can retire on a full pension at 55, and police officers, prison warders and train drivers can retire at 50. A mother with three or more children has the right to retire on a full pension after just 15 years public service.

There's a worsening crisis in state pension funding in France (and most western countries), which has the largest proportion of inactive people over 55 in the EU, high unemployment, one of Europe's highest life expectancies, and over 40 per cent of 18 to 25 year-olds in full-time education. As in many countries, there are plans to transfer the burden from the public to the private sector, although this is likely to create controversy and social unrest.

When you first register with French social security, a record is opened in your name where your payments are recorded. Your insured period is determined from your record and periods of absence from work due to sickness, work accidents, childbirth, unemployment or war are credited for pension purposes. Pensions are calculated according to the following formula: basic wage multiplied by the period insured divided by 160. To receive a full pension you must have contributed for at least 40 years. The period required to qualify for the maximum state pension is 40 years, (there are plans to extend this to 42.5 or even 45 years). If you don't qualify for a full pension, your pension is proportional to the number of quarters you have contributed, e.g. 75 or 80 quarters will earn you a half pension. A reduced pension is equal to 1/160 of the full pension multiplied by the number of quarters' insurance. The maximum pension is equal to 50 per cent of your average earnings in your ten highest paid years (earnings are revalued in line with inflation), which is progressively being increased to 25 years. The maximum full pension is 86,820F a year.

A state pension is paid only when you cease full-time employment. It isn't paid automatically and you must make an application to your regional sickness insurance fund office (*Caisse Régionale d'Assurance Maladie/CRAM*) and complete either a *demande de retraite personelle* or a *demande de retraite progressive* if you continue to work part-time. It's advisable to complete your application three or four months before your planned retirement date. In any correspondence with your local CRAM office you should give your full name, address, social security number and the number of your local social security office.

State pensions are automatically adjusted semi-annually in accordance with the national average wage. If you move to France after working in another EU country (or move to another EU country after working in France), your state pension contributions can be exported to France (or from France to another country). French state pensions are payable abroad and most countries pay state pensions directly to their nationals resident in France. French pensions are indexed to take account of rises in the cost of living. If you plan to retire to France, you should ensure that your income is (and will remain) sufficient to live on, bearing in mind devaluations if your pension or income isn't paid in French francs, rises in the cost of living (see page 306), and unforeseen expenses such as medical bills or anything else that may reduce your income, e.g. stock market crashes.

SUPPLEMENTARY PENSIONS

Most employees in France contribute to a supplementary pension plan (*caisse complémentaire de retraite*), which include both state and private schemes, in addition to the state pension fund. In many industries, complementary pension schemes are provided for employees earning above a certain salary threshold, e.g. 12,000F per month, called *Institutions de Réparation*. Almost every trade or occupation has its own scheme and in many companies it's obligatory for employees to join. In addition to providing a supplementary pension, most schemes are allied to a complementary health insurance fund (*assurance complémentaire maladie*) that pays the portion of medical bills that isn't paid by social security (see page 232).

Executives and managerial staff contribute to a mandatory supplementary pension scheme (*caisse de retraite des cadres ou des cadres supérieurs*). An employee is attributed a number of points each year and the pension rate is based on the number of points accumulated at age 60, although a lower pension may be taken at age 55. A survivor is entitled to 60 per cent of a deceased employee's pension. In most cases your supplementary pension and your state pension provide a pension equal to around 80 per cent of your final salary at retirement, providing that you have contributed for the maximum 40 years. When you change employers in France or become self-employed, your contributions to a supplementary pension scheme are transferable.

If your French employer doesn't provide a supplementary pension scheme or you're self-employed, you may wish to contribute to a private scheme. Note that a self-employed person must pay around 12,500F to 15,000F a year into an obligatory pension fund for a pension that can be as low as 1,500F a month. If you already contribute to a company scheme and are transferred to France, you should make sure that you can continue to contribute while employed in France. Many company pension schemes are 'portable' and can be transferred to another employer or converted into a private pension scheme. Note, however, that contributions to foreign pension schemes aren't usually tax deductible in France.

HEALTH INSURANCE

The vast majority of people in France are covered for health treatment under social security (see page 232). However, most also subscribe to a complementary health insurance fund (*assurance complémentaire maladie*), commonly called a *mutuelle*, that pays the portion of medical bills that isn't paid by social security (the *ticket modérateur*). A *mutuelle* scheme may also provide a supplementary pension (see above).

Almost every trade or occupation has its own *mutuelle* and in many cases it's obligatory for employees to join. Many *mutuelles* base their reimbursements on those of social security (see page 232) and reimburse a patient only after social security has paid a proportion of a fee. Therefore in a case where social security doesn't contribute, e.g. when a medical practitioner isn't approved by social security (*non-conventionné, non-agréé*), a *mutuelle* may also pay nothing. However, some *mutuelles* pay the whole cost or part of the cost for wholly private treatment and for treatment or items that aren't covered or barely covered by social security, such as false teeth and spectacles.

Note that reimbursement applies only to the standard medical charges (*tarif de convention*). For example if a blood test costs 500F and the *tarif de convention* is 400F, your *mutuelle* would normally pay only the 30 per cent of the 400F that isn't refunded by social security. You must pay the 100F charged in excess of the *tarif de convention* yourself. However, you can insure yourself for the actual charge (*frais réels*), which reimburses you for any extra charge above the *tarif de convention*. Most complementary insurance policies offer different levels of cover.

If you aren't (or have never been) employed in France but have a social security card, you can join a *mutuelle*, the premium depending on your income, e.g. around 2,500F a year for someone earning 200,000F a year or from around 1,000F a year for someone who isn't employed. Note that there are two different kinds of *mutuelle*. One is a sort of provident society or sick fund, which is a non-profit organisation that ploughs its profits back into the fund, and the other an insurance company (hopefully) operating at a profit. A provident *mutuelle* provides fixed tariffs regardless of the number of claims and is *infinitely preferable* to an insurance company.

If you're self-employed (*travailleur non salarié*), you must take out a health insurance policy (*assurance au premier franc*) through your social security office or through a professional organisation such as the *Réunion des Assureurs Maladie (RAM)*, 29, rue de Clichy, 75009 Paris (☎ 01.45.96.12.77). Information about insurance for the self-employed can be obtained from the *Caisse d'Assurance Maladie des Professions Libérales d'Ile de France*, 22, rue Violet, 75730 Paris Cedex 15 (☎ 01.45.79.82.15). Note that the medical costs of self-employed persons are repaid at 50 per cent by social security and *not* the 70 per cent, e.g. for doctors and dentists, paid for salaried employees. The self-employed should join an organisation such as the CDCA (see page 36), which has its own low cost health insurance scheme repaying members at 100 per cent (premiums for the self-employed are usually higher than for employees).

When choosing a *mutuelle*, ask your friends, colleagues and neighbours, or simply look under *Mutuelles d'Assurances* in your Yellow Pages. Compare the costs, terms and benefits provided by a number of funds before making a decision. Note that it's usually necessary to have been a member of a *mutuelle* for a certain period before you're eligible to make a claim, e.g. three months for medical claims and six months for dental claims. It's advisable to choose an insurer who's regulated by the *Loi Evan*, which means that after a certain period they aren't permitted to alter your terms and conditions, increase the premiums or refuse to continue your insurance after an accident or illness. Further information about *mutuelles* can be obtained from the *Fédération Nationale de la Mutualité Française*, 255, rue de Vaugirard 75015 Paris (☎ 01.40.43.30.30). A French insurance company cannot cancel your policy or increase your premiums if your health deteriorates with advancing years and increasing needs, providing that you have been insured with the same company for at least two years.

If you aren't covered by French social security you should take out private health insurance. It's an advantage to be insured with a company that will pay large medical bills directly, because if you're required to pay bills and claim reimbursement from the insurance company, it can take you several months to receive your money. All French health insurance companies pay hospital bills directly, unlike some foreign companies such as the American Blue Cross (although Blue Cross *will* pay the American Hospital of Paris and some medical practitioners directly).

Note that the USA doesn't have a reciprocal health agreement with France and therefore American students and other Americans who aren't covered by social security *must* have private health insurance in France. Anyone who isn't covered for health care under social security must provide proof of health insurance when applying for a visa or residence permit (*carte de séjour*). Some foreign insurance companies don't provide sufficient cover to satisfy French regulations, therefore you should check the minimum cover necessary with a French consulate in your country of residence. Most private health insurance policies don't pay family doctors' fees or pay for medication that isn't provided in a hospital or there's a high 'excess', e.g. you must pay the first 500F of a claim, which often exceeds the cost of treatment. Most will, however, pay for 100 per cent of specialist fees and hospital treatment in the best French hospitals. If you already have private health insurance in another country, it may be possible to extend it to cover you in France.

If your stay in France is limited, you may be covered by a reciprocal agreement between your home country and France (see **Medical Treatment Abroad** on page 249). Make sure you're fully covered in France before you receive a large bill. **It's foolhardy for anyone living and working in France not to have comprehensive health insurance.** If you or your family aren't adequately insured, you could be faced with some *very* high medical bills. When changing employers or leaving France, you should ensure that you have continuous health insurance and if you're planning to change your health insurance company, you should ensure that important benefits aren't lost.

DENTAL INSURANCE

It's unusual to have full dental insurance (*assurance dentaire*) in France, as the cost is prohibitive. Basic dental insurance is provided under social security (see **Dentists** on page 243) and by your *mutuelle* insurance. A *mutuelle* may offer additional cover for a higher premium. Most private health insurance companies offer optional dental cover or extra dental cover for an additional premium, although there are many restrictions and cosmetic treatment is excluded. Where applicable, the amount payable by a health insurance policy for a particular item of treatment is fixed and depends on your level of dental insurance. A list of specific refunds is available from insurance companies.

HOUSEHOLD INSURANCE

Household insurance in France generally includes third party liability, building and contents insurance, all of which are usually contained in a multi-risk household insurance policy (*assurance multirisques habitation*).

Third Party Liability (*responsabilité civile propriétaire*): It's a legal requirement in France that property is insured for third party liability at all times or when building work starts on a new home (so that your neighbour can sue you when your chimney stack falls on his head). It's common for a buyer to take over the insurance of the vendor of a property and under French law, third party liability insurance automatically transfers to the new owner unless he takes out new insurance. The insurance must be transferred to the new owner's name on completion or be cancelled. One of the duties of the notary (*notaire*) is to check that a buyer has third party insurance. If you take over the existing insurance you should ensure that it provides adequate cover (many French tend to under-insure) and isn't too expensive.

Building (*bâtiment*): Although it isn't compulsory for owners, it's advisable to take out property insurance covering damage to the building due to fire, water, explosion, storm, freezing, snow, theft, malicious damage, acts of terrorism, broken windows and natural catastrophes. Property insurance is based on the cost of rebuilding your home and is increased each year in line with an industry agreed inflation figure. It also covers you against third party liability to guests and visitors on your property (*responsabilité civile vie privée*). **Make sure that you insure your property for the true cost of rebuilding.**

Contents (*contenu*): Contents are usually insured for the same risks as a building (see above) and are insured for their replacement value. Items of high value must usually be itemised and photographs and documentation (e.g. a valuation) provided. When claiming for contents, you should produce the original bills if possible (always keep bills for expensive items) and bear in mind that replacing imported items may be much more expensive than buying them abroad. Note that contents' policies usually contain security clauses and if you don't adhere to them a claim won't be considered.

Apartments: If you own an apartment as a *copropriétaire*, building insurance is included in your service charges, although you should check exactly what's covered. You must, however, still be insured for third party risks in the event that you cause damage to neighbouring apartments, e.g. through flooding or fire.

Holiday Homes: Premiums are generally higher for holiday homes, due to their high vulnerability, particularly to burglaries, and are usually based on the number of days a year a property is inhabited and the interval between periods of occupancy. Cover for theft, storm, flood and malicious damage may be suspended when a property is left empty for more than three weeks at a time (or if there's no visible forced entry). It's possible to negotiate cover for periods of absence for a hefty surcharge, although valuable items are usually excluded. If you're absent from your property for long periods, e.g. more than 60 days a year, you may also be required to pay an excess (e.g. 1,500F) on a claim arising from an occurrence that takes place during your absence (and theft may be excluded). You should read all small print in policies. **Note that, where applicable, it's important to ensure that a policy specifies a holiday home and not a principal home.**

In areas with a high risk of theft (e.g. some parts of Paris and the French Riviera), you may be required to fit extra locks (e.g. two locks on external doors, one of a deadlock type) and internal-locking shutters or security bars on windows. A policy may specify that all forms of protection on doors must be employed whenever a property is unoccupied, and that all other forms (e.g. shutters) must also be used after 2200 and when a property is left empty for two or more days. Some companies may not insure holiday homes in high risk areas. It's unwise to leave valuable or irreplaceable items in a holiday home or a home that will be vacant for long periods. **Note that some insurance companies will do their utmost to find a loophole which makes you negligent and relieves them of their liability.** While it may be cheaper or more convenient to take out contents insurance abroad, you should be aware that this can lead to conflicts when the building is insured with a French company, e.g. in France door locks are part of the contents and in Britain they constitute part of the building.

Rented Property: Your landlord will usually insist that you have third party liability insurance. A lease requires you to insure against 'tenant's risks', including damage you may make to a rental property and to other properties if you live in an apartment, e.g. due to floods, fire or explosion. You can choose your own insurance company and aren't required to use one recommended by your landlord.

Premiums: Premiums are usually calculated on the size of the property, either the habitable area in square metres or the number of rooms, rather than its value. Usually the sum insured (house and contents) is unlimited, providing the property doesn't exceed a certain size, e.g. 1,200m², and is under a certain age, e.g. 200 years old. However, some companies restrict home insurance to properties with a maximum number of rooms (e.g. seven) and/or a maximum value of contents. e.g. 400,000F. The cost of multi-risk property insurance in a *low-risk* area is around 700F to 800F a year for a property with one or two bedrooms, 1,200F to 1,400F for three or four bedrooms and around 1,500F to 1,700F to a year for five or six bedrooms. Premiums are much higher in high risk areas and increase annually. If you have an index linked policy, your cover is increased each year in line with inflation.

It's possible and legal to take out building and contents insurance in another country for a property in France, although the policy is usually written under French law. The advantage is that you will have a policy you can understand and you will be able to handle claims in your own language. This is usually a good option for the owner of a holiday home in France, although it can be much more expensive than insuring with a French company, so it pays to compare premiums. Always carefully check that the details (*conditions particulières*) listed on a policy are correct, otherwise your policy could be void.

Claims: If you wish to make a claim you must usually inform your insurance company in writing (by registered letter) within two to five days of the incident or 24 hours in the case of theft. Thefts should also be reported to the local police within 24 hours as the police statement (*déclaration de vol/plainte*), of which you receive a copy for your insurance company, usually constitutes irrefutable evidence of your claim. Check whether you're covered for damage or thefts that occur while you're away from the property and are therefore unable to inform the insurance company immediately.

Note that in certain cases, claims for damaged property aren't considered unless the government declares the situation a natural catastrophe or Act of God, as has happened with floods in southern France in recent years. Even so, many people found after the floods that their household insurance didn't cover them for water coming in from ground level, only for water seeping in through the roof. Read the small print, and if floods are one of your concerns, make sure that you're covered. It's particularly important to have insurance for storm damage in France, which can be severe in some areas. Note, however, that if you live in an area that's hit by a succession of natural disasters (such as floods), your household insurance may be cancelled. Household insurance is often combined with third party liability insurance (see below).

THIRD PARTY LIABILITY INSURANCE

It's customary in France to have third party liability insurance (*assurance responsabilité civile*). To take an everyday example, if your soap slips out of your hand while you're taking a shower, jumps out of the window and your neighbour slips on it and breaks his neck, he (or his widow) will sue you for around ten million francs. With third party liability insurance you can shower in blissful security (but watch that soap!).

Third party liability insurance covers all members of a family and includes damage done or caused by your children and pets, for example if your dog or child bites someone. Where damage is due to severe negligence, benefits may be reduced. Check whether insurance covers you against accidental damage to your home's fixtures and fittings. If you have children at school in France, they must also be covered by third party liability insurance. You can also insure your children against accidents on the way to or from school and while at school, for which schools usually provide an insurance proposal form at the beginning of each school year.

Third party liability insurance is usually combined with household insurance (see above). The cost of third party liability insurance when included in household insurance is around 1,000F a year and you may need to pay an excess, e.g. the first 500F to 1,000F of a claim.

HOLIDAY & TRAVEL INSURANCE

Holiday and travel insurance (*assurance voyage*) is recommended for all who don't wish to risk having their holiday or travel spoilt by financial problems or to arrive home broke. As you're no doubt already aware, anything can and often does go wrong with a holiday, sometimes before you even reach the airport or port, particularly when you *don't* have insurance. Travel insurance is available from many sources including travel agents, insurance agents, motoring organisations, transport companies and direct from insurance companies. Package holiday companies also offer insurance policies, **most of which don't provide adequate cover.**

Before taking out travel insurance, carefully consider the level of cover you require and compare policies. Most policies include cover for loss of deposit or holiday cancellation, missed flights, departure delay at both the start *and* end of a holiday (a common occurrence), delayed baggage, personal effects and lost baggage, medical expenses and accidents (including repatriation home if necessary), personal money, personal liability, legal expenses or a tour operator going bust.

Medical expenses are an important aspect of travel insurance and you shouldn't rely on reciprocal health arrangements (see **Medical Treatment Abroad** on page 249). It isn't advisable to depend on travel insurance provided by charge and credit card companies, household policies or private medical insurance, none of which usually provide adequate cover (although you should take advantage of what they offer). The minimum medical insurance recommended by experts is 2,500,000F in France and the rest of Europe and 5,000,000F to 10,000,000F in North America and some other destinations, e.g. Japan. If applicable, check whether pregnancy related claims are covered and whether there are age restrictions for those aged over 65 or 70. Third party liability cover should be around 10,000,000F in Europe and 20,000,000F in North America.

Always check any exclusion clauses in contracts by obtaining a copy of the full policy document (all relevant information isn't included in the insurance leaflet). Skiing and other winter sports should be specifically covered and *listed* in your travel insurance policy. Special winter sports policies are available and are more expensive than normal holiday insurance.

The cost of travel insurance varies considerably, depending on your destination and the duration. Usually the longer the period, the lower the daily or weekly cost, although the maximum period is usually limited to six months. You should expect to pay around 150F for a weeks insurance in Europe, 200F for two weeks and 350F for a month. Premiums are around double for travel to North America, where medical treatment costs an arm and a leg (although they also accept dollars!). Premiums may be higher for those aged over 65 or 70. Many insurance companies offer annual travel policies from around 1,000F that are good value for frequent travellers. **However, carefully check exactly what's covered (or omitted), as these policies may not provide adequate cover.**

Although travel insurance companies gladly take your money, they aren't usually so keen to pay claims and you may have to persevere before they pay up. Always be persistent and make a claim *irrespective* of any small print, as this may be unreasonable and therefore invalid in law. Insurance companies usually require you to report a loss (or any incident for which you intend to make a claim) to the local police (or carriers) within 24 hours and obtain a written report. Failure to do this means that a claim usually won't be considered.

MOTOR BREAKDOWN INSURANCE

Motor breakdown insurance (*assurance dépannage*) in France and other European countries is provided by French car insurance companies (see page 201) and French motoring organisations (see page 223). If you're motoring abroad or you live abroad and are motoring in France, it's important to have motor breakdown insurance (which may include holiday and travel insurance), including repatriation for your family and your car in the event of an accident or breakdown. Most foreign breakdown companies provide multi-lingual, 24-hour centres where assistance is available for motoring, medical, legal or travel problems. Some organisations also provide economical annual motoring policies for those who frequently travel abroad, e.g. owners of holiday homes in France. When motoring in Europe, don't assume that your valuables are safe in the boot of your car, particularly if the boot can be opened from inside. Check that your insurance policy covers items stolen from your car.

LIFE INSURANCE

Although there are worse things in life than death (like spending an evening with a life insurance salesman), your dependants may rate your death **without life insurance** (*assurance vie*) high on their list. Many French companies provide free life insurance as an employment benefit, although it may be accident life insurance only. You can take out a life insurance or endowment policy with numerous French or foreign insurance companies. Note that French policies are usually for life *insurance* and not for *assurance*. An assurance policy covers an eventuality that's certain to occur, for example, like it or not, you must die one day! Thus a life assurance policy is valid until you die. An insurance policy covers a risk that *may* happen but isn't a certainty, e.g. accident insurance (unless you're *exceptionally* accident prone).

In certain cases life insurance premiums are tax-deductible and a life insurance policy can delay the payment of inheritance tax for unrelated persons. For example income from a life assurance policy is exempt from tax providing the policy doesn't mature for at least eight years. This can be in the form of a *plan d'épargne populaire (PEP)* in which a maximum of 400,000F may be invested tax-free. A single taxpayer can have one plan and a couple one for each partner. Not surprisingly, these policies are very popular in France.

The beneficiaries of certain life insurance policies aren't liable for French gift or inheritance tax. Unrelated beneficiaries who are liable for inheritance tax of 60 per cent can delay paying the tax until they are 70. A life insurance policy intended to take advantage of French law is best taken out in France, to ensure that it complies with French law. A life insurance policy can be useful as security for a bank loan and can be limited to cover the period of the loan. Non-smokers are usually offered a 20 per cent reduction on life policies.

Finally, it's advisable to leave a copy of all insurance policies with your will (see page 304) and with your lawyer. If you don't have a lawyer, keep a copy in a safe deposit box. A life insurance policy must usually be sent to the insurance company upon the death of the insured, with a copy of the death certificate.

14.

FINANCE

France is one of the wealthiest countries in the world, with one of the highest per capita Gross Domestic Products (ca. US$25,500 in 1998) per head in the European Union. The French economy is one of Europe's and the world's strongest, with inflation (around 1 per cent in 1998) among the lowest of any industrialised nation. France has greater extremes of wealth and poverty than many other western European countries and a much smaller middle class. As in most western countries, there's a huge and widening gap between the rich and the poor, e.g. the self-employed and the lowest-paid workers, particularly those living in rural areas. The best way to become (and remain) rich in France is to be born with a platinum spoon in your mouth, as a high proportion of wealth and position is hereditary (much more so than in other western nations). The French don't generally flaunt their wealth and many find the subject of money distasteful (especially the seriously rich).

Although French banks aren't renowned for their proficiency (some even make British Chancellors of the Exchequer look competent), they have improved markedly in the last decade and are more competitive than they were in the '70s and early '80s. Competition for your money is fierce and financial services are offered by numerous banks (commercial, co-operative, savings, investment, etc.), the post office, investment brokers and other financial institutions. Compared with many other western countries, particularly Britain and the USA, France isn't a credit economy and the French prefer to pay cash rather than use credit or charge cards. When you arrive in France to take up residence or employment ensure that you have sufficient cash, traveller's cheques, eurocheques, credit cards, luncheon vouchers, coffee machine tokens, gold *napoléons*, diamonds, etc., to last at least until your first pay day, which may be some time after your arrival. During this period you will find an international credit card (or two) useful.

If you're planning to invest in property or a business in France that's financed with funds from abroad, it's important to consider both present and possible future exchange rates (don't be too optimistic!). On the other hand, if you earn your income in French francs, this may affect your financial commitments abroad, particularly if the French franc is devalued. If you wish to borrow money to buy property or for a business venture in France, you should carefully consider where and in what currency to raise finance. Note that it's difficult for foreigners to obtain business loans in France, particularly for new ventures, and you shouldn't rely on doing so.

Wealth Warning: You should ensure that your income is (and will remain) sufficient to live on, bearing in mind devaluations (if your income isn't paid in French francs), rises in the cost of living (see page 306), and unforeseen expenses such as medical bills or anything else that may reduce your income (such as stock market crashes and recessions!). Anyone planning to live in France should take into account the strength of the franc if their income is paid in a foreign currency which has depreciated in value against the franc in recent years, e.g. the $US and £Sterling. Foreigners, particularly retirees, often under-estimate the cost of living and many are forced to return to their home countries after a year or two. France is also one of the highest taxed countries in the European Union when both direct and indirect taxes (including social security) are taken into consideration.

See also **Chapter 13** for information about social security, pensions and life insurance.

FRENCH CURRENCY

On 1st January 1999 the euro (€) was introduced in France (plus Austria, Belgium, Finland, Germany, Ireland, Italy, Luxembourg, the Netherlands, Portugal and Spain) and will eventually become the country's currency. The currencies of all 11 euro countries are locked into a fixed exchange rate (set by the European Central Bank) with the euro and consequently with each other. Euro notes and coins will become legal tender on 1st January 2002 and for six months will circulate alongside the French franc, which will then be withdrawn (euro coins and notes will be introduced earlier in some countries and will circulate alongside the national currency, but they won't become legal currency until 2002). Companies and banks already use Euros for trading, accounts, statements and receipts, and shops, supermarkets and restaurants produce bills in both currencies. Several towns in France have had 'Euro Days', where the new currency is temporarily the only legal tender and (in general) enthusiasm for the Euro among the French is high.

Until the Euro is officially introduced, the French unit of currency remains the French franc, introduced by King Jean le Bon in 1360 to show that his part of France was free of the English, *franc des anglais*. The franc is also the official currency in Monaco, French overseas territories, such as Guadeloupe and Martinique, and many former French colonies. The French franc is divided into 100 centimes and French coins are minted in coins of 5, 10, 20 and 50 centimes and 1, 2, 5, 10 and 20 (introduced in 1993) francs. The 5, 10 and 20 centime coins are copper coloured (*pièces jaunes*) and the 50 centime, 1, 2, and 5 franc coins are silver coloured. Some old French coins are mostly silver and worth a lot more than their face value. The 10F and 20F coins are small silver-centred coins with a copper rim. Note that money is *argent* in French and small change is called *monnaie* (also currency).

French banknotes (*billets*) depict famous Frenchmen and are printed in denominations of 20 (depicting Debussy), 50 (Antoine de St.-Exupéry), 100 (Cézanne), 200 (Gustave Eiffel) and 500 (Marie and Pierre Curie) francs. The size of notes increases with their value (who said size doesn't matter!). **Beware of counterfeit notes, some of which are made with sophisticated colour laser copiers.** However, new notes have been introduced in recent years containing many new anti-counterfeit measures, including a special strip which is reproduced as black if a banknote is photocopied.

The franc is usually written as F, used in this book, or FF. When writing figures, a period (.) is used to separate units of millions and thousands and a comma is used to denote centimes, e.g. 1.500.485,34 is one million, five hundred thousand, four hundred and eighty five francs and 34 centimes (a nice healthy bank balance!). Store and market prices are written with an F after the figure, e.g. 5,50F is five francs 50 centimes. Values below one franc are written with zero francs, e.g. 0,75F is seventy five centimes.

It's advisable to obtain some French coins and banknotes before arriving in France and to familiarise yourself with them. You should have some French francs in cash, e.g. 500F to 1,000F in small notes, when you arrive. It's best to avoid 500F notes, which sometimes aren't accepted, particularly for small purchases or on public transport! This will save you having to queue to change money on arrival at a French airport, although you should avoid carrying a lot of cash.

FOREIGN CURRENCY

Exchange controls in France were abolished on 1st January 1990 and there are no restrictions on the import or export of funds. A French resident is permitted to open a bank account in any country and to export an unlimited amount of money from France. However, if you're a French resident, you must inform the French tax authorities of any new foreign account in your annual tax return. Sums in excess of 50,000F deposited abroad, other than by regular bank transfers, must be reported to the Banque de France. If you send or receive any amount above 10,000F by post, it must be declared to customs. Similarly if you enter or leave France with 50,000F or more in French or foreign banknotes or securities (e.g. traveller's cheques, letters of credit, bills of exchange, bearer bonds, giro cheques, stocks and share certificates, bullion, and gold or silver coins quoted on the official exchange), you must declare it to French customs. **Note that if you exceed the 50,000F limit and are found out, you can be fined an extortionate 10,000F or more (a number of people fall foul of this legalised form of highway robbery each year, which almost certainly contravenes EU law).**

When transferring or sending money to (or from) France you should be aware of the alternatives. One way to do this is via a bank draft (*chèque de banque*), which should be sent by registered mail. Note, however, that in the unlikely event that it's lost or stolen, it's impossible to stop payment and you must wait six months before a new draft can be issued. Bank drafts aren't treated as cash in France and must be cleared, as with personal cheques. One of the safest and fastest methods of transferring money is to make a direct transfer (*transfert*) or a telex or electronic transfer (e.g. via the SWIFT system in Europe) between banks. A 'normal' transfer should take three to seven days, but in reality it usually takes much longer and an international bank transfer between non-affiliated banks can take weeks! A SWIFT telex transfer *should* be completed in a few hours, with funds being available within 24 hours. The cost of transfers vary considerably, not only commission and exchange rates, but also transfer charges (such as the telex charge for a SWIFT transfer). Note that it's usually quicker and cheaper to transfer funds between branches of the same bank than between non-affiliated banks.

When you have money transferred to a bank in France, ensure that you give the name, account number, branch number (*code agence*) and the bank code (*clé rib*). If money is 'lost' while being transferred to or from a French bank account, it can take weeks to locate it. If you plan to send a large amount of money to France or abroad for a business transaction such as buying property, you should ensure you receive the commercial rate of exchange rather than the tourist rate. Always check charges and rates in advance and agree them with your bank (you may be able to negotiate a lower charge or a better exchange rate).

You can also send money by international money order from a post office or a telegraphic transfer, e.g. via Western Union, the fastest and safest method, but also the most expensive. Money can be sent via American Express offices by Amex card holders. It's also possible to send cheques drawn on personal accounts and Eurocheques, although both of these take a long time to clear (usually a number of weeks) and fees are high. Postcheques can be cashed at any post office in France and most credit and charge cards can be used to obtain cash advances (see page 284).

Most banks in major cities have foreign exchange windows and there are banks or exchange bureaux with extended opening hours (see page 278) at airports, major railway stations in Paris and in all major cities. Here you can buy or sell foreign currencies, buy and cash traveller's cheques, cash eurocheques, and obtain a cash advance on credit and charge cards. Note, however, that some French banks refuse to cash traveller's cheques or eurocheques. At airports and in tourist areas in major cities, there are automatic change machines accepting up to 15 currencies including US$, £Sterling, Deutschmarks and Swiss francs.

There are many private *bureaux de change* in Paris and other major cities, with longer business hours than banks, particularly at weekends. Most offer competitive exchange rates and low or no commission (but check). They are easier to deal with than banks and if you're changing a lot of money you can also usually negotiate a better exchange rate. Never use unofficial money changers, who are likely to short change you or leave you with worthless foreign notes rather than French francs. The best exchange rate is usually provided by banks (Banque Nationale de Paris has a reputation for offering the best exchange rate and charging the lowest commission). The French franc exchange rate (*cours de change*) for most European and major international currencies is listed in banks and daily newspapers, and is also given on Minitel (see page 125).

If you're visiting France, it's safer to carry traveller's cheques (*chèques de voyage*) than cash. It's best to buy traveller's cheques in French francs when visiting France, although they aren't as easy to cash as in some other countries, e.g. the USA. They aren't usually accepted as cash by businesses, except perhaps in Parisian hotels, restaurants and shops, all of which usually offer a poor exchange rate. You can buy traveller's cheques from any French bank, usually for a service charge of 1 per cent of the face value. There should be no commission charge when cashing French franc traveller's cheques at any bank in France (you must show your passport). However, charges and rates can vary considerably on traveller's cheques in foreign currencies. Banks usually offer a better exchange rate for traveller's cheques than for banknotes, although they often levy a high commission, e.g. between 20F and 30F per cheque.

Always keep a separate record of cheque numbers and note where and when they were cashed. American Express provides a free, 24-hour replacement service for lost or stolen traveller's cheques at any of their offices worldwide, providing you know the serial numbers of the lost cheques. Without the serial numbers, replacement can take three days or longer. All companies provide local numbers for reporting lost or stolen traveller's cheques.

One thing to bear in mind when travelling anywhere isn't to rely on one source of funds only.

BANKS

There are two main types of banks in France: commercial and co-operative. The largest commercial banks have branches in most large towns and cities and include Crédit Lyonnais, Banque Nationale de Paris (BNP) and Société Générale. All three have now been privatised and in order to compete with other larger European banks, are intent on merging, the latest being a union between BNP and Société Générale. The top four French banks (Crédit Agricole, Crédit Lyonnais, Société Générale and BNP) are among the world's top ten banks. Note that as in many other European countries, the post office serves as the largest banking facility in France.

The largest co-operative banks are Crédit Agricole, Crédit Mutuel and Banque Populaire. They began life as regional, community-based institutions working for the mutual benefit of their clients, although most are now represented nationally and offer a full range of banking services. Unlike commercial banks, each branch office of a co-operative bank is independent and issues its own shares. Anyone can become a member and invest in their shares, which is usually mandatory if you wish to take out a mortgage or loan but isn't necessary to open a current cheque account. Crédit Agricole is the largest co-operative bank and is also the biggest landholder in France. It's the largest retail bank in Europe with around 10,000 branches and some 17 million customers.

There are also savings banks in France such as Caisses d'Épargne with a network of over 400 regional institutions, although they offer a limited range of services compared with commercial and co-operative banks. Foreign-owned banks in France number some 175, more than in any other European country except Britain, although they have a small market share. However, competition from foreign banks is set to increase, as EU regulations now allow any bank trading legitimately in one EU country to trade in another. All banks, including foreign banks, are listed in the Yellow Pages under *Banques*.

Most major foreign banks are present in Paris, but branches are rare in the provinces. In many small villages there are often tiny bank offices (*permanences*) which usually open one morning a week only. Among foreigners in France, the British are best served by their national banks, both in Paris and in the provinces, particularly the French Riviera. The most prominent British bank is Barclays with around 100 branches, including at least one in all major cities. If you do a lot of travelling abroad or carry out international business transactions, you may find that the services provided by a foreign bank are more suited to your needs. They are also more likely to have staff who speak English and other foreign languages. Note, however, that many foreign banks and some French banks such as Banque Paribas, handle mainly corporate clients and don't provide banking services for individuals.

Although banking has become highly automated in recent years, French banks still lag behind banks in many other European countries (notably Britain, Germany, the Netherlands and Switzerland) in terms of efficiency and the range and quality of services provided. Decisions regarding loans and other transactions often aren't made by managers at local level and must be referred to a regional head office.

You must usually press a bell to gain access to a French bank. After deciding that you aren't a robber a staff member presses a button to open the outer door. For security purposes, most banks have two entrance doors, the second of which is opened only after the first has closed (intended to trap potential robbers as they attempt to flee with their booty). French banks usually have a more casual air than banks in many other countries and most use open counters rather than protected teller windows.

Opening Hours

Normal bank opening hours are from 0900 to 1630, Mondays to Fridays, although banks may open anytime between 0830 and 0930 and close between 1600 and 1700. Larger branches may also have late opening until 1900 on certain days. In small towns, banks close for lunch from noon or 1230 until 1330 or 1400. In cities, some branches of major banks remain open until 1830 or 1900. Many banks open on Saturdays, particularly in market towns, although when a bank in a rural area opens on Saturdays it may close on Mondays. Banks are closed on public holidays and when a public holiday falls on a Tuesday or Thursday, banks usually close on the preceding Monday or the following Friday respectively.

At major airports such as Paris' Charles de Gaulle and Orly airports, *bureaux de change* are open from 0700 to 2300 daily. Banks at main railway stations in Paris are open from 0900 until between 2000 and 2300, although they usually have long queues. In Paris and other cities, private *bureaux de change* are usually open from 0900 to 1800, Monday to Saturday.

Opening an Account

You can open a bank account in France whether you're a resident or a non-resident, although a bank can refuse to open an account. However, if you have been refused by two banks, the third must open an account for you (you must obtain proof of refusals in writing). It's best to open a French bank account in person, rather than by correspondence from abroad. Ask your friends, neighbours or colleagues for their recommendations and just go along to the bank of your choice and introduce yourself. You must be aged at least 18 and provide proof of identity, e.g. a passport (be prepared to produce other forms of identification), and your address in France (an EDF bill usually suffices).

If you wish to open an account with a French bank while you're abroad, you must first obtain an application form, available from overseas branches of French banks. You need to select a branch from the list provided, which should be close to where you will be living in France. If you open an account by correspondence you must provide a reference from your current bank, including a certificate of signature or a signature witnessed by a solicitor. You also need a photocopy of the relevant pages of your passport and a French franc draft to open the account.

Non-Residents: If you're a non-resident, you're only entitled to open a non-resident account (*compte non-résident*). A non-resident account previously had many restrictions, including limiting account holders to making deposits from outside France only, although this is no longer the case. There's now little difference between non-resident and resident accounts for deposits up to 50,000F, and you can deposit and withdraw funds in any currency without limit. Non-resident accounts have a ban on ordinary overdrafts (*découverts*), although loans for a car or house purchase are possible. If you're a non-resident with a second home in France it's possible to survive without a French account by using eurocheques, traveller's cheques and credit cards, although this isn't wise and is an expensive option. If you're a non-resident you can have documentation (e.g. cheque books, statements, etc.) sent to an address abroad.

Residents: You're considered to be a resident of France if you have your main centre of interest there, i.e. you live or work there more or less permanently. To open a resident account you must usually have a residence permit (*carte de séjour*) or evidence that you have a job in France.

Note that it isn't advisable to close your bank accounts abroad, unless you're certain that you won't need them in the future. Even when resident in France, it's cheaper to keep money in local currency in an account in a country that you visit regularly, rather than pay commission to convert French francs. Many foreigners living in France maintain at least two accounts, a foreign bank account for international transactions and a local account with a French bank for day-to-day business.

Cheque Accounts

The normal bank account for day-to-day transactions in France is a cheque or current account (*compte de chèque*). When opening a cheque account, you should request a *carte bleue* debit card, which can be used to pay bills throughout France (see page 284). You will receive a cheque book (*chéquier/carnet de chèques*) and your *carte bleue* around two to three weeks after opening an account (although some banks don't issue a cheque book until it has been operated for at least two months). You must usually collect your cheque book and *carte bleue* in person from your branch, although it can be sent to you abroad by registered post at your expense. Note that it usually takes weeks to obtain a new cheque book, so you should keep a spare one. Many French employers pay their employees' salaries into a bank or post office account by direct transfer (*virement*), so make sure that you give your employer your account details.

It's illegal for banks in France to pay interest on current accounts. Most French people deposit their 'rainy day' money in a savings account (see page 282). However, most banks will transfer funds above a certain sum from a cheque account into an interest-bearing savings account. There are no monthly charges on a cheque account and no charges for transactions such as direct debits or (usually) standing orders, except when made overseas. You may withdraw any amount up to the balance (*solde*) of your account by cashing a cheque (*encaisser un chèque*) at the branch where you have your account. At any other branch of your bank, you can usually withdraw up to 3,000F per week and must provide identification and your cheque book. If the branch has a computer link to your branch, you may withdraw any amount up to the balance of your account. When withdrawing cash from a French bank, you may need to go to one counter (*guichet*) for the transaction and then to the cashier (*caisse*) to collect your money (the system was invented by bureaucrats!).

Personal cheques (*chèques*) are widely accepted throughout France and many people use them to buy everything from petrol to food, from restaurant meals to travel tickets. All stores accept cheques. There are no cheque guarantee cards in France and therefore you're usually asked to produce identification, e.g. a passport or *carte de séjour*, when paying by cheque. Usually cheques are crossed (*chèques barrés*) and personal cheques aren't negotiable, i.e. they cannot be signed and endorsed for payment to a third party. They can be paid into an account in the name of the payee only (who must sign the back). This means you cannot cash a cheque unless you have your own bank account. It's possible to obtain 'open' uncrossed cheques (*chèques non-barrés*), although your bank is required to notify the French tax authorities of all uncrossed cheques issued. Because of this rule, few people request uncrossed cheques as they attract the (very) unwelcome attention of the tax inspectors. The main reason that cheques are crossed and cannot be endorsed is to discourage tax evasion, a national sport in France.

The design of a French cheque may be different from what you're used to and looks as if it was designed by a committee! In the top right-hand corner is a box or line where the value of the cheque is written in numerals. The line *payez contre ce chèque* is where the value of the cheque is written in words. Write the name of the payee next to the line marked *à l'ordre de* (or *moi-même* when writing a cheque for cash). The date line is in the lower right-hand corner above the signature position and is preceded by the town where the cheque was written (*lieu de création*). It isn't possible to postdate a cheque in France, as cheques are payable on the date presented irrespective of the date written on them and are valid for one year and one day after this date. At the bottom of the cheque is your name and address.

When writing figures in France, or anywhere on the continent of Europe, the number seven should be crossed (7) to avoid confusion with the number one, written with a tail and looking like an uncrossed seven (1) to many foreigners. The date is written in the standard European style, for example 10th September 1996 is written: 10.9.96, not as in the USA, 9.10.96. If there's a difference between the amount written in figures and the amount written in words, the amount written in words is assumed to be correct. Most banks supply a specimen cheque showing how it's written.

Cheque clearing takes longer in France than it does in most other countries. Under the French system, a cheque paid into your account will show on your account balance the day it's deposited (using the 'value date' or *date de valeur* system), **although it won't have been cleared.** Two dates are usually shown, the date a transaction is recorded and the date it's credited or debited to your account. Always make sure that cheques, including bank drafts (which *aren't* treated as cash in France), have been cleared before making a withdrawal against them. The time needed to clear a cheque depends on whether it's drawn on a bank in the same town (*sur place*) or in another town (*hors place*). A cheque drawn on a different bank in another town may take up to 12 days to clear. Note also that some people are slow to pay in cheques that you have written. When making payments into an account, a distinction is made between cash (*espèces*) and cheques, which must be listed (*versement de chèques*) on the paying-in form.

You should **NEVER** go overdrawn or write 'rubber' cheques in France (called a *chèque en bois* in French, literally a wooden cheque, or *chèque sans provision*). Writing rubber cheques is a criminal offence and there are no cheque cards in France to guarantee them. If you illegally overdraw your account (*en découvert*), your bank will send you a registered letter demanding that the necessary funds be paid into the account within 30 days. You will also be 'fined' around 200F to 300F. In the meantime you mustn't write any more cheques. If the funds aren't deposited within 30 days or if you overdraw your account twice within a 12-month period, your account will be closed! You must return your cheque book to your bank and also cheque books for other bank accounts in France.

Your name will also be entered on a blacklist (*interdit bancaire*) maintained by the Banque de France. You will be unable to operate a cheque account at any bank in France for one year and your name will remain on the blacklist for three years. If you're blacklisted it can make life difficult and can make obtaining a French mortgage or loan impossible for years afterwards. Around one cheque in every 1,500 'bounces' in France and some 750,000 people are forbidden to operate bank accounts. If you can prove that overdrawing your account was due to the fault of another party, you can avoid being blacklisted. Persistent cheque bouncers can be fined from 3,000F to 250,000F and receive prison sentences of from one to five years.

Account statements (*relevé*) are usually sent monthly, although you can usually choose to receive them weekly or quarterly. Your account details (*relevé d'identité bancaire*) such as your bank, branch and account number are printed at the top of statements. This information is required when payments are to be made directly to or from your account, e.g. when electricity and telephone bills are paid by direct debit.

If your cheque book is lost or stolen, you must notify your bank by telephone immediately (☎ 01.42.41.22.22 from 0800 to 2300) and confirm the loss in writing. Once you have informed your bank of a loss, any cheques written after that time cease to be your responsibility.

General Information

The following general points are applicable to most French banks:

• All regular bills such as electricity, gas, telephone, mortgage or rent, etc., can be paid directly by direct debit (*prélèvement automatique*) by your bank. A direct debit instruction form (*relevé d'identité bancaire*) is provided by your bank and they (and standing orders) are made free of charge. This method of payment has the advantage that payments are recorded on your monthly statement. Bills can also be paid via Minitel (see page 125). Note that if you don't pay a bill on time interest (*majoration*) can be charged at 1.5 times the official rate.

• In theory a French trader can refuse to accept a cheque for goods or services costing less than 10,000F and can refuse cash for anything above 10,000F (although most Frenchmen are more than happy to accept any amount of cash at any time). In fact, in order to prevent tax evasion, French law states that rent, office supply services and any work costing over 1,000F *must* be paid by cheque. Some businesses have signs stating that below a certain amount, e.g. 100F, cheques aren't accepted.

• It's difficult to stop the payment (*faire opposition à un chèque*) of a cheque in France and it's possible only if your cheque book is lost or stolen, or the payee loses a cheque or has it stolen. It isn't normal in France to stop a cheque when, for example, goods or services aren't as specified or ordered.

• Buying stocks and shares in France is normally done through your bank, rather than a stockbroker (*agent de change/courtier*). Banks make a charge that's added to the broker's commission, plus value added tax (TVA) of 20.6 per cent. New share issues can usually be bought through newspaper advertisements in newspapers such as *Le Monde*. French banks also sell shares in their own unit trusts.

• Many banks offer customers safe deposit boxes with annual rents ranging from around 500F to 2,000F a year, depending on their size. Note, however, that most banks restrict compensation for losses to around 100,000F.

• Any account holder can create a joint account by giving his spouse (or anyone else) signatory authority. A joint account can be for two or more people. If applicable, you must state that cheques or withdrawal slips can be signed by any partner and don't require all signatures. Note that in the event of the death of a partner, a joint account is blocked until the will has been proven.

Savings Accounts

In addition to a cheque account you can open a savings account (*compte d'épargne sur livret*) or deposit account (*compte à terme*) with commercial, co-operative and savings banks (*caisses d'épargne*). Savings banks are similar to British building societies and American Savings and Loan organisations, and offer savings schemes and loans for property and other purchases, although general banking services are limited compared with other banks. The post office also offers a range of savings accounts (see page 110).

Most financial institutions offer a variety of savings and deposit accounts with varying interest rates and minimum deposits, depending on the type of account and the bank. French residents are permitted to have a savings account where interest is earned tax-free up to a maximum deposit of 100,000F, although the interest rate is low. With deposit accounts (term deposits), you must be prepared to invest for between 1 to 12 months, during which period your money is tied up. The longer the term, the higher the return.

You usually receive a pass book (*livret*) for a savings account, where deposits and withdrawals are recorded. Many Frenchmen have a government subsidised, low-interest savings account called a *Plan d'Épargne Logement (PEL)*. This is designed to accrue credits toward a future low-interest loan to be used exclusively for the purchase of a home or home improvements. The minimum monthly deposit in a PEL is 300F and it must be maintained for at least five years to benefit.

One of the best ways to invest small sums is to buy units in a managed fund organisation called a *Société d'Investissement à Capital Variable (SICAV)* or a *Fonds Commun de Placement (FCP)*. SICAVs and FCPs are offered by most banks and are similar to unit trusts, with unit prices starting low and increasing to around 1,000F. Interest rates are linked to market rates and units can be cashed at any time.

Cash & Debit Cards

Most French banks offer customers a combined cash and debit card called a *carte bleue (CB)*), widely accepted throughout France (ensure that your card will work in cash machines throughout France and not just in your local *département*). Although it's integrated with both the VISA and Mastercard/Eurocard network, it isn't a credit card but a combined cash and debit card that can be used in place of cheques. Purchases and cash withdrawals are automatically debited from your cheque account, although you may have a choice of either instant debit or debit at the end of the month. You don't receive a monthly statement and cannot run up bills. A CB allows holders to withdraw up to 2,000F per week from any cash machine (automated teller machine or *guichets automatiques*) and up to 3,000F a week from a machine operated by your own bank. You can also obtain account balances and mini-statements from a cash machine and write personal cheques for cash at any bank displaying a CB sticker. Some machines offer the option to display instructions in English.

The key benefit of the CB is that it's accepted almost universally throughout France. It can be used to pay for practically everything including *autoroute* tolls, parking, and rail and *métro* tickets. When using your CB in a cash machine or when making a purchase, you simply enter your four-digit personal identification number (PIN). In 'retail outlets' your PIN is entered via a cordless machine. This has eliminated the need to sign bills (and helps prevent fraud) and you can enter your code in restaurants, hotels, petrol stations, supermarkets and many other businesses.

Don't rely entirely on a CB card to obtain cash, as they are sometimes 'swallowed' by cash machines and it may take a few weeks before it's returned to you via your bank. Some machines also refuse foreign cards for no apparent reason (if this happens try another bank). If you lose your *Carte Bleue* you must report it to the central office (☎ 01.42.77.11.90 or 08.36.69.08.80) and inform your bank as soon as possible. Some banks such as the Société Générale and Crédit Agricole issue their own cash cards. **Take care when withdrawing cash from a machine at night as some machines are popular venues for muggers.**

CREDIT & CHARGE CARDS

Credit and charge cards are usually referred to collectively as credit cards in France, although only cards such as Mastercard, Visa and some store cards are real credit cards, where the balance can be repaid over a period of time. The most common French credit card is the *Carte Bleue Visa* card. A *Carte Bleue Visa* debited immediately (*débit immédiat*) costs from 150F to 240F a year. A Carte Premier Visa card (costing 700F to 800F a year) is similar to a gold card and allows a higher credit limit than a standard Visa card, plus travel and medical assistance and insurance benefits.

Visa is the most widely accepted credit card in France and other credit cards such as American Express, Diners Club and Mastercard, aren't as common as in Britain and the USA (the French wisely prefer cash, which cannot be traced by the tax authorities!). Never assume that a business (such as a restaurant) accepts a particular credit or charge card or you may discover to your embarrassment that: 'that *won't* do nicely, sir'! **Note that many French businesses require customers to enter a PIN number via a keypad as with a cash or debit card (see page 283), without which you will be unable to use your credit card.**

French 'smart' credit cards contain a micro-chip, and some foreign cards cannot be used in French cash machines and some businesses refuse to accept British cards without a micro-chip, although they are valid in France. If this happens tell the shopkeeper or clerk *'Les cartes Britanniques ne sont pas des cartes à puce, mais à pistes magnétiques. Ma carte est valable et je vous serais reconnaissant d'en demander la confirmation auprés de votre banque ou de votre centre de traitement.'* ('British cards don't contain microchips, but have magnetic stripes. My card is valid and I would be grateful if you would request authorisation from your bank or processing centre.')

Most credit cards allow you to withdraw cash from machines, e.g. with a Visa card you can usually withdraw up to 2,000F per week from banks and post offices in France, indicated by a *Carte Bleue/Visa* sign and make payments of up to 10,000F or 15,000F per month (limits vary depending on the type of card and your credit limit). American Express also cash personal cheques for card holders. Some credit card issuers provide free travel and accident life insurance, when travel costs are paid with cards. Before obtaining a credit or charge card, compare the costs and benefits, particularly the interest rates charged.

If you maintain a bank account abroad, it's advisable to retain your foreign credit cards. One of the advantages of using a credit card issued abroad is that your bill is usually rendered or your account debited around six weeks later, thus giving you interest-free credit (except when cards are used to obtain cash, when interest is levied immediately). You may, however, find it more convenient and cheaper to be billed in French francs rather than in a foreign currency, e.g. US$ or £Sterling, when you must wait for the bill from outside France and payments may vary due to exchange rate fluctuations.

Major department and chain stores in France issue their own account cards, e.g. ABM, Galeries Lafayette, Monoprix, Printemps and Uniprix, as do mail-order companies (see page 388). Some cards allow credit, where the account balance may be repaid over a period of time, although interest rates are high.

If you lose a bank or credit card, report it immediately to the issuing office. You can insure against losing credit cards or you may be able to pay a fee to the card company, relieving you of any liability. To report lost or stolen credit cards in France telephone 01.45.67.84.84. Credit card thefts are high in France, although they could be completely eradicated if credit cards with a laser-engraved photograph and signature (which have been shown to be fraud-proof) were universally adopted, coupled with the need to enter a Personal Identification Number (PIN). Note, however, that French cashiers rarely check signatures and often hand them back before asking for a signature (partly because French cards are protected by the use of a PIN number).

Even if you don't like credit cards and shun any form of credit, they do have their uses, for example no-deposit car rentals; no prepaying hotel bills; making payments via telephone, Minitel and the Internet; greater safety and security than cash; and above all, convenience. They are particularly useful when travelling abroad. **However, visitors should never rely solely on a credit card to obtain cash in France.**

EUROCHEQUES

Most French banks issue eurocheques and eurocheque cards (*cartes Eurochèque*). The eurocheque card has a variety of uses and can be used as a cash card, debit card and a cheque guarantee card. There's a fee of around 100F for a eurocheque card, which is valid for up to two years. The main advantage of eurocheques is that they can be used as traveller's cheques to obtain cash at some 250,000 bank branches and post offices in Europe, and to pay bills in over five million outlets including shops, hotels, restaurants and garages. Eurocheque cards can also be used to withdraw cash (in local currency) from cash machines in over 20 European countries. The cash amount you can withdraw varies from country to country and is usually the equivalent of 1,000F in local currency per day.

The only disadvantage is the high fees and charges for using a eurocheque card and eurocheques. There's a usage charge plus commission each time a card is used to obtain cash from an ATM and a charge based on the face value of a cheque plus commission and handling fees. When cashing a eurocheque in a bank outside France, there's a handling fee plus a fee of up to 1.6 per cent (the maximum permitted) of the cheque's value, depending on the country. Most banks charge a commission of 2.5 per cent with a minimum charge of around 20F, so don't write eurocheques for small amounts. When sending money within Europe, it's often cheaper to send a post office money order or make a giro transfer.

Although they are widely used and accepted in many European countries, eurocheques aren't popular in France. Many small businesses (hotels, restaurants and shops) either refuse to accept eurocheques drawn on foreign banks or add 5 or 10 per cent because their banks levy a surcharge on non-French eurocheques. Some French banks charge as much as 100F for processing a eurocheque, irrespective of the amount for which it's drawn! Don't take it for granted that a business will accept a eurocheque and ask if you don't see the blue and red EC sign. Note that many French banks also refuse to accept eurocheques!

Issuing banks recommend that you don't keep your eurocheque card and cheques in the same place and that you *never* keep your card with a note of your PIN number. Don't leave them in your car and carry only as many cheques as necessary. If you lose both your card and cheques at the same time, or they are stolen and subsequently cashed, you may find that you're liable due to negligence. **If you lose your EC card, notify your bank as soon as possible.**

LOANS & OVERDRAFTS

All French banks provide loans (*emprunt/prêt*) and overdrafts (*découvert*), although they aren't as free with their money as banks in many other European countries – particularly regarding business loans to foreigners. Loans are subject to your credit rating, income and the amount of debt you already have. French law doesn't permit French banks to offer loans where the repayments are more than 30 per cent of your net (i.e. disposable) income. A few banks allow a cheque account holder whose salary is paid directly into his account to overdraw a specified sum without making special arrangements, when the current overdraft rate applies. Check with your bank.

It pays to shop around for a loan, as interest rates vary considerably depending on the bank, the amount and the period of the loan. Don't neglect smaller banks, as it isn't always necessary to have an account with a bank to obtain a loan. Ask your friends and colleagues for their advice. If you have collateral, e.g. French property or an insurance policy, or you can get someone to stand as a guarantor for a loan, you will be eligible for a secured loan at a lower interest rate than an unsecured loan. Some banks may insist that clients take out a life insurance policy to cover the term of a loan. The interest rate is quoted as the TEG (*taux effectif global*), the French equivalent of the annual percentage rate (APR) used in Britain and the USA.

Borrowing from private loan companies, as advertised in newspapers and magazines is expensive with *very* high interest rates. **Use them only as a last resort, when all other means have been exhausted.** Even then, as a foreigner, you may need to find a homeowner or French citizen to act as a guarantor, in which case you will be able to borrow from a bank. In general, the more desperate your financial situation, the more suspicious you should be of anyone willing to lend you money (unless it's your mum!). The local 'agency for competition, consumption and fraud repression' (*Direction départementale de la Concurrence, Consommation et Répression des Fraudes*) for your department can provide information regarding contracts and agreements.

MORTGAGES

Mortgages (home loans) are available from all major French banks (both for residents and non-residents) and many foreign banks. Most French banks offer French franc mortgages on French property through foreign branches in European Union and other countries. Crédit Agricole is the largest French lender, with a 25 per cent share of the French mortgage market. Most financial advisers advise lenders to borrow from a large reputable bank rather than a small one. French law doesn't permit French banks to offer mortgages or other loans where repayments are more than 30 per cent of your net income. Joint incomes and liabilities are included when assessing a couple's borrowing limit (usually a French bank will lend to up to three joint borrowers). The 30 per cent of income includes existing mortgage or rental payments, both in France and abroad. If the total sum exceeds 30 per cent of your income, French banks aren't permitted to extend further credit. Should they attempt to do so, the law allows a borrower to avoid liability for payment.

Both French and foreign lenders have tightened their lending criteria in the last few years due to the repayment problems experienced by many recession-hit borrowers in the early '90s. Some foreign lenders apply stricter rules than French lenders regarding income, employment and the type of property on which they will lend, although some are willing to lend more than a French lender. It can take some foreigners a long time to obtain a mortgage in France, particularly if you have neither a regular income or assets there. If you have difficulty you should try a bank that's experienced in dealing with foreigners such as the Bank Transatlantique in Paris.

To calculate how much you can borrow in France, multiply your total net monthly earnings by 30 per cent and deduct your monthly mortgage, rent and other regular payments. Note that earned income isn't included if you're aged over 65. The remainder is the maximum amount you can repay each month on a French mortgage. For example:

monthly net income	30,000F
multiplied by 30 per cent	9,000F
less monthly deductions	4,000F
maximum monthly repayments	5,000F

As a rough guide, repayments on a 400,000F mortgage are around 4,000F a month at 6 per cent over 15 years. There are special low mortgage rates for low-income property buyers in some departments.

Mortgages can be obtained for any period from two to 20 years, although the usual term in France is 15 years (some banks won't lend for longer than this). In certain cases mortgages can be arranged over terms of up to 25 years, although interest rates are higher. Generally the shorter the period of a loan, the lower the interest rate. All lenders set minimum loans, e.g. 100,000F to 200,000F, and some set minimum purchase prices. Usually there's no maximum loan amount, which is subject to status and possibly valuation (usually required by non-French lenders).

French mortgages are usually limited to 70 or 80 per cent of a property's value (although some lenders limit loans to just 50 per cent). A mortgage can include renovation work, when written quotations must be provided with a mortgage application. Note that you must add expenses and fees totalling around 10 to 15 per cent of the purchase price on an 'old' property, i.e. one over five years old. For example if you're buying a property for 500,000F and obtain an 80 per cent mortgage, you must pay 20 per cent deposit (100,000F) plus 10 to 15 per cent fees (50,000F to 75,000F), making a total of 150,000F to 175,000F.

Note that when buying a property in France, the deposit paid when signing the preliminary contract (*compromis de vente*) is automatically protected under French law should you fail to obtain a mortgage. Some lenders will provide a mortgage offer within a few weeks of an application. It's possible to obtain a mortgage guarantee or certificate from most lenders, valid for from two to four months, during which period a lender will guarantee you a mortgage, perhaps subject to valuation of the property. There may be a commitment fee of around 1,000F (banks charge fees for everything).

Once a loan has been agreed, a French bank will send you a conditional offer of a loan (*offre préalable*), outlining the terms. In accordance with French law, the offer cannot be accepted until after a 'cooling off' period of ten days. The borrower usually has 30 days to accept the loan and return the signed agreement to the lender. The loan is then held available for four months and can be used over a longer period if it's for a building project.

To obtain a mortgage from a French bank, you must provide proof of your monthly income and all out-goings such as mortgage payments, rent and other loans or commitments. Proof of income includes three months' pay slips for employees, confirmation of income from your employer and tax returns. If you're self-employed you require an audited copy of your balance sheets and trading accounts for the past three years, plus your last tax return. French banks aren't particularly impressed with accountants' (*expert comptable/conseiller fiscal*) letters. If you want a French mortgage to buy a property for commercial purposes, you must provide a detailed business plan (in French).

There are various fees associated with mortgages. All lenders charge an arrangement fee (*frais de dossier*) for setting up a loan, usually 1 per cent of the loan amount. There's usually a minimum fee, e.g. 2,500F (plus TVA) and there may also be a maximum. Many lenders impose an administration fee of around 1 per cent of the loan with minimum (e.g. 500F) and maximum (e.g. 3,500F) fees. Although it's unusual to have a survey in France, foreign lenders usually insist on a 'valuation survey' (costing around 1,500F) for French properties before they grant a loan. Using the above examples, these fees add another 9,000F to the cost of a 400,000F loan.

It's customary in France for a property to be held as security for a loan taken out on it, i.e. the lender takes a charge on the property. If a loan is obtained using a French property as security, additional fees and registration costs are payable to the notary (*notaire*) for registering the charge against the property. Note that some foreign banks won't lend on the security of a French property. If you live in France and borrow from the Crédit Agricole or another co-operative bank, you're obliged to subscribe to the capital of the local bank. The amount (number of shares) is decided by the board of directors and you will be sent share certificates (*certificat nominatif de parts sociales*) for that value. The payment is usually deducted from your account at the same time as the first mortgage repayment. When the loan has been repaid, the shares are reimbursed (if required).

If you're buying a new property off-plan, when payments are made in stages, a bank will provide a 'staggered' loan, where the loan amount is advanced in instalments as required by the *contrat de réservation*. During the period before completion (*période d'anticipation*), interest is payable on a monthly basis on the amount advanced by the bank (plus insurance). When the final payment has been made and the loan is fully drawn, the mortgage enters its amortisation period (*période d'amortissement*).

If you fail to maintain your mortgage repayments, your property can be repossessed and sold at auction (as many foreign homeowners have found to their cost in the last few years). However, this rarely happens as most lenders are willing to arrange lower repayments when borrowers get into financial difficulties.

Types of Mortgages

All French mortgages are repaid using the capital and interest method (repayment), and endowment and pension-linked mortgages aren't offered. As a condition of a French mortgage, you must take out a life (usually plus health and disability) insurance policy equal to 120 per cent of the amount borrowed. The premiums are included in mortgage payments. An existing insurance policy may be accepted, although it must be assigned to the lender. A medical examination may be required, although this isn't usual if you're under 50 years of age. Note that in France, a borrower is responsible for obtaining building insurance (see page 266) on a property and must provide the lender with a certificate of insurance.

French loans can be arranged with a fixed or variable rate. When comparing rates, the fixed rate is higher than the variable rate to reflect the increased risk to the lender. The advantage of a fixed rate is that you know exactly how much you must pay over the whole term. Variable rate loans may be fixed for the first two or more years, after which they are adjusted up or down on an annual basis in line with prevailing interest rates, but usually within a preset limit, e.g. 3 per cent of the original rate. You can usually convert a variable rate mortgage to a fixed rate mortgage at any time. There's normally a redemption penalty, e.g. 3 per cent of the outstanding capital, for early repayment of a fixed rate mortgage, although that isn't usual for variable rate mortgages. If you think you may want to repay early, you should try to have the redemption penalty waived or reduced before signing the agreement. In France, a mortgage cannot be transferred from one person to another, as is possible in some countries.

Mortgages for Second Homes

If you have spare equity in an existing property, either in France or abroad, then it may be more cost effective to remortgage (or take out a second mortgage) on that property, rather than take out a new mortgage for a second home. It involves less paperwork and therefore lower legal fees, and a plan can be tailored to meet your individual requirements. Depending on the equity in your existing property and the cost of a French property, this may enable you to pay cash for a second home. The disadvantage of remortgaging or a second mortgage is that you reduce the amount of equity available in the property. When a mortgage is taken out on a French property, it's based on that property, which could be important if you get into repayment difficulties. Note that French lenders are usually reluctant to remortgage.

It's also possible to obtain a foreign currency mortgage, other than in French francs, e.g. £Sterling, Swiss francs, $US, Deutschmarks, Dutch guilders or Euros. However, you should be extremely wary before taking out a foreign currency mortgage, as interest rate gains can be wiped out overnight by currency swings and devaluations. It's generally recognised that you should take out a loan in the currency in which you're paid or in the currency of the country where a property is situated, i.e. French francs. In this case, if the foreign currency is devalued you will have the consolation of knowing that the value of your French property will ('theoretically') have increased by the same percentage, when converted back into the foreign currency. When choosing between a French franc loan and a foreign currency loan, be sure to take into account all costs, fees, interest rates and possible currency fluctuations. However you finance the purchase of a second home in France, you should obtain professional advice from your bank manager and accountant.

Note that if you have a foreign currency mortgage or are a non-resident with a French franc mortgage, you must usually pay commission charges each time you make a mortgage payment or remit money to France. However, some lenders will transfer mortgage payments to France each month free of charge or for a nominal amount. If you let a second home, you can offset the interest on your mortgage against rental income, but pro rata only. For example if you let a French property for three months of the year, you can offset a quarter of your annual mortgage interest against your rental income.

VALUE ADDED TAX

Value Added Tax (VAT) is called *taxe sur la valeur ajoutée (TVA)* in France (or the 'Voracious Administration Tax') and accounts for around 45 per cent of government revenue (twice as much as income tax!). Most prices of goods and services in France are quoted inclusive of tax (*toutes taxes comprises/TTC*) although sometimes business supplies are quoted exclusive of tax (*hors taxes/HT*). France has the following rates of TVA:

Rate (%)	Applicability
2.1	medicines subject to reimbursement by social security, daily newspapers;
4.0	magazines;
5.5	reduced rate: food (including most beverages and take-away food such as sandwiches), agricultural products, medicines (non-social security), books, public transport, canteens, cinema, theatre, concerts, hotel accommodation and travel agencies;
20.6	standard rate: all services and articles that don't come under a special rate.

Certain goods and services are exempt from VAT including food, children's clothes, medical and dental care, educational services, insurance, banking and financial services, and various transactions subject to other taxes. VAT is payable on goods purchased outside the EU, but not on goods purchased in an EU country where VAT has already been paid, although you may be asked to show a VAT receipt. VAT on imported secondhand goods, on which VAT hasn't previously been paid, is subject to a complex calculation based on their secondhand value.

A service business with an annual turnover of over 400,000F must register for VAT and charge VAT to its customers. If VAT relates to sales, then they must exceed 1,000,000F before registration is necessary. If you're self-employed (*travailleur indépendant*) or a sole-trader, you must register with the appropriate organisation (see **Self-Employment** on page 35) and will automatically be given a VAT number. With the exception of very small businesses, VAT returns must be made monthly and not quarterly as in some other EU countries. VAT refunds aren't paid automatically and must be applied for on certain dates. VAT fraud is rife in France and payments are often made in cash to avoid VAT payments.

See also **Customs** on page 76 and **Shopping Abroad** on page 389.

INCOME TAX

Generally speaking, income tax (*impôt sur le revenu*) in France is below average for EU countries, particularly for large families, and accounts for some 20 per cent of government revenue only. However, when income tax is added to the crippling social security contributions, regarded as a form of tax in France, and other indirect taxes, then French taxes are among the highest in the industrialised world (around 50 per cent). Unlike many other countries, employees' income tax *isn't* deducted at source (i.e. pay as you earn) by employers in France, where individuals are responsible for paying their own income tax. Most taxpayers pay their tax a year in arrears in three instalments, although it can be paid in ten monthly instalments. However, tax is withheld at flat rates and at source for non-residents who receive income from employment and professional activities in France. Non-residents who receive income from a French source must file a statement with the *Centre des Impôts de Non-Résidents* (9, rue d'Uzès, 75094 Paris Cedex 02) each year.

The French have a pathological hatred of paying taxes and tax evasion is a national sport (most Frenchmen don't consider cheating the 'tax man' a crime). It's estimated that around one-third of non-salaried taxpayers don't declare a substantial part of their income. Consequently, if your tax affairs are investigated the authorities often take a hard line if they find you have been 'cheating', even if you made an 'innocent' mistake. If your perceived standard of living is higher than would be expected on your declared income, the tax authorities may suspect you of fraud, so contrive to appear poor (not difficult for struggling authors!). In extreme circumstances, income tax or a higher rate of tax can be arbitrarily imposed by tax inspectors (*régime d'imposition forfaitaire*). The tax authorities maintain details of tax declarations, employers and bank accounts on computers to help them expose fraud, and can now use social security numbers and access all other government computer systems to identify residents and their circumstances.

As you would expect in a country with a 'billion' bureaucrats, the French tax system is inordinately complicated and most Frenchmen don't understand it. It's difficult to obtain accurate information from the tax authorities and errors in tax assessments are commonplace. Unless your tax affairs are simple, it's prudent to employ an accountant to complete your tax return and ensure that you're correctly assessed. The information below applies only to personal income tax (*Impôt sur le Revenu des Personnes Physiques/IRPP*) and not to companies.

Many books are available to help you understand and save taxes and income tax guides are published each January including *VO Impôts* and the *Guide Practique du Contribuable*. You can obtain tax information and calculate your tax using Minitel (3615 IR SERVICE) if you're very smart! You will, however, need to understand French perfectly (and then some) to complete your own tax return.

Liability

Your liability for French taxes depends on where you're domiciled. Your domicile is normally the country you regard as your permanent home and where you live most of the year. A foreigner working in France for a French company who has taken up residency in France and has no income tax liability abroad, is considered to have his tax domicile (*domicile fiscal*) in France. A person can be resident in more than one country at any given time, but can be domiciled only in one country. The domicile of a married woman isn't necessarily the same as her husband's, but is determined using the same criteria as anyone capable of having an independent domicile. Your country of domicile is particularly important regarding inheritance tax (see page 302).

Under the French tax code, domicile is decided under the 'tax home test' (*foyer fiscal*) or the 183-day rule. You're considered to be a French resident and liable to French tax if any of the following apply:

• your permanent home, i.e. family or principal residence, is in France;

• you spend over 183 days in France during any calendar year;

• you carry out paid professional activities or employment in France, except when secondary to business activities conducted in another country;

• your centre of vital economic interest, e.g. investments or business, is in France.

If you intend to live permanently in France, you should notify the tax authorities in your present country (you will be asked to complete a form, e.g. a form P85 in Britain). You may be entitled to a tax refund if you depart during the tax year, which usually necessitates the completion of a tax return. The tax authorities may require evidence that you're leaving the country, e.g. evidence of a job in France or of having bought or rented a property there. If you move to France to take up a job or start a business, you must register with the local tax authorities (*Centre des Impôts*) soon after your arrival.

Double-Taxation: French residents are taxed on their worldwide income, subject to certain treaty exceptions (non-residents are taxed only on income arising in France). Citizens of most countries are exempt from paying taxes in their home country when they spend a minimum period abroad, e.g. one year. France has double-taxation treaties with over 70 countries including all members of the EU, Australia, Canada, China, India, Israel, Japan, Malaysia, New Zealand, Pakistan, the Philippines, Singapore, Sri Lanka, Switzerland and the USA.

Treaties are designed to ensure that income that has already been taxed in one treaty country isn't taxed again in another treaty country. The treaty establishes a tax credit or exemption on certain kinds of income, either in the country of residence or the country where the income is earned. Where applicable, a double-taxation treaty prevails over domestic law. Many people living abroad switch their investments to offshore holdings to circumvent the often complicated double-taxation agreements. If you're in doubt about your tax liability in your home country, contact your nearest embassy or consulate in France. The USA is the only country that taxes its non-resident citizens on income earned abroad.

Leaving France: Before leaving France, foreigners must pay any tax due for the previous year and the year of departure by applying for a tax clearance (*quitus fiscal*). A tax return must be filed prior to departure and should include your income and deductions from 1st January of the departure year up to the date of departure. The local tax inspector will calculate the tax due and provide a written statement. When departure is made before 31st December, the previous year's taxes are applied. If this results in overpayment, a claim must be made for a refund. A French removal company isn't supposed to export your household belongings without a 'tax clearance statement' (*bordereau de situation*) from the tax authorities stating that all taxes have been paid.

Note that moving to France (or another country) may offer considerable opportunities for 'favourable tax planning', i.e. tax avoidance, rather than tax evasion. To take the maximum advantage of your situation, you should obtain professional advice from a tax adviser who's familiar with both the French tax system and that of your present country of residence.

Allowances

Before you're liable for income tax, you can deduct social security payments and certain allowances. The resultant figure is your taxable income. Income tax is calculated upon both earned income (*impôt sur le revenu*) and unearned income (*impôt des revenus de capitaux*). If you have an average income and receive interest on bank deposits only, tax on unearned income won't apply as it's deducted from bank interest before you receive it. Taxable income includes base pay; overseas and cost of living allowances; contributions to profit sharing plans; bonuses (annual, performance, etc.); storage and relocation allowances; language lessons provided for a spouse; personal company car; payments in kind (such as free accommodation or meals); stock options; home leave or vacations (paid by your employer); children's education; and property and investment income (dividends and interest).

Although the tax percentage rates in France are high, your taxable income is considerably reduced by allowances. Note that social security payments *aren't* taxable and are deducted from your gross income before your allowances are applied. Some income such as certain social security benefits, e.g. family and maternity allowances, aren't subject to income tax. Everyone is entitled to a 10 per cent allowance (*déduction forfaitaire normale*) for 'professional' or 'notional' expenses which is a minimum of 2,230F and a maximum of 74,590F. A general allowance of 20 per cent is deducted from the balance of income after deduction of the 10 per cent allowance. It also applies to everyone and is deductible on taxable income up to 680,000F. This is reduced to 10 per cent for the portion of your salary above 478,000F if you own over 35 per cent of the share capital of the company paying your salary.

There are also allowances for pension contributions (up to a maximum amount); major property repairs for your principal French residence; alimony and child support payments; certain support payments to parents and descendants; child-minding costs; life insurance premiums; mortgage interest payments; certain investments in rented property; gifts and subscriptions to charitable, educational, scientific, social and cultural organisations; and certain foreign-source income such as dividends, interest and royalties. Further supplementary allowances of up to 40 per cent are granted to around 100 professions including artists, actors, journalists, models, photographers, travelling sales people, radio hosts, commercial pilots, stewardesses, weavers and certain categories of civil servants. Note that anyone can itemise their actual expenses and claim additional deductions if these exceed their standard deductions.

Calculation

The tax year in France runs for a calendar year from 1st January to 31st December. Families are taxed as a single entity, thus a father's return normally includes his wife's and children's income, although he can elect for a dependant child's income to be taxed separately if this is advantageous. A wife may be taxed separately if she's separated from her husband. The French income tax system favours the family, as the amount of income tax paid is directly related to the number of dependant children.

French tax rates are based on a system of coefficients or parts, reflecting the family status of the taxpayer and the number of dependant children under the age of 18, or handicapped dependants of any age, as shown below:

Parts

No. Of Children	Married/Widow(er)	Single/Divorced/Separated
0	2 (1 or 1.5*)	1 or 1.5*
1	2.5	2
2	3	2.5
3	4	3.5
4	5	4.5
5	6	5.5
+1	+1	+1

* 1 or 1.5 parts apply to widows and widowers with no dependants and ex-servicemen over the age of 75 (who are allowed an extra 0.5 part).

Dependant children are classified as those aged under 18 years and unmarried or handicapped children of any age. However, if children are unmarried and aged under 21, in full-time education and aged under 25, or any age and doing military service, they can be claimed as dependants. A form requesting dependant status must be signed by the child and must be sent with the parents' tax return. All income of dependant children must be included in the parents' tax return.

The income tax rates for a single person (1 part) for 1999 income (2000 tax return) are shown in the table below. Note that taxable income, is income after the deduction of social security contributions and various allowances (listed above). Tax is calculated by multiplying the taxable income within a particular bracket by the tax rate, e.g. $51,340 - 26,100 = 25,240 \times 10.5$ per cent $= 2,651.20$.

Taxable Income (F)	Rate (%)	Portion	Aggregate
below 26,100	0	0.00	0.00
between 26,100 and 51,340	10.5	2,524.00	2,524.00
" 51,340 and 90,370	24	9,367.20	11,891.20
" 90,370 and 146,320	33	18,463.50	30,354.70
" 146,320 and 238,080	43	39,456.80	69,811.50
" 238,080 and 293,600	48	26,649.60	96,461.10
above 293,600	54		

The tax rate for other taxpayers can be calculated using the above table by multiplying the taxable income by the number of parts. For example if you're a married couple with no children (2 parts) simply double the taxable income amounts shown; if you're a married couple with two children (3 parts) treble the taxable income shown (and so on). The following table shows the amount of tax payable for selected taxable incomes from 50,000F to 300,000F (1999 income):

Taxable Income	1	1.5	2	2.5	3	3.5	4	4.5	5
50,000F	2510	0	0	0	0	0	0	0	0
75,000F	8328	3764	2394	1024	346	0	0	0	0
100,000F	15195	9492	5019	3649	2278	908	0	0	0
150,000F	32062	22794	21907	11821	7528	6158	4788	3418	2047
200,000F	53562	39294	35640	17196	25016	14150	10038	8668	7297
300,000F	100043	80346	58826	54488	45585	38150	33313	28479	23643

The following table shows a simple tax calculation:

Item	Sum(F)
gross annual salary	300,000
minus social security payments*	(31,000)
minus 1st standard allowance (10%)	269,000
	(26,900)
minus 2nd standard allowance (20%)	242,100
	(48,420)
	193,680
minus other allowances	(25,000)
Taxable income	168,680F

Examples of tax payable (1999 income):

- single person (1 part)   39,750F
- couple (2 parts)   20,980F
- couple with two children (3 parts)   11,305F

* See the table on page 259.

Self-Employed

Those who qualify as self-employed in France include artisans or craftsmen (*professions artisanales*) such as builders, plumbers and electricians. Others include those involved in trading activities such as shopkeepers, anyone buying and selling goods, agents, brokers and property dealers. There are three ways in which a self-employed person or sole trader can be taxed in France, depending upon his

income or turnover: a flat rate tax (*forfait*), simplified accounts (*bénéfice réel simplifié*) or through regular accounts (*bénéfice réel normal*).
Flat rate tax (*forfait*) is limited to anyone earning less than 500,000F a year. Accounts don't need to be submitted in the usual way and the tax assessment is a flat rate based on the normal net earnings for the type of business. This represents a saving in administration fees for both the taxpayer and tax officials. This arrangement is, however, limited to a maximum of two years with a possible extension for a further year.

Simplified accounts (*bénéfice réel simplifié*) are a compromise between flat rate tax and regular accounts. Businesses that qualify for simplified accounts are those with earnings between 500,000F and 1,500,000F a year. Only simple accounts need be kept, such as a cash book recording receipts and outgoings. All expenditure must, however, be supported by a receipt or an invoice.

Regular accounts (*bénéfice réel normal*) must be submitted by those with earnings in excess of 1,500,000F a year and those who choose not to use the simplified accounts procedure.

Professionals: If you're a professional such as an accountant, doctor or lawyer or a freelance worker such as an artist or writer, you're classified as a *profession libérale* or a *travailleur indépendant*. There are two ways in which you can file your income tax return. You can choose the *déclaration contrôlée* system requiring you to keep accounts of income and expenses, including all related receipts and documents. The second option is the *évaluation administrative* scheme, whereby you must keep a ledger of all income, but the tax department takes care of deductions.

MICRO-BIC & BNC: If you earn less than 120,000F from a commercial but non-salaried source, you can declare it as 'MICRO-BIC' income on your tax return and receive a 50 per cent allowance before paying income tax. The same applies to small earnings from a non-commercial organisation such as a charity, which is declared under the BNC (i.e. non-commercial, micro-earnings regime) and attracts a 25 per cent reduction before tax. If after deducting the allowance your income is below the tax threshold, you will pay no income tax.

Income Tax Return

You're sent an annual tax return (*déclaration des revenus*) by the tax authorities around March of each year. If you aren't sent a form you can obtain one from your local town hall or tax office. The standard return is the 2042N, although there's a simplified form (2042S) for those with uncomplicated tax affairs. There are supplementary forms for non-commercial profits (forms 2035, 2037); property income (2044); foreign source income such as a pension or dividends (2047); capital gains on financial investments (2074); and other capital gains (2049).

The head of a household usually completes the tax return for the whole family's income (*quotient familial*), including his or her spouse and dependant children. There's no independent taxation of married women in France, where taxation is based on the family unit. An unmarried couple living together have a legal status called *concubinage*, providing certain tax advantages. A tax return can be completed by either the husband or wife but must be signed by both, making both jointly responsible for any errors (this also means that both partners know exactly what the other earns!).

A wife living apart from her husband who isn't married in 'community of property' (see page 402) can choose to be assessed separately. A wife's income is assessed separately in the first year of marriage from 1st January to the date of her marriage. It's possible for children under 18 with their own income, e.g. income from an inheritance or their own earnings, to be independently assessed.

The tax return must be filed by 28th February (29th February in a leap year) and is for the current year. Income tax is based on the preceding year's income, taking into account any deductible allowances. For example the return filed in February 1999 was for the calendar year 1998. Late filing, even by one day, attracts a penalty of 10 per cent of the amount due.

French tax returns are complicated, despite attempts to simplify them in recent years. The language used is particularly difficult to understand for foreigners (and many French) and is quite complex. Local tax offices (*bureau des impôts/Hôtel d'Impôts*) are usually helpful and will help you complete your tax return. You can make an appointment for a free consultation with your local tax inspector at your town hall. However, if your French isn't excellent you will need to take someone with you who's fluent. Alternatively you can employ a tax accountant (*expert-comptable/conseiller fiscal*).

If you pay income tax abroad, you must return the form uncompleted with evidence that you're domiciled abroad. Around one month later you should receive a statement from the French tax authorities stating that you have no tax to pay (*vous n'avez pas d'impôt à payer*). The French tax authorities may request copies of foreign tax returns.

Changes in your tax liability may be made by the tax authorities up to three years after the end of the tax year to which the liability relates. Therefore you should retain all records relating to the income and expenses reported in your tax returns, until the expiration of this period, even if you have left France. Penalties for undeclared or understated income and unjustified deductions range from 40 per cent for 'bad faith' errors to 80 per cent for fraud, plus interest on the amount owed.

Tax Bills

Sometime between September and December you will receive a tax bill (*avis d'imposition*) for the current tax year, based on your income tax return for the previous year, e.g. in September 1999 you will receive your tax bill for 1999 based on your 1998 income. There are two methods of paying your tax bill in France: in three instalments (*tiers provisionnels*) or in ten equal monthly instalments (*mensualisation*).

Three Instalments: The most common method of payment is by three instalments. The first two payments, each comprising around one-third (*tiers*) of the previous year's tax liability, are provisional (*acompte provisionnel*) and are payable on 15th February and 15th May each year. For example in 1999, these payments each represent around a third of your total tax bill for 1998. The third and final instalment, the balance of your tax bill, is payable by 15th September. The tax authorities adjust your third payment to take into account your actual income for the previous year. To take a simple example, if you paid 120,000F in income tax in 1997, your first two payments in 1999 (for tax year 1998) would each be for 40,000F, i.e. one-third of your previous bill. If your actual tax liability for 1998 was 150,000F, you would then pay the balance of 70,000F (150,000F minus the 80,000F already paid) in September 1999 as a final payment.

Payment dates are officially 31st January, 30th April and 31st August, but the tax authorities allow you an extra two weeks (or 15 days) to pay bills. If you pay your tax bill late, you must pay a penalty equal to 10 per cent of your annual tax bill. The following schedule shows the tax payment for a new arrival in France:

Year	Tax Return/Bill
1st	(arrival in France) no tax payable
2nd	28th February - file tax return for 1st year's income
	15th September - pay entire tax bill for 1st year
3rd	15th February - pay first instalment of 2nd year's tax
	28th February - file tax return for 2nd year's income
	15th May - pay second instalment of 2nd year's tax
	15th September - pay final instalment of 2nd year's tax
4th	as for 3rd year

During your first year in France you won't have a previous year's tax liability (in France). Therefore the income tax computed with the information contained in the tax return filed on 28th February of your second year is payable in full on 15th September of the same year. In the following year, the normal procedure is applied. Note that if you arrive in France in, for example, September 1999, you won't start paying tax until September 2000. Even then you will have only been resident in France for less than four months of your first tax year (1999) and will pay little or no tax in the year 2000 and won't need to pay any significant income tax until two years after your arrival, i.e. September 2001.

Monthly Instalments: You can choose to pay your tax in ten equal monthly instalments (*Mensualisation*) by direct debit from a bank or post office account. Under this system you pay one tenth of your previous year's tax bill on the 8th of each month from January to October. If your income is less in the current year than the previous year, the tax office will stop payments when it has received the full amount. On the other hand, if you earned more in the previous year than the year before, the tax office will automatically deduct further payments in November and December. Monthly payments are a good budgeting aid, particularly if you're a spendthrift and are likely to rush out and spend your salary as soon as you receive it. However, most Frenchmen prefer to pay in three instalments, with the advantage that you can invest the amount set aside for tax until each payment is due.

RESIDENTIAL & REAL ESTATE TAXES

There are two types of local property taxes (*impôts locaux*) in France: residential tax (*taxe d'habitation*) and real estate tax (*taxe foncière*). Residential tax is payable by anyone who lives in a property in France, whether as an owner, tenant or rent free. Real estate tax is paid only by owners of property in France. Both taxes are payable whether the property is a main or a second home, or the owner is a French or foreign resident. Taxes pay for local services including rubbish collection, street lighting and cleaning, local schools and other community services, and include a contribution to departmental and regional expenses. You may be billed separately for rubbish collection (*ordures*). If your property is a second home (*résidence secondaire*) this should be stated on your bill, which should be reduced accordingly.

Real Estate Tax: Real estate tax (*taxe foncière*) is paid by owners of property in France and is similar to the property tax (or rates) levied in most countries. It's payable even if a property isn't inhabited, providing it's furnished and habitable. Real estate tax is levied on buildings and shelters for persons or goods that are considered to be buildings, warehouses, house boats (fixed mooring) and on certain land. The tax is split into two amounts: one for the building (*taxe foncière bâtie*) and a smaller one for the land (*taxe foncière non bâtie*). Tax is payable on land whether or not it's built on. Real estate tax isn't applicable to buildings and land used exclusively for agricultural or religious purposes, or to government and public buildings.

New and restored buildings used as main or second homes are exempt from real estate tax for two years from the 1st January following the completion date (certain new houses and apartments are exempt for 10 or 15 years). An application for a temporary exemption from real estate tax must be made to your local tax office (*centre des impôts fonciers* or *bureau du cadastre*) before 31st December for exemption the following year. Applications must be made within 90 days of the completion of a new or restored building.

Residential Tax: Residential tax (*taxe d'habitation*) is payable by anyone who resides in a property in France on 1st January, whether as an owner, tenant or rent-free. It's payable on residential properties (used as main or second homes), outbuildings (e.g. accommodation for servants, garages) located less than one kilometre from a residential property, and on business premises that are an indistinguishable part of a residential property. Residential tax is levied by the town where the property is located. Premises used exclusively for business, farming, student lodging and classes, and official government offices are exempt from residential tax. Tax is usually payable on assessment in autumn of the same year.

If a property is your family's main home, there are obligatory deductions for dependants including children, parents, grandparents (depending on their age) and handicapped dependants of any age. Deductions are calculated as a percentage of the rental value and are 10 per cent for each of the first two dependants and 15 per cent for each additional dependant. If you aren't liable for income tax or paid little income tax for the previous year, or your main home has a rental value of less than 130 per cent of the average local rental value, you may be entitled to a reduction. Residential tax isn't paid by residents aged over 60 and others living in their principal home who were exempt from income and wealth tax the previous year. In 1999 new lower income levels were introduced whereby if your 1998 revenue was less than 43,900F (with additional income of 11,740F for each half-part quotient) then you're exempt from Residential Tax. In an effort to stimulate the letting market, residential tax was doubled in recent years (in certain areas only, on an experimental basis) when a property has been left empty for over two years.

Valuation: Residential tax is based on the average (notional) rental value of property in the previous year, adjusted for inflation, as calculated by the land registry (*Service du Cadastre*). It's calculated on the living area of a property, including outbuildings, garages and amenities, and takes into account factors such as the quality of construction, location, renovations, services (e.g. mains water, electricity and gas) and amenities such as central heating, swimming pool, the number of bathrooms, covered terrace, garage, etc. Properties are placed in eight categories ranging from 'very poor' to 'luxurious'. Changes made to a building, such as improvements or enlargements, must be notified to the land registry within 90 days. In principle, the notional rental value is the same for both residential tax and real estate tax. If you think a valuation is too high, you can contest it. The amount of tax due is calculated by multiplying the base figure (50 per cent of the rental value) by the tax rate for the tax year. A nationwide reassessment of property taxes has taken place in recent years and they have been increased considerably.

Payment: Forms for the assessment of both residential and real estate tax are sent out by local councils and must be completed and returned to the regional tax office (*Centre des Impôts*) by a specified date. They will calculate the tax due and send you a bill. You may be given up to two months to pay and a 10 per cent penalty is levied for late payment. It's possible to pay residential tax monthly (in ten equal instalments from January to October) by direct debit from a French bank account, which helps soften the blow.

Residential tax is payable by anyone who occupies a property in France on 1st January and if you vacate or sell a property on January 2nd, you must pay residential tax for the whole year. However, real estate tax is apportioned by the notary between the seller and buyer from the date of the sale. Taxes vary from area to area and are higher in cities and towns than in rural areas and small villages, where few community services are provided. In rural areas, the total residential and real estate tax is around 4,000F a year for an average dwelling, although they range from 750F for a basic small cottage to 10,000F or more for a luxury villa. In some areas a regional or sundry tax (*taxe assimilée*) is also levied, particularly if a property is in a popular tourist area. This is because the local authorities must spend more than usual on amenities and the upkeep of towns (gardens, etc).

WEALTH TAX

A wealth tax (*impôt sur la fortune/ISF*) was introduced on 1st January 1989 (since when billions of francs have disappeared into foreign banks!) and is payable on an individual's net estate when it exceeds 4.7 million francs. If you're domiciled in France, the value of your estate is based on your worldwide assets. If you're resident in France but not domiciled there, the value of your estate is based on your assets in France only. Wealth tax is assessed on the net value of your assets on 1st January each year and is payable by the following 15th June on filing the return (15th July for other European residents and 15th August for all others). On 1st January 1999 the rates were:

Assets (F)	Rate (%)	Liability (F)
up to 4.70m	zero	0
from 4.70m to 7.64m	0.55	16,170
from 7.64m to 15.16m	0.75	54,400
from 15.16m to 23.54m	1.0	83,800
from 23.54m to 45.58m	1.3	286,520
from 45.58m to 100.00m	1.65	897,930
Above 100.00m	1.8	

The amount payable is reduced by 1,000F for each dependant. The taxable estate doesn't include 'professional assets' (*biens professionnels*), which may include shares in a company in which you play an active role, providing they total at least 25 per cent of the equity. It excludes companies with property investment as their main activity.

CAPITAL GAINS TAX

Capital gains tax (*impôt sur les plus values*) is payable on the profit from sales of certain property in France including antiques, art and jewellery, securities and real estate. After paying capital gains tax (CGT), gains are added to other income and are liable to income tax.

Antiques, Art and Jewellery: CGT applies to the sale of antiques, art objects, collector's items, jewellery and precious metals. The tax is paid by the seller, but is withheld by the sales agent, exporter or the buyer. CGT is 7.5 per cent of the sale price of precious metals. The rate for antiques, collector's items, jewellery and *objets d'art* is generally 7 per cent, but is reduced to 4.5 per cent when objects are sold at public auction.

Securities: CGT at 19.4 per cent is payable on the sale of French or foreign quoted or unquoted securities (stock and rights to stock) if the total sale exceeds 100,000F in value or half this amount on certain mutual funds. However, if you or your immediate family members own over 25 per cent of the securities of a company subject to corporation tax, then the exemption from CGT doesn't apply.

Principal Residence: CGT isn't payable on a profit made on the sale of your principal residence in France, providing that you have occupied it since its purchase or for a minimum of five years. You're also exempt from CGT if you're forced to sell for family or professional reasons, e.g. you're transferred abroad by your employer. Income tax treaties usually provide that capital gains on property are taxable in the country where the property is located. Note that if you move to France permanently and retain a home abroad, this may affect your position regarding capital gains. If you sell your foreign home before moving to France, you will be exempt from CGT as it's your principal residence. However, if you establish your principal residence in France the foreign property becomes a second home and is thus liable to CGT when it's sold. **Note that EU tax authorities co-operate in tracking down capital gains tax dodgers.**

Second Homes: Capital gains on second homes in France are payable by both residents and non-residents. Long and short-term gains are treated differently. Short-term gains are classified as profits on the sale of a property owned for less than two years and are taxed at 33.3 per cent for non-residents and as ordinary income for residents. Long-term gains are categorised as gains on a property owned for more than two years and less than 22 years. The taxable gain is the difference between the purchase and sales price reduced by 5 per cent for the third and each subsequent year up to 22 years, and multiplied by an index linked multiplier (*coefficient*) of the sale price. After a property has been owned for 22 years it's exempt from CGT.

Residents are exempt from CGT on a second home in France if they don't own their main residence, i.e. you're a tenant or lease holder. You or your spouse mustn't be the owner of your permanent residence and the sale of the second home must take place more than five years after its acquisition or completion, and more than two years after that of a principle residence. The exemption applies only to the first sale of a second home in France.

Where applicable, CGT is withheld by the *notaire* handling the sale. The tax calculation is made by the *notaire*, although the local tax office can claim further tax if the assessment proves to be incorrect. On the other hand, if the amount withheld is too high, you should (eventually) receive a refund. You may be able to agree with the *notaire* what the CGT should be. Before a sale the *notaire* prepares a form calculating the tax due and appoints an agent (*agent fiscal accredité*) or guarantor to act on your behalf concerning tax. If the transaction is straightforward, the local tax office may grant a dispensation (*dispense*) of the need to appoint a guarantor, providing that you apply *before* completion of the sale. If you obtain a dispensation, the proceeds of the sale can be released to you in full after CGT has been paid. The *notaire* handling the sale must apply for the dispensation.

Everyone is allowed an allowance of 6,000F to set against a short or long-term capital gain. You should keep all bills for the fees associated with buying a property (the *notaire*, agent, surveyor, etc.), plus any bills for renovation, restoration, modernisation and improvements of a second home, as these can be offset against CGT and are index-linked. If you work on a house yourself, you should keep a copy of bills for materials and tools, as these can be multiplied by three and the total offset against CGT. Painting and decorating costs (*embellissement*) cannot be claimed against CGT. Costs relating to the sale can also be offset against any gain, as can part of the interest paid on a loan taken out to purchase or restore a property.

INHERITANCE & GIFT TAX

As in most other western countries, dying doesn't free your assets from the clutches of French tax inspectors. France imposes both inheritance (*droits de succession*) and gift (*droits de donation*) taxes on its inhabitants.

Inheritance Tax: Inheritance tax, called estate tax or death duty in some countries, is levied on the estate of a deceased person. Both residents and non-residents are subject to inheritance tax if they own property in France. The country where you pay inheritance tax is decided by your domicile (see **Liability** on page 291). If you're living permanently in France at the time of your death, you will be deemed to be domiciled there by the French tax authorities. If you're domiciled in France, then inheritance tax applies to your worldwide estate (excluding property), otherwise it applies only to assets located in France. It's important to make your domicile clear, so that there's no misunderstanding on your death.

When a person dies in France, an estate tax return (*déclaration de succession*) must be filed within six months of the date of death and within 12 months if the death occurred outside France. The return is generally prepared in France by a *notaire*. If the estate doesn't have any property or if the sole beneficiary is the spouse and the gross value is less than 10,000F, no return is necessary.

Inheritance tax in France is paid by individual beneficiaries, irrespective of where they are domiciled, and not by the estate. Tax may be paid in instalments over five or, in certain cases, ten years or may be deferred. The rate of tax and allowances vary depending on the relationship between the beneficiary and the deceased. French succession laws are quite restrictive compared with the law in many other countries. The surviving spouse has an allowance of 400,000F (500,000F from 1st January 2000) and the children and parents of the deceased an allowance of 300,000F. After the allowance has been deducted there's a sliding scale up to a maximum of 40 per cent on assets over 11.2 million francs, as shown in the table below:

Tax Rate (%)	Amount (F) Spouse	Children/Parents
5	up to 50,000	up to 50,000
10	50,000 to 100,000	50,000 to 75,000
15	100,000 to 200,000	75,000 to 100,000
20	200,000 to 3.4m	100,000 to 3.4m
30	3.4m to 5.6m	3.4m to 5.6m
35	5.6m to 11.2m	5.6m to 11.2m
40	over 11.2m	over 11.2m

As you can see from the above table, it's best to leave property in France to your spouse, children or parents, in order to take advantage of the relatively low tax rates.

There's an allowance of 100,000F for each brother and sister if the deceased was single, widowed, divorced or separated, over 50 years old, was incapable of working due to a medical condition, *and* the brother or sister had lived continuously with the deceased for at least five years before his death. If the 100,000F allowance isn't applicable, the allowance for brothers and sisters is just 10,000F. After the 100,000F or 10,000F allowance, the tax rate for brothers and sisters is 35 per cent up to 150,000F and 45 per cent above this amount. Mentally or physically handicapped beneficiaries who are unable to earn a living receive a special allowance of 300,000F, in addition to the 100,000F for brothers and sisters (if applicable). Any beneficiary who doesn't benefit from any other allowance has an allowance of 10,000F. Between relations up to the fourth degree, i.e. uncles/aunts, nephews/nieces, great uncles/aunts, great nephews/nieces and first cousins, there's a flat rate tax of 55 per cent. For relationships beyond the fourth degree or between unrelated persons, the tax rate is 60 per cent.

Exemptions from inheritance tax include certain woodlands and rural properties, and legacies to charities and government bodies. Many people take out a life insurance policy to reduce the impact of inheritance tax, as the beneficiaries of life insurance policies aren't liable to inheritance tax. Note that if you're a resident in France and receive inheritance from abroad then you're subject to French inheritance tax. However, if you've been resident for less than six years in France then you're exempt or if you paid the bill in another country then this is deducted from your French tax bill.

Gift Tax: Gift tax is calculated in the same way as inheritance tax, according to the relationship between the donor and the recipient and the size of the gift. A reduction of gift tax is granted depending on the age of the donor (the younger the donor the larger the reduction). If the donor is under 65 years of age the tax is reduced by 50 per cent and for those aged 65 to 75 there's a 35 per cent reduction. Over 75 there's no reduction. Any gifts made before the death of the donor (*inter vivos*) must be included in the estate duty return. Note that gift tax is payable on gifts made between spouses in France and therefore assets should be equally shared before you're domiciled there.

It's important for both residents and non-residents with property in France to decide in advance how they wish to dispose of their French property. This should be decided before buying a house or other property in France. There are a number of ways of limiting or delaying the impact of French inheritance laws including inserting a clause (such as a *clause tontine*) in a property purchase contract (*acte de vente*), officially changing your marital regime (see page 402) in France (e.g. to joint ownership or *communauté universelle*), and by buying property through a civil real estate company (*Société Civile Immobilière*), possibly with a clause *tontine*. The clause *tontine* allows a property to be left in its entirety to a surviving spouse, without it being shared among the children (see **Wills** below). A surviving spouse can also be given a life interest (*usufruit*) in an estate in priority to children or parents through a gift between spouses (*donation entre époux*), although this may not apply to non-residents. Note that French law doesn't recognise the rights to inheritance of a non-married partner, although there are a number of solutions to this problem, e.g. a life insurance policy.

French inheritance law is an extremely complicated subject and professional advice should be sought from an experienced lawyer who understands both French law and that of any other country involved. Your will (see below) is also a vital component in reducing French inheritance and gift tax to the minimum or delaying its payment.

WILLS

It's an unfortunate fact of life that you're unable to take your hard-earned assets with you when you take your final bow (or come back and reclaim them in a later life!). All adults should make a will (*testament*) regardless of how large or small their assets. The disposal of your estate depends on your country of domicile (see **Inheritance & Gift Tax** above). As a general rule, French law permits a foreigner who *isn't* domiciled in France to make a will in any language and under the law of any country, providing it's valid under the law of that country.

Note, however, that 'immovable' property (or immovables) in France, i.e. land and buildings, *must* be disposed of (on death) in accordance with French law. All other property in France or elsewhere (defined as 'movables') may be disposed of in accordance with the law of your country of domicile. Therefore, it's extremely important to establish where you're domiciled under French law. One of the best solutions for a non-resident who wishes to avoid French inheritance laws regarding immovable property located in France may be to buy it through a French holding company, in which case the shares of the company are 'movable' assets and are therefore governed by the succession laws of the owner's country of domicile.

French law is restrictive regarding the distribution of property and the identity of heirs and gives priority to children, including illegitimate and adopted children, and the living parents of a deceased person. Under French law (*code Napoléon*) you cannot disinherit your children, who have absolute priority over your estate, even before a surviving spouse. There are, however, many legal ways to safeguard the rights of a surviving spouse, some of which are mentioned above under **Inheritance & Gift Tax**. The part of a property that must be inherited by certain heirs (*héritiers réservataires*) is called the legal reserve (*réserve legale*). Once the reserved portion of your estate has been determined, the remaining portion is freely disposable (*quotité disponible*). Only when there are no descendants or ascendants is the whole estate freely disposable.

If you die leaving one child, he must inherit one half of your French estate and two children must inherit at least two-thirds. If you have three or more children, they must inherit three-quarters of your estate. If a couple has no surviving children, their parents inherit their estate. The reserve for parents is 25 per cent per parent and if there's only one surviving parent it remains 25 per cent. Brothers and sisters are next in line after children and parents, and can only be disinherited if specified in a will.

There are three kinds of will in France: holographic (*testament olographe*), authentic (*testament authentique*) and secret (*testament mystique*), described below.

A **holographic will** is the most common form of will used in France. It must be written by hand by the person making the will (i.e. it cannot be typewritten or printed) and be signed and dated by him. No witnesses or other formalities are required. In fact it shouldn't be witnessed at all, as this may complicate matters. It can be written in English or another language, although it's preferable if it's written in French (you can ask a *notaire* to prepare a draft and copy it in your own handwriting). It can be registered in the central wills registry (*fichier de dernières volontés*).

An **authentic or notarial will** is used by some 5 per cent of French people. It must be drawn up by a *notaire* in the form of a notarial document and can be handwritten or typed. It's dictated by the person making the will and must be witnessed by two *notaires* or a *notaire* and two other witnesses. Unlike a holographic will, an authentic will is automatically registered in the central wills registry.

A **secret will** is rarely used and is a will written by or for the person making it and signed by him. It's inserted and sealed in an envelope in the presence of two witnesses. It's then given to a *notaire* who records on the envelope a note confirming that the envelope has been handed to him and that the testator has affirmed that the envelope contains his will.

A gift between spouses (*donation entre époux*) can be used to leave property to a spouse and delay the inheritance of an estate by any surviving children. It must be prepared by a *notaire* and signed in the presence of the donor and the donee. For anyone with a modest French estate, for example a small property in France, a holographic will is sufficient. Note that where applicable, the rules relating to witnesses are strict and if they aren't followed precisely they may render a will null and void. In France, marriage doesn't automatically revoke a will, as in some other countries, e.g. Britain. A holographic or secret will must be handed to a *notaire* for filing. He sends a copy to the local district court where the estate is administered. Wills aren't made public in France and aren't available for inspection.

Under French law, the role of the executor is different from many other countries and his duties are supervisory only and last for a year and a day. He's responsible for paying debts and death duties and distributing the balance in accordance with the will. On your death, the executor who's dealing with your affairs in France must file a *déclaration de succession* within one year of your death. At death your property passes directly to your heirs and it's their responsibility to pay any outstanding debts and their own inheritance tax. Note that winding-up an estate takes much longer than in many other countries and is usually given a low priority by *notaires*.

It's possible to make two wills, one relating to French property and the other to foreign property. Opinion differs on whether you should have separate wills for French and foreign property, or a foreign will with a codicil (appendix) dealing with your French property (or vice versa). However, most experts believe it's better to have a French will from the point of view of winding up your French estate (and a will for any country where you own immovable property). If you have French and foreign wills, make sure that they don't contradict one another (or worse still, cancel each other out, e.g. when a will contains a clause revoking all other wills). Note that a foreign will written in a foreign language must be translated into French (a certified translation is required) and proven in France in order to be valid there.

Keep a copy of your will(s) in a safe place and another copy with your solicitor or the executor of your estate. Don't leave them in a bank safe deposit box, which in the event of your death is sealed for a period under French law. You should keep information regarding bank accounts and insurance policies with your will(s), but don't forget to tell someone where they are!

Note that French inheritance law is a complicated subject and it's important to obtain professional legal advice when writing or altering your will(s).

COST OF LIVING

No doubt you would like to try to estimate how far your French francs will stretch and how much money (if any) you will have left after paying your bills. Inflation in France in 1998 was around 1 per cent and the French have enjoyed a stable and strong economy in recent years, reflected in the strong French franc. Salaries are generally high and the French enjoy a high standard of living, although some 5.5. million people live below the poverty threshold (those with a monthly net income of less than half the average national income). Social security costs are very high, particularly for the self-employed, and the combined burden of social security, income tax and indirect taxes make French taxes among the highest in the EU.

Anyone planning to live in France, particularly retirees, should take care not to underestimate the cost of living, which has increased considerably in the last decade. France is a relatively expensive country by American standards, particularly if your income is earned in $US. You should be wary of cost of living comparisons with other countries, which are often wildly inaccurate (and often include irrelevant items which distort the results). It isn't just residents who need to watch the *centimes*, as in recent years many visitors have found it difficult or impossible to remain within their budgets. The cost of living in France is similar to that of Germany and some 25 per cent lower than in Britain and around 25 per cent higher than the USA.

It's difficult to calculate an average cost of living in France as it depends on each individual's particular circumstances and life-style. With the exception of Paris and other major cities, where the higher cost of living is offset by higher salaries, the cost of living in France is around average for western European countries. The actual difference in your food bill will depend on what you eat and where you lived before arriving in France. Food in France costs around 50 per cent more than in the USA, but is similar overall to most other western European countries, although you may need to modify your diet. From 2,000F to 2,500F should feed two adults for a month, excluding fillet steak, caviar and alcohol (other than a moderate amount of inexpensive beer or wine). Shopping for selected 'luxury' and 'big-ticket' items such as stereo equipment, household apparatus, electrical and electronic goods, computers and photographic equipment abroad can result in significant savings.

A list of the approximate **MINIMUM** monthly major expenses for an average single person, couple or family with two children are shown in the table below (most people will no doubt agree that the figures are either too HIGH or too LOW). When calculating your cost of living, deduct **at least** 15 per cent for social security contributions (see page 258) and the appropriate percentage for income tax (see page 291) from your gross salary. The numbers (in brackets) refer to the notes following the table.

MONTHLY COSTS (F)

	Single	Couple	Couple with 2 children
Housing (1)	2,500	3,500	4,500
Food (2)	1,300	2,250	2,800
Utilities (3)	300	500	700
Leisure (4)	600	1,000	1,200
Transport (5)	600	600	800
Insurance (6)	400	700	800
Clothing	300	600	1,200
TOTAL	6,000	9,150	12,000

(1) Rent or mortgage payments for a modern or modernised apartment or house in an average suburb, excluding Paris and other high-cost areas. The properties envisaged are a studio or one-bedroom apartment for a single person, a two-bedroom property for a couple and a three-bedroom property for a couple with two children.

(2) Doesn't include luxuries or liquid food (alcohol).

(3) Includes electricity, gas, water, telephone, cable TV and heating costs.

(4) Includes entertainment, restaurant meals, sports and vacation expenses, plus newspapers and magazines.

(5) Includes running costs for an average family car plus third party insurance, annual taxes, petrol, servicing and repairs, **but excludes depreciation or credit purchase costs.**

(6) Includes 'voluntary' insurance such as supplementary health insurance, disability, home contents, third party liability, legal, travel, automobile breakdown and life insurance.

15.

LEISURE

When it comes to leisure few countries can match *la belle France* for the variety and excellence of its attractions, from its outstanding physical beauty to the sophistication and grandeur of its cities. France is the world's most popular tourist destination, attracting over 60 million visitors a year, and tourism is the country's most important industry (the Eiffel Tower in Paris is the most visited admission-charging monument in the world, attracting some six million visitors a year).

France is one of the most beautiful countries in Europe, if not *the* most beautiful, and has the most varied landscape. It's a country of infinite variety, offering something for everyone: magnificent beaches for sun-worshippers; beautiful and spectacular countryside for nature lovers; mountains and seas for sports fans; vibrant Parisian night-life for the jet set; vintage wines for connoisseurs; *haute cuisine* for gourmets; an abundance of culture, art and serious music for art lovers; and tranquillity for the stressed. In France, the pursuit of *la bonne vie* is a serious business and even *bon viveurs* are spoilt for choice (most Frenchmen rate the pursuit of pleasure and style way ahead of success and wealth). Nowhere else in the world is there such an exhilarating mixture of culture and climate, history and tradition, sophistication and style.

France provides a wealth of leisure and entertainment facilities. Paris is one of the world's great cities and a treasure house of national monuments. It's also one of the least expensive and cleanest major capitals in the world (on the negative side, watch out for pickpockets and bag snatchers). There's much to be enjoyed that's inexpensive or even free, not least its beauty and the extravagant street entertainment, both cultural and sartorial. Paris dominates the cultural scene in France, even more so than capital cities in other European countries, such as London and Rome. France spends an enormous amount of public money promoting the arts, particularly in Paris, widely recognised as the art capital of Europe. Cultural policy is a political priority and the government even appoints a Minister of Culture (the mayor of Paris and the state government compete to see who can spend the most on the arts).

Naturally there's much more to France than just Paris, and the provinces accentuate a land of great culture. Many towns have a cultural centre (*maison de la culture*) where exhibitions, theatre, music festivals, debates and art classes are held. There are many excellent provincial art galleries and museums, and art and music festivals are staged in all regions and major towns in France. Traditional folk festivals are held throughout the country, most notably in the south (France boasts more festivals than any other European country).

Information regarding local events and entertainment is available from tourist offices, and is published in local newspapers and magazines, plus many foreign publications such as the English-language *France* magazine (see **Appendix B**). In most cities there are magazines and newspapers devoted to entertainment, and free weekly or monthly programmes are published by tourist organisations in major cities and tourist centres. Many city newspapers publish weekly magazines or supplements, containing a detailed programme of local events and entertainment. The Paris Tourist Office provides a 24-hour recorded information service in English for performances and shows in Paris (☎ 01.49.52.53.56).

GUIDE BOOKS

The main aim of this chapter, and indeed the purpose of the whole book, is to provide information that isn't found in standard guide books. General tourist information is available in numerous French and foreign guide books including a range of indispensable books produced by Michelin, all of which complement each other. The Michelin *Green Guides* encompass some 25 books, around 15 published in English, each covering a different area in detail. They contain a wealth of information about local history, architecture and geology, and numerous maps and plans. The *Michelin Blue Guide to France* contains detailed itineraries and is culturally oriented for the art lover.

The annual *Michelin Red Guide* is the most comprehensive hotel and restaurant guide available anywhere, and is priceless for both residents and visitors. It's an institution in France and many French people won't stay or eat anywhere without consulting the latest *Red Guide*. It contains all the necessary information including prices, opening times, facilities (including special facilities for children and the handicapped), town maps, and useful references to other Michelin guides. Although published in French only, the *Red Guide* contains an introduction and an explanation of symbols in English and other languages. It takes a while to decipher and recognise all the symbols, but it's well worth the effort. Michelin also produce many excellent maps (see page 221).

Although you may prefer to buy a foreign guide book written by a fellow countryman, French guides such as the *Michelin Red Guide*, the *Gault-Millau Guide de la France* (see page 341) and the *Logis de France* guide (see page 315) are unrivalled for their breadth of up-to-date information. Good general English-language guide books include the *Baedeker Guide to France, Birnbaum's France,* the *Blue Guide France, Fodor's France, Let's Go France* and *France: The Rough Guide* (see **Appendix B** for a comprehensive list).

Among the best Paris guides are the *Time Out Paris Guide,* the *Rough Guide to Paris,* the *Paris Mode d'Emploi/User's Guide* (Paris Tourist Office) and *Pauper's Paris* for those on a tight budget. The best map of Paris is the *Plan de Paris par Arrondissements,* containing detailed maps of each *arrondissement,* the *métro,* bus maps and a comprehensive street index. A free Paris map is available from French Government Tourist Offices (FGTO) and the Paris tourist office distributes a free monthly booklet, *Paris Sélection.* There are many weekly entertainment guides to Paris including *Pariscope* (which contains a section in English), *L'officiel des spectacles* and *7 à Paris.* There's also an English-language *Paris City Magazine* available free from bookshops and public offices in Paris, or on subscription from Paris City magazine, 9, Impasse d'Antin, 75008 Paris.

TOURIST OFFICES

Most French towns have a tourist office (*syndicat d'initiative* or *office de tourisme*), located in town centres and at main railway stations. A directory containing some 3,400 offices is published by the *Fédération Nationale des Offices de Tourisme et Syndicats d'Initiative,* 280, Bd. St Germain, 75007 Paris (☎ 01.40.59.43.82). Around 45 major cities and tourist areas have an *Accueil de France* tourist office open every day of the year which make hotel bookings for personal callers (for a small fee) anywhere in France, up to eight days in advance. For information contact *Accueil de France,* 127, Champs Elysées, 75008 Paris (☎ 01.49.52.53.54, Internet: www.paris-promotion.fr).

Many departments provide official booking services under the name *Loisirs-Accueil,* where you can book a hotel, *gîte,* campsite, or a special activity or sports holiday. Departments also have local tourist committees and the 16 regions of France have regional tourist authorities. Over 500 villages and towns meeting certain standards relating to natural attractions, accommodation, leisure facilities, shops and information facilities, plus general appearance and cleanliness, are listed in the *Guides des Stations Vertes* (guide to country resorts) obtainable from *La Fédération Française des Stations Vertes*, Hôtel du Départment de la Sarthe, 72040 Le Mans.

Tourist offices in the main cities are open daily, including Saturdays and Sundays. Telephone the tourist office or consult a guide book to check the precise business hours. In major towns, reduced opening hours are in operation during winter, while in smaller towns and resorts, tourist offices close for lunch (e.g. noon to 1400) and may be open during the summer or winter (e.g. in ski resorts) seasons only.

The main tourist office in Paris is the *Office de Tourisme de Paris*, 127, avenue des Champs Elysées, 75008 Paris (☎ 01.49.52.53.54), which is open from 0900 to 2000. Paris also has a free bilingual (English/French) telephone information service (*Paris Mode D'Emploi Par Telephone*) where you can obtain cultural, gastronomic, practical and entertainment details (☎ 01.44.29.12.12). There are tourist offices at all of Paris' main railway stations open daily from 0800 to 2100 from May to October and from 0800 to 2000 from November to April (except for Gare d'Austerlitz which opens from 0800 to 1500 Mondays to Fridays and from 0800 to 1300 on Saturdays). Many of France's regions also have tourist offices in Paris. The Paris tourist office (and many others) will find you a hotel or hostel room in Paris or in other parts of France for a fee, e.g. 10F to 40F, depending on the standard. Many tourist offices change foreign currency. There are also tourist offices at international airports in Paris and other cities, where you can make hotel reservations. In Paris, official interpreters are available on the streets during the main tourist season and wear armbands indicating the languages they speak.

Outside France, the French Government Tourist Office (FGTO) or *Maison de la France* is a mine of information and has offices in Austria, Belgium, Brazil, Canada, Denmark, Finland, Germany, Hungary, Ireland, Italy, Japan, Luxembourg, the Netherlands, Norway, Portugal, Spain, Sweden, Switzerland, the United Kingdom and the USA. The *Maison de la France*, 8, ave de l'Opéra, 75001 Paris (☎ 01.42.96.10.23) provides tourist information about most regions of France and will mail information. It's open on Mondays to Fridays from 0900 to 1900.

Among the plethora of information published by the FGTO, one of the most useful booklets is *The Traveller in France and Reference Guide*. It contains a comprehensive list of hotel groups; self-catering accommodation; package and special interest holiday companies (including caravan and camping, touring and sporting holidays); helpful hints; maps and guides; motoring tips; and a list of local addresses. FGTO publications include *The Short Break Traveller*, *The Touring Traveller*, *The Winter Traveller*, *France for Active Holidays* and *France Youth Travel*. The FGTO also publishes *Festive France*, an annual directory of festivals, light and sound shows, and other events throughout France.

If you write to a local tourist office for information, you should include an international reply coupon and shouldn't expect a reply in English, although most offices have staff that can understand letters written in English.

HOTELS

There are thousands of hotels in France (including *hôtels de ville* and *hôtels de police!*), with some 1,500 in Paris alone. France offers an unrivalled choice of hostelries for travellers and caters for all tastes and pockets, from sumptuous 'five-star palaces' and *châteaux* to a profusion of small family hotels. If you want to meet the real French, start at the bottom rather than the top of the accommodation chain. The country is abundantly provided with comfortable family-run hotels, offering good food and accommodation, and good value for money (although they aren't as good value as they once were). One of the delights of travelling in France is discovering the hidden gems off the beaten track. The hoteliers of France are an education and their hotels are usually an extension of their characters with the ambience of a country home. Children and animals are usually welcome.

French hotels are classified from one to four star de luxe (five stars on the international star-rating system) by the French Ministry of Tourism, depending on their facilities and the type of hotel. This provides a guarantee of standards directly related to the price. Note, however, that stars are based on facilities, e.g. the ratio of bathrooms to guests, rather than quality, meaning you can often find excellent ungraded and one-star hotels. Two star hotels are usually small and friendly, family-run hotels, providing the backbone of French tourism. A *rough* guide to room rates is shown below:

Star Rating	Price Range (F)	Class
L****	1,000-1,500 ++	luxury (*hôtel hors classe, palace*)
****	600-1,300	top class (*hôtel très grand confort*)
***	300-800	very comfortable (*hôtel de grand tourisme, grand confort*)
**	200-400	comfortable (*hôtel de tourisme, bon confort*)
*	150-250	average comfort (*hôtel de moyen tourisme*)
None	150-200	basic (*hôtel de tourisme/simple*)

The prices quoted above are for a double room with bath for one night (prices in France are usually quoted per room and *not* per person). Prices include services and government taxes (TVA) but not *taxe de séjour* (e.g. 1F to 7F per day in Paris) that's added to the bill in some areas. Room prices don't usually include breakfast. Rates must, by law, be prominently displayed where prospective guests can see them and must include seasonal rates and state whether the price includes tax and service. Room rates should be displayed in rooms, except in the case of four-star hotels, where if you need to ask the price, you cannot afford it! Many hotels in popular resorts have slightly higher room rates during July and August (the best time to visit Paris) and a minimum stay of three nights. Out of high season, hotels may offer a discount for stays of three nights or longer. Many hotels provide off-season discounts, particularly during the winter and early spring months, which may include three nights for the price of two or two nights for the price of one at weekends. You can book a room in around 50 (mainly three star) Paris hotels through Abotel, 1, Villa

Boissière, 75016 Paris (☎ 01.47.27.15.15) and receive a discount of from 20 to 40 per cent, depending on the season.

French hotels are among the cheapest in the western world, including Parisian hotels, where you can still get an attractive double room for 400F to 500F per night (you can also rent some rooms by the hour!). The same standard room in the country costs as little as 250F. However, you can easily pay 2,500F a night for a room in a luxury 'palace' hotel on the French Riviera or in Paris, which has more luxury hotels than any other city in the world including the Bristol, Crillon, Plaza-Athénée and the Ritz. A superior room (or suite) in a top-class hotel on the French Riviera can run to 4,000F or more a night in high season. Prices at beach resorts increase in July and August and are generally higher the closer you are to the beach. Many of France's best restaurants are found in top class hotels.

In most towns a single room costs from 150F to 200F and a double room from 150F to 300F. As in most countries, single rooms are only marginally cheaper (if at all) than doubles. Room rates in Paris are up to 100 per cent more expensive than in the provinces, although still relatively inexpensive compared with some other European capitals (e.g. London). Many hotels have rooms for three or four guests at reduced rates or provide extra beds for children in a double room free or for a small charge. A double room may contain one or two 'double' beds, although they may not be full-size double beds; often a room will have a double bed and one or two single beds. When travelling *en famille* the French like to pack as many people as possible into one room, thus reducing the cost considerably. Many hotels don't have single rooms and are reluctant to give a double room to one person.

One and two-star hotels abound in Paris, with prices starting at around 150F, although you must be prepared to share bathroom facilities. In the cheapest places you may be charged extra to use a shared bath or shower. Note that staff in inexpensive hotels may not speak English. Inexpensive singles without a bathroom or shower can be found in Paris from around 125F (or 150F with a shower) and from around 100F (125F with a shower) in other cities. Inexpensive hotels are usually found close to main railway stations in major cities. Not many hotels have private parking. If you're staying at a hotel without a car park, ask the hotel staff to recommend a safe place to park your car, i.e. safe from both thieves *and* parking wardens!

Room rates don't usually include breakfast (*petit déjeuner*), but do include service and tax (*service et taxes compris/STC* or *toutes taxes comprises/TTC*). This is because room rates are controlled by the government and charging for breakfast and other meals is how small hotels make much of their profit. Breakfast times vary considerably, so check in advance. Breakfast costs from 15F to 65F (average 25F to 35F), depending on the class of hotel, e.g. 20F per person in small hotels (around 30F in Paris) and around 50F in large medium class hotels, often served buffet style. In some hotels, children under 16 sharing their parents' room receive a free breakfast. You can usually choose from coffee, tea or hot chocolate, accompanied by croissants and rolls, butter and jam, and perhaps orange juice. High class hotels offer a choice of expensive cooked breakfasts, although it's cheaper to find a local café or brasserie. Many hotels don't provide a very appetising or good value-for-money breakfast, which may consist of half a *baguette* and weak coffee only. If you're staying in or near a small town it's often better to have breakfast at a local café.

Many French hotels insist that guests eat dinner in the hotel before they let a room. Although it's officially illegal to insist on half-board (*demi-pension*), i.e.

breakfast and dinner, or full board (*pension complète*), which includes all meals, it's sometimes the only way to obtain a hotel room in a popular resort during the high season. Usually with half or full board you must stay for a minimum of three days. You should ask to see the menu before signing up for half or full board, as the cost of meals (and particularly wine) may make a room prohibitively expensive. Note that the smaller the establishment, generally the better the food.

You should be shown a room. No Frenchman would dream of accepting a room without inspecting it first, especially the bed, which may be hard or lumpy. Often beds have long, hard, sausage-shaped bolsters (*traversin*) that serve as pillows, running across a double bed. Usually the bottom sheet runs around them and substitutes for pillow-cases. Most foreigners find bolsters uncomfortable, although they are quite happily used by most French guests. There may be pillows (*oreiller*) in the wardrobe, which like bolsters, usually have no slips and are placed under the bottom sheet. Duvets are common.

Most hotels have central heating in winter and are, if anything, too warm. Air-conditioning is generally found only in luxury hotels and large modern hotels, particularly in the south. Although windows are usually double-glazed, if you're staying in a city it's advisable to ask for a quiet room. Some rooms have no curtains and are fitted with shutters or blinds, possibly located *outside* the window. Modern hotels have electric roller shutters. Hotel rooms in France aren't always equipped with a radio or TV, irrespective of the price, with the exception of modern and luxury hotels. Satellite TV is provided in top class hotels. All top class hotels provide tea and coffee-making facilities; a radio and colour TV; bathroom or shower; telephone; room service; and a mini-bar or refrigerator. Drinks from a hotel mini-bar are expensive, but it's handy for storing your own food and drinks.

Hotel bulbs are usually dim and it's often wise to take a 60 or 100 watt bulb or a clip-on reading lamp (and a long lead) if you like reading in bed. Power points above wash basins are usually suitable only for electric razors. If you want to use a non-French hairdryer or travel iron, you must provide a French adapter and try to locate a suitable power point, which may be outside the room. Rooms without a shower or bath usually have a washbasin. Rooms with a private bath or shower may not have a WC. Most French hotel rooms have a *bidet* (see page 412). Don't expect to find soap or a decent towel in a cheap hotel (or a bedtime mint on your pillow!).

The backbone of the French hotel network is the *Logis et Auberges de France*, the world's largest hotel consortium, whose trademark is a green and yellow sign of a fire burning in a hearth. *Logis* members include over 5,000 privately run hotels in the French countryside (none in Paris). Members must conform to strict standards of comfort, service, hygiene, safety, quality of food and price. Most are one or two-star hotels in popular locations, with prices ranging from 150F to 400F per night for a double room. The *Logis* guide is available from FGTOs (see page 312), many of which operate a video desk service where personal callers can select a hotel. A number of *Logis* hotels can also be booked through the 'Logis Stop' service offered by *Gîtes de France* (see page 320). Contact the *Fédération Nationale des Logis et Auberges de France*, 83, Ave d'Italie, 75013 Paris (☎ 01.45.84.70.00) for further information. A *Logis de France* handbook is available from bookshops and FGTOs.

In addition to the thousands of small family-run hotels, France also has its share of soulless 'business' hotels, such as Ibis, Mercure, Novotel and Sofitel, although many have been refurbished and updated in recent years. International chains including Hilton, Holiday Inn, Intercontinental and Trust House Forte are represented in Paris and other major cities. One advantage of staying at chain hotels is that the standards and facilities are consistent in any hotel in the chain, each of which can book you a room at any other hotel in the chain. In general, French hotels don't cater well for business travellers, and business centres with secretarial staff and translation services are usually confined to a few luxury hotels in Paris and the French Riviera. However, most hotels have photocopy, telex and fax facilities for their guests' use. Few French hotels have swimming pools, private parking, and health and sports facilities such as gymnasiums. Most top class hotels have a restaurant, coffee shop and bar.

If you wish to indulge yourself, then you need look no further than the *Relais et Châteaux* chain of over 250 independently-owned elegant three and four star hotels (many occupying châteaux and other former stately homes) and exquisite restaurants (*relais*). They produce a guide detailing their establishments throughout the world available from FGTOs or the Centre d'Information, *Relais & Châteaux*, 9, avenue Marceau, 75116 Paris (☎ 01.47.23.41.42). They also publish a free map of France showing their hotels. It's also possible to stay in many private *châteaux*, manors, abbeys and priories, some 70 of which are listed in the *Château Accueil* directory available from FGTOs or direct from Château du Plessis, 49220 La Jaille-Yvon (☎ 02.41.95.12.75). A *Bienvenue au Château* guide is also available from the FGTO. An excellent association of privately-owned two to four star hotels where you're assured of peace and tranquillity is *Les Relais du Silence*, 17, rue Quessant, 75015 Paris (☎ 01.44.49.90.00).

At the other end of the market are a number of budget hotel chains such as *Formule 1*, which are common on the outskirts of major towns and cities (often close to *autoroutes*). From around 150F per night up to three people can share a modern room with a double and single bed and a colour TV. Shared toilets and showers are available in the corridors. Breakfast costs around 25F per person. You can arrive at any time of day or night and if there are no staff on duty you can pay for a room via a credit card machine at the entrance. If you arrive late you can obtain the number of your room and the entry code by inserting your credit card (used to book the room) into the automatic reception machine (press the key indicated by a Union Jack and instructions are displayed in English). The machine will issue a receipt with a code number, allowing you to access both the hotel and your room. If you leave your room, e.g. to have dinner, don't forget to take your receipt with you! If the machine won't accept your card, press the *appel d'urgence* button located near the entrance and a staff member will open up for you. For a list of Formule-1 hotels, write to Chain des Hôtels Formule 1, 29, promenade Michel Simon, 93166 Noisy le Grand Cedex (☎ 01.43.04.01.00, bookings 08.36.68.56.85). Other reasonably priced *autoroute* chains include Etap (owned by Formule 1), Mister Bed (☎ 01.46.14.38.00), Première Classe (☎ 01.64.62.46.46) and Village Hotels (☎ 03.80.71.50.60).

It's advisable to book a room during the high season months of July and August, on public holiday weekends, and during international trade fairs, conventions and festivals. At most other times it's usually unnecessary, particularly in rural areas and small towns. Note that many family hotels close for two to three weeks between May and September for their holidays (nothing interferes with the 'Great French Holiday' – even business!). Some hotels in villages and small towns also close their restaurants for one or two days a week, e.g. Sunday and/or Monday. On closing days, no breakfast or other meals are served. Seasonal closing and weekly closing days are shown in the *Michelin Red Guide* (see page 310).

When booking by post for a period of a week or longer, you're usually asked to send a deposit (*arrhes*). Don't book and pay for a long period in advance, as you won't receive a refund if you leave early. It's advisable to make reservations at least two to three months in advance for summer in major cities (such as Paris), and around two weeks in advance at other times. Hotels can also be booked through Minitel, the Internet and many tourist offices (for a small fee). Always honour reservations or call and cancel your booking. If you have paid a deposit and the booking is cancelled due to the landlord's fault, you will receive double your deposit in compensation.

A hotel is required to keep a booked room until 1800 or 1900 only, after which time it can be let to someone else unless you have paid in advance. If you plan to arrive later than this, you should advise the hotel of your estimated arrival time. Some hotels close overnight, therefore if you plan to arrive late, e.g. after 2300, notify the hotel 24 hours in advance and they will arrange to have someone meet you. You're required by French law to show your passport or identity card and complete a registration form (*fiche policière*) when registering.

Checkout time is usually noon at the latest and if you stay any later you may be charged for an extra day. If you're staying in a small hotel and wish to leave early in the morning, it's best to pay your bill (*note*) the evening before and tell the proprietor when you plan to leave (check your bill carefully for errors). Otherwise you may find the hotel locked up like Fort Knox and no-one around to open the door.

Most guide books contain a selection of hotels and there are numerous French hotel guides. The most comprehensive hotel (and restaurant) guide available is the *Michelin Red Guide*, which includes both the humblest and poshest of establishments (see page 310). Other good guides include *Les Routiers Guide to France* (Alan Sutton Publishing), *The Good Hotel Guide* by Hilary Rubinstein (Papermac) and the *Guide to Hotels and Country Inns of Character and Charm in France* (Rivages). A complete list of hotels and pensions is published annually by the FGTO (*Annuaire des Hôtels et Pensions de Famille de Tourisme à prix homologués*).

BED & BREAKFAST

France has numerous 'bed and breakfast' (*chambres d'hôte*) establishments, particularly in villages and on farms, where French families let their spare rooms to visitors. Many *chambres d'hôte* operate under the sponsorship of *Gîtes de France* and are classified according to their comfort and environment with one to three ears of corn (*épi*). The cost is usually around 300F per night for two people with breakfast, and possibly a private bath or shower. In addition to single and double rooms, many *chambres d'hôte* have accommodation for families and most serve meals (*table d'hôte*). The standard of *chambres d'hôte* is usually high and the home-cooked food is invariably delicious, with fresh local produce in abundance. All regions produce annual listings of *chambres d'hôte*.

Café-Couette (C&C), meaning literally coffee and a duvet, is similar to a bed and breakfast. Accommodation is in private homes ranging from a small suburban house to a luxury *château*. The main advantage of C&C is that most owners treat their guests as family friends rather than faceless strangers, and go out of their way to help you enjoy your stay. The motive of many French families to open their homes to guests isn't to get rich, but to make friends and meet people from different walks of life. C&C properties are graded and awarded a number of coffee pots. Rates are around 150F per person per night for a double or triple room (200F for a single) in a 'two coffee pot home', 225F per person (300F single) for three coffee pots and 300F per person (400F single) for four coffee pots. There's no charge for children under two sharing their parents' room. Reservations can be made only for a minimum of 600F or 1,000F in July and August. For bookings and a copy of the C&C annual guide, contact Café-Couette, 8, rue d'Isly, 75008 Paris (☎ 01.42.94.92.00).

There are many guides to bed and breakfast in France including *French Country Welcome* (Gîtes de France); Karen Brown's *French Country Bed & Breakfast* (Travel Press); Alistair Sawday's *Guide to French Bed & Breakfast* (Alistair Sawday Publishing); *Bed & Breakfast of Character and Charm in France* (Fodor's Rivages); *French Entrée Bed and Breakfast in France* by Patricia Fenn & Rosemary Gower-Jones (Quiller Press); and *Charming Small Hotel Guides: France Bed & Breakfast* by Paul Wade & Kathy Arnold (Duncan Petersen Publishing). When staying in bed & breakfast accommodation, it helps if you speak some French as your hosts may not speak English.

SELF-CATERING

France has an abundance of self-catering accommodation and the widest possible choice. You can choose from literally thousands of cottages (*gîtes*), apartments, villas, bungalows, mobile homes, chalets, and even *châteaux* and manor houses. The most luxurious dwellings have private swimming pools, tennis courts and acres of private parkland, although you may need to take out a second mortgage to pay the bill! Self-catering is particularly popular in skiing areas and along the Atlantic and Mediterranean coasts, where there's a wealth of purpose-built apartments. Standards vary considerably, from dilapidated ill-equipped cottages to luxury villas with every modern convenience. You don't always get what you pay for and unless a company or property has been highly recommended, it's best to book through a reputable organisation such as *Gîtes de France* (see below).

Cottages (*Gîtes*): The word *gîte* means simply a home or shelter, but is nowadays widely used to refer to any furnished self-catering holiday accommodation. A typical *gîte* is a small cottage or self-contained apartment with one or two bedrooms (sleeping four to eight and possibly including a sofa bed in the living-room), a large living-room/kitchen with an open fire or stove, and a toilet and shower room. There are usually shutters on the windows (possibly no curtains), stone or wooden floors with a few scatter rugs or carpets and possibly bare stone walls. The maintenance-free surfaces are designed to facilitate cleaning. There's usually a garden with garden furniture and possibly a swimming pool (if it's a shared swimming pool, ask how many people or dwellings will be sharing it). In certain parts of France, notably the overcrowded French Riviera, *gîtes* may be no more than purpose-built concrete rabbit hutches, built to a basic standard and strictly regulated. Most *gîtes* in rural areas have a septic tank (*fosse septique*) and items such as sanitary towels, paper (other than **French** toilet paper), disposable nappies, condoms, and anything made of plastic, mustn't be flushed down the toilet.

Equipment: Properties are generally well-equipped with cooking utensils, crockery and cutlery, although you're usually required to provide your own bed linen and towels (they can be rented for an extra charge, but can be expensive). Equipment and facilities may include central heating, a washing machine, dishwasher, microwave, covered parking and a barbecue. Some owners provide bicycles, and badminton and table tennis equipment. If you need a cot or a high chair, mention it when booking. Some basic food stuffs (salt, pepper, sugar) and essentials such as toilet paper and soap may be provided, but don't count on it. Most people take a few essential foods and supplies with them and buy fresh food on arrival. Some things that may come in handy are a decent cook's knife, a teapot (if you make tea in a pot), and a few of your favourite foods such as tea (French tea is terrible), instant coffee (although most *gîtes* have filter coffee machines) and relishes you cannot live without.

Costs: The cost is normally calculated on a weekly basis (Saturday to Saturday) and depends on the standard, location, number of beds and the facilities provided. Minimum standards usually ensure that a *gîte* has running water, a shower, an indoor toilet, and shuttered or curtained windows. The rent is higher for a *gîte* with a pool. The rent for a *gîte* sleeping six is typically from 1,000F to 2,000F per week in June and September, and 1,500F to 2,500F in July and August. The rest of the year may be classified as the low season, when rents are slightly lower. If you're making a late booking, try to negotiate a lower price as it's often possible to obtain a large reduction (if you're into brinkmanship it may pay you to leave it until the last minute).

Sometimes the year is divided into low, mid and high seasons, although many owners offer accommodation from June to September only. Electricity, gas and water charges aren't always included, particularly outside the high season (June to August), and may be charged at exorbitant rates. There's usually a charge for cleaning, e.g. 200F to 400F per week, although this may be waived if you leave the place spotless (where applicable, the cost is usually deducted from your deposit). Heating (if necessary) is also usually extra and can be expensive. You may also need to pay a local tax (*taxe de séjour*).

Booking & Deposits: It may be necessary to book six months in advance for popular areas in July or August, when there may be a minimum two-week rental period. Outside the high season it's possible to find a *gîte* on the spot in most areas. When booking, you're usually required to pay a 'damage' deposit (*caution*), which cannot be more than 25 per cent of the rental charge and cannot be requested more than six months in advance. A deposit is termed either *des arrhes* or *acompte*. When it's *des arrhes*, you can back out of the agreement and forfeit your deposit and if the owner cancels he must pay you double the deposit. When a deposit is *acompte* it means that you have a binding contract. If you back out of the agreement you must still pay the full rental fee, although you can claim damages if the landlord cancels your booking.

Luxury Houses & Villas: You can pay up to 50,000F per week in the high season for a luxury villa sleeping eight to ten people on the Côte d'Azur – for 'a few thousand' francs more you could *buy* your own cottage! A luxury house in the Dordogne with swimming pool and sleeping eight rents for between 8,000F and 12,000F per week in July and August. All luxury properties have outdoor private swimming pools and some even have indoor heated pools.

Cities: Self-catering serviced apartments are provided in Paris and other major cities. Rates vary considerably and may be per person, per night (e.g. 125F), or a fixed rate per night irrespective of the number of guests, e.g. 650F for a studio sleeping four. Rates usually decrease for longer stays, e.g. 2,500F per week for a studio. See also **Temporary Accommodation** on page 84.

Holiday Villages: Holiday villages and Club resorts (such as Club Méditerranée) are an increasingly popular choice among holidaymakers. They are usually self-contained with everything available on site including shops, restaurants, swimming pools, and a wide range of sports and entertainment facilities. Children's clubs keep the kids happy, leaving parents free to indulge themselves. Inexpensive holiday village accommodation is available through *Villages-Vacances-Familles*, a non-profit organisation created in 1958 to provide holidays for low-income families. *Villages-Vacances-Familles* holiday villages provide child-minding and entertainment for children and are open to foreign visitors.

Holiday parks are similar to club resorts, except that sports and leisure facilities may be housed in a temperature-controlled (e.g. 21°C) plastic dome, e.g. CenterParcs. Guests stay in villas set in attractive country locations or by the sea. There are also many mobile home holiday centres in France, usually located on superb sites with similar facilities to holiday villages. Camping in fully-equipped 'permanently' erected family tents is another self-catering option.

Finding Accommodation: Outside France, the best place to start looking for self-catering accommodation is your local travel agent or French Government Tourist Office. Many properties are let by holiday companies and associations, often as part of an inclusive holiday package, e.g. including the cost of a ferry from Britain. Properties are also let directly by owners through ads. in French property magazines (see **Appendix B**) and newspapers. Many *gîtes* are second homes and are let for most of the year through organisations such as *Gîtes de France*, although many owners prefer to let them themselves. Note that if you rent directly from the owner, you may find it difficult to receive satisfaction or redress if you have a complaint.

The biggest and most reputable French self-catering organisation is *Gîtes de France*, handling over 45,000 properties. Properties are called *gîtes ruraux* and are classified and approved (standards are guaranteed by the local *Relais départemental des Gîtes de France*). *Gîtes ruraux* are classified according to their comfort and environment, and are awarded one to four ears of corn (*épi*). For more information contact the *Fédération Nationale des Gîtes Ruraux de France, 59 rue de Saint Lazare, 75009 Paris* (☎ 01.49.70.75.75), who publish *Les Nouveaux Gîtes Ruraux*.

Gîtes can be booked through the FGTO in many countries, where *Gîtes de France* may also have an office. A handbook containing a selection of over 2,500 *gîtes* is published by the FGTO in Britain and is provided 'free' in return for a token annual membership fee that also entitles you to use a computerised booking system to reserve a *gîte*. Most French *départements* publish a list of local *gîtes* (write to the tourist office in the local departmental town). One of the most popular guides to self-catering in France is *Guide des Locations Vacances Loisirs*, published quarterly.

There are a number of books for self-caterers in France including *Self-Catering France* by John P. Harris and William Hedley (Collins), *The Gîtes Guide* (FHG Publications Ltd.) and *Gîtes et Refuges en France*, available from *Éditions Créer*, rue Jean Amariton, Nonette, 63340 St-Germain Lembron.

HOSTELS & DORMITORIES

There's a variety of inexpensive accommodation in France including youth hostels (often with dormitory rooms), although fewer than in many other European countries.

Youth hostels are open to all members of the International Youth Hostel Federation (IYHF) and affiliated organisations. IYHF membership is available in France at the Paris office of FUAJ (see below) or at any hostel and costs around 100F a year, or 70F if you're under 26. One-night membership of the IYHF is available for around 20F. There are no age restrictions. Hostels fill early in July and August, when you should book in advance if possible, although some hostels *don't* accept reservations and restrict stays to a maximum of three or four nights. French hostels are classified into three grades with accommodation usually in single-sex rooms and dormitories with two to eight beds. The cost is usually from 25F to 80F per night (there are usually cheaper rates for groups), plus an additional rental charge for a sheet sleeping sack if you don't provide your own. Some hostels allow you to use your own sleeping bag. Breakfast costs from around 15F.

Although inexpensive, hostels aren't always cheaper than budget hotels for two or three persons sharing a room, particularly in major cities. They may also be situated on the edge of town, thus necessitating an additional train or bus fare. The main advantage for budget travellers is that most hostels have cooking facilities or inexpensive cafeterias, allowing savings to be made on meals. All hostels have a curfew from 2200 or 2300 (from between midnight and 0200 in Paris) and are usually closed between 1000 and 1700, although some are flexible. There are restrictions on smoking and alcohol consumption and guests may be required to help with household chores. There are two French youth hostel associations: the *Fédération Unie des Auberges de Jeunesse* (FUAJ), 27, rue Pajol, 75018 Paris (☎ 01.44.89.87.27), operating over 200 youth hostels, and the *Ligue Française pour les Auberges de Jeunesse* (LFAJ), 67, rue Vergniaud, 75013 Paris (☎ 01.45.48.69.84). There are three youth hostels in Paris requiring IYHF membership. You need to arrive early to guarantee a bed.

In major cities there are hotels for young people (*hôtels de jeunesse*), somewhere between a hotel and a youth hostel, and *Foyers des Jeunes Travailleurs/Travailleuses*, which are residential hostels for students and young workers. The *Union des Centres de Rencontres Internationales de France (UCRIF)* links *foyers* throughout France. UCRIF publish a complete list of members and services, available from *Maison de l'UCRIF*, 27, rue de Turbigo, 75002 Paris (☎ 01.40.26.57.64). Room rates are usually from around 75F to 125F per night for singles and 150F to 200F for doubles. *Foyers* usually have an inexpensive cafeteria or canteen. During July and August you can also stay in student accommodation at most French universities. Rates are from around 50F per night and you can book through the *Centre Régional des Oeuvres Universitaires* (CROUS), 39, av. Georges-Bernados, 75231 Paris (☎ 01.40.51.36.00). In Paris, *Accueil des Jeunes en France (AJF)*, 119, rue St-Martin, 75004 (☎ 01.42.77.87.80) guarantees to find low-cost accommodation with an immediate reservation for at least one night. They have 8,000 beds available year round and over 11,000 in summer. The AJF books rooms free of charge in their own *foyers* and charges 10F for other establishments (they also provide a free hotel booking service).

In country areas there are unmanned hostels or simple shelters providing dormitory accommodation called *gîtes d'étapes*. They are listed in footpath guides and marked on IGN walkers' maps (see page 356), and are usually reserved for walkers, cyclists, horse riders and skiers crossing France along the *grandes randonnées*. As a basic standard they have bunks, showers and cooking facilities, although some are very comfortable. *Gîtes d'étapes* are often run by local communities and the key is usually kept by a local caretaker (who may be the local mayor) at a nearby house or by the local tourist office (*syndicat d'initiative*). The rate per night is usually from 60F to 70F. A list of *gîtes d'étapes* is included in *Accueil à la Campagne* (together with places offering bed and breakfast and farm campsites) available from the *Fédération Nationale des Gîtes Ruraux de France* (see page 320). *Gîtes et Refuges en France* lists over 1,600 places providing inexpensive accommodation for outdoors lovers (available from Éditions Créer, rue Jean Amariton, Nonnette, 63340 St-Germain-Lembron).

The most common form of shelter in remote hill and mountain areas is a primitive mountain hut called an *abri*. Information can be obtained from local *Bureau des Guides* or tourist offices. In many areas there are country guesthouses providing dormitory accommodation from around 35F per night. Many monasteries and convents also accept paying guests and are listed in the *Guide des Monastères* available from *La4*, 3, rue de Mézières, 75006 Paris (☎ 01.44.39.03.03).

CAMPING & CARAVANS

Camping and caravanning are extremely popular in France, with both the French and the many thousands of tourists who flock to France each year to spend their holidays in the open air (*en plein air*). The French have elevated *le camping* to a high level of sophistication and chic, and are the most camping-conscious nation in Europe, with over 11,500 campsites including over 2,000 rural and farm sites.

Campsites vary considerably from small municipal sites (*camping municipal*) with fairly basic facilities to luxury establishments with a wide range of facilities and amenities. Rates range from around 20F per night at a municipal site up to 200F or more at a four-star site for a family of three or four, a car, plus a caravan position or camping space (*emplacement*). A 'night' is usually from noon to noon and some sites charge extra to use showers, sports facilities (such as tennis courts) and other amenities such as ironing facilities or use of a freezer. Most sites have different rates for high (*haute saison*) and low (*basse saison*) seasons. Although site reductions for low season are usually minimal, out of season package holidays often yield considerable savings. Many campsites are open from June to September only and most have less than 150 places. Like hotels, campsites are classified from one to four stars:

Star Rating	Cost (F)*	Standard
****	30-40 +	luxury (*très grand confort*)
***	25-35	high (*grand confort*)
**	20-30	medium (*confort*)
*	15-20	standard (*confort moyen*)

* Approximate cost per person, per night during the high season, including camping or caravan space, car parking and use of facilities. Note that prices can vary considerably between campsites with the same star rating.

A four-star rating indicates a comfortable low-density site with a wide range of amenities and electricity hook-ups for one-third of spaces or even all spaces at a top site. There's a range of indoor recreation areas, showers, sauna, toilets, washing machines, shops, lock-up storage for valuables, and a wide choice of sports facilities. These usually include a swimming pool (outdoor and/or indoor) and tennis courts, and may also have facilities for golf or crazy golf, volleyball, cycling, table-tennis, trampolining, canoeing, fishing and boating. Many sites are situated in popular hiking and climbing areas. Large campsites usually have a restaurant and a bar (or a selection).

Three-star sites are roughly the same as four but with slightly fewer amenities, less camping space, and fewer electricity hook-ups, e.g. just 10 per cent of spaces. Only basic amenities such as toilets, hot and cold water, public telephone and electric razor power points are provided at one and two-star sites, although some one-star sites may not have hot water. Some sites have special facilities for the disabled, which is usually noted in guide books. French campsites are usually extremely clean.

Booking is usually possible at three and four-star sites and is essential during the peak season of July and August, particularly for sites situated on the coast and near lakes and waterways (inland camps aren't usually too crowded). In fact the high season is best avoided altogether, if possible, as it's very crowded, particularly on the French Riviera. It's important to book if you have a caravan and require an electricity hook-up. Outside peak periods you can usually find a campsite without difficulty on the spot, but don't leave it too late in the day if you're in a popular area (after noon is too late at some sites). Many campsites have tents, caravans, mobile homes and bungalows for hire, and some provide special winter accommodation. Some also provide ready-erected fully furnished luxury canvas 'houses' with all modern conveniences including fully-sprung mattresses, refrigerators, four-burner stoves and electric lighting.

Permission is required to park or camp on private property or anywhere outside official campsites. Note that it's strictly illegal in most regions to camp on private or public land (including beaches) without permission. On private land, a farmer may shoot first and ask questions afterwards! You need permission from the local *Office des Eaux et Forêts* to camp in state forests (*forêts domaniales*). Off-site camping (*camping sauvage*) is restricted in many areas, particularly in the south of France, due to the danger of fires. You can also camp on a farm (*camping à la ferme*) in rural areas, although there are generally no facilities. A maximum of six camping spaces are permitted on farm land or in a park near a *château* (castle-camping).

Some sites are classified as natural camping areas (*aire naturelle de camping*) and are for naturists. France has the best facilities in Europe for naturists and has a huge number of superbly equipped naturist camping centres (for those who don't want to bother with laundry while on holiday). If you aren't a member of a naturist association in another country, then you must join the French Naturist Federation (*Fédération Française de Naturisme*), 65 rue de Tocqueville, 75017 Paris (☎ 01.47.64.32.82). You need a colour (full-frontal?) photograph for your naturist 'passport'. Campers usually need an international camping carnet (20 to 25F), available from French (see below) and foreign camping and motoring associations. You must be 18 years of age to obtain a carnet, which is a personal identity card and includes third party liability insurance for up to 12 people (depending on where you buy it) at all authorised sites in Europe.

The French Federation of Camping and Caravanning produce a *Guide Officiel* describing in detail the facilities at around 11,500 sites, including naturist camping areas, farm camping and country camping. It's available direct from *La Fédération Française de Camping et de Caravanning (FFCC)*, 78, rue de Rivoli, 75004 Paris

(☎ 01.42.72.84.08) and from bookshops and camping, caravanning and motoring organisations. The FFCC also offer special insurance for campers and caravanners and an international camping carnet.

Many sites are members of associations or groups which include *Camping Qualité France*, 105, rue la Fayette, 75010 Paris (☎ 01.48.78.13.77), with around 220 sites throughout France, *Sites et Paysages de France*, BP33, 38520 Bourg d'Oisans (35 members) and *Airotels*, BP8, 33950 Lège, Cap-Ferret. For a really lavish campsite you need look no further than *Castels & Camping Caravaning*, BP301, 56008 Vannes Cedex (☎ 02.97.42.55.83), which have around 50 sites situated in the grounds of a beautiful *château* or manor, around a small village, or in an exceptional natural setting. When writing to sites from abroad, you should enclose an international reply coupon.

In France, camping and caravanning guides are published for all areas and are available from local regional tourist offices. There are also many national camping guides including Alan Rogers' *Good Camps Guide, France* (Deneway Guides); the *Michelin Green Guide - Camping and Caravanning*; *Caravan and Camping in France* by Frederick Tingey (Mirador); and *Camping à la ferme* (farm camping) published by *Gîtes de France*. The FGTO (see page 312) publish an excellent free booklet, *The Camping Traveller in France*. If you wish to rent a mobile home, caravan or tent on site then Alan Rogers' France *Rented Accommodation on Quality Sites in France* (Deneway Guides) provides a comprehensive list.

If you're a newcomer to camping and caravanning it's advisable to join a camping or caravan club, which usually provide useful information (e.g. the best guides to campsites), approved sites, caravan and travel insurance, travel services, rallies, holidays, reservations and a range of other benefits. Clubs include the Camping and Caravanning Club, Greenfields House, Westwood Way, Coventry CV4 8BR, UK (☎ 01203-694995) and the Camping Club de France, 218, bd Saint-Germain, 75007 Paris (☎ 01.45.48.30.03).

THEME PARKS

France has some 60 theme parks of varying size and scale. The most famous is Disneyland Paris at Marne-la-Vallée 32km (20mi) east of Paris, which opened in April 1992 (where M stands for Mickey Mouse, Marketing, Merchandising and MONEY!) and is the fourth most-visited attraction in the world. The latest addition to the Disney theme parks is smaller than existing Disney parks, but a number of expansions have taken place in recent years and more are planned. The 56-acre park contains five theme 'lands', all with their own attractions (around 40), shops and restaurants. There are six hotels on site and an 18-hole golf course. The best way to get to Disneyland from Paris is via the RER express suburban railway (see page 180) on Line A terminating at Marne-la-Vallée/Chessy (a special RER station was built for Disneyland Paris).

Disneyland is open year round, from 0900 until 2300 in spring and summer (in autumn and winter from 1000 to 1800 daily, except for Saturdays and Sundays when it closes at 2300). Check opening and closing times as they are liable to change. Obtain a guide book, arrive early and make for the most popular rides with the longest queues first (you will spend lots of time queuing). Avoid French public holidays and weekends like the plague. Picnics are banned to increase profits at the restaurants (which now sell wine) and fast-food outlets and bags are sometimes searched for illicit sandwiches (you can always stuff your pockets full of choc bars and drink from free fountains). There's a left luggage area (for picnic hampers) at the entrance with a picnic area outside. The entrance fee depends on the season and is 220F for adults and 170F for children aged 3 to 11 (since when have 12-year-olds been adults?) during the high season (April to September plus the Christmas and New Year holiday periods). Fees are reduced from October to March. You can buy a pass for two or three days and if you're totally addicted you can even buy an annual pass.

When you visit Disneyland it's sometimes difficult to imagine that you're still in France. The squeaky-clean staff wear obligatory permanent plastic smiles (like Mormons on a day out) and endlessly parrot 'have a nice day', albeit in French. The main difference between Disneyland Paris and the American Disney parks is that in North America it's hot and sunny most of the time (pixie dust loses its magic sparkle in the rain and cold, although you can buy a Mickey Mouse plastic raincoat). Some travel analysts reckon it's better, and possibly even cheaper for Europeans, to travel to Disney World in Florida, where you're guaranteed sunshine.

There's a surfeit of Disneyland Paris guides including the Michelin Plan-Guide Disneyland Paris and Green Guide Disneyland Paris, Fodor's Disneyland Paris, Disneyland Paris: The Guide (Harmsworth) and Disneyland Paris Berlitz (Berlitz). Further information can be obtained direct from Disneyland Paris, BP 100, 77777 Marne la Vallée Cedex 4 (☎ 01.49.41.49.10).

One of the most unusual and popular theme parks in France is Futuroscope near Poitiers, dubbed the 'European Park of the Moving Image'. Attractions include the Omnimax room where a film is projected onto the inside of a domed ceiling 17 metres in diameter (800m²/8,611ft²), the Kinémax housing a cinema with a 600m² (6,458ft²) flat screen that's higher than a seven-storey building, the Dynamic Motion Theatre where the seats move in tune with the action (e.g. motor racing and bobsleigh), the Magic Carpet with a 700m² (7,534ft²) screen in front and another beneath your feet, a 360° Cinema with wrap-around films, a 3D cinema and much more. Admission is 145F per day (280F for two days) for adults and 130F (220F for two days) for children under 16. If your French isn't fluent you can obtain free headphones that provide an English translation. Futuroscope (☎ 50.49.49.30.80) is open year round and has its own hotels (you should allow two days to see everything).

For a traditional 'real' French theme park try Parc Astérix in the Jean-Jaques Rousseau forest near the Charles-de-Gaulle Paris airport (170F adults, 120F children under 12, under 5's free), open from April to October. If you haven't much time and wish to see France in one day, visit Le Pays France Miniature at Elancourt outside Paris (75F adults, 50F children). France boasts many excellent aquariums including the modern Nausicaä at Boulogne, one of the largest and most comprehensive aquariums in the world, and one of France's most popular attractions (around 45F adults, 30F children). Watersport theme parks are popular, such as the Walibi parks at Agen, Lyon, Metz and Roquefort (around 95F adults, 85F children). Traditional travelling fun fairs are installed each year at the Bois de Vincennes in Paris. The French also love the circus and travelling circuses are common throughout France.

MUSEUMS, ART GALLERIES, ETC.

France has a wealth of museums and important collections. There are over 100 museums in and around Paris alone, ranging from the largest in the world, the *Musée*

National du Louvre, to some of the smallest and most specialised (oenophiles and inebriates may be interested in the *Musée de Vin*). The *Louvre*, which celebrated 200 years in 1993, is the most important museum in France and among its many famous exhibits are the *Mona Lisa* and the *Venus de Milo*. It takes around a week to see everything in the *Louvre*, which is also the world's largest (ex) royal palace and a national treasure itself. Other important Paris museums and galleries are the *Musée National d'Art Moderne*, the *Centre National d'Art et de Culture Georges Pompidou*, the *Galerie de Jeu de Paume*, *Musée Rodin*, *Musée Picasso*, *Musée d'Orsay* and the *Cité des Sciences et de l'Industrie*.

One of Paris' most popular art venues is the Pompidou Centre, housing the National Museum of Modern Arts, the Public Reference Library, with over one million French and foreign books, the Institute of Sound and Music and the Industrial Design Centre. In addition to its national galleries, Paris boasts around 300 commercial galleries displaying the most innovative modern and contemporary art (admission is free). Parisian galleries are open from Tuesday to Saturday from 1400 to 1900. All private galleries close on Sundays and Mondays.

National museums usually open from 1000 until 1800 and close on Tuesdays with the exception of *Versailles, Trianon Palace*, the *Musee d'Orsay* and the *Cité des Sciences et de l'Industrie/la Géode* at La Villette, which close on Mondays. The *Musée du Louvre* is open from 0900 to 1800 (except Tuesdays) and Wednesdays until 2145. Other Parisian museums stay open until 2000 on Thursdays, which is the best time to visit in summer when they are practically deserted, or at lunchtimes, when the French are busy eating. Most Parisian museums offer free entrance or substantial reductions during late afternoon. Municipal museums have the same opening hours as national museums, but are closed on Mondays. Smaller collections may close during August. Most museums close on public holidays, an irritating continental habit.

The entrance fee for those aged 26 to 59 is usually 15F to 45F, with half price or free entry on Sundays (entrance to the *Louvre* costs 45F before 1500 and 26F after 1500). Most museums offer free entry to those aged under 18 and a 50 per cent reduction for those aged 18 to 25 and 60 or over. National museums are half price on Wednesdays and Sundays. Entrance to the *Musée d'Orsay* is free on Sundays and the *Louvre* is free on the first Sunday of the month. Tickets at many museums and galleries must be purchased from a complex multi-lingual ticket machine, yet another example of the French love affair with ticket machines. Entrance to provincial museums is free on Sundays and to those aged under 7 and over 60 at all times.

A museum and monument card (*la carte musées et monuments*) allows entry to over 60 museums and monuments in the Paris area. It's valid for one (80F), three (190F) or five (240F) consecutive days. You need to visit a few museums to get your money's worth, but it's good value for 'culture vultures'. It's obtainable from participating museums, the Paris tourist office, *métro* stations and FGTO offices abroad. The *carte* allows you to bypass queues and ticket offices (or machines) and enter via a 'group admission' door. Most museums and special exhibitions charge half-price to holders (aged 60 or over) of the *Carte Senior* rail card (see page 177). Current museum and gallery exhibitions in Paris are listed in weekly entertainment magazines such as *Pariscope* and *l'Officiel des Spectacles*.

France also has a wealth of provincial museums devoted to such varied subjects as farming, local history, industry, crafts, cultural heritage, transport, archeology, art, textiles, folklore, war, technology, pottery and nature. You can also visit numerous grand country homes and *châteaux* throughout France. When visiting *châteaux* and other country houses, try to arrive early before the coach parties. Note that most *châteaux* and other stately homes are open during the high season only, from May or June to September. Many are closed one day a week and most close during lunchtimes from noon until 1400. Always check opening times in advance. The FGTO publish a brochure, *Châteaux, Museums, Monuments*, listing 200 cultural attractions in France. Visiting grand gardens isn't particularly popular in France, although there are a number of notable gardens well worth seeing. A leaflet listing 128 gardens in France is available from French Government Tourist Offices and keen gardeners may also be interested in *Les Guides des Jardins de France* by Michael Racine (Guides Hachette).

It's also possible to visit numerous businesses in France, particularly those connected with the food and drink industry such as vineyards, distilleries, breweries, mineral water springs, farms and dairies, while technology enthusiasts may prefer to visit a hydroelectric dam or a nuclear power station.

CINEMAS

French *cinéma* (the 'seventh art') has resisted the threats from French TV (which is generally dreadful) far better than most other western countries. The French are huge film fans and Paris is the cinema capital of the world, with some 350 cinemas, most of which are packed every day (Parisians buy some 80 per cent of all cinema tickets sold in France). Some American-made films are even shown in Paris before they are screened in North America, although they are often released at the same time. In Paris you can literally see a different film every day of the year and every film you ever wanted to see (and lots more that you wouldn't watch for free) is usually showing somewhere. Film lovers shouldn't miss the special cinema days (*journée du cinéma*) in summer, when films are shown non-stop for 24 hours at low prices. There are also private *ciné-clubs* in most French cities.

Many cinemas in Paris show old films or reruns (*reprises*) of classics and many hold seasons and festivals featuring a particular actor, director or theme. France has a dynamic and prosperous film industry which receives the bulk of its funding from a tax levied on cinema tickets (which critics claim allows French film-makers to produce poor films that nobody wants to watch). Many French films sell less than 10,000 seats compared with over one million for blockbuster American movies (around 60 per cent of all films screened in France are American made). However, it's common for a cinema to be showing a film from Eastern Europe or Asia alongside the staple French/American fare.

In Paris and other major French cities, foreign films are shown in their original version (*version originale/VO*) with French subtitles (*sous-titres français*). Dubbed films are labelled VF (*version française*). You may come across VA (*version anglaise*), denoting an English-language film made by a French-speaking director. Note that French translations of English film titles often bear little relationship to the original. Films are classified and entrance may be prohibited to children under 18, 16 or 12, listed as *interdit aux moins de 18 (16, 12) ans*. Children who look younger than their years may be asked to prove their age and should carry some form of identification showing their photo and age. Most cinemas list two show times for each performance, the first of which is for 10 to 40 minutes of commercials and trailers of coming films. Usually you can give them a miss, although on weekends or when a film is a new release, you should arrive early to make sure of a seat. Some cinemas sell tickets in advance. In Paris, performances are usually continuous from 1400 until around midnight or 0100. The last performance usually starts around 2200 from Sunday to Thursday and at midnight on Fridays and Saturdays. Most old large cinemas have been replaced by a number of smaller theatres. Among the best places to see the latest hits in Paris are the Gaumont Grand Écran, the Forum Horizon and the Max Linder Panorama, with their superb optics and stunning (THX) sound systems. Cinemas listed as *grande salle* or *salle prestige* have a large screen (*grand écran*), comfortable seats and high projection and sound standards. Smoking isn't permitted in cinemas, some of which are air-conditioned (a blessed relief in high summer).

Ticket prices range from 40F to 50F (average around 40F) in Paris and the same prices are usually charged for reruns of old classics as for the latest hits. Cinema chains such as Gaumont and UGC offer season tickets (*cartes privilèges*) for frequent customers. The *cartes Gaumont* costs around 185F for five entries and the *UGC carte privilège* around 175F for five entries from Sunday to Friday, and 200F for seven entries. Some independent cinemas offer a free ticket after five or six visits, while others sell reduced price cards for a number of admissions.

Tickets are reduced by 20 to 30 per cent on Mondays and/or Wednesdays in many cinemas. Midday (or 1100) screenings are also reduced and usually cost around 25F. Reduced price tickets (30 to 50 per cent) are available for students, senior citizens, the unemployed, military personnel and families with three or more children. Children and students must produce a student card and senior citizens (over 60) a passport, identity card or *Carte Senior* rail card (see page 177). It's usual to tip the usher 2F to 5F per person in many cinemas in France, where ushers may rely largely on tips for their income. However, ushers at major cinema chains such as Gaumont, Pathé and UGC no longer expect tips.

Europe's largest and most important film festival is the Cannes Film Festival (since 1946), where the top prize is the *Palme d'Or*. In a move that no doubt received the unanimous backing of the *Académie Française*, the French Academy of Cinematic Art and Technology banned foreign-language films from eligibility for its annual *César* awards, the French equivalent of the Oscars. There are many French magazines devoted to films including *Studio*, *Première* and *Positif*. English-language film magazines are also available from international news kiosks.

THEATRE, OPERA & BALLET

High quality theatre, opera and ballet performances are staged in all major cities, many by resident companies. In the provinces, performances are often held in theatres that are part of a cultural centre (*maison de la culture* or *centre d'animation culturelle*). In total over 400 theatre companies receive state subsidies, including 150 in Paris. In addition to the large and luxurious state-funded theatres, there are many good medium and small-size theatres where performance quality varies considerably. Performances aren't always top quality, but there's a huge variety from which to choose.

Parisian theatres include the famous *Comédie Française* (classics), founded over three hundred years ago by Louis XIV, and the *Théâtre National Populaire* (contemporary). Most French-language shows are translated hits from London and New York. There are also many café-theatres, where although performances may not always be memorable, they are usually lots of fun. Children's theatres in Paris and other cities perform straight plays, pageants and magic shows. There are also a number of English-language theatre venues in Paris including the Théâtre Marie Stuart, ACT, Theatre Essaion, Voices and the Sweeney Irish Pub.

Tickets usually cost between 30F and 150F for national theatres and between 50F and 100F for private theatres. Midweek matinee subscriptions are available at reduced cost. The *Kiosque Théâtre* (pl de la Madeleine, 75008 Paris) in Paris sells half-price tickets (Tuesdays to Saturdays from 1230 to 2000) for shows on performance days and many theatres offer student discounts. Just before a show starts, seats are often available at huge discounts. Students can also obtain reduced price tickets from the *Centre Régional des Oeuvres Universitaires et Scolaires/CROUS* (see page 163). Obtaining theatre tickets in advance is difficult in Paris, where many theatres operate a system whereby reservations and sales are permitted only one or two weeks in advance. Many theatres don't accept telephone reservations and don't use ticket agencies. As in cinemas, ushers expect a small tip and smoking isn't permitted. Performances usually start at 2030 or 2100 and theatres close one day a week.

Sound and light (*son et lumière*) shows are held at historic sites throughout France during summer including *les Invalides* in Paris, the *Palais des Papes* in Avignon, and at many *châteaux* and stately homes, particularly in the Loire valley. One of the most spectacular is performed at the ruined *Château du Puy du Fou* in the Vendée twice a week from June to August and features 700 actors and 50 horsemen. It's much more than just another sound and light show and is well worth making a detour. Drama festivals are also popular and include the world-renowned Festival d'Avignon in July/August, encompassing drama, dance, film, concerts, exhibitions and many other events.

The *Paris Opéra Ballet* has a history going back three centuries and is one of the world's foremost ballet companies (it no longer stages opera). Its leading ballerina, Syvie Guillem, is one of the most sought-after dancers in the world. Under the direction of the late Rudolf Nureyev in the '80s, the *Paris Opéra Ballet* was the best ballet company in the world, although its crown has slipped since he left. Although tickets are cheaper than in London and New York, they are hard to obtain as most seats are sold by subscription months in advance. Contact the theatre directly for tickets: Paris Opéra, Théâtre de l'Opéra, Service Location par Correspondance, 8, rue Scribem 75009 Paris (☎ 08.36.69.78.68, Mondays to Saturdays from noon to 1800).

The new *Opéra de la Bastille* (2bis, Place de la Bastille, 75012 Paris, ☎ 01.40.01.16.16, 1100 to 1900 Monday to Saturday) is France's major opera venue, although it has been plagued by problems (e.g. lack of funding, sackings and strikes) since its opening. In contrast, the Paris *Théâtre du Châtelet* is one of the most celebrated opera venues in Paris. France also has 12 regional opera companies, of which Bordeaux, Lille, Lyon and Toulouse are among the best. Modern and contemporary dance thrives in France and the *Centre Georges Pompidou* stages some interesting avant-garde programmes by French and international dance companies. Many small dance companies perform in small theatres and dance studios.

MUSIC

France boasts some five million amateur musicians and stages over 300 music festivals a year. However, the French don't have a reputation as music lovers and there's a dearth of classical music in Paris compared with many other capital cities (France has no world-renowned orchestras). Fortunately international orchestras and soloists regularly tour France and there are frequent concerts in Paris and the provinces by the *Orchestre de Paris*, the *Orchestre Philharmonique de Radio France*, and various other national and provincial orchestras (among the best are Lille, Lyon and Toulouse). The Parisian concert season runs from October to June, where the main venue is the *Salle Pleyel*. There are discounts at classical music concerts for senior citizens on production of identification or a *Carte Senior* (see page 177). The main agency for tickets to almost any concert or cultural event in Paris is the *Fédération Nationale d'Achat des Cadres* (FNAC) at 136, rue de Rennes, 75001 Paris (☎ 01.45.44.39.12) or Forum des Halles Level 3, 1-5, rue Pierre-Lescot, 75001 Paris (☎ 01.40.41.40.00). You can also buy tickets from the Virgin Megastore, 52, ave des Champs Elysées, 75008 Paris (☎ 01.49.53.50.00).

Open air music festivals are common and popular in summer throughout the country, many of which are staged in spectacular venues such as cathedrals and *châteaux*. Music festivals embrace all types of music including classical, opera, chamber music, organ, early music, piano, popular, jazz and folk, many of which are listed in a booklet, *Festive France*, available from the FGTO. In Paris, *AllôConcerts* provides 24-hour telephone information (in French) about free open-air concerts in Parisian parks (☎ 01.42.76.50.00) and classical students from the *Conservatoire National* perform regularly in the Paris *métro* and on the city's streets. Recitals of organ and sacred music are held in churches and cathedrals such as the *Notre Dame* in Paris, and many churches sponsor concerts with good soloists and excellent choirs. Paris also has a number of music halls where top international artists regularly perform.

French popular music is generally poor and unoriginal (even the imitators are bad) and the rock music scene is usually a 'few decades' behind London and New York. This is reflected in the fact that the '60s rock star Johnny Hallyday, who's now over 50, remains one of France's biggest music stars (can you name a French pop star?). Foreign bands are much better known to French fans than any French group. Most rock venues can be divided into those where you sit and listen and dance clubs (the liveliest places). Tickets for club dates cost around 100F and concerts 150F or more. Drinks are expensive in music clubs and may run to 80F for a beer. Because of its lack of vast stadiums, Paris isn't an automatic stop on a top band's European concert tour. French rock has never been exported to Britain or the USA, although France has a wealth of excellent musicians and attracts the finest musicians from the Francophone world, particularly North and West Africa.

What Paris lacks in popular music it makes up for with the superiority of its jazz clubs. It's easily Europe's leading jazz venue and attracts the world's best musicians. France is also the venue for many excellent jazz festivals including the Festival de Jazz in Paris in autumn, the Antibes-Juan-les-Pins Festival and the Nice Jazz Festival in July, one of the most prestigious jazz and blues festivals in Europe. France even has a nationally-funded National Jazz Orchestra. Most jazz is performed in cellar clubs, where there's usually a cover fee and expensive drinks. Music starts at around 2200 and lasts until around 0400 at weekends and includes everything from trad to be-bop, free jazz to experimental. French music magazines include the *Guide des Concerts* and *Les Activités Musicales*.

SOCIAL CLUBS

There are many social clubs and organisations in France catering for both foreigners and the French. These include Ambassador clubs, American Women's and Men's Clubs, Anglo-French clubs, Business Clubs, International Men's and Women's clubs, Kiwani Clubs, Lion and Lioness Clubs and Rotary Clubs. Expatriates from many countries have their own clubs in major cities, a list of which is often maintained by embassies and consulates in France. For example a free *Digest of British and Franco-British Clubs, Societies and Institutions* is published by the British Community Committee and is available free from the British embassy in Paris (see **Appendix A**).

Many local clubs organise activities and pastimes such as chess, bridge, art, music, sports activities and sports outings, theatre, cinema and local history. Joining a local club is one of the easiest ways to meet people and make friends. If you want to integrate into your local community or French society in general, one of the best ways is to join a local French club. Ask your local town hall for information.

NIGHT-LIFE

French night-life varies considerably depending on the town or region. In small towns you may be fortunate to find a bar with music or a *discothèque*, while in Paris (which has the most varied night-life of any city) and other major cities you'll be spoilt for choice. Paris by night is usually as exciting and glamorous as its reputation, and it offers a wide choice of entertainment including jazz clubs, cabarets, discos, sex shows, music clubs, trendy bars, nightclubs and music halls. The liveliest places are the music clubs, which are infinitely variable and ever-changing with a wide choice of music including zouk, reggae, jazz, funk, rock, techno and rai. Jazz clubs are popular, particularly in Paris. The most popular clubs change continually and are listed in newspapers and entertainment magazines. The action starts around 2300 or midnight and goes on until dawn (0500 or 0600). The admission fee to Parisian clubs is usually high, e.g. from 100F to 150F (possibly less on certain days when women may be offered free entrance), and generally includes a 'free' drink. Some clubs offer free entry but drinks are expensive.

A traditional and entertaining night out in Paris is dinner and cabaret at one of the city's many venues, which include the *Crazy Horse Saloon*, the *Folies Pigalle*, the *Lido* and the *Moulin Rouge* (the celebrated *Folies Bergère* closed its doors in 1992 after 125 years). The entertainment features an endless stream of titillating, topless, teasers (breasts, breasts and more breasts) and plenty of sexy men for the ladies. It doesn't come cheap and runs to between 400F and 800F per head, including dinner. Cabaret is unfortunately a dying art and nowadays caters mainly to foreign tourists.

Paris also has many fashionable and expensive nightclubs and discos for members or regulars only. High-tech discos are popular, where lasers and high decibels (not to mention drugs) combine to destroy your brain. Note that drunkenness and rowdy behaviour are considered bad taste in France and bouncers are often over-eager to flex their muscles (soccer hooligans beware!). Old style dance halls (*bal musette*), where dancing is to a live orchestra, are making a comeback in Paris and are popular with both young and old. The French have even discovered the 'art' of making fools of themselves in public (politicians do it all the time) through karaoke, which is becoming increasingly popular in Paris and other cities.

GAMBLING

Gambling is a state-controlled monopoly in France (established by Louis XIV), where nearly everyone has a flutter on the national lottery and horse racing. The French spend some 65 billion francs on gambling each year. Over 20 million people regularly play LOTO, France's national lottery (*loterie nationale*), on which billions of francs are wagered annually. The lottery draw is made live on TV and takes precedence over all other 'news'. Gambling on horse racing is also popular, with betting on the tote system controlled by the *Pari Mutuel Urbain (PMU)*, which has branches (around 7,500) at cafés throughout France. The most popular bet is the *tiercé*, which entails forecasting the first three horses to finish in the correct order; you can also choose four (*quarté*) or five (*quinté*) horses. Sunday is the most popular day for race meetings.

France has casinos in all the major cities and popular tourist resorts such as Aix-les-Bains, Biarritz, Cannes, Deauville (biggest gross in France thanks to its five-franc one-armed bandits, rarely legal in France), Divonne and Evian. The most famous casino of all is that of Monaco (which is almost French). Blackjack and roulette are the most popular casino games. Punters must be aged over 18.

BARS & CAFES

There's at least one bar or café in every village and town in France, although the number has fallen from over 500,000 at the turn of the century to around 60,000 today. In major towns and cities, watering holes include wine bars, café-bars, brasseries, bar-brasseries and tea-rooms (*salons de thé*).

Bars: A bar (or *bar-comptoir*) sells alcoholic drinks and perhaps coffee and snacks, but doesn't usually serve complete meals. Bars have been rapidly disappearing in Paris (*les limonades* or *zincs*, named after the zinc counters of the original cafés), where over 30,000 have closed in the last decade. However, don't despair, there are still plenty left to slake your thirst. Traditional bars are increasingly being replaced by modern establishments with TVs, video games, pin-ball machines (*flipper*) and piped music. There are also typical English and Irish pubs in Paris and other cities serving a range of British and other imported beers and 'authentic' pub food (hopefully better!). There are gay and lesbian bars and cafés in Paris and other major cities, listed in gay magazines.

Wine Bars: There are wine bars in Paris and some other cities, where fine wines are served by the glass and snacks are available, although they are expensive and aren't common or popular in France.

Cafés: A café (or café-bar) serves alcoholic drinks, soft drinks, and hot drinks such as tea and coffee. They usually serve snacks (e.g. sandwiches) and ice-cream all day, and may serve meals at lunch time. If you just want a drink, don't sit at a table with a table cloth, which indicates that it's reserved for customers wishing to eat. Some cafés are best avoided during lunchtimes, e.g. between noon and 1400, when they are extremely busy (although it's usually an excellent sign). Most cafés have outside tables or terraces on the street, depending on the season and the weather.

Cafés are a marvellous institution throughout France and have been called the life support system of French culture (there are over 10,000 in Paris alone). They aren't simply places to grab a cup of coffee or a bite to eat, but are meeting places, shelters, sun lounges, somewhere to make friends, talk, write, do business, study, read a newspaper or just watch the world go by. Although they don't have a reputation as hard drinkers, the French spend a lot of time in bars and cafés, perhaps nursing a single drink (locals often use them as their sitting rooms). Usually nobody will rush you to finish your drink, unless it's the height of the tourist season and people are waiting for tables. A popular card game in bars and cafés is *Belote*, a mixture of bridge, rummy and solo, played with a standard card pack minus all cards below nine. Like restaurants, cafés are supposed to provide no-smoking areas, although the law is openly flaunted. All cafés must display a tricoloured 'Licence IV' plaque bearing a number, permitting the proprietor to sell alcohol at any time of day.

Brasseries: A brasserie or bar-brasserie serves a wider selection of food than a café and is regarded more as a café-restaurant. The main distinction between a brasserie and a restaurant is that a brasserie serves meals and snacks throughout the day, while restaurants stick to traditional meal times.

Tea-Rooms: A *salon de thé* is a tea-room serving tea and coffee, sandwiches, cakes and pastries, but no alcohol. Tea-rooms are fashionable in Paris (e.g. Angelina and Ladurée) and other major cities, and are more expensive than cafés or brasseries. Afternoon tea (*goûter* or *le five o'clock*) isn't usually served in France.

Coffee: A coffee (*café*) is a small black coffee or an expresso (*express*) made with an expresso machine. A *café noir double* is a double expresso, for those with strong hearts. A *café au lait* is an expresso with steamed milk and comes in small (*petit crème*) and large (*grand crème*) sizes. If you don't specify a small coffee, many places will serve a large one. The French often dunk their croissants in their *café au lait* (or hot chocolate) at breakfast time. A *café allongé* (or *café long*) is an expresso with extra hot water and a *café serré* is an extra strong expresso with half the usual amount of water (guaranteed to wake you up!). Decaffeinated coffee (*déca*) is also widely available. Weak milky coffee, as drunk by the average American or Briton, is aptly referred to as sock juice (*jus de chaussettes*).

Cost: The cost of all drinks varies considerably depending on the establishment and its location. A bar or café must display its prices (*tarif de consommations*). At café terraces on major boulevards such as the Champs Elysées or the rue de Rivoli in Paris, you're charged double or triple the price in a less fashionable street. A bar or café may serve drinks at the counter (*au comptoir*), at a table inside (*en salle*) or an outside table (*en terrasse*). You pay more for sitting at a table than standing at the bar and there's usually an even higher charge for a table outside. If you order a drink at the bar and sit down to drink it, it costs more. The price of drinks may also increase after 2000. The cost of a coffee varies from around 7F (average around 10F) for a small *café au lait* standing at the bar to 25F or more for a large one seated in a Parisian tourist spot. Beware of high prices at railway stations, airports and in tourist areas, where overcharging is rife.

Tea: Tea is usually drunk black (*thé nature*) and is often Lipton's, unless you specify tea with lemon (*thé au citron*) or milk (*thé au lait*). French 'black' tea is often terrible. Herbal teas (*tisanes*) are popular and include camomile (*camomille*), mint (*menthe*), lime blossom (*tilleul*) and verbena (*verveine*). Hot chocolate (*chocolat chaud*) is a popular drink and iced tea and coffee are popular in summer.

Soft Drinks: Popular soft drinks include flavoured syrups (*sirop*), such as *menthe* and *grenadine*, cola (*coca*) and freshly-squeezed lemon or orange juice (*citron/orange pressé*). Sparkling (*gazeuse/pétillante*) and still (*non-gazeuse/plate*) mineral waters are popular and most people have their particular favourites such as

Badoit, Evian, Perrier or Vichy. Mineral water and soft drinks are often more expensive than wine or beer.

Beer: Beer is popular in all areas, although most is consumed in the north and east. French beer is usually of the export lager variety and among the most popular French brands are Fischer/Pêcheur, Kanterbräu, Kronenbourg, Météor, Millbrau, Mützig, Pelforth, Slavia, '33' Export and Valstar. Foreign beers such as Stella Artois (Belgium) are available in major towns and are expensive (around double the cost of French beer). You can order a *bock* (half a 25cl glass), a *demi* (not a half litre as you may expect, but 25cl), a *sérieux* (50cl) or a *formidable* (a litre). Draught beer (*pression*) is sold in 25cl glasses for around 12F. Expect to pay three to five times the supermarket price for a 25cl beer in a bar. A shandy is a *panaché* or a *bière limonade*. Cider is a popular drink in Brittany and Normandy, although it isn't drunk much in other parts of the country and is more expensive than wine.

Wine: Wine is commonly drunk in cafés and bars, although it's rarely drunk in fashionable places. It's usually served in small (*petit*) and large (*ballon*) sizes, and can also be ordered in a small quarter-litre (25cl) pitcher (*pichet*). You usually order simply a red (*rouge*) or a white (*blanc*). Don't expect vintage wine, except in wine bars where it's appropriately priced. Champagne is popular in fashionable places, but *very* expensive.

Spirits: Gin and tonic and scotch whisky (particularly malt whisky) are popular and have a certain *cachet* among the fashionable set. Popular *apéritifs* (or *apéros*) include *kir*, a mix of white wine with crème de cassis (a blackcurrent liqueur), *kir clair*, white wine with just a drop of cassis, and *kir royal*, made with champagne (instead of white wine) and cassis. *Pastis*, an aniseed or liquorice flavoured drink diluted with water and usually ice, is popular in the south (popular brands include Berger, Pernod and Ricard).

Other popular drinks include Cinzano, Dubonnet, Martini (out of a bottle, not dry with an olive), white port, Cognac, Armagnac, Calvados (apple brandy) and a wide variety of liqueurs such as Bénédictine, Chartreuse, Cointreau and Grand Marnier. Alcohol flavoured with fruit and other things is common throughout France and every region has its own variations such as crème de cassis, crème de menthe and crème de cacao. The French aren't renowned for their drink-mixing ability, with the exception of bartenders in expensive cocktail bars in top class hotels, where prices start at around 50F (some have a 'happy hour' when drinks are half price). Not surprisingly, many fashionable (i.e. expensive) bars accept credit cards, particularly in Paris. Cafés serve much the same range of alcoholic drinks as bars (except cocktails).

Snacks: Bars and cafés usually serve a range of snacks including a *croque monsieur* (toasted cheese and ham sandwich); a *croque madame* (the same as a *croque-monsieur* but with a fried egg on top); omelettes (plain, ham, mushroom); crêpes (the savoury buckwheat variety, *galettes*, are served as a main course, sweet white flour type as a dessert); sandwiches (15 to 25F) usually consisting of around a third of a baguette filled with ham, cheese or *paté*; and filled croissants. Many cafés and fast food outlets accept coupons provided by employers, similar to luncheon vouchers and called *ticket restaurants*. Establishments accepting them have stickers on their windows (don't expect to find them on Michelin-starred restaurants!). Note that a snack in a bar can cost as much as a three-course lunch in a modest little bistro.

Opening Hours: There are no licensing hours in France and alcohol can sensibly be sold at any time of the day or night, although an official permit is required.

Generally a bar or restaurant closes when the *patron(ne)* decides it does (e.g. when the last customer falls off his bar stool). Most bars and establishments selling alcohol open sometime between 0600 and 1100 and close between midnight and 0200. Many Parisian cafés open at 0700 or 0800 and close around 1400. Most brasseries and cafés open around 1100 and remain open until 2300 or later. Cafés and bars close to markets often keep the same hours as the market. Like restaurants, most bars and cafés close on one day a week (*jour de repos*), usually shown on the door.

Paying: In a bar or café each drink is usually presented with a cash register receipt. You usually pay for your drinks when you leave, although you may be asked to pay when you're served if it's very busy or you're in a tourist spot (tourists cannot be trusted!). If your waiter is going off duty, he'll also ask you to pay. When you have paid, your receipts are torn or crumpled by the waiter. Service and tax is included in the price and it's unnecessary to tip, although Frenchmen often leave a few small coins. At the counter you usually receive your change in a little plastic dish that's upturned to signify that you've paid.

Drinking Age: The legal age for drinking in public establishments in France is 16, although there's virtually no enforcement and children are readily served and sold alcohol everywhere. Officially unaccompanied children under 16 aren't allowed into establishments serving alcohol. When accompanied by an adult, children aged 14 to 16 may drink beer or wine, but nothing stronger.

RESTAURANTS

One of the prerequisites for a happy and rewarding life in France is a love of good food and wine. No other country is so devoted to good food and the French are among the world's biggest eaters (the French don't snack but eat civilised meals). The average Frenchman spends around 20 per cent of his food budget in restaurants and eats out an average of three times a week. Whether it's a family meal at home, a snack at a little bistro, or a gastronomic feast at a three-star Michelin restaurant (where eating is a *very* serious business), the French *really enjoy* good food and wine. They like nothing more than to talk about food and wine (sex and politics lag way behind), and will do almost anything in the name of the God Gastronomy. Good French food is noted for its freshness, lack of artificial ingredients and preservatives, and exquisite presentation. French cooking is an art form and master chefs such as Paul Bocuse are national heroes, although French food reflects not only the expertise of its chefs but also the attitude of the customers, who are the most discerning in the world.

Foreigners are often surprised at how French restaurants can serve such excellent food at such modest prices (the French aren't telling). Almost everyone can afford to eat out in France and culinary treats await you around every corner. Paris is widely recognised as the gastronomic capital of the world and has more restaurants than any other city, although Lyon has more Michelin-starred chefs and is rated by many as the centre of French cuisine. Note, however, that not all restaurants offer good value for money (*rapport qualité-prix*) and it's possible to eat badly in France. One simple rule to help avoid the bad restaurants is to frequent establishments packed with local residents, although it isn't necessary to eat the same dishes (frogs' legs, snails, offal, etc.). Eating houses in France encompass a wide range of establishments including auberges, bistros, brasseries, buffets, fast-food and take-away outlets, hostelleries, pizzerias, relais or relais routiers, restaurants and rôtisseries. Some of the most common establishments are described below.

An **auberge** (or *hostellerie* or *relais*) was originally a coaching-inn or hostelry. Today it's generally an alternative name for a restaurant and may no longer provide accommodation. An *auberge de jeunesse* is a youth hotel.

A **brasserie** (or bar-brasserie) is a down-to-earth café-restaurant serving meals throughout the day and often remaining open until the early hours of the morning, particularly in Paris. See also **Bars & Cafés** on page 332.

A **bistro** is generally a small, simple restaurant (or café-restaurant), although they can be trendy and expensive, particularly in Paris and other cities. The traditional hallmark of a bistro is basic French cuisine at reasonable prices. They also provide venues for artists, a place to meet and talk and a stage for musicians. Unfortunately, like cafés, bistros have long been in decline and their numbers have fallen dramatically in the last few decades.

A **buffet** is a self-service restaurant, usually found in railway stations and airports. A *libre-service* (or a *self*) establishment is a self-service cafeteria often found in hypermarkets, on *autoroutes* and in city centres. There are many American-style fast food joints in Paris and other French cities including McDonalds (which has even invaded the Champs Elysées in Paris and the Promenade des Anglais in Nice) and Burger King. Other 'fast food' and take-away (take-out) establishments include pizzerias and *crêperies*. American-style, fast-food outlets account for around 10 per cent of restaurant turnover in France and are fast threatening the survival of cafés and bistros.

A **relais routier** is literally a transport café, although they have none of the connotations of 'greasy spoon' establishments in other countries, being excellent, value-for-money, roadside restaurants patronised by all travellers, particularly truck drivers. Transport cafés along the *routes nationales* offer good value for money and a long line of trucks outside any establishment is usually a good sign.

A **restaurant** is a serious eating place that serves meals at normal meal times and isn't somewhere for just a drink or snack, unless it's a café-restaurant.

A **rôtisserie** is a grill or steakhouse specialising in grills, although it may also serve a wide range of other dishes.

Although the French eat much the same meals as people in most other countries, they may have different emphasis.

Breakfast isn't important to most Frenchmen and usually consists of just coffee, which is freshly brewed, strong and drunk out of enormous vat-sized cups with milk. When eaten, breakfast is usually of the continental variety consisting of croissants or rolls (or a *baguette*), butter and jam, accompanied by tea, coffee or hot chocolate. French families are increasingly eating breakfast cereals, thus confirming they don't *always* have good taste.

Lunch is sacred and the most important meal of the day. However, contrary to popular belief, some 75 per cent of the workforce takes less than a hour for lunch, not two or three hours, although long lunch breaks are still common in the provinces where life proceeds at a more leisurely pace. Lunch is generally served from noon until 1400, when nearly everything closes in rural areas, although most people lunch around 1230 in the provinces and at 1300 in Paris. You will find it difficult to get a hot meal almost anywhere in rural areas after 1400 or 1430.

Dinner is usually served from 1900 until 2130 or 2200, although in the main cities many restaurants stay open until after midnight (in Paris, a few are even open

24 hours). In the provinces people usually eat between 1900 and 2000, or between 2000 and 2100 in the extreme south. You will be lucky to get dinner after 2100 or 2130 in most places or perhaps *à la carte* meals only will be served. Usually dinner is a lighter meal than lunch, particularly in the provinces, although judged by most standards it's certainly no snack. There's often little difference between lunch and dinner menus, except perhaps in small village restaurants. In small villages, restaurants may serve dinner by prior arrangement only. A meal eaten late in the evening, perhaps after a cinema or theatre visit, is called supper (*souper*) and may be eaten as late (or early) as 0200.

French cooking is divided into a range of categories or styles including *haute cuisine, nouvelle cuisine, cuisine régionale, cuisine bourgeoise* and *cuisine minceur*.

Haute cuisine is the cream of French cooking and naturally the most expensive, although it isn't as popular as it once was. It comprises a huge repertoire of rich and elaborate sauces made with butter, cream and wine, and a variety of exotic ingredients such as truffles (sauces were originally added to disguise the poor quality of the main ingredients).

Nouvelle cuisine is a healthier version of *haute cuisine* with the emphasis on freshness, lightness and tiny helpings, i.e. pretty food in small portions artfully arranged on large plates. The accent is on minimum cooking to retain natural flavours, with sauces designed to enhance rather than hide the taste of the main ingredients. Chefs are encouraged to experiment and create new dishes, indeed if master chefs wish to retain their ratings in the gastronomic bibles, it's mandatory. *Nouvelle cuisine* has become less fashionable in recent years as its popularity has spread and many top class restaurants have abandoned it.

Cuisine régionale (or *cuisine des provinces/cuisine campagnarde*) is cooking that's indigenous to the different regions of France, each of which has its own unique style of cooking and specialities, often influenced by the surrounding countries. *Cuisine régionale* was traditionally based on the availability of local produce, although many popular regional dishes are becoming increasingly difficult to find in restaurants.

Cuisine bourgeoise (or *cuisine paysanne/cuisine traditionelle*) consists of excellent but plain fare such as meat or game stews and casseroles made with wine, mushrooms and onions, with a liberal dose of garlic and herbs. *Cuisine bourgeoise* cooking is common in *relais* and middle class restaurants, and although sometimes lacking in imagination it's universally popular, particularly among those with hearty appetites.

Cuisine minceur is gourmet food for slimmers (invented by Michel Guérard) and is the most delicious slimming food in the world. It's similar to *nouvelle cuisine* but with the emphasis on the avoidance of fat, sugar and carbohydrates, and using substitute fat-free ingredients.

Reservations: Always book for popular restaurants, inexpensive restaurants offering exceptional value for money, and any restaurant in a popular resort. Top class restaurants, such as Parisian *grands restaurants* with two or three Michelin stars or three or four Gault-Millau *toques* (see page 341), are often booked up months ahead. There are usually less than 20 restaurants in the *whole of France* with three Michelin stars. If you're eating in one of these gastronomic temples you should reconfirm your booking the day before. Many gourmet restaurants are located in top class hotels. Sunday lunch is the main gastronomic event of the week for French families and often lasts over three hours. Many restaurants put on a special Sunday menu for an extra charge and inexpensive set meals are usually unavailable. It's important to book in advance or to arrive early, e.g. by noon. Any later and you'll be lucky to find a seat at a popular restaurant. Note, however, that many restaurants are closed on Sunday evenings and in Paris many are closed on Sundays.

Menus: Menus with prices must be displayed outside restaurants, with the exception of small village restaurants without a menu, where you're offered whatever is being served on a particular day. All restaurants *must* offer a fixed-price menu (*menu à prix fixe/menu conseillé/menu formule*) with from three to seven courses (the average is four). Menu prices are legally required to include tax and service, although some restaurants still add 15 per cent for service (see **Tipping** on page 411). You can also order *à la carte* dishes from the menu, which are much more expensive (in France *la carte* is the menu and *le menu* is a fixed-price meal).

Most restaurants offer a choice of fixed-price menus, usually including a choice of starter (*hors d'oeuvre*), a main course (often called the *entrée*) and dessert. Generally the more expensive the fixed-price menu, the wider the choice of dishes and the larger the number of courses. A *menu dégustation* or *menu gastronomique/menu affaires* is often served in a top class restaurant. It consists of many small portions of the specialities of the house, designed to display the chef's expertise, each of which may be served with a complimentary wine. Often the best value-for-money set menus are the lunch menus offered by top restaurants, which at 300F to 400F are around half the *à la carte* cost.

In humble village restaurants the fixed-price menu contains no choices and usually includes wine. No *à la carte* food may be served and it's often the menu or nothing. This may be written on a blackboard outside the restaurant or there may be no written menu at all (in which case you need to be adventurous or starving, particularly if your French isn't fluent). The sign of good food in an unpretentious establishment is often a hand-written menu, which is an indication that the dishes change frequently. Generally the shorter the menu, the better the food. Neighbourhood bistros are usually good because they have a regular clientele who complain loudly if standards fall.

Generally it's best to avoid tourist menus (*menus touristiques*) and places catering largely to tourists (check the cars in the car park). Some restaurants have a children's menu (*menu d'enfants*) and many local restaurants provide a free (or make a nominal charge) place setting (*couvert*) for a young child eating from his parents' order. Some restaurants cater especially for babies and children. French restaurants generally love children and are more than happy to cater for them.

Fixed menu prices range from as little as 50F per head in a village café/restaurant up to 1,000F or more at a two or three-star Michelin gastronomic shrine (excellent places to dine providing someone else is paying!). In between these two extremes are numerous restaurants with menus between 75F and 200F, where good restaurants abound. Note that although a meal for around 50F can be excellent in some rural establishments, you shouldn't expect too much for this sum in Paris and other cities, where well-heeled French families happily spend 1,000F a head on a meal!

Although menu prices are low compared with many other countries, many restauranteurs have compensated by increasing the price of wine, coffee and other drinks. Prices for an identical *plat du jour* costing 50F in a rural restaurant may cost three times as much on the French Riviera and other fashionable areas. Note that many restaurants serve huge portions and it's often possible to order less and share. Those on a tight budget and with limited time may prefer to eat in a self-service restaurant (*le self*) such as *Mélodine*, where you can eat well for around 40F or less. Most large department stores, hypermarkets and shopping centres also have self-service restaurants.

Courses: The composition and number of courses of a meal can vary greatly and there are often surprises. The first course (starter or *hors d'oeuvre*) may vary from a hearty soup in a no-menu establishment to a range of exquisite mouth-watering concoctions in a top-class restaurant. The second course (or *entrée*) may be served only in medium or top-class restaurants and usually consists of fish, although it can also be an omelette, chicken, rabbit, frogs' legs or snails. You can order an *entrée* for your main course (it's often difficult to distinguish between the two). The main course is traditionally a meat course, although you can choose fish. In a village or country restaurant the main course is usually automatically accompanied by French fries (*frites*) and a common vegetable such as peas, green beans or carrots. In most restaurants the main course is served with vegetables (*garni*), although they may be served separately, particularly in the south. Note that in inexpensive restaurants it's common to use the same knives and forks throughout a meal.

A green salad may be served as a separate course after the main course. All restaurants serve delicious and unlimited amounts of bread as part of a meal, which isn't cut with a knife but broken with your hands. The cheese course is served after the main course and precedes the dessert. A good cheese board contains cheeses made from cow's, goat's and possibly even sheep's milk, many of which will be local and unfamiliar. The dessert course is usually undistinguished in humble establishments, consisting perhaps of ice-cream, sorbets, cream caramel, peach melba or simply fruit. However, in first-class restaurants it will be as elaborate and delicious as the rest of the meal. Finally you'll be served small cups of strong black coffee, possibly accompanied by a bowl of *petits-fours*. Coffee isn't usually included in a fixed-price menu. Brandy and liqueurs are often drunk with coffee.

Note that meat in France is usually served rare, unless specified otherwise. The various degrees of cooking steak in France are very rare (*bleu*), rare (*saignant*), medium (*à point*) and well done (*bien cuit*). For the British and others who prefer their meat cremated, the French offer a further degree: BBC (*bien bien cuit*). The French have an unsympathetic attitude towards vegetarians, who are thin on the ground in France and as rare as dieters in a Michelin-starred restaurant (not eating meat in France is akin to having a contagious disease). You need to be courageous to be a vegetarian in France, where the number of carnivores (per capita) is exceeded in Europe only by Belgium. If you're a vegetarian you should stick to self-catering in France as there are only a few vegetarian restaurants in the major cities, although crêperies and pizzerias usually serve vegetarian dishes.

Wine: In France, wine is regarded as a necessary accompaniment to even the humblest of meals and in rural restaurants it's even included in fixed-price menus (the French believe 'a meal without wine, is like a day without sunshine'). To a Frenchman, wine adds a further dimension to the enjoyment of food, and symbolises conviviality, bonhomie and *joie de vivre*, although consumption is now down to a *mere* 25 bottles per person per year, compared to 90 bottles a generation ago. Generally the better the restaurant, the better the range and quality of the cellar, particularly in major wine-producing areas such as Bordeaux, Burgundy and the Rhône valley. Some restaurants have a wine list 'a mile long' with up to 1,000 varieties, while modest rural restaurants may offer just a limited selection of local wines, although they usually complement the local food and are mostly good value and palatable.

If wine is included in a fixed-price menu it's shown on the menu (*vin compris*) and includes, within reason, as much wine as you want (a modest table wine and not *Château Lafite* 1970!). You must pay for drinks other than wine. When drinks are included (*boisson comprise*), you can usually choose between wine, beer or mineral water, but must usually pay for anything more than a quarter of a litre of wine or a small bottle of beer or water per head. Although 'free' wine can be quite good, if you're a wine buff you may prefer to order something better. In restaurants serving good food, the cheapest house wine (*vin de la maison/vin du patron*) is often good. In cheaper eating-places house wine can be ordered by the glass or *carafe* (a litre), *demi-carafe* (a half litre) or a *quart* (a quarter litre). 'Quality' wine is ordered by the half-bottle or bottle, although the cheapest bottles may be inferior to the house wine. Wine may also be served in a jug or pitcher (*pichet*).

If there's no house wine or wine by the carafe, wine will be expensive, particularly when compared with the modest cost of the food. A bottle of wine usually costs from 50F for a quality that's probably no better than carafe wine. The cost of a good bottle of wine is generally around three times the supermarket price, although the mark up is higher on cheaper wines than on more expensive wines (which can cost up to 5,000F a bottle in top restaurants!). This is because many restaurants make little profit on their food and must make up for it with the wine. Not surprisingly, there are no BYO (bring your own wine or other drinks) restaurants in France. Usually it's quite safe to order the cheapest wine on the menu as no half decent restaurant would serve 'bad' wines. The vast majority of Frenchmen aren't wine snobs or particularly knowledgeable about wine and most happily drink house wine.

Although you *can* drink any wine with any food (even some Frenchmen drink strong red wine with fish), particular wines complement certain food. The *patron(ne)* or wine waiter (*sommelier*) will be happy to suggest a wine to complement a particular dish. Even a modest restaurant will have a wine list (*carte des vins*), although with the notable exception of top class restaurants it's usually short and simple. Champagne in restaurants is only for the seriously rich (500F to 700F a bottle). When staying in a hotel with a restaurant, it's common practice to have a bottle of wine recorked and kept for your next meal. Although French children often drink wine at home, children under 14 aren't permitted to drink alcohol in a restaurant.

Other Drinks: It isn't mandatory to drink wine with a meal and you can drink water (tap or mineral), beer or nothing at all. If you want a free carafe of water, ask for a *carafe d'eau fraîche*, which must be provided by law, otherwise you may be served mineral water. Drinks such as beer and mineral water have the same mark-up as wine, with prices depending on the brand (N.B. beer *isn't* an inexpensive alternative to wine). If you dare, you can even order a Coke, tea or coffee *with* your food, although you risk being thrown out on your ear or at the very least being regarded with disdain. In France, coffee or tea is *never* served with a meal and savoury and sweet foods are rarely mixed.

Food to Avoid? The French have a recipe (or half a dozen) for everything that walks, crawls, slithers, jumps, swims or flies – no living thing is safe from the French cooking pot! If you're a bit squeamish or fussy about eating certain things (the 'ugh!' factor) such as frogs and snails, or the entrails and extremities of assorted animals, it's wise to learn what to avoid. However, irrespective of how repulsive something may be in its natural state, the French usually contrive to make it taste (and possibly even look) delicious. Nevertheless, if you're adventurous, you're bound to get a few unpleasant surprises.

Things you may wish to avoid could include frogs' legs (*cuisses de grenouilles*), snails (*escargots*), bird's wing (*aile*), little eels (*anguillette*), brain (*cervelle*), tripe (*gras double/tripes*), lung (*mou*), brawn or boar's head (*hure*), sweetbreads/pancreas (*ris*, rice is *riz*), calf's innards (*fraise de veau*), kidney (*rognon*), liver (*foie*), pig's head/brawn (*fromage de porc/tête*), calf's head (*tête de veau*), testicles (*rognons blancs/animelles*), horsemeat (*cheval*, France is Europe's second largest consumer after Belgium), pig's trotters (*pieds de porc*), pig's ears (*oreilles de porc*), pig's tail (*queue de porc*), and a variety of songbirds such as blackbirds (*merles*), buntings (*ortolans*) or warblers (*beguinettes*). If you don't like garlic, avoid anything that's *à l'ail* (although it's good for you).

Given the quality and variety of French cooking, it's little surprise that foreign restaurants are somewhat thin on the ground in France (except for Paris) compared with most other European countries. In Paris, the abundance of African, Middle Eastern, Vietnamese and West Indian restaurants reflect the colonial history of France. Among the most common foreign restaurants here are Algerian, Chinese, Greek, Indian, Italian, Japanese, Korean, Lebanese, Moroccan, Russian, Vietnamese and West Indian. However, foreign restaurants rarely make the top grade.

Most restaurants close one day a week, often on Sundays or Mondays, although many open every day, particularly those in tourist resorts and large cities. Always check in advance, as some restaurants close on unexpected days, e.g. Saturdays. Most restaurants also close for one or two months a year (*fermeture annuelle*) for their annual holidays. Restaurants in winter holiday resorts may close for part or the whole of the summer, while those in summer resorts generally close in winter. In Paris, restaurants close at various times of the year and many close for part of the annual summer evacuation in July and August at the height of the tourist season. Many top class Paris restaurants close for the whole of August to avoid the hordes of plebeian foreign tourists.

You should wait to be seated by a waiter or the proprietor in any establishment. Although many Frenchmen do it, it's considered by many to be bad manners to call the waiter *garçon*. Waiters should be called *monsieur* and waitresses *madame* or *mademoiselle* (if obviously young). Snapping your fingers to attract the waiter's attention is also bad manners. When you wish to pay the bill ask for *l'addition*. Note that *not* all restaurants accept credit cards. Since November 1992, restaurants have been required to provide an area for non-smokers. However, many establishments either ignore the law or create a non-smoking section or floor (Siberia) where most non-smokers usually have no wish to sit or even be seen dead. Before the new law, few restaurants in France voluntarily created a non-smoking area. Restaurants are wary of doing anything that may deter customers and apart from a few pretentious places in Paris that insist on a jacket and tie, most don't impose dress restrictions. Most French don't dress to eat and smart casual dress is usually good enough for even for the best of restaurants. Somewhat surprisingly, dogs are permitted in most restaurants in France, as are children, although you should check first.

Two invaluable books for gourmets and gourmands are the *Michelin Red Guide* (see page 310) and the *Gault-Millau Guide de la France*. The *Gault-Millau* (published only in French) is primarily a restaurant guide, but includes a selection of hotels. It isn't as comprehensive as the *Michelin Red Guide* but makes up for it with its mouth-watering and vivid descriptions of gastronomic delights. Michelin restaurants are rated by their number of 'rosettes' (usually called stars) and Gault-Millau by the number of *toques* (chefs' hats). If you want good French food without breaking the bank, try those awarded a single knife and fork and marked with a red 'R' (*repas*) in the *Red Guide*.

The annual *Guide des Relais Routiers* is a guide to the excellent *Relais Routiers* inexpensive roadside restaurants (or transport cafés) found throughout France. A priceless little book packed with useful information and containing an excellent dictionary of French menu terms is *The Pocket Guide to French Food and Wine* by Tessa Youell & George Kimball (Carbery). If you have trouble deciphering the menu, obtain a copy of *Bon Appétit* by Judith White (Peppercorn), a handy pocket-size menu dictionary. Guides to local restaurants are published in all areas and are available free from tourist offices.

LIBRARIES

France isn't well served by its libraries (*bibliothèque*) and has a poor library service compared, for example, with Britain and the USA. Most Frenchmen don't do a lot of reading and most homes possess few books. Consequently libraries aren't very popular, which is reflected in the poor public library system. However, libraries have improved in the last ten years, particularly the semi-private *bibliothèques pour tous*. Paris is better served than most cities with 55 municipal public libraries open from Tuesday to Saturday (closed on Sundays and Mondays), many with a selection of English-language books. Most libraries have photocopy machines.

If you're lucky enough to find a library in a small town, it will usually have limited opening hours, perhaps no more than ten hours per week, a poor selection of books and probably nothing in foreign languages. Many libraries are reference (*consultation sur place*) rather than lending libraries and don't allow members to borrow books. Often you don't have direct access to books, but must complete a form describing what you want. It can take as long as 20 minutes to obtain a book, which is collected from a distribution point (like most things in France, the system is designed to keep the maximum number of civil servants in 'employment').

When you're allowed to borrow books, the number is strictly limited, e.g. two books at a time, and there's unlikely to be a section where you can study or work. To borrow books you need a library membership card (provided free). A valid ID with a photo is required, proof of your address, e.g. an electricity bill showing your current address, and possibly two photographs (plus a pint of blood). Under 18s require parental authorisation. Some reference libraries insist that you register and obtain a membership card just to enter and look at books.

Some libraries, such as the *Bibliothèque Nationale* in Paris, which contains a copy of every book published in France, are open only to graduate students and bona fide researchers. The *Bibliothèque de France* in Paris, one of the late President Mitterrand's *grands projets* completed in 1995, is the world's largest library. It has a total surface area of 365,000m² and will eventually house 12 million volumes. A day pass costs 20F and the library is open Tuesdays to Saturdays from 1000 to 1900, and from noon to 1800 on Sundays. In addition to public libraries there are private libraries in Paris and other major cities. The American Library in Paris (open Tuesdays to Saturdays from 1000 to 1900) houses the largest collection of English-language books in France. Annual membership costs around 570F for individuals (460F for students) and 750F for families. Membership of the British Council Library in Paris (Mondays to Fridays from 1100 to 1800) costs around 250F a year or 30F a day and allows you to take out six books at a time. Other English-language libraries include the Benjamin Franklin Documentation Centre and the Canadian Embassy Special Library. The English Language Library for the Blind (35, rue Lemercier, 75107 Paris, ☎ 01.42.93.47.57) provides over 1,000 American and British books on cassette for blind and partially sighted persons. Cassettes are mailed post-free throughout Europe in return for a small annual membership fee.

DAY & EVENING CLASSES

Adult day and evening classes are run by various organisations in all cities and large towns in France. In addition to formal adult and further education (see page 164), day and evening classes offer courses and lectures in everything from astrology to zoology. The range and variety of subjects offered is endless and includes French and foreign languages, handicrafts, hobbies and sports, and business-related courses. Many expatriate clubs and organisations also organise day and evening classes in a variety of subjects, such as the Women's Institute for Continuing Education (20, bd du Montparnasse, 75015 Paris, ☎ 01.45.66.75.50). Some expatriate organisations provide special classes for children (e.g. English), particularly during school holidays. French universities run non-residential language and other courses during the summer recess.

Among the most popular classes with foreigners are those concerned with cooking (and eating), which have enjoyed increasing popularity in recent years. Most courses are taught by master chefs in their own kitchens and vary from a weekend to a week. Some courses take you through everything from buying food at markets, devising the menu, selecting the wine and cheese, and not least, preparing and cooking the food. Others teach students about good food and wine through savouring the results of someone else's labour, rather than slaving over a hot stove (much more enjoyable). A full list of companies offering cookery courses and gastronomic breaks is provided in the *Reference Guide to Travellers in France* available from the FGTO. The most famous French cookery school is the *École Cordon Bleu* (8, rue Léon Delhomme, 75015 Paris, ☎ 01.53.68.22.50) and many famous French chefs have also founded cookery schools including Paul Bocuse, Auguste Escoffier, Michel Guérard and Roger Vergé.

Adult further education programmes are published in many cities and regions, and include courses organised by local training and education centres. Local newspapers also contain details of evening and day courses. See also **Further Education** on page 164 and **Language Schools** on page 165.

16.

SPORTS

Sports facilities in France are usually good, although lacking in some rural areas. France isn't generally noted for its famous sportsmen and sportswomen and recreational sports don't play an important part in most French lives. School and university sports are low key compared with many other countries and schools aren't the breeding ground for professional sports that they often are abroad. However, an increasing number of people have taken up sports and regular exercise in recent years, as the fashion for a healthy lifestyle has gathered momentum.

With few exceptions, when participating in sports the French generally prefer solo to team sports. Among the most popular sports are *boules*, cycling, fishing, golf, hiking, horse riding, hunting, swimming, tennis, skiing and squash. France is a mecca for watersports enthusiasts and canoeing, sailing, waterskiing, surfing and wind-surfing have a large following, as do aerial sports such as hang-gliding, paragliding and gliding. Team sports such as basketball, soccer and rugby are popular, although most people prefer to watch rather than participate. The most popular spectator event in France (and the world) is the annual *Tour de France* cycle race. Many less well-known sports are popular in the summer in the French Alps and the Pyrénées including rock climbing, white water rafting, glacier skiing, mountain biking, grass-skiing and four-wheel driving.

Many sports have class connotations such as boules, soccer and rugby (working class), tennis and skiing (middle class), and golf (upper class). When the French decide to take a sport seriously they do it with a vengeance, as is the case with skiing and tennis, where France has unrivalled facilities. The latest sport to get the treatment is golf, which although still exclusive is one of the fastest growing sports in France. Many sports facilities have grown on the back of the tourist revolution, particularly skiing and golf. There are few community sports facilities or centres in France, where sports clubs often insist that overseas visitors are members of a club or association in their home country. Participation in many sports is expensive, although costs can be reduced through season tickets, annual membership or by joining a club. Fashion is all important in France and whether you're skiing, playing tennis or sailing, it's more important to look the part than perform like a champion.

The FGTO (see page 312) and other tourist offices are an excellent source of sports information and can provide you with information about almost any sport. The FGTO publishes a free brochure, *France for Active Holidays*, describing many of France's sports attractions, plus a range of other sports information. Many publications promoting special sports events and listing local sports venues are available from regional and local tourist offices. Information can also be obtained from the *Direction du Temps Libre et de l'Education Populaire*, Direction des Sports, 78, rue Olivier de Serres, 75739 Paris Cedex (☎ 01.48.28.40.40). Sports fans may be interested in the all-sports daily newspaper *L'Équipe*, which publishes fixtures, results and details of all sports events in France, plus major events abroad.

FOOTBALL

Football or soccer (*le foot*) is France's national sport with over seven million players and the country has firmly established itself as a major force in recent years, which culminated in winning the World Cup in 1998 (which was hosted by France). At club level, France has had little European success and Marseille are the only French team to have won the European Champions' Cup (in 1993). The club was later embroiled in a bribery scandal and stripped of its 1993 league title, banned from the

Champions' Cup and relegated to the French second division. The French soccer league has four divisions and teams also take part in a national cup competition (*coupe de France*). The French first division has 20 teams and top clubs include Bordeaux, Marseille, Monaco and Paris St. Germain. French football takes a break from Christmas eve until the end of January, in common with many other European countries. French clubs import many foreign players, mostly from Africa, although it also loses its best players to foreign clubs (e.g. England's Arsenal). In recent years a number of first division clubs have run up huge debts and some have even been relegated as a result.

RUGBY

France is unusual among continental countries in that rugby is hugely popular and the national team is one of the best in the world (thanks to the British, who introduced rugby during World War I). France (*les tricolores*) plays in the annual five nations championship (*tournoi des cinq nations*) along with England, Ireland, Scotland and Wales (plus Italy from the 1999/2000 season), with international games played at the *Parc des Princes* in Paris. The national team traditionally plays with a flair and open entertaining style reminiscent of the All Blacks (New Zealand). French rugby owes its popularity (and existence) to clubs rather than schools or universities, as, for example, in Britain. It has its stronghold in the southwest of the country (the Midi), where every town has a team. Among the most famous clubs are Agen, Bayonne, Béziers, Brive, Narbonne and Toulouse. French clubs compete in an annual European Cup competition with British clubs. Most rugby in France follows the rugby union code (15 players a side), although rugby league rules (13 players a side) are also popular, particularly in Carcassonne and Perpignan.

SKIING

Both alpine or downhill (*alpin*) and cross-country skiing (*ski de fond/ski nordique*) are widely practiced in France, although alpine skiing is by far the most popular. France is Europe's number one destination for serious downhill skiers and some 15 per cent of the French population also ski regularly. The French mountain ranges have the largest number of resorts and the most extensive network of ski lifts in the world (over 4,000). France boasts over 3,000km² (over 1,150mi²) of skiing areas spread over six mountain ranges. The ski season runs from December to April (or May in the higher resorts, which are the best choice for early or late season skiing).

Skiing areas include a number of vast inter-linked regions with over 300km (186 miles) of *pistes* and some with over 600km (372mi) of *pistes*, e.g. the *Portes du Soleil* and the *Trois Vallées*, providing the largest linked skiing areas in the world. In the *Trois Vallées* you can ski for two weeks without using the same lift or skiing the same run twice! There are many long runs including the *Vallée Blanche* at Chamonix (24km/15mi), the *Aiguille Rouge* at Les Arcs and the *Sarenne* at Alpe d'Huez (both 16km/10mi). A number of French resorts are linked with Italian and Swiss resorts, thus allowing experienced off-*piste* skiers even further scope to get lost.

The French invented the purpose-built ski resort, where you jump out of bed in the morning directly onto the *piste* (but put your pants and skis on first!). However, there's more to France than purpose-built ski resorts, which are mostly lacking in character and charm (many are downright ugly), and the country also has many traditional village resorts rivalling the best in Austria and Switzerland. The main advantages of purpose-built resorts are that they are situated at high altitude where there's reliable snow and are designed so you can ski from door-to-door (in some resorts almost all runs start and finish in the village). The trend nowadays is away from monolithic concrete blocks and back to traditional wooden chalets.

The biggest and most famous French ski resorts include Alpe d'Huez, Les Arcs, Argentières, Avoriaz, Chamonix, Courcheval, Les Deux Alpes, Flaine, Les Menuires, Megève, Méribel, Morzine, La Plagne, Tignes, Val d'Isère, Valmorel and Val Thorens, the highest resort in Europe. Chamonix, Courcheval and Megève are France's most fashionable ski resorts. Many French resorts are situated at high altitude and have excellent snow records, even when most of the rest of the Alps is snow-less. Many resorts also boast snow cannons, enabling them to guarantee skiing throughout most of the season. In addition to the French Alps, there's also skiing in some 35 resorts in the French Pyrénées, e.g. Barèges and Cauterets, although they cater mostly for beginners and intermediates rather than experts. It's generally cheaper to ski in the Pyrénées than the Alps. Most resorts have a range of ski lifts including cable cars, gondolas, chairlifts and draglifts. Draglifts are usually *pomas* for single riders, rather than two-person T-bars, which many people find difficult to ride, particularly when on their own. Lifts are marked on *piste* plans as are all runs, which are graded green (beginners), blue (easy), red (intermediate) and black (difficult) in France.

Alpine or downhill skiing is an expensive sport, particularly for families. The cost of equipping a family of four is around 8,000F for equipment and clothing, or around 2,000F per person. If you're a beginner it's better to hire ski equipment (skis, poles, boots) or buy secondhand equipment until you're addicted, which if it doesn't frighten you to death, can happen on your first day on the *pistes*. Most sports shops have pre-season and end of season sales of ski equipment. Ski passes cost between 600F and 1,000F (e.g. *les Trois Vallées*) for six days. Ski hire costs 250 to 400F and boots 125 to 250F for six days, although they are often cheaper in the smaller resorts. Some resorts have low and high season rates for ski passes and ski and boot hire.

Ski resorts provide a variety of accommodation including hotel, self-catering apartments and chalets. Accommodation is more expensive during holiday periods (Christmas, New Year and Easter), when ski-lift queues are interminable and *pistes* are overcrowded. During public and school holiday periods (see page 146) the crowds of school children may drive you crazy, both on and off-*piste*. These periods are best avoided, particularly as the chance of collisions are greatly enhanced when *pistes* are overcrowded.

If you get bored with all those 'easy' black *pistes*, you may like to try something different such as bob-sleighing, freestyle or mogul skiing, mono-skiing, snowboarding (surfing), off-*piste* skiing, ski-bobbing, ski touring, speed skiing or tobogganning. Mono-skiing and snow-boarding are particularly popular in France and are taught in most resorts. The French also invented extreme skiing, which involves negotiating slopes steeper than 60 degrees (only for the seriously foolhardy). Other activities may include paragliding, parasailing, hang-gliding, snow-shoe walking, sleigh rides, climbing, archery, dog sleighs, dog-sledding, ice-hockey, and snow scooters and snowmobiles (fortunately still relatively thin on the ground in Europe).

Heli-skiing, where helicopters drop skiers off at the top of inaccessible mountains, is illegal in France. However, powder hounds can ski into unnavigable areas and be picked up by helicopter and can also be dropped off by helicopter in Italy or Switzerland (where heli-skiing is legal) and ski back to France. It costs around 1,000F a drop. Summer skiing is available in la Plagne, Tignes, Val d'Isère, Val Thorens, les Deux Alpes and the Alpe d'Huez, and can be combined with other sports such as tennis, swimming, golf, horse riding, grass skiing, fishing, watersports, hiking, climbing and a range of other activities.

Most winter resorts also provide a variety of mostly indoor activities including tennis, squash, ice-skating, curling, heated indoor swimming pools, indoor golf, tenpin bowling, gymnasiums, fitness centres, saunas and solariums. There's an excellent choice of restaurants and bars in most resorts, although they can be expensive. Other entertainment includes discos, cinemas, night clubs and casinos.

For further information about skiing and other winter sports in France contact the *Club Alpin Français*, 24, Ave de Laumière, 75019 Paris (☎ 01.53.72.87.00), the *Fédération Françaises de Ski*, 50, rue Marquisats, 74000 Annecy (☎ 04.50.51.40.34) or the *Association des Maires des Stations Française de Sports d'Hiver* (also known simply as SkiFrance) 61, bd Haussmann, 75008 Paris (☎ 01.47.42.23.32, Internet: www.skifrance.fr). The latest weather and snow conditions are available via Minitel, TV teletext, daily newspapers and direct from resorts. The FGTO publishes a *Winter Holiday Guide*.

Safety

Safety is of paramount importance in any sport but it's particularly important when skiing, where the possibility of injury is ever present. In recent years, skiing-related deaths and serious injuries have increased considerably as slopes have become more crowded. Around 200 skiers die each year in Europe and thousands more are injured, many seriously. Unless you're an expert skier, it's best to avoid skiing in poor weather and snow conditions. When snow conditions are bad, the danger of injury increases considerably, particularly for beginners and intermediates, who often find it difficult or impossible to control their skis. Young children should wear safety helmets in all conditions as soon as they are able to use normal *pistes* and lifts. However, skiing isn't necessarily a dangerous sport and medical studies show that the risk of injury while skiing is much less than many other sports and only marginally higher than playing table tennis (sounds unbelievable)!

Equipment: While it's unnecessary to wear the latest ski fashions, it's important to have suitable, secure and safe equipment – particularly bindings and boots. Although the latest high-tech bindings are a great help in avoiding injuries, the correct settings are vital. They should be set so that in the event of a fall you part company with your skis before your leg (or part thereof) parts company with your body (or tries to). Beginners' bindings must be set so that they release fairly easily, but not so easily that they open every time a turn is attempted. It's important to have your skis and bindings serviced each season by a qualified ski mechanic. If you're using hired skis, double check that the bindings are set correctly and that they release freely in all directions. If you aren't entirely happy with hired equipment, never hesitate to request adjustments or an exchange.

Avalanche Warnings: **NEVER** ignore avalanche warnings (*danger d'avalanches*), denoted by black and yellow flags, signs or flashing lights, or attempt to ski on closed (*barré*) *pistes* or anywhere there's a danger of avalanches. Avalanches on open *pistes* are extremely rare, as overloaded slopes overlooking *pistes* are blasted with explosives to remove excess snow. Don't ski off-*piste* unless you're an experienced skier and never on your own. In an unfamiliar area it's important to hire an experienced local ski guide (*moniteur de ski*). Only ski where it's permitted; in some areas, off-*piste* skiing is forbidden to protect the wildlife habitat. Each year many skiers are killed in avalanches, usually when skiing off-*piste* (there have also been a number of deaths as a result of chalets being buried by avalanches). You can buy a small radio transmitter, e.g. an avalanche transceiver, to help rescuers locate you if you're buried in an avalanche. They are expensive, although sensible off-*piste* skiers consider their lives are worth the cost and most guides insist that their clients have them. You can also wear an Avalanche Balloon System (ABS) air balloon rucksack, which can be inflated like a car air-bag to protect you in the event of an avalanche (although experts are undecided about its effectiveness).

Ability and Injuries: Try to ski with people of the same standard as yourself or with an experienced skier who's willing to ski at your pace and don't be in too much of a hurry to tackle those black runs. It isn't obligatory to ski from sunrise to sunset, although some fanatics may try to convince you otherwise. Stop skiing and rest when you feel tired, a sure sign of which is when you keep falling over for no apparent reason (unless you've had a large liquid lunch). **It's better to ride down in the cable-car than on a stretcher.** Most ski accidents happen when skiers are tired. If you injure yourself, particularly a knee, stop skiing and seek medical advice as soon as possible. If you attempt to ski with an injury or before an injury has had time to heal, you risk aggravating it and doing permanent damage.

Skiers' Highway Code

As the ski slopes become more crowded, the possibility of colliding with a fellow skier has increased considerably. Happily, the result of most clashes is simply a few bruises and dented pride; nevertheless the danger of serious injury (or even death) is ever present. You cannot always protect yourself from the lunatic fringe, e.g. the crazy novice who skis way beyond his limits and the equally loony 'expert' who skis at reckless speeds with a total disregard for other skiers. The following guidelines from the International Ski Federation's (FIS) Code of Conduct may help you avoid an accident:

Respect for others: A skier must behave in such a way that he neither endangers nor prejudices others.

Control of speed and skiing: A skier must adapt his speed and way of skiing to his own personal ability and to the prevailing conditions of terrain and weather.

Control of direction: A skier coming from above, whose dominant position allows him a choice of path, must take a direction that assures the safety of the skier below. **Failure to observe this rule is the cause of most accidents.**

Overtaking: A skier should leave a wide enough margin for the overtaken skier to make his turn. As when motoring, the most dangerous skiing manoeuvre is overtaking.

Crossing the *piste*: A skier entering or crossing a *piste* must look up and down to make sure that he can do so without danger to himself or others. The same applies after stopping.

Stopping on the *piste*: Unless absolutely necessary, a skier must avoid making a stop on the *piste*, particularly in narrow passages or where visibility is restricted. If a skier falls, he must clear the *piste* as soon as possible.

Climbing: A climbing skier must keep to the side of the *piste* and in bad visibility keep off the *piste* altogether. The same goes for a skier descending on foot.

If you get hit by a reckless skier you can sue for damages under France's civil negligence laws or equally you can be sued if you're the guilty party. There's no foolproof way of avoiding accidents. Obey the FIS code and make sure that you're well insured for both accidents and private liability (for a minimum of 10,000,000F). Skiers must obey signs and markings, assist at accidents, and provide their names and addresses when required.

Learning to Ski

If you're a newcomer to downhill skiing, it's worthwhile enrolling in a ski school for a week or two to learn the basics. It's also much safer than simply launching yourself off the nearest mountain, particularly for other skiers. Good skiing is all about style and technique and the value of good coaching cannot be over-emphasised. France has some 11,000 instructors and all French resorts have ski schools (*Écoles de Ski Français*) where classes are organised at all levels, from beginner to competition. Ski school costs from 300F to 500F for six half days, usually three hours morning or afternoon, or from around 600F to 1,000F for six full days, usually six hours per day. Individual lessons are available for 100F to 200F per hour. Note that in some resorts, many instructors don't speak English. English-speaking instructors are more common in the most popular resorts such as Chamonix, Meribel, Tignes and Val d'Isère. It's worth noting that ski instructors in France have priority at lifts and hiring an instructor can save you a lot of time queueing.

There's no better country in which to learn to ski than France, particularly if you're an adult. If you're a complete beginner, the best way to learn is with the French short-ski method (*ski-evolutif/ski moderne*) of instruction. As a learning method for adults it's unbeatable and is highly recommended by most experts. As a beginner you want to be able to turn easily and you *don't* want to go fast. Short skis provide both these advantages plus better balance and allow beginners to start learning parallel turns immediately. Beginners start on skis of around one metre in length and usually progress to 1.60 metre skis within a week, by which time most are making 'adequate' parallel turns. *Ski-evolutif* is taught in many French resorts and was invented in Les Arcs.

If you plan to take young children on a skiing holiday, you should choose a resort with a *crèche* or kindergarten and good non-skiing facilities such as Courcheval, Flaine, La Plagne, Valmorel and Val Thorens. Most resorts have nurseries for infants aged six months to three years old, while older children can attend a ski school. A nursery costs around 200F per day including lunch (or 1,000F for six days) and skiing kindergarten from 650F to 1,100F for six days, depending on the resort and whether a supervised lunch is included. Tourist offices organise baby-sitters in many resorts.

It may pay you to invest in a good skiing book such as the *Sunday Times We Learned to Ski* (Collins), which is an excellent choice, not only for beginners but for any skier. It's expertly researched and written and cannot be too highly recommended, **and according to many experts it's simply the best book ever written about learning to ski!**

Cross-Country Skiing

Cross-country skiing (*ski de fond/ski nordique*) doesn't have the glamorous (and macho) jet-set image of alpine skiing, but it's nevertheless a popular sport in France. It appeals to both young and old, particularly those whose idea of fun is a million miles away from careening down a hill at 100kph, with a thousand metre drop on one side and a glacier on the other. Cross-country skiing can be enjoyed at any pace and over any distance and therefore has great appeal to both the unfit and the keen athlete. It's exhilarating, particularly if you make the effort to learn the correct technique and persevere beyond the beginners' stage.

Compared with alpine skiing, cross-country skiing has the advantages of cheaper equipment, lower costs, far fewer broken bones, no queues *and* no expensive ski-lift passes. Essential equipment costs as little as 750F to 1,000F for skis, bindings, poles, boots and gloves. No special clothing is necessary (apart from gloves and boots), providing you have a warm pullover and a tracksuit. Trails, usually consisting of two sets of tracks (*pistes de ski de fond*), are made on specially prepared and sign-posted routes. Some resorts have floodlit trails for night skiing. You can enjoy cross-country skiing anywhere there's sufficient snow, although using prepared trails is easier than making your own.

BOULES

Boules or *pétanque* has been unkindly referred to as a 'glorified game of marbles', probably by some poor foreign loser. *Pétanque* is actually quite a different game from *boules* and was developed in southern France from an earlier *boules* game called *jeu provençal*. The main difference between *boules* and *pétanque* is that in *boules* you release the ball (*boule*) when moving up to the 'launch' spot and in *pétanque* (from *pieds tanqués*, meaning 'feet together') you stand still with your feet together when you throw. It's generally recognised that *pétanque* is easier to play as no special playing area is required, the 'court' is smaller than for *boules* and the rules are simpler. There are also various other variations played throughout the country (there's even a game played with square *boules* in the south of France!).

For most people *boules* is a pastime or social game, rather than a serious sport. However, it managed to earn recognition as an Olympic demonstration 'sport' in the Barcelona Olympics in 1992, so perhaps it deserves to be taken seriously. The forerunner to *boules* was possibly invented in Britain and played with cannon balls (Sir Francis Drake was playing *boules* and not bowls when the Spanish Armada interrupted play). It's played mostly in the south of France, where most village squares have a pitch (*piste*) and many towns have a special arena called a *boulodrome*. It also isn't unusual to find people playing in the middle of the road! The pitch should be around 3 by 12 metres (they vary considerably) and the more uneven the surface the better (although grass is totally unsuitable). The other essential requirement is an unlimited supply of *pastis*.

It's usually played by two teams comprising two (*doublettes*), three (*triplettes*) or four (*quadrettes*) players (a singles match is a *tête a tête* or head-to-head). A member of the starting team throws a small wooden marker ball or jack, called the *cochonnet* (piglet in French, although many other names are used depending on the area), up the pitch, between six and ten metres from the throwing point. The object is for players to pitch their balls as close to the *cochonnet* as possible. Players usually fall into two schools: *pointeurs*, who aim to get as close to the *cochonnet* as possible, and *tireurs*, who aim to scatter their opponents' *boules* to all corners of the land (which is quite legitimate). An all-rounder (usually the captain) with an eye to tactics is called a *milieu*. In the 'version' of *boules* called *pétanque* the thrower stands in a circle of 35 to 50cm (14 to 20in) diameter, just large enough for both feet, and launches his *boule* from a stationary crouching position. Another version of the game allows three steps to build up momentum and is called *à la longue*.

After one player from each team has thrown, the next thrower is decided by whose *boule* finished closest to the *cochonnet*. The team farthest away from the *cochonnet* continues to throw until they get a closer *boule* than the other team or until they have no more *boules*. The players on the other side then throw the rest of their *boules*. When both teams have finished the points are counted. The team whose *boule* (or *boules*) lies closest to the *cochonnet* wins the 'end'. When *boules* are too close to call, a piece of string is used to measure the distance from the *cochonnet*. One point is earned for each *boule* lying closer to the *cochonnet* than the closest *boule* of the opposing team. For example if the three closest *boules* belong to the winning team, they earn three points. A player on the winning team then starts the next end by throwing the *cochonnet*. A match continues until a team scores 11 points (a *partie*). A second or return match in a series of three is called *la revanche* and when each side has won one match, the deciding match is called *la belle*.

You can buy plastic sets of *boules*, but they are just for children and tourists. Serious competition players play with stainless steel *boules*, which must have their weight (in grammes) and the manufacturer's registration number stamped on them. There are a variety of finishes, weights and even colours of *boules*, so take advice before buying a set. Those who find bending a problem can buy a magnetic device to pick up their *boules* while standing (although standing can also be a problem after a surfeit of *pastis*). In a singles or doubles game, each player has three *boules* (two each in triples). In the last decade the number of registered players has doubled and the *Fédération Française de Pétanque (FFP)* has over 500,000 members. Although traditionally a male dominated game, many young players are female. Beware of hustlers and never play the locals for money!

CYCLING

France is one of Europe's foremost cycling countries, where cycling is both a serious sport and a relaxing pastime. French motorists usually give cyclists a wide berth when overtaking (apart from Parisians, who respect nobody else's right to use the road), although tourists aren't always so generous, particularly those towing caravans. Bicycles aren't expensive in France, where you can buy a men's 18-speed racing bike or a women's 'shopping' bike for around 650F and a 21-speed mountain bicycle (*vélo tout terrain/VTT*) for as little as 700F from many supermarkets and hypermarkets (children's mountain bikes cost from around 500F). Note that mountain-biking is a serious sport in France with sponsored events and even professional riders. There are special VTT bike trails in many areas, although bikes aren't permitted on hiking tracks. Bicycles should be fitted with an anti-theft device such as a steel cable or chain with a lock. If your bicycle is stolen you should report it to the local police, but don't expect them to find it.

Safety: Cycling in Paris and other cities can be dangerous and isn't recommended (except perhaps on Sunday mornings between 0500 and 0600). Cyclists must use cycle lanes (*piste cyclable*) where provided (there are few in France) and mustn't cycle in bus lanes or on footpaths. If you cycle in cities you should wear reflective clothing, protective head gear, a smog mask and a crucifix. It isn't necessary to wear expensive sports clothing when cycling, although a light crash helmet is advisable, particularly for children, and is much cheaper than brain surgery. Head injuries are the main cause of death in bicycle accidents, most of which don't involve accidents with automobiles, but are a result of colliding with fixed objects, or falls. Always buy a quality helmet that has been approved and subjected to rigorous testing. Take *particular* care on busy roads and don't allow your children onto public roads until they are experienced riders. Under new safety rules introduced in 1995, cycles must be roadworthy and be fitted with a horn or bell and front and rear lights.

Transporting Bikes: You can travel with your bicycle (as 'hand' baggage) on any day of the week on over 2,000 short-distance trains (subject to space), marked with a bicycle symbol in timetables. In many regions, e.g. the Ile-de-France, you can transport your bicycle free anytime on Saturdays, Sundays and public holidays, and during off-peak times on other days, i.e. outside the hours of 0630 and 0930 and 1630 and 1900 (you're responsible for loading and unloading it from the luggage van). Bicycles must be transported separately on most long-distance trains (French trains don't have a guard's van) and must usually be registered for each journey (delivery usually takes around five days). They can be insured during transportation and can also be delivered to your home. There's a transportation fee of 135F for an unpacked cycle and 170F for a packed cycle on national lines. A bicycle can be stored with the SNCF baggage service for around 35F per day.

Renting Bikes: Bicycles can be rented from over 200 SNCF stations in the principal tourist regions, particularly on the coasts. The SNCF usually provides three types of bicycle: a traditional bicycle with a 'unisex' frame, adjustable seat and handlebars, with or without gears; a touring model with ten speeds, with either a 'unisex' or a men's frame; and an all-track 'mountain' bike with six-speed gears. The rates for one or two days are around 50F a day for a traditional bike and around 60F a day for a touring or mountain bike (there are reductions for longer periods).

You must show a passport or driving licence and pay a 1,000F deposit for a traditional bike and 1,500F for touring or all-track bikes. Payment can be made in cash, by cheque or by credit card (e.g. Carte Bleue, Carte Bleue Visa, Eurocard, Mastercard or Access) at certain stations, when no deposit is necessary. Payment is made when you return the cycle, which can be to the station you rented it from or any other station renting cycles. Bicycle rental is subject to availability and bikes can be reserved in advance in person. A list of stations where you can rent a bike is contained in a brochure, *Guide Train + Vélo*, available from SNCF stations. Some *métro* and RER stations in Paris also rent bikes. Bicycles can also be rented from bicycle shops (*marchand de vélos*) in Paris and other cities and towns, but it's expensive, e.g. from 25F an hour in Paris or 100F per day (around double the rate charged by the SNCF).

Tour de France: The *Tour de France* is the ultimate challenge on wheels and is among the toughest sporting events in the world. It's also France's and the world's biggest annual sporting event and is watched by some 20 million people along the route. It has its own radio station, bank and telephone exchange, and is administered by a 3,000 strong organisation team. The *Tour de France* is held in July and consists of three weeks of almost continuous cycling (around 100 hours) totalling over 4,000km (2,175mi) on the toughest roads of France and its neighbouring countries (there have even been stages in England and Ireland). The route and length of the race changes each year, with towns paying handsomely to be a 'stage-town'. The race finishes at the Champs Elysées in Paris.

The race leaders wear various distinctive jerseys including a yellow jersey (*maillot jaune*) for the overall race leader, a green jersey (*maillot vert*) for the most consistent rider based on placings gained in each stage, and a white jersey with red polka dots (*maillot à pois*) for the leading mountain climber ('king of the mountains'). The pack, i.e. the bunch of riders at the front of the race, is called the *peloton*. France has other important road races including the Paris-Nice in March. Professional track racing is also popular and includes the *Six Jours Cycliste de Paris*.

Associations & Clubs: Keen cyclists may wish to join the *Fédération Française de CycloTourisme (FFCT)*, 8, rue Jean-Marie Jégo, 75013 Paris (☎ 01.44.16.88.88). The FFCT sells a wide range of articles for cyclists including maps, books, camping carnets and cycling accessories. There are cycling clubs in all medium to large towns including *Le Bicyclub de France*, 7, rue Ambroise Thomas, 75009 Paris. Cycling tours are arranged in most cities and many tourist areas. When going on a day tour or longer, take drinks, first-aid and tool kits, a puncture repair outfit and a good map. Among the best maps for cycling are the Michelin yellow maps (scale: 1cm = 2km).

Many books are written for cyclists in France including *Cycling France* by Jerry H. Simpson (Bicycle Books), *Cycle Touring in France* by Richard Neillands (Oxford Illustrated Press), *France by Bike* by Karen and Terry Whitehill (Cordee) and *Cycling in France* by Susi Madron (George Philip). Susi Madron also operates Britain's biggest French cycling holiday company, 'Cycling for Softies', 2 & 4 Birch Polygon, Manchester M14 5HX, UK (☎ 0161-248 8282).

HIKING

France has some of the finest hiking (*tourisme pédestre*) areas in Western Europe. Almost nowhere else offers the combination of good weather, variety and outstanding beauty that's commonplace in France. Spring and autumn are the best seasons for hiking, when the weather is cooler and the routes less crowded, although the best time for mountain flowers is between May and August. Although there are some pleasant walks in northern regions, most northern areas have few hills and present no challenges for serious walkers, most of whom head for the Alps, Pyrénées, Vosges, Auvergne and Jura mountains.

France has the finest network of walking trails in Europe including some 30,000km (18,600mi) of footpaths known as *Grande Randonnée (GR)*. A *GR de pays* is a country walk and a *Promenade Randonnée (PR)* an excursion from a GR for one-day or weekend walks. Routes are marked with white/red or yellow/red bars placed on trees, rocks, walls and posts. Tracks are mostly public and are accessible to all over ten years of age. The GR network was started in 1947 and has since been expanded into every corner of France under the guidance of the *Fédération Française de la Randonnée Pédestre (FFRP)*, Sentiers et Randonnée, 14, rue Riquet, 75019 Paris (☎ 01.44.89.93.90). The FFRP issues permits and provides insurance, although these aren't compulsory.

Trails include the 605km (375mi) GR1 (*Sentier Tour de l'Ile de France*), circling Paris, and the 800km (500mi) GR65 (*Sentier St Jacques*) following the old pilgrim road to Santiago de Compostela from Le Puy to the Spanish frontier. The basic source of information for the GR network is the *Institut Géographique National (IGN)* map number 903 'long distance footpaths' (*Sentiers de Grandes Randonnée*), showing all GR trails. One of France's most famous long-distance walks is the *Tour de Mont Blanc*, a two-week ramble around the Mont Blanc massif. It begins in Chamonix and runs through France, Switzerland and Italy before returning to the foot of the Vallée Blanche.

In mountain areas there are mountain refuge huts on the main GR routes, although these are usually open in summer only. They are basic but much better than being stranded in a storm. The cost is around 50F to 70F per night or less if you're a member of a climbing association or a club affiliated to the *Club Alpin Français*. France has six national parks, all with an inner zone where building, camping and hunting are prohibited, and 85 state-run natural reserves created to preserve the most-threatened areas of national heritage.

The FFRP publishes a series of topographic guides (*Topo-guides*) covering all of France's long-distance footpaths and an annual *Rando Guide*. Most *Topo-guides* are available in English and French and contain 1:50000 scale maps, describe routes, explain how to get to the start, and include a wealth of information about accommodation, restaurants, shops and attractions along routes. The Michelin 1,100 orange series (scale 1:50,000 or 1cm = 500m) are good for walking, although for the ultimate in detail, you need the IGN blue series of 2,000 maps. The scale is 1:25,000 with one centimetre equalling 250 metres (or 2.5in = 1mi), which is detailed enough to show individual buildings.

Orienteering is a popular sport in France and is a cross country race where competitors use a map and a compass to navigate between control points, visited in sequence. There are several variations in addition to walking including running, cross-country skiing, mountain-biking and even snow-shoeing. It can be enjoyed as a serious top-level sport or as a fun activity for all ages. Ask the FGTO or a local hiking club for information. There are hiking clubs in most areas, all of which organise local walks, usually on Sundays. Local footpaths include forest paths (*routes forestières*) and 'little walks' (*petites randonnées*), usually between 2km and 11km.

Wherever you walk in France, you need to be alert for savage dogs. In rural areas it seems that almost everyone keeps a fierce dog to deter unwelcome strangers (many are no doubt warm and cuddly when you get to know them, but it pays not to take chances). Carry a stick or walking cane to defend yourself (pointing it at a dog is usually enough to prevent it attacking you). Don't venture too far off the path during the hunting season, when you risk being shot by an over-zealous farmer (if the dogs don't get you first!).

Among the best English-language books for French hikers are *Walking in France* by Rob Hunter (Oxford Illustrated Press), *Walking Through France* by Robin Neillands (Collins) and *Classic Walks in France* by Rob Hunter and David Wickers (Oxford Illustrated Press).

Safety

The following notes may help you survive a walk on the wild side.

- Don't over-exert yourself, particularly at high altitudes where the air is thinner. Mountain sickness usually occurs only above 4,000m (13,000ft), but can happen at lower altitudes. A few words of warning for those who aren't particularly fit: take it easy and set a slow pace. It's easy to over-exert yourself and underestimate the duration or degree of difficulty of a hike. If the most exercise you usually get is walking to the pub and crawling back, then start slowly and build up to those weekend marathons. If you're unfit, use chair-lifts and cable-cars to get to high altitudes.

- Never attempt a major hike alone as it's too dangerous. Notify someone about your route and destination, and your estimated time of return. Check the conditions along your route and the times of any public transport connections, and take into account the time required for both ascents and descents. If you're unable to return by the time expected, let somebody know (if possible). If you realise you will be unable to reach your destination, e.g. due to tiredness or bad weather, turn back in good time or take a shorter route.

- Check the local weather forecast (see page 394). Generally the higher the altitude, the more unpredictable the weather. If you get caught in a heavy storm, descend as quickly as possible or seek protection.

- Hiking, even in lowland areas, can occasionally be dangerous, so don't take unnecessary risks. There are enough natural hazards including bad weather, rockfalls, avalanches, rough terrain, snow and ice, and wet grass, without adding to them. Don't walk on closed tracks at any time (they are signposted). This is particularly important in the spring, when there may be a danger of avalanches or rockfalls. If in doubt about whether a particular route is open, ask at the local tourist office.

- Take sun protection, for example a hat, sunglasses, and sun and barrier cream. This is particularly important if you're hiking at high altitude, where you will burn more easily due to the thinner air. Use a total sunblock cream on your lips, nose and eyelids, and take a scarf or handkerchief to protect your neck from the sun. You will also need to protect yourself against ticks and mosquitos in some areas.

- Take a water bottle. This is much appreciated when you discover that the restaurant that was just around the corner is still miles away because you took the wrong turning!

- If you're gathering mushrooms, present them to your local pharmacist, who's also an official 'mushroom inspector'. Some species are deadly poisonous and people die each year from eating them.

MOUNTAINEERING, ROCK-CLIMBING & CAVING

Those who find hiking a bit tame may like to try mountaineering (*alpinisme*), rock-climbing or caving (subterranean mountaineering), all of which are popular in France. France has the best rock-climbing and some of the best mountaineering in Europe. The French have always been avid climbers and France has some of the world's leading exponents, including the best female freestyle climber, Catherine Destiville, whose exploits are largely responsible for increasing the sport's popularity. If you're an inexperienced climber it's advisable to join a club and 'learn the ropes' before heading for the mountains. Information about clubs is available from the *Club Alpin Français*, 14, ave de Lumière, 75019 Paris (☎ 01.53.72.88.00).

You will also need a guide when climbing in an unfamiliar area, particularly when climbing glaciers (don't, however, follow your guide too closely – if he falls down a crevice it isn't necessary to accompany him!). Guides are available at mountaineering schools and in many smaller resorts and should be members of the guides association (UIAGM) which has strict standards. If you find a guide other than through a recognised school or club, you should make sure that he's qualified. Mountain guides are available in the main climbing areas including Briançon, La Chapelle, Embrun, La Grave and Pelvoux for the high Alps; Chamonix and St-Gervais for the Savoie-Dauphiné; Gavarnie, Luchon and St-Lary for the mid-Pyrénées; and Bastia for Corsica. Chamonix is the centre of French climbing and its *Compagnie des Guides* is renowned as the world's oldest (established 1821) and best association of mountain guides. There are mountain refuge huts on the main GR routes (see page 355) in mountain areas.

Many climbers lose their lives each year in France, many of whom are inexperienced and reckless (or just plain stupid). Many more owe their survival to rescuers, who risk their own lives to rescue them. Mont Blanc, Europe's highest peak at 4,800m/15,780 feet, has seen a record number of deaths in recent years and over 1,000 in the last 20 years (more than 80 in 1997 alone). **Needless to say, it's extremely foolish, not to mention highly dangerous, to venture into the mountains without proper preparation, excellent physical condition, adequate training, the appropriate equipment and an experienced guide.**

RACQUET SPORTS

Racquet sports are very popular in France, particularly tennis. Squash is much in vogue and gaining in popularity, but badminton isn't widely played and facilities are generally poor. France invented the game of tennis, or so they would have you believe, and has over 2½ million players and some 10,000 clubs. Tennis' popularity has grown tremendously in the last few decades and there are courts in most towns and villages, although in small villages there may be one court only. Courts are usually hard (*court en dur*), although clay courts (*court en terre battue*) are also popular; many courts are floodlit. One of the reasons for the popularity and high standard of tennis in France is that there are hundreds of covered and indoor courts, enabling tennis to be played year round.

There are two main kinds of racquet clubs in France: sports centres open to allcomers and private clubs. Sports centres require no membership or membership fees and anyone can book a court. In Paris and other cities, there are huge tennis complexes with as many as 24 courts, open from 0700 to 2200 daily. Costs are reasonable and are around 50F an hour for an indoor court, 25F an hour for an outdoor court or 35F if it's floodlit. Most towns and villages have municipal courts that can be rented for 20F to 30F an hour.

Tennis was long regarded as an elite sport in France and remains that way in many private clubs, which are usually expensive and exclusive and rarely accept unaccompanied visitors. Membership runs into thousands of francs a year and most clubs have long waiting lists. At an elite private club you can pay 200F an hour for a court. France has many tennis schools and resorts such as the renowned Pierre Barthes Tennis Resort in Cap d'Agde, the largest tennis school in the world, with 62 outdoor hard courts plus indoor tennis and squash facilities. Many tennis clubs provide saunas, whirl-pools, solariums and swimming pools, and most have a restaurant. Some hotels have their own tennis and squash courts, and organise coaching holidays throughout the year. Information is available from racquet clubs, travel agents and tourist offices.

The French Open tennis tournament is one of the world's four 'grand slam' (*grand chelem*) events, along with the US and Australian Opens and Wimbledon. It's held during the last week of May and the first week of June at the *Stade Roland-Garros* in Paris, and is the only grand slam event staged on clay courts. The French won the Davis Cup in 1991, defeating the much-fancied Americans in the final (they compensated by losing ignominiously to Switzerland the following year). France has a number of women players ranked in the world's top 20, but they are still seeking another male superstar since Yannick Noah (the last Frenchman to win the French Open) retired.

There are squash clubs in most large towns in France, although some may have only one or two courts. There are also many combined tennis and squash clubs. The standard of squash in France is low due to the lack of experienced coaches and top competition, although it's continually improving. Racquets and balls can be hired from most squash clubs for the American version of squash, called racquet ball, played in France on a squash court. Some tennis centres also provide badminton courts and there are badminton clubs in many areas.

SWIMMING

Not surprisingly, swimming (*natation*) is one of France's favourite sports and pastimes, with its glorious summer weather, miles of beautiful sandy beaches (*plage*), and numerous public swimming pools (*piscine*). Beaches vary considerably in size, surface (sand, pebbles, etc.) and amenities, and most are notable for their elegance, neatness and order. Most resorts provide beach clubs for the young (*clubs des jeunes*) and all but the smallest beaches have supervised play areas where you can leave young children for a fee. Deck chairs and umbrellas can be hired on most beaches. Most beaches are free, although there are private beaches in some areas, particularly along the Mediterranean. In a few areas, public beaches are dirty and overcrowded, although this is very much the exception.

Almost 90 per cent of French beaches were in the top two EU 'blue flag' (*pavillon bleu*) standards (A and B) for the quality of their water in 1997, although many that failed the tests were dangerously polluted. The dirtiest beaches are on the northern coast between Calais and Cherbourg, the cleanest around Nice (although not all). The pollution count must be displayed at the local town hall: blue = good quality water, green = average, yellow = likely to be temporarily polluted, and red = badly polluted. Up to date information can be obtained by dialling 3615 INFOPLAGE on Minitel.

Swimming can be dangerous at times, particularly on the Atlantic coast, where some beaches have lethal currents. You should observe all beach warning signs and flags. Most beaches are supervised by lifeguards who operate a flag system to indicate when swimming is safe. When a beach is closed it's shown by a sign (*baignade interdite*). There are stinging jellyfish in parts of the Mediterranean and along the Atlantic coast.

Most French towns of any size have a municipal swimming pool (*piscine municipale*), including heated indoor pools (*piscine chauffée couverte*) and outdoor pools (*piscine en plein air*). Public pools open from around 1030 to 1300 and 1500 to 1900 – yes, even pools close for lunch! Opening hours may vary from day-to-day and most municipal pools aren't open during the evenings. Heated indoor pools are open year round and outdoor pools are open during the summer only, e.g. from 15th June to 31st August. Note that many hotel and public pools may be open in July and August only. Admission to municipal pools is usually 10F to 20F for adults and 10F to 15F for children.

Public pools in cities are usually overcrowded, particularly when children aren't at school, e.g. Wednesdays, weekends and school holidays. Pools in hotels and health clubs are less crowded, although expensive. It's compulsory to wear a swimming cap in a public pool. In country areas, lakes, rivers and canals are employed as swimming pools (*piscine naturelle*), although you should avoid those flowing through urban areas which are often polluted. Most swimming pools and clubs provide swimming lessons (all levels from beginner to fish) and run life saving courses. France also has a number of huge watersports centres with indoor and outdoor pools, waterslides, flumes, wave machines, whirlpools and waterfalls, plus sun-beds, saunas, solariums, jacuzzis and hot baths.

The French are also the best undressed people on the beach and France is the naturist capital of Europe (having supplanted the former Yugoslavia), with numerous naturist beaches, villages and over 60 holiday centres, including campsites. Topless bathing is common almost anywhere (St. Tropez is a lecher's paradise), even in Paris along the banks of the Seine, but nude bathing should be confined to naturist beaches. The main naturist areas include Aquitaine, Brittany, Corsica, Languedoc, Provence and the Midi-Pyrénées.

Information about naturist holidays can be obtained from the FGTO, who publish *France, a Land for all Naturisms*. If you aren't a member of a naturist association in another country, then you must join the French Naturist Federation (*Fédération Française de Naturisme*), 65, rue de Tocqueville, 75017 Paris, ☎ 01.47.64.32.82), or pay a fee covering the duration of your stay. Cape d'Agde on the Languedoc coast is the biggest naturist resort in the world, with a population of 40,000 from Easter to September. Naked day trippers are allowed, although most centres don't allow single male visitors (sexist!).

WATERSPORTS

France is a paradise for watersports enthusiasts, which is hardly surprising considering its immense coastline, numerous lakes, and thousands of kilometres of rivers and canals. Popular watersports include sailing, windsurfing, water-skiing, jet-skiing, rowing, canoeing, kayaking, surfing, barging, rafting and subaquatic sports. Wet suits are recommended for windsurfing, waterskiing and subaquatic sports, even in summer. Rowing and canoeing are possible on most lakes and rivers, where canoes and kayaks can usually be rented. France has Europe's best surfing beaches, huddled on the extreme southwest Atlantic coast, including Biarritz (the capital of European surfing), Capbreton, Hossegor and Lacanau. Skin-diving and snorkelling are popular, particularly around the coasts of Brittany, the French Riviera and Corsica. There are clubs for most watersports in all major resorts and towns throughout France, where instruction is usually available.

Be sure to observe all warning signs on lakes and rivers. Take particular care when canoeing, as even the most benign of rivers have 'white water' patches that can be dangerous for the inexperienced. It's wise to wear a life-jacket, whether you're a strong swimmer or a non-swimmer. On some rivers there are quicksand-like banks of silt and shingle where people have been sucked under.

France has over 7,500km (4,660mi) of inland waterways and it's possible to navigate from the north coast to the Mediterranean along rivers and canals. Canals aren't just for pleasure craft and millions of tonnes of freight are transported on them annually. Life on France's waterways continues at a leisurely pace, not least due to the maximum speed limit, which is 10kph on canals and 5kph on rivers. The principal inland boating areas are Alsace, Brittany, Burgundy, Champagne and Picardy-Flanders. The most popular waterway is the *Canal du Midi* in the south of France. Note that some rivers have strong currents and require considerable skill and experience to navigate. Except for parts of the Moselle river, all French waterways provide free access.

Boating holidays are popular in France. The style of boats vary from motorboats for two to four persons to barges or houseboats (*pénichettes*) with accommodation for 10 to 12 persons. A boat with six to eight berths costs around 5,000F per week in low season and 10,000F per week in high season. If you prefer to let someone else do the work, there are even hotel barges, some with heated swimming pools, air-conditioning, and suites with four-poster beds! The FGTO publish a free booklet, *Boating on the Waterways*.

Sailing has always been a popular sport with the French and there are some 750,000 yacht owners in France. The French have a long tradition of seafaring and are prominent in international yachting, particularly long-distance races. In 1993, Frenchman Bruno Peyron was the first sailor to circumnavigate the world in under 80 days. Boats of all shapes and sizes can be hired in most resorts and ports, where there are also sailing clubs and schools. If you have a few francs to spare and wish to impress your friends, you can even rent a luxury yacht with crew for a modest 750,000F to 1,250,000F per week (plus tips). French residents must have a 'sea certificate' to pilot power boats of 6 to 50 horsepower within five nautical miles of a harbour, in addition to a sea licence (*permis mer*). If you're inexperienced, you should steer well clear of jet-skis, which can be deadly in the wrong hands.

From 1993, the 'wandering yacht' has no longer been able to escape VAT, which must be levied on yachts in EU countries at the time of sale. Previously owners could escape VAT by keeping their yachts harboured for less than six months a year in any EU country. Buyers from non-EU countries remain exempt, providing they export their yachts to non-EU waters. It pays to shop around for the lowest VAT rate when buying a yacht as rates vary considerably. EU resident owners aren't permitted to register their vessels abroad simply to avoid paying VAT and any vessel registered outside the EU must be located there (and is liable to import duties if it's berthed in an EU port).

If you wish to berth a boat in France, you need to find a caretaker (*gardien/ne*)) to look after it. The cost of keeping a yacht on the Atlantic coast is much cheaper than on the Mediterranean, although even here it needn't be too expensive providing you steer clear of the most fashionable ports. Mooring fees vary considerably, e.g. from around 100F per day in Normandy to 1,000F per day in St. Tropez. France has hundreds of harbours, 20 of which (from Normandy to the Mediterranean) have formed *France Station-Voile* to promote their attractions. A book which may be of interest to boat owners is *The French Alternative: The Pleasure and Cost-Effect of Keeping your Boat in France* by David Jefferson (Waterline). Wherever you berth your yacht, it should be fully insured. A growing number of luxury yachts disappear each year in France, particularly on the French Riviera, although the police believe this is due more to insurance fraud than theft.

AERIAL SPORTS

France has an historical and abiding passion for aviation; from the Montgolfière brothers and Blériot to the present day, it has always been at the leading edge of aeronautics. The love affair extends to all aerial sports including light-aircraft flying, gliding, hang-gliding, paragliding, parachuting, sky-diving, ballooning and microlighting. The most important assets for aerial sports enthusiasts are madness and money, both required in abundance to fulfil man's ultimate ambition. The Alps and Pyrénées are excellent venues for aerial sports, particularly hang-gliding and paragliding (*parapente*), due to the updrafts and the low density of air traffic. Paragliding, which entails jumping off a steep mountain slope with a parachute, is technically easier than hang-gliding. The Pyrénées are reckoned to be the best mountains in Europe for paragliding, with their warm summers and wide valleys. Participants must complete an approved course of instruction, after which they receive a proficiency certificate and are permitted to go solo.

There are flying clubs at most airfields in France, where light aircraft and gliders (and helicopters for prison escapes) can be hired. Parachuting and freefall parachuting (sky-diving) flights can also be made from many private airfields in France. The south of France is an excellent place to learn to fly, as flying is rarely interrupted by bad weather. The latest American craze to have (literally) taken off in France is microlight (*ultra-léger motorisé/ULM*) flying. A microlight (or ultralight) is a low-flying go-cart with a hang glider on top and a motorised tricycle below, and is one of the cheapest and most enjoyable ways to experience real flying. For information contact the *Fédération Française de Vol à Moteur*, 6, rue Galilée, 75008 Paris (☎ 01.47.20.93.02) or the *Fédération Française de Vol à Voile*, 29, rue de Sèvres, 75006 Paris (☎ 01.45.44.04.78).

The first manned hot-air balloon flight was made in France in 1783 by Montgolfière and ballooning remains popular with a large number of participants. There are balloon meetings throughout France, particularly in summer. It is, however, an expensive sport and participation is generally limited to the wealthy (lawyers and politicians get a reduction for supplying their own hot air). Those who prefer to keep their feet firmly planted on terra firma may prefer to fly a kite (especially recommended for politicians), which has increased dramatically in popularity in recent years in Europe. A huge nylon kite can cost 25,000F or more. The biggest European kite-flying festival is held in Dieppe.

Before taking up aerial sports (apart from kite-flying), you're advised to make sure that you have adequate health, accident and life insurance and that your affairs are in order. Why not try fishing instead? A nice, sensible, SAFE sport (unless, of course, you're a fish).

FISHING

Although not particularly well-known internationally, France is a paradise for fishermen, with over 4,800km (3,000mi) of coastline, 240,000km (150,000mi) of rivers and streams, and 120,000 hectares (300,000 acres) of lakes and ponds. Enough to keep even the keenest of anglers busy for a few weeks! There's excellent fishing in rivers, lakes and ponds throughout France, many of which are stocked annually with trout, grayling and pike. Fishing (*pêche*) is enjoyed regularly by around four million French anglers and irregularly by some 20 per cent of the population, and is claimed by many to be France's national sport (soccer fans would disagree).

Fishing rights in France may be owned by a private landowner, a fishing club or the local community. Almost all inland waters, from the tiniest stream to the largest rivers and lakes, are protected fishing areas, where a permit (*permis de pêche*) is required. Signs such as *pêche réservée/gardée* are common and denote private fishing. Many of the best fishing waters are in private hands, although it may be possible to obtain permission to fish from the owners. Often stretches of a river are divided between local clubs and anglers must join a local fishing club to fish there. In addition to club fees, you may also have to pay an annual fee (e.g. 100 to 200F) to the local federation of clubs. You need a passport-size photograph for your membership card. Club membership entitles you to fish in club waters throughout France under reciprocal arrangements with other clubs.

Fishing rights for waters on public land are the property of the state and a special tax (*taxe piscicole*) is levied. Permits are sold by fishing tackle shops, who can also advise you of the best local fishing spots, and in some cases by local cafés. Once you have a permit, you're automatically a member of the *Association de Pêche et de Pisciculture (APP)*. Permits are issued for a full season and permits for short periods of one or two weeks aren't available, although daily cards can be purchased for some lakes and ponds.

There are various categories of permits for public waters, denoted by excise stamps. Stamp one (around 100F) is the compulsory standard excise stamp (*timbre fiscal de base/à la ligne*), allowing you to fish with one rod, one float and one hook in coarse fish rivers (*2ème catégorie*). Stamp two (150F) is a supplementary stamp (*timbre supplément*) allowing you to fish in rivers, streams, coarse fish rivers and game fish rivers, using any fishing method (e.g. fly-fishing, float-fishing, ledgering, live-bait and spinning) and with a maximum of three rods. You can catch all fish except salmon. Stamp three (150F) is a reciprocity excise stamp (*timbre halieutique*) allowing you to fish in all the departments of southern France. You can buy this stamp only when you have stamps one and two and it should be purchased in the same department, otherwise it costs double. Stamp four (*timbre saumon*) is for sea trout and salmon fishing (costing from around 100F to over 600F for salmon), although salmon have become rare in France's rivers. Always carry your fishing permit with you as wardens (who patrol most waters) may ask to see it.

Rivers are divided into two categories. First category (*première catégorie* or *salmonidés dominants*) covers headwaters and rivers suitable for salmon, trout and grayling, where maggots are banned as bait. The second category (*deuxième catégorie* or *salmonidés non dominants*) usually includes the lower stretches of rivers populated mainly by coarse fish, where bait can include practically anything except fish-eggs. You must pay an annual supplement of around 100F to fish in category one waters.

The fishing season varies depending on the area and type of fish, but is typically from around 1st March to 15th September for the first category (*1re catégorie*) and from 15th January to 15th April for the second category (*2e catégorie*). You're permitted to fish from half an hour before sunrise until half an hour after sunset and night fishing is forbidden on all rivers (although permitted in certain lakes and ponds). Fishing regulations vary from department to department. There are limits on catches in most areas. Boats can be hired on inland waters and from sea ports, where deep-sea fishing expeditions are organised. Sea fishing is better in the Atlantic than the Mediterranean.

Up-to-date information on fishing areas, regulations, competitions and weather forecasts can be obtained via Minitel. For further information contact the *Conseil Supérieur de la Pêche*, 134 av. Mabakoff, 75011 Paris (☎ 01.45.02.20.20) or the *Union National des F.A.A.P.P.*, 17, rue Bergère, 75009 Paris (☎ 01.48.24.96.00). A brochure, *Angling in France*, is available from the FGTO. Information about local fishing areas and fishing permits is available from local tourist offices and town halls.

HUNTING

Hunting (*chasse*) is popular in France, which has some 1.6 million registered hunters (*chasseurs*), more than all other European countries combined. A licence isn't required for a shotgun, which can be bought by mail order or over the counter in your local hypermarket. Hunting is a key part of the masculine culture and women are discouraged (less than 2 per cent of hunters are women). It's even a way of doing business (*chasses d'affaires*) in France and companies often invite their most important clients to shoots. Popular prey includes wild boar (*sangliers*), deer, partridge, pheasant, duck, snipe, pigeon, rabbit and hare.

French hunters are notoriously bad marksmen and many are killed each year in hunting accidents. Many are inexperienced and some are downright dangerous, especially if they've been at the bottle before taking to the land. Although they won't deliberately shoot you (unless you're a conservationist or *garde-chasses*), it's advisable to steer clear of the countryside during the hunting season. Hunters must have comprehensive accident insurance and hunting within 200m of a house is forbidden. The minimum age for hunting in France is 16 and a permit (*permis de chasse*) is necessary costing around 200F a year. Permits for non-residents are available from local *préfectures*, for which you require two passport-sized photographs, a passport and a shotgun licence (with a French translation). Permits are severely restricted and are expensive (e.g. around 1,000F) due to the scarcity of game and the already fierce competition among local hunters.

Hunting is legal from September to February, although the actual dates vary depending on the department and the prey (e.g. the close season for snails is 1st April to 30th June). No hunting is permitted during the breeding and early-nurturing periods, and the species and numbers of game that can be shot is carefully controlled. There are plans to shorten the hunting season (to the end of January) to protect migrating birds during their return to breeding grounds, although this is hotly contested by hunters. Although hunters don't have the right to hunt on private land (*Propriété privée*) without permission, when land has traditionally been used by hunters they won't bother to ask (country people regard hunting as a sacred right). Where hunting is forbidden it's usually shown by a sign (*chasse interdite/gardée*).

Hunting rights are jealously guarded in France where hunters pay 10,000F a year or more for hunting rights in some areas.

There isn't a tradition of conservation in France. Although most hunters claim to be nature lovers, tending the land and conserving wildlife, they are inclined to shoot anything that moves (including each other). Many millions of birds are shot illegally each year, most being shot for 'sport' rather than the table. However, poachers do a thriving business providing songbirds for private 'gourmet' dining clubs and restaurants (don't, however, expect to find blackbird pie or grilled robin on the menu). Fortunately for France's hapless wildlife, many French hunters spend more time trying to find their dogs than actually hunting.

For further information contact the *Office Nationale de la Chasse*, 85 bis, avenue de Wagram, 75017 Paris (☎ 01.44.15.92.28). There are many magazines devoted to hunting in France. Skeet, clay pigeon and range shooting are also popular.

GOLF

Golf is one of the fastest growing sports in France, where there are over 200,000 registered players and the second highest number of golf courses (over 500) in Europe after Britain, the majority of which were built in the last decade. Most courses are located in magnificent settings (seaside, mountain and forest) and many are linked with real estate development. Properties on or near golf clubs, which may include life membership, are becoming increasingly popular with foreigners seeking a permanent or second home in France.

Most golf clubs are found in Normandy, Brittany, the Centre, Pays de la Loire, Poitou-Charentes, Aquitaine, Languedoc, Roussillon, the Côte d'Azur, Savoie Mont-Blanc and the Paris region. France stages a number of international golf tournaments as part of the European tour including the French Open, the Mediterranean Open, the Cannes Open and the Lâncome Trophy. The country has courses to suit all standards, although there are few inexpensive public courses and golf is considered a rich man's sport. Most private clubs accept 'green fees' players and most French golfers prefer to pay and play, rather than pay an annual membership fee. The minimum handicap requirements are usually 24 for men and 28 for women, although some are as high as 35 for both sexes or offer free access. Green fees (18 holes) may vary depending on the season, e.g. 200-300F during high season and as little as 100F during the low season. Fees at clubs are higher at weekends and on public holidays than during the week.

Golf holidays are popular in France and are a major source of revenue for golf clubs. Most courses welcome visitors and some clubs have special rates. A golf pass is available in some areas and allows visitors to play at a number of courses in a particular area. Due to the relatively small number of players, golf is a more relaxed game in France than in many other countries and queues are virtually unknown. Most French players make some famous professional snails look like hares and many treat a game as a leisurely stroll after lunch. Dress regulations are almost non-existent.

Most clubs have driving ranges, practice putting greens, bunker practice areas, a clubhouse (possibly a *château*), restaurant and bar. Many clubs are combined with country or sporting clubs boasting a luxury hotel, restaurant, swimming pool, gymnasium, tennis courts, billiards, croquet and *boules*. You can hire golf clubs, a golf trolley (around 20F a round) and possibly a golf buggy (150F to 200F a round or

300F a day) at all clubs. In major cities there are indoor driving ranges where membership costs from 450F to 550F per month or 2,000F to 3,000F a year.

The FGTO publish a brochure, *Golf in France*, containing a comprehensive list of travel companies offering golf holidays, including leading British companies such as BDH Golf and Fairways of France (Brittany Ferries also offer golf packages). The *Institut Géographique National* (IGN) publishes a general (ref. 910) golf map of France. For more information about golf in France contact the *Féderation Française de Golf*, 69, avenue Victor-Hugo, 75016 Paris (☎ 01.44.17.63.00).

OTHER SPORTS

The following are a selection of other popular sports in France:

Athletics: Most French towns have local athletics clubs organising local competitions and sports days. Paris hosts an annual marathon attracting over 15,000 runners. Jogging isn't as popular in France as it is in many other countries.

Basketball: Basketball is surprisingly popular in France, where CSP Limoges became the first French team to win the European Clubs' Championship in 1993, Europe's top basketball title. There are amateur clubs in large towns and cities.

Billiards and Snooker: Many hotels, bars and sports clubs have billiard or snooker tables, and there are billiards clubs in the larger towns where facilities may include French billiards, British snooker and American pool. French billiards is played on a table with no pockets. In Paris, some billiard halls are as elegant as art galleries, e.g. the Clichy Montmartre billiards club.

Bungee Jumping: If your idea of fun is jumping off a high bridge or platform with an elastic rope attached to your body or limbs to prevent you merging with the landscape, then bungee jumping may be just what you're looking for. Although late starters, the French have taken to bungee jumping with a vengeance. Most venues use purpose-built platforms and cranes, rather than natural locations.

Gymnasiums or Health Clubs: Where masochists go to torture themselves. The number of health clubs in France has mushroomed in recent years and there are gymnasiums (*gymnase*) and health clubs in most towns. Most have tonnes of expensive bone-jarring, muscle-wrenching apparatus, plus pools, saunas, jacuzzis and steam baths. Fees are from around 500F a month or 1,500F to 5,000F a year, plus a registration fee. Most clubs permit visitors, although there's usually a high hourly or daily fee. Some clubs are small and extremely crowded, particularly during lunch hours and early evenings. Some first class hotels also have fitness rooms. Dance, training and exercise classes are provided by sports centres and clubs throughout France.

Handball: Played indoors on a pitch similar to a five-a-side soccer pitch. Handball players pass the ball around by hand and attempt to throw it into a small goal (it's popular among footballers with two left feet). There are over 300,000 players in France and dozens of local leagues. It's also played professionally in France and the French national champions compete in the European championships.

Horse Racing: France has some 265 racecourses headed by Longchamps (the world's longest track), Chantilly, Deauville and St. Cloud. There are large provincial courses in Bordeaux and Marseille, but the majority of courses are small. The annual prize money of 800 million francs is the highest in Europe and turnover from race betting is greater than from the national lottery. All legal betting is via the *Pari Mutuel Urbain (PMU)* monopoly totaliser system (there are no bookies in France).

Chantilly is the centre of French horse racing and stages the French Derby in June. The top flat race in Europe (if not the world) is the *Prix de l'Arc de Triomphe*, held the first weekend in October at Longchamps in Paris. Trotting is also popular in France, where the top race is the *Prix d'Amérique* held at Vincennes in Paris, attracting a greater following than the *Prix de l'Arc de Triomphe*.

Horse Riding: Horse riding is widespread in France, which has thousands of kilometres of groomed bridlepaths (*randonnées équestres*). The French are passionate about horses (they also like to eat them) and there's a large horse population in France, where horses are cheaper to buy and keep than in most other European countries. There are thousands of riding schools, equestrian centres and pony clubs in France, and hundreds of horse shows are staged throughout the year. In addition to cross country riding, dressage, hurdles and show jumping are also popular. Cross-country riding holidays and horse trekking are popular, with riders staying overnight in *gîtes*. One of the most beautiful areas to enjoy a riding holiday is in the Camargue, riding the famous Camargue white horses. For more information contact the *Association Nationale pour le Tourisme Équestre et l'Équitation de Loisirs*, 15, rue de Bruxelles, 75009 Paris (☎ 01.42.81.42.82).

Motor Racing: Motor racing is very popular in France (particularly on public roads), which is famous for the Le Mans 24-hour sports car race (founded in 1923) held in June and the Monte Carlo rally in January (founded in 1913), the most famous of all road rallies (although upstaged by the arduous Granada-Dakar race in recent years). France also stages many other international motor races, including the French Formula One Grand Prix. The Monaco Formula One Grand Prix in May is the most popular on the circuit, so popular in fact that owners of apartments overlooking the course are able to charge up to 250,000F rent for the two days of the meeting. Racing on two or three wheels also has a strong following including motor cycling, motocross, side-car racing and scrambling.

Ten-Pin bowling: There are ten-pin bowling centres in all major French cities, usually open from around 1500 until 0300 or 0400. Ten-pin bowling and skittles (*jeu de quilles*) can also be played in many hotels and restaurants.

Miscellaneous: Many French and foreign sports and pastimes have a group of expatriate fanatics in France including American football, baseball, boccia, bullfighting, cricket, croquet, pelote (pelota/jai-alai) and polo. Cricket is popular in some parts of France, although it's mainly played by deranged expatriates (exposed to too much sun) with a few token eccentric Frenchmen to make up the numbers (the French ought to take to cricket like ducks to water, particularly when it comes to stopping for lunch and tea!). There are some 25 cricket clubs in France participating in an annual cup competition. For information about local expatriate sports facilities and clubs enquire at tourist offices, town halls, embassies and consulates (see **Appendix A**).

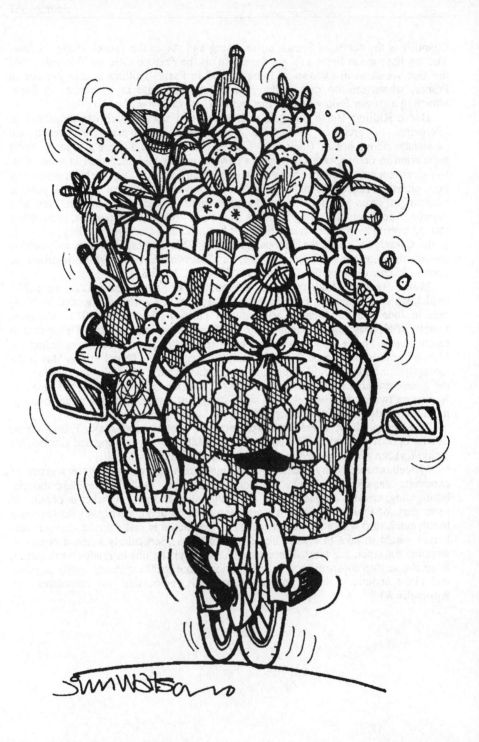

17.

SHOPPING

France is one of Europe's great shopping countries and French shops are designed to seduce you with their artful displays of beautiful and exotic merchandise. Paris is a shoppers' paradise, where even the shop windows are a delight, although it isn't the best place to find bargains and is generally no place for budget shoppers. Nevertheless, Paris attracts an army of foreign shoppers keen to pay for top quality French labels such as Chanel, Dior, Hermès and Louis Vuitton. French products are distinguished by their attention to detail, elegance, flair and quality, particularly good clothes (not to mention their high prices). However, unless you have money to burn, don't even think about buying imported branded goods in France!

Most French towns of any size have a supermarket or two and on the outskirts of large towns there are huge shopping centres with hypermarkets, do-it-yourself stores and furniture warehouses (there's a constant battle between town centres and out-of-town shopping centres). In many city centres there are pedestrian streets (*rues piétonnes*) where you can walk and shop without fear of being run down by a speeding motorist. French retailers are among the world's most competitive and have smaller profit margins than many other countries. Price fixing isn't permitted in France, with the exception of books, where the price is fixed to protect small bookshops from 'unfair' competition from large retailers. Many retailers do, however, accept recommended prices as a condition of supply by manufacturers and the price of bread and pharmaceuticals are controlled by the government.

As in most countries, it's important to shop around and compare prices, which can vary considerably (not only between small shops and hypermarkets, but also between different supermarkets and hypermarkets in the same town). Note, however, that price differences usually reflect different quality, so make sure that you're comparing similar products. Some products are particularly expensive in France and are worth importing. These include electronic and audio equipment, cameras, cosmetics, furniture, books and almost anything that's imported from outside the EU. Among the best buys in France are pottery, decorative glass, kitchenware, quality clothes (including children's), fashion accessories, toys, domestic electrical equipment, wines, liquors, luxury foods, perfumes and handicrafts.

You should beware of fake goods as some 70 per cent of all fake products are copies of French brands (perfumes are a favourite target). Even French truffles, which cost around 7,000F a kilo for the black variety, have been substituted by inferior Chinese truffles in recent years! You should also be aware that bringing counterfeited goods into France is now a criminal offence. In theory having a pirated Cartier watch or fake Louis Vuitton handbag can result in a jail sentence, although in practice it will usually just be confiscated. Having more than one item, however, carries a fine of up to one million francs and two years in prison!

Hard-hit Parisian department stores have held early sales in recent years in a bid to attract reluctant shoppers and sales and special offers are commonplace. In general, French shops are limited to just two sales (*soldes/fins de série*) a year, each for a maximum of two months' duration. Items sold in sales must show the lowest price offered during the previous month and the sale price. Note that a *liquidation totale* isn't a closing down sale, but a clearance sale. The main sales are held in the first two weeks of January and July. It's also possible to buy goods direct from factories in France, with discounts of between 30 and 70 per cent, although factory shops aren't nearly as common as in the USA. Keen bargain hunters may be interested in *The Factory Shop Guide for Northern France*, Gillian Cutress & Rolf Stricker (1 Rosebery Mews, Rosebery Road, London SW2 4DQ, UK). Other books of interest to shopaholics are Frommer's *Born to Shop France* by Suzy Gershman and *Paris Pas Cher* (Flammarion).

French shopkeepers are usually honest and won't try to rob you, although you should check your change. In some stores you don't pay the person serving you but a cashier, who may be the owner. The French don't usually make good servants and store staff are often surly and unhelpful. Rude sales staff are commonplace, particularly in department stores, where you can wait ages to be served while staff chat among themselves and ignore customers (in France the customer often comes last). French stores rarely allow customers to exchange unwanted goods or offer a money-back guarantee. If you break something in a store, you're legally liable to pay for it, although the shopkeeper may not wish to enforce the law. In Paris and other cities, or anywhere there are lots of tourists, you *must* be wary of pickpockets and bag-snatchers. *Never* tempt fate with an exposed wallet or purse, or by flashing your money around.

For those who aren't used to buying articles with metric measures and continental sizes, a list of comparative weights and measures is included in **Appendix C**.

SHOPPING HOURS

Shopping hours in France vary considerably depending on the city or town and the type of shop. Food shops cannot legally open for more than 13 hours a day and other shops are limited to 11 hours a day (there are also restrictions on the number of hours employees can work each week). Food shops in the provinces (such as bakers) open from as early as 0630 or 0700 until noon or 1230, and again from between 1500 and 1600 until 1900 or 2000. Non-food shops usually open from 0900 or 1000 to noon, and from 1400 until 1830 or 1930. Small shops tend to tailor their opening hours to suit their customers rather than their staff.

Large stores and hypermarkets remain open at lunchtime, although smaller supermarkets usually close, except perhaps on Fridays and Saturdays. Most hypermarkets are open from 0900 until 2100 or 2200 Monday to Saturday. France is generally closed on Sunday, although some village shops, particularly *boulangeries*, *charcuteries* and *pâtisseries*, open on Sunday mornings until noon. There's widespread opposition to Sunday trading from the unions and small shopkeepers, although French stores *are* permitted to open on five Sundays a year and those in designated 'tourist' areas (e.g. coastal and ski resorts) can open on any Sunday. Many shops are closed on Monday mornings or all day Mondays, particularly shops that open on Sundays. In many cities and towns, stores are open late one evening a week, e.g. Wednesdays in Paris, until between 2000 and 2200.

Most Parisian department stores open at 0930 and close at 1830 or 1900. Paris has food shops that stay open until 2200 or midnight and a few that open 24-hours. Many small Parisian boutiques close on Monday mornings and open at around 1000 or 1030 on other days until 1900 or 1930. Some shops in Paris close for the whole of August or for another month in the year. Shops and restaurants often use abbreviations to indicate the days they are open or closed, e.g. every day (*TLJ* or *tous les jours*), except Monday (*sauf lundi*), and Saturdays, Sundays and holidays (*S, D & F* or *samedis, dimanches et fêtes*). All shops close on 1st January, 1st May, 14th July and 25th December, but some are open on other public holidays.

SPECIALIST FOOD SHOPS

Buying food is a serious business in France, where the range and quality of fresh food is without parallel (nobody ever starved to death in modern France). The French have a passion for eating and shopping for food is a labour of love and not to be rushed. When she has time, the French housewife usually prefers to shop in small specialist food shops and markets, rather than in large soulless supermarkets and hypermarkets. Consequently, she spends more time shopping than her counterpart in other western countries, although less than previously. Somewhat surprisingly, despite the intense competition from supermarkets and hypermarkets, traditional small family-run shops still thrive in villages and towns throughout France, and control some 60 per cent of the general retail trade and around 50 per cent of the food trade. Although their numbers are decreasing, more as a result of the depopulation of rural areas than competition from supermarkets, they survive by offering friendly and personal service (advice, tastings, etc.) and high quality.

If you live in France, one of the best ways to integrate (ingratiate?) with the local community is to support local businesses. The quality and range of food provided by small shops varies considerably, so shop around to find those you like best and become a regular customer. In small towns and villages in rural areas there are mobile shops (*marchands ambulants*) travelling around the country selling bread, meat, fish, dairy products, fruit and vegetables. They usually visit villages on one or two days a week. Ask your neighbours what days they call and listen for their horns, which are usually loud enough to wake the dead.

The French quality designation *appellation d'origine contrôlée* (AOC or AC) applies to food as well as wines, which are protected from 'inferior' imitations both nationally and internationally. Like wine and spirits, an AC specifies not only the area of production but also the ingredients or feed, variety of breed (in the case of meat or poultry), and the methods of production and manufacture. Foods covered by an AC include cheese, butter, poultry, fruit and vegetables. In France, food is sold by the kilo or pound (*livre* which is 500g), or parts thereof, and by the piece (*pièce*).

Farmers and producers throughout France sell their produce direct to the public and you will often see signs, e.g. *produits de la ferme – vente directe*, in country areas for fruit, vegetables, wine (and other beverages), cheese, *paté de fois gras*, honey, eggs and other foods.

France has a much wider selection of specialist food shops than many other countries, including the following:

Boucherie (butcher's shop): Most villages and all towns have a butcher's shop selling all kinds of meat including pork, although generally speaking pork is the preserve of the *charcuterie* (see below). A *boucherie* doesn't sell horse meat (*cheval*), which is sold by a specialist horse butcher (*boucherie chevaline*), denoted by a sign with a horse's head (it's also sold by supermarkets and hypermarkets). Horse meat is similarly priced to beef and is eaten in most European countries including Belgium, Germany and Spain (many people believe it's the best of all meats). A butcher may also sell poultry, although this is sold exclusively by specialist poultry shops (*volailler*) in some towns. Butchers will often cook meat purchased from them at little extra cost and many also sell spit-roasted chickens and other cooked meats.

The French are voracious carnivores and are second in Europe only to the Belgians in the quantity of meat they consume. When the French kill an animal for food nothing is wasted, not even the ears and tail, not to mention its innards and private parts (one man's poison is another man's delicacy!). Every part of an animal is sold, including offal of every description, which is highly prized in France. The French are puzzled by many foreigners' aversion (squeamishness) to eating certain parts of an animal. Unless your French is particularly good, you're better off buying your meat pre-packed from a supermarket. However, if your French is up to the task, your local butcher is the best choice and is usually an excellent source of cooking tips. Butchers often open on Sundays and are closed on Mondays or Monday mornings. Supermarkets and hypermarkets have a meat counter and are open on Mondays.

Boulangerie (baker's shop): The French love their daily bread (many old country homes have a bread oven), although consumption has fallen from some 84kg per head, a year in 1965 to around 40kg today (or from 900g to around 150g a day). Thanks to a 19th century law, all towns and villages above a certain size must have a *boulangerie* or a *dépôt de pain*, which is an outlet selling bread, e.g. a café, newsagent, supermarket or petrol station. The weight and price of bread is government regulated and is uniform throughout the country. French bread *must* be freshly made (and is best when still warm) as it goes stale quickly, and therefore bakers bake twice or even three times a day (although much bread has been deep frozen at the dough stage or after being three-quarters baked). The types of bread offered by bakers often vary considerably and many bake special loaves to their own recipes. You should try a few bakers until you find one that's to your taste.

When foreigners refer to French bread they usually mean a *baguette*, although there are many other varieties. *Pain* (or *pain parisien/gros pain*) is the thickest and longest, while the narrowest and shortest is the *ficelle* (literally a 'piece of string'). Other common names are *flûte* and *bâtard*. Wholemeal bread is called *pain complet/intégral*. Village bakers don't sell a lot of different types of 'wholemeal' bread, although you can usually find *pain de campagne* (country bread, usually made with a blend of white, wholemeal and rye flour), *pain de seigle* (rye and wheat bread) and *pain au son* (with added bran). Unlike a *baguette* these can be kept for a few days. Wholemeal or mixed grain *baguettes* are available from some bakers. *Pain de mie* is a tasteless sandwich loaf used for toast. You can ask for almost any bread to be sliced for an extra franc or two, although it's impossible to slice fresh bread while it's still warm. Most bakers also bake a range of special breads made with raisins, nuts (e.g. almonds, hazelnuts or walnuts) and chocolate.

A *boulangerie* also sells delicious *croissants*, small cakes (called *brioches*) and chocolate *croissants* (called *pain au chocolat*), plus a limited range of cakes and biscuits, although for real fancy cakes you must go to a *pâtisserie* (see below). Like bread, *croissants* vary considerably in quality and taste, and it's well worth shopping around for the best. The most delicious are made with lashings of butter (*croissants au beurre*) and are distinguished by their pointed ends. *Croissants* made with margarine are cheaper and have their ends curled towards the middle. In cities and large towns, a *boulangerie* is sometimes combined with a *pâtisserie* and/or *confiserie*, although this is rare in country areas. Bakers usually close one day a week, although in a town with more than one they won't all close on the same day. When the only baker in a village closes, bread is usually available from another outlet, such as the village café. Supermarkets have been accused of selling bread at a loss to attract customers in recent years, which prompted the government to introduce large fines for offenders.

Charcuterie: A *charcuterie* is a delicatessen or pork butcher's shop. It sells mostly cooked meats, including delicious ham, bacon, roast beef, sausages, salami and black pudding, plus paté, pies, quiches, omelettes, pizzas, salads and prepared dishes. Each region has its own pork specialities, as does each *charcutier*. A *charcuterie* may also have a *rôtisserie*, where mouth-watering meat and poultry is spit-roasted to perfection. A *charcutier* may also be a caterer (*traiteur*) who can create delicious dishes for two or a banquet for 100. This is the crafty way to provide your guests with *cordon bleu* food and enjoy lavish praise, without so much as cracking an egg (an increasing number of French hostesses use caterers and modestly accept the praise for the gourmet food).

Confiserie: A *confiserie* is a high class confectioner, not to be confused with a common sweet shop. Every town has a *confiserie* where you can buy scrumptious hand-made chocolates and confectionery made with every fattening (and expensive) ingredient under the sun. They may also make excellent home-made ice-cream (*Glacier*). A *confiserie* isn't the place to buy children's mass-produced sweets, bought in bulk at the supermarket, but confectionery to win somebody's heart (or placate your mother when you have forgotten her birthday!). A *confiserie* may be part of a cake shop (*pâtisserie*).

Crémerie (dairy): A *crémerie* sells butter, cream, cheese, eggs, yoghurt, ice cream, and a variety of other foods, many having nothing to do with milk. Surprisingly, a *crémerie* doesn't usually sell fresh milk. They are usually found in rural areas where there are lots of cows, such as Normandy or the Jura. Both salted (*demi-sel*) and unsalted (*doux*) butter (*beurre*) is available, made from both pasteurised and unpasteurised milk. Low fat margarine-like spreads are available in supermarkets, although they aren't usually used as a substitute for butter.

A *crémerie* also sells dozens of different cheeses, many of which cannot be found elsewhere. When choosing Brie or Camembert (or a similar cheese), state whether you want it ripe (*fait*) or unripe (*pas fait*). France produces around 400 varieties of cheese (the actual number is disputed). Cheese made from unpasteurised milk is under threat from Brussels' eurocrats, although under the French AC system, it's actually illegal to make cheeses from pasteurised milk! Many thousands of cases of food poisoning are attributed to cheese each year, although nobody knows for sure whether the cheese is infected before, during or after it's made. Imported cheeses are rare in France and are usually found only in supermarkets, although the French have adopted some foreign cheeses as their own, including Emmental and Gruyère from Switzerland. Goat's cheese is popular in France. If a *crémerie* doesn't sell cheese, it means there's usually a cheese shop (*fromagerie*) nearby.

L'épicerie/l'alimentation générale: An *épicerie/alimentation générale* is a grocer's or general store (an *épicerie* is literally a 'spice shop'). It sells most everyday foods including butter, cheese, coffee, fruit, vegetables, wine and beer, plus a range of preserved and pre-packaged foods. Many general stores are now self-service (*libre-service*). With the exception of market stalls, there are few specialist greengrocers or fruit and vegetable shops in France. In Paris and other cities, many grocers stay open late in the evening, e.g. 2200. Ethnic food shops abound in Paris and other cities including shops selling American, Arabic, British (e.g. Marks & Spencer, which is increasingly popular with the French), Chinese, Greek, Hebrew, Indian, Italian and Japanese specialities.

Pâtisserie: A *pâtisserie* is a cake shop selling wonderful (but expensive) home-made pastries, fruit tarts and chocolate éclairs too beautiful for consumption, and perhaps home-made ice-cream. It's possible to buy just one or two pieces of a fruit tart or flan. Every town and region tends to have its own specialities. Like a *confiserie*, which may be part of a *pâtisserie*, it isn't a safe place for dieters or anyone with a sweet tooth. They will make cakes to order for special occasions and ice a name or greeting, usually in unintelligible English. All creations are beautifully wrapped, even when buying a single small tart.

Poissonnerie (fishmonger's): *Poissonneries* are rare in inland France compared with other food shops, although fish stalls are common in indoor markets. France has unrivalled seafood (*fruits de mer*) and in Europe only the Portuguese eat more fish. Fish isn't, however, an inexpensive alternative to meat, although it's reasonably priced in fishing ports. Most foreigners find it difficult to identify the myriad types of fish sold in France (French fishermen don't throw *anything* back, except foreign fishermen), which vary from region to region. The most common species include sole, turbot, eel, trout, salmon, bass, whitefish, sole, pollack, tuna, whiting, monkfish, John Dory, turbot, sardine, anchovy, mackerel, mullet, octopus, squid and cuttlefish. Fish are cleaned, scaled and 'topped and tailed' free on request.

Common shellfish include lobster, crawfish, crab, oysters, scallops, clams, mussels, cockles, shrimps and prawns. Crabs and shrimps are often pre-cooked. In France, oysters (*huître*) aren't just for millionaires and cost as little as 15F to 20F a dozen in fishing ports, depending on the size and variety, and up to twice as much in markets and supermarkets. The prejudice against eating oysters in the summer (months without an 'r') is a throwback to the time when they couldn't be kept fresh and is irrelevant today (although they breed in summer which often makes them cloudy and may affect their flavour).

MARKETS

Markets are a common and welcoming sight in towns and villages throughout France, and are an essential part of French rural life, largely unaffected by competition from supermarkets and hypermarkets. They are colourful, entertaining and an experience not to be missed, even if you don't plan to buy anything. The *raison d'être* of the French market is its fresh meat, fruit, vegetables, fish, cheese, bread and other foods, although it's generally more expensive than supermarkets. In many markets a wide range of live 'food' is also available including snails, lobsters, crabs, ducks, chickens, guinea fowl, pigeons and rabbits. A variety of other goods are commonly peddled in markets including flowers, plants, clothes and shoes, ironmongery, crockery and hardware. Specialist markets (particularly in Paris) include antiques, books, clothes, stamps/postcards, flowers, birds and pets. There are generally three kinds of markets in France: indoor markets, permanent street markets and travelling open-air street markets that move from neighbourhood to neighbourhood on different days of the week or month. Many small towns hold a market or fair once a month, usually on the same date each month.

When buying fruit and vegetables, whether from a market or a supermarket, it's best to buy what's local and in season. Few fruit and vegetables are imported, and when available imported produce is usually expensive. Most country food markets have a selection of stalls run by organic farmers. All produce is clearly marked with its price per piece or per kilogramme. When shopping for food in markets, most vendors object to customers handling the fruit and vegetables, although you needn't be shy about asking to taste a piece of cheese or fruit (markets are the best place to taste the flavour of the real France). It's wise to take a bag when buying fruit and vegetables, as paper bags aren't always provided, although carrier bags may be sold. The best buys are often found when stallholders are preparing to close for the day, particularly on Saturdays and Sundays.

Antique and flea markets (*Marché aux Puces*) are common in France, the largest being held at Saint-Ouen in Paris, with 7km of shops selling secondhand goods, antiques and curios (*brocante*). It's open every Saturday, Sunday and Monday from 0730 until 1900. Paris also has a number of smaller flea markets. Don't expect to find many (or any) bargains in Paris, where anything worth buying is snapped up by dealers. However, in provincial flea markets you can turn up some real bargains, particularly fine china (e.g. Limoges) and bric-a-brac.

To find out when local markets are held, ask at your local tourist office or town hall. The most popular days for markets are Wednesdays and Saturdays, although they can be found somewhere every day of the week except Mondays. In the provinces, markets are often held in the mornings only, from around 0600 until noon or 1300 (shrewd shoppers get there before 0900). You need to get up with the birds to shop at some wholesale markets (e.g. in Paris), open from around 0400 to 0800. Every district (*arrondissement*) in Paris has at least two or three weekly street markets, some of which close for lunch, e.g. from 1300 to 1600, and continue until 1900 or 2000. There are Sunday morning markets in many towns. Market days may be listed on a sign when entering a town.

DEPARTMENT & CHAIN STORES

France invented the department store (*grand magasin*) and it has many excellent stores, although they have suffered falling sales in recent years and a number have failed. Among the most famous department stores are *Au Bon Marché* (the first department store in France, founded in 1852), *Au Printemps* (best for perfumes), *Galeries Lafayette* (famous for high fashion) and *La Samaritaine*, the largest department store in Paris. Fashion is the forte of most Parisian department stores, many of which stage regular fashion shows. Most also specialise in cosmetics and provide money changing services, export discounts, a travel agency, and theatre and concert ticket sales. Some department stores such as *Au Printemps* give visitors a 10 per cent discount on all purchases. Many department stores also have a food (*alimentation*) department.

If you're making a number of purchases from different departments, you can often obtain a *carnet d'achats* and pay for everything at the same time. Most department stores deliver goods within a certain radius and also send goods overseas (for a fee). Department stores don't close for lunch and are usually open from 0930 to 1830 or 1900 Monday to Saturday, with late-night shopping one day a week until 2100 or 2200.

Chain stores are relatively rare in France compared with most other European countries, although there are exceptions such as the shoes stores Bally and Eram, FNAC (audio, books and video) and Darty (household appliances). Department stores such as *Au Printemps, Au Bon Marché, Trois Quartiers, La Samaritaine* and *Nouvelles Galeries* are also chain stores. Department chain stores such as *Monoprix* and *Prisunic* (subsidiaries of *Galeries Lafayette* and *Au Printemps* respectively) and *Uniprix* are budget stores (*magasins populaires*) with outlets throughout France.

There are also a number of foreign chain stores operating in France including the Body Shop, C & A, Habitat, Gap, Jaeger, Ikea, Marks & Spencer, WH Smith, Bretanos, Esprit, Zara, Virgin Megastore and Toys 'R' Us.

SUPERMARKETS & HYPERMARKETS

There are supermarkets (*supermarchés*) and hypermarkets (*hypermarchés*) in (or just outside) most towns in France. A hypermarket is officially defined as a supermarket with over 2,500m² (27,000ft²) of floor space. Hypermarkets are often located in a shopping or commercial centre (*centre commercial*) with many smaller shops, cafés and restaurants (often including a self-serve restaurant), toilets, telephone booths, a huge free car park, and a petrol station (the cheapest source). Many supermarkets have instant photo booths.

Hypermarkets are similar to department stores and sell everything you would expect to find in a supermarket plus books, CDs and cassettes, TVs and stereo equipment, cameras, furniture, textiles, household goods, gardening equipment and furniture, domestic electrical equipment, do-it-yourself, white goods (refrigerators, freezers, washing machines), sports equipment, jewellery, bicycles, tools, kitchenware, clothes and shoes, toys, and magazines and newspapers (including foreign newspapers). France even has funeral supermarkets (Roc'Eclerc), where you can choose your coffin and headstone at your leisure (what a pleasant thought!).

The first hypermarket was opened by Carrefour in 1963 and there are now over 600 throughout France, accounting for some 50 per cent of food sales. Among the leading supermarket and hypermarket chains are Auchan, Carrefour, Casino, Champion, Continent, Euromarché, Intermarché, Leclerc, Mammouth, Montlaur, Prisunic, Rallye and Super U/Hyper U. All supermarket and hypermarket chains publish regular brochures and leaflets. Leclerc are famous for their low prices and their battles to abolish price monopolies on a range of products including wine, petrol, cars and coffins. They also campaigned long and hard to sell pharmaceutical products, books and jewellery in their stores.

The cost of food in France is about average for Western Europe and a couple with two children can expect to spend around 700F per week on food (including a modest amount of inexpensive alcohol). Most supermarkets and hypermarkets have food counters for meat, fish, bread and cheese. The French generally don't like to buy pre-packaged meat, fish, fruit or vegetables and prefer to buy them to order. Supermarkets sell excellent fresh fruit and vegetables, the best and cheapest usually being local produce (French farmers do their utmost to ensure that inexpensive foreign produce never reaches the stores). Some supermarkets have a salad bar. Fruit and vegetables may be weighed by an assistant or you weigh them yourself on scales with buttons depicting the various produce. They *aren't* weighed at checkouts.

There's a huge choice of tinned vegetables (and tinned meats) in French supermarkets, most superior to foreign varieties, but few frozen vegetables. While the French have excellent fresh food, they generally have a poor choice of frozen and convenience foods and microwave meals are rare. Although the production of frozen foods in France has increased fivefold in the last decade, there's still a poor choice compared with American and British supermarkets (which to the French, simply confirms what poor taste they have!). Frozen and convenience foods are expensive, although the French are consuming more fast foods than ever (to the detriment of traditional foodstuffs) and buy around four times more diet foods than previously.

French supermarkets sell few foreign foods with the exception of biscuits, confectionery, preserves, Chinese foods, delicatessen foods (e.g. *charcuterie*) and perhaps a few cheeses.

Coffee is cheaper and better in France than most countries. Arabica is reckoned to be among the best for a mild full flavour, while Robusta is cheaper and makes a good strong cup. Decaffeinated coffee (*café décaféiné*) is widely available. Don't even *think* about buying 'French' tea bags, which are expensive and taste dreadful, no matter how familiar-sounding the brand. Most supermarkets sell fresh milk (often sold in plastic sacs), although most French people buy UHT long-life milk (which initially tastes awful in tea but most British people get used to it). It usually comes in skimmed (*écrémé*) and semi-skimmed (*demi-écrémé*) versions and is sold in one litre cartons. Note that 'fresh' milk may be days old when purchased and consequently goes sour quickly (the French don't drink milk and sensibly prefer wine). It's common to find food in supermarkets that has exceeded its 'sell-by' date (*date limite de vente*), so don't forget to check. The use of bar-codes isn't universal and items may be individually marked with their price.

Checkout staff routinely ask you to open your bags to see whether you have pinched half a dozen frogs' legs or snails and usually have a counter, called a *consigne*, where you can leave bags and goods purchased elsewhere. You can usually pay with a debit card such as a *carte bleue*, where you enter your personal ID number on a numeric pad. You can also pay with credit cards such as Mastercard and Visa, although authorisation can take ages. You should provide your own bags, as apart from flimsy plastic bags (*poches/sacs*), supermarkets don't provide free bags, although they can usually be purchased for a few francs. Checkout staff don't bag your purchases and take them out to your car for you. Note that it's essential to have a 10F coin to use a trolley. You insert the coin in a slot to release the trolley and when you have finished with it return it to the trolley park, lock it into another trolley and your 10F coin is returned.

Hypermarkets are generally open all day from 0800 until 2100 or 2200 from Mondays to Saturdays and don't close for lunch. Supermarkets generally open at 0800 or 0900 and close earlier than hypermarkets, e.g. 1900 or 1930, or perhaps later on Fridays. Some supermarkets close for lunch, e.g. 1230 to 1500, although not usually on Saturdays.

ALCOHOL

Drinking is an integral part of everyday life in France, where most people have a daily tipple. Whatever your poison, you should find something to your taste among the numerous wines, beers, spirits and liqueurs produced in France. France is of course most famous for its wines and one of the essential features of a civilised home is a large cellar (*cave*). The laws governing the production of wine in France are the strictest in the world (although abuses are becoming increasingly common) and French wine is classified under four categories, officially recognised and enforced by the French government and EU wine legislation.

Vin de table: *Vin de table* is the lowest wine classification in France. It's produced from any number of different varieties of grapes, and may also be a blend of wines from different regions and even different countries. However, the designation *vin de table* isn't necessarily an indication of inferior quality and some *vin de table* wines are better quality than AC wines. Producers of VDQS and AC wines (see below) may be limited in the amount they can sell under that classification and the rest becomes *vin de table* or *vin de pays*. Although widely referred to as *vin ordinaire*, this isn't an official classification but a generic term used to refer to inexpensive table wine.

Vin de pays: *Vin de pays* (literally 'country wine') is produced from specified types of grapes and grown in a particular area (indicated on the label) and isn't a blend. It was instituted in 1973 and formerly meant *vin ordinaire*, along with *vin de table*, although it now represents the top end of the everyday table wine market. As with *vin de table* wines, quality varies considerably. Both *vin de pays* and VDQS wines (see below) must undergo official annual independent tastings to be awarded or retain their classifications. They are often sold in returnable litre bottles on which there's a deposit (*consigne*), possibly denoted by stars embossed near the shoulder. Some *vins de table* and *vins de pays* are sold in bottles with plastic stoppers, which isn't usually a sign of good quality.

Vin Délimité de Qualité Supérieure (VDQS): Introduced in 1945, a VDQS classification serves as a proving ground for quality wines before being awarded full AC status (see below). The classification is now rare as an increasing number of quality wines attain AC status. Like wines classified as AC, VDQS wines must satisfy rules governing the method of growth and production. Producers are restricted in the amount of wine that they can produce under a VDQS label.

Vin à Appellation d'Origine Contrôlée (AOC or AC): AC wines comprise some 40 per cent of total output and are subject to stringent regulations established by the *Institut National des Appellations d'Origine des Vins et Eaux-de-Vie (INAO)*. They are produced in a strictly-defined area under exacting regulations including the types of grape used, the quantity of vines planted per hectare, vine pruning methods, the quantity of wine produced per hectare, and the minimum alcohol content of the wine. All fine wines have an AC classification. Note, however, that it isn't a guarantee of quality and a good *vin de pays* is often better than a second-rate AC wine. In areas such as Bordeaux and Burgundy, where there's a concentration of top producers, wines from top-ranking vineyards are further categorised into growths (*crus classés*) such as *grand cru* and *premier cru*, denoting the highest quality and most expensive wines.

Note that in recent years many AC wines (usually at the cheaper end of the market) have been found to contain wine from outside the certified regions printed on their labels and many are also spiked with sugar. An AC designation is unfortunately no assurance of quality and your best guarantee is the reputation and integrity of the producer.

Champagne: Champagne is produced in the area of the same name centred around the towns of Reims and Epernay. It's the favourite tipple of the *bourgeoisie*, although this often has more to do with its snob appeal than taste. Champagne costs around 50F a bottle from an 'anonymous' producer or from around 100F from a top house. You pay a premium for the famous names (*grandes marques*) and champagne from smaller producers (*petits champagnes*) is usually excellent and better value. Prices fell dramatically in the early '90s due to falling sales and a supermarket price war, although they have now recovered. Many other sparkling wines are made by the champagne method (*méthode champenoise*) and sold in champagne bottles, including Vouvray (from Saumur) and Blanquette de Limoux (Roussillon), both excellent and costing around half the price of inexpensive champagne.

Production Areas: Nearly every region of France produces wine, from the simplest *vin de table* to the finest vintage wines. The best French wines come from Alsace, Bordeaux, Burgundy, and the Loire and Rhône valleys. The vast majority of everyday table wines (*vin de table* or *vin ordinaire*) are grown in the Languedoc-Roussillon region, the biggest wine-producing area in the world. However, this area has been transformed in the last decade or so and wines such as *Corbières, Faugères, Fitou, Coteaux du Languedoc, Minervois* and *Côtes du Roussillon* are much improved and excellent value for money. There are also good wines from smaller areas such as Bergerac, Corsica, Jura, Provence (mostly rosé) and Savoie. Early or new (*primeur* or *nouveau*) 'first pressing' wines are produced in most areas and include the famous Beaujolais *nouveau* (more correctly termed Beaujolais *primeur*). If you know little about French wine, it's generally best to stick to wines from the best-known areas such as Bordeaux, Burgundy, Languedoc-Roussillon and the Rhône valley for red wines, and Alsace, Bordeaux, Burgundy and the Loire for white wines. Some people insist that wines with the prettiest labels are best, such as Château Mouton Rothschild!

Wine Merchants: There are few specialist wine merchants (*marchand de vins/caviste/négociant*) in France, although there's usually at least one in most large towns. There are, however, a few chains of wine shops (such as Nicolas), where prices are fixed throughout the chain, and independent wine shops and local chains in Paris, such as Le Repaire de Bacchus. Most wine shops will deliver if you buy more than a few bottles. A good *épicerie* or *charcuterie* usually also sells fine wines and they aren't usually any more expensive than supermarkets.

Supermarkets: Most people buy their wine from supermarkets and hypermarkets, although the quality and range of wines on offer isn't usually outstanding. Some supermarkets and hypermarkets have a poor choice and stock few inexpensive or vintage wines. Different branches of the same supermarket or hypermarket often stock completely different wines, even when located in the same region. Among the best for wine are Auchan and Leclerc (Intermarché also stock a good selection). Some supermarkets sell good wines under their own label and most have special offers. However, you should avoid buying expensive *châteaux* wines from a supermarket, as they are generally badly stored (e.g. upright and at the wrong temperature).

Nowhere are the French more parochial and nationalistic than when it comes to selling wine. Most supermarkets and hypermarkets stock a wide selection of local wines, but may stock little from other regions of France apart from the most expensive fine wines. Foreign wines are rare and expensive in France and you're likely to find few (if any) in your local supermarket. Note that although French wines generally offer unbeatable value for money, vintage wines can cost more in France than in some other countries (e.g. Britain). You should be selective when buying wine, particularly when buying in hypermarkets in or near Channel ports, where some supermarkets off-load mediocre wine at not so mediocre prices onto unsuspecting British shoppers.

Buying Direct: Buying direct is the best way to buy wine in France, where many wine lovers buy the bulk of their wine direct from growers, either by making an annual visit to vineyards or by mail order. Vineyards selling wine direct usually have signs inviting you to free tastings (*dégustation gratuite* or *dégustation et vente*), with the hope of selling you a few bottles or cases. Most vineyards and distillers are geared to receive visitors, particularly the great champagne and cognac houses, who often make a small charge for a conducted tour and tastings. When free tastings are offered, you can leave without buying if you don't like anything, although it sometimes takes a lot of courage and determination (there's an unwritten rule that you buy something). Some producers operate a better system, whereby you pay a nominal tasting fee that's returned if you buy six bottles or more. Some producers sell only half-dozens or dozens. Bottles of wine purchased from a grower may be no cheaper than from a supermarket, although you have the advantage of tasting it and an assurance of quality.

If you're serious about buying wine for your cellar, you should go to a recommended producer rather than take pot luck. One way is to consult *Le Guide Hachette des Vins*, an authoritative 950-page annual wine directory that lists producers in all regions with their addresses, telephone numbers and opening hours. Most importantly, it also lists the wines for sale and provides a quality rating. Another way is to obtain recommendations from local experts such as wine waiters or the regional *maison du vin*. One of the delights of living in France for wine lovers is being able to visit a vineyard on a sunny day and celebrate *la culture du vignoble*. Note that appointments must be made to visit some *châteaux* and most are closed during lunch times. The quality of wines you're invited to taste often depends on your ability to make the right comments (and whether you appear to be rich!). Wine tasting has its own unique vocabulary and if you aren't an expert it's best to stick to *bon, très bon* and perhaps *très très bon* if you're really impressed.

Buying in Bulk: Those who are in the know often buy their wine in bulk (*en vrac*) direct from producers such as wine co-operatives (*caves coopératives*) and wine-growing unions (*unions des viticulteurs*). If you buy in bulk you may pay as little as 5F per litre for a good *vin de pays*, costing around 10F in a labelled bottle in a supermarket. Note, however, that AC wines are rarely sold in bulk. When buying in bulk, you'll usually need some large white plastic jerricans (for wine, not petrol!) with a spout, available from *drogueries* (hardware stores) and supermarkets. The best size are five or ten-litres (keen bulk buyers never go anywhere without a few empty cans in the boot of their car). You can also buy a collapsible plastic cube (*cubitainer*) with a tap (like a wine box) holding 10 to 20 litres. Wine bought in bulk should be bottled or drunk within a few months, or immediately if you extract some from the container. You'll need a good supply of bottles, corks, a corking machine, labels and storage racks (corks and labels are provided free by some co-operatives). Wine can also be stored in demijohns that hold around six bottles. Some co-operatives sell wine in large 5 or even 12-litre bottles (just the right size for a quiet drink with 'a few' friends).

When buying in bulk, the grower must fill in a VAT form (*acquit*), obtainable from local tax offices. This form states the type of wine, the quantity, the date it left the producer, the registration number of the vehicle, its destination and even its planned arrival date. It must accompany all shipments of wine no matter how small, although it's intended to stop growers from increasing their output of Château Superior by adding some cheap plonk. In a country less bedevilled by bureaucracy the small buyer would be exempt (but rules are rules). Keen bulk buyers may be interested in *Buying French Wine from the Château and Vineyard* by Hilary Wright (Mandarin).

Education: As even teetotallers are no doubt aware, there's more to wine than its colour, which may be red, white, pink or even yellow (*vin jaune* from the Jura). It's a well known fact that the more you know about wine, the more you will enjoy it.

There are numerous excellent books about wine including Hugh Johnson's *Pocket Wine Book, World Atlas of Wine* and *The Story of Wine* (all published by Mitchell Beazley). Other good books include *Oz Clarke's Wine Guide* (Webster's), The Sunday Telegraph *Good Wine Guide* (Pan), the *Which? Wine Guide* (Hodder & Stoughton) and for those who don't know when they've had enough, *Floyd on Hangovers* (Michael Joseph). A number of holiday companies offer tours of the major wine growing areas for both oenophiles and novices wishing to learn something about wine (you may even learn something of the 'secret language' used by experts when describing wine). Finally, one thing every red wine drinker should know is that if you spill red wine on your carpet or clothes, the best way to *guarantee* that it won't leave a stain is to immediately soak it liberally in white wine. So even if you rarely drink white wine, keep a bottle (cheap plonk will do) handy for those little emergencies. White wine doesn't usually stain.

It's Official! Drinking red wine is medically recognised as an aid to reducing heart and other diseases, a fact that has been confirmed by a number of studies in recent years. Those who need convincing may like to read *Your Good Health: The Medicinal Benefits of Wine Drinking* by Dr. E. Maury (Souvenir Press). However, drinking excessive amounts of red wine (or any alcohol) can destroy your brain and cause liver failure! As French producers sometimes warn buyers: *l'abus d'alcool est dangereux pour la santé, consommez avec modération* (alcohol abuse is dangerous for your health, consume in moderation). Despite the popular view of the French as great drinkers, their alcohol consumption per head is relatively low (and wine consumption has reduced by a third in the last 25 years) and there's a growing anti-alcohol lobby.

Beer: French beer is usually of the export lager variety and mainly comes from France's two main beer-producing regions, the northeast (Alsace and Lorraine) and the northwest (Picardy, Artois and Flanders). Among the most popular French brands are Fischer/Pêcheur, Kanterbräu, Kronenbourg, Météor, Millbrau, Mützig, Pelforth, Slavia, '33' Export and Valstar. Many excellent and strong beers (e.g. top-fermented *bières de garde*) are brewed by small farmhouse breweries. Beer is usually sold in packs of 6 to 24 small 25cl bottles and is much cheaper than in most other countries, an average pack of 24 x 25cl bottles costing around 25F in a supermarket, or just one franc per bottle. Supermarkets have frequent special offers on beer and some brands can be bought in returnable one litre bottles, which works out even cheaper than small bottles. Bottles can be returned to any store. Supermarkets usually have a special store (*bouteilles consignées/verres consignés*) where you return your empties, although in small shops you simply hand in the empty bottle when buying a new one. In a supermarket you receive cash or a credit to be used at the checkout. Note that beer prices in village shops are up to 50 per cent higher than in supermarkets.

Other Drinks: Among the many other popular alcoholic drinks in France are cider (brewed in Brittany and Normandy), pastis, Dubonnet, cognac, armagnac, calvados and a wide variety of liqueurs such as Bénédictine, Chartreuse, Cointreau and Grand Marnier. Alcohol flavored with fruit and other things is common throughout France and every region has its own variations such as crème de cassis, crème de menthe and crème de cacao. Aniseed liqueurs such as Berger, Pernod and Ricard are brewed in the south. France even produces its own gin and whisky, although they are usually terrible (and conspicuous by their silly names). Spirits are cheaper in France than in many other European countries, although more expensive than in Italy and Spain. Imported gin and scotch whisky (unknown brands) are available in France for around 40F to 50F a bottle.

TOBACCONISTS

Tobacconists (*tabac*), indicated by a stylised cigar sign, are a unique institution in France. Not only are they the sole authorised vendors of cigarettes and other tobacco products, but they are also mini-stationers and the source of official government forms. A *tabac* also sells postage stamps at face value, postcards, single envelopes and writing paper, gifts and souvenirs, cigarette lighters, photographic film, and other odds and ends. It also sells lottery tickets and may be an agent for PMU off-track betting (see page 332) and is usually combined with a bar, café or newsagent's.

A *tabac* is the official outlet for road tax *vignettes* (see page 204) and fiscal stamps (*timbre fiscal*) used to pay fines (e.g. parking tickets), government taxes and official fees such as those required for a residence permit (*carte de séjour*). Note that few *tabacs* stock the whole range of fiscal stamps and you may need to try a few to get the one you need. A few Parisian *tabacs* are open 24-hours.

FASHION

Fashion (or style) is a huge business in France, where women have a seemingly effortless chic and the ability to look as if they have just stepped out of a fashion magazine on any budget (a true *Parisienne* won't even venture to the corner shop without 'The Look'). Whether students, housewives or models, French women have a formidable sense of style and are the best dressed in the world (the men aren't far behind). Paradoxically, the French actually spend a smaller proportion of their income on clothes than many other Europeans. The fashion industry is France's second largest employer, accounting for some 375,000 jobs and worth around 170F billion a year. Children's fashion is also big business and there are fashion shops in the major cities devoted exclusively to children. Clothes outlets in France include couture houses, elegant boutiques, department stores and street bazaars.

The flagship of the French fashion industry is *haute couture*; made-to-order clothes employing the best designers, craftsmanship and materials. The fortunes of *haute couture* (unkind critics call it 'fancy dress') fashion houses have made a strong recovery in recent years after a lean spell in the early '90s, despite being outrageously expensive (garments cost from 20,000 to 50,000F or more), elitist and an anachronism in today's world. The worldwide clientele for *haute couture* clothing is estimated to number no more than a few thousand people, with just a few hundred regular customers. Many designs are spectacles created solely for the catwalk, although they would cause a sensation at the office party! The real business of the top fashion houses is perfumes and cosmetics, which represent an estimated 80 per cent of turnover and keeps them afloat. Some designers also 'lend' their names to a variety of other (often 'tacky') products.

Clothes tend to be expensive in France, mainly due to the lack of inexpensive imported clothes available in most other countries. When buying clothes, the French generally prefer quality rather than quantity. Although expensive, the best French 'classic' clothes are made to last and never go out of fashion. However, half the clothes bought by the French are mediocre in design and quality. One of the best value-for-money ready-to-wear labels is Tati, who have their flagship store at boulevard Rochechouart in Paris and branches in a number of other cities. French women spend a huge sum on accessories (e.g. Fogal, Hermès and Prada) and they are also the largest buyers of shoes in Europe, buying an average of over five pairs a year. Top shoe shops include Bally, Charles Jourdan, and for the seriously rich, Stephane Kélian. As with quality clothes, good shoes are expensive (and difficult to find in wide fittings).

However, bargains can be found in the cities if you're willing to hunt around or wait for the sales. Last season's designer labels are usually sold at a 50 per cent reduction. Most Parisian boutiques hold sales in January and at the end of June, and bargains can be found year round in Alésia, the major discount shopping district in the 14th *arrondissement*. The *Forum des Halles* in Paris is a giant subterranean shopping centre where you can find every kind of clothing at bargain prices (finding your way out is something else). Popular women's ready-to-wear shops include Benetton, Cacharel, Caroll, Franck et Fils and Infinitif. Top men's shops include Cacharel, 100,000 Chemises, Kenzo, Charles Le Golf, New Man, Alain Figaret and Cerrutti 1881. Many fashionable (and wealthy) Frenchmen have a penchant for classic British clothes from Aquascutum, Burberry, Jaeger and Pringle. Among the young, American clothes are all the rage, particularly jeans, sweatshirts and trainers.

There are also many thriving 'vintage' (secondhand) or *bis bis* (gently used) clothes shops in Paris such as the *magasin du troc*, which sells slightly used couture clothes and accessories, perhaps worn only by models. Here you can pick up a Chanel suit for as little as a third of the new price and a bit of judicious haggling can knock the price down even further. Vintage clothing stores for both men and women are becoming increasingly popular among chic Parisians. If you're anti-fashion, you will also feel at home in Paris, where the young have taken to grunge (*le look cradingue/le grunge*). Costume hire and formal wear rental is possible from many shops in Paris and other cities. There are many excellent women's fashion magazines in France including *Modes et Travaux*, *Dépêche Mode Professional* and *Vogue*.

NEWSPAPERS, MAGAZINES & BOOKS

There are over 200 daily, weekly and monthly newspapers and magazines in France, not including trade magazines and reviews. However, there are no national daily newspapers, which are usually published for a region such as *Sud-Ouest* and *Ouest-France*. Consequently circulation figures are low in comparison with newspapers in countries with national newspapers. *Ouest-France*, published in Rennes, is the biggest-selling daily paper, with almost double the sales (800,000) of any Parisian newspaper. The French aren't great newspaper readers and only one household in four buys a newspaper. French newspapers aren't good value for money and are more expensive and smaller than many foreign newspapers. Like most things in France, newspapers receive a multi-billion franc annual subsidy from the government in the form of tax breaks, reduced distribution costs via the state-owned postal service, subsidised newsprint and direct payments.

The two best-known newspapers are *Le Monde* (independent, liberal/centrist), published in Paris in the afternoon and given the following day's date (which can be confusing!) and *Le Figaro* (moderate right, conservative). *Le Monde* is the most intellectual and respected of all French newspapers as well as the best-selling. It's also the most drab and carries few photographs and advertisements, shuns colour, and is printed in a style that went out of fashion in the 19th century. *Le Parisian* is the local Parisian daily newspaper with regional editions renamed *Aujourd'Hui* in 1995. *France-Soir* is a scandal sheet more concerned with accounts of murder, rape and pillage, than 'serious' news.

Other popular newspapers include *l'Humanité*, the recently revamped, official organ of the foundering French Communist Party, *Libération* (known colloquially as *Libé*), an intellectual and one-time fashionable tabloid of the centre-left, and *L'Équipe*, a daily newspaper devoted entirely to sport. *La Croix* is a Catholic newspaper. There are also a number of economic newspapers including *les Echos* and *La Tribune* (France's *Financial Times* or *Wall Street Journal*). Surprisingly, Sunday newspapers are almost unknown apart from the undistinguished *Le Journal du Dimanche* and *L'Humanité Dimanche*. Distribution of Paris newspapers is mainly confined to Paris and the Ile-de-France region. Many newspapers provide excellent weekly magazines and reviews, and free local weekly newspapers are delivered to homes in many areas.

Where the French really excel is in the field of magazines and they produce a larger number than any other European country. Popular weekly current affairs magazines include the best-selling *Paris Match, Le Nouvel Observateur* (left), *L'Express* (right of centre), *Le Point* (middle-of-the-road) and *Marianne* (left, tabloid-like). Other popular magazines include *Figaro Magazine, Jours de France* and *Le Canard Enchaîné* (satire). France has strict laws regarding personal privacy, although this hasn't prevented the publication of a number of new scandal sheets in recent years including *Minute* and *Voici*. Free English-language magazines include *Paris Free Voice, France-USA Contacts* and the *Paris City Magazine*, distributed through bookshops, expatriate organisations and clubs in Paris.

Newspapers and magazines are sold at tobacconists (*tabac*), newsagents (e.g. *Maison de la Presse*), railway station kiosks, and in supermarkets and hypermarkets. Major foreign European newspapers are available on the day of issue in Paris and a day or two later in the provinces. Some English-language daily newspapers are widely available on the day of publication including *USA Today, International Herald Tribune* (edited in Paris), *Wall Street Journal Europe*, the *Guardian* and the *European Financial Times*, printed in Frankfurt. Many English and foreign newspapers produce weekly editions including the British *International Express*, the *Guardian Weekly*, and the *Weekly Telegraph*, some of which publish French editions. The price of foreign newspapers sold in France is stated in the newspaper, usually on the front or back page.

France also has a number of British expatriate English-language monthly newspapers and magazines including *Boulevard, Riviera Reporter, Blue Coast, The News* and *The Recorder*. Most are available in many *Maison de la Presse* and major supermarket chains and available on subscription (see **Appendix B** for addresses). Note that many French and foreign newspapers can be purchased on subscription, usually at a large saving over local retail prices.

Imported English-language books are expensive in France (except for this one, which is an absolute bargain!), usually costing around double their 'recommended' home country price. Americans in particular will be appalled. There are no discount bookshops (*librairies*) in France. It used to be cheaper to buy best-selling books, such as Michelin guides, from hypermarkets. However, the French government introduced fixed prices to protect small bookshops from going out of business, thus restricting the availability of most books. In small towns there are usually a few small shops selling a limited selection of books, rather than one well-stocked large bookshop. Most French bookshops don't stock English-language books.

There are, however, English-language bookshops in most large towns and cities in France. English-language bookshops in Paris include the Abbey Bookshop, Librairie Albion, Attica, Bretanos, Galignani, Nouveau Quartier Latin, Shakespeare & Co, WH Smith & Son, Tea and Tattered Pages, and the Village Voice. There are also other foreign-language bookshops in Paris and other cities including African, Arabic, German, Indian, Italian, Japanese, Polish and Portuguese. Secondhand and rare bookshops and markets are common in Paris, notably the *bouquinistes* stalls along the left bank of the river Seine. Many expatriate organisations and clubs run their own libraries or book exchanges and some French public libraries keep a small selection of English-language books (see **Libraries** on page 342).

FURNITURE & FURNISHINGS

Furniture (*meubles*) is generally quite expensive in France compared with many other European countries. Generally the choice is between inexpensive budget furniture and high quality expensive furniture, with little in between. Exclusive modern and traditional furniture is available everywhere, although not everyone can afford the exclusive prices, including bizarre pieces from designers such as Gaultier for those with money to burn. Many regions of France have a reputation for quality handmade furniture. If you're looking for antique furniture at affordable prices, the best bargains are to be found at antique and flea markets in rural areas. However, you must drive a hard bargain as the asking prices are often a joke. You can often buy good secondhand and antique furniture at bargain prices from a *depôt-vente*, where people sell their old furniture and courts sell repossessed household goods. Look under *Dépôts-vente ameublement et divers* in your local Yellow Pages.

Modern furniture is popular in France and is often sold in huge stores in commercial centres. Inexpensive chain stores include But, Conforama and Fly. Furniture can also be purchased from large hypermarkets, some of which provide the free loan of a van. Pine furniture is inexpensive and popular. Beware of buying complicated home-assembled furniture with indecipherable French instructions and too few screws. If you want reasonably priced, good quality, modern furniture, you need look no farther than Ikea, a Swedish company manufacturing furniture for home assembly with a 14-day money-back guarantee (note that the price of Ikea furniture varies depending on the country and most items are much cheaper in France than, for example, in Britain).

The kind of furniture you buy may depend on a number of factors including the style and size of your home, whether it's a permanent or holiday home, your budget, the local climate, and not least, your personal taste. If you intend to furnish a holiday home with antiques or expensive modern furniture, bear in mind that you will need adequate security and insurance. If you intend to move permanently to France in a number of years and already have a house full of good furniture abroad, there's little point in buying expensive furniture in France. It may pay you to compare the cost of buying furniture abroad with that in France. If you're buying a large quantity of furniture, don't be reluctant to ask for a reduction as many stores will give you a discount.

HOUSEHOLD GOODS

Household goods in France are generally of good quality with a large choice, which although not as wide as in some other European countries, has improved considerably in the last decade. Prices are also more competitive than previously, with bargains to be found at supermarkets and hypermarkets such as Carrefour, Mammouth and Rallye. Apart from hypermarkets, one of the best stores for household appliances is Darty, which has outlets in most towns. No-interest credit or deferred payment is common and goods can usually be paid for in ten monthly instalments. Not surprisingly for a nation that spends much of its time in the kitchen (the rest is spent eating!), French kitchenware is excellent and among the best in the world.

Bear in mind when importing household appliances that aren't sold in France, that it may be difficult or impossible to get them repaired or serviced locally. If you bring appliances with you, don't forget to bring a supply of spares and refills such as bulbs for a refrigerator or sewing machine, and spare bags for a vacuum cleaner. Note that the standard size of kitchen appliances and cupboard units in France *isn't* the same as in other countries, and it may be difficult to fit an imported dishwasher or washing machine into a French kitchen. Check the size *and* the latest French safety regulations before shipping these items to France or buying them abroad, as they may need expensive modifications.

If you already own small household appliances, it's worthwhile bringing them to France as usually all that's required is a change of plug. However, if you're coming from a country with a 110/115V electricity supply, such as the USA, you'll need a lot of expensive transformers and it's better to buy new appliances in France. Small appliances such as vacuum cleaners, grills, toasters and electric irons aren't expensive in France and are of good quality. Don't bring your TV without checking its compatibility first, as TVs from many countries won't work in France (see page 130)

If you need kitchen measuring equipment and cannot cope with decimal measures, you will need to bring your own measuring scales, jugs, cups and thermometers. Foreign pillow sizes (e.g. American and British) aren't the same as in France and the French use duvets and not blankets to keep warm in winter (besides more 'natural' methods!).

LAUNDRY & DRY CLEANING

All large towns have dry cleaners (*nettoyage à sec/pressing*), most of which also do minor clothes' repairs, invisible mending, alterations and dyeing. Dry cleaning is expensive and you must usually pay in advance. Cleaning by the kilogramme with no pressing is possible in some places and you can also save money by having your clothes brushed and pressed (*pressing/blanchisserie*) by a valet service, rather than cleaned. Thanks to the French obsession to always look their best, there are more dry-cleaners and valet services in Paris alone, than in the whole of many other European countries. Express cleaning may mean a few days rather than hours, even at a dry cleaners where cleaning is done on the premises. Some shops will collect and deliver items for a small fee.

With the exception of Paris, there are few self-service launderettes (*laveries automatiques*) in France (most people have washing machines), although most dry cleaners do laundry. Launderette machines are usually operated by tokens (*jetons*) marked with the price and purchased from an attendant. Machines usually take around seven kilos of washing, although there are often machines of different sizes. Washing powder and softeners are available from vending machines, although it's much cheaper to provide your own. Launderettes have heavy duty spin-dryers (*super-essorage*) that reduce the time required to dry clothes. Dryers are usually very hot, so take care with delicate items requiring little drying.

In some villages, women still prefer to do their washing or a final rinse at a communal clothes-washing place (*lavoir*). These are usually located by a river or near a spring and have stone troughs, scrubbing surfaces and communal drying lines.

HOME SHOPPING

Shopping by mail-order and phone has long been popular in France and shopping via the Internet is expected to take off in a big way in the next few years. Electronic shopping is expected to dominate retailing in future, whether in-store or from home, and TV shopping is also becoming increasingly popular and is worth around one billion francs a year. Shopping via Minitel is also popular, although it's expected to be replaced by the Internet in the next decade.

Mail-Order Catalogues: The French mail-order (*vente à domicile*) business is the third largest in Europe after Germany and Britain. Mail-order is the fastest growing branch of the French fashion business. The leading companies include *La Porte Blanche*, *La Redoute*, *Les Trois Suisses* and *Quelle*, most of which also have stores in major cities and collection points throughout the country. Companies such as *Les Trois Suisses* have an up-market, modern image, particularly when compared with the rather old-fashioned image of mail-order in some countries. The main selling points of mail-order companies are high-quality, affordable prices and guaranteed delivery times. Goods can be ordered directly from home via catalogue databases and paid for with credit cards (most companies issue their own credit cards).

Although most foreign mail-order companies won't send goods abroad, there's nothing to stop you obtaining catalogues from friends or relatives and ordering through them. Many foreign companies also publish catalogues and will send goods anywhere in the world, for example Fortnum & Masons, Habitat and Harrods in Britain. Most provide account facilities or payment can be made by international credit cards. If you're an addicted mail-order shopper, Shop the World by Mail, PO Box 1599, Sarasota, FL-34230-1599, USA and Shop America, 25 McLean Drive, Sudbury, MA 01776, USA may be the answer to your prayers.

Internet Shopping: Shopping via the Internet is the fastest-growing form of retailing and although it's still in its infancy. Shopping on the Internet is *very* secure (secure servers, with addresses beginning https:// rather than http://, are almost impossible to crack) and in most cases safer than shopping by phone or mail-order. There are literally thousands of shopping sites on the Internet including Taxi (www.mytaxi.co.uk), which contains the Internet addresses of 2,500 worldwide retail and information sites, www.enterprisecity.co.uk, www.iwanttoshop.com, www.shopguide.co.uk. and www.virgin.net (which has a good directory of British shopping sites). With Internet shopping the world is literally your oyster and savings can be made on a wide range of goods including CDs, clothes, sports equipment, electronic gadgets, jewellery, books, CDs, wine and computer software, and services such as insurance, pensions and mortgages. Huge savings can also be made on holidays and travel. Small high-price, high-tech items (e.g. cameras, watches and portable and hand-held computers) can usually be purchased cheaper somewhere in Europe or (particularly) in the USA (for cameras try www.normancamera.com), with delivery by courier within as little as three days.

Buying Overseas: When buying goods overseas ensure that you're dealing with a bona fide company and that the goods will work in France (if applicable). If possible, *always* pay by credit card when buying by mail-order or over the Internet, which provides you extra protection as the credit card issuer may be jointly liable with the supplier. When you buy expensive goods abroad, have them insured for their full value. When buying overseas, take into account shipping costs, duty and VAT. If you purchase a small item by mail from outside the EU you may need to pay VAT (TVA) on delivery or at the post office on collection.

SHOPPING ABROAD

Shopping abroad makes a pleasant change from all those 'boring' French shops full of tempting and expensive luxuries (although the information in this section applies equally to foreign residents shopping in France as it does to French residents shopping abroad). It can also save you money and makes a pleasant day out for the family. Don't forget your passports or identity cards, car papers, dog's vaccination papers and foreign currency. Most shops in border towns eagerly accept French francs, but will usually give you a lower exchange rate than a bank. Many families, particularly those living in border areas, take advantage of lower prices outside France, particularly when it comes to buying alcohol (e.g. in Andorra, Belgium and Italy). Whatever you're looking for, compare prices and quality before buying. Bear in mind that if you buy goods that are faulty or need repair, you may need to return them to the place of purchase.

From 1993 there have been no cross-border shopping restrictions within the European Union for goods purchased duty and tax paid, providing goods are for personal consumption or use and not for resale. Although there are no restrictions, there are 'indicative levels' for certain items, above which goods may be classified as commercial quantities. For example, persons entering Britain aged 17 or over may import the following amounts of alcohol and tobacco without question:

- 10 litres of spirits (over 22° proof);
- 20 litres of sherry or fortified wine (under 22° proof);
- 90 litres of wine (or 120 x 0.75 litre bottles/ten cases) of which a maximum of 60 litres may be sparkling wine;
- 110 litres of beer;
- 800 cigarettes and 400 cigarillos and 200 cigars and 1kg of smoking tobacco.

There's no limit on perfume or toilet water. If you exceed the above amounts you may have to convince the customs authorities that you aren't planning to sell the goods. Thousands of Britons have got into the habit of popping across the Channel to do some shopping in the last few years, particularly for alcohol and tobacco. The vast complex *Cité Europe*, situated just two minutes from Eurotunnel's terminal is one of Europe's biggest shopping centres with more than 150 shops and restaurants (attracting over 17 million visitors a year). A number of books have also been published on the subject including the *The Cross-Channel Drinks Guide* by Tom

Stevenson (Absolute Press); *A Bootful of Wine* by Alec King (Mandarin); and *The Calais Beer, Wine & Tobacco Directory* by Alan Kelly and Kim Whitaker (Euro Publishing). The huge difference in the price of alcohol and tobacco between Britain and France has been called 'a bootleggers' charter', although there are huge fines for anyone caught selling duty-paid alcohol and tobacco in Britain, which is classed as smuggling.

Never attempt to import illegal goods into France and don't agree to bring a parcel into France or deliver a parcel in another country without knowing exactly what it contains. A popular confidence trick is to ask someone to post a parcel in France (usually to a poste restante address) or to leave a parcel at a railway station or restaurant. **THE PARCEL USUALLY CONTAINS DRUGS!**

DUTY-FREE ALLOWANCES

Duty-free (*hors-taxe*) shopping within the EU is set to end on the 30th June 1999, although it will still be available when travelling further afield. Duty-free allowances are the same whether or not you're travelling within the EU or from a country outside the EU. From 1st January 1993, for each journey to another EU member state travellers aged 17 or over (unless otherwise stated) are entitled to import the following goods purchased duty-free:

● one litre of spirits (over 22° proof) *or* two litres of fortified wine (under 22° proof) *or* two litres of wine;

● two litres of still table wine;

● 200 cigarettes *or* 100 cigarillos *or* 50 cigars *or* 250g of tobacco;

● 60ml of perfume;

● 250ml of toilet water;

● 500g of coffee (*or* 200g coffee extract) and 100g tea (*or* 40g tea extract) for persons aged 15 or over;

● other goods including gifts and souvenirs to the value of 300F (150F for those aged under 15).

Duty-free allowances apply to both outward and return journeys, even if both are made on the same day, and the combined total (i.e. double the above limits) can be imported into your 'home' country. Since 1993, duty-free sales have been 'vendor-controlled', meaning that vendors are responsible for ensuring that the amount of duty-free goods sold to individuals doesn't exceed their entitlement. Duty-free goods purchased on board ships and ferries are noted on boarding cards that must be presented with each purchase. Ferry companies usually have a number of special offers providing additional savings.

If you live outside the EU you can obtain a VAT refund on purchases if the total value (excluding books, food, services and some other items) amounts to 2,000F or more. Large department stores, particularly in Paris, often have a special counter where non-EU shoppers can arrange for the shipment of duty-free goods. An export sales invoice (*bordereau pour détaxe*) is provided by retailers, listing all purchases and comprising three pages (each of which must be signed), two pink and one green. When you leave France your purchases must be validated by a customs officer who will retain the two pink pages and return a copy to the vendor responsible for reimbursing the VAT. The third (green page) is stamped and returned to you and is your receipt. At major airports (e.g. in Paris) there are special *douane de détaxe* offices where you can obtain a VAT refund on the spot, but you must show your purchases so don't pack them in your checked baggage. Note that French bureaucracy ensures that the process takes at least an hour to complete. If the refund is made by the vendor it can take up to six months.

RECEIPTS

When shopping in France, insist on a receipt (*quittance/ticket*) and keep it until you have left the shop or have reached home. This isn't just in case you need to return or exchange goods, which may be impossible without the receipt, but also to verify that you have paid if an automatic alarm sounds as you're leaving a shop or any other questions arise. Generally speaking, a complaint won't be entertained without a receipt. Under the French Civil Code, all products sold must be suitable for the use for which they are intended. If they aren't, you're entitled to exchange them or obtain a refund and it's illegal for traders to use 'small print' (*clauses abusives*) to try to avoid liability. You have the same legal rights whether goods are bought at the recommended retail price or at a discount during a sale.

It's advisable to keep receipts and records of all major purchases made while you're resident in France, particularly if your stay is for a limited period only. This may save you both time and money when you finally leave France and are required to declare your belongings in your new country of residence.

CONSUMER ASSOCIATIONS

There are strict consumer protection laws in France, where the price of goods and services must be clearly displayed and indicate whether tax and service is included (as applicable). Every department has an official 'directorate of competition and prices' (*la Direction Départementale de la Concurrence et des prix*), whose job is to prevent consumers being cheated by dishonest vendors. Simply the threat of an official complaint will often have the desired result.

The *Institut National de la Consommation (INC)* (80, rue Lecourbe, 75015 Paris, ☎ 01.45.60.20.20) is the umbrella organisation for all French national consumer associations. It can provide you with the name of an appropriate consumer association if you require information or have a particular complaint or problem. The INC publishes a monthly magazine *50 Millions de Consommateurs* containing comparative product tests, practical and legal information, loan calculations and insurance surcharges. It's available on subscription and from newsagents. Other French consumer associations include the *Union Fédérale des Consommateurs Que Choisir*, 11, rue Guénot, 75011 Paris (☎ 01.43.48.55.48) and the Union Fédérale de Consommateurs, 13, rue de Turbigo, 75002 Paris (☎ 01.43.48.55.48).

18.

ODDS & ENDS

This chapter contains miscellaneous information, including everything you ever wanted to know about tipping and toilets (but was afraid to ask). Most of the topics covered are of general interest to anyone living or working in France, although admittedly not all are of vital everyday importance. However, buried among the trivia are some fascinating snippets of information.

CITIZENSHIP

There are three ways you can acquire French citizenship: by being born in France, through marriage or through naturalisation. A child born in France of foreign parents who doesn't automatically receive the nationality of his parents can apply for French nationality between the ages of 16 and 21 (they no longer automatically become French citizens at 18). This applies, for example, to children born in France of American parents. The marriage of a non-French citizen to a French citizen entitles him or her to French citizenship after two years of marriage.

To obtain French citizenship through naturalisation, as opposed to acquisition through marriage, you must have lived in France for at least five years and must satisfy the authorities that you're of good character and have sufficient knowledge of the French language. The period of residence may be reduced if you have attended certain French institutions of higher education or have rendered special services to the country (e.g. consumed prodigious amounts of French wine!). An application for naturalisation takes around 18 months to two years to be processed and must be made to the *préfet* of your local *département*. He will pass your file to your local mayor for investigation and if you haven't committed any mass murders and have paid your taxes, your application is sent to Paris with the *préfet's* recommendation. The minister's decision is final and there's no appeal against a refusal to grant naturalisation. Naturalisation confers French nationality upon the applicant, his spouse and his children aged under 18.

CLIMATE

France is the only country in Europe that experiences three distinct climates: continental, maritime and Mediterranean. It isn't easy to generalise about French weather (*temps*), as many regions and areas of France are influenced by surrounding mountains, forests and other geographical features, and have their own micro-climates. If you're planning to live in France and don't know whether the climate in a particular region will suit you, it's advisable to rent accommodation until you're absolutely sure, as the extremes of hot and cold in some areas are too much for some people. If you're seeking 'guaranteed' sun you need to head south. Generally the Loire river is considered to be the point where the cooler northern European climate gradually begins to change to the warmer southern climate. Spring and autumn are usually fine throughout France, although the length of the seasons vary depending on the region and altitude. In Paris, it's rare for the temperature to fall below minus 5°C (41°F) in winter or to rise above 30°C (86°F) in summer. However, Paris gets its fair share of rain. The expression 'raining cats and dogs' (*il pleut chats et chiens*) was coined here, when during periods of heavy rainfall, dead cats and dogs were flushed out of the sewers into the streets!

The west and northwest (e.g. Brittany and Normandy) have a maritime climate tempered by the Atlantic and the Gulf Stream, with mild winters and warm summers, and most rainfall in spring and autumn. The area around La Rochelle in the west enjoys a pleasant micro-climate and is the second sunniest area of France after the French Riviera. Many people consider the western Atlantic coast has the best summer climate in France, with the heat tempered by cool sea breezes. The Massif Central (which acts as a weather barrier between north and south) and eastern France have a moderate continental climate with cold winters and hot and stormy summers. However, the centre and eastern upland areas have an extreme continental climate with freezing winters and sweltering summers. The northern Massif is prone to huge variations in temperature and it was here that an amazing 41°C (106°F) minimum/maximum temperature difference was recorded **in one day** (on 10th August 1885).

The Midi, stretching from the Pyrénées to the Alps, is hot and dry except for early spring, when there's usually heavy rainfall; the Cévennes region is the wettest in France with some 200cm (79in) of rain a year. Languedoc has hot dry summers and much colder winters than the French Riviera, with snow often remaining until May in the mountainous inland areas. The Riviera enjoys a Mediterranean climate of mild winters, daytime temperatures rarely dropping below 10°C (50°F), and humid and very hot summers, with the temperature often rising above 30°C (86°F). The average sunshine on the French Riviera is five hours in January and 12 hours in July. Note, however, that it isn't always warm and sunny on the Riviera and it can get quite cold and wet in some areas in winter.

The higher you go, the colder it gets, so if you don't like cold and snow, don't live up a mountain, e.g. in the Alps, Pyrénées, Vosges, Auvergne or Jura mountains. The mountains of the Alps and Pyrénées experience extremes of weather with heavy snow in winter and hot summers, although the western Pyrénées have surprisingly mild winters. The natural barrier of the Alps disrupts normal weather patterns and there are often significant local climatic variations. Central and eastern France have the coldest winters and consequently the highest heating bills. One of the most unpleasant aspects of very cold winters is motoring. If you need to commute in winter, bear in mind that roads are inevitably treacherous at times and can be frightening if you aren't used to driving on ice and snow (fog is also a particular hazard).

France occasionally experiences extreme and unpredictable weather (it's all the fault of the politicians), which has become a favourite topic of conversation in some areas. Freak conditions combined to create violent storms in the south of France in recent years, e.g. in 1992 winds of 150km (93mph) an hour and flash floods resulted in over 40 deaths, and 63 communes being declared disaster areas. They were the worst storms in living memory and of a ferocity experienced only once every 50 years. In some areas 30cm (12in) of rain fell in three hours and half the annual rainfall for the region fell in just ten hours. Wherever you live in France, if you're anywhere near a waterway you should ensure that you have insurance against floods.

France experiences many violent cold and dry winds (*vent violent*) including the *Mistral* and the *Tramontane*. The *Mistral* is a bitterly cold wind that blows down the southern end of the Rhône valley into the Camargue and Marseille. The *Tramontane* affects the coastal region from Perpignan, near the Pyrénées, to Narbonne. Corsica is buffeted by many winds including the two aforementioned plus the *Mezzogiorno* and *Scirocco*.

Average daily maximum/minimum temperatures for selected cities in Centigrade and Fahrenheit (in brackets) are:

Location	Spring	Summer	Autumn	Winter
Bordeaux	17/6 (63/43)	25/14 (77/57)	18/8 (64/46)	9/2 (48/36)
Boulogne	12/6 (54/43)	20/14 (68/57)	14/10 (57/50)	6/2 (43/36)
Lyon	16/6 (61/43)	27/15 (81/59)	16/7 (61/45)	5/-1 (41/30)
Nantes	15/6 (59/43)	24/14 (75/57)	16/8 (61/46)	8/2 (46/36)
Nice	17/9 (63/48)	27/18 (81/64)	21/12 (70/54)	13/4 (55/39)
Paris	16/6 (61/43)	25/15 (77/59)	16/6 (57/43)	6/1 (43/34)
Strasbourg	16/5 (61/41)	25/13 (77/55)	14/6 (57/43)	1/-2 (37/28)

A quick way to make a *rough* conversion from Centigrade to Fahrenheit is to multiply by two and add 30 (see also **Appendix C**). Weather forecasts (*météo*) are broadcast on TV and radio stations and published in daily newspapers. You can obtain the weather forecast for a particular department by telephoning 08.36.68.02 followed by the department number, e.g. 24 for Dordogne. Forecasts are also available via Minitel (3615 *météo*) and the Internet.

CRIME

France has a similar crime rate to most other European countries and in common with them crime has increased considerably in recent years. Stiffer sentences have failed to stem the spiralling crime rate and the prison population in France has doubled to some 60,000 in the past decade, creating a crisis in the overcrowded jails. Although most crimes are against property, violent crime is increasing, particularly in Paris. Mugging is on the increase throughout France, although it's still relatively rare in most cities. In some towns in southern France pensioners have been the target of muggers and even truffle hunters have been robbed of their harvest at gun point. Sexual harassment (or worse) is common in France and women should take particular care late at night and never hitchhike alone. Some 'experts' recommend that women carry a tear gas aerosol, although it's officially illegal.

Thefts are soaring and housebreaking and burglary have reached epidemic proportions in some areas ('holiday' or second homes are a popular target). Many people keep dogs as a protection or warning against burglars (*attention: chien méchant*) and have triple-locked and steel-reinforced doors. However, crime in rural areas remains relatively low and it's still common for people in villages and small towns not to lock their homes and cars. Car theft and theft from cars is rife in Paris and other cities. Foreign-registered cars are a popular target, particularly expensive models, which are often stolen to order and spirited abroad.

Pickpockets and bag-snatchers have long been a plague in Paris, where the 'charming' street urchins (often gypsies) are a highly organised and trained bunch of pickpockets. They try to surround and distract you, and when your attention is diverted pick you clean without you noticing. Keep them at arm's length, if necessary by force, and keep a firm grip on your valuables. Always remain vigilant in tourist haunts, queues and on the *métro*. *Never* tempt fate with an exposed wallet or purse or by flashing your money around and hang on tight to your shoulder bag. One of the most effective methods of protecting your passport, money, traveller's cheques and credit cards, is with an old-fashioned money belt. Tourists and travellers are the targets of some of France's most enterprising criminals, including highwaymen (see page 217) and train robbers.

The worst area for crime is the Mediterranean coast (one of the most corrupt and crime-ridden regions in Europe), particularly around Marseille and Nice, where most crime is attributable to the vicious underworld (*Milieu*) of the Côte d'Azur racketeers and drug dealers. Marseille is notorious for its links with organised crime such as drug-trafficking (the *French Connection*), money-laundering, robbery and prostitution. There's a growing use of guns in urban crime and gang killings are fairly frequent in Marseille and Corsica, where separatist groups such as the *Front Libéral National Corse (FLNC)*, *Cuncolta Naziunalist* and the *Mouvement pour l'Autodétermination (MPA)* have become increasingly violent in recent years. In Paris there's a threat from bombs planted by Algerian Islamic militants, which have killed a number of people in the last few years.

Although the increase in crime isn't encouraging, the crime rate in France is relatively low, particularly violent crime. This means that you can usually safely walk almost anywhere at any time of day or night and there's usually no need for anxiety or paranoia about crime. However, you should be 'street-wise' and take certain elementary precautions. These include avoiding high-risk areas at night, particularly those frequented by drug addicts, prostitutes and pickpockets. Street people (*clochards*) in Paris and other cities may occasionally harass you, but they are generally harmless. You can safely travel on the Paris *métro* (and other *métros* in France) at any time, although some stations are best avoided late at night. When you're in an unfamiliar city, ask a policeman, taxi driver or other local person whether there are any unsafe neighbourhoods – and avoid them! See also **Car Theft** on page 217, **Security** on page 94, **Household Insurance** on page 266, **Legal System** on page 400 and **Police** on page 406.

GEOGRAPHY

France, often referred to as *l'héxagone* due to its hexagonal shape, is the third largest country in Western Europe after Russia and the re-unified Germany. It covers an area of almost 550,000km² (213,000mi²), stretching 1,050km (650mi) from north to south and almost the same distance from west to east (from the tip of Britanny to Strasbourg). Its land and sea border extends for 4,800km (around 3,000mi) and includes 2,700km (1,677mi) of sea coast. France also incorporates the Mediterranean island of Corsica (*Corse*) situated 160km (99mi) from France and 80km (50mi) from Italy, covering 8,721km² (3,367mi²) and with a coastline of 1,000km (620mi). France is bordered by Andorra, Belgium, Germany, Italy, Luxembourg, Spain and Switzerland, and the opening of the Channel Tunnel in 1994 connected it with Britain (although only by rail). Its borders are largely delimited by geographical barriers including the English Channel (*la Manche*) in the north, the Atlantic Ocean in the west, the Pyrénées and the Mediterranean in the south, the Alps and the Rhine in the east.

The north and west of France is mostly low-lying and the Paris basin in the centre of the country occupies a third of France's land area. France is noted for its extinct agricultural regions. The Massif Central in the south and southeast of France volcanoes, hot springs and many rivers. In ranges (Alps, Auvergne, Jura, are mountainous, although despite its many a lowland country with most Massif Central, Pyrénées and Vosges), F of its area less than 200 metres above sea level. Almost 90 per cent of the land is productive, with around one-third cultivated, one-quarter pasture and one-quarter forest.

France has a comprehensive network of rivers and canals comprising some 40 per cent of European waterways, including the Garonne, Loire, Rhine, Rhône and the Seine. The Loire, 1,020km (634mi) in length, is France's longest river. The Massif Central has many peaks rising above 1,500m (5,000ft) and Europe's highest mountain, Mont Blanc (4,810m/15,781ft), is situated in the French Alps.

France also has a number of overseas territories, four of which are classified as overseas departments: Guadaloupe, Guyane, Martinique and Réunion. Although situated within France, Monaco is an independent principality and isn't governed by France. France has 22 regions and 95 *départements*, shown on the map on page 444.

GOVERNMENT

France has a republican form of government dating from 1792, three years after the French revolution, although it has been much modified and refined over the years. Since 1792 there have been five republics (new constitutions) lasting from three to 70 years: first (1792-1795), second (1848-1851), third (1870-1940), fourth (1946-1958) and fifth (1958-). Since 1870, the government has been headed by a president with a prime minister and two houses of parliament. France's rulers are bound by a written constitution detailing the duties and powers of the president, government and parliament, and the conditions of election. The central government is divided into three branches: the executive, legislature and the judiciary. The executive is headed by the president, who's the head of state. The legislative branch is represented by parliament, comprising the national assembly and the senate. The constitution is protected by a nine-member constitutional council.

The President: Under the fifth republic, instituted by President de Gaulle in 195?, the French president wields more power than his American counterpart and can assume dictatorial powers in a national emergency. He 'leads and determines the policy of France' and appoints the prime minister and government. He can dissolve the house (once a year) should it pass a vote of no confidence against his prime minister as he has considerable powers in the fields of foreign affairs and defence. The French president lives, appropriately, like a king in the Elysée palace.

All French citizens aged 23 or older are eligible as candidates for the presidency (providing they have a big nose) or parliament. The president is directly elected by the people every seven years and must have an absolute majority. Should a candidate not achieve an absolute majority on the first ballot, which is unusual, a second ballot is held two weeks after the first ballot between the two candidates with the highest number of votes one week for the first ballot two weeks' campaigning is allowed for the first ballot and please note!). A president and there's also a strict limit on election expenses (USA president can dissolve can be elected for a maximum of two terms. Although the passed by parliament, ment and call new elections, he cannot block legislation

Many people believe appeal directly to the people by calling a referendum. from its present seven, residential mandate should be reduced to five years end the need for *cohab* with the national assembly. This would theoretically different (and usually hos hen the president presides over a parliament of a al persuasion, which has happened three times in recent years.

Parliament: Parliament plays a secondary role in France compared with many other democracies, and it meets in two sessions for a total of just 120 days a year. It has two houses, the National Assembly (*Assemblée Nationale*) and the Senate (*Sénat*). The National Assembly is the senior lower house, to which its 577 deputies (*députés*) are directly elected by the people every five years. Although well paid, many deputies have other jobs as well. Unlike most other countries, when a deputy is appointed a minister, he must give up his seat to a previously nominated substitute (*adjoint*). The Senate (upper house) is indirectly elected by a college of some 130,000 local councillors. It consists of 318 senators (mostly local politicians) with a nine-year mandate, one third of whom are elected every three years. The Senate has limited powers to amend or reject legislation passed by the National Assembly; when an impasse is reached the National Assembly has the final decision.

The French employ a modified first-past-the-post system, proportional representation being abandoned in 1988. As with presidential elections, unless a candidate receives over 50 per cent of the votes on the first ballot, there's a second ballot one week later. Only candidates who received at least 12.5 per cent in the first round are eligible, although usually only the top two candidates contest the second round. Thanks to the two-round voting system, the Gaullists' (RPR) 20 per cent of the vote in the 1993 elections won them 242 seats, while almost the same percentage of the vote shared by the National Front and the Green alliance gained them *none*.

Political Parties: The main political parties in France are the *Rassemblement pour la République* (RPR), the conservative Gaullist party founded by de Gaulle, the Union for a Democratic France (*Union pour la Démocratie Française/UDF*), incorporating the Republican Party (*Parti Républicain*) founded by former president Giscard d'Estaing, the Socialist Party (*Parti Socialiste*), the Communist Party (*Parti Communiste*) and the National Front (*Front National*). The influence of the Communist Party, once the largest political party in France, has been decimated in recent years and it's still trying to come to terms with the collapse of communism in eastern Europe. The main policy platform of the racist and xenophobic, extreme right-wing National Front, led by Jean-Marie Le Pen, is the repatriation of immigrants from France (*France for the French* is their battle cry). It won a frightening 35 seats in the national assembly in 1981, although it lost them in 1988 when proportional representation was abandoned. Other fringe parties include the Green (*Les Verts*) and Ecology (*Génération Ecologie*) parties, although they have yet to win any seats in the National Assembly. Most French citizens are apathetic towards politics and abstentionists are the biggest electoral group.

Local Government: For political and administrative purposes, France is divided into 22 regions, 95 *départements*, 3,509 cantons and 36,394 communes. The regions were created in 1972, each consisting of a number of *départements* (see map on page 444) with a directly elected regional council (*conseil régional*). Many correspond to the old provinces of France such as Burgundy, Normandy and Provence. Each region has its own elected assembly and executive, with its seat the region's designated 'capital' town (*chef-lieu*). Regional elections take place in March and the term of office is six years. Regions are responsible for adult education and certain aspects of culture, tourism and industrial development. The state retains control of general education, justice and health services.

Departments: Each *département* has an elected council whose seat is the prefecture (*préfecture*) run by a prefect (*préfet*). *Départements* are responsible for welfare, social services and law enforcement. They are numbered in alphabetical order with a two-digit number, from Ain (01) to Val d'Oise (95). There are also four overseas departments: Guadaloupe (951), Martinique (972), Guyane (973) and Réunion (974). The *département* number comprises the first two digits of post codes and the last two digits of vehicle licence plates. Departmental elections are held every six years.

Communes: Communes vary in size from large cities to tiny villages with a handful of inhabitants and are governed by a municipal council and a mayor (*maire*). They control their own town-planning, including granting building permits, buildings and environment. The town hall also functions as a registry of births, marriages and deaths; passport office; citizens advice bureau; land registry; council headquarters; tourist and information office; and registrar's office (for conducting civil marriages).

Mayors: The town hall, called the *hôtel de ville* in cities and large towns, and the *mairie* in small towns and villages, is the seat of the mayor and France's top school for public life. Almost all prime ministers and presidents of France have been mayors of their home towns. France has three times as many mayors as any other EU country and they have wide powers. They are important political figures and are both the elected head of the municipal council and representatives of the state. Most central government ministers, 80 per cent of deputies and 90 per cent of senators are also mayors of their home towns. Municipal elections are held to elect the local mayor, whose term of office is six years. Mayors are frequently re-elected and often serve a number of terms of office. The mayor works in conjunction with the municipal council (*conseil municipal*). Fraud, corruption and sleeze are even more widespread in local municipal politics than at the national level and in recent years there has been an increasing number of scandals involving mayors (a number of whom have absconded with public funds). In addition, many towns and cities have been forced to increase taxes to pay for grandiose schemes embarked upon by megalomaniac mayors, costing local taxpayers millions of francs.

Paris: Paris is unique in that it's divided into 20 districts, called *arrondissements*, each with its own mayor. Since 1977, Paris has also had an elected mayor, chosen by the 163 councillors of the municipal council. Paris is both a *département* and a commune, and therefore its council sits as both a departmental council and a municipal authority. *Arrondissements* are shown on post codes (e.g. 75001 signifies the 1st *arrondissement*) and are also written as 1e, 2e, 3e (1st, 2nd, 3rd) or Xe, XVe and XXe (10th, 15th, 20th).

Eligibility to Vote: Only French citizens aged 18 or older are permitted to vote in French elections, sensibly always held on a Sunday. To register to vote you must have been resident for at least six months in a community. Foreign EU citizens resident in France are eligible to vote in elections to the European Parliament and local municipal elections, and may also stand as candidates for councillors in municipal elections, but not as mayors or deputy mayors.

LEGAL SYSTEM

The French legal system is based entirely on written civil law. The system of administrative law was laid down by Napoléon in 1789 and is appropriately called the *code Napoléon* (Napoleonic code). The code governs all branches of French law and includes the *code civil*, the *code fiscal* and the *code pénal*. However, in 1994 a new criminal code was introduced to replace the *code Napoléon* and included clauses on sexual harassment, ecological terrorism, crimes against humanity and a maximum jail sentence of 30 years. France has two judicial systems: administrative and judiciary. The administrative system deals with disputes between the government and individuals, while the judiciary handles civil and criminal cases. France doesn't have a jury system (abolished in 1941) but a mixed tribunal made up of six lay judges and three professional judges, with convictions decided by a two-thirds majority.

Under the French criminal law system, cases are heard by a variety of courts, depending on the severity of the alleged offence. A *tribunal de police* is a court dealing with minor contraventions such as parking fines and other fixed penalty offences. A *tribunal d'instance* is a magistrates' court handling minor criminal cases (*délits*), and a *cour d'assises* is a criminal court that tries major cases (*crimes*). Civil cases involving amounts up to a maximum of 30,000F are also heard in a *tribunal d'instance*, above which amount cases go before a high court (*tribunal de grande instance*). Commercial cases are heard by a special *tribunal de commerce*.

It's unnecessary to employ a lawyer or barrister (*avocat*) in a civil case heard in a *tribunal d'instance*, where you can conduct your own case if your French is up to the task. If you use a lawyer, not surprisingly, you must pay his fee. In a *tribunal de grande instance* you *must* employ a lawyer. An *avocat* can act for you in almost any court of law. A legal and fiscal adviser (*conseil juridique et fiscal*) is similar to a British solicitor and can provide legal advice and assistance on commercial, civil and criminal matters, as well as tax, social security, labour law and similar matters. He can also represent you before certain administrative agencies and in some courts. A bailiff (*huissier*) deals with summonses, statements, writs and lawsuits, in addition to the lawful seizure of property ordered by a court. He's also employed to officially notify documents and produce certified reports (*constats*) for possible subsequent use in legal proceedings, e.g. statements from motorists after a road accident.

A public notary (*notaire*, addressed as *maître*) is a public official authorised by the Ministry of Justice and controlled by the *Chambre des Notaires*. Like a *conseil juridique* he's also similar to a British solicitor, although he doesn't deal with criminal cases or offer advice concerning criminal law. *Notaires* have a monopoly in the areas of transferring real property, testamentary and matrimonial acts, which by law must be in the form of an authentic document (*acte authentique*), verified and stamped by a *notaire*. In France, conveyancing is strictly governed by French law and can be performed only by a *notaire*. A *notaire* also informs and advises about questions relating to administrative, business, company, credit, family, fiscal and private law. In respect to private law, a *notaire* is responsible for administering and preparing documents relating to leases, property sales and purchases, divorce, inheritance, wills, loans, setting up companies, and buying and selling businesses. He guarantees the validity and safety of contracts and deeds, and is responsible for holding deposits on behalf of clients, collecting taxes and paying them to the relevant authorities.

In France, the accused has the right to silence and anyone charged with a crime is presumed innocent until proven guilty, although the burden of proof is generally on the accused to prove his innocence. Although rare, suspects are sometimes held for months without access to a lawyer. A radical and controversial reform of France's arrest and indictment procedure was instituted in 1993, under which suspects are entitled to see a lawyer within 20 hours of their arrest, a person under judicial investigation must be notified in writing, and an examining magistrate may no longer remand suspects in custody in a case he's investigating. Under France's inquisitorial system of justice, suspects are questioned by an independent examining magistrate (*juge d'instruction*).

Never assume that the law in France is the same as in any other country as this often *isn't* the case. For those whose French is up to the task, there are many books explaining the intricacies of French law including *Un an de Chronique Juridique* and *Le Guide Juridique*, both published by VO Editions. If you need an English-speaking lawyer, you can usually obtain a list of names from your country's embassy or a local consulate in France (see **Appendix A**). Certain legal advice and services may also be provided by embassies and consulates in France, including an official witness of signatures (Commissioner for Oaths).

MARRIAGE & DIVORCE

Somewhat surprisingly for a Catholic country, marriage is becoming increasingly unpopular in France, where only some 50 marriages are performed each year for every 10,000 citizens (the lowest per capita number in Europe). Over seven million French citizens live without a partner, around one million of whom are divorcees, and the number is growing each year. Many couples don't bother to get married and simply live together as man and wife (*union libre*). Living with an unmarried partner is popular in France and is officially recognised (called *concubinage*). The number of married couples in France has declined substantially in the last few decades (only the Swedes are less keen on marriage in Europe), while the number of unmarried couples living together has more than doubled to around two million. It's estimated that 40 to 50 per cent of couples who get married have already cohabited for up to two years.

Since the '70s, unmarried couples living together have received the same privileges in law as married couples, including social security. A free certificate is available from town halls testifying that a couple are living together as man and wife. The major disadvantage of *concubinage* is that it isn't recognised under French inheritance laws, and therefore partners can inherit only the amount allowed to non-relatives (see **Wills** on page 304) and they receive no state pension when their partner dies. An unmarried mother (*mère célibataire*) is paid a generous allowance by the state. Illegitimacy no longer carries the stigma it once did and illegitimate children have the same rights as legitimate children. Over a quarter of French children are born out of wedlock and a fifth to single-parent homes.

A civil wedding ceremony, presided over by the mayor or one of his deputies, must be performed in France to legalise a wedding. Although around 50 per cent of couples choose to undergo a church 'blessing' ceremony, it has no legal significance and must take place after the civil ceremony. There's no fee for a marriage in France, although most town halls make a collection in aid of local charities. The legal age of consent for marriage in France is 18, although girls aged over 15 can get married with the consent of at least one parent. Before marrying, a couple must undergo a mandatory medical examination (*certificat d'examen médical prénuptial*), including a blood test and chest X-ray, no more than two months prior to marriage. The cost is reimbursed by social security. The medical was originally intended to check compatibility between the blood groups of a couple, although with the advent of Aids it has taken on a new significance. The results are confidential and cannot prevent a wedding from taking place. If a divorced or widowed woman wishes to remarry within 300 days of the divorce or death, she must provide a medical certificate verifying that she isn't pregnant.

To arrange a marriage in France, either partner must apply at least one month in advance to the town hall where they normally live and must have lived there for at least 40 days (30 days residence plus ten days for publication of the banns). The bride and groom must each provide at least one witness and may provide a maximum of two, the names of whom must be given to the *mairie* when the wedding is arranged. Both partners must also provide birth certificates (stamped by their country's local consulate), proof of residence in France, and a medical certificate issued within the previous two months (originally to establish that a couple didn't have incompatible blood groups). A divorced or widowed woman must provide a divorce or death certificate (translated into French, if necessary). Notification of an impending wedding (*bans*) must be published ten days prior to the ceremony at the town hall where the wedding is to take place, and also where the couple have their residence(s). Copies of the marriage certificate can be obtained at the *mairie*. Married couples are given a 'family book' (*livret de famille*) in which all official family events such as the birth of children, divorce or deaths are recorded.

Marriages are performed under a marital regime (*régime matrimonial*) that defines how a couple's property is owned during marriage or after divorce or death, i.e. separately or in common. If you're married in France, the rules of the marriage *régime* apply to all your land or land rights in France, irrespective of where you're domiciled, and your total assets if you're domiciled in France (see **Liability** on page 291). There are two *régimes*: joint ownership of all assets (*communauté universelle*) or separate ownership (*régime de la séparation des biens*), where each spouse retains legal ownership of his or her own assets. If you're married under *séparation des biens*, assets owned before the marriage or acquired through inheritance during the marriage remain the private property of each partner, and assets acquired during the marriage belong to both partners. In France, it's usual for those married under *séparation des biens* to detail how their assets are to be disposed of in a notarised contract.

If you don't understand the implications of France's marriage *régimes*, you should seek legal advice from a *notaire* (see page 400) before getting married. If you were married abroad and are buying a house in France, your *notaire* will ask you which matrimonial system you were married under and whether there was a marriage contract. If there was no marriage contract, you will usually be deemed to be married under the statutory *régime* of joint ownership of all assets. You can legally change your marital *régime*.

As in most other western countries, the divorce rate has risen alarmingly in France in the last decade (around a third of marriages end in divorce) and has even spawned a best-selling *Divorce* magazine. You can be divorced under French law only when either spouse is a French citizen or when two non-French spouses are resident in France. To be divorced 'by mutual consent' (*divorce par consentement mutuel* or *divorce sur demande conjointe*), you must have been married for at least six months. The grounds for a divorce needn't be disclosed, providing both parties agree on the repercussions such as the division of property, custody of children, alimony and maintenance. A divorce is usually granted automatically by a judge, although he may order a delay of three months for reflection. A divorce becomes final one month after judgement or two months if it has gone to appeal.

Other types of divorce are 'consent to divorce but not to consequences' (*divorce sur demande acceptée*), divorce based on fault (*divorce pour faute*) such as adultery, and divorce based on termination of married life (*divorce pour rupture de la vie commune*). A contested divorce must be decided by a court of law.

MILITARY SERVICE

France is the leading nuclear power (*force de frappe*) in Western Europe, where the size of its armed forces are second only to Germany's. In 1995, France incensed millions of people and created a diplomatic storm in the Pacific region by a resumption of nuclear tests in the South Pacific. However, following its tests France announced plans to sign a test ban treaty in 1996. French defence spending accounts for some 15 per cent of the state budget and around 3.5 per cent of GDP. France formed a Eurocorps with Belgium and Germany in 1993 and is a member of NATO.

Compulsory military service is in the process of being phased out in France and French males born after 1st January 1979 are no longer required to serve as conscripts. Instead they (females will also be required to attend from 2000) attend a one day compulsory military training course, *Rendezvous Citoyen* or *Appel de préparation à la défense*. The day's course consists of lectures on the army and the country's defence systems and literacy and numeracy tests. If proof of attending the course cannot be provided, then you face a variety of sanctions ranging from being excluded from public examinations at school or university to being unable to obtain a driving licence, or a fishing or hunting licence. The idea of 'citizenship' is to be reinforced by lessons on citizenship at secondary schools.

PETS

If you plan to take a pet (*animal domestique*) to France, it's important to ascertain the latest regulations. Make sure that you have the correct papers, not only for France but for all the countries you will pass through to reach France. Particular consideration must be given before exporting a pet from a country with strict quarantine regulations, such as Britain. If you need to return prematurely, even after a few hours or days in France, your pet must go into quarantine, e.g. for six months in Britain, which apart from the expense is distressing for both pets and owners. Norway and Sweden abolished quarantine on 1st May 1994 and Britain plans to replace quarantine in 1999 or 2000 with a new system under which animals must be microchipped and have a 'passport' listing their vaccinations. It will be restricted to animals imported from rabies-free countries and countries where rabies is under control (e.g. Western Europe and possibly North America), but the quarantine law will remain in place for pets coming from Eastern Europe, Africa, Asia and South America. The new regulations are expected to initially cost pet owners £150 a year plus £60 a year for follow-up vaccinations and around £20 for a border check.

You can take up to three animals into France at any one time, one of which may be a puppy (three to six months old), although no dogs or cats under three months of age may be imported. Two parrot-like (psittacidaes) birds can be imported into France and up to ten smaller species; all require health certificates issued within five days of departure. Other animals require special import permits from the French Ministry of Agriculture. There's generally no quarantine period for animals in France. However, there are strict vaccination requirements for dogs, although France has almost eradicated rabies in the last 20 years by vaccinating foxes and it could disappear in the next few years.

If you're importing a dog into France, it must be vaccinated against rabies and have a certificate (*certificat contre la rage*) or have a health certificate (*certificat de bonne santé*) signed by an approved veterinary surgeon issued no more than five days before your arrival. British owners must complete an *Application for a Ministry Export Certificate for dogs, cats and rabies susceptible animals* (form EXA1), available from the Ministry of Agriculture, Fisheries & Food (☎ 0181-330 4411). A health inspection must be performed by a licensed veterinary officer before you're issued with an export health certificate. If you're transporting a pet to France by ship or ferry, you should notify the ferry company. Some companies insist that pets are left in vehicles (if applicable), while others allow pets to be kept in cabins. If your pet is of nervous disposition or unused to travelling, it's best to tranquillise it on a long sea crossing. Pets can also be transported by air.

For visitors with pets, a rabies vaccination is compulsory only for animals entering Corsica, being taken to campsites or holiday parks, or participating in shows in a rabies-affected area. Where applicable, the rabies vaccination must have been given between 30 days and less than a year before arrival in France. If you intend to live permanently in France, most vets recommend that you have a dog vaccinated against rabies before your arrival, which saves you having to get your dog vaccinated on arrival in France. Resident dogs must also be vaccinated against distemper and hardpad and need an annual rabies booster. Cats aren't required to have regular rabies vaccinations, although if you let your cat roam free outside your home it's advisable to have it vaccinated annually. Cats must, however, be vaccinated against feline gastro-enteritis and typhus. All vaccinations must be registered with your veterinary surgeon (*vétérinaire*) and be listed on your pet's vaccination card or health certificate.

France is a nation of dog-lovers with around 17 dogs to every 100 people, one of the highest ratios in the world, and an unofficial dog population of some ten million (over 500,000 in Paris alone). Around 40 per cent of French men and women list their dogs as the most important thing in their lives (even more important than their lovers!) and the French spend some 22 billion francs on them annually (chic 'poodle-parlours' abound). Some 500,000 people are bitten by dogs each year, 60,000 of whom are hospitalised, although there's no plan to muzzle dogs. Around 60,000 dogs are also stolen each year and another 100,000 are abandoned by their owners, many at the start of the long summer holiday or after the hunting season is over (so much for pet lovers!).

All dogs in France must be tattooed with an identity number inside one of their ears, enabling owners to quickly find lost pets and also preventing a rabies or other vaccination certificate from being used for more than one dog. Tattooing is done by vets and costs around 250F. The identity numbers are kept in a central computer controlled by the French Society for the Protection of Animals (*Société Protectrice des Animaux/SPA*). Contact the nearest SPA office if you lose your pet. Dogs and cats don't wear identification discs in France and there's no system of licensing.

No other nation pampers its dogs more than the French, except perhaps rich Americans. There are many kennels and catteries (*pensions/refuges pour animaux*) in France, where fees are around 40F per day for cats and 60F per day for dogs. If you plan to leave your pet at a kennel or cattery, book well in advance, particularly for school holiday periods. French hotels usually quote a rate for pets (e.g. 50F per night), most restaurants allow dogs and many provide food and water (some even allow owners to seat their pets at the table!). There are even exclusive dog restaurants in France. Although food shops make an effort to bar pets, it isn't unusual to see a supermarket trolley containing a dog (the French don't take much notice of 'no dogs' signs). There's usually no discrimination against dogs when renting accommodation, although they may be prohibited in furnished apartments. Paris has a pet cemetery (*cimetière des chiens*) at Asnières founded in 1899 and there are others in Nice, Toulouse and Villepinte.

Veterinary surgeons are well trained in France, where it's a highly popular and well paid profession. Emergency veterinary care is available in major cities, where there are also animal hospitals (*hôpital pour animaux*) and vets on 24-hour call for emergencies. A visit to a vet usually costs 150F to 200F. Some vets also make house calls, for which there's a minimum charge of 400F to 500F. Taxi and ambulance services are also provided for pets. Health insurance for pets is available from a number of insurance companies and it's common practice in France to have third party insurance in case your pet bites someone or causes an accident. This is usually included in general third party liability insurance (see page 268). Dogs must be kept on leads in most public parks and gardens in France and there are large fines for dog owners who don't comply. Dogs are forbidden in some parks, even when on leads. On public transport, small pets must usually be carried in a basket or cage if a fare is to be avoided (the SNCF charges half 2nd class fare for uncaged dogs weighing over 6kg).

The unpleasant aspect of France's vast dog population is abundantly evident on the streets of French towns and cities every day, where dogs routinely leave their 'calling cards'. You must *always* watch where you walk in France. Most dog owners don't take their pets on long country walks, but just to a local park or car park or simply let them loose in the streets to do their business. In Paris, there are laws against fouling footpaths, although most French ignore the 'pooper-scooper' law requiring them to clean up after their dogs. At the very least owners are required to take their pets to the kerb to relieve themselves (you're reminded by dog silhouettes on the footpath in Paris and other cities). Signs also encourage owners to teach their dogs to use gutters (*Apprenez-lui le caniveau*), which are regularly cleaned and disinfected. There are dog toilet areas in Paris and some other French cities. In Paris and some other towns there are patrolmen on motorised pooper-scoopers (*caninettes*), a motorbike-cum-vacuum cleaner equipped with suction tubes, brushes and disinfectant (they pick up four tonnes of doggy-do from the streets of Paris alone, every single day). Although it's of little consolation, it's supposedly good luck to tread in something unpleasant!

If you want to take your pet from France to a country without rabies, it may need to go into quarantine for a period. This applies, for example, to Australia, Britain and Ireland. Check with the authorities of the country concerned. For the latest regulations regarding the importation and keeping of pets in France contact *Sous Direction de la Santé et de la Protection Animales*, 175, rue du Chevaleret, 75646 Paris Cedex 13 (☎ 01.45.84.13.13). If you wish to import an exotic pet or more pets than the standard quota, contact the *Direction Générale des Douanes*, 23bis, rue de l'Université, 75007 Paris.

POLICE

There are three main police forces in France: the *police nationale*, the *gendarmerie nationale* and the *Compagnie Républicaine de la Sécurité (CRS)*. French policemen are addressed formally as *monsieur l'agent* and colloquially called *flics* (cops), although there are many less polite names. The *police nationale* are under the control of the Interior Ministry and are called *agents de police*. They deal with all crime within the jurisdiction of their police station (*commissariat de police*) and are most commonly seen in towns, distinguished by the silver buttons on their uniforms. At night and in rain and fog, they often wear white caps and capes.

The *gendarmerie nationale/gardes-mobiles* is part of the army under the control of the Ministry of Defence, although they are at the service of the Interior Ministry. *Gendarmes* wear blue uniforms and traditional *képis*, and are distinguished by the gold buttons on their uniforms. They deal with serious crime on a national scale and are responsible for *autoroute* patrols, air safety, mountain rescue, and air and coastal patrols. *Gendarmes* include police motorcyclists (*motards*), who patrol in pairs.

The CRS are often referred to as riot police, as they are responsible for crowd control and public disturbances, although they also have other duties including patrolling beaches as life-savers in summer. Over the years they have acquired a notorious reputation for their violent response to demonstrations (*manifestations*) and public disturbances, although often under extreme provocation (they routinely have paving stones and barricades thrown at them). Just their appearance at a demonstration is enough to raise the temperature, although they have been trying to improve their public image.

In addition to the three kinds of police mentioned above, most cities and medium-size towns also have their own municipal police (*police municipale/corps urbain*) who deal mainly with petty crime, traffic offences and road accidents. They traditionally wore a *képi* (like *gendarmes*), although this has been replaced by flat peaked caps. All French police are armed, although municipal police have only rubber bullets. Special police forces include the CSP anti-terrorist police who guard embassies and government buildings in Paris. They wear blue windcheaters, carry machine guns and *aren't* the best people to ask for directions.

In general, the police (of whatever hue) aren't popular with the French public and have an unenviable reputation, particularly among ethnic groups. Police 'brutality', usually directed towards racial minorities, has resulted in violent race riots in some areas. A Council of Europe commission recently stated that suspects in France ran a 'not inconsiderable risk' of being mistreated while in police detention.

The police can stop you and demand identification at any time (called *un contrôle*), so it's advisable to carry your passport or residence permit (*carte de séjour*). If you don't have any identification you can be arrested and if you aren't in possession of at least 10F you can also be charged with vagrancy (although if you have a gold American Express card they may let you off!). The police can hold you in custody for 48 hours without charge, although after 24 hours they need the authority of a public prosecutor or investigating magistrate. If the offence under investigation involves state security, two further 48-hour extensions can be granted, making a total of six days. The police don't prosecute criminal cases in France, which is performed by a public prosecutor. Police can fine offenders on-the-spot for motoring offences such as speeding and drunken driving, and fines must be paid in cash (see **Traffic Police** on page 208).

If you're arrested, your rights aren't as clearly defined in France as in many other western countries. Unless your French is fluent, you should make it clear that you don't understand French and ask permission to call your lawyer or embassy. Someone from your embassy should be able to provide a list of English-speaking lawyers. If you're arrested, you're required to state your name, age and permanent address only. *Never* make or sign a statement without legal advice and the presence of a lawyer. If you're accused of a serious offence, such as possession or trafficking in drugs, it may be difficult to obtain bail.

If you need to contact the police in an emergency, dialling 17 will put you in touch with your local *gendarmerie* or *commissariat de police*, listed at the front of your local telephone directory. If you lose anything or are the victim of a theft, you must report it in person at a police station and complete a report (*déclaration de vol/plainte*), of which you will receive a copy. This must usually be done within 24 hours if you plan to make a claim on an insurance policy. Don't, however, expect the police to be the slightest bit interested in your loss.

POPULATION

The population of France is some 59 million, with an average population density of around 100 people per km² (260 per mi²), one of the lowest in Europe. However, the population density varies enormously from region to region. Paris is one of the most densely populated cities in the world, with over 20,000 inhabitants to the km² (over 52,000 per mi²), while in many rural areas there are just a handful. When Paris is excluded, the population density for the rest of the country drops to around 50 people per km² (130 per mi²). Over 70 per cent of the French population lives in the urban areas of the north, east and the Rhône valley. France has few large cities compared with other European countries with comparable populations and only Paris (2.5m), Lyon (1.2m), Marseille (1.1m) and Lille (1.05m) have over one million inhabitants. The greater Paris area has a population of nearly 11 million, while some 32,000 of France's 36,394 communes have less than 2,000 inhabitants.

In the last 20 years there has been a shift away from the industrial regions of the north to the sunny south (who said the French weren't smart!). There's also a drift away from the mountainous areas of central France and for the first time in history there's a shift away from Paris, as young executives and technocrats head for Avignon, Grenoble, Lyon, Montpellier, Nice and Toulouse. France has had a declining population for many years and today the birth rate is barely sufficient to maintain current population levels. There are various government incentives to encourage families to have more children, including generous family allowances, allowances for unmarried mothers and tax breaks. However, inducements haven't had much affect on the size of the average family of 1.8 children.

The average age of the population is around 37 years, with some 15 per cent of the population aged over 65. Along with many other countries, France is finding it increasingly difficult to fund its state pensions and lavish social security benefits, due to its declining workforce. The average life expectancy in France is 81 for women and 73 for men and increasing (wine *must* be good for you!). France is also becoming increasingly popular with retirees, particularly those from Britain, Germany, the Netherlands and Scandinavian countries.

RELIGION

France has a long tradition of religious tolerance and every resident has total freedom of religion without hindrance from the state or community. The majority of the world's religious and philosophical movements have religious centres or meeting places in Paris and other major cities. France is a Christian country with the vast majority of the population belonging to the Catholic faith and less than 5 per cent Protestants. France is also home to some 700,000 Jews, the highest number of any European country, and over one million Muslims, mostly immigrants from North Africa. Both Jews and Muslims have been the targets of bigots and racists in recent years.

Religion in France isn't as strong as in the past and attendance at mass has dropped to around 10 per cent in Paris and some 15 per cent throughout the country (attendance is lowest among those aged 18 to 35). Only some 50 per cent of marriages are consecrated in a church and 60 per cent of babies baptised. Parish priests have lost much of their traditional influence and there's a serious shortage of recruits for the priesthood. However, few Frenchmen are atheists, despite the successes of the Communist Party in the last few decades, although belief in God is equivocal. The most important religious shrine in France is that of Our Lady at Lourdes, which receives hundreds of thousands of visitors a year in search of a miracle cure.

Church and state were officially divorced in 1905 and direct funding of the church by the state is illegal. The Catholic church is prominent in education, where it maintains many private schools separate from the state education system, although largely funded by the state. The debate over public and parochial (church) education occasionally causes controversy. An attempt to abolish state funding for religious schools by the Socialists in the '80s generated fierce opposition and was quickly abandoned.

Many churches and cathedrals provide (often free) organ, choral and classical concerts throughout the year. For information about local places of worship and service times, contact your local town hall or information office. Churches and religious centres are listed in the Yellow Pages under *églises* and *culte*, and include American and English churches in Paris and other major cities.

SOCIAL CUSTOMS

All countries have their own particular social customs and France is no exception. As a foreigner you will probably be excused if you accidentally insult your host, but you may not be invited again. Note that the French are much more formal than most foreigners imagine and newcomers should tread carefully to avoid offending anyone.

• When you're introduced to a French person, you should say good day (*bonjour madame* or *bonjour monsieur*) and shake hands (*le shake-hand*, a single pump is enough). *Salut!* (hi or hello) is used among close friends and young people. When saying goodbye, it's a formal custom to shake hands again. In an office everyone shakes hands with everyone else on arrival at work *and* when they depart. It's also customary to say good day or good evening on entering a small shop and goodbye (*au revoir madame/monsieur*) on leaving (friends say cheerio or *à bientôt*). *Bonjour* becomes *bonsoir* around 1800 or after dark, although if you choose *bonsoir* (or *bonjour*), don't be surprised if the response isn't the same. *Bonne nuit* (good night) is used when going to bed or leaving a house in the evening. On leaving a shop you may be wished *bonne journée* (have a nice day) or variations such as *bon après-midi, bon fin de l'après-midi, bon dimanche* or *bon weekend*.

The standard and automatic reply to *merci* is *je vous en prie*, which is the equivalent of the American 'you're welcome'.

• Titles should generally be used when addressing or writing to people, particularly when the holder is elderly. The president of a company or institution should be addressed as *monsieur (madame) le président (la présidente)*, a courtesy title usually retained in retirement. The mayor must be addressed as *Monsieur le Maire* (unless he tells you otherwise).

• To kiss or not to kiss, that is the question. It's best to take it slowly when negotiating this social mine-field and to take your cue from the French. You shouldn't kiss (*bise*) when first introduced to an adult, although young children will expect to be kissed. If a lady expects you to kiss her, she will offer her cheek. The 'kiss' is deposited high up on the cheek, never on the mouth (except between lovers). It's usually not really a kiss, more a delicate brushing of the cheeks, although some extroverts plant a great wet smacker on each side of the face. There must *never* be one kiss. Two is the standard number, although many people kiss three or four times. It depends where you are. A rough guide is two in Paris (Parisians think more is vulgar), three in the provinces, and four in the south and between the young (and among family members). Note that kissing takes place only once a day on the first meeting!

Which cheek you start on is a matter of choice, although it's customary to start with the right cheek in Lyon and Paris. When two groups meet, such as two families, each male member of each group must seek out the male members of the other group and shake hands. The females kiss each other on the cheeks as do men and women. With the exception of relatives and close friends, men don't usually kiss or embrace each other in France, so it isn't compulsory to kiss your hoary neighbour.

• When talking to a stranger, use the formal form of address (*vous*). Don't use the familiar form (*tu/toi*) or call someone by their Christian name until you're invited to do so. Generally the older or more important person will invite the other to use the familiar *tu* form of address (called *tutoiement*) and first names. The familiar form is used with children, animals and God, but almost never with your elders or work superiors. However, the French are becoming less formal and the under 40s often use *tu* and first names with colleagues, unless they are of the opposite sex, when *tu* may imply a special intimacy! Note that some people remain *vous*, such as figures of authority (the local mayor) or those with whom you have a business relationship, e.g. your bank manager, tax officials and policemen.

• If you're invited to dinner by a Frenchman (which is a rare occurrence), take along a small present of flowers, a plant or chocolates. Gifts of foreign food or drink aren't generally well received unless they are highly prized in France such as scotch whisky; foreign wine, however good the quality, isn't wise! Some people say you must never take wine, although this obviously depends on your hosts and how well you know them.

• If you take flowers, there should be an odd number and you should unwrap them before presenting them to your hostess. Flowers can be tricky, as to some people carnations mean bad luck, chrysanthemums are for cemeteries (they are placed on graves on All Saints' Day) and roses (particularly red ones) signify love and are associated with the Socialists. Perhaps you should stick to plastic, silk or dried flowers – or a nice bunch of weeds.

● The French say good appetite (*bon appétit*) before starting a meal. If you're offered a glass of wine, wait until your host has made a toast (*santé*) before taking a drink. If you aren't offered a (another) drink, it's time to go home. You should, however, go easy on the wine and other alcohol, as if you drink to excess you're unlikely to be invited back!

● Although the French are often formal in their relationships, their dress habits, even in the office, are often extremely casual. Note, however, that the French tend to judge people by their dress, the style and quality being as important as the correctness for the occasion. You aren't usually expected to dress for dinner (although you should wear something!), depending of course on the sort of circles you move in. In invitations, formal dress (black tie) is *smoking exigé/tenue de soirée* and informal dress is *tenue de ville*.

● Always introduce yourself before asking to speak to someone on the telephone. Surprisingly it's common to telephone at meal times in France, e.g. noon to 1400 and around 2000, when you can usually be assured of finding someone at home. If you call at these times, you should apologise for disturbing the household. It isn't always advisable to make calls after 1400 in the provinces, when many self-employed workers have a siesta.

TIME DIFFERENCE

Like most of the continent of Europe, France is on Central European Time (CET), which is Greenwich Mean Time (GMT) plus one hour. The French change to summer time in spring (usually at the end of March) when they put their clocks forward one hour. In autumn (usually September) clocks are put back one hour for winter time. Time changes are announced in local newspapers and on radio and TV, and take place at 0200 or 0300.

Times in France, for example in timetables, are usually written using the 24-hour clock, when 10am is written as 10h and 10pm as 22h. Midday (*midi*) is noon and midnight (*minuit*) is 2400; 7.30am is written as 7h 30 or 07.30. The 24-hour clock is often also used in speech, for example 7pm (*sept heures du soir*) may be referred to as *dix-neuf heures* (1900). In some French towns, clocks strike twice, with a minute's pause in between, just in case you miss it the first time (so make sure you don't live too close to the town clock!). The international time difference in winter between Paris and some major international cities is shown below:

PARIS	LONDON	JO'BURG	SYDNEY	AUCKLAND	NEW YORK
1200	1100	1300	2200	2400	0600

TIPPING

Tipping (*pourboire*, literally 'for a drink') is common in France, although it isn't as widespread as in the USA, where tipping is a way of life. In some places you may even come across signs forbidding tipping (*pourboire interdit*)! Tipping may depend on whether a service charge has already been included in the price. Service included, written on a restaurant menu as *service compris (SC)*, *service et taxe compris (STC)* or *prix nets/toutes taxes compris (TTC)*, means that prices are inclusive of service and value added tax (TVA), and that no extra tip is necessary (although always welcome). If tax is included and service is extra, *service non compris (SNC)* or *service en sus* will usually be written on the menu, and 10 to 15 per cent will be added to the bill. In some restaurants the service charge is shown on the menu, e.g. *service 12 or 15 per cent*. In rare cases when service isn't included or levied, *Service à l'appréciation du client* may be written on the menu, and you 'can' tip 10 to 15 per cent if you were pleased with the service and food. Unless otherwise noted on the menu, service and tax are usually included, but check with the waiter. In hotels a 15 per cent service charge is usually included in the bill.

In bars and cafés, prices usually include service when you sit at a table, but not when you stand at the bar (it should be shown on the menu or bill or the *tarif des consommations*). It's normal to leave your small change on the bar or a small tip in the dish provided when you stand at the bar. Those who are usually tipped include porters (5 to 10F per bag, which may be a fixed fee), toilet and cloakroom attendants (2F), ushers (2 to 5F), tour guides (5 to 10F), waiters (10 to 15 per cent), taxi drivers (10 to 15 per cent) and hairdressers (10 per cent). In top class hotels it's normal to tip a bell boy, porter, chambermaid or other staff members if you ask them to perform extra services. In public toilets where there's an attendant, there's usually a fixed charge and you aren't required to tip, although when no charge is displayed, it's usual to leave one or two francs. It's usual to tip the usher 2F to 5F per person in many cinemas, theatres and sports stadiums in France, where they may rely solely on tips for their income. This custom is, however, being discontinued and ushers at many cinema chains (e.g. Gaumont, Pathé and UCG) no longer expect tips. It's unnecessary to tip a petrol station attendant (*pompiste*) for cleaning your windscreen or checking your oil, although they are poorly paid and are pleased to receive a small tip.

Christmas is generally a time of giving tips to all and sundry including the postman, rubbish collector and local firemen. The size of a tip depends on how often someone has served you, the quality and friendliness of the service, and your financial status. Generally tips range from 10F to 100F or more, particularly for the *concierge/gardienne* of your apartment block (it pays to be nice to him/her). If you're unsure who or how much to tip, ask your neighbours, friends or colleagues for advice, who will probably all tell you something different! Large tips are, however, considered ostentatious and in bad taste (except by the recipient, who will be your friend for life).

TOILETS

French public toilets vary considerably in their antiquity and modernity, and in addition to some of the world's worst, France (always a country of stark contradictions) also has some of the best. The French use a variety of names to refer to a toilet including *toilettes*, *WC*, *lavabos*, *cabinets*, *petit coin* (the little corner) and colloquially *chiottes* (the crapper). Public toilets are labelled *messieurs/hommes* (men's) and *dames* (ladies).

The old *vespasiens* (named after the Emperor Vespasian, who introduced it to ancient Rome) or *pissoir/pissotière* are thankfully no more. They have been replaced in most cities and towns by unisex 24-hour coin-operated *sanisettes* or 'superloos', cylindrical metal booths topped with a *toilettes* sign. They cost a rather expensive 2F, which makes a mockery of the expression 'to spend a penny', although a number of people can use them in the allotted time. You have up to 15 minutes to do your business before it automatically flushes and the whole cubicle is chemically cleaned (not a good time to get caught with your pants down!). You shouldn't permit small children (e.g. under the age of 10) to use them on their own, as they may be unable to open the door and can be dangerous (a small child was once swept into the sewer by the cleaning process and drowned!).

The Turkish type of loo (*cabinets à la turque/siège turc*) is still found on basic campsites, at *autoroute* rest stops, and in many cheap bars and restaurants. It consists of a square basin set into the floor with two raised islands either side for your feet and a pull-chain for the flush. Care must be taken when flushing it, as it tends to soak the floor, and it's often difficult to keep your clothes and feet dry. In many restaurants and bars, men and women share a common WC and a urinal may be placed next to the hand-washing facilities. In cheap bars and restaurants there may be no toilet paper. In some rural areas you're given a key or even a detachable door handle to the toilet. Some toilets have no light switch and the light is operated automatically when you lock the door (this harks back to the days when electricity was expensive in France). Note that some cafés and bars don't like non-customers using their toilets as a public convenience, although you're entitled to use them free of charge by law (but it's polite to buy a drink).

In cities and towns, public toilets are also found at railway and bus stations, parking garages and in the street. In towns there are often public toilets with attendants (*Dame Pipi*) where there's a fixed charge of 1F to 2F. If no charge is displayed, it's normal to leave 50 centimes or one franc. Toilet paper may be dispensed (piece by piece) by the attendant. In rural areas, the lack of public toilets is no obstacle to many Frenchmen, who are happy to relieve themselves by the side of the road whenever the urge strikes them. In Paris, it's common to see young children (assisted by their parents) relieving themselves in the gutter (*caniveau*), which is where dogs are also supposed to do their business (the gutters are swept and washed daily).

In private residences, Americans should ask for the toilet and not the bathroom (*salle de bains*), as the toilet is often separate from the bathroom. Most French bathrooms have a *bidet* in addition to a toilet bowl, which are for 'intimate ablutions' and aren't footbaths, drinking fountains or toilets! They are also common in hotels, where rooms may have a wash basin and a *bidet* but no toilet bowl, although they are going out of fashion (apparently the bottom has dropped out of the market!).

French toilets employ a variety of flushing devices including a knob on top of the cistern which is pulled upwards, a chain, a push button on the cistern behind the bowl, or even a foot-operated button on the floor (in public toilets). Note that if a building has a septic tank (*fosse septique*), certain items must *never* be flushed down the toilet including sanitary towels, paper (other than **French** toilet paper), disposable nappies (diapers), condoms or anything made of plastic. French toilet paper is narrow, thin and of poor quality, and is designed for use in systems with septic tanks. **You should also never use standard bleaches, disinfectants and chemical cleaners in systems with septic tanks (special brands are available for septic tanks), as they can have a disastrous affect on its operation and create nasty smells!**

19.

THE FRENCH

Who are the French? What are they like? Let's take a candid and totall prejudiced look at the French people, tongue firmly in cheek, and hope the forgive my flippancy or that they don't read this bit, which is why it's hidden away the back of the book. (**French readers please note: This chapter isn't supposed t be taken *too* seriously!**)

The typical Frenchman is artificial, elitist, hedonistic, enigmatic, idle, civilise insular, a hypochondriac, bloody-minded, spineless, a suicidal driver, misunderstoo inflexible, pseudo-intellectual, modern, lazy, disagreeable, seductive, complaining, philosopher, authoritarian, cultured, gallant, provincial, educated, sophisticate aggressive, flirtatious, unsporting, egocentric, unbearable, paternalistic, insecur racist, an individual, ill-disciplined, formal, cynical, unfriendly, emotional, irritatin narrow-minded, charming, unhygienic, obstinate, vain, laid-back, a socialist *and* conservative, serious, long-winded, indecisive, convivial, unloved, callou bad-tempered, garrulous, inscrutable, ambivalent, infuriating, anti-America incomprehensible, superior (inferior), ignorant, impetuous, a gastromaniac, blinkere decadent, truculent, corpulent, mono-lingual, romantic, extravagant, reckles sensuous, pragmatic, aloof, chauvinistic, capitalistic, courteous, chic, patrioti XENOPHOBIC, proud, passionate, fashionable, nationalistic, bureaucrati conceited, arrogant, dishonest, surly, rude, impatient, articulate, chivalrous, brav selfish, imaginative, amiable, debauched, boastful, argumentative, elegant, a lous lover, egotistical, cold, a good cook, sexy, private, promiscuous, contradictor political, intolerant, inhospitable, brusque, handsome, an Asterix fan, and above all insufferably French!

You may have noticed that the above list contains 'a few' contradictions (as doe life in France), which is hardly surprising as there's no such thing as a typic Frenchman. Apart from the numerous differences in character between th inhabitants of different regions of France, the population encompasses a potpourri c foreigners from all corners of the globe. However, while it's true that not *a* Frenchmen are stereotypes (some are almost indistinguishable from 'normal' people I refuse to allow a few eccentrics to spoil my arguments . . .

Living among the French can be a traumatic experience and foreigners are ofte shocked by French attitudes. One of the first things a newcomer needs to do i discover where he fits into the picture, particularly regarding class and status. I many ways the French are even more class and status conscious than the British (i was the Normans who introduced class into Britain), with classes ranging from th aristocracy (*les grandes familles*, otherwise known as the guillotined or shortene classes) and upper bourgeoisie, through the middle and lower bourgeoisie to th workers and peasantry. The French class system is based on birthright rather tha wealth and money doesn't determine or buy status (so ill-bred *nouveau riche plouc* needn't apply).

The French are renowned for their insularity (worse than the Japanese!) an cannot stand foreigners. The butt of French jokes (not that there are many) are th Belgians and Swiss, whom the French poke fun at out of jealousy for their refine French accents and superior cultural heritage. However, if it's any consolation, th French reserve their greatest enmity for their fellow countrymen (everybody hate Parisians – even other Parisians). The French are Alsatians, Basques, Burgundians Bretons, Corsicans, Normans, Parisians, Provençal or whatever first and French distant second. Parisians believe that anybody who doesn't live in Paris is a peasan and beneath contempt. Paradoxically, most Parisians (half of whom are interlopers have a yearning to live in the country (*la France profonde*) and escape to it at every opportunity. Fortunately the French don't travel well, for which the rest of the world can be truly thankful.

There's a love-hate relationship between the French and Germans (the French *love* to hate the Germans), although they reserve their greatest animosity for *les Anglo-Saxons*, i.e. the very same foreigners who rescued them TWICE from the dreaded Hun. France owes its liberty, independence and status as a great (small 'g') power to American and British intervention in two world wars, a humiliating fact they would prefer to forget (although it doesn't hurt to remind them now and again!). Although it's understandable when you've had your butt kicked by the Krauts three times in succession that you prefer not to dwell on it, they're still an ungrateful shower (next time the Germans can keep the damn place!).

Every setback is seen as part of an international conspiracy (naturally concocted by *les anglo-saxons*) to rob France of its farms, jobs, culture and very identity. The French bemoan the American influences creeping (hurtling?) into their lives such as *le fast food*, language, TV and films, and worst of all, American 'culture', as depicted by Disneyland Paris (which patriotic Frenchmen are praying will go broke). However, French youth devours everything American including its clothes, films, music, food, coke, toys, technology and culture. McDonald's 'restaurants' (the word is used *very* loosely) have become a favourite target for rampaging farmers and self-styled cultural 'guardian angels', battling to prevent the Americanisation of France.

Which brings us to a subject dear to every Frenchman's heart – food. As everyone knows, food was a French invention (along with sex, the guillotine and VAT) and eating is the national pastime (more important than sex, religion and politics combined). The French are voracious carnivores and eat anything that walks, runs, crawls, swims, or flies. They are particularly fond of all the obnoxious bits that civilised people reject including hoofs, ears, tails, brains, entrails and reproductive organs (the French are anything but squeamish). They also eat repulsive things such as snails and frogs' legs (but what do they do with the bodies?). The French are also partial to barbecued British lamb, which they prefer cooked alive over the embers of a burning truck. A nation of animal lovers, the French are particularly fond of the tastier species such as horses and songbirds, which are usually eaten raw with garlic (it's essential to develop a tolerance to garlic if you're to live in France). The French have an ambivalent attitude towards animals and those they don't pamper as pets are often treated abominably.

The French also know a thing or two about drinking and are among the world's most prolific consumers of alcohol (only the Luxembourgeois drink more), although you rarely see a legless Frenchman. As every Frenchman knows, intelligence, sexual prowess and driving skills are all greatly enhanced by a few stiff drinks. Not surprisingly, the French are obsessed with their livers (when not eating those of ducks) and bowel movements, both of which have an intimate relationship with food and drink. The customary treatment for a liver crisis (*crise de foie*) and most other ailments is the suppository, used to treat everything from the common cold to a heart attack (the French are a nation of hypochondriacs and when not eating are popping pills).

Frenchmen are never happier than when they are complaining about something, and protests (*manifestations*) are commonplace and an excuse for a good riot (the French are descended from a tribe called the Vandals). Civil disobedience is the national sport and the French take to the barricades at the drop of a beret. France has numerous self-help groups (called anarchists in other countries) and many Frenchmen, e.g. fishermen, farmers and truck drivers, are a law unto themselves. Observing senseless edicts such as motoring laws, prohibitive signs (e.g. no parking, no smoking, no dogs, no riots, etc.) and other trivial rules is a matter of personal choice in France. Although France is ostensibly a country of written rules, regulations and laws, they exist solely to be waived, bent or adapted (*système débrouillard*) to your own use.

Kind-hearted French farmers are famous for their love of animals and they often take their cows and sheep for a day out to Paris and other cities (they also regularly distribute free produce on the city streets for the poor town folk). The French, who are difficult to govern during the best of times, are impossible to rule in bad times. France always seems to be teetering on the edge of anarchy and revolution, and mass demonstrations have a special place in French political culture. The CRS (riot police) are the only people capable of communicating with rioting Frenchmen, which they do by whacking them on the head with a large baton (when not looking the other way). Not surprisingly, the French are the world's leading consumers of tranquillisers, not to mention aspirins to counter the effects of being frequently bashed on the head.

The French complain loud and long about their leaders and the merest mention of politics is a cue for a vociferous argument. They're contemptuous of their politicians, which isn't surprising considering they're an incompetent, licentious and corrupt bunch of buffoons who couldn't organise a *soûlerie* in a vineyard. They rate lower than prostitutes in the French social order and the public service they provide (French prostitutes have morals and principles and do a sterling job – ask any politician!). French politics are a bizarre mixture of left and right, although paradoxically most Frenchmen are extremely conservative. The French (through Jean Monnet) invented the European Union (EU), a fact which should be patently obvious to anyone, considering it's one of the most bureaucratic and dictatorial organisations in the world. The French believe that the EU was a splendid institution while it pursued French ambitions and was led by France, but are ambivalent since all the rabble were admitted. General de Gaulle was adamant that the intractable British shouldn't be allowed to join the club and the last few decades have shown that he certainly had a good case!

France is the most bureaucratic (*le mal français*) country in the world, with almost twice as many civil servants as Germany and three times as many as Japan. In order to accomplish anything remotely official in France, 98 forms must be completed in quintuplicate, each of which must be signed by 47 officials in 31 different government departments. Only then do you get your bus pass! When dealing with civil servants you must *never* show your impatience, which is like a red rag to a bull. It's the fault of all those French cheeses; as de Gaulle so succinctly put it: "it's difficult to rule a nation with 365 cheeses" (or possibly 265, 400 or even 750). It's even harder to govern a country that has no idea how many cheeses it has!

The French aren't exactly noted for their humility and variously describe France (*la Grande Nation*) as the most cultured of countries, the light of the world, and a nation destined by God (who's naturally a Frenchman) to dominate the continent. Not surprisingly, Paris is the capital of civilisation and the city of light. France lives on its past glories (*la gloire*) and clings tenaciously to its colonies (which it uses as a testing ground for its nuclear weapons) long after other colonists have seen the light. French history is littered with French delusions of grandeur (*la grandeur française*), which spawned such infamous megalomaniacs as Charlemagne, Napoleon, de Gaulle, and the most famous Frenchman of all, Asterix. France yearns for foreign adulation, the predominance of the French language and culture (Johnny Hallyday aside), and to be hailed as the undisputed leader of Europe. The Frenchman's favourite word is appropriately *supérieur* (nobody **ever** accused the French of being modest).

The French language has divine status in France and is the language of love, food and the Gods. The French cling to their language as their last vestige of individuality and its propagation by the foreign service is sacrosanct (mock it at your peril!). The French love their language and habitually use it as a blunt instrument to intimidate uneducated foreigners, i.e. anyone who doesn't speak French (only in France are tourists treated with contempt for not speaking the language). To fully understand the French you need an intimate knowledge of their beautiful and romantic language, which is the key to their spirit and character. In practice this consists of learning just two words, *merde!* and *NON!*, which can be used effectively to deal with every situation, as was aptly demonstrated by General de Gaulle (see also *le bras d'honneur* below). The French say no to everything and only afterwards consider the question.

As every educated person knows, the best way to communicate with foreigners is to shout at them in English at close quarters. On the rare occasion that this doesn't work you should resort to sign language, a scientific and highly developed art form in France. The supreme gesture is *le bras d'honneur*, meaning 'up yours' (or something less printable!). It's executed with your right arm outstretched and your left hand smacking your right bicep, followed immediately by your right forearm springing upwards. It isn't advisable, however, to make this gesture in the general direction of a *gendarme* or anyone with a gun.

Most Frenchmen pretend not to speak English, usually because they speak it excruciatingly badly and nobody can understand them anyway (if the French weren't so damned nationalistic they would speak English and dispense with this *français* nonsense). The French appropriately have a gigantic inferiority complex about the English language, which they blame for the decline of the French language and empire (the ability to speak French is no longer the sign of a civilised person). However, French youth increasingly speak perfect English, which to the older generation merely confirms the country's cultural decline.

When not eating the French are allegedly making love. They are obsessed with sex and have a long tradition of debauchery. French men think they are God's gift to women and are in a permanent state of unbridled eroticism. They see every attractive woman as a potential conquest, particularly foreign women, some of whom have a reputation for being 'easy' prey (if you *really* want to know how good your wife is in bed, ask your French friends!). The French use sex to sell everything from cars to mineral water (what foreigners find sexist, the French find sexy) and lack modesty in all things, discarding their clothes at every opportunity. French women enjoy being objects of desire (bimbos) and most care little for women's liberation and are quite happy with the status quo. Flirting is an art form in France, where sexual overtones are part and parcel of professional life.

The French are renowned for their sexual peccadilloes and are credited with inventing sadism (the Marquis de Sade), brothels (bordellos), French letters (named after the French town of Condom?), masturbation and adultery. In France, *c'est normal* for a woman to seek lovers and for a man to have mistresses. If a married man is a philanderer it's a source of pride and a mark of respect and nothing to be ashamed of (it's a real vote-catcher for politicians!). A mistress is a status symbol, the absence of which casts grave doubts on a man's virility and sexual predilections. As a by-product of this rampant free love, the French have record numbers of illegitimate children, whom they have been forced to legalise (along with their concubines). The French even have the gall to call homosexuality 'the English vice' (*le vice anglais*), although everyone knows why Paris, which is famous for its transvestites, is called *gay* Paris (France is the only country where the men wear more perfume than the women!).

Despite not washing, living on garlic and wearing their socks for weeks on end, Frenchmen have amazingly established a reputation for suave, seductive charm (surely women aren't attracted by the likes of Alain Delon, Gérard Depardieu and Sacha Distel?). However, despite his formidable reputation, the Frenchman's performance in bed is similar to that of his army; an excess of pomp and ceremony, but when the pantaloons are down he empties his cannon out of range and rolls over. Fittingly, the national symbol of France is the resplendent cockerel, which seduces and impregnates the submissive hens and then crows (*cocorico!*) triumphantly, even when it has nothing to boast about (after which it's cooked in wine and eaten). However, despite the undeniable fact that the rooster services many hens, the evidence is that he doesn't satisfy them (around half of French women declare their sex lives to be unsatisfactory).

The French are formidable sportsmen and have produced a long line of sporting heroes (although their names are difficult to recall). Among the most popular French sports are sex; beating the system (e.g. fare evasion, cheating the tax man, claiming unlawful social security and defrauding the EU); stock-car racing on public roads; corruption, fraud and sleaze; falling off skis; running (away from the Germans); falling off bicycles while following Americans, Belgians, Spaniards and assorted other foreigners around France; losing at football (1998 was a temporary aberration); falling off bar stools; boules (a form of marbles played by southerners plastered on pastis); rioting; horse riding (to escape from rampaging Germans); shooting themselves in the feet; tennis; and sex. It's widely acknowledged that the French are cheats, poor losers and have absolutely no notion of *le fair play*. After all, how can a nation which doesn't play cricket *or* baseball possibly be trusted to play by the rules?

Enough of this frivolity, let's get down to serious business. Like most capitalist countries, France is a sorely divided nation. While the elite and privileged *bourgeoisie* luxuriate in the sun, the inhabitants of the poor suburbs and immigrant ghettos remain permanently in the shade, plagued with poor transport, soaring crime, extremist politics, and an acute sense of dereliction and hopelessness. France has a festering racial problem with the suppressed and disadvantaged Africans and Arabs (enticed to France as cheap labour in the '50s to '70s) locked in a vicious cycle of poverty and racism.

The increasingly destitute farming communities and thousands of rural villages are also firmly anchored in second class France. The human fallout from *la bonne vie* and the '90s recession inhabit the streets and *métro* tunnels of French cities (it's estimated that around 100,000 people live on the streets of Paris alone). France also suffers from increasing drug abuse, alcoholism, violence and mounting unemployment, which is a vast and enduring problem and likely to lead to social unrest unless it's drastically reduced. However, by far the biggest challenge facing France's leaders is how to reform the economy (e.g. debt-ridden public companies, a burgeoning social security deficit and soaring taxation) without provoking a (another) revolution. In the last few years the French have been deeply disillusioned, with unemployment and anxiety about the country's future prosperity infecting the whole of society.

To be fair (who the hell's trying to be fair?), the French do have a few good points. France is blessed by a superb climate and outstanding natural beauty, augmented by the charm and splendour of French cities and towns. The French enjoy the best cuisine in the world and many of the world's great wines. They have superb public services, fine schools, excellent social security benefits (although the country cannot afford them), superb hospitals (no waiting lists), excellent working conditions and employee benefits, and a first-class transportation system with magnificent *autoroutes* and among the world's fastest trains. The country enjoys a high standard of living, low inflation, a relatively healthy economy (despite the gloom) and one of the strongest currencies in the world. The French (unlike many other nations) haven't turned their backs on their roots and strong family ties and loyalties are a prominent feature of French life.

France is one of the most cultured countries in the world and the French are renowned for their insatiable appetite for gastronomy, art, literature, philosophy and music. Paris houses some of the world's greatest museums, monuments and architectural treasures, and is one of the world's most attractive and romantic cities and its cleanest major capital (London and New York please note). France is highly competitive on the world stage, notably in foreign affairs, business, technology, sport and culture, and is one of the few western countries with the vision and boldness to conceive and execute grandiose schemes. The French are justifiably proud of their achievements (critical foreigners are simply jealous) and France is no longer an island unto itself, its traditional insularity having been replaced by a highly developed sense of international responsibility. It remains one of the most influential nations in the world and a positive power for good, particularly in the field of medicine, where *Médecins sans Frontière* and *Médecins du Monde* do exemplary work.

While doing battle with French bureaucracy is enough to discourage anybody, the real French people usually couldn't be more welcoming. If you're willing to meet them half way and learn their language, you'll invariably be warmly received by the French, who will go out of their way to help you. Contrary to popular belief they aren't baby-eating ogres (except for Parisians) and providing you make an effort to be friendly they're likely to overwhelm you with kindness. Anyone planning to make their permanent home in France should bear in mind that assimilation is all-important. If you don't want to live *with* the French and share their way of life, language, culture and traditions, then you're probably better off going somewhere else. Although it's difficult to get to know the French, when you do you invariably make friends for life.

The mark of a great nation is that it *never* breeds indifference in foreigners – admiration, envy, hostility or even blind hatred – but never indifference! Love it or hate it, France is a unique, vital, civilised, bold, sophisticated and sometimes disturbing country. In the final analysis the French enjoy one of the world's best lifestyles and what many believe is the finest overall quality of life (French civilisation has been described as an exercise in enlightened self-indulgence). Few other countries offer such a wealth of intoxicating experiences for the mind, body and spirit – and not all out of a bottle! Whether francophiles or francophobes, most foreigners agree that France is a great place to live. *Vive la différence! Vive la République! Vive la France! Vive les Français!*

ON SECOND THOUGHTS,
I'D PREFER IT OVER THERE

20.

MOVING HOUSE OR LEAVING FRANCE

When moving house or leaving France, there are numerous things to b considered and a 'million' people to be informed. The checklists contained i this chapter will make the task easier and may even help prevent an ulcer or nervou breakdown – providing you don't leave everything to the last minute.

MOVING HOUSE

When moving house *within* France the following items should be considered:

- If you're renting accommodation, you must usually give your landlord at leas three months notice (refer to your contract). Your resignation letter must be ser by registered mail (*lettre recommandée avec avis de réception*).

- Inform the following, as applicable:

  - Your employer.

  - Your present town hall and the town hall in your new community within on month of taking up residence. They will change the address on your *carte d séjour*.

  - Your local social security (*Caisse Primaire d'Assurance Maladie/CPAM*) an family allowance (*Caisse d'Allocations Familiales*) offices.

  - Your local income tax office (*centre des impôts*).

  - If you have a French driving licence or a French registered car and ar remaining in the same department, you must return your licence and ca registration document (*carte grise*) and have the address changed (see pag 196). If you're moving to a new department you must inform both your curren and new *préfectures*. You must re-register your car (see page 196) and obtain new licence (see page 200) from your new *préfecture* within three months o taking up residence.

  - Your electricity, gas and water companies.

  - France Télécom (and other phone companies) if you have a telephone and you regional TV licence centre (*Centre Régional de la Redevance Audiovisuelle*) i you have a TV licence.

  - Your insurance companies, e.g. health, car, house contents and private liability hire purchase companies; lawyer; accountant; and local businesses where yo have accounts. Obtain new insurance, if applicable.

  - Your banks and other financial institutions such as stockbrokers and credit card companies. Make arrangements for the transfer of funds and the cancellation o alteration of standing orders (regular payments).

  - Your family doctor, dentist and other health practitioners. Health records should be transferred to your new practitioners.

  - Your children's and your schools. If applicable, arrange for schooling in your new community (see **Chapter 9**). Try to give a term's notice and obtain copies of any relevant school reports and records from current schools.

  - All regular correspondents, subscriptions, social and sports clubs, professional and trade journals, and friends and relatives. Arrange to have your mail redirected by the post office by completing a permanent change of address card (*order de réexpédition définitif*). Change of address cards are available from post offices.

- Your local consulate or embassy if you're registered with them (see page 79).

● Return any library books or anything borrowed.

● Arrange removal of your furniture and belongings (or rent transportation, if you're doing your own removal)

● If you live in rented accommodation, obtain a refund of your deposit from your landlord.

● Ask yourself (again): 'Is it really worth all this trouble?'.

LEAVING FRANCE

Before leaving France for an indefinite period the following items should be considered *in addition* to those listed above under **Moving House:**

● Check that your own and your family's passports are valid!

● Give notice to your employer, if applicable.

● Check whether any special entry requirements are necessary for your country of destination by contacting the local embassy or consulate in France, e.g. visas, permits or inoculations. An exit permit or visa isn't required to leave France.

● You may qualify for a rebate on your income tax (see page 291) and social security payments (see page 254). Tax rebates are normally paid automatically.

● If you have contributed to a supplementary pension scheme, a percentage of your contributions will be repaid (see page 264), although your pension company will require proof that you're leaving France permanently.

● Arrange to sell anything you aren't taking with you (house, car, furniture, etc.) and to ship your belongings. Find out the procedure for shipping your belongings to your country of destination (see page 95). Check with the local embassy or consulate in France of the country to which you're moving. Special forms may need to be completed before arrival. If you have been living in France for less than a year, you're required to re-export all imported personal effects, including furniture and vehicles (if you sell them, you may be required to pay tax or duty).

● If you have a French registered car that you intend to take with you, you can drive on your French registration plates for a maximum of three months.

● Pets may require special inoculations or may need to go into quarantine for a period (see page 404), depending on your destination.

● Contact France Télécom (see page 114) and anyone else well in advance if you need to recover a deposit.

● Arrange health, travel and other insurance (see **Chapter 13**).

● Depending on your destination, you may wish to arrange health and dental checkups before leaving France. Obtain a copy of your health and dental records and a statement from your health insurance company stating your present level of cover.

• Terminate any French loan, lease or hire purchase contracts, and pay all outstanding bills (allow plenty of time, as some companies are slow to respond).

• Check whether you're entitled to a rebate on your road tax, car and other insurance. Obtain a letter from your French motor insurance company stating your no-claims bonus.

• Make arrangements to sell or let your house or apartment and other property in France.

• Check whether you need an international driving licence or a translation of your French or foreign driving licence for your country of destination.

• Give friends and business associates in France a temporary address and telephone number where you can be contacted abroad.

• If you will be travelling or living abroad for an extended period, you may wish to give someone 'powers of attorney' over your financial affairs in France, so they can act on your behalf in your absence. This can be for a fixed period or open-ended and can be limited to a specific purpose only. **You should, however, obtain expert legal advice before doing this.**

• Buy a copy of *Living and Working in* ******** before leaving France. If we haven't published it yet, drop us a line and we'll get started on it right away!

  Bon Voyage!

APPENDICES

APPENDIX A: USEFUL ADDRESSES

Embassies

Embassies are located in the capital Paris and many countries also have consulates in other cities (British provincial consulates are listed on page 433). Embassies and consulates are listed in the Yellow Pages under *Ambassades, consulats et autres représentations diplomatiques*. Note that many countries have more than one office in Paris. Before writing or calling you should telephone to confirm that you have the correct address.

Albania: 131, rue Pompe, 16e (☎ 01.45.53.51.32).

Algeria: 50, rue Lisbonne, 8e (☎ 01.53.93.20.20).

Angola: 19, av Foch, 16e (☎ 01.45.01.58.20).

Argentina: 6, rue Cimarosa, 16e (☎ 01.45.53.22.25).

Armenia: 9 rue Viète, 17e (☎ 01.42.12.98.00)

Australia: 4, rue Jean Rey, 15e (☎ 01.40.59.33.00).

Austria: 6, rue Fabert, 7e (☎ 01.45.56.97.86).

Bahrain: 3015 pl Etats-Unis, 16e (☎ 01.47.23.48.68).

Bangladesh: 5, sq Pétrarque, 16e (☎ 01.45.53.41.20).

Belgium: 9, rue Tilsitt, 17e (☎ 01.44.09.39.39).

Benin: 87, av Victor Hugo, 16e (☎ 01.45.00.98.82).

Bolivia: 12, av Président Kennedy, 16e (☎ 01.42.24.93.44).

Bosnia Herzegovenia: 194 rue Courcales, 17e (☎ 01.42.67.34.22)

Brazil: 34 Cours Albert 1er, 8e (☎ 01.45.61.63.00).

Brunei Darussalam: 4, rue Logelbach, 17e (☎ 01.42.67.49.47).

Bulgaria: 1, av. Rapp, 7e (☎ 01.45.51.85.90).

Cambodia: 4 rue Adolphe Yvon, 16e (☎ 01.45.03.47.20)

Cameroon: 73, rue Auteuil, 16e (☎ 01.47.43.98.33).

Canada: 35, av Montaigne, 8e (☎ 01.44.43.29.16).

Central African Republic: 30, rue Perchamps, 16e (☎ 01.42.24.42.56).

Chad: 65, rue Belles Feuilles, 16e (☎ 01.45.53.36.75).

Chile: 2, av La Motte Picquet, 7e (☎ 01.44.18.59.60).

China: 11, av George V, 8e (☎ 01.47.23.36.77).

Colombia: 22, rue Elysée, 8e (☎ 01.42.65.46.08).

Comoros: 20, rue Marbeau, 16e (☎ 01.40.67.90.54).

Congo: 37 bis, rue Paul Valéry, 16e (☎ 01.45.00.68.57).

Costa Rica: 78, av Emile Zola, 15e (☎ 01.45.78.96.96).

Cote d'Ivoire: 102, av Raymond Poincaré, 16e (☎ 01.53.64.62.62).

Croacia: 79, av Georges Manbel, 16e (☎ 01.53.70.02.80)

Cyprus: 23, rue Galilée, 8e (☎ 01.47.20.86.28).

Czech Republic: 15, av Charles Floquet, 7e (☎ 01.40.65.13.00).

Cuba: 16, rue Presles, 15e (☎ 01.45.67.55.35).

Denmark: 77, av Marceau, 16e (☎ 01.44.31.21.21).
Djibouti: 26, rue Emile Menier, 16e (☎ 01.47.27.49.22).
Ecuador: 34, av Messine, 8e (☎ 01.42.56.22.59).
Egypt: 56, av Léna, 16e (☎ 01.53.67.88.30).
El Salvador: 12, rue Galilée, 16e (☎ 01.47.20.42.02).
Estonia: 14, bd Montmartre, 9e (☎ 01.48.01.00.22).
Ethiopia: 35, av Charles Floquet, 7e (☎ 01.47.83.83.95).
Finland: 2, rue Fabert, 7e (☎ 01.44.18.19.28).
Gabon: 26 bis, av Raphaël, 16e (☎ 01.44.30.22.60).
Gambia: 17, rue St Lazare, 8e (☎ 01.42.94.09.30).
Germany: 13, Ave F.D. Roosevelt, 8e (☎ 01.53.83.45.00).
Ghana: 8, villa Said, 16e (☎ 01.45.00.09.50).
Greece: 17, rue Auguste Vacquerie, 16e (☎ 01.47.23.72.28).
Guatemala: 73, rue Courcelles, 8e (☎ 01.42.27.78.63).
Guinea: 51, rue Faisanderie, 16e (☎ 01.47.04.81.48).
Guinea-Bissau: 94, rue St. Lazare, 9e (☎ 01.45.26.18.51).
Haiti: 10, rue Théodule Ribot, 17e (☎ 01.47.63.47.78).
Honduras: 8, rue Crevaux, 16e (☎ 01.47.55.86.43).
Hungary: 5 bis, sq Avenue Foch, 16e (☎ 01.45.00.41.59).
Iceland: 8, av Kléber , 16 (☎ 01.44.17.32.85).
India: 15, rue Alfred Dehodencq, 16e (☎ 01.40.58.70.70).
Indonesia: 49, rue Cortambert, 16e (☎ 01.45.03.07.60).
Iran: 4, av Léna, 16e (☎ 01.40.69.70.00).
Ireland: 41, rue Rude, 16e (☎ 01.44.17.67.00).
Israel: 3, rue Rabelais, 8e (☎ 01.40.76.55.00).
Italy: 51, rue Varenne, 7e (☎ 01.49.54.03.00).
Jamaica: 60, av Fich, 16e (☎ 01.45.00.62.25).
Japan: 7 av Hoche, 8e (☎ 01.48.88.62.00).
Kenya: 3, rue Cimarosa, 16e (☎ 01.45.53.35.00).
Korea: 125, rue Grenelle, 7e (☎ 01.47.53.01.01).
Kuwait: 2, rue Lubeck, 16e (☎ 01.47.23.54.25).
Laos: 74, av Raymond Poincaré, 16e (☎ 01.45.53.02.98).
Latvia: 6, Villa Saïd, 16e (☎ 01.53.64.58.10).
Lebanon: 42, rue Copernic, 16e (☎ 01.40.67.75.75).
Liberia: 12, pl Général Catroux, 17e (☎ 01.47.63.58.55).
Libya: 2, rue Charles Lamoureux, 16e (☎ 01.45.53.40.70).
Lithuania: 14, bd Montmartre, 9e (☎ 01.48.01.00.33).
Luxembourg: 33, av Rapp, 7e (☎ 01.45.55.13.37).
Madagascar: 4, av Raphaël, 16e (☎ 01.45.04.62.11).
Malawi: 20, rue Euler, 8e (☎ 01.40.70.18.46).
Malaysia: 32, rue Spontini, 16e (☎ 01.45.53.11.85).
Mali: 89, rue Cherche Midi, 6e (☎ 01.45.48.58.43).

Malta: 92, av Champs Elysées, 8e (☎ 01.45.62.53.01).
Mexico: 9, rue Longchamp, 16e (☎ 01.42.61.51.80).
Monaco: 22, bd Suchet, 16e (☎ 01.45.04.74.54).
Morocco: 35, rue Le Tasse, 16e (☎ 01.45.20.69.35).
Mozambique: 82, rue Laugier, 17e (☎ 01.47.64.91.32).
Myanmar: 60, rue Courcelles, 8e (☎ 01.42.25.56.95).
Nepal: 45 bis, rue Acacias, 17e (☎ 01.46.22.48.67).
Netherlands: 7, rue Eblé, 7e (☎ 01.40.62.34.66).
New Zealand: 7 ter, rue Léonard de Vinci, 16e (☎ 01.45.00.24.11).
Nicaragua: 34, av Bugeaud, 16e (☎ 01.44.05.90.42).
Niger: 154, rue Longchamp, 16e (☎ 01.45.04.80.60).
Nigeria: 173, av Victor Hugo, 16e (☎ 01.47.04.68.65).
Norway: 28, rue Bayard, 8e (☎ 01.53.67.04.00).
Oman: 50, av Léna, 16e (☎ 01.47.23.01.63).
Pakistan: 18, rue Lord Byron, 8e (☎ 01.45.62.23.32).
Panama: 145, av Suffren, 15e (☎ 01.47.83.23.32).
Paraguay: 1, rue St Dominique, 7e (☎ 01.42.22.85.05).
Peru: 50, ave Kléber, 16e (☎ 01.53.70.42.00).
Poland: 1, rue Talleyrand, 7e (☎ 01.45.51.49.12).
Portugal: 3, rue Noisiel, 16e (☎ 01.47.27.35.29).
Qatar: 57, quai Orsay, 7e (☎ 01.45.51.90.71).
Romania: 3, rue Exposition, 7e (☎ 01.45.51.42.46).
Russia: 40, bd Lannes, 16e (☎ 01.45.04.05.50).
Rwanda: 12, rue Jadin, 17e (☎ 01.42.27.36.31).
San Marino: 21, rue Auguste Vacquerie, 16e (☎ 01.47.23.78.05).
Saudi Arabia: 5, av Hoche, 8e (☎ 01.47.66.02.06).
Senegal: 14, av Robert Schuman, 7e (☎ 01.47.05.39.45).
Seychelles: 51, rue Mozart, 16e (☎ 01.42.30.57.47).
Sierra Leone: 16, av Hoche, 8e (☎ 01.42.56.14.73).
Singapore: 12, sq Avenue Foch, 16e (☎ 01.45.00.33.61).
Somalia: 26, rue Dumont d'Urville, 16e (☎ 01.45.00.76.51).
South Africa: 59, quai Orsay, 7e (☎ 01.53.59.23.23).
Spain: 22, av Marceau, 8e (☎ 01.44.43.18.00).
Sri Lanka: 15, rue Astorg, 8e (☎ 01.42.66.35.01).
Sudan: 56, av Montaigne, 8e (☎ 01.42.25.55.73).
Sweden: 17, rue Barbet de Jouy, 7e (☎ 01.44.18.88.00).
Switzerland: 142, rue Grenelle, 7e (☎ 01.49.55.67.00).
Syria: 20, rue Vaneau, 7e (☎ 01.47.05.92.73).
Tanzania: 13, av Raymond Poincare, 16e (☎ 01.53.70.63.66).
Thailand: 12, rue Lord Byron, 8e (☎ 01.42.89.89.44).
Togo: 15, rue Madrid, 8e (☎ 01.44.70.04.39).
Tunisia: 25, rue Barbet de Jouy, 7e (☎ 01.45.55.95.98).

Turkey: 16, av Lamballe, 16e (☎ 01.45.24.52.24).
Uganda: 13, av Raymond Poincaré, 16e (☎ 01.53.70.62.70).
United Arab Emirates: 3, rue Lota, 16e (☎ 01.45.53.94.04).
United Kingdom: 35, rue Fauberg St. Honoré, 8e (☎ 01.44.51.31.02).
United States of America: 2, rue St Florentin, 1e (☎ 01.43.12.23.47).
Uruguay: 15, rue Le Sueur, 16e (☎ 01.45.00.81.37).
Venezuela: 11, rue Copernic, 16e (☎ 01.45.53.29.98).
Vietnam: 62, rue Boileau, 16e (☎ 01.44.14.64.00).
Yemen: 25, rue Georges Bizet, 16e (☎ 01.47.23.61.76).
Yugoslavia (Republic of): 54, rue Faisanderie, 16e (☎ 01.40.72.24.24)
Zaire: 32, cours Albert, 1er, 8e (☎ 01.42.25.57.50).
Zambia: 34, av Messing, 8e (☎ 01.45.61.05.08).
Zimbabwe: 5, rue Tilsitt, 8e (☎ 01.53.81.90.10).

British Provincial Consulates

Biarritz, British Consulate (Hon.), 7, ave Edouard VII, Barclays Banks SA, 64202 Biarittz Cedex (☎ 05.59.24.21.40).

Bordeaux, British Consulate-General, 353, bd du Président Wilson, BP 91, 33073 Bordeaux Cedex (☎ 05.57.22.21.10).

Boulogne-sur-Mer, British Consulate (Hon.), c/o Cotrama, Tour Administrative, Hoverport, 62200 Boulogne-sur-Mer (☎ 03.21.87.16.80).

Calais, British Consulate, c/o P&O European Ferries, 41, place d'Armes, 62100 Calais (☎ 03.21.96.33.76).

Cherbourg, British Consulate (Hon.), c/o P&O European Ferries, Gare Maritime, 50101 Cherbourg (☎ 02.33.44.20.13).

Dinard, British Consulate (Hon.), La Hulotte, 8, bd des Maréchaux, 35800 Dinard (☎ 02.99.46.26.64).

Dunkerque, British Consulate (Hon.), c/o L. Dewulf, Cailleret & Fils, 11, rue des Arbres, BP 1502, 59383 Dunkerque (☎ 03.28.66.11.98).

Le Havre, British Consulate (Hon.), c/o Lloyds Register of Shipping, 124, bd de Strasbourg, 76600 Le Havre (☎ 02.35.42.27.47).

Lille, British Consulate-General, 11, square Dutilleul, 59800 Lille (☎ 03.20.12.82.72).

Lyon, British Consulate-General, 24, rue Childebert, 69288 Lyon Cedex 1 (☎ 04.72.77.81.70).

Marseille, British Consulate-General, 24, ave du Prado, 13006 Marseille (☎ 04.91.15.72.10). Also deals with **Monaco.**

Nantes, British Consulate (Hon.), L'Aumarière, 44220 Couëron (☎ 02.40.63.16.02).

Nice, British Consulate (Hon.), 8, rue Alphonse Kerr, 06000 Nice (☎ 04.93.82.32.04). Also deals with **Monaco.**

Toulouse, British Consulate (Hon.), c/o Lucas Aerospace, Victoria Center, 20, chemin de Laporte, 31300 Toulouse (☎ 05.61.15.02.02).

APPENDIX B: FURTHER READING

The lists contained in this appendix are only a selection of the hundreds of books written about France. In addition to the general and Paris guides listed below, there are also numerous guides covering individual regions of France. The publication title is followed by the author's name and the publisher's name (in brackets). Note that some titles may be out of print but may still be obtainable from bookshops and libraries. Books prefixed with an asterisk (*) are recommended by the author.

General Tourist Guides

*Allez France, Richard Binns (Chiltern House)
Berlitz Traveller's Guide France (Berlitz)
*Birnbaum's France, (Houghton Mifflin)
*The Blue Guide to France (A&C Black)
Collins Eurotunnel Weekend Guide (Harper Collins)
*Cruising French Waterways, Hugh McKnight (A&C Black)
Exploring France, Peter & Helen Titchmarsh (Jarrold)
Family France, Frank Barrett (Boxtree)
Fielding's France, Gary Krant (Fielding Morrow)
*Franc-Wise France, Richard Binns (Chiltern House)
*France: Landscape, Architecture, Tradition (Michelin)
*French Leave Encore, Richard Binns (Chiltern House)
*Frommers France (Prentice Hall Travel)
*Holiday Which? Guide to France, Adam Ruck (Consumers' Association and Hodder & Stoughton)
*Lets Go France (MacMillan)
*Lonely Planet: France (Lonely Planet)
*Mapaholics France, Richard Binns (Chiltern House)
*Michelin Blue Guide to France
*Michelin Green Guides
Off The Beaten Track, France (Moorland Publishing)
On the Waterfront in France, Gill Charlton (Fontana)
*The Penguin Guide to France (Penguin)
RAC Gault Millau 'The Best of France' (Andre Gayot)
*The Rough Guide to France, Kate Baillie & Tim Salmon (Rough Guides)
Secret France (AA)
Slow Boat Through France, Hugh McKnight (David & Charles)
Visitor's Guide France (Moorland)
Watersteps Through France, Bill & Laurel Cooper (Methuen)

Paris Guides

Blue Guide Paris (Black/Norton)
*David Gentleman's Paris (Hodder & Stoughton)
Essential Paris, Susan Grossman (AA)
Eyewitness Travel Guide: Paris (Dorling Kindersley)
The Footloose Guide to Paris, Deidre Vine (Simon Price)
Guide to Impressionist Paris, Patty Lurie (Lilburne Press)
Lonely Planet: Paris (Lonely Planet)
Michael's Guide Paris (Inbal Travel)
Michelin City Plans, Paris
*Pauper's Paris, Miles Turner (Pan)
Paris, Julian Green (Marion Boyars)
Paris, Vivienne Menkes-Ivry (Christopher Helm)
Paris Confidential, Joseph R. Yogerst (Roger Lascelles)
Paris for Free (or Extremely Cheap), Mark Beffart (Mustang)
Paris de Luxe: Place Vendôme, Alexis Gregory (Thames & Hudson)
*Paris Inside Out, David Applefield (Frank Books)
*Paris Mode d'Emploi/User's Guide (Paris Tourist Office)
*The Rough Guide to Paris (Rough Guides)
*Time Out Paris Guide (Penguin)
The Woman's Travel Guide Paris, Catherine Cullen (Virago Press)

Living & Working in France

*A Bull by the Back Door, Anne Loader (Léonie Press)
The Dreamer's Guide to Living in France, John Hodgkinson (Breese Books)
Emplois d'Eté en France - Summer Employment in France (Vacation Work)
*An Englishman in the Midi, John P. Harris (BBC)
*Can We Afford the Bidet?, Elizabeth Morgan (Lennard Publishing)
*The Duck With a Dirty Laugh, Anne Loader (Léonie Press)
French Dirt, Richard Goodman (Pavilion Books)
French or Foe, Polly Platt (Culture Crossings)
*How to Get a Job in France, Mark Hempshell (How To Books)
Home and Dry in France, George East (La Puce Publications)
At Home in France, Christopher Petkanas (Weidenfeld)
*A House in the Sunflowers, Ruth Silvestre (WH Allen)
Living as a British Expatriate in France (French Chamber of Commerce)
*More From an Englishman in the Midi, John P. Harris (BBC)
*A Normandy Tapestry, Alan Biggins (Kirkdale Books)
Paradise Found, Jim Keeble (Carnell)
*Perfume from Provence, Lady Fortescue (Black Swan)

*René & Me, George East (La Puce Publications)
*Some of My Best Friends are French, Colin Corder (Shelf Publishing)
*Sunset House, Lady Fortescue (Black Swan)
To Live in France, James Bentley
*Toujours Provence, Peter Mayle (Pan)
*Understanding France, John P. Harris (Papermac)
*A White House in Gascony, Rex Grixell (Victor Gollancz)
*Working in France, Carol Pineau and Maureen Kelly (Frank Books)
*A Year in Provence, Peter Mayle (Pan)

Property & Business

At Home in France, Christopher Petkanas (Weidenfeld and Nicolson)
At Home in France, Jane Hawking (Allegretto)
**Buying a Home in France, David Hampshire (Survival Books)
Buying Residential Property in France, Bertrand Defournier (French Chamber of Commerce)
Buying and Renovating Property in France, J. Kater Pollock (Flowerpoll)
Buying & Restoring Old Property in France, David Everett (Robert Hale)
English-French Building and Property Dictionary, J. Kater Pollock (Flowerpoll)
*French Country, Buchholz & Skolnik (Aurum Press)
*The French Farmhouse, Elsie Burch Donald (Little, Brown & Co.)
French Housing, Laws & Taxes, Frank Rutherford (Sprucehurst)
French Real Property and Succession Law, Henry Dyson (Robert Hale)
The French Room, Elizabeth Wilhide (Conran Otopus)
French Style, Suzanne Slesin and Stafford Dliff (Thames and Hudson)
The French Touch, Daphné de Saint Sauveur (Thames & Hudson)
A Guide to Renovating Your Home in France, Janine Paul (199 Amyand Park Road, Twickenham, Middx. TW1 3HN).
Letting French Property Successfully, Stephen Smith & Charles Parkinson (PFK Publishing)
Maison Therapy, Alastair Simpson (New Horizon)
The Most Beautiful Villages of the Dordogne, James Bentley
Really Rural, Marie-France Boyer (Thames & Hudson)
Setting Up a Small Business in France (French Chamber of Commerce)
Traditional Houses of Rural France, Bill Laws (Collins & Brown)

Food & Wine

ABC of French Food, Len Deighton (Arrow)
The A-Z Gastronomique, Fay Sharman & Brian Chadwick (Papermac)
*Bistro Cooking, Patricia Wells
*Bocuse's Regional French Cooking, Paul Bocuse (Flammarion)

*Bon Appétit, Judith White (Peppercorn)

Brittany Gastronomique, Kate Whiteman (Conran Octopus)

Château Cuisine, Willan & Baker (Conran Octopus)

*Floyd on France, Keith Floyd (Michael Joseph).

*Floyd on Hangovers, Keith Floyd (Michael Joseph).

The Food Lover's Guide to Paris, Patricia Wells

*The Food Lover's Companion Guide to France, Marc & Kim Millon (Little, Brown)

Food from France, Quentin Crewe & John Brunton (Ebury Press)

France: A Feast of Food and Wine, Roger Voss (Mitchell Beazley)

La France Gastronomique, Anne Willan (Pavilion)

France: The Vegetarian Table, Georgeanne Brennan (Chronicle)

The French Cheese Book, Major Pat Rance (Papermac)

*Le French Cookbook (Bay Books)

*The French Food & Drink Dictionary, Robyn Wilson (Sphere)

*French Vineyards, Michael Busselle (Pavilion)

*Gault-Millau Guide de la France

*Les Routiers Guide to France (Alan Sutton)

Mastering the Art of French Cooking, Simone Beck, Louisette Bertholle & Julia Child (Penguin)

*Michelin Red Guide France (Michelin)

*The Pocket Guide to French Food and Wine, Tessa Youell & George Kimball (Carbery)

*The Taste of France, Robert Freson (Webb & Bower)

*Time Out Eating & Drinking in Paris (Penguin)

*Vegetarian France, Alex Burke & Alan Todd (Editions La Plage)

The Vineyards of France, Don Philpott (MPC)

*Wine Atlas of France, Hugh Johnson & Hubrecht Duijker (Mitchell Beazley)

The Wines of France, Clive Coates (Random Century)

Wining and Dining in France, Robin Neillands (Ashford, Buchan & Enright)

Woman of Taste, Pamela Vandyke Price (John Murray)

*Your Good Health: The Medicinal Benefits of Wine Drinking, Dr. E. Maury (Souvenir Press)

Miscellaneous

**The Alien's Guide to France, Jim Watson (Survival Books)

*Cambridge Illustrated History: France, Colin Jones (Cambridge University Press)

*Cultural Atlas of France, John Ardagh (Facts on File)

Fragile Glory, Richard Bernstein (Bodley Head)

*France in the New Century: Portrait of a Changing Society, J. Ardagh (Viking)

Francwise France, Harvey Elliot (Chiltern House)

*The French, Theodore Zeldin (Harvill)
*Good Camps France, Alan Rogers (Deneway Guides)
*Hannibal's Footsteps, Bernard Levin (Sceptre)
The Identity of France, Fernand Braudel (Fontana)
The Legal Beagle Goes to France, Bill Thomas (Quiller)
The Making of Modern France - Politics, Ideology and Culture, Emmanuel Todd (Blackwell)
*The Man Who Broke Out of the Bank, Miles Morland (Fontana)
Mapaholics' France, Harvey Elliot (Chiltern House)
The Nature Parks of France, Patrick Delaforce (Windrush Press)
*On The Brink, Jonathan Fenby (Little Brown)
*Paris Chic, Dominique Brabec & Eglé Salvy (Thames & Hudson)
Portraits of France (Hutchinson)
Searching for the New France, James Hollifield & George Ross (Routledge)
Taxation in France, Charles Parkinson (PFK Publishing)
Terence Conran's France (Conran Octopus)
That Sweet Enemy, Christopher Sinclair-Stevenson (Jonathan Cape)
*Writers' France, John Ardagh (Hamish Hamilton)
*Xenophobe's Guide to the French, Nick Yapp & Michel Syrett (Ravette Books)

English-Language Newspapers & Magazines

Blue Coast, 32, rue Maréchal Joffre, 06000 Nice, France. Monthly magazine.

Boulevard, Mediatime France SA, 68, rue des Archives, 75003 Paris, France. Paris lifestyle magazine.

France Magazine, Dormer House, Stow-on-the-Wold, Glos. GL54 1BN, UK. Monthly lifestyle magazine.

France-USA Contacts, FUSAC, 3 rue La Rochelle, 75014 Paris, France. Free weekly magazine.

French Property News, 2A Lambton Road, London SW20 0LR, UK. Monthly property newspaper.

Focus on France, Outbound Publishing, 1 Commercial Road, Eastbourne, East Sussex BN21 3XQ, UK.

Living France, 79 High Street, Olney MK46 4EF, UK. Monthly lifestyle/property magazine.

The News, Brussac, 3, chemin La Monzie, 24000 Perigueux, France. Monthly newspaper.

Paris Free Voice, 65, quai d'Orsay, 75007 Paris, France. Free weekly newspaper.

The Riviera Reporter, 56, chemin de Provence, 06250 Mougins, France. Monthly free magazine.

APPENDIX C: WEIGHTS & MEASURES

Although most countries officially use the metric system of weights and measures, if you're from Britain or the USA (and a few other places) you may be more familiar with the imperial system, in which case the tables on the following pages will be of help. Comparisons shown aren't exact but are close enough for the accuracy required in most everyday calculations.

Clothes sizes, apart from the different measurement systems used, can vary wildly depending on the manufacturer (as we all know only too well!). Try all clothes on before buying. Don't be afraid to return something if, when you try it on at home, you decide it doesn't fit or it's a different colour from what you imagined. French shops will exchange most goods or give a refund.

Women's clothes:

Continental	34	36	38	40	42	44	46	48	50	52
UK	8	10	12	14	16	18	20	22	24	26
USA	6	8	10	12	14	16	18	20	22	24

Pullovers:

	Women's						Mens					
Continental	40	42	44	46	48	50	44	46	48	50	52	54
UK	34	36	38	40	42	44	34	36	38	40	42	44
USA	34	36	38	40	42	44	Sm	Medium		large		exl

Note: sm = small, exl = extra large

Men's Shirts

Continental	36	37	38	39	40	41	42	43	44	46
UK/USA	14	14	15	15	16	16	17	17	18	

Men's Underwear

Continental	5	6	7	8	9	10
UK	34	36	38	40	42	44
USA	small	medium	large	extra large		

Children's Clothes

Continental	92	104	116	128	140	152
UK	16/18	20/22	24/26	28/30	32/34	36/38
USA	2	4	6	8	10	12

Children's Shoes

Continental	18	19	20	21	22	23	24	25	26	27	28
UK/USA	2	3	4	4	5	6	7	7	8	9	10

Continental	29	30	31	32	33	34	35	36	37	38
UK/USA	11	11	12	13	1	2	2	3	4	5

Shoes (Women's and Men's)

Continental	35	35	36	37	37	38	39	39	40	40
UK	2	3	3	4	4	5	5	6	6	7
USA	4	4	5	5	6	6	7	7	8	8

Continental	41	42	42	43	44	44
UK	7	8	8	9	9	10
USA	9	9	10	10	11	11

Weights:

Avoirdupois	Metric	Metric	Avoirdupois
1 oz	28.35 g	1 g	0.035 oz
1 pound	454 g	100 g	3.5 oz
1 cwt	50.8 kg	250 g	9 oz
1 ton	1,016 kg	1 kg	2.2 pounds
1 tonne	2,205 pounds		

Note: g = gramme, kg = kilogramme

Length:

British/US	Metric	Metric	British/US
1 inch =	2.54 cm	1 cm =	0.39 inch
1 foot =	30.48 cm	1 m =	3.28 feet
1 yard =	91.44 cm	1 km =	0.62 mile
1 mile =	1.6 km	8 km =	5 miles

Note: cm = centimetre, m = metre, km = kilometre

Capacity:

Imperial	Metric	Metric	Imperial
1 pint (USA)	0.47 l	1 l	1.76 UK pints
1 pint (UK)	0.568 l	1 l	0.265 US gallons
1 gallon (USA)	3.78 l	1 l	0.22 UK gallons
1 gallon (UK)	4.54 l	1 l	35.211 fluid oz

Note: l = litre

Temperature:

Celsius	Fahrenheit	
0	32	freezing point of water
5	41	
10	50	
15	59	
20	68	
25	77	
30	86	
35	95	
40	104	

The Boiling point of water is 100 degrees Celsius, 212 degrees Fahrenheit.

Oven temperature:

Gas	Electric	
	F	**C**
-	225-250	110-120
1	275	140
2	300	150
3	325	160
4	350	180
5	375	190
6	400	200
7	425	220
8	450	230
9	475	240

For a quick conversion, the Celsius temperature is approximately half the Fahrenheit temperature.

Temperature Conversion:

Celsius to Fahrenheit: multiply by 9, divide by 5 and add 32.
Fahrenheit to Celsius: subtract 32, multiply by 5 and divide by 9.

Body Temperature:

Normal body temperature (if you're alive and well) is 98.4 degrees Fahrenheit, which equals 37 degrees Celsius.

APPENDIX D: REGIONS & DEPARTMENTS

The map opposite shows the 22 regions and 95 departments of France, which are listed below. The departments are (mostly) numbered alphabetically from 01 to 89. Departments 91 to 95 come under the Ile-de-France region, which also includes Ville de Paris (75), Seine-et-Marne (77) and Yvelines (78), shown in detail opposite.

01 Ain	33 Gironde	65 Hautes-Pyrénées
02 Aisne	34 Hérault	66 Pyrénées-Orientales
03 Allier	35 Ille-et-Vilaine	67 Bas-Rhin
04 Alpes-de-Hte-Provence	36 Indre	68 Haut-Rhin
05 Hautes-Alpes	37 Indre-et-Loire	69 Rhône
06 Alpes-Maritimes	38 Isère	70 Haute-Saône
07 Ardèche	39 Jura	71 Saône-et-Loire
08 Ardennes	40 Landes	72 Sarthe
09 Ariège	41 Loir-et-Cher	73 Savoie
10 Aube	42 Loire	74 Haute-Savoie
11 Aude	43 Haute-Loire	75 Paris
12 Aveyron	44 Loire-Atlantique	76 Seine-Maritime
13 Bouches-du-Rhône	45 Loiret	77 Seine-et-Marne
14 Calvados	46 Lot	78 Yvelines
15 Cantal	47 Lot-et-Garonne	79 Deux-Sèvres
16 Charente	48 Lozère	80 Somme
17 Charente-Maritime	49 Maine-et-Loire	81 Tarn
18 Cher	50 Manche	82 Tarn-et-Garonne
19 Corrèze	51 Marne	83 Var
20 Corse	52 Haute-Marne	84 Vaucluse
21 Côte-d'Or	53 Mayenne	85 Vendée
22 Côtes-d'Armor	54 Meurthe-et-Moselle	86 Vienne
23 Creuse	55 Meuse	87 Haute-Vienne
24 Dordogne	56 Morbihan	88 Vosges
25 Doubs	57 Moselle	89 Yonne
26 Drôme	58 Nièvre	90 Territoire de Belfort
27 Eure	59 Nord	91 Essonne
28 Eure-et-Loir	60 Oise	92 Hauts-de-Seine
29 Finistère	61 Orne	93 Seine-Saint-Denis
30 Gard	62 Pas-de-Calais	94 Val-de-Marne
31 Haute-Garonne	63 Puy-de-Dôme	95 Val-d'Oise
32 Gers	64 Pyrénées-Atlantiques	

APPENDIX E: SERVICE DIRECTORY

This **Service Directory** is to help you find local businesses and services in France and the UK, serving residents (and visitors) in France. Note that when calling France from abroad, you must dial the international access number (e.g. 00 from the UK) followed by 33 (the country code for France, **shown in the telephone numbers listed below**) and the subscriber's number. Please mention *Living and Working in France* when contacting companies.

AGENTS (PROPERTY)

KBM Consultancy, North End House, Ashton Keynes, Wiltshire SN6 6QR, UK (☎ 01285-861026, fax 01285-862767). Contact: Karen Mulcahy. Family-run business specialising in helping families to find their holiday 'home from home'. **See advertisement on page 88.**

Regent St. Properties, Suite 401, 302 Regent Street, Mayfair, London W1R 6HH, UK (☎ 0181-289 9697/0171-580 4242, mobile 0958-606533). Contact: Patrick O'Connell. Specialising in properties in Brittany, Normandy and Provence (£30,000 - £150,000). Research undertaken for your ideal home.

BUILDING SERVICES

Welby S.A.R.L., La Benardais, 22100 Léhon, France (☎ +33 02.96.83.26.22, fax +33 02.96.88.22.94, e-mail: anne.welby@wanadoo.fr). Contact: Mike Welby. Drawings, planning permission and all trades through to the finished house. The complete building service.

INSURANCE

A.T.O.B. Agents Travellers & Owners Bureau, PO Box 5169, Leicester, LE4 8ZF, UK (☎ 0116-2644609, e-mail: information@A-2-B.com). Contact: Simon Hawkesley MLIA (dip), principal. Insurance for main residence, second and holiday homes, buildings, contents, legal liability, annual, travel, medical, personal possessions, etc.

LANGUAGE SCHOOLS

Alliance Française, 1, Dorset Square, London NW1 6PU, UK (☎ 0171-723-6439, fax 0171-224 9512). Contact: Mr. Barillet (director of courses). The world's largest educational and cultural association. French tuition for individuals and companies. English-French translations. **See advertisement on page 459.**

LEGAL SERVICES

Coopers Solicitors, Farrow House, Thursley Road, Elstead, Surrey GU8 6DH, UK (☎ 0800-266568, fax 01252-703711, e-mail: legalline@coopers-solicitors.co.uk). Contact: Stephen Cooper (senior partner). Buying property, wills and succession, accidents, business advice in France. *Nous avons le savoir-faire!*

De Pinna Notaries, 35 Piccadilly, London W1V 0PJ, UK (☎ 0171-208 2900, fax 0171-208 0066). Contact: Martin Scannall or Robert Urquhart. Specialists in French legal services and taxation.

Penningtons, Bucklersbury House, 83 Cannon Street, London EC4N 8PE, UK (☎ 0171-457-3000/01256-406300, fax 0171-457-3240, e-mail: brookscm@penningtons. co.uk). Contact: Charles Brooks (partner, solicitor/avocat). Advice on French property, inheritance, wills and related subjects available from English lawyers qualified in French law.

Sean O'Connor & Co., 4 River Walk, Tonbridge, Kent TN9 1DT, UK (☎ 01732-365378, fax 01732-360144. Contact: Sean O'Connor (solicitor). Heavy French legal jargon is our business. We understand it fully. Spot on. Alert.

Simone Paissoni, Solicitor, 22, avenue Notre Dame, 06000 Nice, France (☎ +33 04.93.62.94.95, fax +33 04.93.62.95.96, e-mail: spaissonirad@magic.fr). Contact: Simone Paissoni. English qualified solicitor will assist clearly and comprehensibly with all aspects of property ownership/acquisition.

MORTGAGES

MFS Partners, Cair, Deviock, Torpoint, Cornwall PL11 3DN, UK (☎/fax 01503-250272, Internet: www.mfspartners.com). Contact: Marcus Connell (senior partner). French mortgages are different – find out how! Ring for advice or free leaflet.

Templeton Associates, 9 Rivers Street Place, Julian Road, Bath BA1 2RS, UK (☎ UK 01225-422282 or France +33 05.58.79.06.33, fax 01225-422287, e-mail: templeton@cableinet.co.uk, Internet: www.templeton-france.com). Contact: Michele Templeton (director). Mortgages arranged with major French banks for purchase, renovation, building, refinance and equity release.

PUBLICATIONS

Focus on France, Outbound Publishing, 1 Commercial Road, Eastbourne, East Sussex BN21 3XQ, UK (☎ 01323-412001, fax 01323-649249, e-mail: outbounduk @aol.com).

RELOCATION ADVISORS

ndh conseil, 220-224, boulevard Jean Jaurès, 92773 Boulogne Cedex, France (☎ +33 01.55.20.08.28, fax +33 01.46.21.07.67, e-mail: ndhconseil@aol.com). Contact: Joëlle Touhadian. A wide range of services tailored to meet the needs of families or companies facing international relocation. **See advertisement inside front cover.**

REMOVALS

Delahaye Moving Ltd., 27 Wates Way, Mitcham, Surrey CR4 4HR, UK (☎ 0181-687 0400, fax 0181-687 0404, e-mail: move@delahaye.keme.co.uk). Contact: F. P. Delahaye. Family business. International removals, storage and shipping. Personalised and effortless from start to finish.

The Old House (Removals & Warehousing) Ltd., 1/2/3 Pelham Yard, High Street, Seaford, East Sussex BN25 1PQ, UK (☎ 01323-892934, fax 01323-894474, e-mail: oldhouseremovals@compuserve.com). Contact: Mr. P. R. Barrett (managing director). Fully bonded member of B.A.R. Overseas. Moving to Europe over 35 years. Full and part loads. Free quotations and advice.

Richman-Ring Ltd., Eurolink Way, Sittingbourne, Kent, ME20 3HH, UK (☎ 01795-427151, fax 01795-428804, e-mail: info@richman-ring.com). Contact: Tony Richman (director). International movers. See also our Internet website: www. richman-ring.com.

TEMPORARY ACCOMMODATION

Allô Logement Temporaire, 64, rue du Temple, 75003 Paris, France (☎ +33 01.42.72.00.06, fax +33 01.42.72.03.11, e-mail: alt@claranet.fr). Contact: Georg Riediger. Intermediary agency working to bring together apartment owners and prospective renters.

TRAVEL

Flightclub, Guildbourne Centre, Chapel Road, Worthing, West Sussex BN11 1LZ UK (☎ 01903-215123, fax 01903-201225, e-mail: vos@clubs.itsnet.co.uk). Low cost worldwide flights. Instant availability. Property owner incentives – earn extra revenue from your rentals (01903-215123).

INDEX

D

E

N

O

P

SUGGESTIONS

Please write to us with any comments or suggestions you have regarding the contents of this book (preferably complimentary!). We are particularly interested in proposals for improvements that can be included in future editions. For example did you find any important subjects were omitted or weren't covered in sufficient detail? What difficulties or obstacles have you encountered which aren't covered here? What other subjects would you like to see included?

If your suggestions are used in the next edition of *Living and Working in France*, you will receive a free copy of the Survival Book of your choice as a token of our appreciation.

NAME: _____

ADDRESS: _____

_____

_____

Send to: Survival Books, PO Box 146, Wetherby, West Yorks. LS23 6XZ, United Kingdom.

My suggestions are as follows (please use additional pages if necessary):

OTHER SURVIVAL BOOKS

There are other 'Living and Working' books in this series including America, Australia, Britain, Canada (summer '99), London (autumn '99), New Zealand, Spain and Switzerland, all of which represent the most comprehensive and up-to-date source of practical information available about everyday life in these cities and countries. We also publish a best-selling series of 'Buying a Home' books that include Buying a Home Abroad plus buying a home in Britain (autumn '99), Florida, France, Ireland, Italy, Portugal and Spain.

Survival Books are available from good bookshops throughout the world or direct from Survival Books. If you aren't entirely satisfied simply return them to us within 14 days of receipt for a full and unconditional refund. Order your copies today by phone, fax, mail, e-mail from: Survival Books, PO Box 146, Wetherby, West Yorks. LS23 6XZ, United Kingdom (tel/fax: +44-1937-843523, e-mail: orders@survival books.net, Internet: survivalbooks.net).

BUYING A HOME IN . . .

Survival Book's 'Buying a Home' series of books are essential reading for anyone planning to purchase a home abroad and are designed to guide you through the jungle and make it a pleasant and rewarding experience. Most importantly, they are packed with valuable information to help you avoid the sort of disasters that can turn your dream home into a nightmare! Topics covered include:

- Homework & Avoiding Problems
- Choosing the Region
- Finding the Right Home & Location
- Real Estate Agents
- Finance, Mortgages & Taxes

- Home Security
- Utilities, Heating & Air-Conditioning
- Moving House & Settling In
- Renting & Letting
- Permits & Visas

- Retirement, Working & Starting a Business
- Travelling & Communications
- Health & Insurance
- Renting a Car & Driving
- And Much, Much More!

Survival Books are the most comprehensive and up-to-date source of practical information available about buying a home abroad. Whether you're seeking a mansion, villa, farmhouse, townhouse or apartment, a holiday or permanent home, these books will help make your dreams come true. Buy them today and save yourself time, trouble <u>and</u> money?

BUYING A HOME IN FRANCE

CONTAINS <u>EVERYTHING</u> YOU NEED TO KNOW TO FIND, BUY AND ENJOY YOUR DREAM HOME IN FRANCE!

Buying a Home in France is essential reading for anyone planning to purchase property in France and is designed to guide you through the jungle and make it a pleasant and enjoyable experience. Most importantly, it is packed with vital information to help you avoid the sort of disasters that can turn your dream home into a nightmare! Topics covered include:

- Avoiding Problems
- Choosing the Region
- Finding the Right Home and Location
- Real Estate Agents
- Finance, Mortgages and Taxes
- Home Security
- Utilities and Heating
- Moving House and Settling In
- Renting and Letting
- Permits and Visas
- Travelling and Communications
- Health and Insurance
- Renting a Car and Driving
- Retirement, Working and Starting a Business
- And Much, Much More!

Buying a Home in France is the most comprehensive and up-to-date source of information available about buying property in France. Whether you want a villa, farmhouse, townhouse or an apartment, a holiday or a permanent home, this book will help make your dreams come true.

Buy this book and save yourself time, trouble and money!

Order your copies today by phone, fax, mail or e-mail from: Survival Books, PO Box 146, Wetherby, West Yorks. LS23 6XZ, United Kingdom (☎/fax: +44-1937-843523, e-mail: orders@survivalbooks. net, Internet: survivalbooks.net).

THE ALIEN'S GUIDE TO FRANCE

Here at last is a guide for visitors to France who are mystified and maybe a little daunted by all those funny little foibles and idiosyncrasies which make the French so endearingly FRENCH!

This book will help you avoid the newcomer's most serious gaffes and help you appreciate more fully the rich *bouillon* of the French *joie de vivre*. Vital topics covered include:

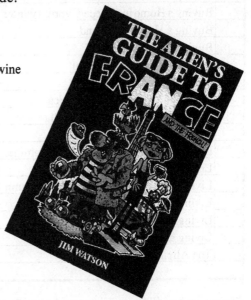

- All you need to know about French wine
- History without mystery
- Useful sign language
- French culture for barbarians
- French cuisine and eating anything
- Basic French etiquette
- French cars and driving badly
- Regional characters
- Shopping 'til you're dropping
- Sensitive areas
- And much, much more

So straighten your beret, slip into a little black dress and cast off the corset of timidity – with a copy of this book in your pocket you can visit France with poise and confidence, secure in the knowledge that you too can live the life *au français*.

***The Alien's Guide to France* is required reading for all visitors to France – whatever planet you are from!**

Order your copies today by phone, fax, mail or e-mail from: Survival Books, PO Box 146, Wetherby, West Yorks. LS23 6XZ, United Kingdom (☎/fax: +44-1937-843523, e-mail: orders@survivalbooks. net, Internet: survivalbooks.net).

ORDER FORM

Qty	Title	Price*			Total
		UK	Europe	World	
	Buying a Home Abroad	£11.45	£12.95	£14.95	
	Buying a Home in Britain (summer 1999)	£11.45	£12.95	£14.95	
	Buying a Home in Florida	£11.45	£12.95	£14.95	
	Buying a Home in France	£11.45	£12.95	£14.95	
	Buying a Home in Greece/Cyprus (winter 1999)	£11.45	£12.95	£14.95	
	Buying a Home in Ireland	£11.45	£12.95	£14.95	
	Buying a Home in Italy	£11.45	£12.95	£14.95	
	Buying a Home in Portugal	£11.45	£12.95	£14.95	
	Buying a Home in Spain	£11.45	£12.95	£14.95	
	Living and Working in America	£14.95	£16.95	£20.45	
	Living and Working in Australia	£14.95	£16.95	£20.45	
	Living and Working in Britain	£14.95	£16.95	£20.45	
	Living and Working in Canada (summer 1999)	£14.95	£16.95	£20.45	
	Living and Working in France	£14.95	£16.95	£20.45	
	Living and Working in London (autumn 1999)	£11.45	£12.95	£14.95	
	Living and Working in NZ	£14.95	£16.95	£20.45	
	Living and Working in Spain	£14.95	£16.95	£20.45	
	Living and Working in Switzerland	£14.95	£16.95	£20.45	
	The Alien's Guide to France	£5.95	£6.95	£8.45	
				TOTAL	

Cheque enclosed/Please charge my Access/Delta/Mastercard/Switch/Visa* card,

Expiry date _____ No. _ _ _ _   _ _ _ _   _ _ _ _   _ _ _ _

Issue number (Switch only) _____ Signature: _____

* Delete as applicable (price for Europe/World includes airmail postage)

NAME: _____

ADDRESS: _____

_____

_____

Send to: Survival Books, PO Box 146, Wetherby, West Yorks. LS23 6XZ, United Kingdom **or tel/fax/e-mail credit card orders to 44-1937-843523.**